Civil Society & Peacebuilding

Civil Society & Peacebuilding

A Critical Assessment

edited by
Thania Paffenholz

Viva Books

New Delhi | Mumbai | Chennai | Kolkata | Bengaluru | Hyderabad | Kochi | Guwahati

First Indian Edition 2011

VIVA BOOKS PRIVATE LIMITED

- 4737/23 Ansari Road, Daryaganj, New Delhi 110 002
  E-mail: vivadelhi@vivagroupindia.net, Tel. 42242200
- 76, Service Industries, Shirvane, Sector 1, Nerul, Navi Mumbai 400 706
  E-mail: vivamumbai@vivagroupindia.net, Tel. 27721273, 27721274
- Jamals Fazal Chambers, 26 Greams Road, Chennai 600 006
  E-mail: vivachennai@vivagroupindia.net, Tel. 28290304, 28294241
- B-103, Jindal Towers, 21/1A/3 Darga Road, Kolkata 700 017
  E-mail: vivakolkata@vivagroupindia.net, Tel. 22836381, 22816713
- 7, Sovereign Park Apartments, 56-58, K. R. Road, Basavanagudi, Bengaluru 560 004
  E-mail: vivabangalore@vivagroupindia.net, Tel. 26607409, 26607410
- 101-102 Mughal Marc Aptt., 3-4-637 to 641, Narayanguda, Hyderabad 500 029
  E-mail: vivahyderabad@vivagroupindia.net, Tel. 27564481, 27564482
- First Floor, Beevi Towers, SRM Road, Kaloor, Kochi 682 018, Kerala
  E-mail: vivakochi@vivagroupindia.net, Tel: 0484-2403055, 2403056
- 232, GNB Road, Beside UCO Bank, Silpukhuri, Guwahati 781 003
  E-mail: vivaguwahati@vivagroupindia.net, Tel: 0361-2666386

Published by arrangement with

Lynne Rienner Publishers, Inc.
1800 30th Street, Boulder
Colorado 80301

ISBN : 978-81-309-1856-3

Published by Vinod Vasishtha for Viva Books Private Limited, 4737/23, Ansari Road, Daryaganj New Delhi - 110 002. Printed and bound by Anand Sons, Delhi.

Contents

Preface

The importance of civil society to peacebuilding efforts has been increasingly acknowledged since the mid-1990s, attending a massive rise in civil society peacebuilding initiatives overall. The proliferation of such initiatives, however, has not been matched by research on the nexus between civil society and peacebuilding. Thus, we know little about what civil society means to peacebuilding—and how effective it can be for ending armed conflicts and sustaining peace.

In response, a three-year research project was initiated under the auspices of the Geneva-based Center on Conflict, Development, and Peacebuilding (CCDP) at the Graduate Institute of International and Development Studies. The results of that project are presented in this book. The overarching objective here is to contribute to a better understanding of the role of civil society in support of peacebuilding, both during and after armed conflict. The key research questions that we address are: What are the constructive functions of civil society in support of peacebuilding? What are the main factors that support those functions? And what are the main obstacles that hinder their fulfillment?

We adopt a broad definition of *civil society;* the term encompasses a range of actors, from professional associations, clubs, unions, faith-based organizations, and nongovernmental organizations to traditional and clan groups and other community groups. We do not include members of political parties or the media (with the exception of their associations). The analysis focuses on local and national groups; we do not look explicitly at global civil society campaigns. Nor have we looked at international NGOs and other civil society groups that are not part of the national or local arena. We do, however, explore the links between national civil society groups and their international partners.

We likewise adopt a broad definition of *peacebuilding,* embracing a definition that acknowledges existing differences yet remains workable. Put simply, *peacebuilding* aims at preventing and managing armed conflict and at sustaining peace after large-scale organized violence has ended. It is a multidimensional effort, incorporating all of the activities that are linked directly to that objective. Thus, peacebuilding should create conditions that are conducive to economic reconstruction, development, and democratization, but the term should not be equated and confused with such activities.

We employ quantitative and qualitative methodologies, developing a comprehensive analytical framework as the basis for systematically assessing the relevance and effectiveness of civil society in peacebuilding in a series of case studies. This framework allows our results to be compared across different cases.

This book is organized into three parts. Part 1 sets out the theoretical underpinnings of the project, exploring the historical and conceptual development of the concept of civil society (Chapter 1), the relationship between civil society and the state (Chapter 2), and the relationship between civil society and peacebuilding theories and activities (Chapter 3). Chapter 4 presents a comprehensive framework for the analysis of civil society peacebuilding efforts. Part 2 (Chapters 5 to 15) consists of country case studies, eleven in all, organized geographically by region, moving roughly clockwise from Central America. In Part 3, we elaborate on our overall findings with regard to the implementation, relevance, and effectiveness of the seven civil society peacebuilding functions (Chapter 16); identify a number of key enabling and disenabling factors (Chapter 17); and present general conclusions (Chapter 18).

* * *

I would like to take this opportunity to thank the many organizations and individuals that made this project possible. First, I am grateful to our main donors, the Norwegian and Swiss Ministries of Foreign Affairs. Special thanks go to Ivar Evensmo of the Norwegian Agency for Development Cooperation and Cristina Hoyos and Jean-François Cuénod of the Swiss Agency for Development and Cooperation for their ongoing engagement, encouragement, and important reflections on the policy relevance of this work. Thanks also to the World Bank's Social Development Department for supporting the first phase of the project, to Reiner Forster and Mark Mattner for initiating this research when they were at the World Bank, and to all the experts who were part of the review panels at the World Bank. I likewise thank the German Federal Ministry for Cooperation and Development (BMZ) and the German Technical Cooperation (GTZ) for their support, and especially Kirsten Garaycochea (BMZ), Uwe Kievelitz, Gabriele Kruk, and Annette Backhaus (all GTZ) for their comments on the policy relevance of the project.

My appreciation goes to the Scientific and Technological Research Council of Turkey, as well as to the International Studies Association, for additional workshop funding. Thanks also to our partner institutions: American University of Beirut; Bilkent University in Ankara; Davidson College in North Carolina; the Department of Peace and Development Research at the School of Global Studies, Göteborg University; International Peace Research Institute; Institute for Conflict Analysis and Resolution, George Mason University; Institute for Development and Peace, University of Duisburg; Institute for Peace and Development, American University, Washington, D.C.; Institute of Applied Media Studies, Zurich University of Applied Sciences; International Crisis Group, Nepal; Life and Peace Institute, Uppsala/Nairobi/Bukavo; Nordic Africa Institute, Uppsala; Queens University, Belfast; Sabancı University, Istanbul; University of California–Irvine; and University of Massachusetts–Boston.

I am extremely grateful to my colleagues at CCDP at the Graduate Institute of International and Development Studies for all their support. Special acknowledgment goes to Mariya Nikolova, Oliver Jütersonke, Riccardo Bocco, Meghan Pritchard, and Sandra Reimann. Many thanks also to Daniel Paffenholz for his readiness to help with the quantitative and qualitative assessment of the case studies.

I would like to thank all of the researchers involved in the project, as well as all of our reviewers and advisers. I owe special gratitude to John Darby, Siegmar Schmidt, Neclâ Tschirgi, and Jaco Cilliers. Many thanks also to Esra Çuhadar for organizing the Antalya conference in 2007.

A very special word of gratitude goes to Christoph Spurk for all of his conceptual support in the development and application of the framework, the many substantial comments he gave on a number of chapters, the training in quantitative coding he provided, his input at workshops, and his ongoing moral support.

—Thania Paffenholz

Civil Society & Peacebuilding

PART 1

Context: What We Already Know

1

Understanding Civil Society

Christoph Spurk

Citizen participation in the processes of political decisionmaking is seen as a core requirement of functioning democracies. Civil society is one institution that has gained importance in its perceived ability to facilitate regular and sustained participation by the citizenry, beyond simply voting in general elections. Increasingly, therefore, civil society is viewed by more and more researchers and practitioners as a basic pillar of democracy.

The concept of civil society, however, is diverse and can carry many meanings, necessitating some clarification. This chapter has two main purposes: to depict the diversity of civil society concepts, along with their applications in different contexts; and to elaborate on a new functional model of civil society in order to facilitate a better understanding of civil society's contributions to democratization and other political goals.

In light of these debates, we can identify two models for understanding civil society: *actor-oriented* and *function-oriented*. The benefits and shortcomings of each are explained, and a new extended functional approach is proposed.

History, Philosophical Roots, and Basic Concepts

Civil society is a widely used term in modern scholarship, "the big idea on everyone's lips" (Edwards 2004, 2). Despite this, there is no commonly agreed-upon definition, beyond the basic idea of civil society being an arena of voluntary, uncoerced collective action around shared interests, purposes, and values (Merkel and Lauth 1998, 7). A survey of the literature makes it clear that civil society as a concept contains elements that are diverse, complex, and above all, contentious. Some of the literature even questions whether this fuzziness explains the popularity of civil society, in that "it can be all things to all people" (Glasius 2004, 3).

Major European philosophers such as Aristotle, Rousseau, and Kant articulated a notion of civil society as being synonymous with the state or political society (Keane 1988, 36). "Civil" was seen as the opposite of the state of "nature" and also of "uncivilized" forms of government, such as despotism. Civil society, according to this conception, expresses the growth of civilization to the point where society has become "civilized" (Kumar 1993, 377).

In the second half of the eighteenth century, however, a major shift in conceptualizing civil society was introduced by writers such as Adam Ferguson and Thomas Paine, among others (Keane 1988). During this period, a concept of civil society was slowly developed that differentiated it from the state, endowing civil society with its own forms and principles. From this time onward, civil society was seen not only as oriented toward the state but also as acting as a limit on (and sometimes even a counter to) state powers. Essentially, then, civil society, as it became defined in a different way, was a means of defense against despotism and other potential abuses by political leaders (Bratton 1994, 53–54).

Under this penumbra, thinkers conceptualized the relationship between civil society and the state in somewhat different ways. John Locke (1632–1704), for example, was the first modern philosopher to stress that civil society should be understood as a body in its own right, separate from the state. Locke argued that people form a community in which their social life develops and in which the state has no say. This sphere is pre- or unpolitical. The first task of civil society, according to Locke, is to protect the individual—specifically individual rights and property—against the state and its arbitrary interventions (Merkel and Lauth 1998, 4; Schade 2002, 10).

Charles de Montesquieu (1689–1755) elaborated on his own model of the separation of powers (*De l'esprit des lois,* 1748), whereby he distinguished, similarly to Locke, between political society (regulating the relations between citizens and government) and civil society (regulating the relations between citizens). Montesquieu, however, presents a far less sharp contrast between the two spheres. Instead, his philosophy stresses a balance between central authority and societal networks (*corps intermediaries*), in which the central authority (monarchy) must be controlled by the rule of law and limited by the countervailing power of independent organizations (networks) that operate inside and outside the political structure (Merkel and Lauth 1998, 5).

G. W. Friedrich Hegel (1770–1831) viewed civil society as the historical product of economic modernization (and not as a natural expression of freedom) and the bourgeoisie-driven economy, positioned between the two spheres of family and state (Keane 1988, 50–55). For Hegel, civil society comprised a huge variety of actors, including the market economy, social classes (including the bourgeoisie), corporations, intellectuals, and civil servants—essentially all societal actors not directly dependent on the state apparatus. Hegel emphasized that civil society actors are not always in harmony but rather are in conflict, as the burghers followed mainly selfish interests. Therefore, in Hegel's view civil society must be controlled by a strong state that is supposed to act in the "universal interest of the population" (Keane 1988, 53).

Karl Marx (1818–1883) states that "civil society as such develops only with the bourgeoisie," and he defines the concept as comprising "the entire material interactions among individuals at a particular evolutionary stage of the productive forces" (Marx, quoted in Bobbio 1988, 82). As with Hegel, Marx's definition accommodates a huge diversity of actors, including the economy and the market. In contrast to Hegel, however, Marx states that civil society is the base of the capitalist domination model, regulating and subordinating the state, which thus becomes an institution of the dominant class (Bobbio 1988, 75–76; Kumar 1993, 377). To put it in Marxist terms, civil society is the structural base, and the state belongs to the superstructure that ensures capitalist domination by force.

The exclusive link between civil society and capitalist development was questioned by John Keane (1988). He emphasizes that the modernization of the idea of civil society, and the separation of civil society from the state, were primarily political developments rather than being economic in nature. This view was driven by the fear of state despotism, something that led political thinkers and many nonentrepreneurial groups to develop civil society as a different counteracting entity. These people and groups were critical as well to capitalist development, and many feared the inequalities caused by the growth of commodity production (Keane 1988, 63–66).

Alexis de Tocqueville (1805–1859) placed more emphasis on the role of independent associations as civil society in his two-volume masterwork *De la démocratie en Amérique* (usually translated as *Democracy in America*). He saw associations as schools of democracy in which democratic thinking, attitudes, and behavior are learned by individual citizens, the aim being to protect and defend individual rights against potentially authoritarian regimes and tyrannical majorities within society. Associations are, additionally, a balancing force against a central state inclined to form a power monopoly (Keane 1988, 60). According to de Tocqueville, these associations should be built voluntarily and at all levels (local, regional, national). Thus, civic virtues like tolerance, acceptance, honesty, and trust are actually integrated into the character of civic individuals. They contribute to trust and confidence, or as Putnam later phrased it, social capital (Putnam 2000, 19–26).

Antonio Gramsci (1891–1937) focused on civil society from a Marxist theoretical angle while reversing the Marxist viewpoint in various ways. In contrast to Marx, Gramsci saw civil society as part of the superstructure in addition to the state, but with a different function: the state served as the arena of force and coercion for capitalist domination, and civil society served as the field through which values and meanings were established, debated, and contested. Civil society thus produces noncoercive consent for the system (Kumar 1993; Bratton 1994, 54–55; Bobbio 1988). According to Gramsci, civil society contains a wide range of organizations and ideologies that both challenge and uphold the existing order. The political and cultural hegemony of the ruling classes and societal consensus is formed within civil society.

Another divergence from Marx is seen in the relationship of civil society to the state. Gramsci argues that initiatives for change could start from this superstructure sphere of civil society, with its values and ideologies. In traditional Marxism, changes can only come from basic structures, such as economic relations (Bobbio 1988, 86–88). This might be one reason why Gramsci's ideas influenced subsequent resistance to totalitarian regimes in Eastern Europe and Latin America (Lewis 2002).

Jürgen Habermas focused on the role that civil society should play within the communication process in the public sphere. Generally, communication as a social act plays a decisive role according to Habermas's basic "theory of communicative action." This theory states that legitimacy and consensus on political decisions are provided through open communication, that is, by the unbiased debate of social actors. In this understanding, the political system (state, government, and political society) needs the articulation of interests in the public space to put different concerns on the political agenda. Usually, established institutions, such as political parties, would perform this articulation. However, it cannot be left entirely to institutions alone, argues Habermas, as political parties and parliaments need to "get informed public opinion beyond the established power structures" (Habermas 1992, 374). Therefore, the ability to organize as civil society is needed particularly by marginalized groups as a means to articulate their interests.

Habermas's concept of civil society has been contested as highly normative and idealistic. Bent Flyvbjerg (1998) claims that a more realistic approach needs to consider the societal context in which this kind of communication takes place. Based on Michel Foucault's understanding of power in society, one must analyze the different relations among social actors in society and their power imbalances to obtain a realistic picture of civil society's limited potential.

The Structure and Positioning of Civil Society: A Definition

From this overview, we can see that major shifts in how civil society is conceptualized have taken place over time. This includes the change from equating civil society with the state itself toward viewing the two as opposing forces, as well as the change from a purely economic understanding of civil society to a noneconomic, political understanding. Such variations notwithstanding, we can identify some common ground for understanding the structure and positioning of civil society within society at large.

Civil society is seen as a sector on its own. It consists of a huge variety of mainly voluntary organizations and associations that maintain different objectives, interests, and ideologies. Oftentimes, they compete with one another.

Although not driven purely by private or economic interests, they are nonetheless viewed as autonomously organized, interacting within the public sphere.

Civil society is seen as *different from both the state* (comprising executive government institutions, bureaucracy, administration, judiciary) *and the political sphere* (legislature, political parties) due to the fact that civil society is making political demands toward the state and others, but is not running—as politicians and parties do—for political office in government. Thus, civil society is formally and legally independent from state/political society, but it is oriented toward and interacts closely with the state, the political sector, and the economic sector.

Civil society is seen as *differentiated from the market and the business sector (economic sphere)* (but see Glasius 2004, 1), as well as from the family/ private realm (see Figure 1.1a).

These sectors can also be viewed as partially overlapping in the sense that boundaries are sometimes blurred. Some authors emphasize this reality by considering how some actors can operate in various spheres or sectors simultaneously (Croissant 2003, 240).

Some of the research stresses that specific actors are in general attributed to specific sectors, but occasionally they, too, can also act as civil society. For example, business entrepreneurs (belonging to the business sector) are acting within civil society when they demand tax breaks from the state. This understanding also helps us uncover other actors who may have a role as civil society,

Figure 1.1 The Position of Civil Society

a. Civil society as a sector b. Civil society as an intermediate sphere

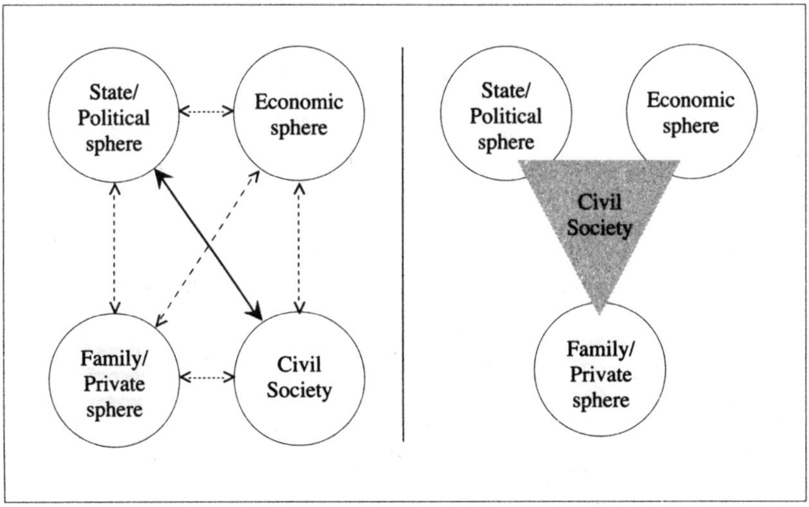

such as traditional groups in Africa (Croissant et al. 2000, 18). In this conception, authors may prefer to characterize civil society *as the space between the sectors* (Merkel and Lauth 1998, 7). Civil society is thus the public realm between state, business, and family (see Figure 1.1b).

To clarify who belongs to civil society, it is helpful to consider the processes of *articulation* and *negotiation* of political interests within society. Typically, various intermediaries act as connectors between the private sphere (ordinary citizens who are only occasionally directly involved in politics) and the political-administrative system (running the country with little or no direct contact with the population). Intermediaries—including political parties, associations, social movements, and the media—establish contact and feedback among these distant spheres. And among these intermediaries, only associations and social movements belong to civil society. Political parties are seen as part of the political society sphere, as their representatives usually compete for running political offices in government. Civil society makes demands to the political society or state, but it does not aspire to assume office. However, civil society often provides staff out of its ranks for political society and its institutions.

The media's role is even more contentious. Some scholars and practitioners see media as part of civil society (van Tongeren et al. 2005; Berger 2002), whereas others see media as executing a different role in society. Christoph Spurk (2007) argues that media do not belong to civil society because the mass media comprise professional organizations and not voluntary ones, thus belonging to the economic sphere. Additionally, the role attributed to the media in a democratic environment requires them—at least ideally—to report comprehensively and impartially without serving specific interests. Thus, a free and pluralistic media have a role on their own (Voltmer 2006). Their task is to enable public debate, and they should not represent specific interests that are held by civil society and organizations. Yet, some media might not consider these to be limitations, and they are better viewed as part of the state/political society, like state or party media, or as part of advocacy/communication strategies of specific organizations. In contrast, people working in the media sector (journalists, publishers) can form their own associations, which then act as civil society, similar to any other association. Media fulfilling their public task might support civil society in its endeavor to confront the state, as this usually involves opening further access to the public sphere (Spurk 2007). The media as a whole are generally not considered to be part of civil society.

All of the above considerations can be condensed into the following definition:

> Civil society is a sphere of voluntary action that is distinct from the state, political, private, and economic spheres, keeping in mind that in practice the boundaries between these sectors are often complex

and blurred. It consists of a large and diverse set of voluntary organizations—competing with each other and oriented to specific interests—that are not purely driven by private or economic interests, are autonomously organized, and interact in the public sphere. Thus, civil society is independent from the state and the political sphere, but it is oriented toward and interacts closely with them.

Civil Society Discourses in Different Contexts

Civil society has been debated in very different contexts. Within political science research, the main focus has been civil society's role in the political transition toward democracy in different regions of the world. Based on this debate, civil society gained importance as well in international cooperation, in terms of practitioners' discourse on development cooperation, as well as in the policy discourse on violent conflict in developing and transition countries. The sections below review the main strands of these debates and examine how civil society concepts have been interpreted in politics and practice in different contexts and geographical regions.

Civil Society in Political Transition and Democratization

As we have alluded to previously, civil society has been an almost purely Western concept, historically tied to the political emancipation of citizens from former feudalistic ties, monarchies, and the state during the eighteenth and nineteenth centuries. Other notions of civil society (i.e., those that might have existed in other regions or at different times) barely surface in the international debate about civil society (Appiagyei-Atua 2002, 2–3; Pouligny 2005, 498). As a result, there is still much debate over whether Western concepts of civil society are transferable to non-Western countries or other historical contexts with different levels of democracy and economic structures (Lewis 2002; Harneit-Sievers 2005).

Western Europe: From exclusiveness to inclusion. In its early phase, civil society in Western Europe (the eighteenth and early nineteenth centuries) was driven by economic and academic elites who demanded civil and human rights, as well as political participation. In its second phase (the nineteenth and early twentieth centuries), civil society widened its areas of activity and potential. New actors entered civil society—for example, the social movements of the working class, farmers, and churches—who not only engaged in social welfare but also articulated political and societal claims. In their view, these new actors were less universal than the earlier elites, focusing instead on specific interests, sometimes stressing societal conflict and deprivation. The third phase of civil society began with the emergence of new social movements in the 1960s, such as women's liberation, in addition to the student, peace, and ecology movements. These new movements and agendas considerably expanded both the range and scope of civil society activities and, likewise, the reasons for being part of civil society in its many manifestations (Lauth 2003, 229).

The United States and Western Europe: Social capital debate. Starting in the United States, a rich debate emerged in the 1990s regarding the performance of major social institutions, including representative government, and its relation to political culture and civil society. Robert Putnam sees social capital—social networks, a rich associational life, along with the associated norms of reciprocity and trustworthiness—as the core element of civil society. This affirms that the characteristics of civil society and civic life affect the health of democracy and the performance of social institutions (Putnam 1993; Putnam 2002, 14). Putnam's research argues that there exists a tremendous decline of social capital in the United States. His work has since spurred considerable research on various forms of social capital (Putnam 2000; Putnam 2002, 14–25) and its conduciveness to democracy.

Eastern Europe: Challenges of a threefold transition. Most countries in Eastern Europe faced a threefold transition: the political transformation from dictatorship to democracy, the economic transformation from a state to a market economy, and sometimes the state transformation due to the disintegration of the Soviet Union (Merkel 1999, 377). Eastern Europe's transition drew much interest, mainly from European researchers and practitioners. Numerous case studies showed that, in most countries, civil society played a major role, although not the only role, in overcoming authoritarian regimes and establishing democratic structures (Merkel 1999, 397–441).

Research demonstrates that civil society plays different roles in various transition phases. Its success seems contingent on many factors, such as its strength and its capacity to fulfill the right functions at the right time; the incorporation of democratic procedures in its own structure and organization, especially after immediate system change; and the extent of bridging societal divides by inclusive membership as well as the "civility" of its actions. All this must be viewed within the context of other factors and power structures within which civil society interacts (Merkel 2000; Lauth 2003).

Civil society in the South: Is the concept applicable? In Latin America, Africa, and Asia, we find very different debates on the subject, due to different historical, political, and economic developments.

1. Latin America. In Latin America, the concept of civil society gained importance mainly in the fight against military dictatorship at the end of the 1960s. Peter Birle (2000, 242–261) described a high diversity of civil society groups, based on his analysis of the development of civil society in five Latin

American countries under military dictatorship and in the recovering of democracy. He identified various types of civil society according to the main focus of action. The *antiauthoritarian civil society* consists of groups fostering the protection of human rights and tolerance and facilitated nonviolent resistance to military regimes in Latin America. *Gramscian civil society,* as put forward by other research, renewed the thinking of the traditional leftist groups after the revolutionary armed liberation in Latin America had failed and opened up new spaces of discussion. *Neoliberal groups of civil society* focused on individual freedom and were part of neoliberal deregulation and privatization development strategies. Neoliberalism stressed that private initiatives need to be liberated from all sorts of ties and supports, mainly originating from private business. Other groups, characterized under the general label *new social movements,* were greatly skeptical of established political parties and favored an entirely new egalitarian and participative order. And finally, *social networks* attempted to increase the practical quality of governance, working toward renovating education systems or improving citizen participation in general (Birle 2000, 232–234).

Robert Pinkney (2003, 102–103) sees civil society's role as very limited, stating that civil society in Latin America "extended to greater resistance to authoritarianism" but failed to develop a major role for itself once democracy had been restored. Pinkney presumes that social movements and loose groupings are suitable for resisting dictatorship but less so for the "mundane processes of sustaining democracy." In contrast, Birle highlighted the fact that, despite military dictatorship, a reduced civil society could and did still survive. Hardships under dictatorships provoked the engagement of groups that normally would not engage as civil society. Even after democratic systems were reinstalled, a growing pluralism in civil society developed, countering earlier assumptions that civil society would diminish once democracy was established.

2. Africa. The main question in Africa—as for other regions in the global south—is whether the concept of civil society is applicable in the geographical context. It must be understood that conditions for Western-type civil society (e.g., a self-confident urban citizenship that has already gained some autonomy from state structures) are mostly absent in Africa.

Among the varying positions within the literature, one states that due to colonial rule—fostering a small urban elite in African cities and oppressing a large majority of the population by leaving them as subjects of traditional despotic rulers in rural areas—Africa knows only traditional associations but has no space for a civil society that aims at participatory governance. Because this pattern largely continued in the postcolonial phase, there was no civil society of this type in Africa (Lewis 2002, 567–577; Maina 1998, 135–137). Others argue that the weak development of civil society is partly due to the generally low level of development that hinders societies to further differentiate and to offer opportunities for civil society activities (Schmidt 2000, 301).

This is reflected in skepticism over whether civil society can work in Africa in the way that Western donors expect as they try to foster democracy. Nelson Kasfir (1998) states that some concepts exclude specific "uncivil" organizations, such as ethnic and religious associations, that are important to political struggles in Africa. Moreover, organizations are usually included only if they are deemed to show "civil" behavior, conceived as being autonomous of social interests and not bound into neopatrimonial networks. This way, important elements of the public sphere in Africa become excluded by definition. Additionally, Kasfir doubts whether these kinds of independent organizations can be sustained in Africa without the support of government or foreign donors. He is skeptical as to whether the Western participatory model of competing interests in the public sphere can really be institutionalized in Africa today. He sees politics there as being dominated by neopatrimonial relations in which state officials have no need to respond to citizens' concerns but distribute resources to their often ethnically organized clients (Kasfir 1998, 130–133).

A second viewpoint sees little problem in applying the concept of civil society to Africa and considers almost all existing nonstate actors as civil society (Harneit-Sievers 2005, 2). For example, Michael Bratton (1994) sees a role (albeit a limited one) for civil society—at least for the transition period from authoritarian to more democratic rule. He identified circumstances that have yielded various configurations of civil society and resulted in different roles in the democratization process, as shown by the cases of Kenya and Zambia in the 1990s. He distinguishes among the material dimension (economic crisis stimulates the founding of self-help groups and popular protests), the organizational dimension (the existence and nature of an organization leading the civil society movement), and the ideological dimension (the goals of civil society). The transition to democratic rule will be successful even when middle-class organizations (teachers, entrepreneurs, state employees, as well as church leaders and lawyers) leave the regime, join protests, and elaborate a shared vision for an alternative regime. Normally, after transition and with new elections, the political actors then take the leading role, and the civil society actors step back.

Bratton emphasizes that civil society exists in Africa under all regimes. In times of authoritarian rule, independent thinkers take refuge within civil society as a sphere beyond the reach of the state. Nevertheless, some politicians soon evacuate civil society and reenter political society, when circumstances permit the formation of parties. Thus, this two-way transfer—from civil to political society and back—is viewed as typical (Bratton 1994, 57; Merkel and Lauth 1998).

A third viewpoint straddles the middle, stressing the need to adapt the concept of civil society to Africa (Lewis 2002, 578–580). Africa's civil society is seen as different from Western conceptualizations, but also as having executed similar functions (albeit in a rudimentary way). Jean-François Bayart (1986), for example, defines civil society precisely in Western contexts—in the opposition to authoritarian states. Essentially, it is seen "as the process by which society seeks to 'breach' and counteract the simultaneous 'totalization' unleashed by the state" (Bayart 1986, 111). It then becomes necessary to look at various organizations (such as traditional associations and male youth groups) that were not acknowledged as civil society but already worked in traditional society as controllers of traditional government. Examples include elders and chiefs (Appiagyei-Atua 2002, 6). Other traditional institutions can equally be seen as cells of civil society (Harneit-Sievers 2005, 5–9).

Kasfir raises the point that some independent organizations behave aggressively and confront the state directly. He doubts whether such civic organizations will always make the state more democratic, as they could also undermine the state's capacity to reconcile different interests. Only when political institutions are strong might an aggressive civil society serve to strengthen democracy; when weak, they might have the opposite effect (Kasfir 1998, 141).

His claim for including all voluntary organizations, instead of excluding some by definition, is joined by Mahmood Mamdani and Ernest Wamba-dia-Wamba (1995). They show that, in various case studies, many groups in Africa—traditional, ethnic, and/or religious—take part in or are dominated by political struggle and thus need to be included in research on civil society in order to come closer to reality and to enrich common knowledge. Some authors directly favor including groups with involuntary membership and kinship relations, although such would not be the case for Western conceptions of civil society (Lewis 2002, 578–579).

Many authors assess the impact of Africa's civil society on democratization as very limited, because it has been fragmented and because links between civil society organizations (social self-help groups, urban intellectuals) and the formal political system are sometimes weak (Pinkney 2003, 104–105; Schmidt 2000, 321–323).

Chris Allen (1997) questions whether NGOs are really contributing to democratization as expected by donors. He seeks to show that NGOs normally have no revolutionary drive and are only able to empower people. According to this viewpoint, civil society aimed at democratization requires organizations that claim direct political reform, something that is not common in Africa.

3. Asia. In Asia, civil society has been far less discussed. This could be due in part to the presence of authoritarian regimes throughout Asian history. Additionally, Asian values are unique, thereby making the Western concept of civil society less applicable in Asia (Alagappa 2004, xii). Civil societies in Asia are highly diverse in their composition, resources, and goals. Although a rise of civil society organizations in Asia became noticeable during the 1980s, a closer look at the history demonstrates that, in many Asian countries, communal networks existed even during precolonial times (Alagappa 2004, xii). Under colonial regimes, civil society organized mostly along lines of ethnicity

and religion—thus the philanthropic engagement by Buddhist groups in Myanmar, Christian groups in the Philippines, and Muslim groups in Indonesia and Malaysia (Guan 2004, 24). The role of the church has remained central to the development of community-based organizations at the local level in the Philippines, Indonesia, and Thailand.

Throughout the 1950s and 1960s, civil society in Southeast Asia gradually organized in opposition to colonial and repressive regimes. Since then an exposure to democracy and modernity within many Southeast Asian countries penetrated the structures of family, religion, community, cultural association, caste, and class and introduced a model of association based on "rational will" (Dahal 2001a, 7). The effects of this paradigm shift have been diverse throughout Asia. In some cases (Nepal, India, China), the historical asymmetries that accumulated along lines of class, gender, and caste led civil society projects to focus on initiating social dialogue and expressing the grievances of marginalized constituencies (Howell 2004, 121–129; Dahal 2001a, 7; Chandhoke 2007, 32).

In Central Asia and the Caucasus, in contrast, civil society involvement was similar to the Eastern European model. Thus, the emergence of civil society became linked to the empowerment of dissident opposition movements to counter suppressive regimes in Central Asia and the Caucasus (Babajanian et al. 2005, 212). Later, some opposition movements even assumed a political role (Ruffin and Wangh 1999, 27–31). In addition, civil society organizations based on the communal concept of informal ties (clan, family, neighborhood) or neopatrimonial structures continued to exist. In the case of Georgia and Armenia, the church continues to play an important role in helping nurture those ties (Babajanian et al. 2005, 214). One caution, however, is that religion also has the potential to create more tensions between the state and civil society actors.

A common strand among countries in Asia is that civil society is still not protected, as the state continues to be the central, and often the most repressive, actor in the region. Political and economic interests steered democratization toward a type of social organization that placed state institutions, special interest groups, and economic sectors into a single associated sphere. As the Asian financial crisis unfolded in the late 1990s, hopes were high for a more active civil society involvement in negotiating a distinct atmosphere for organization and discourse. Today the relationships among state, religion, social organization, and communal links in Asia remain tense. Empirical studies, however, tend to show a unique role for civil society organizations and their potential to create synergies between traditional models of association and the Western concept of civic organization.

4. The Middle East. The literature generally identifies the absence or weakness of civil society in this region to counter strong and authoritarian regimes. It also highlights the rejuvenation of NGOs. Intermediate powers and autonomous social groups are dependent on state patronage (Abootalebi 1998) in societies that have been organizing political actions along family and clan

lines for decades. Still, one can glimpse a gradual opening of political space under some authoritarian states due to increasing pressure from citizens (Norton 1995, 4–8).

One peculiarity is that civil society is differentiated between a "modern" part, in the form of human rights organizations, and the "traditional" part, in the form of Islamic movements. After September 2001, Arab human rights organizations redoubled efforts in the quest for democracy and offered, in the view of some scholars, an alternative Arab discourse on governance (Nefissa 2007, 68). Nevertheless, they tend to be elitist and lack a genuine social basis (Nefissa 2007, 70). The social mass basis is the cause celebre of Islamic movements, traditionally active in the areas of social work and charity (Melina et al. 2005), but they are less likely to tackle political issues, at least openly.

5. Global civil society. The 1990s saw an increase in NGO activities worldwide, especially in transnational NGOs and networks that placed important issues on the international agenda, launched international campaigns (e.g., on landmines and blood diamonds), and participated in key international conferences (UN 2003). Thus they advocated for and spoke on behalf of people who were neglected. International NGOs also conducted large and well-organized campaigns on development issues and presented alternative viewpoints to those of official governments and development agencies. Their involvement in the UN system has been acknowledged, and recommendations have been made for continuing relations and interactions into the future (UN 2003, 19–21).

The concept of a global civil society (Kaldor 2003) is debated intensively in the literature. Some see the debate as a reflection of globalization (Cardoso 2003), with the potential to influence the framework of global governance by promoting debate and bridging existing societal divides (Clark 2003). Critics of the global civil society tend to focus on NGOs' lack of legitimacy, dominance by Western organizations in quantitative and qualitative terms, and (although valuing the expertise and competence of international NGOs) their claim of being "representatives of the world's peoples" (Anderson and Rieff 2004, 35).

Civil Society in Development Cooperation

Civil society and its actors have gained an important role not only in the debate over political transition but also in the practice of development cooperation, at least from the mid-1980s. This shift is seen in voluntary agencies' and NGOs' increased involvement in development cooperation. And it can be attributed to the neoliberal development model (Debiel and Sticht 2005, 9) of the 1980s, which encouraged skepticism toward the state and favored privatization of state welfare and infrastructure services. Thus, NGOs took on new assignments, especially within social sectors, for which the state had theretofore been responsible. They increasingly took over operational tasks, in line with efforts to reduce the role of the state and when state weakness became pervasive (Abiew and Keating 2004, 100–101).

A series of UN world conferences during the 1990s encouraged the formation of new NGOs and the expansion of existing ones. NGOs were presented as alternative implementers of development assistance when states and governments in partner countries were weak or poorly performing. This ascendance of NGOs was due to their perceived political independence, their flexibility, and their effectiveness in reaching beneficiaries, in contrast to bureaucratic state apparatuses. Funding of official development assistance channeled through NGOs increased from an average of US$3.1 billion from Organization for Economic Cooperation and Development (OECD) countries in 1985–1986 to US$7.2 billion in 2001 (Debiel and Sticht 2005, 10). Other sources mention even higher figures (Schmidt 2000, 302).

The debate regarding developing countries was similar to discourses in the industrialized world about the so-called third sector. The third sector gained considerable attention in the 1990s as it started to operate outside the confines of the state and the market, and by extension, outside government control and beyond the profit motive. Despite some heterogeneity, the entities of the third sector include the same range of nonprofit voluntary institutions as does civil society. With many common features (Salamon and Anheier 1999, 4), they provide services to members and clients (Badelt 1997, 5).

However, there are also differences between the third sector and civil society. As the third sector becomes a significant economic force, the debate centers on the types of services that can be provided and the types of organizations (Salomon and Anheier 1997, 12–19 and 20–25). In contrast, the civil society debate focuses on the political, social, and cultural effects of civil society organizations, especially for democratic development.

Against this background, the shift in funding through NGOs can be identified as strengthening the third sector to become a more efficient alternative for service delivery. This shift did not aim to support the establishment of a vibrant civil society, although such support was often identified and labeled as civil society support.

The political angle of civil society gained momentum at the beginning of the 1990s as a means to improve governance and democratization. As the cold war ended, there arose the opportunity to establish principles of good governance, respect for human rights, and the rule of law—priority objectives in development cooperation. Thus, a vibrant civil society was considered an important pillar for establishing democracy, and support for it became an obvious aim of democratization (Schmidt 2000, 312). Almost all international donors mention civil society as an important factor to "influence decisions of the state" (BMZ 2005, 3), also highlighting civil society's responsibility for a democratic state and its "dynamic role . . . in pushing for social, economic and political change" (DFID 2005a; 2001b) or stressing its role in encouraging open debates on public policy (USAID 2005; Kasfir 1998).

In practice, donors mix third sector and civil society approaches through a combination of service delivery and advocacy. Beyond noting general and positive connotations of civil society, only a few donors undertake specific tasks. The World Bank highlights advocacy, monitoring, and direct service delivery as three main functions of civil society (World Bank 2003a, 3). Other donors justify combining these tasks, given their interconnectedness. The potential of community-based organizations to advocate for the poor is enhanced by the legitimacy provided by the effective delivery of services (DFID 2001a, 5).

NGOs' involvement in development cooperation, and especially in civil society, has been widely acknowledged but also criticized (Debiel and Sticht 2005, 11). Critics point out that funding for civil society has concentrated on NGOs, that NGOs are less independent from governments, and that accountability to local people and communities is weak. A main critique is that support for civil society has been concentrated on international and national NGOs (Stewart 1997, 26) at the expense of other civil society actors that have broader membership. For example, trade unions and other mass organizations could guarantee more participation than NGOs with a very limited membership base (Bliss 2003, 198). NGO performance in democratization can also be questioned, because some NGOs are personally or institutionally tied to the government, thus making it difficult to become a counterweight to existing regimes.

Political scientists also argue that international NGOs are not as independent from donor governments as they often claim. As donors at least partly outsource the implementation of development cooperation, official and nongovernment aid become closely intertwined (Debiel and Sticht 2005, 12), raising doubts about the actual independence of NGOs.

The legitimacy of NGOs is also questioned, largely due to the prevailing division of labor. Funds are channeled from donor governments to northern NGOs, which then subcontract implementation to southern NGOs (Neubert 2001, 61). It has been observed that southern NGOs are accountable only to their northern counterparts rather than local constituencies. Thus, many NGOs are regarded as consultants or small businesses with purely economic interests (Bliss 2003, 198; Schmidt 2000, 306). The modern southern NGO represents a new type of organization: nonprofit, but acting like a commercial consulting firm (Neubert 2001, 63) financed by external mandates. Some critics fear that commercialization of civil society, especially the commercialization of advocacy or public policy work, discourages more legitimate local actors that are not receiving funds (Pouligny 2005, 499) from participating or becoming more active. Civic engagement is at risk of being dominated by the commercial NGOs, which in the long run weakens the development of a vibrant civil society.

Civil Society and Armed Conflict

Armed conflict has become a major factor in foreign policy and international cooperation. The following section reviews the general aspects of civil society

this vacuum to defraud communities (World Bank 2005, 16). Furthermore, they developed higher responsiveness upward to donors rather than downward to beneficiaries (World Bank 2005, 16).

Two Different Research Approaches to Analyze Civil Society

Based on this account of civil society discourse and practice in different contexts, and in light of the relevant literature, two approaches for analyzing civil society can be identified: actor-oriented and functional.

Actor-Oriented Approaches

Actor-oriented approaches concentrate on the performance and features of civil society actors. These research designs have major shortcomings.

They often use only one civil society model (typically, inspired by one of the above-mentioned philosophers) and then examine it. However, there are many civil society models (or functions; see below) that are of equal importance; at the very least, no single approach can be prioritized. Thus, some performances of civil society might remain hidden by actor-oriented research.

Actor-oriented research often also examines only organizations with specific objectives and sometimes even specific "civil" behavior. Other organizations are—more or less arbitrarily—excluded by definition from being considered within the definition of civil society. Thus, important players are either overlooked or given short shrift, and the role of not-so-important players can actually be overestimated (Kasfir 1998, 127). This will conceal rather than explain realities. One example is the case of ethnic groupings or fundamentalist religious organizations that are excluded for reasons not made entirely transparent (Kasfir 1998) or due to the perception that they are "uncivil." This perception stems from the requirement among some authors that civil society actors must respect the values of nonviolence and mutual tolerance to fit the criteria (Merkel and Lauth 1998, 7). This is also the case for research concentrating only on modern, urban NGOs, thereby inadvertently failing to consider traditional, rural groupings (see, e.g., DAC 2005, equating civil society with NGOs).

To exclude by definition some potential actors, and to systematically neglect functions of civil society actors that might actually play important roles, limit the findings of relevant research.

For empirical research to produce relevant findings on how civil society works within society and for political transformation, a different and much more open approach is necessary. This can be found in the functional approach.

Functional Approaches

In contrast to actor-oriented models, the functional approach concedes that various models or concepts of civil society exist, none of which is prioritized over others. The concepts can be distinguished by the function that civil society performs. The two main authors who have elaborated functional approaches are summarized below.

Merkel and Lauth's function model. One school of thought, from German political scientists, presents a model of five specific functions of civil society. These functions are identified from research on system transformation in Eastern Europe and enriched by practical case studies on the role of civil society in different contexts (Merkel and Lauth 1998; Merkel 2000; Croissant et al. 2000; Lauth 2003). This model views civil society not as a specific historic form, but as an analytical category. This decoupling from history helps to distill the functions of civil society as they relate to democracy and to analyze different regional or cultural contexts and societal conditions. The five essential functions of civil society are:

1. *Protection.* Civil society is the social sphere beyond the state in which citizens, endowed with rights, are free to organize their lives without state interference. The state has to ensure protection of the private sphere. The task of civil society is to remind the state of this warrant and, if needed, compel the state to honor it.
2. *Intermediation between state and citizens.* Civil society must ensure a balance between central authority and social networks, a precondition for safeguarding the rule of law. This function focuses on the permanent exchange of self-organized associations with the state in order to control, limit, and influence the activities of the state.
3. *Participatory socialization.* This function stresses that civil society and associations are schools of democracy. People learn how to execute their democratic rights, even on a basic level. People will acquire the capacities of being citizens, participating in public life and developing trust, confidence, tolerance, and acceptance. This also supports the decentralization of power and the creation of solidarity among citizens, both of which act as defense mechanisms against possible attacks on freedoms.
4. *Community-building and integration.* Civil society is seen as a catalyst for civil virtues or as an antidote to individualism and retreat to family and statism. Thus, participation in social organizations helps to bridge societal cleavages, to create civil virtues, and to foster social cohesion. It also satisfies the needs of individuals to develop bonds and attachments. One precondition is that the self-organization of civil society does not take place purely under ethnic, religious, or racist premises.
5. *Communication.* Public communication is the core function of civil society in deliberative democracy models. It stresses the importance of a free public sphere, separated from the state and the economy, where people have room for debate, participation, and democratic decisionmaking.

> Civil society and its associations—besides political parties and parliaments—have a major role to establish this "democratic public" and to act as watchdog. Actors of spontaneous groups, organizations, and social movements are able to articulate concerns and problems and transfer them from the private sphere to the political agenda.

Comparative empirical research has demonstrated that these five functions are not mutually exclusive but rather tend to complement one another in fostering democracy. Depending on the context, it also suggests that some functions seem to be more basic (e.g., protection), in that they are essential during the immediate phase of democratic system change. Other functions (integration) gain more importance only in the later stages of consolidating democracy (Croissant et al. 2000, 37–41). Further research is needed to see whether the internal organization of civil society groups will determine whether they are able to perform their functions not only in immediate system change but also in a consolidated democratic society. In this phase, community-building and integration usually play important roles that are seemingly difficult to achieve by organizations with undemocratic organizational setups (Lauth 2003, 225–227).

Edwards's roles model. Michael Edwards made a similar attempt to structure the meanings of civil society. Out of the diversity of concepts offered by multiple actors regarding civil society, and "recognizing that civil society does indeed mean different things to different people" (Edwards 2004, 3), he elaborated three roles.

- Civil society as associational life. Civil society is the world of voluntary associations that act as "gene carriers" for developing values such as tolerance and cooperation. This is the central role that the "neo-Tocquevillian school" ascribes to a rich associational life (Edwards 2004, 18–36).
- Civil society as the good society. The second role sets this rich associational life in context, fostering positive norms and values and emphasizing that activities must be geared toward specific social and political goals (Edwards 2004, 37–53). By this, Edwards, like many others, excludes the "uncivil" side of civil society by definition and highlights the learning of democratic or social behavior.
- Civil society as the public sphere. The third role of civil society is to provide a public sphere wherein citizens can debate the great questions of the day and negotiate a constantly evolving sense of common good and public interest. This role is central for finding proper solutions and decisionmaking in society. It is central for civil society and crucial for

> democracy to interact fairly in the public sphere. This means a willingness to cede some territory to others, to develop shared interests, and to deliberate democratically. (Edwards 2004, 54–71)

Edwards's main hypothesis is that each of these roles alone cannot achieve effective social change and other positive outcomes normally attributed to civil society. Thus, he calls for the integration or synthesis of the different roles and to consider them comprehensively when supporting civil society initiatives (Edwards 2004, 10). This will balance the weaknesses of each role with the strengths of the others. Edwards's model concurs with most of those suggested in Merkel and Lauth's model.

Additional Functions in Development Cooperation

Reviewing the models for civil society in development cooperation, we can see that much more emphasis is given to service delivery. Donors assign service delivery a higher priority under the guise of improving living conditions (SIDA 2005). This reflects the fact that the third sector approach is equated with civil society democracy discourse. Even though Edwards highlights the service provision role of NGOs in "deliberate substitution for the state" (2004, 14), democracy theory attributes no role to service delivery, seen as not directly related to democratization (Merkel and Lauth 1998, 10).

In addition, monitoring government activities, holding institutions to account, and fostering transparency and accountability (World Bank 2003a, 3) can be considered as separate functions of civil society that go unmentioned in Merkel and Lauth's model, yet they are closely related to communication and protection functions.

The other functions mentioned in the context of development cooperation can be attributed to civil society functions under Merkel and Lauth's model. Stimulating a dialogue between civil society and government (DFID 2001a, 4–5) can be equated with the intermediation function, whereas advocating on behalf of the poor and channeling the views of the people to the political system (DFID 2001b, 11) clearly belong to Merkel and Lauth's public communication function.

It is important to emphasize that civil society is considered a positive force in the development cooperation discourse. The "dark" or "uncivil" side of civil society does not seem to be considered in analysis or project design.

An Extended Functional Approach: Seven Basic Functions of Civil Society

Combining Merkel and Lauth's five functions, which already encompass those of Edwards's roles model, with two new functions contributed by development cooperation practice, a new model of civil society is achieved. This model is composed of seven functions and enables an in-depth understanding of civil society's detailed role in political, social, and development processes. The seven functions are:

1. *Protection of citizens.* This basic function of civil society is protecting lives, freedom, and property against attacks and despotism by the state and other authorities. It is based on the work of Locke.
2. *Monitoring for accountability.* This function consists of monitoring the activities of central powers, state apparatuses, and government. This is also a way to control central authorities and hold them to account. Monitoring can refer to human rights, public spending, corruption, and primary school enrollment. The function is based on Montesquieu's separation of powers, but it is enhanced by development cooperation perspectives.
3. *Advocacy and public communication.* An important task of civil society is its ability to articulate interests—especially of marginalized groups—and to create channels of communication in order to bring them to the public agenda, thereby raising public awareness and facilitating debate. In development cooperation, this Habermasian function is described as advocacy.
4. *Socialization.* With its rich associational life, civil society contributes to the formation and practice of democratic attitudes among citizens. People learn to develop tolerance, mutual trust, and the ability to compromise through democratic procedures. Thus, democracy is ensured not only by legal institutions but also by citizens' habits.
5. *Building community.* Engagement and participation in voluntary associations also has the potential to strengthen bonds among citizens, building social capital. In cases where associations include members from other ethnic or social groups, it also bridges societal cleavages and contributes to social cohesion.
6. *Intermediation and facilitation between citizens and state.* Civil society and its organizations fulfill the role of balancing the power of, and negotiating with, the state at different levels (local, regional, national). It establishes diverse relations (communication, negotiation, control) among various interest groups or between independent institutions and the state. This role echoes the work of Montesquieu.
7. *Service delivery.* The direct provision of services to citizens is an important activity of civil society associations, such as self-help groups. Especially in cases where the state is weak, it becomes essential to provide shelter, health, and education. Although organizations executing civil society functions also provide services to members and clients, the functional model centers on *political* functions and objectives—in

> contrast to the third sector debate that focuses on services and economic objectives. Thus, service delivery as a *function* is considered an entry point for other civil society functions, but this should be based on a careful assessment of whether the specific service is indeed a good entry point for those objectives.

Comparing the two main approaches, the functional model (more so than the actor-oriented model) is conducive to developing an in-depth analysis and understanding of civil society's influence. The functional approach comprises all potential civil society actors, including nonurban, religious, and ethnic organizations, as well as actors belonging to other sectors (e.g., business) but sometimes playing a civil society role (e.g., the business association making a political demand on the government). Breaking down activities by function takes into account the performance of other actors; it also adds detail and depth of knowledge. And it enables cross-country comparisons due to the fact that functions can be more easily compared than actors in different contexts.

Limitations and Clarifications of the Functional Model

The scope of civil society functions. Constructive civil society functions are not exclusively provided by civil society actors. They are also provided by other actors in society. Protection, for example, should be primarily provided by the state, the judiciary, and law enforcement authorities. Yet, democratic attitudes are also learned in voluntary associations, as well as in the classroom, family, and community. Additionally, public communication is organized by an independent and diverse media, an actor belonging to the economic sector or the state; civil society usually provides only small contributions.

"Uncivil" or bad civil society actors. Although Merkel and Lauth require that civil society needs to be civil—thereby excluding groups that show uncivil behavior—the functional model includes "uncivil" actors and tries to identify constructive as well as destructive performances.

Obviously, many civil society actors might not fulfill one or more of the constructive functions, but instead develop uncivil behaviors, such as preaching hatred against others, being violent, and destroying life and property. Associations and organizations can be destructive, but they can also have integrative and disintegrative potential. On-the-ground knowledge and sound analysis are required to determine the nature of actors and the functions they perform. Roberto Belloni (2006, 8–10) provides a range of examples from Africa, Sri Lanka, and Northern Ireland in which civil society actors focused only on strengthening their bonding ties, based on a sense of belonging and kinship that were later channeled destructively. He presumes that the less bridging ties are built, the more likely it is that influence is to be detrimental. Although additional research is needed on the conditions under which civil society organizations act positively and negatively, it is important to keep in mind the potential for detrimental effects.

The discussion and emphasis on civility are akin to Putnam's distinction between good (or positive) and bad (or negative) social capital. Good social capital is built when associations develop strong bridging ties—such as including members from other ethnic or social groupings—whereas bad social capital is characterized only by bonding ties or strong inward social capital. Such social capital is usually evident when only members from the same ethnic or social grouping are included. They are more inclined to act violently against others in comparison to associations that have stronger bridging ties (Putnam 2000, 22–23).

The role of civil society toward the state and within society. The constructive civil society functions do not describe the enabling environment in which they operate. However, it is clear that civil society should not replace the state and other actors within political society. Rather, it should improve the interplay of citizens with the state and achieve a greater level of effectiveness and responsiveness for state institutions (Croissant et al. 2000, 17; Merkel and Lauth 1998, 7; Kumar 1993). Thus, especially when the state is fragile or authoritarian, external support may need to focus, at least initially, on improving the enabling environment for civil society. This might encompass capacity-building for state structures and enforcement of the rule of law.

Service delivery as an entry point. The above-mentioned functions aim to improve the interplay between political and economic systems and the people, thus ensuring democratic, participatory decisionmaking in society. Thus, service delivery is only seen as a function in its own right when used as an entry point for political civil society functions, which in any event should be based on a careful assessment of whether the service is indeed a good entry point for wider functions and objectives.

* * *

This chapter summarizes the history of the concept of civil society, as well as the debates on civil society in various contexts, mainly political transition, development cooperation, and violent conflict. It distilled the main approaches for analyzing and understanding civil society. On this basis, the chapter elaborates on an extended functional approach that captures the different meanings of civil society in one model for conducting empirical research on civil society's contribution for different purposes.

Note

The author thanks Thania Paffenholz for the intensive discussions and inspiring comments on the analysis and understanding of civil society. Special thanks go to Siegmar Schmidt and Roberto Belloni for their in-depth comments, to Mariya Nikolova for her assistance with the sections on civil society in Asia and the Middle East, and to Reiner Forster for his initiative in starting this research.

2

Civil Society and the State

Kjell Erling Kjellman
and Kristian Berg Harpviken

Within the peacebuilding paradigm, there has been a strong focus on strengthening and building state institutions, with parallel initiatives aimed at promoting civil society. This is not surprising given that the modern democratic state is seen as both a logical unit of analysis and a solution to political disorder, a notion that became entrenched during the second half of the twentieth century as Western states enhanced their standing following World War II (Milliken 2003). Reinforced by scholarly thinking in the 1950s and 1960s, leaders of burgeoning democracies in Latin America and Asia came to believe in the power of the state to shape societies and economies. Great expectations regarding the creation of bureaucratic state organizations became the recipe for achieving social order, with an emphasis on the power of a state independent of powerful social groups. The belief in the sweeping capacities of governance institutions remained prominent well into the 1980s, informed in part by the efforts of social scientists (Migdal 2001).

The concept of civil society has a long tradition within the social sciences and has experienced a resurgence given its presumed role in facilitating development, harnessing the power of governments, and enacting social change more generally (Colás 2002). Among policymakers, renewed interest in the interaction between the state and civil society finds its roots in Western liberal theory and the concept of "liberal peace."

This focus on states and civil society has occurred in tandem with the intensified involvement of the international community in attempting to rebuild so-called failed states and to lay the institutional groundwork to promote economic development (Bates 2008; Englebert and Tull 2008; Tschirgi 2004, 4–5; Milliken 2003). The eagerness of the international community, however, has not necessarily been guided by a research-based understanding of the challenges and potential pitfalls facing such efforts. Within scholarly research, the state has figured heavily by virtue of its presumptive capacity to shape political processes, its role vis-à-vis society writ large, and its relative strength in various policy domains, as well as in response to the need to account for the factors that have shaped the formation and organization of states in different parts of the world (Evans et al. 1985). As Thania Paffenholz and Christoph Spurk (2006) have pointed out, the effectiveness of civil society as a positive force in peace-building is reliant on the framework of a functioning state.[1] Simultaneously, the state, in all its constituent parts, is itself deeply embedded in civil society.

The role of the state and its relationship to civil society raise a central concern. Although research tends to operate with a clear separation, focusing exclusively either on the state or on civil society, this is more often a point of emphasis than empirical reality. From the sociohistorical perspective, lines between the state and civil society are blurred, with each being integral in shaping the other. There is broad recognition that civil society–state interaction was vital in the formation of European nation-states, as well as in non-Western contexts. Nonetheless, there has been a tendency to conceive of the state and civil society as two autonomous spheres (see Chapter 1 in this volume), a view that implicitly informs parts of the present-day statebuilding agenda. In reality, where states have developed as a result of sociohistorical processes, they bear the imprint of civil society. State institutions, for instance, will tend to be structured as a result of the enfranchisement of civic actors, embodied in legal rights, political representation, and interest mediation. Furthermore, even though the role of civil society has figured heavily in the discourse on statebuilding, this is far less frequently reflected in practice. Rather, the emphasis has tended to be on the engagement of political elites and the construction of recognizable—at least from a Western perspective—political institutions (Paris and Sisk 2008).

In this chapter we seek to provide an understanding of why statebuilding by external actors is often problematic; we discuss the relationship between states, statebuilding, and the role of civil society in postconflict situations. We sketch out how social science analyses have conceived of the development of modern states and review externally driven statebuilding projects. In the final sections, we reflect on the linkages between the state and civil society, indicating the manner in which conflict transforms the relationship between the state and civil society across the political, economic, and security dimensions.

State Formation in Historical Perspective

Writing at the beginning of the twentieth century, Max Weber formulated the most enduring definition of the state. In Weber's formulation, a state can be most concisely conceived of as a central authority structure with legitimate means over coercion within a given territory (Weber 1978). In extending this definition, a decisive criterion for the modern, democratic nation-state is that there is a break between governmental authority and inherited privilege in the hands of elites—in essence a separation between the social structure and the exercise of judicial and administrative functions. This includes the expansion of a uniform central authority across the entire national territory through the construction of a modern bureaucratic infrastructure, replacing patrimonial practices and personnel (Bendix 1977, 128). In an ideal sense, fully functioning states have the ability and the capacity to enforce political decisions through hierarchic steering with authoritative decisionmaking and material sovereignty (Risse and Lehmkuhl 2006, 9).

Social-science analyses of state formation have been varied and far-reaching. For Weber, state formation resulted from the struggle between patrimonial rulers and their staffs over control of the "means of administration," such as the rights to and income from offices (Weber 1978). War and preparations for war are seen as having played a key role in consolidating state institutions. One of the earliest state theorists, Otto Hintze, argues that military pressure—war itself as well as the threat of war—was what drove rulers in medieval and early modern Europe to concentrate power in their own hands through the construction of professional bureaucracies capable of administering standing armies and the infrastructure to support them (Hintze, 1970 [1906]). Financing standing armies encouraged the growth of urban economies and accompanying bureaucracies as rulers needed a means to extract taxes in order to finance standing armies. This, in turn, proved instrumental to the development and expansion of administrative, financial, military, and judicial infrastructures as a way to administer preparations for war (Tilly 1990 [1975]).

A somewhat different line of reasoning points to state formation as the product of class struggle and the advancement of modern capitalism. In the early modern period, capitalism was sustained through the formation of a stable political and institutional framework that could foster and sustain economic interests. This process, in part, entailed the deliberate efforts of elites as a way to promote representation and their own legitimacy. There is little consensus as to what makes a state legitimate in the eyes of its citizens; therefore, one of the tasks facing states has been to find ways in which to legitimate its standing, such as through increased (real or perceived) democratization—for instance, by creating democratic institutions and including previously disenfranchised groups. One important example: states in post–World War II Europe sought to strengthen legitimacy by granting new rights to previously excluded groups (Milliken and Krause 2003). Disenfranchised groups have also sought to expand the institutional role and domain of the nation-state, claiming new rights based on previously excluded identities or claims, such as through social mobilizations from below in the quest for equal citizenship (Bendix 1977).

Scholarly work on state formation outside Europe and North America has, to a greater extent, recognized the role of civil society in shaping state institutions. In contrast to Europe at the time of state formation, nations in other parts of the world have been characterized by somewhat more complex divisions along tribal, kinship, ethnic, and religious lines. Whereas the class structure in Europe tended to consolidate the position of elites, rulers in developing countries resorted to the use of despotic power due to their inability to create efficient state administrative apparatuses, thus limiting the development of infrastructural power, a problem exacerbated by the legacy of colonialism. The composition of society found in many non-Western contexts—with the fragmented patterns of kinship and tribal organization—also makes it far more difficult for states to consolidate power and implement a prefectoral system. As Joel S. Migdal (1988) has argued, strong postcolonial states emerged in cases where the colonial power encouraged the consolidation of groups under a single aegis; in instances where the colonial power pursued a strategy of fragmenting social control at the local societal level, a weak state emerged (Thomas 2003). At the same time, it has often been noted that the conceptualization of civil society in non-Western contexts tends to operate with a somewhat restricted notion of civil society, focusing primarily on its more visible and readily recognizable—at least from a Western perspective—elements (Kasfir 1998; Harpviken and Kjellman 2004).

The State-in-Society

A problem is that many state-oriented scholars have followed Weber's emphasis of the state as an autonomous organization vested with the means through which to dominate, but in the process they neglected the role of civil society. This view still holds sway with respect to present statebuilding efforts. State formation processes are by definition ongoing and incomplete: "even modern Western European states today do not always reach the Weberian pinnacle in which a rationalized central bureaucracy enjoys a monopoly of organized violence over a given territory and population" (Milliken and Krause 2003, 3). This point is even more relevant in other parts of the world. States labeled as "failed" states on the African continent never resembled the ideal type of the modern Western polity even prior to their disruption (Englebert and Tull 2008, 111–112).

In practice, however, what we now conceive of as civil society played an active role in shaping state formation, although in a very different form from what we recognize in contemporary societies; states, in turn, played a key role in shaping civil society. The formation of states, as many of these accounts point out, resulted from a process of contestation among ruling elites and societal interests, a feature that characterizes modern Western democracies as well as those in non-Western contexts to the present day. As a result, what we now consider developed states—such as those in Europe—became so through a continual process of contestation and negotiation, engaging statemakers and various societal groups. In this respect, the key to understanding state formation lies in the interaction between those seeking power, organized societal interests, and the composition of social cleavages.

While Weber sought to describe an ideal-type state, a lofty level of functioning that few would in reality attain, scholars and practitioners have often conflated the ideal with reality: "Weber's use of an ideal type state monopolizing legitimate force and ruling through rational laws gives scholars precious few ways to talk about real-life states that do not meet this ideal. Weber's definition has the state firing on all cylinders, and, while he certainly did not mean the ideal type to be taken as the normal type, this is precisely what has happened in subsequent scholarship" (Migdal 2001, 14). As Migdal goes on to argue, the problem arises because states are continually measured against an ideal that few are likely to achieve. Moreover, it provides little room to theorize about the negotiation, interaction, and practice that goes on in society, and it provides no space for conceiving of arenas of competing sets of rules apart from casting them as negatives, conceptualized as failures, nonstates, or weak states (Migdal 2001, 15). Although the elite-capitalism perspective goes somewhat farther in according societal groups an active role in state formation, it nevertheless places the role of elites and the ruling class at the forefront.

Conceiving of the state as embedded in a matrix of social interaction can provide a way out of this somewhat myopic view. While theorists such as Otto Hintze and Max Weber conceptualized the state as an autonomous actor within society, elite-capitalists argued for a more society-centered view of the state. The so-called state-in-society approach extends this line of reasoning and, in the process, posits an alternative to Weber's classic conceptualization. Migdal (2001, 15–16) defines the state-in-society as "a field of power marked by the use and threat of violence and shaped by (1) *the image of a coherent, controlling organization in a territory, which is a representation of the people bounded by that territory,* and (2) *the actual practices of its multiple parts.*"[2] Here, the state is seen in terms of two key aspects: images and practices. The *image* of a state refers to the perception of a dominant, integrated, autonomous entity that maintains control over a territory, establishing rules or permitting others to make rules in certain circumstances (e.g., business, clubs, and organizations). *Practices* are the repeated acts of states and leaders over time that serve to reinforce and validate the territorial element of state control, as well as the social separation between the state and other social institutions (Migdal 2001, 18).

The state-in-society perspective has a number of implications for understanding the relationship between civil society and the state. It contends that the state is embedded in societal and cultural practices and is rooted in broader societal traditions. It is, therefore, difficult to divorce the way the state is composed from its broader context; the focus on images suggests that the way in which citizens will perceive the state differs between contexts. From an analytic standpoint, this opens the door for making contestation between ruling elites, political actors, and various societal actors—including civil society actors—the unit of analysis. States may not be as cohesive and unitary, as is often posited by the Weberian ideal. Thus the focus shifts to the dynamic interaction between societal groups as they compete for political power and influence, viewing the outcomes of this contestation as the key in state formation. Moreover, the focus on contestation is consistent with present-day democratization processes, as, for example, social movements mobilize in order to increase citizens' rights and privileges, or as European states attempt to incorporate new ethnic and religious minorities.

The experience of statehood in non-Western contexts underscores the perspective that Migdal introduced. Approaches that seek to posit a clear separation between the state, on the one hand, and civil society on the other, whereby civil society is seen purely as playing a mediating role between the state and citizens, do not capture the negotiation process that characterizes state formation (Skocpol et al. 2000; Evans 1995; Janoski 1998). Civil society is often portrayed as creating the social capital (cooperation and trust) for effective state performance. The ability of civil society to mediate between state institutions and the concerns of citizens, as well as generating civic cooperation and trust, is dependent on a state that is effective in formulating rules and regulations that allow civil society to develop (Jalali 2002, 123). In other words, the involvement of civil society groups in decisionmaking and policymaking processes is contingent on institutional guarantees for participation, along with state structures democratic enough to facilitate a constructive role for civil society. Although the role of civil society varies from context to context, some of the more central tasks of civil society (emphasized by Spurk in Chapter 1 of this volume) are the articulation of citizen concerns, advocacy, community-building, and the provision of necessary services. Institutional analysts have further pointed out that creative government action has the potential to foster social capital, and the linking of mobilized citizens to public agencies can promote government efficacy through a combination of strong public institutions and organized communities (Evans 1995, 30).

The state-in-society approach can be instrumental in understanding the oft-posited dichotomy between "strong" and "weak" states. In this view, states are not inherently strong or weak as a function of their institutional composition, but rather as a reflection of the underlying social structure. In societies with fragmented social control, states are likely to be characterized by the control of so-called strongmen: local leaders who exert an undue influence on institutions, bureaucrats, and officials. When such structures are weak, state officials are provided a greater opportunity to apply uniform rules and policies—those of the state—and are more able to pursue broad policy and social agendas. In this respect, weak or ineffective political institutions are not random or necessarily geographically determined. Rather, they are systematic from the standpoint of how power, wealth, and social control are distributed in society (Migdal 2001, 58–94). Thus, constructing political organizations with the hope that they will evolve into effective and democratic institutions with time is not sufficient. Instead, the key to building viable state institutions lies in addressing underlying issues of power disparities and social control.

"Creating" New States Through Statebuilding

Although the collapse of the Soviet bloc may have defused the potential for conflict between the world's superpowers, it precipitated a new wave of unrest and civil conflict in other parts of the world (Harbom and Wallensteen 2007). The result was a series of civil conflicts that led to extended interventions by the international community. Since the end of the cold war, the number of states under postconflict international tutelage has subsequently been on the rise (Hänggi 2005). International actors have frequently operated with a comprehensive—and often self-imposed—mandate to influence social and political affairs in postconflict contexts (Caparini 2005). One central critique of many initial peacebuilding schemes is that they failed to build institutional foundations for sustainable governance (Paris 2004). Thus, agencies such as the United Nations began to emphasize the construction of legitimate state institutions in an effort to promote lasting peace and to prevent the resumption of violence. This has occurred in tandem with—at least at the policy level—promoting the role of civil society, recognizing that states are rarely effective in the absence of strong societies, whereby local ownership and local-level processes come to be seen as integral components in promoting the efficacy of governments (Paris and Sisk 2008; Evans 1995, 30).

These efforts can be said to be anchored in a Weberian notion of the state, emphasizing state development at the institutional level, focused on the rule of law and legitimacy. Current statebuilding initiatives are based on the notion that cooperation between international and domestic leaders, the mobilization of sufficient resources, and the involvement of citizens represent the key to building democratic national institutions (Ghani and Lockhart 2008). However, statebuilding endeavors tend to rely heavily on quick fixes such as rapid elections and economic privatization. Efforts have been aimed largely at securing optimal institutional conditions for promoting liberal economic reforms and transitioning to democracy as quickly as possible. The emphasis has thus been on the promotion of institutional reforms, good governance, multiparty elections, constitutionalism, the rule of law, human and minority rights, gender equality, economic liberalization, and security-sector reform (Tschirgi 2004; Kolås and Miklian 2008).

On the African continent, for example, there has been a notable failure to build functioning democracies despite concerted efforts to build political institutions as well as civil society. As Nelson Kasfir (1998) has argued, the problem in large part stems from the fact that promoting civil society has entailed a Western bias of what these civil society organizations should be, in the process excluding many ethnic organizations, as some of these are seen as politically unpalatable. However, it is these ethnic organizations that constitute the most vital part of civil society in many parts of Africa. Thus, the failure to promote democracy in Africa has stemmed partially from a failure to recognize and accept social realities (even though supporting them may present donors and other external actors with a dilemma) and the need for political institutions and civil society to reflect one another.

In the statebuilding discourse during the twenty-first century, there has been considerable attention paid to the potential role of civil society (Posner 2004). However, this has not necessarily been converted into practice (Harpviken and Kjellman 2004). Much of the statebuilding exercises can be characterized as elite-driven: attempts at building national institutional frameworks from the top down. This critique feeds into the question of how power is distributed within society. The institutional route to statebuilding preferred by donors and the international community is, at first glance, attractive, as countries with strong institutions are able to regulate power among competing societal groups, at least in the long term. As Marina Ottaway points out, this may prove fallible in the short term: "The model chosen by the international community is a shortcut to the Weberian state, an attempt to develop such an entity quickly and without the long, conflictual and often brutal evolution that historically underlies the formation of states. The advantage of such streamlined transformation is obvious; but the reality suggests that these attempts often stumble on the unresolved issue of power" (Ottaway 2003, 248).

In this sense, newly created institutions possess limited political authority; therefore they are not effective in regulating the power of different political factions. Elections, for example, are not particularly effective in regulating entrenched power struggles in society. States do not fail or become weak because they do not have functioning institutions; rather, they fail because the creation of institutions is not necessarily effective in addressing underlying disparities in power between societal groups (Ottaway 2003; Lake forthcoming).

The new wave of externally driven statebuilding has also triggered a concern that it represents a new form of colonialism, a capitalist exploitation of vulnerable societies. International actors have tended to emphasize the temporary nature of their missions as a way to offset this critique. This, however, is far simpler in cases where the political trajectory of the operation is clearly understood by all parties; it is considerably more problematic where the political trajectory is less evident and where the very presence of international agencies comes under question by local political actors (Chesterman 2007). Two important examples are Afghanistan and Iraq, where the viability of the statebuilding enterprise is under threat as significant parts of civil society express a lack of confidence in foreign benefactors. A more moderate position is taken by other commentators, who argue that long-term commitment to statebuilding is at best tantamount to creating "cultures of dependency" and that an international presence runs contrary to the aim of self-sufficiency (Paris and Sisk 2008).

Nevertheless, discussions do not so much focus on whether the international community should engage in rebuilding postconflict societies and states; instead the focus is on how the international community should engage in rebuilding. There are a number of debates as to the best way forward, what considerations must be taken into account, and whose normative values are promoted (Chandler 2006). External actors can set up organizations, but such organizations can become institutions only to the extent that relevant actors come to believe that they provide solutions to real problems. The dilemma arises when institution-building is defined primarily on the basis of imported blueprints rather than indigenous needs and what local actors perceive as the most prominent issues (Ottaway 2003).

Civil Society and the Conflictual State

Armed conflict almost invariably results in a breakdown in the capacity of state functions. The enduring character of conflicts such as those in Angola, Burundi, the Sudan, Afghanistan, and Sierra Leone, for example, have demonstrated the debilitating effects of conflict on state institutions, resulting from the fact that much of the violence was directed against the existing government or regime (Rotberg 2004). Robert H. Bates (2008) has demonstrated how armed conflict, mediated by a series of underlying factors such as poverty, ethnic composition, and political participation, impact and facilitate the onset of failure on the part of state institutions. The weakening of the capacity and willingness of the state has often been couched in terms of "state failure," although the term *disruption* more accurately captures the various ways in which the state and society are transformed by conflict (Maley et al. 2003; Englebert and Tull 2008).

Disruption as a consequence of armed conflict can refer to the implosion of the state, thereby rendering it vulnerable to actors who seek to gain political influence and authority; the deployment of the power of the state in one's own interest; political competition among groups bearing arms; and the transformation of political parties into military bands controlled by political elites (Bates 2008, 2). A common characteristic is a government's loss of physical control over its territory, or the lack of monopoly on the legitimate use of force. Other traits include the weakening of authority to make and enforce decisions, the inability to provide public services, and the degradation in relationships with other states. Further indicators are human rights abuses, large-scale migration, economic decline, and the delegitimization of the state (Iqbal and Starr 2006). In conflict-ridden states, regimes prey on constituents, resorting to patrimonial rule dependent on a patronage-based system of extraction from citizens; there is a further increase in insecurity among ordinary citizens, in terms of oppression by governments, increased criminal violence, deterioration of infrastructure, and neglect of educational and health systems. Political institutions degrade to the point where only the executive functions, and the legislative branch merely serves to rubber-stamp decisions by the executive. Corruption flourishes, and opportunities for economic gain become rife for a select few, at the expense of society at large, while the state loses its legitimacy—among its own citizens as well as internationally (Rotberg 2004, 5–10). The sum is a set of features that entails a weakening in states' willingness and capacity to act across three critical dimensions: political, economic, and security. Below we explore the consequences for civil society.

In the political dimension, the involvement of civil society in various aspects of political decisionmaking (e.g., policy advice and formulation) is contingent on a degree of policy coherence in the administrative arena, both horizontally (e.g., geographically) and vertically through the various levels of government. During conflict, the state may assume a more authoritarian stance and place restrictions on civil society, such as by redefining the institutional framework. In weak or failed states, the impact on civil society is obviously much different. A lack of state functionality curtails the representation of citizens, rendering institutions less responsive and incapable of formulating and implementing policy or of ensuring democratic rights, effectively constricting the ability of civic groups to channel issues into the political process. Conflict can exacerbate existing cleavages in society, and these can manifest themselves further in civil society, such as in ethnic polarization. One result can be that civil society becomes organized into monoethnic associations, primarily concerned with advancing their own highly politicized agendas, with little contact across societal cleavages (Orjuela 2003). The tendency may be especially pronounced when whole regions are controlled by oppositional groups, as in Sri Lanka, where the regulatory regime in areas controlled by the Liberation Tigers of Tamil Ealam was very different from that of the government (Uyangoda 2008).

Similar issues can manifest themselves along the economic dimension and thereby also have an indirect effect on civil society. Although the relationship between the state and the market has varied greatly in time and space, the state nevertheless performs a number of core functions in regulating and securing the market. First and foremost, the state seeks to establish institutional guarantees and a predictable set of rules for the expansion and transfer of capital in various forms. When these institutional conditions are disrupted, there is a greater risk for the informalization of economic transactions, thereby allowing elites to more easily secure resources for self-enrichment (Ghani and Lockhart 2008, 149–156). Economies of societies in conflict and postconflict situations may also display a greater propensity toward providing goods and services directly and indirectly related to the conflict. This may assume a legal nature, become a part of the so-called gray-sector economy, or enter the illegal black market. NGOs, for example, may be drawn into becoming providers of intelligence and also be used as vehicles for trafficking drugs and laundering money. At the extreme, a potential consequence of a breakdown of institutional market regulation is the emergence of an economic sector that operates parallel to the legal financial market. The emergence of such "war economies" may motivate influential actors to want to maintain a certain level of insecurity and restrict the space in which civil society actors can operate. Alternatively, actors that are economically successful may come to dominate the political discourse, silencing civil society voices that represent genuine interests (Harpviken and Kjellman 2004).

The state's capacity and willingness to provide security for its citizens can also impact civil society at large. During the cold war, "security" was largely conceived in terms of national security, defined in military terms. Since the collapse of the Soviet bloc, however, there has been a rapid shift to broaden the concept of security to include social, political, humanitarian, economic, and environmental concerns. There is thus a growing recognition that the state alone should not be the sole object of security, but must also take into account the security needs of communities and individuals, giving rise to concepts such as "human security" (Burgess and Owen 2004). Strengthening human security by the state is dependent on the capacity and willingness to mobilize political resources (Bryden and Hänggi 2005). In functional states, the civic sphere has become increasingly vital to good-governance practices, providing state institutions responsible for management of the security apparatus with alternative expertise and input to policy while advocating for the security needs of citizens (Florini 2005; Bryden and Hänggi 2005; Caparini 2005; Burgermann 2001).[3]

When states are unable or unwilling to provide for the security of citizens, the role of civil society is jeopardized. Bruce Baker and Eric Scheye (2007) have noted that it is a fallacy to assume that the state is always the main actor in security and justice, as these are functions often carried out by private or informal entities.[4]

Nevertheless, a fundamental assumption in functioning democracies is that the state is entrusted with the task of protecting its citizens. The presence of nonstate military forces capable of challenging the state army, the transformation of the political process into armed conflict, and heightened crime and violence all effectively serve to constrict the space for civil society. The loss of institutional and political control over the military by states reduces civil society's political role while increasing the influence of military actors in defining the security agenda—what would otherwise be the domain of civic actors. Moreover, the freedom that the public sphere enjoys in an ideal democratic state is also undermined, and the state may utilize force to control opposition and dissent rather than to provide citizens with security.

Fostering and building civil society are challenging under the best of circumstances and are obviously rendered far more difficult when the basic functions of the state break down. In disrupted states, norms of reciprocity and trust are often low. Ideally, the state functions as a guarantor for civil society to flourish; in disrupted states, state institutions may either be weak or controlled by special-interest groups. In an ideal setting, individual citizens tend to be more willing to devote time and resources to the associational life that characterizes civil society. However, in the face of lawlessness, lack of public services, ineffective security, and so forth, individuals will be far more likely to focus on providing basic needs for themselves and their households, thereby further undermining the potential growth of civic life. More problematical, the civil society organizations likely to emerge tend to be more uncivil than civil. With the collapse of a central authority, opportunities are provided for criminal networks and the emergence of militia groups (Posner 2004).

Somewhat paradoxically, disrupted states can also provide an opportunity for civil society to grow. On one level, while civil society is torn apart by conflict, it also provides citizens with a source of support. Traditional structures become more important as people seek refuge in the familiar when facing upheaval (Harpviken and Kjellman 2004). Civil society is, in this respect, resilient, and new structures will emerge and some existing civil society forms will be reinforced (Harvey 1998, 206–207). In a somewhat different way, civil society can flourish in the absence of the state, provided that the state in question was either repressive or ineffective in the first place. That is, the assumption that states necessarily provide guarantees for civil society is a retreat to the Weberian ideal, one that is actually achieved by few states. In some cases, disruptions to the state can provide the space for civil society groups to emerge and flourish. In Somalia, for instance, it appears that the absence of government has proven better than the repressive institutions that characterized Mohamed Siad Barre's government, allowing local economies and organizations to blossom (Menkhaus 1998; Posner 2004, 247–248).

Positing such different impacts on civil society as a result of state disruption may seem both contradictory and confusing. However, when looking at the way in which civil society is impacted by the state, it is vital to understand the type of state under discussion. For example, disruptions to predatory or authoritarian states may help civil society, whereas disruptions to a developmental state that offers support to civil society are detrimental. Other variables also figure in this process. State disruptions characterized by the emergence of warlords with access to lootable resources, or by external support coupled with minimal local accountability, are likely to lead to the erosion of civil society (Harpviken 2009). States in which the breakdown of government does not lead to widespread chaos can, in contrast, serve to stimulate the development of civil society groups (Posner 2004, 248–249).

Across the political, economic, and security dimensions, therefore, disruptions to the state have the reciprocal effect of altering the relationship between it and civil society. In general, this reduces the space for civic actors to perform their functions, while in other instances it compromises the idealized role of civil society as actors that articulate the concerns of citizens, and channel these into the political process. The relationship between states and civil society, however, is complex. In countries such as Congo, Somalia, Angola, and Ethiopia, the relatively stunted civil society in each nation lacked the unity of purpose needed to resist dictatorship, rendering it more vulnerable to repression and manipulation (Musah 2003). There is also the issue of the relationship between civil society and warlords, whereby a weak civil society is in competition with armed actors vying for political power (Giustozzi 2005). From the perspective of analysis, this challenges social scientists to move beyond linear thinking on the relationship between states and civil society and instead recognize the complex matrix in which the state is a site of contestation by opposing groups (including those in control of the state apparatus) versus actors in civil society. It would be beyond the scope of this chapter to establish all the possible variants of this often confounding logic; what we have sought to do is point out the main ways in which conflict disrupts the functioning of the state and how these in turn impinge on civil society. The task for scholars and practitioners alike is to further develop the necessary tools for understanding, and eventually for constructively intervening in, this complex relationship.

Concluding Remarks: The Way Forward

The divergent paths to statehood in European nations described by social scientists, as compared to those in non-Western contexts, have had significant implications for the formulation of statebuilding practice. The Weberian view, with its strong focus on institutions and the rule of law, has come to predominate. Policymakers have tended to conflate Weber's ideal type with reality, failing to recognize that most states will reflect deviations from this ideal. This view has also tended to inform policy. A focus on the state and its relation to existing societal cleavages, organization, and composition allows for a more nuanced understanding of what is possible. In non-Western contexts, fragmented societies have made strong state structures difficult to achieve. Cleavages—be they ethnic, religious, tribal, or through power or economic disparities—present a significant challenge for the international community in rebuilding states in the aftermath of conflict. Given the manner in which conflict disrupts the relationship between civil society and the state in terms of the political, economic, and security dimensions, peacebuilding efforts face an even steeper challenge.

A number of practical lessons can be drawn from the discussion presented here. As Paffenholz and Spurk (2006) have stressed, there is a need for a "holistic approach," understanding civil society and states in relation to one another. Other elements, such as the presence of militias, or the overall nature of societal cleavages (e.g., linguistic, ethnic, religious, economic), are also key to analyses. Our review of state formation tells us that the path to a functioning state may be long, unpredictable, and inherently conflictual. These are insights suggesting that statebuilding efforts cannot necessarily create a recipe for intervention based on historical state-formation experiences. The dominant peacebuilding paradigm emphasizes building strong state institutions; however, this may also underestimate the extent to which that paradigm is also a reflection of a civil society that may be weak and divided, yet engaged in contestation for political power. The insight that a state, to be viable, must ultimately mirror the society that it represents brings to the fore several dilemmas that scholars and practitioners have barely begun to address. The state-in-society approach offers a way to recognize the interlinkages that exist between the state and civil society.

Notes

We are grateful for comments on earlier drafts of this chapter from Roberto Belloni, Mariya Nikolova, Thania Paffenholz, and Christoph Spurk. The authors are fully responsible for any errors or omissions.

1. See also Harpviken and Kjellman (2004).

2. Emphasis in original.

3. In describing this relationship, scholars have invoked concepts such as "multilevel governance" (Sikkink 2005; Marks and McAdam 1999).

4. For instance, in Africa, customary courts are the dominant form of regulation of disputes (Baker and Scheye 2007, 512).

3

Civil Society and Peacebuilding

Thania Paffenholz

Within peacebuilding theory and practice, the involvement of civil society seems to be undisputed.[1] While the origins of the notion of civil society are found in democracy theory and in Western philosophy (see Chapter 1 in this volume), the understanding of civil society as it applies specifically to peacebuilding has yet to be adequately explored.

Any attempt to unpack our understanding of civil society's role in peacebuilding is challenging for many reasons. First, the essential meaning of peacebuilding is contentious in both theory and practice. Differing understandings of the underlying concept of peace determine the ways in which to achieve peace. Moreover, the concepts of peace and peacebuilding are deeply embedded in societies with varying cultural practices, which might in turn influence the understanding of those concepts. Second, because the dominant concept for international peacebuilding today is the Western concept of liberal peace—especially as applied in so-called postconflict societies—other concepts are often difficult to distinguish. Third, and as a consequence of the aforementioned, civil society can take different roles in contributing to peacebuilding depending on the context and understanding of peacebuilding. Fourth, we face a real deficit of theories about the concept of civil society in peacebuilding. Fifth, there is little empirical evidence about the relevance and effectiveness of civil society in peacebuilding, as it is a concept strongly permeated by normative values. Essentially, civil society is often seen as the "good society," inevitably contributing to peacebuilding in a positive way. Thus, any attempt to approach the issue in question needs to unpack existing hypotheses in theory and practice and to confront them with the scant empirical evidence that we find in the existing research.

The objective of this chapter, therefore, is to provide an overview of the state of affairs in understanding the role of civil society in peacebuilding theory and practice. The chapter is organized into four parts: an overview of the origins of the concept of peacebuilding, focusing on civilian forms of peacebuilding; a discussion of theoretical notions of peacebuilding; a look at the practice of civil society peacebuilding, based on the existing empirical evidence originating in debates found in the literature and among practitioners (as there is no explicit theory of peacebuilding);[2] and a call for greater theorizing and for more empirical evidence that will allow the testing of existing hypotheses against the realities of civil society peacebuilding.

Understanding Peacebuilding

Peacebuilding is essentially the process of achieving peace. Depending on one's underlying understanding of peace, peacebuilding differs considerably in terms of approaches, scope of activities, and time frame. The term *peacebuilding* and related concepts are used in research and practice with varying understandings and definitions.[3]

Although all societies from early history onward have created mechanisms and institutions to build peace, be they councils of elders or religious leaders or other organized forums,[4] the institutionalization of peacebuilding in international law emerged only in the late nineteenth century.[5] This process started with the Hague peace conference in 1898, was followed by the foundation of the League of Nations in the wake of World War I, and finally resulted in the creation of the United Nations at the end of World War II, with the main objective to monitor and support world peace through mediation, facilitation, good offices, and arbitration between states. The main protagonists involved in this process were nation-states, as the organization of the United Nations reflected (Cortright 2008, 40–43; Chetail 2009, introduction). Civil society engagement, especially in the context of international conflicts, was originally considered to complicate the peacebuilding efforts of professional diplomats (Berman and Johnson 1977). One exception was the involvement of the Quakers (Curle 1971).

The notion of peacebuilding in the twentieth century was also influenced by the nonviolence and peace movements. The roots of these movements date to the Enlightenment and the religious-inspired moral reform movements in Great Britain and the United States. The peace movement itself gained momentum before and during the two world wars and was later reshaped in the form of antiwar (e.g., Vietnam) and disarmament movements during the cold war (Cortright 2008, 23–180; Barash and Webel 2002, 28–55 and 512–636).

The debate over peacebuilding gained additional momentum with the establishment of peace research. Although scholars had long carried out peace research within a range of academic disciplines, it was not until the late 1950s and early 1960s that peace research was established as a normative, interdisciplinary policy-oriented academic field. This was exemplified by the foundation of related academic journals.[6] Pioneers in the field were Kenneth and Elise

Boulding in the United States, Johan Galtung in Norway, Adam Curle in the United Kingdom, Ernst-Otto Cziempiel and Dieter Senghaas in Germany, and John Burton in Australia. From its inception, peace research confronted an inherent dilemma. As a policy-oriented science, "peace research must meet the needs of the decision-makers"; this makes proposals for change in the international system practically impossible—"only adaptive change within the system is possible" (Schmid 1968, 229). This statement from the late 1960s holds true today. The contemporary peacebuilding debate is characterized by a strong policy-oriented practitioner discourse within the United Nations and other organizations that tends to incorporate all moderate critiques from research and to ignore the fundamental ones (Heathershaw 2008).

The term *peacebuilding* was first used by Johan Galtung in a 1975 essay. He defined the term as one of three approaches to peace: peacemaking, peacekeeping, and peacebuilding (Galtung 1975, 282–304). His understanding of peacebuilding is based on his conceptual distinction between negative peace (the end of violence) and positive peace (peaceful society at all levels). Galtung developed this concept from an analysis of violence. Whereas negative peace achieves the absence of physical violence through peacekeeping, only positive peace can achieve the absence of structural violence through peacemaking and peacebuilding. Peacemaking in a conflict resolution understanding (discussed later in this chapter) aims at removing the tensions between the conflict parties in addressing the causes of violence. Peacebuilding achieves positive peace by creating structures and institutions of peace based on justice, equity, and cooperation. In consequence, peacebuilding addresses the underlying causes of conflict and prevents their transformation into violence (Galtung 1975, 297–304; Gawerc 2006, 439). Most definitions and understandings of peacebuilding reflect these two antipodes of positive and negative peace as introduced by Johan Galtung.

The use of the term *peacebuilding* started proliferating with its rebirth in a 1992 UN Secretary-General report, titled *An Agenda for Peace*. Many scholars and almost all policy practitioners trace the beginning of peacebuilding to this document, often referring to peacebuilding as a "new" concept (e.g., Heathershaw 2008, 600). *An Agenda for Peace* proposed a new framework to manage international armed conflicts. The Secretary-General's agenda was introduced in light of the stronger UN role after the end of the cold war and the increasing amount of UN-led peacekeeping operations aimed at stabilizing countries after war. In this understanding, peacebuilding is described as "post-conflict peacebuilding."[7] The 1992 UN report focuses on stabilizing negative peace and presents a narrow definition of peacebuilding (Paffenholz and Spurk 2006, 15), that is, preventing the recurrence of violence immediately after armed conflicts and helping a country set parameters for beginning the journey to positive peace. The activities to achieve this goal are: disarming, destroying weapons, repatriating refugees, training security forces, monitoring elections, and advancing the protection of human rights. These measures, which are for the most part associated with short- to medium-term international interventions, do *not* carry with them the notion of sustained efforts to achieve "peace on a durable foundation," as noted in the report. Thus, already in *An Agenda for Peace,* which became the main reference document for the peacebuilding debate to come, peacebuilding emerged as a less than clear concept and has remained so ever since (Haugerudbraaten 1998).

An Agenda for Peace, however, must be seen in light of the historical context during the early 1990s. A number of long-term armed conflicts were being resolved (e.g., Namibia, Mozambique, Cambodia, and El Salvador), and there was hope that the world would become a more peaceful place due to the perception that most past conflicts had been proxy conflicts of the cold war. The wars in Somalia and Yugoslavia and the genocide in Rwanda brought such optimism to a harsh end. The result was a reconceptualization of peacebuilding with a wider understanding of the concept as exemplified in the 1995 supplements to *An Agenda for Peace.* In those documents, peacebuilding is understood to include preventative measures (Boutros-Ghali 1995), which are not necessarily related to peacekeeping operations. Thus, peacebuilding as a concept acquired a broader meaning. The international discussions in research and policy practice ever since have focused mainly on two different understandings of peacebuilding, both of which reflect the two antipodes of peace as defined by Galtung.

Liberal and Sustainable Peacebuilding

The understanding of *liberal peacebuilding,* which came out of the debates during the mid-1990s, is a follow-up to the concepts in *An Agenda for Peace.* As such, it focuses on the democratic rebuilding of states after armed conflict and is based on the concept of the democratic/liberal peace going back to the works of Immanuel Kant. In his 1795 work, *Zum Ewigen Frieden* ("Perpetual Peace"), Kant laid the foundation for understanding peacebuilding between states based on democratic values (Kant 1995). He argued that the democratic constitution of states correlates with their relatively peaceful behavior vis-à-vis other states. Confirming Kant's arguments, an impressive amount of quantitative research makes a clear, positive causal linkage between democracy and peace (Chan 1997; Ray 1998; Russett and Starr 2000). Democracies do not fight each other (Rummel 1979; Doyle 1983a and 1983b; Small and Singer 1976), because democracies' shared norms of compromise and cooperation prevent conflicts of interests from escalating into violence.[8] R. J. Rummel (1997) extended this research to armed violence *within* states, coming to similar conclusions: democracies have by far the lowest level of internal armed conflict. Interestingly, repressive authoritarian states also have a relatively low level of armed violence, but for different reasons. States in the transitional phase between authoritarian and inclusive democratic governance have the highest levels of armed violence (Hegre et al. 2001). A variation of the "democratic peace" is the debate on "liberal peace," based on the 1776 works of Adam Smith. In his book *An Inquiry into the Nature and Causes of the Wealth of Nations* (A. Smith 1904), he suggested a possible correlation among democracy, economic liberalization, and peace (i.e., the higher the level of a free-market economy in combination with a democratic political system, the higher the chances for peace). Today, liberal peace is an integral part of the democratic peace debate (Xenias 2005, 360), as most democracies are liberal market economies.

Peacebuilding is therefore equated with statebuilding,[9] and the debates focus on the period after large-scale armed violence has ended. Peacebuilding in the largest sense came to entail the quick establishment of security, democratic political structures, and economic reforms. In this understanding, peacebuilding ends when a postconflict country is perceived by the international community as able to guarantee minimum security to its people (thus allowing outside peacekeeping forces to exit), as well as its ability to establish working democratic structures (usually understood as a national government legitimized through internationally observed and recognized elections).

Two lively research discourses surround liberal peacebuilding. The first looks at how effective peacebuilding can be achieved (mainly focusing on short- to medium-term strategies), exemplified in different debates around reaching and implementing peace agreements (Stedman 1997; Walter 1997; De Soto and Del Castillo 1994; Paffenholz 2001a; Fitzduff 2002; Hampson 1996; Call and Cousens 2008) and achieving human security (Owen 2004).[10] The second discourse criticizes the entire concept of liberal peacebuilding. Within these critical debates we find more moderate critics (Paris 1997 and 2004; Lund 2003) and more fundamental ones (David 1999; Featherstone 2000; Duffield 2001; Bendaña 2003; Pugh 2004; Richmond 2005; Mac Ginty 2006; Heathershaw 2008).

Sustainable peacebuilding can be attributed to John Paul Lederach, who developed a framework based on an understanding of peacebuilding that centers on sustainable reconciliation within societies. Thus, according to Lederach, peacebuilding can be achieved through the establishment of structures, processes, and training of people within a generation-long time frame (Lederach 1997). The limitation of this understanding lies in the unclear end and scope of peacebuilding. It allows for almost any activity at any given time (more on this below).

Development cooperation entered the peacebuilding debates in the early 1990s as development actors took on new tasks in response to the challenges posed by postconflict peacebuilding.[11] In the aftermath of the tragic events in Rwanda, research showed that aid *can* actually do harm in conflict situations and may inadvertently have negative effects on conflict dynamics (Uvin 1998; Anderson 1999; Andersen 2000). Thus, the development community has engaged in debates over the links among armed conflict, peace, security, and development. We find here policy/operational–oriented frameworks that explore the development-conflict-peace nexus and provide processes, approaches, and tools to integrate a peacebuilding lens into development interventions (Bush 1998; Anderson 1999; Paffenholz and Reychler 2007).

Moreover, there is a debate on aid effectiveness in fragile and conflict countries. This discourse is based on the assumption that aid is effective only when recipient countries adopt sound policies and nurture effective institutions (OECD-DAC 2005). The Paris Declaration on Aid Effectiveness argues that so-called fragile countries—many of them emerging from a war—need special attention. The proposed approach is to "stay engaged, but differently," and to find the best way to deliver support by taking into account the specific development environment (OECD-DAC 2005, 7). This debate is closely linked to the liberal peacebuilding conceptualization.

The development community's involvement in the peacebuilding discourse carries implications. First, many peacebuilding approaches and tools, such as conflict analysis frameworks, were imported into the development field. Second, development actors started to fund or implement interventions that were directly aimed at peacebuilding. This contributed to an increase in peacebuilding activities and the involvement of new actors, mainly NGOs,[12] which also gave rise to the professionalization and commercialization of peace work (Orjuela 2004; Pouligny 2005). Third, the definition and understanding of peacebuilding have been stretched in scope and duration.

During the late 1990s, after almost a decade of intensive debate and practice in peacebuilding, a discussion started on the lessons learned from peacebuilding. This discussion gained importance with the growing reluctance of donors to fund peace interventions that cannot prove a positive impact on the peace process. Many interventions claim long-term impacts on peace processes without being able to demonstrate specific results. As a consequence, donor organizations have become more critical. The Hewlett-Packard Foundation, for example, was one of the largest sources in the United States of funds for research and NGO peace initiatives before it stopped this funding stream. Donor concerns have been expressed in numerous conferences and reports, and as a result many donors are currently drafting evaluation guidelines for peacebuilding interventions (Paffenholz 2005b).

Unlike in the development field, the issue of evaluation has only entered the field of peacebuilding since the late 1990s (Church and Shouldice 2002 and 2003; Fast and Neufeldt 2005).[13] A number of projects have assessed peacebuilding experiences, such as the Joint Utstein Study (D. Smith 2003), which analyzed the peacebuilding efforts of different governments, and the Reflecting on Peace Project, which evaluated the lessons from NGO[14] peacebuilding efforts (Anderson, Olson, and Doughty 2003). There are also several proposals and frameworks on how to evaluate peacebuilding more generally (Fast and Neufeldt 2005; Paffenholz 2005b; Paffenholz and Reychler 2005c; Church and

Rogers 2006) and individual peacebuilding initiatives in particular (D' Estree et al. 2001; Çuhadar 2004).

The relationship among research, experts, and policy practice has also changed since the mid-1990s. There exist different types of peacebuilding experts: there are peace researchers, on the one hand, and experts working for consultancy firms, peacebuilding INGOs, donor organizations, and agencies on the other. Although few researchers are heavily involved in policy practice as advisers and ghostwriters of essential policy papers, experts from consultancy firms and peacebuilding NGOs are more likely to be involved in planning and evaluation processes and in designing operational tools. However, people also shift between these worlds, working for a few years in one sector and then the other. Some are also fully absorbed into donor and NGO institutions. Researchers from the South are also taking part in this enterprise, often performing the role of local consultants to international assessment and evaluation missions. John Heathershaw argues that this intertwined relationship among research, experts, and policy practitioners has led to a pragmatic peacebuilding practice that takes all moderate critique into consideration (Heathershaw 2008, 613–618). Others (Paffenholz and Spurk 2006, 26) have argued that this has additionally led to an increasing emphasis on quick results, at the expense of greater conceptual understanding of issues, sound research, and critical academic reflection.

Making Sense of the Debate

In summary, the evolution of the peacebuilding discourse is connected to an underlying understanding of peace. Thus, varying understandings of peacebuilding have emerged, reflecting the tension between negative and positive peace (i.e., taking a narrow or wide understanding of peacebuilding). We find two main paradigms: *sustainable peacebuilding* with a wide understanding, and *liberal peacebuilding* with a short- to medium-term understanding, akin to statebuilding. Although sustainable peacebuilding has received the most attention since the 1990s, liberal peacebuilding is the livelier dispute today. It is important to note that these concepts also have overlapping elements. Although the time frames are different, and the explicit goal of liberal peacebuilding is the establishment of liberal peace, sustainable peacebuilding approaches also reflect many liberal elements of the "good society," based on the work of Kant.

Thus, any attempt to define peacebuilding is almost impossible when acknowledging existing differences. I have decided to use a working definition balancing between the two extremes while also allowing for flexibility:

Peacebuilding aims at preventing and managing armed conflict and sustaining peace after large-scale organized violence has ended. It is a multidimensional effort; its scope covers all activities that are linked directly to this objective across five to ten years. Peacebuilding should create conducive conditions for economic reconstruction, development, and democratization as preconditions for legitimate democratic order, but should not be equated and thus confused with these concepts.

Peacebuilding Theory and Civil Society

In this section I identify how peacebuilding plays within various international relations theories and elaborate on "middle-level theories": conflict management, resolution, and complementary, transformation, and alternative discourses. Finally I trace the role of civil society within these two bodies of theories.

Peacebuilding Within IR Theory

In a nutshell, the focus of all international relations theories is on regulating the international system of states and thus maintaining peace as security, order, or justice.[15] *Realism* focuses on the balance of power among sovereign nation-states based on an understanding that the international system is anarchic and states are driven by interest rather than by idealistic norms. Peacebuilding within realism refers to maintaining stability through hegemonial power and the preservation of interests. In contrast, *idealism* advocates a world regulated by international organizations, norms, and standards. Peacebuilding, therefore, aims at achieving peace between nations based on the establishment of norms and standards and through a super-entity like the United Nations, which can help in regulation and monitoring. A Marxist-inspired *structuralist* IR analysis focuses on justice and equality and critically analyzes the power relations within the system. Peacebuilding in this context is a revolutionary approach to mobilize the masses in order to achieve radical change in the international system. *Poststructural* IR looks into issues of justice, equality, and power relations but emphasizes marginalized actors and discourses. Here, peacebuilding is not about a common meta-narrative but about understanding differences and including the discourses on the everyday peace of ordinary people in international debates in an emancipatory sense.

Peacebuilding within IR theory is often not explicit. The framing of IR theories has, however, inspired the middle-level theories, which deal more explicitly with peacebuilding (even if not all of them refer to the very term).

The Different Schools Within Middle-Level Theories

In previous publications, I have identified four schools of thought that can be distinguished here (Paffenholz and Spurk 2006, 26). Oliver Richmond has also identified four generations of peacebuilding discourses (Richmond 2002 and 2005, 85–123). Merging my own with Richmond's clustering,[16] I will present five schools, which can be viewed as the middle-level theories of peacebuilding. These schools use different terminologies and have different conceptual understandings, approaches, scopes, and actors. Their histories are closely related to the history and evolution of the field of peacebuilding. The different schools have had different influences on peacebuilding, and practice has tended to adopt elements from different schools. The conceptual frameworks and terminologies often create confusion, and the origins are at times unclear. These five schools are: conflict management, conflict resolution, complementary, conflict transformation, and the emerging school of alternative discourse in peacebuilding.[17]

Since the end of the Cold War in the early 1990s, mediation was the dominant approach to peacebuilding, but from the mid-1990s onward it became clear that peacebuilding required additional approaches. Therefore, the first three schools originally focused on mediation.

The conflict management school. The approach of conflict management is to end wars through diplomatic initiatives. This is the oldest school of thought, closely linked to the institutionalization of peacebuilding in international law. Peacebuilders, according to the logic, are external diplomats from bilateral or multilateral organizations. The theoretical approach is referred to as "outcome-oriented." It aims to identify and bring to the negotiating table leaders of the conflict parties. Its main focus is the short-term management of the armed conflict. Recent examples include the Sudan and the Aceh peace accords (Miall et al. 1999, 158–168; Paffenholz 1998, 22–41 and 2001a, 75–81; Richmond 2005, 89–96).

Power mediation is a special form of conflict management, with the same criteria as the outcome-oriented approach but including the possibility of exerting external power on the parties, including financial "carrots" and/or military "sticks" (Trouval and Zartman 1985, 263). Examples include the 1995 US-mediated peace treaty for Bosnia, when the United States linked reconstruction support to a peace agreement and threatened the bombing of the Bosnian-Serb artillery if no agreement was reached. Another example is Haiti, when former US president Jimmy Carter mediated an agreement as US troops prepared to intervene.

The largest contribution of the conflict management school is its focus on those in power who have the ability to end large-scale violence through negotiated settlement. The conflict management school has been criticized because mediators tend to concentrate solely on the top leadership of the conflict parties (Lederach 1997); often ignore the need for facilitation by different internal and external actors before, during, and after negotiations (Paffenholz 1998 and 2000); are not always neutral in internal conflicts (Ropers and Debiel 1995); and overlook deeper causes, thus being unable to guarantee the long-term stability of any peace agreement (Hoffmann 1995). Conflict management approaches today move beyond the exclusive concern with securing a peace agreement to focus on conditions for the successful implementation of postconflict peacebuilding. Thus, it is now possible to distinguish between first-generation (Crocker, Hampson, and Aal 2001) and second-generation approaches to conflict management (Stedman 2002).

The conflict resolution school. The conflict resolution school aims at solving the underlying causes of conflict and to rebuild destroyed relationships between parties. Here, relations need to be rebuilt not only between the top representatives of the conflict parties but also within society at large. This school was established within academic research during the 1970s, adopting strategies from sociopsychological conflict resolution at the interpersonal level. Early on, peacebuilders were mainly Western academic institutions carrying out conflict resolution workshops with nonofficial actors close to the conflict parties (Fisher 1997; Kelman 1992).

Workshops were designed to rebuild relationships between the representatives of the conflict parties and to work with them to solve the causes of the conflict. The theoretical foundations of the approach are to be found in John Burton's concept of human needs (Burton 1969) and Azar's concept of protracted social conflicts (Azar 1990).

As the approach evolved, the scope of actors was broadened. An elite-based civil society approach became a general civil society and grassroots approach, including a range of actors, from individuals to communities to organized civil society groups.[18]

Given the inclusion of more actors and the broadening scope of activities, it has become difficult to trace the trajectory of this approach. The common features of modern (second-generation) conflict resolution approaches can be identified as follows: All involved actors aim to address the root causes of conflict with relationship-building and long-term resolution-oriented approaches; and they do not represent a government or an international organization (Bailey 1985; Stedman 1993). The main suppliers are international NGOs, often working with national and local NGOs. The main activities are dialogue projects between groups or communities, peace education, conflict resolution training to enhance peacebuilding capacity of actors from one or different groups, and conflict resolution workshops.

The biggest contribution of the conflict resolution school is its perspective on peacebuilding as identifying human needs and—perhaps most important, as Richmond notes (2005, 100)—listening to the voices of unofficial and ordinary people. The conflict resolution school has been criticized from a conflict management perspective. Improving communications and building relationships between conflict parties do not necessarily result in an agreement to end the war (Bercovitch 1984). The approach was also criticized for assuming that working with civil society and the grassroots does not automatically spill over to the national level (Richmond 2001). Another critique states that the approach does not acknowledge cultural or other societal differences (Richmond 2005, 99), does not make participants sufficiently aware of issues of structural violence, and is essentially a part of the liberal peace toolkit (Richmond 2005, 100–101).

The complementary school. This school focuses on the possible congruence between the conflict management and conflict resolution schools. By putting the strength of these two schools together, the logical inference is that peacebuilding is needed both from the top and from below. In the early to mid-1990s, different approaches sought to overcome the dichotomy between conflict management and conflict resolution. The first was Ronald Fisher and Loraleigh Keashly's (1991) "contingency model for third party intervention in armed conflicts," which aimed at identifying the appropriate third-party method and the timing of interventions. Based on Friedrich Glasl's (1982 and 1990) "conflict escalation model," the approach is to deescalate the conflict from phase to phase. When a conflict is in the early escalation phase, it is the appropriate time for resolution-oriented approaches; in contrast, conflict management approaches, like official mediation, should be used when the conflict has already escalated. After a peace accord has been reached, it is time to revert to resolution-oriented approaches.

Based on quantitative empirical research, Jacob Bercovitch and Jeffrey Z. Rubin (1992) developed an approach similar to the contingency model but shifted the perspective from approaches to actors. In this approach it is not important which mediators are the most effective, but rather who is more effective at different stages of the conflict. The results are similar to those of Fisher and Keashly in that the more the conflict escalates, the more powerful the third party should become.

The "multi-track diplomacy" approach by Louise Diamond and John McDonald (1996), while recognizing that different approaches and actors are needed to reach peace, seeks to draw a clearer distinction between the different approaches and actors by adopting a "track" concept. Track 1 involves diplomatic peacebuilding initiatives by governments and is in line with the conflict management school. Track 2 represents the original conflict resolution school. The other tracks try to cluster other relevant actors.

The complementary school received attention in scholarly circles for overcoming the conflict management–conflict resolution dichotomy (Nan 2008). The main critique of this approach points out that, in practice, different types of interventions can take place at the same time (Bloomfield 1995; Webb et al. 1996; Paffenholz 1998 and 2000; Fitzduff 2000)[19] and it does not fully address the issue of coordination (Paffenholz 1998).

The conflict transformation school. This school focuses on the transformation of deep-rooted armed conflicts into peaceful ones, based on a different understanding of peacebuilding. It recognizes the existence of irresolvable conflicts and therefore suggests replacing the term *conflict resolution* with the term *conflict transformation* (Rupesinghe 1995). John Paul Lederach developed a comprehensive and widely discussed transformation-oriented approach (Lederach

1997). Building on the complementary school, Lederach also sees the need to resolve the dilemma between short-term conflict management and long-term relationship building, as well as the resolution of the underlying causes of conflict. His proposal was to build "long-term infrastructure" for peacebuilding by supporting the reconciliation potential within societies. In line with the conflict resolution school, he sees the need to rebuild destroyed relationships, focusing on reconciliation within society and on strengthening society's peacebuilding potential. Third-party intervention should concentrate on supporting internal actors and coordinating external peace efforts. Sensitivity to the local culture and a long-term time frame are also necessary.

This approach focuses on peace constituencies by identifying midlevel individuals and groups and empowering them to build peace and to support reconciliation. Empowerment of the middle level is assumed to influence peacebuilding at the macro and grassroots levels. Lederach divides society into three levels, which can be approached through different peacebuilding strategies. Top leadership can be accessed by mediation at the level of states (Track 1) and by the outcome-oriented approach. Midlevel leadership (Track 2) can be reached through more resolution-oriented approaches, such as problem-solving workshops or peace commissions, and with the help of partial insiders (i.e., prominent individuals in society). The grassroots level (Track 3), however, represents the majority of the population and can be reached through a wide range of peacebuilding approaches, such as local peace commissions, community dialogue projects, or trauma-healing.

Building on a decade of work in the Horn of Africa, the conflict transformation approach of the Swedish Life and Peace Institute adopts a community-based, bottom-up peacebuilding approach, expanding Lederach's midlevel approach to the grassroots track. This also combines in-country peacebuilding with peacebuilding advocacy at the international level and thus conceptually relates to the debate on global civil society (Paffenholz 2003 and 2006b).

The largest contribution of the conflict transformation school is its shift in focus from international to local actors. It therefore puts even more emphasis on civil society and ordinary people than does the resolution school. Whereas in the resolution school these actors are subject to outsiders' interventions, within the conflict transformation school they are at the center of peacebuilding. The role of outsiders is thus limited to supporting internal peace constituencies, rather than playing a key intervening role. However, with the development of second-generation conflict resolution approaches starting in the mid-1990s, the difference has become marginal. The conflict transformation school has not been subjected to any fundamental critique for a while.[20] On the contrary, it has become the leading school for scholar-practitioners and the international peacebuilding NGO community (see below). This author, when analyzing the validity of the approach in the Mozambican (Paffenholz 1998) and Somali peace processes (Paffenholz 2003 and 2006b), points to several deficiencies: first, the linkage between the tracks is not sufficiently elaborated, as conflict management is still necessary but underconceptualized in Lederach's approach; second, external actors should not only support insiders directly but also consider the wider peacebuilding arena, and they might also lobby for peacebuilding vis-à-vis other actors like regional or international governments (Paffenholz 1998, 213–215); third, civil society organizations can also take up a conflict management approach, as exemplified by the churches in the Mozambican peace process (Paffenholz 1998, 213–215); fourth, there is a need to understand traditional values and local voices in peace processes as already emphasized in Lederach's approach (however, it needs also to be critically analyzed, for these structures are often transformed by modern developments; Paffenholz 1998, 76); and fifth, the main focus on the middle level might not work in all societies, and the option to work directly with the grassroots in a bottom-up community peacebuilding approach should be better conceptualized, as exemplified by the work of the Life and Peace Institute in Somalia (Paffenholz 2003 and 2006b).[21]

John Heathershaw adds another critical dimension: as Lederach's approach is essentially based on a Christian religious understanding of peace derived from the New Testament—which he explores in more detail in his later works (Lederach 2005)—Heathershaw argues that Lederach's approach has transplanted the "religious fringes into the secular mainstream" (Heathershaw 2008, 608). A. B. Featherstone points to the lack of a power analysis in Lederach's approach (Featherstone 2000, 207). Other critiques have also elaborated on some of the negative consequences of the practical application of the approach (Paffenholz and Spurk 2006, 23–26; Richmond 2005, 103–104).

The alternative discourse school. There is an emerging literature analyzing peacebuilding through the lens of discourse analysis and advocating for an alternative approach to peacebuilding (Featherstone 2000; Richmond 2005; Mac Ginty 2006; Heathershaw 2008). By deconstructing the theory and the international practitioners' discourse, they show that the peacebuilding discourse is trapped in the "liberal imperative" (Richmond 2005, 208), as only one model for peacebuilding is normatively accepted, that is, the liberal peace. These authors claim that this kind of peacebuilding has become a self-referential system, which has long lost its connection to the real world and the needs of people. In line with Michel Foucault, the alternative discourse school does not present a meta-alternative[22] but instead points to the need to refocus on the everyday peace of ordinary people (Featherstone 2000; Bendaña 2003; MacGinty 2006, 33–57; Richmond 2005). A. B. Featherstone and Alexandro Bendaña deliver the most radical interpretations: with a power analysis based on Foucault, Featherstone considers the peacebuilding schools as "part of an apparatus of power which attempts to discipline and normalize" (Featherstone 2000, 200). On the basis of an analysis of Southern voices, Bendaña comes to similar conclusions by emphasizing that peacebuilding becomes an inherently conservative undertaking, which seeks managerial solutions to fundamental conflicts over resources and power. Peacebuilding thus attempts to modernize and relegitimize a fundamental status quo respectful of a national and international market economy (Bendaña 2003, 5).

The alternative approach suggested here is one of transformative peacebuilding that leads to a posthegemonic society (Featherstone 2000, 213–214), in which oppressed voices are listened to and respected. It therefore also implies structural changes and the acknowledgment that peacebuilding is mainly a Western enterprise that needs to engage in a serious South-North dialogue. Here we find a resemblance to Habermas's concept of the Herrschaftsfreie Gesellschaft[23] ("a society free of hegemony"; Habermas 1981) and Foucault's concept of *gouvernmentalité*[24] ("governmentality"; Foucault 2004), as well as a Marxist IR reading.[25]

The biggest contribution of this emerging alternative-discourse peacebuilding school is its focus on ordinary people, oppressed voices, the analysis of power structures, and an assessment based on realities instead of normative assumptions. There is one main criticism that can be established: while the need to give voice to alternative, oppressed actors is clearly stated within the writings of the above-mentioned authors, most of them[26] do not actually analyze these alternative voices. This seems an inherent contradiction to the very alternative discourse for which these authors advocate. The main focus of these studies is the liberal peace and actors of the international community therein (i.e., Western governments and NGOs, the UN, etc.).

The Role of Civil Society Within the Different Theories

The role of civil society within IR theories and middle-level theories of peacebuilding varies considerably.

In the realist-inspired conflict management school, civil society plays a limited role as nonstate issues are ignored (Richmond 2005, 89; Paffenholz and Spurk 2006, 18). There are exceptions, in which international civil society institutions act as mediators, such as the Comunita di Sant'Egidio in the Mozambique peace negotiations or the Geneva Centre for Humanitarian Dialogue in the first Aceh peace negotiations. When civil society actors become official mediators, their actions and behavior are not different from those of official governmental mediators (Paffenholz 1998, 213–215; Paffenholz and Spurk 2006, 23). Civil society, however, rarely has a seat at the negotiation table based on the assumption that the smaller the number of actors involved, the easier it is to reach agreement. Negotiation theories, especially those based on game theory and the theory of effective communication, confirm this assumption. However, a quantitative research analyzing twenty-two peace negotiations over fifteen years shows a positive correlation between the degree of civil society involvement in peace negotiations and the sustainability of peace agreements (Wanis–St. John and Kew 2006).[27]

Nevertheless, it is a challenge to ensure a broad-based peace process without having too many actors involved in the actual negotiations. One way out is the establishment of parallel civil society forums, as seen in Guatemala during 1994–1996 (Armon et al. 1997; Molkentin 2002) and in the Afghanistan negotiations in 2001 in Germany (Paffenholz 2006a). In both cases, parallel civil society forums had an official mandate to discuss issues and give recommendations to the Track 1 negotiations. Their positions considerably influenced the peace agreements. The selection of civil society representatives, the ample time allowed, and the coordination between the negotiations and the civil society forum were essential to the legitimacy, acceptance, and influence of this type of forum. Although in Guatemala a locally driven process influenced the peace agreement, the case of Afghanistan shows that an externally driven civil society involvement can also be effective,[28] including the ability to play an important role in the postsettlement phase (Paffenholz 2006).

Other approaches try to link the population to the official mediation process through broad information campaigns or public opinion polls (Barnes 2002). Although it is relatively easy to organize communication from the conflict parties to the population, a more serious challenge is the communication flow from the population to the negotiations.

Global civil society can also play an important role by exerting pressure on donors in their home countries to address specific issues of international peacebuilding, to protect national civil society through international awareness, or to support their functioning through knowledge transfer and funding.

Civil society actors are the key protagonists in the idealist-inspired conflict resolution and conflict transformation schools.[29] The latter are additionally being inspired by alternative discourses. The focus of both schools is on the roots of conflict and on relationships between conflict parties and society, and the understanding within both is that such issues can best be addressed by nonstate actors. The main difference is that the resolution school tends to focus on external actors, whereas the transformation school looks mainly at internal actors. Civil society also plays an important role within alternative discourses on peacebuilding. Here more emphasis is put on grassroots emancipation; cultural, gender, and other differences; as well as structural changes of the system through international dialogue and possibly also revolutionary change. Here an emancipated civil society becomes the agent of change through social movements and public communication. In all three schools, there is a linkage among global, national, and local civil society to bring the needs and concerns of ordinary people to national and international agendas. This role is therefore closely linked to Jürgen Habermas's concept of public communication and his understanding of civil society (Habermas 1981 and 1992; see Chapter 1 in this volume).

In summary, civil society plays a role in peacebuilding within most theories. However, the idealist, alternative discourse and Marxist-inspired, middle-level theories put more emphasis on civil society than does the realist-inspired conflict management school; and second-generation conflict management starts to reflect on the involvement of nonstate actors in the negotiation process. Comparing the conceptualization of civil society in political philosophy with the one in democracy theory (see Chapter 1), we see a lack of theorizing around civil society in peacebuilding. Civil society is often seen as one core actor in many of the theories to achieve positive peace. Nevertheless, the underlying reasoning for civil society's peacebuilding role remains largely unclear.

Civil Society Peacebuilding in Practice

This section looks at the practice of civil society peacebuilding, linking the aforementioned discussions to the evidence we find from the implementation of civil society peacebuilding to date.[30]

The first observation is that the rapid growth in civil society peacebuilding initiatives from the mid-1990s onward is not matched by an accompanying research agenda. Only a few publications explicitly deal with the subject. We find the following types of studies:

- Actor-oriented, lessons-learned studies that aim to understand who is doing what (van Tongeren et al. 2005)
- Single actor–oriented studies that analyze the role of particular civil society actors (mostly NGOs) in peacebuilding (Aall 2001; Barnes 2005; Pouligny 2005; Debiel and Sticht 2005; Richmond and Carey 2006; Goodhand 2006)
- Studies that analyze civil society as an actor within the framework of the liberal peace (Bendaña 2003; Paris 2004, 179–211 and 2006; Richmond 2005, 127–148; Heathershaw 2008, 607–609 and 616–618)
- Studies assessing the effectiveness of NGO peace work in general (Anderson, Olson, and Doughty 2003) or evaluating the impact of specific (mostly conflict resolution workshops) civil society initiatives (D'Estrée et al. 2001; Çuhadar 2004; Ohanyan with Lewis 2005; Atieh et al. 2005); moreover, a number of assessments and evaluations of particular projects have taken place (most of them, however, are not publicly available[31])
- Country case studies: Folley (1996) on El Salvador; Paffenholz (2003) on Somalia and (1998) on Mozambique; Belloni (2001) on Bosnia-Herzegovina; Patrick (2001) on Timor-Leste; Orjuela (2003) and (2004) on Sri Lanka; Challand (2005) on Palestine

The existing studies, however, address different research questions and methodologies, complicating the comparison of results and the drawing of conclusions in any meaningful way. Nevertheless, a very general analysis of the above-mentioned studies reveals three main trends.

First, the practice of civil society peacebuilding seems to be influenced by the two previously identified peacebuilding paradigms: liberal peacebuilding and sustainable peacebuilding. Within the framework of liberal peacebuilding, civil society has a clear space as an alternative service delivery supplier when the government is not able to deliver, and also as a guarantor of basic democratic values and principles, such as issues related to human rights and peacebuilding through civil education, training, and advocacy. Thus, the framework of liberal peace gives justification for civil society support, whereas the framework of sustainable peacebuilding gives practitioners directions for how to support civil society. These directions (i.e., theories/hypotheses of change) are strongly linked to the practitioner's interpretation of Lederach's conflict transformation approach. Lederach has offered a complex, comprehensive approach to peacebuilding (Lederach 1997), yet it is mainly his middle-out approach, focusing on the three tracks, that has become reflected in practice. Thus, the empowerment of the midlevel leadership under Track 2 has had considerable influence on the practice of civil society peacebuilding. This has led to a common set of underlying assumptions about what is perceived as working in support of effective civil society peacebuilding. For instance, all sorts of Track 2 initiatives (in practice, these are mainly different conflict resolution approaches performed by national and international NGOs and a few others) will automatically influence peacebuilding at the macro level (in support of the establishment or implementation of peace agreements). This has led to a mushrooming of conflict resolution training and dialogue initiatives, executed mostly by international and national NGOs, which receive the majority of funding.

Second, most studies confirm that there is now general acceptance that national actors should play the leading role in peacebuilding and that the role of outsiders should be limited to support. There is also agreement that civil society peace initiatives are as important as official or unofficial diplomatic efforts. External funding and capacity-building have provided great opportunities for many local organizations (Aall 2001), enabling many new initiatives. Civil society organizations in conflict zones have shown concerns with social justice and development (Richmond 2005, 147). There are many civil society peacebuilding success stories, some of them presented in different studies. Unfortunately, most of them are not based on clear success criteria and transparent methodologies.

Third, besides many positive achievements, most existing studies are critical of NGO[32] peacebuilding initiatives. The main findings point to the crowding out of local efforts and actors (Folley 1996; Paffenholz 2001b, 8–9; Patrick 2001; Belloni 2001 and 2006, 21; Orjuela 2004; Jeong 2005, 215–219; Bendaña 2003; Bush 2005; Pouligny 2005, 499) and the weak membership base and lack of transparency vis-à-vis donors and local constituencies of most new national urban NGOs (Orjuela 2004, 256; Debiel and Sticht 2005, 16–17; Neubert 2001, 63), leading to the conclusion that donor-driven NGO civil society initiatives have limited the capacity to create domestic social capital and ownership for the peace process (Belloni 2006, 21–2). Studies looking into the effectiveness of NGO peace initiatives point to the fact that the assumed theory of change (i.e., supporting Track 2 initiatives automatically goes to the top) does not hold per se. Studies analyzing single conflict resolution workshop initiatives stress the fact that change of individual attitudes does not impact on a wider societal change, as it does not change collective-foe images of the other group in the conflict (Çuhadar 2004; Ohanyan with Lewis 2005). The Reflecting on Peace Project found that only under specific conditions can these initiatives have an impact: either key people must be supported or, alternatively, there must be a large enough number of people to create a critical mass for peacebuilding (Anderson, Olson, and Doughty 2003). Studies explicitly analyzing the practice of civil society peacebuilding with reference to liberal peacebuilding (Paris 2004, 179–211 and 2006, 425; Richmond 2005, 127–148; Heathershaw 2008, 607–609, 616–618; and Bendaña 2003) come to the conclusion that civil society organizations are part and parcel of the *gouvernmentalité* of the liberal peacebuilding grand narrative, as they serve the purpose of implementing the liberal peacebuilding agenda.[33] Heathershaw states that in upholding the principle of impartiality, understood pragmatically as "do no harm," civil society organizations have lost their ability to advocate for radical social change (Heathershaw 2008, 609). Bendaña notes that "liberal donors and accompanying NGOs have evolved sufficiently to now recognize that short and medium term 'conflict-sensitive development' do not, in and of themselves, bring us closer to sustained engagement to long term structural problems and attainment of positive peace" (Bendaña 2003, 20). Roland Paris nevertheless opts for promoting "good civil society" alongside statebuilding (Paris 2004, 194–196).

In summary, although there has been a remarkable growth of civil society peacebuilding, in addition to specific achievements, we often see many critical findings about the effectiveness of NGO peacebuilding. What is missing, however, is a coherent and more systematic picture as to what exactly civil society actors (beyond and including NGOs) can actually contribute to peacebuilding and what main supporting and limiting factors exist.

The Need for Theory and Evidence

Civil society has emerged from a marginal actor in peacebuilding during the cold war (with some exceptions) to an accepted key actor in almost all peacebuilding theories, even more so in peacebuilding policy discourses and practice.

Two main peacebuilding paradigms have emerged: *sustainable peacebuilding* and *liberal peacebuilding*. Both of these concepts are permeated by normative values. Thus, this chapter has tried to unpack the underlying hypotheses in theory and practice and to confront them with the scant empirical evidence found in the existing research. This has revealed some important results.

Although most theories tend to place importance on the role that civil society can play in peacebuilding, Marxist- and alternative discourse–inspired middle-level theories tend to put more emphasis on this role than would be allowed by a more realist-inspired model of conflict management. Despite the fact that second-generation conflict management has started to reflect on the involvement of nonstate actors in the negotiation process, we still lack well-developed theories addressing the relationship between civil society and peacebuilding. This is especially true when looking at the well-developed conceptualization of civil society in political philosophy and democracy theory (see Chapter 1 in this volume). Civil society is often considered within many peacebuilding theories to be a core actor in the attainment of positive peace. Yet, the underlying theory framework by which civil society–driven peacebuilding can be achieved remains largely unclear.

A look at the practice of peacebuilding shows that civil society has a role to play and is an accepted player in peacebuilding. There has even been a proliferation of civil society peacebuilding initiatives. Most studies focus on the role of NGOs and arrive at critical conclusions on the linkages between donors, NGOs, and their local partners. The professionalization of civil society peacebuilding has sidelined indigenous local efforts for social change and peace and has created dependencies from outside interventions. Thus, it becomes difficult to analyze the role and impact on peacebuilding of other civil society actors like unions, associations, and traditional and religious leaders. Moreover, as existing studies address very different research questions, it is difficult to compare their results and draw substantial conclusions on the role of civil society in peacebuilding.

Michael Lund (2003) states that peacebuilding is an undertheorized and overconceptualized concept. The same holds true for civil society peacebuilding, which also lacks sufficient empirical evidence to generate conclusions about its relevance and effectiveness.

To counterbalance these deficiencies, Chapter 4 establishes the theoretical framework for systematically analyzing the role of civil society in peacebuilding, setting the stage for the country case studies in Part 2.

Notes

I would like to thank John Darby, Siegmar Schmidt, Riccardo Bocco, Roberto Belloni, and Christoph Spurk for their comments, as well as Mariya Nikolova, Meghan Pritchard, and Luc-Frédéric Jotterand for their assistance.

1. This chapter follows the definition of "civil society" introduced by Christoph Spurk in Chapter 1 of this volume. It is important to note that civil society comprises much more than NGOs and that some actors are *not* part of civil society (i.e., political parties, the media, and businesses, with the exception of professional associations). It is, however, also important to note that the boundaries are often blurred between the civil, private, political, and business spheres. Nevertheless, for analytical clarity the distinction is necessary.

2. The review of research literature assessing the role of civil society in peacebuilding is based on a study conducted in 2006 (Paffenholz and Spurk 2006). Our project's empirical research started thereafter; see the Preface in this volume.

3. For a survey of different uses of the term within twenty-four governmental and intergovernmental bodies, see Barnett et al. (2007).

4. Most of these mechanisms have focused on community, individual, and societal peacebuilding. For an overview of "traditional conflict resolution" see Boege (2006) and Zartman (2000).

5. For an overview of the institutionalization of peacebuilding in international law, see the introduction in Chetail (2009).

6. The first academic journals were founded in 1957 (*Journal of Conflict Resolution*) and 1964 (*Journal of Peace Research*).

7. The term *postconflict* is somewhat at odds with the notion that conflict is inevitable in any society and can be constructive. Moreover, in many societies after large-scale violence, continuing violence and crime can exist. Therefore, some scholars use the term *postsettlement*. This term is, however, also problematic, because after war there is not always peace agreement (settlement) in place, even though large-scale organized violence has ended. The analysis in this chapter sometimes uses the term *postconflict,* while recognizing its limitations, or refers to "the end of large-scale violence."

8. The Peace Research Institute in Frankfurt (PRIF) is using Kant's framework as an umbrella for the institute's research with the objective to identify antinomies within the concept of democratic peace.

9. The main bulge of literature is taking "An Agenda for Peace" as the starting point for the concept of peacebuilding and the debate surrounding it (Paris 2004, 13–39); see also Heathershaw (2008) and Cousens (2008).

10. For a narrow understanding of the concept of human security, see, e.g., Krause (2004) and Mack (2002); for a wider understanding, see Hampson and Hay (2002) and Alkire (2003).

11. For an overview of the debate, see Paffenholz (2006c). For a more elaborate version in French and German, see *L'Annuaire Suisse de politique de développement* (2006, 19–47).

12. "Civil society" means the civil society at large, including different kinds of actors; see Spurk in Chapter 1 of this volume. In contrast, "NGO" refers to only this specific civil society actor.

13. For an overview of the debate, see Çuhadar, Dayton, and Paffenholz (2008).

14. The focus of the case studies is international NGOs working in conflict zones.

15. For an overview of international relations theories, see Goldstein et al. (2005). For an attempt to conceptualize peace in international relations theory, see Richmond (2008).

16. Richmond distinguishes conflict management, resolution, peacebuilding, and the emerging alternative approaches based on discourse analysis. Although he provides an in-depth analysis of the first two generations, he does not analyze the complementary approaches (cf. Fisher and Keashly 1991; Bercovitch and Rubin 1992, Diamond and McDonald 1996), nor does he analyze the conflict-transformation school as a separate generation. When discussing peacebuilding, he merges theory with the practitioner discourse immediately, thereby moving to a critique of the liberal international peacebuilding agenda (Richmond 2005, 102–111).

17. For summaries of the schools, see Paffenholz (1998, 18–77 and 2000); Paffenholz and Spurk (2006, 20–23); Miall et al. (1999); and Richmond (2005, 90–96).

18. The literature sometimes contains a distinction between more elite-based approaches, focusing on the original concept of high-level conflict resolution workshops (Track 1.5); approaches involving organized civil society (Track 2) and grassroots engagement (Track 3) build on Lederach's track distinction; see discussion below.

19. When analyzing the peace process in Northern Ireland, Bloomfield (1995) and Fitzduff (2000) concluded that the existence of parallel activities of different kinds of actors made the process successful. Paffenholz (1998) comes to the same conclusion in her study on the Mozambique peace process.

20. There has been criticism, but most of it has either not been published or is not in English (Paffenholz 1998, 213–215). Paffenholz's Ph.D. work was published in German, and the English summary in *Peacebuilding: A Field Guide* (Reychler and Paffenholz 2000) does not elaborate on the critique. There had also been many discussions about the applicability of the approach in Somalia among the staff of the Life and Peace Institute's Horn of Africa Program from 1995 to 2000 (Paffenholz 2003).

21. It should be mentioned here that Lederach is very much grassroots-oriented in his fieldwork.

22. "Meta-alternative" refers to an overall normative theoretical explanation of the world, like idealism, realism, or Marxism.

23. Habermas, in his 1981 opus *Theory of Communicative Action* (*Die Theorie des Kommunikativen Handelns*), developed a theory of democratic public space where institutions enable citizens to debate matters of public importance that contribute to an ideal type of society in which actors are equally endowed with the capacities of discourse and recognize each other's basic social equality, and in which speech is undistorted by ideology or misrecognition, which leads to a posthegemonic society with discourses "free of hegemonic and power relations" (in German: *herrschaftsfreier Diskurs in einer herrschaftsfreien Gesellschaft*).

24. Foucault developed his concept of *gouvernmentalité* ("governmentality") during his courses at the Collège de France in 1977 (Foucault 2004). He often defines governmentality as the "art of government" in a wide sense that is linked to the concept of "power and knowledge" (*pouvoir et savoir*), i.e., with an idea of "government" that is not limited to state politics alone. Power can manifest itself positively by producing knowledge and certain discourses that are internalized by individuals and guide the behavior of populations. This leads to more efficient forms of social control, as knowledge enables individuals to govern themselves. In the case of neoliberal governmentality (a kind of governmentality based on the predominance of market mechanisms and the restrictive action of the state), the knowledge produced allows the construction of autoregulated or autocorrecting selves.

25. For the latter, see Galtung (1971).

26. Partly with the exception of Bendaña, as he presents Southern academic, but not necessarily Southern oppressed, voices.

27. It must, however, be mentioned that this is not based on in-depth empirical research and does not define the understanding and criteria for sustainability of a peace agreement.

28. In this understanding of "effectiveness," civil society had a role to play and could bring some relevant issues to the table and to important policy forums concerned with the implementation of the peace agreement.

29. I am not mentioning the complementary school here, as the same arguments hold as for the conflict management and resolution schools.

30. This chapter presents empirical evidence existing until 2006, before the civil society peacebuilding project started empirical testing; a few new studies have been added.

31. For a clustering of the types of evaluations available, see Çuhadar, Dayton, and Paffenholz in Sandole et al. (2008, 383–395).

32. This includes NGOs only; for civil society organizations, see Chapter 1 in this volume.

33. The authors do not all mention the concept of *gouvernmentalité;* however, it implicitly drives their analysis. See Richmond (2005, 18).

4

A Comprehensive Analytical Framework

Thania Paffenholz and Christoph Spurk

The previous chapter points up the need for a theoretical base that facilitates a comparative analysis of civil society peacebuilding activities across different contexts and phases of conflict. In this chapter, we present a framework for just such analysis. Applying this framework to various cases should reveal insights—specifically in relation to under what conditions and during what phases of the conflict—that civil society can contribute to peacebuilding.

This framework was first developed in 2006 (Paffenholz and Spurk 2006). The seven civil society functions as identified from democracy theory and the development cooperation/third-sector discourse (see Chapter 1 in this volume) have been applied to the context of civil society peacebuilding. This resulted in an analytical framework that thereafter was pilot tested in a few case studies in early 2007.[1] By then, we had identified a number of inherent limitations of a purely functional approach in our 2006 study, which include:

- The focus on the constructive role of civil society, which runs the risk of applying a normative agenda of the "good" civil society, overlooking the fact that civil society might also show "uncivil" behavior or act as a spoiler (Paffenholz and Spurk 2006, 13–14)
- The scope of the functions: actors other than civil society might have important roles within a function, which could explain, for example, why civil society is active or not
- The underrepresented role of the state as a crucial actor that influences the space civil society can take up

The pilot testing of the framework confirmed these limitations and additionally pointed to the fact that a functional approach does not sufficiently explain why certain functions are performed or not. It is crucial to also analyze the context, as it is the enabling and disabling environment for civil society peacebuilding.

Taking the limitations of the original framework into consideration, a "Comprehensive Framework for the Analysis of Civil Society Peacebuilding" was established and subsequently applied in a series of case studies (see Part 3 of this book). The four major elements of the framework—which are *context, functions, assessment,* and *conclusions*—are presented below.

Understanding the Context of Peacebuilding

The objective of the context analysis is to understand the role of civil society within its own environment, as a means to analyze enabling and disabling factors that determine civil society's role in peacebuilding. First, it is necessary to depict each country case study in light of the sociopolitical, cultural, economic, regional, and global environments in which the conflict is taking place. This requires presenting the character of each state, including its political regime, as well as the main characteristics of the media and other main actors in society (which might include, for example, a clarification of gender roles in society). All of these characteristics should be seen as independent variables.

The context analysis requires us also to clarify the understanding of peacebuilding within the country being studied. Essentially, this takes into account the parties to the conflict and the role played by other strata of society, as well as the impact of regional and international actors. It becomes possible thereby to develop a more robust understanding of peacebuilding in the given context, as well as the needs for peacebuilding in the short term (i.e., ending the violence), medium term, and long term in light of the various interpretations and perceptions by different actors from within and outside of the country (including internationals).

The next step in the context analysis is to assess the status of civil society within the country being studied. This includes the composition of civil society (traditional and faith-based organizations, unions, associations, sports clubs, self-help groups, social movements, NGOs, communities, etc.); questions regarding the membership base (including gender and youth proportions); financial resources; specific characteristics of civil society (e.g., violence); the internal organization of civil society (values, culture, gender); existing power relations; and the enabling environment for civil society (legislation, regulation, etc.).

Understanding the Functions of Peacebuilding

Within our comprehensive framework, the second element is identifying and analyzing the seven civil society functions of peacebuilding. Below we present our basic understanding of civil society's peacebuilding functions. The seven functions are:

1. Protection
2. Monitoring
3. Advocacy and public communication
4. In-group socialization
5. Social cohesion
6. Intermediation and facilitation
7. Service delivery

Function 1: Protection

Within the established discourse on civil society, known generally as democracy theory or democratic theory, dating to the work of John Locke and others, the protection of citizens and communities against the despotism of the state is a core civil society function. During and after armed conflict, protection becomes almost a precondition for fulfilling other roles and functions, as civil society actors are hindered from taking up peacebuilding roles when threatened by armed groups (Aall 2001; Orjuela 2004; Barnes 2005; Jeong 2005). This is particularly true because states, once weakened by armed conflict, cannot properly fulfill even a self-protection function. As a result, the Reflecting on Peace Project indicates, the provision of security and the reduction of violence (i.e., as an NGO function) are necessary for effective peace work (Anderson and Olson 2003; see Chapter 3).

In peacebuilding, protection needs to be secured not only vis-à-vis a despotic state but also against any armed actor, ranging from the national army to local groups. The concept is linked to a narrow understanding of peace in line with Johan Galtung's notion of negative peace (Galtung 1969). The main activities for civil society within this protection function are: international accompaniment, watchdog activities, the creation of "zones of peace," humanitarian aid, and civil society initiatives for human security.

The protection function is often ascribed to external NGOs that support national or local civil society actors either indirectly (e.g., as a watchdog through a presence on the ground, facilitating humanitarian or development service delivery; Orjuela 2003, 47) or directly (e.g., through international accompaniment). A good example of the latter is the work of Peace Brigades International, an international NGO that sends outsiders into conflict zones to protect national peace or human rights activists so that they can fulfill their work (Eguren 2001). We find, however, that local civil societies also take up protection functions for their own communities. For example, communities in the Philippines and Colombia have negotiated zones of peace, within which arms are not allowed (Barnes 2005; Orjuela 2004; Eviota 2005).

The protection function can also come in the form of support given to security-related interventions, such as landmine removal and the demobilization, disarmament, and reintegration of former combatants. In general, however, this is not a civil society function per se, as it can be implemented by other actors such as the state, the United Nations, or business enterprises (mainly in the case of landmine removal by contractors). Nevertheless, in exceptional cases, civil society might take up some elements of protection interventions when it concerns their own community. For example, churches in Mozambique launched a demobilization campaign after the official UN demobilization process ended, having concluded that too many weapons continued to threaten the populace.

Besides these options for protecting citizens, individual case studies often assume that civil society cannot fully replace the state's protection function. This is especially important when a weak state gives space to armed nonstate actors like militias, paramilitaries, and mafia-like criminal organizations.

Function 2: Monitoring

Monitoring is a precondition to the protection and the advocacy/public communication functions; monitoring is also a key function in democratization as a means for holding governments accountable. The monitoring function is based on Montesquieu's separation of powers, but it is also enhanced by development-cooperation perspectives.

Within the context of peacebuilding, monitoring remains closely related to protection, advocacy, and early warning as a means for action. International and local groups monitor conflict situations and give recommendations to decisionmakers, and they provide information to human rights and other advocacy groups.

The main activities related to the monitoring function are the creation of political early-warning systems and reporting on human rights abuses. In both, we see increasing cooperation among local groups and outsiders, including not only national and international NGOs but also regional organizations. In Nepal, national human rights organizations, which also have close links to Amnesty International, cooperate closely with local groups. These ties among different actors create safe spaces for local groups to fulfill monitoring tasks. In the context of early warning, examples of cooperation among local, national, and regional entities can be seen in Africa. Early-warning systems developed by regional organizations (e.g., CEWARN in the Horn of Africa) cooperate with local civil society groups to conduct the actual monitoring. In West Africa, UN OCHA, the regional organization ECOWAS, and a regional NGO peace network have signed a memorandum of understanding for joint early warning.

Function 3: Advocacy and Public Communication

Advocacy is a core function within democracy discourse, often referred to as "communication," as it entails civil society promoting relevant social and political themes on the public agenda. Advocacy is considered to be one of the core functions of peacebuilding (Aall 2001; Paffenholz 2003a). Its peacebuilding roots can be traced to the early works of peace researchers such as Johan Galtung (1969) and Herman Schmid (1968), who stated that peace research is an effort to bring the oppressed voices of people in conflict countries onto the public agenda. Such understandings are also based upon the work of Jürgen Habermas.

The main activities within this function are: agenda-setting by local civil society actors, such as bringing themes to the national agenda in conflict countries (road map projects, awareness workshops, public campaigns); lobbying for civil society involvement in peace negotiations; and creating public pressure (mass mobilization for peace negotiations or against the recurrence of war). Also important is international advocacy for specific conflict issues (e.g., banning landmines, blood diamonds, and child soldiers) or for specific countries that are in conflict.

The advocacy function can be taken up by both national and international civil society. Primarily, however, it is a function for national civil societies. An interesting example is the 2006 mass mobilization against the Nepali king, which started as a political movement of the parties and the armed faction (Maoists) before developing into a countrywide peace and democracy movement.

We can distinguish two types of advocacy:

1. Nonpublic advocacy. Here, civil society actors communicate with the political apparatus *in private,* bringing issues to the negotiation agenda in peace talks through informal dialogues, diplomatic channels, or political elites. Informal advocacy brings specific issues to the negotiation or postagreement agenda (e.g., through the establishment of a truth commission) or, in the general form of informal advocacy, sets up the negotiations themselves. (The latter is mainly seen as facilitation and will be discussed as it relates to that function; see below.)
2. Public communication. Here the focus is on *public* advocacy, which means that claims and demands are made in public via demonstrations, press releases, petitions, or other statements in support of a specific demand. The strongest form of public communication is mass movements and street agitation.

Previous research suggests that the advocacy function is relevant to all phases of armed conflict. However, different issues might be more or less important at different times. For example, during armed conflict civil society can advocate for achieving a peace agreement, against violence and human rights violations, for broad-based participation in the peace process, as well as for other relevant themes. Civil society can be linked to the official negotiation process through broad-based information campaigns, public opinion polls (Barnes 2002), and more direct involvement. During the official peace negotiations in

Guatemala from 1994 to 1996 and for Afghanistan in 2001 in Germany, official parallel civil society forums were established (Armon, Sieder, and Wilson 1997; Molkentin 2002; Stanley and Holiday 2002; Greiter 2003; Paffenholz 2006) that gave recommendations to the official Track 1 negotiations. During the peace process in Northern Ireland, civil society organizations organized "Yes" campaigns for public support of the peace agreement.

During the postconflict phase, civil society can advocate against the recurrence of violence, for the proper implementation of peace agreements, for important themes on the postconflict agenda, and for building a culture of peace within society (Orjuela 2004, 51–53; Jeong 2005, 120–121).

Function 4: In-Group Socialization

Socialization is a key civil society function that supports democratic behavior and upholds democratic attitudes and values within society. Democratic behavior is realized through citizens' active participation in associations, networks, and movements. The foundations of this theory can be traced to Alexis de Tocqueville, Robert Putnam, and Antonio Gramsci. Naturally, this becomes a civil society function in the context of peacebuilding that aims at inculcating a "culture of peace," especially within divided societies. The objective is to promote attitude changes within society by developing peaceful conflict resolution and reconciliation. The difference between *socialization* and *social cohesion* (see below) is that socialization takes place only within groups and not between or among former adversary groups. In the conflict and postconflict settings, in-group bonding ties are strengthened. Every national and local association that practices peaceful coexistence and decisionmaking has the capacity to contribute to this function. Yet, this function is often supported from outside. For example, Interpeace, the Geneva-based international NGO, supports groups on different sides of the Israel-Palestine conflict and works to strengthen each group in its efforts for achieving peace. The construction of in-group social capital can also be fostered through peace education, including radio, TV soap operas, street theater, peace campaigns, schoolbooks, poetry festivals, and the like, or through more traditional training in conflict resolution and negotiation.

We can identify two types of in-group socialization:

1. The culture of peace. Socialization for democratic attitudes and for handling conflicts peacefully entails activities that aim at enhancing a culture of peace and constructive conflict resolution for society at large, or for single groups within society or to the conflict (e.g., conflict resolution training or capacity-building offered to different groups or to a single group in the conflict).
2. Socialization toward building or consolidating in-group identity, which aims at strengthening the identity of a particular group, mostly oppressed

> or marginalized groups in asymmetric conflicts Here, it is crucial to analyze whether a group is working toward strengthening its in-group identity actively against others or is socializing certain types of behavior that are not threatening to other groups. Moreover, it is also important to assess how these groups are perceived by other groups (e.g., a Tamil group might get together to strengthen cultural identity, but in doing so, it is perceived by Sinhala nationalists as a nationalist Tamil group).

Many civil society initiatives designed to support attitude change within adversarial groups have been implemented to foster a culture of peace in conflict countries. Research related to a series of dialogue projects within the context of the Israel-Palestine conflict indicates that developing a link between local micro-initiatives and the macro peace processes is difficult to achieve. Such culture-of-peace initiatives work at the individual level, rather than targeting society at large (Atieh et al. 2004). Nevertheless, the main idea behind strengthening in-group identity is that empowered groups will be able to engage in bridging the divide between (former) adversary groups. The question remains, however, whether and how this process works.

Based on the available literature, we can conclude that the current practice of in-group socialization as a civil society function shows a number of weaknesses: most culture-of-peace activities are often too sporadic (Aall 2001, 373), lack coordination, and fail to create a critical mass movement for change. The evaluation of the United Nations Development Program (UNDP) Peace Fund in Nepal (Paffenholz et al. 2004) confirms and illuminates these findings. First, many initiatives have demonstrated positive effects at the local level but failed to impact the macro-level peace process because the initiatives were scattered or were not coordinated and thus failed to create a peace movement that could put significant pressure on leaders. Second, the local impact was limited because it proved extremely difficult to mobilize people for a long-term culture of peace when they lacked basic human needs (e.g., food and security). A comparative international study examined both the positive and negative effects of education on conflict and peacebuilding. Lynne Davies (2004) concluded that education in general contributes more to conflict than to peace. She found that schools in the North and the South are dominated by an education system that enhances difference, mistrust, fear, and the acceptance of aggression.

Function 5: Social Cohesion

In the democratic civil society discourse, integration (or social cohesion) is seen as an important civil society function that ensures the building of community. The main influences here are Gramsci and Tocqueville; later, Putnam elaborated on the concept of "bridging ties."

This is an essential civil society function within the context of peacebuilding, as "good" social capital is often destroyed during war and thus needs to be rebuilt, mainly in order to reconstruct trust and to prevent "uncivil virtues." It is also important to the revitalization of active civic engagement (Paffenholz 2003a; Orjuela 2004, 46–47; Jeong 2005, 120). Therefore, it is crucial to build "bridging ties" across adversarial groups, not just "bonding ties" within specific groups (Putnam 2002). The objective of this function is to help groups learn how to live together in peaceful coexistence.

We can identify three types of social cohesion–oriented activities:[2]

1. Relationship-oriented cohesion for peace. This means bringing together representatives and/or members of (former) conflicting groups to foster relationships aimed at peaceful behaviors. People are brought together, and workshops, dialogues, and exchange visits are held, based on the expectation of long-term attitude change toward the "other."
2. Outcome-oriented cohesion for peace. This means bringing together representatives and/or members of (former) conflicting groups to go beyond building relationships, attempting to reach a larger outcome, such as an initiative for peacebuilding. The main initiatives can include conflict resolution workshops aimed at producing an outcome for peacebuilding (e.g., participating in peace negotiations), and are usually accomplished through the participation of key actors.
3. Outcome-oriented cohesion for business or development work (nonpeace). Here social cohesion is achieved by bringing together the conflicting groups for some objective other than peace. Examples are multiethnic chambers of commerce and water-user groups that consist of two or more conflicting groups. These initiatives are not developed to build peace but to run services, such as a water system. This way, new trust and social capital are built up almost unconsciously. For example, a study in India (Varshney 2002) shows that ethnically integrated organizations, including business, trade, and other associations, have been an effective means for building ties across ethnically divided groups, even leading to an "institutionalized peace system." These organizations have been able to facilitate the control of violence (Varshney 2002, 46).

Existing evidence indicates that attitude change might not be necessary for behavior change. One qualitative and quantitative research evaluation of the impact of peace education on attitude change (Ohanyan with Lewis 2005) looked at peace camps that involved groups from both sides of the Georgian-Abkhazian conflict. This study found evidence that little attitude change was achieved through peace education initiatives over a period of four years. However, initiatives promoting and implementing joint work initiatives were still possible and were perceived by the adversarial groups as fruitful even without any attitude change. This case gives evidence for the assumption that the third type of cohesion initiative (i.e., outcome-oriented/nonpeace social cohesion) is more effective than other types.

Schools are an institution that can contribute importantly to social cohesion. A research project undertaken by the International Bureau of Education assessed curriculum policies in seven countries following armed intergroup conflicts and came to a similar conclusion. Schools have an essential influence in building social cohesion within societies, but schools can also contribute to the formation of adversarial and segregated attitudes that form the basis for future adversarial behavior in support of intergroup violence (Tawil and Harley 2004; *Palestine-Israel Journal of Politics, Economics, and Culture* 2001). Davies (2004) further points out that most of the practice in peace education training and curricula development seldom enters formal schooling, and is relegated to scattered pilot examples. Consequently, she recommends that research and practice pay much more attention to the structural and institutional dimensions of "conflict education instead of mainly assessing the . . . peace education examples."

Function 6: Intermediation and Facilitation

The intermediation function of civil society within the democracy discourse, which is based on the work of Montesquieu, highlights the role of civil society as an intermediator/facilitator between citizens and the state. In the peacebuilding context, facilitation can also be an important function that takes place between or among groups (not only between state and citizens) and at different levels of society.

The main activities within this function are facilitation initiatives (whether formal or informal) between armed groups, between armed groups and communities, and among armed groups, communities, and development agencies.

The contribution of civil society to diplomatic conflict management activities is, however, limited (Aall 2001) and is taken up only in exceptional cases, as conflict management is a government function best undertaken by states or the United Nations. In the rare case when civil society actors take up this function, we see the involvement of external civil society actors, such as international NGOs, international networks, and research institutions. For example, the Catholic lay organization San Egidio mediated the Mozambique peace negotiations in Rome from 1990 to 1992 (Paffenholz 1998), and the Center for Humanitarian Dialogue, a Geneva-based international NGO, facilitated the initial negotiations between the parties in Aceh (Indonesia).

One activity with wide support is the provision of conflict resolution and negotiation training to key civil society actors as a means to strengthen their potential facilitation role.

Local civil society can often facilitate:

- Between civil society and warring parties on the village or district level. In the conflict zones of Nepal, civil society representatives have successfully negotiated the release of citizens from custody by armed groups (Paffenholz, Damgaard, and Parasain 2004).

- Between warring parties to negotiate peace zones (see function 1, above) or violence-free days, as negotiated by churches during the war in El Salvador in order to ensure a child vaccination campaign (Kurtenbach and Paffenholz 1994).
- Between international or national aid agencies and the warring parties as a means to ensure delivery of goods and services to communities (Orjuela 2004, 48).
- Between international or national aid agencies and local civil society. NGOs often become the de facto providers of services within war zones and unstable postconflict settings, as delivery cannot be implemented through government structures. Because NGOs are usually not acquainted with the local context, they are in need of facilitators to negotiate with local communities as well as armed groups (Jeong 2005, 218).

Function 7: Service Delivery

During armed conflicts, the provision of aid and services by civil society actors (mainly NGOs, but sometimes associations and faith-based organizations) increases as state structures are destroyed or weakened. There is no doubt that this is extremely important to helping war-affected populations. We often find that the same actors are providing services and other peacebuilding functions simultaneously. Nevertheless, the question remains whether, and under which circumstances, service delivery is also a civil society function in peacebuilding.

In assessing the service-delivery function for the objective of peacebuilding, we find many different arguments. Some authors see aid delivery as a separate function of civil society, because it saves lives and thus creates preconditions for civil society to exist (Barnes 2005). Another line of thinking, following democracy discourse, views service delivery as fulfilling an economic, social, or humanitarian objective (Salomon and Anheier 1997, 12–19). Therefore, it is argued, these types of activities should not be labeled as civil society support per se (see Chapter 1). A third argument states that aid delivery can be important for civil society peacebuilding *only* if donors and agencies are aware of this role and explicitly try to find entry points for peacebuilding via aid intervention (Anderson 1999). In Sri Lanka, an emergency education project for the most conflict-affected areas in the north was started in the immediate aftermath of the cease-fire agreement. A project management committee was formed and included the two conflict parties on the district level that had not previously engaged in dialogue with one another (Paffenholz 2003b). Here, service delivery served as an entry point for the "conflict-sensitive social cohesion" function of civil society peacebuilding.

In sum, it remains unclear whether or not aid delivery is a function that supports peacebuilding. For empirical testing, we apply an exploratory approach to ascertain whether service delivery can provide entry points for peacebuilding by civil society actors, or whether it has been an obstacle to peacebuilding by distracting energy from other functions.

Assessing Civil Society Functions in Peacebuilding

Having defined our understanding of the seven functions of civil society peacebuilding, below we present the analytical steps within our general framework. We consider each function in light of the hypotheses above. All the functions will then be assessed comprehensively, so that conclusions can be drawn for each case study in question.

1. Understand each function *in context.* What does each function mean for peacebuilding in the specific context of the country or conflict? While the meaning of each function is explained by the framework (see above), it is necessary to contextualize each function within a given context.
2. Assess the *relevance* of each function for peacebuilding based on context analysis. Given the context, would the function be relevant for peacebuilding independently of whether civil society actors have actually performed that function?
3. *Identify the activities* of civil society actors along defined phases of conflict. Here we must examine civil society actors in terms of the initiatives that have actually been implemented, attributing the activities to specific functions. It is important to analyze the activities of other actors in the context of each function as a means to assess the effectiveness of civil society's performance vis-à-vis these other actors.
4. Assess the *effectiveness* of civil society activities in each function against clear criteria defining what constitutes the threshold for effectiveness. For our project we assess the effectiveness of each function against the objective of peacebuilding in each phase (i.e., contribution to the reduction in violence, a negotiated agreement or medium- to long-term sustainability of the peace agreement between the main conflict parties, as well as reduction of violence or establishing conditions for treating the conflict constructively in society at large). Within each function, different methodologies can be applied to assess effectiveness. These methodologies include the content analysis of peace agreements to verify whether themes advocated or discussed by civil society groups or conflict-resolution workshops have been taken into account, evaluation studies and results from public opinion polls that assess attitude changes among groups at particular times of an initiative or process, and interviews conducted specially for this project. Here it is possible to link the functional approach back to actors by analyzing which civil society actors have been more effective within each function.

It must be noted that it is difficult to assess the effectiveness of an activity within a function without taking into account the context and a comprehensive assessment (see below).

Comprehensive Assessment of All Functions: Some Conclusions

After assessing each function individually, it is necessary to assess all functions comprehensively in order to draw conclusions for the case study. Below we summarize how this is done throughout the chapters in Part 2.

1. Assessing the *importance* of functions (i.e., assess the most relevant functions in each case according to peacebuilding needs, as well as the most often executed and most effective ones).
2. *Relations* between functions (i.e., assess whether some functions are mutually reinforcing, complementary, or counterproductive as they relate to other functions).
3. *Causation* (i.e., link the analysis to the context: which context variables, such as state, media, armed groups, violence, composition of civil society, external actors, or donor supporters have been enabling or disenabling factors for civil society peacebuilding).
4. *Overall conclusions* for each case study analyze variables to paint a comprehensive picture of the role that civil society plays in peacebuilding within a specific case (i.e., major achievements, which actors contributed the most, and the primary supporting and hindering factors for effective civil society peacebuilding).

Notes

1. These cases have been Bosnia-Herzegovina, Sri Lanka, the Kurdish conflict, Nigeria, and Israel/Palestine.

2. The authors are grateful to Çuhadar and Dayton (2008) for help in further conceptualizing these distinctions.

PART 2

Case Studies: Applying the Framework

5

Guatemala: A Dependent and Fragmented Civil Society

Sabine Kurtenbach

Civil society organizations played a major role in the transition processes from authoritarian to democratic political systems in many Latin American countries, but their record in peacebuilding is mixed.[1] In Guatemala during its civil war, actors throughout civil society played important roles in the preparation of and run-up to the peace accord signed on December 29, 1996. During and after Central America's longest and most violent war, monitoring and advocacy were the most important functions being fulfilled; to a lesser degree, civil society was able to organize some rudimentary forms of protection. For the organizations of civil society, the shared aim of terminating the conflict was the central factor leading to cohesion, integration, and mobilization.

Postaccord peacebuilding proved to be much more difficult. Although the end of military violence opened new spaces and possibilities for civil society activities in Guatemala, civil society was not strengthened but fragmentized, contrary to hopes and assumptions. Although the political violence waned, Guatemala remains a violent country, with homicide rates increasing every year.[2] Criminal networks control parts of the state apparatus and prevent structural reforms for peacebuilding. More than ten years after the end of war in Guatemala, peace is low-intensity at best. Although different civil society actors did try to confront this situation, they were able neither to develop a joint strategy nor to form a concerted political or social force.

The following analysis focuses on the different roles and functions that Guatemala's civil society has fulfilled during the war and in the postaccord years. Any positive role that actors could perform during the war was dependent on support and cooperation from external actors that wanted the war to end. After this central aim was accomplished, Guatemala's civil society passed through a process of fragmentation over issues and priorities, as well as along ethnic lines.[3] Although international actors still provide aid to Guatemalan civil society, the complexity of the current conflict does not allow for coherent and coordinated strategies.

Context

Guatemala is the largest country in Central America and shares borders with Mexico, Belize, Honduras, and El Salvador. Today it has a population of about 12 million, with a high percentage of indigenous populations (statistics vary from 45 percent to 69 percent), mostly Maya descendents. Guatemala's history is and has been dominated by the descendants of Spanish colonialists and partly by *los ladinos* (the mestizos); the indigenous populations have been excluded from the country's wealth. At the end of the nineteenth century, the cultivation of coffee led to a concentration of landownership and displaced indigenous populations to higher and less fertile regions. During the first decades of the twentieth century, Guatemala was a prime example of the banana republic, in which a foreign company—in this case, the United Fruit Company (UFCo)—constructed a parallel state subordinating development according to its own necessities.

After an urban-based coalition of middle-class groups emerged, reform-oriented junior military officers and university students ousted dictator Jorge Ubico in 1944; the country enjoyed a period of reform and political liberalization. But when the government tried to increase taxes on land—including UFCo's fallow holdings—a CIA-supported military coup put reforms to an end and installed an authoritarian regime that would last until 1985. The main lines of conflict since then are access to land, the role of the state in the development process, and the racist exclusion of marginalized (mostly indigenous) populations.[4]

Guatemala's civil war belongs in the category of the most protracted and violent of wars. It was, however, the least internationalized among the three Central American armed conflicts of the 1980s. It had different phases, beginning in the east during the early 1960s, with the uprising of young, reform-oriented military officers against the fraud and manipulation of elections by the authoritarian civil-military regime. During the 1970s the regime—now openly militarist—nearly destroyed the armed groups with a harsh strategy of counterinsurgency. The remaining cells moved to the western highlands, where Guatemala's indigenous Maya population lives. At the end of the 1970s (during the Sandinista victory in Nicaragua and reform-oriented military and popular upheaval in El Salvador), they succeeded in reorganizing armed resistance. The mobilization of parts of Guatemala's indigenous majority caused a deep-rooted fear among the white and mestizo status quo–oriented actors and led to racist responses that equated being indigenous with supporting the insurgency. But Guatemala's conflict was not ethnic in the strict sense, as the difference between the indigenous (mostly Maya) and the mestizo (*ladino*) populations was based on cultural differences and reflects self-perceptions between rural and urban livelihoods.[5]

The military strength of the guerrillas (unified since 1982 in the Unidad Revolucionaria Nacional Guatemalteca, URNG) never reached a level that endangered the status quo, but between 1981 and 1983 the military regime reacted with a brutal campaign, destroying more than 400 Maya communities in the highlands, forcing a million men into "civilian self-defense patrols" (Patrullas de Autodefensa Civil, PACs), and creating military-controlled settlements in so-called development poles. Although the Maya population suffered most from the violence, the affected *ladinos* mostly belonged to different social movements (*campesinos,* unions, etc.), to human rights groups, or to those urban sectors of civil society that formed the core of critical public opinion. In 1985 the military organized a controlled process of democratic opening (1985 elections for a constituent assembly, 1986 elections for parliament and president) but remained the dominant actor, introducing a series of authoritarian enclaves within a formally democratic political system.[6]

For the next decade, internal and external actors undertook initiatives to negotiate an end to the war. A regional peace initiative led to a Central American peace treaty in 1987 and served as the basis for mediation by the Christian churches. A series of dialogues among various Guatemalan actors (guerrillas, political parties, churches, civil society organizations, entrepreneurs) took place with the assistance of the Lutheran World Federation and the Catholic bishops' conference. But it was only after the wars in Nicaragua and El Salvador had ended that enough pressure from the US government and those of the so-called Group of Friends (as well as mediation from the United Nations) led to the signing of the comprehensive 1996 peace accord (Arnson 1999; Jonas 2000; Molkentin 2002).

The implementation of fundamental provisions of the peace accord, however, was in crisis after the failure of a constitutional referendum in May 1999. Although the armed conflict had ended, and the guerrilla groups had demobilized and reintegrated, peacebuilding in Guatemala failed in one essential area: violence overall was not eliminated or even reduced to a significant degree. Homicide rates have grown from year to year, and though most violence is related to organized and unorganized crime, political violence against civil society organizations, human rights defenders, independent journalists, and social movement leaders is common and on the rise. This has been a central factor inhibiting the full implementation of the peace accord, as well as a cause for the debilitation and fragmentation of civil society organizations and activities.

Six phases of conflict and peace can and should be distinguished:

1962–1968: A period of low-intensity war in the east, ending with the military defeat of the insurgent guerrilla groups.

1969–1978: Limited military action, but with growing mobilization and restructuring of opposition forces in the face of increasing repression by the military regime.

1979–1985: The second phase of warfare, with a geographical focus on the western highlands, where repression by the state apparatus reached acts of genocide during 1981–1983.

1986–1996: Democratic opening of the political system and peace process after the regional peace accord, followed by direct negotiations under the mediation of the Christian churches (1989–1993) and the United Nations (after 1993). Violence was more selective after the political opening, yet some internationally notorious massacres happened during those years.[7]

1996–1999: This was the immediate postaccord phase, ended by the defeat of the referendum on constitutional reforms in May 1999.

1999–2009: A period of low-intensity peace, with a level of daily violence that is higher than the average wartime casualties (except for the years 1981–1983).

The stakeholders in this conflict have been and still are the traditional oligarchy, the military, and civil society organizations. Although political parties did play a larger role after democratization in 1985, and after the signature of the peace accord in 1996, they mostly lack a substantial social basis. The vacuum created between the relevant social forces and the political system is one of the main reasons for persistent instability and the continuing influence of spoiler forces. Although the picture is more complex than this, this analysis will focus on three categories of stakeholders.

The oligarchy is not unified, but compared to the other actors in Guatemala it is still the most coherent group, united by the interest to maintain the social and economic status quo. To this end it used the military but allowed for the controlled and limited political opening in the mid-1980s.

The military has been a central pillar of the Guatemalan society for most of its history after the Spanish conquest, as it was—alongside the Catholic Church—the only institution with a meaningful presence in the rural countryside. The armed conflict enabled the military to establish control over the country's frontiers and to maintain veto power over internal politics up to 1996, when the peace accord was signed. Since then the military has been displaced from the core of the state apparatus, but it still is an important spoiler of pacification and democratization.

Most of Guatemala's civil society organizations sprang from war and violence, with self-identification resting on opposition to the military. Thus human rights groups and victims' organizations dominated activities for a long time. After the formal retreat of the military in 1985, space opened for activities by NGOs and other organizations. The heyday of civil society groups was during the peace negotiations in the Assembly of Civil Society.

The political, social, and economic features of Guatemala are shaped by a market economy with a high degree of social inequality and exclusion that are quantitatively and qualitatively extensive and structurally ingrained. Social exclusion reflects the main divisions within society. The small, rich, urban-oriented *ladino* oligarchy controls most of the resources while the vast majority of the indigenous rural populations live below the poverty line. The stable macroeconomic development since 1996 has helped to increase the Human Development Index slightly but has not transformed historical exclusion patterns.[8] Although there has been some diversification, the economic model rests on the extraction of natural resources (gold, silver, copper, oil, etc.), with a low need for labor in the formal sector; the majority of the population survives in the informal sector. According to the Second Regional Report on Human Development (PNUD 2003, 67), only 19.9 percent of Guatemalans work in the formal sector, while 41 percent work in the informal sector and 39.1 percent in the agricultural sector. Money transfers from migrants to relatives in Guatemala (*remesas*) alleviate social problems and are of increasing importance to the economy (IAD 2004).

The repressive capacities of the Guatemalan state have been strong for most of its history, but the authoritarian government (and those controlling it) lacked the political will to construct capacities for social integration. The armed forces have been the main institution throughout the country. Democratization and the peace process displaced the military as an institution from the center of the state institutions, but it remains a central veto actor and spoiler. Due to the ongoing rivalries and power struggles between reform-oriented actors and spoilers, as well as the capture of parts of the administration by criminal networks,[9] Guatemala qualifies today as a so-called fragile state. Although basic state infrastructure extends throughout the entire territory, its operational capacity is deficient, mainly due to lack of professionalism, arbitrary use of power, corruption, and the influence of personal and criminal networks. The civilian police—a new institution created by the peace accord—is not only unable to confront the growing levels of violence; in some cases it participates in violence. There has been some progress in securing the independence of the judiciary, although political pressure, intimidation, and corruption remain serious problems, not to mention the overall immunity to prosecution that endangers the rule of law and thwarts peacebuilding and civil mechanisms for conflict resolution.

Guatemala's society is dominated by men, and today's women's organizations were mostly established as a response to war and repression at the end of the 1970s and during the 1980s. The democratic opening after 1986 created political space for gender debate and the formation of women NGOs, but the diversity of the women's movement in Guatemala reflects the dividing lines in society. Women succeeded in having gender issues included in the peace accord, which called for gender equality and created the National Women's Forum to develop a platform for action. At the same time, however, any cooperation with the state deepened existing divisions along social and ethnic lines. Whereas middle-class *ladino* women were able to enhance their roles and positions, poor indigenous women could participate only in a subordinated or client role. There are some exceptions to this rule in public office, the economy, and academia, where prominent persons like Nobel laureate Rigoberta Menchú Tum and Rosalina Tuyuc have sway.[10]

Guatemala is a young country, demographically speaking. People between 15 and 29 years old make up a full quarter of the population (PDH 2004). Youths mirror the cultural and ethnic differences between the mestizo and indigenous peoples. There is a strong tradition of youth organization in Guatemala City (Levenson-Estrada 1988). The revolution of 1944 started with student demonstrations; after the countercoup in 1954, students and pupils of secondary schools were the first to reorganize (fighting against a counterreform in the education system and in support of the Cuban revolution of 1959). Many young people became leaders of guerrilla groups in the 1960s and were the main protagonists of the 1978 uprising against an increase of bus tariffs in Guatemala City (with more than fifty juvenile victims). The political opening of 1985 led to a resurgence of youth organizations, but they lacked an obvious political orientation. Youth gangs are considered a major problem for postwar public security, although their share in violence is mostly overrated in government statements and the media, and they often serve as scapegoats for the failures of the transformation process (UNODC 2007; PDH 2006; UCA 2001–2004; Kurtenbach 2008b).

The characteristics and changes in the political regime are connected directly to the war.[11] During the first phase in the 1960s the military secured its position as the central pillar of the state. The defeat of the armed opposition and the international environment widened the scope for unarmed forces. But political mobilization was followed by repression and violence, mostly against indigenous populations in the western highlands. The military regime's first steps toward opening political and civil spaces in 1984 were motivated by internal differences in the military, as well as by fears among the traditional oligarchy that the military might become autonomous and out of control. The democratization that followed was initiated and controlled by the armed forces. The constitutional convention in 1984 was followed up by parliamentary and presidential elections in 1986. However, the spectrum of political actors in these elections remained limited, with the political left largely being excluded. The controlled opening allowed the military to maintain many enclaves of power, particularly in internal security. The peace accord of 1996 had important provisions lifting restrictions on democracy. Of central importance were the Accord on Strengthening Civilian Power and the Role of the Army in a Democratic Society (signed September 1996), the Accord on Constitutional and Electoral Reforms (December 1996), and the Accord on the Rights of Indigenous Peoples (March 1996).

In the immediate postaccord years the political regime liberalized, and options for civilian and political actors increased. The political transformation process today remains closely tied to implementation of the peace accord. Although there is some progress on formal rights and liberties, as well as legal possibilities for participation, the political regime remains unstable. Informal influences of the traditional status quo–oriented actors remain high; in part, their interests coalesced with emerging criminal and illegal networks that gain influence through violence and corruption.[12]

The party system is fragile and fragmented and reflects a diffuse polarization, a highly volatile electorate, and minimal anchoring in society. As yet, no incumbent governing party has been returned to office. Few substantive differences among the parties can be identified, with the personalities of the top candidates taking precedence. The indigenous population has up to now organized only at the municipal level.

Guatemala's political culture is shaped by a tradition of personalism and clientelism. Asymmetrical personal relations are much more common than interest-based solidarity. Freedom of opinion and freedom of the press are guaranteed, but the media are linked to the main economic interest. As related to peacebuilding, the mass media played a disastrous role in the run-up to the referendum for constitutional reforms in 1999. (Most of the media sponsored the opposition campaign.) There is an emerging independent public discourse, and there are some independent publications (e.g., the *Inforpress Centroamericana* weekly) whose circulations are restricted mostly to the urban intellectual elites and the international community.

Status of Civil Society

A first phase of civil society mobilization led to the overthrow of the Ubico regime in 1944 but was mostly restricted to the capital. Repression after the overthrow of the reform-oriented government in 1954 ended this phase, yet the decade of reform in between is the main political reference point for armed and unarmed opposition to authoritarian and military regimes afterward. Social change, war, and repression led to new forms of organization as well as to a polarization of civil society during the 1960s and 1970s. The fractures inside the Catholic Church are a case in point. José Luis Chea (1988, 149) distinguishes four currents inside the Catholic Church: "traditionalists," who aligned with the military and the oligarchy; "reformists," who acknowledged the existence of social problems and repression, worked with social organizations in favor of change, but were against the use of violence; "rebels," who favored social reforms but whose criticism was directed mostly against the hierarchy inside the church; and "revolutionaries," who aligned with the social movements and sometimes with the armed insurgency.

Nevertheless, since the 1970s a range of civil society organizations were established, but either their traditions were weak or they originated in the experience of war and widespread violence.[13] Most today work on specific local issues and are strong at the local level. At the national level, a few strong interest groups dominate, yet there are severe power imbalances between different actors. The most effective organization is the entrepreneur association Comité Coordinador de Asociaciones Agrícolas, Comerciales, Industriales y Financieras (CACIF). There are a number of professional NGOs, mostly based in the capital, who have some influence, and there are numerous groups lobbying for social and economic changes (at the national level as well as in rural areas) with only limited political influence. The ability of civil society to organize on its own is unbalanced and hindered by politicocultural and socioeconomic barriers. The organizations tackle isolated problems and are short-lived because they, too, are fragmented by the cult of personality. The problems civil society organizations face are threefold: (1) they lack a solid social basis; (2) they hardly cooperate inside a broader agenda of change along common issues of interest; and (3) they have weak or rather limited relations with the party system.

These problems are not only inhibiting a stronger role of civil society in peacebuilding; they are also factors endangering governability and the deepening of democracy. Serious problems arise, for example, when agreements between civil society and government are turned down in the legislature (as happened in various circumstances). This leads to disenchantment with democracy and democratic participation, as well as to a growing mistrust in parliament, as opinion polls show.

Self-organization in civil society encounters many barriers that reflect social divisions. Conflict and mutual distrust lead to fragmentation of civil society along various fissures. Traditionally there is an urban bias toward the organization of NGOs, whereas unions have a history of trying to organize laborers working in the primary natural resources (bananas, sugar, etc.). Reform-oriented civil society organizations organize around specific issues, or on a local or regional basis; some do try to bridge existing cleavages, and others perpetuate traditional conflict. Civil society organizations show a degree of volatility and are dependent on financial assistance from international NGOs and donors.[14]

There has been a lack of organization among the indigenous people up to the 1990s, when—as a consequence of war and widespread violence—the movement for indigenous rights and empowerment began to spread.[15] Coordination among civil society is based on a sector-oriented approach along thematic lines (e.g., human rights, *campesinos*) and limited cooperation during specific political situations (e.g., the Asamblea de la Sociedad Civil, ASC). The peace processes supported coordination at the time but did not introduce or change existing patterns of fragmentation and personalistic structure. The fragmentation of civil society and other organized interest groups renders cooperation, compromise, and participation inside society even more difficult. Most cooperation between civil society organizations is not institutionalized and depends on personal contacts, sympathies, and other factors.

Leaders of social movements, unions, human rights advocacy organizations, and the independent media have been prime targets for state and paramilitary violence. Since the end of the war, groups and individuals who promote accountability for past violence and the rule of law have been specifically targeted. Violence against civil society was worst during the period of military conflict, as the state's repressive apparatus (and its civilian allies) tended to conflate social organizations with guerrillas. Thus during the period when a peacebuilding role for civil society was most needed, it was least possible.[16]

The opening of the political system and democratization after 1985 enlarged the political options for civil society actors and enabled international NGOs and donors to cooperate more closely with civil society. Although these processes remained fragile, they were historically important because civil society gained some public space for repressed opinions and debates.

Along with violence, another important factor shaping the possibilities and limits of peacebuilding was the relationship between civil society organizations and armed actors. The right-wing military and its allies (the PACs) used open as well as selective violence to hinder autonomous organization and to intimidate members. But the URNG also tried to instrumentalize civil society organizations to enhance their influence. This led to splits and quarrels over dominance and subordination as well as strategy, alignments, and coordination among the different groups. The indigenous and Maya organizations are a case in point: there were serious debates between groups who favored a "cultural" approach—demanding bilingualism, for example—and those who advocated for a comprehensive reform of the social, political, and economic systems. For the guerrilla groups, the ethnic-cultural conflict between the indigenous people and the *ladinos* was a conflict subordinated to socioeconomic and political struggles. This led to division within the Maya organizations at the beginning of the 1990s. Comité de Unidad Campesina (CUC) is another example: repression forced CUC members to go underground in 1980 and to align with the Ejército de Guerra Popular (EGP) (although the EGP could not really provide protection). At the same time, this limited autonomy and options for action.[17]

Civil society entered a crisis after the failed referendum on the constitutional reforms in May 1999, which were necessary for implementing the peace accord. This was followed by a process of "disenchantment" with the possibilities for change through the peace process, as well as growing internal conflicts among different organizations over strategies and priorities. Partly this led to a fragmentation along ethnic lines between *ladino* and *indígena* organizations. At the same time, continuing violence involving "hidden powers" or paramilitaries weakened and endangered civil options. Such violence undermines democracy as well as civil forms of conflict regulation. At the same time, it inhibits overcoming distrust of the state from civil society organizations based on the experience of direct state repression and lack of state protection.

After the peace accord was signed and the URNG transformed into a political party that could act legally inside Guatemala, the conflict between URNG and civil society actors changed and became more overt. URNG tried to monopolize the political space, thereby reducing the options and influence of civil society organizations. The very limited success of the URNG in the elections after war's end in 1996 solved this problem in a certain way. Although there have been discussions on a political project, the reform-oriented forces of Guatemalan society have yet to reach a consensus on the contents, scope, and goals of such an endeavor.

In the postaccord years there has been a process to transform social movements into NGOs to gain access to funds from the international donor community.[18] Although this supported a process of professionalization in think tanks and NGOs, it also had some rather negative or problematic effects.

- It rendered cooperation between different organizations more difficult due to the competition for funds.
- It mainstreamed (and thus transformed and depoliticized) the discourse and priorities of the organizations to those of the international community, creating a certain distance between leadership and social basis.
- Professionalization happened mostly at the level of leadership and technical staff of the organizations, opening (or widening) the gap between them and their original constituency.

Peacebuilding Functions

The following section compares the seven different functions: protection, monitoring, advocacy, socialization, social cohesion, intermediation and facilitation, and service delivery.

Until the 1990s the concept of peacebuilding was not discussed in Guatemala or on the international level.[19] During the 1960s and 1970s, revolution was the central topic; discussion of democratization and/or war termination occurred during the 1980s. But even if one tries to reread the accounts of political and societal organization during those decades, it is hard to find many activities that resemble peacebuilding until the regional peace processes began in the mid-1980s.[20] Different sectors of Guatemala's society have different perceptions or concepts of peacebuilding, ranging from an end to war to social justice and rehabilitation for the last 500 years of oppression. There are shades in between.[21]

During the first two phases of the conflict (1962–1968 and 1969–1978) there was no significant activity by civil society organizations in relation to peacebuilding. Two factors help to explain this. First, during the 1960s, repression and violence by the military as well as by paramilitary death squads were directed against the leaders of social organizations and the opposition in general. This generated an environment in which opposition to the government was equated with sympathy for communists and armed opposition. Although the political regime had a civilian façade, the counterinsurgency strategy rested on a militarization of the countryside through *comisionados militares* (serving as vigilantes and informants of the military) and repression (Schirmer 1998). Second, civil society during the 1960s was nascent; even as autonomous and independent organization and mobilization became more important, the few existing initiatives were mostly directed toward the organization of marginalized social groups like landless *campesinos* or in the trade union sector. Activities of different church organizations (like Acción Católica) were directed toward development problems (introduction of new crops, support for merchandise, education, etc.).[22]

Peacebuilding activities in a broader sense (initiatives to confront and end violence and repression as well as activities to deal with the causes and consequences of war) began only during the most violent phase of armed conflict (1979–1985). Humanitarian NGOs addressed the needs of the sectors most affected by violence and displacement, and victims began to organize (partly clandestinely). The most important activities were directed at publicizing the military's atrocities at the national and international levels, thus trying to get some protection from international actors.[23] The most active and visible phase of civil society peacebuilding began with the military deescalation and the political opening after 1985 until the signature of the peace accord in 1996 and the first three years afterward until 1999. This was a time of open organization by various human rights groups, indigenous and women's organizations, and campesino movements. Monitoring and advocacy were the primary functions to press for a negotiated end of the war and to introduce some fundamental reforms in the country's power structures. With the defeat of the proreform forces in the referendum for constitutional reforms in May 1999, civil society and its peacebuilding activities entered a crisis that has not been overcome today.[24]

Protection

Protection in the case of Guatemala refers mostly to protecting the noncombatant society from direct violence and repression by armed actors. As the war was not fought openly but with insurgent tactics and harsh repression, civilians paid a high price. Due to the asymmetric power relations shaping the conflict, society protection could not be provided by civil society organizations that stood outside the control of the military. Thus subordination to and cooperation with the military were a strategy to protect oneself, one's family, or the community. Another option was migration. There was large-scale migration and displacement inside the country to the capital or the coastal region; a small group went to the mountains and founded "communities in resistance" that survived military repression. Others left the country and tried to reach the United States via Mexico or stayed in the refugee camps established by the United Nations in Mexico on the border with Guatemala. Refugees in the Mexican camps, as well as in the communities of resistance, had a high level of organization. They got accompaniment, support, and protection from the United Nations as well as from international solidarity organizations. Already in 1993—that is, before the war ended—the first return of 2,500 refugees to Guatemala was organized under the protection of CAREA (Cadena para un Retorno Acompañado, or "Chain for an Accompanied Return").[25]

Another form of at least rudimentary protection was provided by the political umbrella of the Catholic Church. As the Catholic Church itself was divided over the future of the country, its activities for dialogue and negotiations (which began during the mid-1980s) were accepted by all actors. A similar function was fulfilled by international NGOs, although their work was sometimes decried as support for insurgency. Nonetheless, cooperation with the Catholic Church, international NGOs, and (after 1994) the United Nations Field Mission (Misión de Naciones Unidas en Guatemala, MINUGUA) allowed a rudimentary form of protection. A sad example for the limits of church protection is the murder of Bishop Juan Gerardi after the publication of the Recuperación de la Memoria Histórica (REMHI) report in 1998.[26]

Monitoring

Monitoring meant the observation of political developments related to the causes of war (i.e., structural inequalities, rural problems, etc.), the dynamics of the armed confrontation (displacement, refugees, military repression), and human rights violations in general. Human rights groups, namely the Human Rights Office of the Archbishop of Guatemala (ODHAG), were most active in this field and fulfilled an important function in disseminating information and analysis inside the country as well as at the regional and international levels. Another important group is independent academia. Guatemala has research institutes and think tanks that are internationally honored for their professionalism and quality of work. Among these are Facultad Latinoamericana de Ciencias Sociales (FLACSO), Asociación para el Avance de las Ciencias Sociales en Guatemala (AVANCSO), and the Fundación Mack.

These functions were supported by national and international churches as well as other international actors, such as the United Nations Mission in Guatemala (monitoring human rights between 1994 and 2004), the field office of the United Nations High Commissioner on Human Rights (UNHCHR) since 2004, the United Nations Development Program, and other international human rights organizations (Americas Watch, Amnesty International). Monitoring became institutionalized with the signature of the Accord on Human Rights in 1994, which was the only treaty that came into force immediately. This was an important step, as it provided the work of national and international actors with a secure and common basis of operation. Cooperation between national and international actors was essential; international organizations had much more leverage with the government and the military than did national NGOs (UN 2005). At the same time, there have been many conflicts between local and international actors. While most local groups wanted the internationals to support their positions, the internationals had to respect some diplomatic conventions if they wanted to stay in the country. A case in point: accusations by human rights groups that MINUGUA was taking a soft stance with the government.

After war's end, the second focus of monitoring by civil society organizations was directed toward implementing the peace accord. A clear division of labor can be seen inside civil society as the different sectors monitored those accords that were thematically related to their work. But there was no intent or capacity within civil society to make a comprehensive analysis of the implementation process or to look for crosscutting problems. This strengthened the centrifugal tendencies of civil society and enabled status quo forces to use a policy of divide and conquer to reduce civil society's influence.[27]

Advocacy

Advocacy meant trying to influence the politics of other internal and external actors through public as well as nonpublic channels. This function was most important after the political opening in the mid-1980s and was used by civil society organizations as well as by other actors, although with different and sometimes contradicting goals. While civil society organizations tried to build alliances with other internal and external actors, other actors and spoilers used it to maintain and secure the social status quo.

During the peace process, nonpublic advocacy was an instrument mostly of unarmed spoilers. The most influential actor has been CACIF, which used its access to the governments of Alvaro Arzú (1996–2000) and Oscar Berger (2004–2008) to prevent fundamental reforms of the existing political and socioeconomic status quo. As both presidents were members of the economic oligarchy, the main channel of influence was in personal relations and family ties. Guatemala's oligarchy has an impressive unity concerning fundamental reforms that might endanger the economic and social status quo.[28] Civil society organizations could use nonpublic advocacy with the government to a much lesser degree. The peace accord established a series of "peace institutions" for the implementation of the peace accords (e.g., the Peace Secretariat, known under its Spanish acronym SEPAZ, Secretaría para la Paz). Members of civil society were often named to positions in these institutions. Although these institutions did not have much leverage inside the government, they served as a link to civil society. But cooptation also produced conflicts inside civil society and thus deepened divisions and fragmentation.

Public communications was one of the most important functions of civil society during every phase of conflict. The majority of the demands related to the underlying causes of the conflict (land possession, labor conditions, exclusion) or to the consequences of violence and repression (human rights violations, forced conscription, displacement). Public communications was a central instrument to draw attention to the generalized impunity for homicide and other gross human rights violations. In 1980, the occupation of the Spanish embassy by a group of Mayas from CUC, to protest the massacre of Panzos and the following violence of the military, was an important turning point for international coverage of violence in Guatemala (which up to then had been overshadowed by developments in Nicaragua and El Salvador). The public denunciation of this by Rigoberta Menchú (whose father was one of the victims) and others was essential for the organization of international support for Guatemala's human rights organizations.[29] A similar example is the work of Fundación Mack, an NGO founded by Helen Mack, the sister of the murdered anthropologist Myrna Mack. The foundation is today one of the most recognized (internally and internationally) think tanks specializing in legal issues, public security, and civil-military relations.[30]

With the start of the official peace negotiations, public communications became an important factor for upholding the process as well as for formulating concrete demands on the so-called substantial themes agreed to in the basic document between the government and guerrillas. During this phase, civil society organizations influenced the agenda-setting, which was institutionalized during the Asamblea de la Sociedad Civil (ASC) from May 1994 until shortly before the peace accord was signed in December 1996.[31] The different sectors published documents on topics that were then discussed in the assembly. After a consensus was reached inside ASC, the documents were passed to the UN mediator and the parties in negotiation. Although this was an important form to link civil society organizations at least indirectly to the negotiations, the impact of these documents on the final accord varied significantly, as proposals were nonbinding. Most influential was the Asamblea's paper on the Acuerdo sobre Identidad y Derechos de los Pueblos Indígenas (AIDPI), where the main provisions followed the ASC's draft. At the same time, the influence of the indigenous umbrella organization COPMAGUA (Consejo del Pueblo Maya de Guatemala) was at its peak; it fell apart afterward due to differing priorities. However, after signature, the implementation of this treaty has been most deficient.

After war's end some civil society organizations and think tanks worked as formal or informal consultants for government institutions on a more institutional level. Public policies were discussed in a series of dialogues, with different results. The general idea is that concert between government and civil society is most difficult in relation to "hard" topics (tax reform, land use, etc.);

even if public policy is formulated, the problems of implementation arise as soon as a legal basis is necessary. Parliament has been a bottleneck for reform and implementation. An interesting form of institutionalized consultancy from civil society is the Consejo Asesor de Seguridad (CAS), founded to advise the president on security matters. In 2007, after the scandal on the involvement of police forces in criminal networks, CAS designed a reform for the security system. Whether this reform will be implemented remains to be seen.[32]

Socialization

Socialization meant the internal consolidation of group identity reflecting a common history, shared experiences, and goals. Most civil society organizations (at least those that have not disappeared during the process) passed through a process of learning. In the first years of the armed conflict, literacy and basic Spanish-language education programs by Catholic organizations like Acción Católica and the Maryknoll priests helped empower a generation of rural civil society leaders. During the peak of violence, repression was a shared experience that socialized different groups of civil society toward a common goal: end the military regime and repression. This was important for different sectors (Mayas, *campesinos,* trade unions), as many leaders were killed or had to flee the country. This shared experience helped consolidate groups working on indigenous, *campesino,* and trade union issues but rarely included activities to bridge existing cleavages.

The consolidation of group identity was a major theme for indigenous organizations. During the war there were differences between those groups advocating merely cultural rights and those promoting fundamental socioeconomic and political reforms; after the war there was a tendency toward "ethnization" of many conflicts. Some Maya activists argue that they have to establish (and/or reinvent) Maya identity before they can cooperate on the same level with the rest of society. But generally there is a process of fragmentation, including among the indigenous organizations; as the extremely low support for the candidacy of Nobel laureate Rigoberta Menchú in the presidential elections of September 2007 shows, a series of other causes also played a role.[33]

An important learning process was the ability to formulate demands and to define positions, as well as to discuss them and then compromise. The most important activities for democratic ideals were the protests against the self-coup of President Jorge Serrano in May 1993. The resistance to backslide into an authoritarian regime was the one and only occasion bringing together all civil society organizations from CACIF to *campesinos* on the streets. This exemplifies the minimalist consensus reached in Guatemalan society: existing constitutional procedures should stay intact and not be overthrown.

The capacity to define positions and to compromise was enhanced by the sector-oriented methodology of the peace process during the National Dialogue as well as in the ASC. But after the war, the ability to compromise seems to have suffered due to the loss of a shared goal or enemy. The experiences of the Maya organizations and the consensus-making procedures in the Maya Assembly are a case in point, although they did not overcome fundamental conflicts or impede divisions. During the conflict and afterward, those who could not achieve acceptance for their positions often did not subordinate themselves to the majority but left the organization. The separation of Coordinadora Nacional Indígena y Campesina (CONIC) from CUC is an example (Bastos and Camus 2006).

During the conflict there was little promotion of civil conflict regulation and a culture of peace. After 1996, UNESCO, the Christian churches, and some NGOs—mostly in universities and think tanks—began to work on these issues. In the direct postaccord phase, campaigns on small arms and other issues in public security and crime and violence (IEPADES, FLACSO, etc.) were important. One of the few Guatemalan organizations working on the culture of peace directly is Fundación PROPAZ, an NGO working on processes for dialogue between civil society and the state.[34] It provides training courses in mediation and negotiation; it offers a diploma in dialogue promotion and works as a facilitator at the municipal level. The main problem is that any impact is restricted mostly to the projects, and networking is very difficult.

Social Cohesion

In the Guatemalan context, social cohesion is promotion of bridging ties between the different groups. The experience of war and violence led to bridging between human rights groups and women's organizations. But after the war, fragmentation along social as well as ethnic-cultural lines inhibited the joint reform agenda. As for initiatives of conflict-sensitive social cohesion, they were restricted to the preparatory phase of the peace process when churches provided space for private and informal dialogues between the guerrillas and different sectors of Guatemala's society (including the government, high military officers, and CACIF; see below). After the end of the war there have been some community-level activities, mostly in donor-sponsored projects of reconciliation or around the communal development councils (which do not have a direct relation to peacebuilding). Those micro initiatives lacked national impact, and the high level of postwar violence and general impunity rendered relationship-oriented social cohesion very difficult.

Intermediation and Facilitation

Intermediation and facilitation in Guatemala were directed to promoting dialogue first, negotiations later, between guerrillas and the state. Participation of civil society in this process had different forms. Following the regional peace accord, the government organized a national committee of reconciliation under the leadership of the Catholic Church. The Catholic bishops' conference promoted a direct dialogue between the government and guerrillas during the annual meeting on January 29, 1988, and shortly afterward the archbishop of Guatemala volunteered to serve as mediator. This initiative did not succeed. In 1989, forty-seven organizations (including trade unions, human rights organizations, etc.) participated in the National Dialogue. The establishment of fifteen thematic commissions created a space for dialogue among social actors and the government on democracy, human rights, security, and indigenous peoples. The impact of the National Dialogue on peacebuilding was limited due to lack of participation by important players like CACIF and due to repression by the security forces and paramilitary networks against participants. Nonetheless, the National Dialogue was a basis for the dialogue process between guerrillas and society, as well as for the constitution of the ASC.

From 1990 to 1993 the Catholic Church and some Protestant churches organized a series of dialogues between the URNG and different organizations in civil society, the economy, the political system, and churches. This was possible due to the support of the Lutheran World Federation. The talks were a basis for the indirect inclusion of civil society in the formal negotiations through the ASC.[35]

Service Delivery

Although nearly all the sector-oriented civil society organizations have been working in service delivery, this was rarely used as an entry point to peacebuilding. The focus of service delivery was on the regions with the highest levels of poor and indigenous populations, where it was an important contribution to survival in violence-affected communities. Although humanitarian NGOs were highly politicized, the tight military control during the war made it difficult and dangerous to address issues beyond humanitarian relief. After the war there were more possibilities. Most of all, psychological support and trauma work with victims were important in indigenous communities. International donors supported local capacity-building (e.g., a diploma in mental health). But even then, possibilities to use this as an entry point for a broader process of reconciliation and reconstruction were limited. Again the main reasons for this were existing power relations and a justice system that left former perpetrators mostly untouched.

At the same time, the government has a focus on macroeconomic stability and a minimalist role in service delivery and social affairs. Not even coordinated and joint pressure from civil society and international donors was able to make the implementation of the fiscal part of the peace accord possible. The central benchmark for this is that an increase of the tax rate to 12 percent (still very low) was never achieved. As long as the Guatemalan state does not mobilize internal resources for service delivery, civil society as well as international cooperation will have a compensatory function.

Assessment

Overall the most important functions for peacebuilding of civil society (quantitatively and qualitatively) were monitoring and advocacy. To a lesser degree, civil society organizations could organize rudimentary protection and serve as intermediaries between citizens and the state as well as between citizens and armed groups. In most of these functions civil society depended on the cooperation of the Catholic Church as well as international actors (most of all the United Nations Mission in Guatemala, MINUGUA, and the Group of Friends). Both had an important role as a facilitating actor whose cooperation enhanced the legitimacy of civil society organizations while serving as a protective umbrella against the violent behavior of spoilers.

Specific Patterns

A limited form of protection could be provided by the Catholic Church and the international community due to the asymmetric power relations between the guerrillas and the military. The militarization of the western highlands led to the establishment of new forms of social control, subordinating indigenous rural populations to the counterinsurgency strategy of the military. In the so-called development poles this included even food, as communities were unable to sustain a traditional subsistence economy and had to earn their livings in work-for-food programs. In these programs the population had to construct infrastructure, a necessary condition for the exploitation of natural resources like oil (mostly in Petén and the Franja Transversal del Norte). Due to tight military control in these regions, there was limited possibility for independent organization; even service delivery by civil society actors not collaborating with the military was difficult until the political opening in the mid-1980s.

Monitoring and advocacy were mostly concentrated in the urban areas (especially the capital) for three reasons. First, authoritarian mechanisms of social control were not as strict. Second, civil society has an urban tradition and was better organized than in rural regions. And third, the presence of international actors (diplomatic corps, international organizations, media) served to protect these functions. Information on the situation in the countryside came to the capital mostly through the Christian churches that had a presence all over the country and were thus able to link urban and rural actors. After its establishment in 1985, the Bureau of the Human Rights Ombudsman (Procuraduría de Derechos Humanos, PDH) was another increasingly important local actor for monitoring.

The experience of war and violence served as an important reference point for socialization, mostly for indigenous communities. Before the war indigenous peoples were divided into the twenty-four language groups, and communities were mostly isolated from one another. Repression was collective and served as a basis for the development of joint perceptions that the Maya people were reinventing a common identity. This process has no equivalent in the *ladino* population, which suffers from a crisis of identity that deepened after the war. So while it was important to enable formerly marginalized and excluded sectors of society to participate, this process reinforced existing cleavages and divisions that must be overcome for long-term peacebuilding. Donors played an ambivalent role. As they concentrated support in the poorest (mostly indigenous) regions in the postwar years, there has been overaiding despite the necessities. This might be partly responsible for deepening cleavages, as poor *ladinos* perceive that they are left out of the peace dividend.

There were no relevant activities for social cohesion. This is mostly due to the traditional divisions in Guatemalan society reinforced by war. At the same time, the division between the indigenous and the *ladino* populations is based on self-affiliation along cultural lines (clothes, traditions, cosmology); bridging forms of social cooperation are very difficult to establish under the premise of adherence to Maya identity. Self-affiliation is dependent on context. After the political opening, and due to the manifold support of international donors for the indigenous population, there was a process of "Mayanization"; its impact on everyday life and beyond has yet to be seen.

Relevance of Civil Society Functions

Three provocative theses can be formulated concerning the relevance of civil society functions in different conflict phases. First, the activities of civil society were monodimensional and restricted to monitoring and advocacy, although other functions would have had a higher priority in peacebuilding. During the most violent phases of the conflict, protection and service delivery (independent from the military) would have been central for the rural population. As civil society leaders and organizations were a main target of violence and repression, they were able to protect neither themselves nor others. Thus other functions (advocacy, monitoring) were necessary but had only limited impact.

Second, in a certain way peacebuilding activities of civil society lagged behind the dynamic of the conflict. That is, when social cohesion was a central peacebuilding need during the immediate postwar years, civil society organizations stuck to a sector-oriented approach providing socialization. Advocacy and monitoring were necessary but had limited impact.

Third, civil society organizations lacked a long-term vision and strategy during most phases of conflict and peace. This is reflected not only in the sector-oriented approach but also in the narrow and short-term activities. Only after 1999 (after the peace process entered crisis) did the more professional NGOs begin to develop and pursue long-term strategies. In the first decades there was no mutual consent over political peacebuilding needs. While some civil society organizations opted for revolutionary change (Nicaragua-style), others opted for liberal democracy. This made comprehensive approaches toward medium- and long-term needs extremely difficult. Mutual consent (including not all but most actors of the civil society) about liberal democracy as the frame for peacebuilding emerged only after the failed autogolpe in 1993.[36] For other relevant topics (the role of the state in development, interethnic relations between indigenous people and mestizos, and the use of natural resources) such a consensus is still missing.

During the immediate postaccord years, and in the current phase of generalized violence and selective repression, protection is a central peacebuilding need. But again, civil society organizations rely only on monitoring and advocating changes in the police and judicial systems. This might be a necessary long-term strategy, but it does not resolve short-term needs to protect human rights defenders and leaders of social movements who are targeted for violence by the "hidden powers." Even international organizations like Peace Brigades International (PBI) are not able to protect people against such forms of violence, as these groups do not mind murdering international observers. As the generalized violence endangers the transformation as well as peacebuilding, the development of strategies to cope with this violence is a pressing need. Youths are another cohort suffering from the short-term thinking on peacebuilding. Neither government nor civil society actors saw the need to integrate young people into society; in relation to the high level of violence (for which youth gangs are only partly responsible) young males became the new enemy.

Effectiveness and Impact

The main approach of the majority of actors in civil society peacebuilding was sector- and issue-oriented. Peacebuilding and the end of the war were not goals but ways to promote policy change on specific topics (land, labor rights, indigenous rights, etc.). Human rights and victims' organizations did not really have a different strategy, although the termination of violence was their common core demand.

Cooperation and networking patterns among the different organizations reflect this approach. Cooperation was initiated by the peace process when the National Dialogue, the dialogue with the URNG, as well as discussions inside the ASC, were organized by sectors. The proposals and demands elaborated were closely related to the demands of specific constituencies (indigenous groups, *campesinos,* women, etc.). This historically important process brought up issues that were mostly taboo (like equal status for indigenous populations). But it did not overcome divisions or help to find a comprehensive vision and strategy of inclusive nation-building between these organizations. While a broad set of issues was discussed and agreed to in the peace accord, civil society was not capable of formulating priorities or strategies for the implementation of historic goals.

The only exceptions were directed against serious setbacks in the political context, when the multisector platforms confronted the autocoup of President Serrano in 1993: the Foro Multisectorial Social (FMS), which included human rights organizations; San Carlos University; *campesino* organizations and Maya groups; and the Instancia Nacional del Consenso (INC), organized by CACIF with the collaboration of political parties; right-wing unions; and others. The central demands of both platforms were a return to the constitutional order, the purge of the state apparatus, including the legislature and the judiciary, as well as the participation of civil society in the search for a way out of the crisis. This laid the foundation for the participation of the civil society organizations in the peace process via the ASC.

But at the same time, the ASC returned to the sector-oriented approach. Although this might have been necessary as a working methodology, it was one of the basic reasons for the fragility of civil society peacebuilding and for the fragmentation, division, and loss of influence of civil society after the peace accord and the defeat of the constitutional referendum.

A crucial problem for the ASC was that it mirrored the fundamental divisions of Guatemalan society. The self-exclusion of CACIF and the departure of the small and medium business sector in 1995 are cases in point. The accusations by government representatives, high military officials, CACIF members, and the right-wing press that the ASC inclined toward the positions of the URNG are another example.

Intermediation and facilitation were relevant during conflict as a necessary condition for the termination of the war through formal international negotiations. It was mostly taken up by traditional sectors of civil society, namely the Catholic Church. Due to asymmetric power relations, these sectors needed to enhance their leverage by aligning with international actors (the Vatican and the Lutheran World Federation). Service delivery did play an indirect role in formal negotiations, because it enabled international development cooperation to verify the monitoring and advocating of civil society organizations in the field.

Conclusion

An evaluation of Guatemala's civil society peacebuilding record is mixed. Success came in two important areas. Civil society actors played an important role in the preparation of the negotiated settlement, although the context was unfavorable, as the military saw itself as the victor in the war. Here monitoring and advocacy were fundamental instruments to persuade international actors to step into the process. The democratic opening during the mid-1980s (notwithstanding its deficits and the prerogatives of the military in the internal conflict) was an important factor, enhancing the possibilities of civil society actors to align with international actors and increasing the influence of international actors in favor of peacebuilding. After 1986 the succeeding Guatemalan governments, at least on a rhetorical level, were committed to the validity of international humanitarian law. Thus opinions of the international community became more important after the political opening, and they could enhance the influence of national NGOs through cooperation and/or alignment. This is also valid for the Christian churches that had international support either from the Lutheran World Federation or from the Vatican (Pope John Paul II visited Guatemala 1993 and called for an end of violence). At the same time, this dependency on international engagement limited peacebuilding to war termination—a notion shared by many international actors. Even if this would have been different, after the war ended the political context of formal democracy limited the political role of international actors with reference to "ownership" of reforms and the discourse of donor alignment. As the international community had an uncritical perception of the political context, this was an important obstacle for long-term peacebuilding goals and the transformation of the structural causes of the conflict.

The second success was to bring the structural and historical problems of exclusion, marginalization, and racism to the public agenda. Here, in-group socialization was an important process, as it enabled change-oriented sectors of civil society to develop consensual goals. Although these were important achievements, they were not enough for the establishment of a peacebuilding process in the broader sense. This was due to existing power asymmetries, a fragile state, and the lack of political will to make the necessary fundamental reforms. The high level of postwar violence is a result of (as well as another cause for) this development.

The Guatemalan case shows how all the functions civil society actors did and did not perform were heavily influenced by context. Here, three factors—existing patterns of social organization, political context, and the characteristics of the state—are of utmost importance.

1. The division of Guatemala's society along social and ethnic-cultural lines shaped the structure and the capabilities of civil society organizations, as well as their self-limitation to cooperate with each other. Repression and violence during the war led to a high degree of cooperation between different organizations of civil society; experiences with Guatemala's ASC show that the existing cleavages do not necessarily hinder participation. But after the formal end of the war this capacity was reduced, individuality and fragmentation prevailed, and divisions prevented the necessary alliances and limited the leverage of civil society actors toward the political system and other actors. This is a major reason for failure of the peace accord, which depended to a larger extent on power relations in society.
2. Changes in the political context had a direct impact on the options available to all civil society actors. Monitoring and advocacy are a case in point: the freedom of action for civil society organizations to fulfill these functions is enlarged or reduced by the form of the political regime. While human rights groups or victims' organizations assume important functions, accusing someone of violence was much more dangerous during the authoritarian and repressive regimes before 1985 than after the

political opening. After the democratic opening and the end of the war, a strategy to cooperate with or influence political parties would have been essential for the implementation of the peace accord. Since then, civil society organizations were able to use the public space to negotiate public policies in different areas, but most policies were not passed in parliament, which has been the main bottleneck to reform. Here the lack of bridging capabilities, as well as the lack of strategic vision, is evident.

3. Both developments are the central cause for the third development: the fragile and hybrid process of transformation of an authoritarian and repressive regime to a democratic state. After the end of the war, this process seems to be stuck, with persisting social inequality and the dominance of informal and asymmetric power relations. This enables powerful members of the oligarchy to use informal channels to pursue their personal (or group) interests, while most civil society organizations are not part of these networks. Thus the promotion of transparency, accountability, and the rule of law are fundamental strategies to improve governance and to pass significant measures to enhance civil society influence in formal politics. Although the peace accord designed a series of new state institutions (e.g., the civilian police), these were not allowed to fulfill their stated functions.

In sum, the official termination of the war resulted in the loss of a common "enemy" of civil society organizations and did not lead to the development or formulation of a common vision for postwar society but instead to a process of fragmentation and omnipresent violence. The Guatemalan state, as well as civil society organizations and international donors, was incapable of confronting the violence in the grey zone between war and nonwar. A few research institutes and think tanks have begun to monitor these developments and to develop strategies to confront postwar violence. Guatemala shows that civil society's peacebuilding capacities are intimately linked to and influenced by not only the dynamics of political violence but also violence in general. External actors have important roles in the protection of civil society peacebuilding activities and as promoters of peacebuilding networks. This is important not only during violence (defined as war) but also in other contexts of generalized violence; this is the fundamental impediment to achieving democratic governance. The central peacebuilding challenge in the years to come is to develop comprehensive strategies capable of confronting violence at the intersection between political and criminal forms of violence.

Notes

This chapter is based on the analysis of the literature cited, as well as a series of research and consultancy field trips to Guatemala since 1995 that gave me the opportunity for many conversations and discussions with researchers, as well as with civil society activists, members of different administrations, politicians, and entrepreneurs. Thanks to everybody for the shared insights. Different drafts of this chapter were discussed and commented on during the conferences for the project, and I received comments from external reviewers. My thanks go to the group, as well as to John Darby, Bill Stanley, and Jenny Pearce, for their suggestions to strengthen the arguments. All shortcomings and faults remain my responsibility, of course.

1. Internal wars ended in Nicaragua in 1990, in El Salvador in 1992, and in Guatemala in 1996. In Colombia there have been various peace processes during the last twenty years, but the war is still ongoing. In Mexico there are different armed conflicts at the regional level; in Peru the government succeeded in marginalizing Sendero Luminoso militarily.

2. According to a UN study (UNDP 2007, 19) using data from the Guatemalan police, there were 3,619 homicides in 1996 (the year the peace accords were signed). In the years thereafter, the lowest number of homicides was in 1999 (2,655); since then the number more than doubled, reaching 5,885 in 2006.

3. The term *ethnic conflict lines* will be used, although the conflict in Guatemala is primarily not an ethnic but a social and cultural conflict; the social and cultural divisions of Guatemalan society are nearly identical with the divisions between the Maya and the *ladino* and white populations. The affiliation to one group or the other depends on self-perception as well as on social and economic status.

4. For an overview on Guatemalan history, see Handy (1984), Jonas (1991), Casaús (1992), Kurtenbach (1998a), Paige (1998), CEH (1999), REMHI (1998), and Molkentin (2002), among others.

5. As most of Guatemala's poor live in the countryside, poverty and ethnic-cultural discrimination form part of the everyday life of the indigenous population (National Report on Human Development in Guatemala, PNUD 2005). Indigenous people leaving rural communities and migrating to cities used to lose most of their indigenous heritage. After the end of the war, there is a process of "Mayanization" and a growing self-identification among indigenous populations.

6. On the strategic plan of the military and civil-military relations, see Schirmer (1998) and (2002); Aguilera (1989) and (1994); Arévalo, Doña, and Fluri (2005); and Pearce (2006).

7. The most renowned cases that led to international protest were the murders of anthropologist Myrna Mack in 1990 and of the UCN political leader Jorge Carpio Nicolle (cousin of then-president Ramiro de León) in 1994, as well as the massacres in El Aguacate and Santiago Atitlán at the end of 1990 and in Xamán in October 1995.

8. Slightly more than 56 percent of the national population lives below the poverty line; in indigenous departments the percentage is much higher. The HDI was 0.617 in 1995 and 0.673 in 2004 (UNDP 2006).

9. The "hidden powers" consist of at least three groups: parts of the status quo–oriented oligarchy, retired and active military officers, and groups linked to transnational organized crime. On the postwar violence, see Peacock and Beltrán (2004), WOLA (2000), Vela et al. (2001), and UNODC (2007).

10. On gender issues in Guatemala, see Berger (2006).

11. On the political development, see Dunkerley (1988), Solórzano (2001), and Jonas (1991), among others.

12. On the formation of those networks, see Peacock and Beltrán (2004). These "hidden powers" include legal as well as illegal actors, and the borders between them are difficult to define.

13. The first ones to organize were the Grupo de Apoyo Mutuo (GAM) and the organization of war widows CONAVIGUA (Bastos and Camus 2006); on civil society in war and postwar years in Guatemala, see Krznaric (1999), C. Smith (1990), Pearce

(2007), and Dudouet (2007). For a general overview of the discussion on civil society in Latin America, see Hengstenberg, Kohut, and Maihold (1999) and, in relation to civil society peacebuilding, Jácome, Milet, and Serbín (2005).

14. UNDP coordinated two projects for the participation of NGOs in the implementation of the peace accords, mostly with funds from the Scandinavian countries; from 2004 to 2006 the budget was US$7 million (Bulloven 2007). On private European aid for civil society, see Bieckart (1999).

15. For an overview of Maya mobilization and organization, see Bastos and Camus (2006); for the development of the relations between *ladinos* and Maya populations, see Adams and Bastos (2003).

16. The most comprehensive documentation of the gross human rights violations are REMHI (1998) and CEH (1999); for following years, see the annual reports of Human Rights Watch Americas or the reports of the Ombudsman's office (PDH); on the PAC, see Saenz de Tejeda (2004).

17. For the history and development of the different civil society organizations and NGOs during the 1980s, see Arias (1985), Menchú (1984), Davis (1983), and Bastos and Camus (2006).

18. On key problems in the relationship between donors and civil society in Guatemala, see Howell and Pearce (2001, 160ff). At the level of personal communications there is a critical discourse on the relationship between international donors and NGOs from both sides, but this has not been systematized. On international cooperation in postaccord Guatemala, see the evaluation reports of different projects, e.g., the abovementioned UNDP project (Bulloven 2007) or, under a human rights perspective, Instituto de Derechos Humanos (2006).

19. This is not an all-inclusive accord on activities of civil society organizations; only the most important organizations that work more or less on a national scale have been included.

20. This caveat notwithstanding, I will use the term *peacebuilding* throughout the different phases for activities of civil society organizations that are directed toward the termination and/or reduction of violence.

21. Interestingly, the Spanish term *justicia* has a double meaning of justice as well as law, which makes it difficult to explain that law and rights are not the same as justice and that the rule of law always reflects the power relations of a society.

22. See Brintall (1988) for the development in the Aguacateca region of Huehuetenango and AVANCSO and González (2002) for the Quiché.

23. This was accompanied by a growing body of academic as well as activist literature on the consequences of war and repression; see Handy (1984), Black et al. (1984), Carmack (1988), and Manz (1988).

24. For developments after 1996, see the reports of the UN MINUGUA mission on different topics as well as Sieder (1998) and Kurtenbach (2003 and 2006), among others.

25. There were many press reports and NGO reports on the returnees; for an academic study with a focus on the Ixcan region, see Garbers (2002).

26. On the role of the Christian churches, see Kurtenbach (1996) and (2008a); on the murder of Bishop Gerardi, see Goldman (2007).

27. A case in point is the discourse on the indigenous population as the group that benefits mostly from the peace accords.

28. See Casaús (1992) and Segovia (2004).

29. See Burgos (1984) and the cites in note 16 above.

30. The website contains regular comments and assessments on political and legal questions (Fundación Myrna Mack).

31. On the dynamics inside the ASC, see Bastos and Camus (2006) and Ponciano (1996).

32. On the different experiences of dialogue, see the documentations of the organizations involved, e.g., in the security sector (UNDP 2006a; Arévalo et al. 2005; FLACSO et al. 2002).

33. This process led to a research project by FLACSO and CIRMA under the name "Mayanización y vida cotidiana"; view details at www.flacso.edu.gt/etnicos/docs/investigacion/mayanizacionyvidacotidiana.pdf.

34. See Fundación ProPaz for details and Zepeda López (2004, 191–263) for projects on culture of peace.

35. On the activities of the churches, see Kurtenbach (1994) and (2008a).

36. In 1993 then-president Serrano tried to dissolve the parliament and to break with the existing constitutional order (following the example of the Peruvian president, Alberto Fujimori). But unlike in Peru, in Guatemala this so-called self-coup ended in the displacement of Serrano and the election of Ombudsman for Human Rights Ramiro de León as president for the remaining term of office.

6

Northern Ireland: Civil Society and the Slow Building of Peace

Roberto Belloni

Northern Ireland is rich in associational life. Thousands of voluntary organizations provide citizens with opportunities for engagement in all areas of social, economic, and political life. Many take advantage of these opportunities or organize autonomously to address issues of concern. Since the late 1960s, when the conflict in the province began to escalate, civil society organizations have mitigated some of the worst consequences of violence by supporting individuals under threat, by rallying communities into demanding a settlement to the dispute, and by monitoring both the state's behavior and the actions of violent nonstate actors. Although civil society was not the key player in the peacemaking process, it nonetheless contributed ideas and support to Track 1 negotiators. In the early 1990s, civil society involved the grassroots in the debate about the province's future. When in early 1998 a tentative agreement between the parties was reached, civil society campaigned effectively for its adoption; and since the 1998 Good Friday Agreement was voted into law, civil society has contributed to its implementation, most notably by supporting the reintegration of former paramilitaries into civil life.

Yet, despite these achievements, the defining feature of civil society in Northern Ireland is represented by its sectarian and violent streak. Since the early 1970s, paramilitary groups have imposed their authority on poor and marginalized areas. Initially motivated by the need to provide security and protection to communities in danger, these groups also repressed dissent, controlled illegal activities, and imposed arbitrary and violent forms of "informal justice." In addition to these uncivil, violent groups, there exist organizations—the majority, even—that in most cases abide by the law but remain organized along ethnonational lines. Individuals are often socialized into the values and norms of their own community and remain distrustful of the "other side." Established patterns of segregated education and residential living further complicate the development of cross-community social capital. This chapter argues that civil society in Northern Ireland has provided a positive contribution to the peace process, but primarily by operating in the background, circulating and developing alternative ideas and approaches to managing conflict.

Context

The origin of the conflict in Northern Ireland is commonly dated to the early seventeenth century, when the Plantation of thousands of English and Scottish settlers in Ireland led to the development of two groups with diverse religious and cultural values and conflicting political allegiances. Over three centuries the settlers turned into a working- and middle-class population that identified with the British Empire. The national/ethnic stratification of society developed throughout this period, and it continued into the twentieth century with the consolidation of patterns of economic and political discrimination. Although there are religious aspects to the dispute, the conflict has always been more about discrimination than religion per se.

In 1921, the Republic of Ireland gained independence, with the six counties that now form Northern Ireland remaining part of the United Kingdom. Of the nearly 1 million Protestants in Northern Ireland today, most are *unionists,* meaning they want to preserve the link between the six Northern Irish counties and the British crown. By contrast, most of the approximately 700,000 Catholics in the province identify with the Republic of Ireland, and many are *nationalists,* meaning they want the six counties[1] to be part of the Republic. Both groups have paramilitary factions, known respectively as *loyalists* and *republicans,* who have used violence in the name of their alternative political allegiances. The British state has attempted to address the problem through both military and political means. It has waged a long but unsuccessful war against republican paramilitaries. At the same time, London has couched the conflict as one arising from essentially local roots. As such, it has favored a series of reforms aimed at improving the political, economic, and social conditions of working-class areas, especially of the long-neglected Catholic minority.

The relationship between the Protestant and Catholic communities in Northern Ireland has never been harmonious, although there have been periods of peaceful coexistence. The latest outbreak of the "Troubles" started in the late 1960s, when the Catholic minority, inspired by the US civil rights movement, began protesting discrimination in the allocation of jobs and houses by the Protestant-controlled Northern Ireland government (Cameron Report 1969). Nonviolent Catholic marches were disrupted by unionists and by the Royal Ulster Constabulary (RUC), the overwhelmingly Protestant police force, with some demonstrations ending in violent and bloody clashes. In August 1969, the government in London abandoned its laissez-faire attitude toward Northern Ireland and deployed the British Army in an attempt to reestablish order. Nonetheless, the conflict continued to escalate, with a growing number of casualties on both sides. During twenty-five years of conflict, more than 3,500 people were killed and some 37,000 injured. The economy also suffered considerably during this time (Mac Ginty and Darby 2002, 125–127), as seen in the 40 percent decline in the manufacturing sector. Given that the banking, finance, and business sectors provided only 9 percent of jobs (half of the average for the rest of the United Kingdom), this decline was especially devastating. These conditions were exacerbated by the fact that the tourism industry never developed to its potential, making it unable to fill the gap left by the manufacturing industry. On average, throughout the Troubles the unemployment rate was about 50 percent higher than in the rest of the United Kingdom. Poor areas with high unemployment were prone to violence. More than 40 percent of all deaths during the Troubles occurred in West and North Belfast, where 45 percent of Northern Ireland unemployed workers are found (Hall 2001, 16).

The introduction of legislation in August 1971 authorizing the internment without trial of those suspected of contributing to violence only made the violence dramatically worse, peaking with 479 deaths in 1972. In March 1972, the spike in violence led the British Parliament to abolish the one-sided Northern Ireland government and to replace it with direct rule from London coordinated by a British secretary of state responsible for Northern Ireland affairs. Violence dropped, but casualties remained near 300 deaths per year until the failed policy of internment was abandoned in December 1975, after nearly 2,000 had been detained, 95 percent of them Catholics (CAIN 2008). Violence dropped further over the ensuing years, but thereafter it simmered at roughly eighty deaths per year until 1998, with the signing of the Good Friday Accord. About 50 percent of the conflict deaths occurred before 1977; 95 percent occurred before 1995 (Melaugh, 2007; Sutton, 2007).

During the 1970s and 1980s, a peace movement emerged but was unable to change the course of events in an immediate or easily discernable manner. Cross-community rallies protesting against violence were common but relatively unsuccessful. These rallies reflected a sense of frustration and a drive to counter violence in the streets, but they lacked a clear political agenda. For example, Peace People was a large-scale movement established in 1976 in response to an Irish Republican Army (IRA) operation, which caused the death of three children. Through vigils and street demonstrations, it achieved widespread, cross-community support against violence. Its founders, Mairead Corrigan and Betty Williams, were honored with the Nobel Peace Prize. Despite its visibility, however, Peace People was not able to sustain interest among the general population or to influence political events. By mobilizing the propeace middle class without a political platform or a proposal for negotiation, its momentum quickly waned amid disillusionment about political engagement (Cochrane and Dunn 2002, 163; Fearon 2000, 3).

Seven attempts to reach an agreement between the two communities from 1972 to 1993 failed, although they were broadly valuable in laying foundations for successful peacemaking in the 1990s. Most notably, the 1985 Anglo-Irish

Agreement gave the Irish government a consultative role in the province, in return for Dublin's acceptance that Northern Ireland should remain part of the United Kingdom as long as doing so was expressed in the will of the majority. The agreement augmented the capacity of both governments to address the conflict jointly; thus, despite unionists' opposition, it proved to be "an extremely important key to the development of an eventual political solution" (Fitzduff 2002, 12). In December 1993, British prime minister John Major and Irish taoiseach (head of government) Albert Reynolds issued the Downing Street Declaration, which reiterated the principle of consent and invited the IRA to refrain from violence and participate in peace talks. In August 1994, the IRA announced a complete cease-fire, followed in October by similar announcements of loyalist groups. Talks between the parties began, but the disarmament of all paramilitary organizations remained the most important stumbling block. In February 1996, the IRA put an end to its cease-fire with a massive bomb in London's Canary Wharf.

The May 1997 election of the Labour Party in Britain gave new momentum to the peace process. Labour dropped the demand of decommissioning, thus allowing Sinn Féin, the political wing of the IRA, to join the peace talks. They were joined shortly thereafter by the Ulster Unionist Party (UUP), the political representative of moderate Protestantism. Despite continuing extremist violence, in the small hours of Saturday, April 11, 1998, the parties reached the Northern Ireland Peace Agreement, also commonly known as the Good Friday Agreement. In May 1998, 71 percent of citizens in the North and 94 percent in the Republic voted the agreement into law. In Northern Ireland, an overwhelming majority of nationalists voted in favor of the agreement; only a narrow majority of unionists were supportive. In the Republic of Ireland, citizens endorsed the agreement and voted to change articles 2 and 3 of the Irish Constitution to remove the territorial claim on Northern Ireland.

Three strands were included in the deal. First, a 108-member Northern Ireland Assembly was created to terminate direct rule from London and restore local self-government. The initial Assembly elections in June 1998 were won by the UUP and by the moderate, predominantly Catholic Social Democratic and Labour Party (SDLP). Second, a North-South Ministerial Council was established to address cross-border issues such as transportation, urban planning, tourism, and programs under the European Union. Third, the British-Irish Council operated to address east-west issues involving the entire British Isles (Wilford 2001). The Good Friday Agreement also provided for the establishment of a consultative sixty-member Civic Forum, comprising "representatives of the business, trade unions and voluntary sector, and other such sectors as agreed by the First Minister and Deputy First Minister," and tasked with expressing opinions on "social, economic and cultural matters." Established in October 2000, and touted as a key arena for the development of a new, participatory, and inclusive governance, Civic Forum has had negligible political impact. The Civic Forum was resisted by many politicians as a challenge to their power, especially by the hard-line Democratic Unionist Party (DUP), which raised issues of representativeness, legitimacy, and effectiveness of decisionmaking inherent to this unelected body. The Assembly has been able to muffle the new institution through its control of appointments and funding (McCall and Williamson 2001).

In the postagreement period, the peace process has moved forward with advances and setbacks, but without a return to significant violence. November 1999 was marked by the reinstatement of a power-sharing administration after twenty-seven years of direct rule from London, but it was suspended again in October 2002 amid mutual accusations. The release of paramilitary prisoners under the terms of the agreement proved to be demoralizing for the families of the victims of violence. A violent feud within the ranks of unionist paramilitaries for the control of illegal activities further complicated daily life in the most deprived areas of Belfast. Police reform and paramilitary decommissioning remained subject to conflicting interests and were implemented slowly. In 2001, a new police force called the Police Service of Northern Ireland (PSNI) was created, but it took another six years, until January 2007, for Sinn Féin to provide its endorsement. In July 2005, the IRA announced an end to its armed campaign, and in October the Independent International Commission on Decommissioning reported that IRA weapons were "put beyond use." In the following years, similar announcements were made by other paramilitary groups. These moves proved to be helpful confidence-building measures, and since May 2007 a new power-sharing government has been in place.

The parties to the conflict, however, maintain alternative interpretations of the peace process, its achievements, and future challenges. Much of the unionist community has always been lukewarm about making concessions to people they describe as terrorists. Unionists maintain their allegiance to the British crown and fear greater Irish involvement in Northern Ireland affairs. By contrast, nationalists maintain their ultimate goal of reuniting the island, now via political rather than violent means. The higher Catholic demographic growth, they believe, will facilitate reaching this goal. In 1961, Protestants were 63 percent of the population and Catholics 35 percent; by 2001, the Protestant percentage dropped to 53 percent while the Catholic had grown to nearly 44 percent. In this context, most voluntary groups, statutory bodies, and international actors (notably the European Union) interpret "peacebuilding" as a process aimed at "reconciling" the two communities while building a "shared society." Reconciliation between Protestants and Catholics can be described as a voluntary act involving five related strands: developing a shared vision of an interdependent and fair society; acknowledging and dealing with the past; building positive relationships; achieving significant cultural and attitudinal change; and realizing substantial social, economic, and political change (Hamber and Kelly 2008, 8–11). This view of peacebuilding is not universally shared.

Some nationalists and unionists fear that the peacebuilding agenda either neglects the role of the state or represents a first step toward a united Ireland, as explained below.

Status of Civil Society

The origin of civil society activism in Northern Ireland is closely connected to the political situation dominated by a Protestant-led local government between 1921 and 1969 (Fearon 2000). The Catholic community, often excluded and disempowered, developed its own social network based on the teachings of the Catholic Church and aimed at developing mutual assistance and cooperation. Catholics were effective in organizing themselves and were eventually successful in pressuring for change. In response, Protestant self-help groups were also gradually formed within working-class areas in order to fill a gap of autonomous organizing, but their growth was much slower. Protestants were used to seeing the state as their protector and tended to see civil society as an anti-state, Catholic phenomenon. This attitude began to change as working-class Protestants realized that the state was no longer biased in their favor, and also that a partnership between civil society and the state had become the dominant means of community development. Gradually, Protestant unionists learned from the Catholic nationalist experience, and they began claiming a real or perceived situation of disadvantage in order to obtain funding. Despite Protestants' advances in community development, most Protestants feel they are less well organized than Catholics and that a significant imbalance remains.

For Catholics as well as Protestants, pressing local needs were the main reason for the development of civil society activism. The outbreak of the Troubles caused various levels of damage to housing and infrastructure, human dislocation, and the breakdown of social services. The suspension of local self-government in 1972 provided the voluntary sector with another opportunity to fill the vacuum left by conventional politics. Voluntary groups were created to address destitution, but for the most part they lacked a clear political analysis and perspective. Activists have been motivated primarily by the need "to do something," rather than by a clear political objective (Cochrane and Dunn 2002, 97–121). To date, most groups continue to identify their activities as social and communal in nature, not as political. Yet, as we shall see below in the discussion covering civil society functions, there has been growing political engagement to augment the pursuit of social and communal goals.

Throughout the Troubles, civil and uncivil groups developed in tandem. The outbreak of violence led to the creation and development of paramilitary organizations in working-class areas. Loyalist and Republican groups proliferated and came to enforce their control over their respective communities. Thus, a defining characteristic of civil society in Northern Ireland is the coexistence of civil and uncivil groups, whose main difference in this context is represented by their attitudes toward violence; whereas uncivil groups are willing to endorse and employ violence, civil groups are not. Since the signing of the Good Friday Agreement in 1998, some paramilitary organizations have degenerated into criminal gangs involved in drug dealing, racketeering, robbery, and smuggling. Also, young people are widely perceived as a threat to community safety, and youths are at higher risk of being killed. Almost 26 percent of all victims of the conflict were twenty-one years old or younger, but most of those were in earlier generations. About 32 percent of youths aged fourteen to eighteen have witnessed someone being killed or seriously injured, but this is almost entirely a result of crime. Violence related to the societal conflict has dwindled to a trickle (Hansson 2005, 5).

During the 1980s, relations between voluntary organizations and the government were tense, with civil society organizations subjected to vetting by security forces. The British government enacted a policy denying access to public funds to any voluntary groups alleged to have connections to paramilitary organizations. Nationalist groups in Catholic West Belfast were hit particularly hard by the policy. The 1990s saw a rapprochement with the government (Birrell and Williamson 2001). The vast majority of civil society organizations, including republican groups opposed to British sovereignty on Northern Ireland, are now funded, to different degrees, by governmental bodies. State funding increased from less than £17 million in 1988–1989 to more than £70 million in 2001–2002 (Acheson et al. 2006, 13). Since the 1997 New Labour victory, this funding reflected the government's view of the third sector as important to ensuring social cohesion by identifying and addressing locally experienced social problems. The Labour government has seen the voluntary sector as a crucial "third way" between the state and the market and as a means to foster greater civic engagement of marginalized groups. In 1998, the publication of the "Compact between Government and the Voluntary and Community Sector" set the values and principles underpinning the partnership between the two (Building Real Partnership 1998). "Consultation" was highlighted as a key element in facilitating effective collaboration in policy formulation.[2] However, despite the focus on partnership, the government has set the terms of its relationship with civil society, identifying the sector's main task as one of service delivery. In April 2006, the UK government created a new role (formally titled Minister for the Third Sector) in the Cabinet Office, signaling the intention to work more closely with civil society groups.

In addition to gaining financially from government support, the civil society sector benefited from significant European resources. The European Union introduced its Special Support Programme for Peace and Reconciliation in 1994, committing 667 million ECU. The European Union stressed the importance of developing partnerships involving the voluntary sector in policymaking and implementation. District partnership councils were established in each of the twenty-six local government areas, connecting government councilors, members of the voluntary sector, and representatives of statutory agencies, private business, and trade unions, in collectively deciding how to distribute the funds. The first phase of the Programme for Peace and Reconciliation stimulated the creation and implementation of only a small number of genuinely cross-community projects. The sectarian nature and/or links of many of the single-community projects funded during this period generated controversy regarding any actual contribution to peace. At the same time, these partnerships not only increased the visibility and legitimacy of the voluntary sector but also contributed to the slow development of an inclusive and cross-community ethos (Williamson, Scott, and Halfpenny 2000).

The peace program was extended for seven years (2000–2006) with a financial commitment of 1,154 million euros. The program's overall aim remained the same but focused more on "addressing the legacy of conflict" and "taking the opportunity arising from peace." In a period of political uncertainty, the program was successful in facilitating a sense of ownership over the peace process and in supporting contact between the two communities (NICVA 2004). The third version of the peace program spans the 2007–2013 period. Peace III, as it is known, promised 200 million euros to carry forward the main aspects of the previous programs, placing a strong emphasis on promoting cross-community relations and understanding (EUPTC 2007). Likewise, other grantmaking and charitable organizations disbursed considerable resources to support the peace process. Among these organizations, the Community Foundation for Northern Ireland stands out for its assistance to most of the community development work in the province, including much of the postagreement work with former political prisoners (see below).

In addition to benefiting from extensive financial support, civil society benefits from the existence of political rights and press freedoms that allow voluntary groups to operate unimpeded. The wider socioeconomic context is also enabling, although Northern Ireland still lags behind the rest of the United Kingdom (CIVICUS 2006). Combined, these favorable conditions have facilitated the growth of the voluntary sector. According to the Northern Ireland Council for Voluntary Action (NICVA 2005), this sector consists of organizations that are self-governing, independent, and nonprofit; benefit from a meaningful degree of philanthropy; are established for the wider public benefit; and are nonsacramental religious bodies. On the basis of these criteria, approximately 4,500 organizations operate in Northern Ireland, employing almost 29,000 people (4.4 percent of the workforce). Three out of five adults are associated with a voluntary and civic organization. Most of these organizations work in community development and education and training. Main beneficiaries are the general public (23.6 percent), older people (8.7 percent), and children (8.6 percent). One-quarter of these organizations are based in the Belfast City Council area, and almost 50 percent operate in the most deprived regions (NICVA 2005).

Although this sector is numerically strong, its ability to address Northern Ireland's problems remains contentious. About three-quarters of all organizations have management committees entirely or primarily from one community, and more than one-quarter of them are either wholly Protestant or wholly Catholic. As discussed below, in some notable cases civil society organizations support and develop strong bonding ties among their members, but this comes at the cost of preserving and perpetuating differences and suspicions between the two communities. The organizations' single-identity origins, combined with the segregated nature of residential living, constitute a strong barrier to cross-community engagement (Acheson et al. 2006). Moreover, the growth and increasing professionalization of the third sector are problematic. Occasionally, both the media and even some members of the third sector voice cynicism about the emergence of a "community relations industry" led by middle-class professionals with a nine-to-five mindset, and with limited knowledge of and connections to the most troubled areas (McVeigh 2002; Mitchell 2009).

Peacebuilding Functions

The following section compares the seven different functions: protection, monitoring, advocacy, socialization, social cohesion, intermediation and facilitation, and service delivery.

Protection

Paramilitary violence has been a significant problem since the outbreak of the Troubles, with a handful of deaths still occurring per year even now. In some cases, civil society groups negotiated "peace zones." The Forthspring Inter-Community Group, whose facility is adjacent to a gate in a peace wall in Belfast, was able to secure safety for frontline intercommunity programs. Other groups, such as The Junction in Derry, have taken advantage of relatively safe areas in the city center to declare themselves open to both sides; still others have created safe intercommunity spaces farther removed from the violence, such as Corrymeela's facility in the countryside (see below).

In addition to enduring intercommunity violence, citizens in many working-class areas suffered significant violence and intimidation from paramilitaries within their own community, who played the role of local authorities, and whose approval one was wise to seek before engaging in any civic activity. Both during and after the Troubles, paramilitaries have meted out punishments (including beatings, kneecapping, spine shooting, expulsion from the community, and murder) to all those who break the community's rules. In particular, hard-line, working-class republican districts with high rates of unemployment and marginalization have become "no-go" areas for the RUC, seen as an instrument of the hostile British state. In these areas, paramilitaries assumed the role of a de facto police force controlling community crime. Those involved in "antisocial" criminal activities have been subjected to violence (Knox and Monaghan 2002). Because the victims of this "informal justice" system are often seen by the community as "deserving" their fate, paramilitaries have enjoyed various degrees of support.

A few organizations have attempted to mobilize public opinion against the paramilitaries, particularly following actions leading to the death of innocent victims. As mentioned above, Peace People successfully mobilized public opinion against violence but failed to articulate a proactive alternative political agenda. Families Against Intimidation and Terror (FAIT), created in 1990, attempted to use the media in order to highlight the victims' suffering and thus embarrass political/military republicanism and loyalism (Cochrane and Dunn 2002, 14–15). Throughout its nine years of existence, this group was successful in attracting media attention. In addition, the voluntary sector has organized direct, concrete support to those targeted by paramilitaries. In 1990, the Northern Ireland Association for the Care and Resettlement of Offenders (NIACRO) started the Base 2 program, designed to help individuals under threat. From 1994 onward, when paramilitaries began relying more on banishments than physical violence, Base 2 provided advice, transport, and accommodation for people "expelled" from their communities. Despite the lukewarm attitude of statutory bodies, which often have seen such service providers as implementing "a social exclusion policy for paramilitaries" (Knox and Monaghan 2002, 103), this program has been successful in helping hundreds of individuals under threat (McEvoy 2001, 236–237).

An important, indirect protection function is currently performed by engaging former political prisoners in conflict transformation. The total number of former prisoners is estimated at 15,000 for republicans and 5,000 for loyalists. At least one organization whose members were released under the terms of the Good Friday Agreement (the Ulster Defense Association) turned into a criminal group involved in drug dealing and racketeering. In order to support former prisoners in the process of reintegration into the family and community, EU funding has assisted in the creation of sixty-one groups of former politically motivated prisoners. Groups such as EPIC (for loyalists) and Tar Isteach (for republicans) were created as professional organizations providing a range of services, from counseling to employment training. Some of their members have also engaged in dialogue and cooperation between segregated and estranged working-class communities. In some instances, particularly in Republican areas, they have been instrumental in reducing tensions at interface areas and in persuading young people of the value of nonviolent means of conflict management (Shirlow et al. 2005; Shirlow and McEvoy 2008).

At the same time, *restorative justice* projects are under way at the community level to provide an alternative to paramilitaries' "informal justice" (McEvoy and Mika 2002). In both republican and loyalist communities, the focus of these programs is to repair the harm done by a crime. Victim and offender are brought together through the assistance of a community mediator. A community panel supports them in the process of agreeing to an appropriate form of justice. The cases addressed usually concern petty crimes involving quarrels between neighbors and within families. Although these programs may have offered a valuable alternative to punishments delivered through paramilitaries, shootings and beatings have continued even in the postagreement period. However, distinct patterns between republican and loyalist violence exist. Whereas the former has decreased, the latter has increased, perhaps reflecting the fact that not all unionist paramilitaries support restorative justice (Knox and Monaghan 2002, 125; Shirlow and McEvoy 2008, 123–137). Overall, despite fears that restorative justice may be a continuing sectarian substitute for the state's law enforcement and justice systems (Eriksson 2006), in communities where state legitimacy remains contested, these programs are a useful alternative to paramilitary punishment and violence (Shirlow and McEvoy 2008, 126–127).

On balance, civil society's protection initiatives have been innovative and often effective in limiting violence. In addition to supporting individuals under threat, these programs are commendable for their efforts to demonstrate the possibility and means of achieving nonviolent solutions, thus undermining the rationale for the existence of paramilitary organizations and contributing to build a less violent culture.

Monitoring

Since the misery of World War II, most human rights organizations have understandably focused their attention on monitoring and condemning state abuses. In Northern Ireland, however, approximately 90 percent of the violence has been carried out by paramilitaries. Thus, after much debate in the 1990s, leading organizations such as Amnesty International and Human Rights Watch broadened their remit to scrutinize the activities of paramilitaries as well.[3] Although these NGOs' condemnation of punishment beatings and shooting contributed to the public and political recognition of the problem, it had no noticeable impact on limiting attacks on civilians and security forces (McEvoy 2001, 229–230).

In addition to monitoring paramilitary violence, human rights NGOs have concentrated on state abuses. Since the introduction of internment without charge in 1971, the treatment of detainees became an issue of special concern. Detention centers throughout Northern Ireland have been used for the interrogation of people suspected of terrorism. The conditions in these centers have been exposed and criticized by local and international human rights organizations alike. Since the early 1970s, Amnesty International has published a number of reports denouncing the mistreatment of detainees. These reports' findings were confirmed by international legal organs such as the European Court of

Human Rights, which on several occasions has found the British government in violation of its obligations under the European Convention on Human Rights.

Not only have human rights groups monitored state actions; they have also identified state abuses as one of the key reasons for the conflict and its continuation (Mageean 1997). Northern Ireland's leading human rights NGO (the Committee on the Administration of Justice), as well as international NGOs such as Human Rights Helsinki Watch and Amnesty International, have published numerous reports examining the British government's legislation and policy implementation on issues pertaining to prisoners' rights, equality, employment discrimination, policing, and social inclusion—among others. The work of these human rights groups was instrumental in bringing these issues from the margin to the mainstream of the peace process. In particular, a coalition of organizations engaged in a "parallel peace process" (McCrudden 2001, 87) and was able to get at least some human rights and equality issues on the official agenda for negotiation between the parties (Mageean and O'Brien 1999). Thus the monitoring function was merged in an advocacy role, discussed below.

Since the signing of the 1998 Good Friday Agreement, civil society has played a minor role in monitoring. Currently, the most important monitoring organization is an intergovernmental body (the Independent Monitoring Commission) set up by the British and Irish governments in January 2004. Its tasks include monitoring the activities of paramilitary groups, monitoring the commitment of the British government to a package of security normalization measures, and handling claims by parties in the Northern Ireland Assembly when a minister or other party is not committed to peaceful and democratic means or is not respecting the terms of the pledge of office. Similarly, the Equality Commission is responsible for monitoring the process and procedures that public bodies should adopt in preparing equality schemes, and the Human Rights Commission is tasked with reviewing the adequacy and effectiveness of laws and practices. These commissions have fundamentally changed the context in which human rights organizations operate. On balance, although in the preagreement period civil society was vocal in monitoring and criticizing the state, since the establishment of the institutions created by the Good Friday Agreement, civil society's work in these areas has lost much visibility. In both the pre- and postagreement periods, civil society's monitoring role has had an overall limited impact on changing government policies.

Advocacy

The most visible contribution of civil society to the peace process has been advocacy. In the 1990s, civil society contributed to a settlement between the two communities by lobbying in favor of adopting the Good Friday Agreement (explained below). However, throughout the Troubles, most civil society initiatives were not equally valuable. As noted, groups such as Peace People attracted widespread attention in their demands to stop violence but were unable to articulate a viable political view. By contrast, in the mid-1970s loyalist civil society was effectively mobilized against the first notable attempt at a peace settlement. In 1974, the first power-sharing experiment between the two communities was brought to an end due to a strike by loyalist workers. The uncompromising and sectarian side of civil society prevailed.[4]

Civil society reemerged in the late 1980s and early 1990s to provide a positive contribution, by favoring a constructive dialogue between the parties and by helping to move human rights issues from the margins to the mainstream of the peace process (Mageean and O'Brien 1999). Furthermore, civil society successfully involved the grassroots in the debate on the way forward. In 1992–1993, an independent citizens' group solicited the views of citizens on the issue. Around 3,000 people submitted 554 written and taped submissions. A group of seven prominent commissioners, chaired by Norwegian professor Torkel Opsahl, analyzed the submissions and published an ambitious report addressing a range of issues, from constitutional matters to law, justice, and security, from economic and social issues to religious and cultural ones (Pollack 1993). A number of the recommendations were later adopted in the Good Friday Agreement, including a power-sharing formula (Pollack 1993, 112). Its most lasting contribution, however, was the introduction of a key principle underlying subsequent peace negotiations, something that would change the terms of the political discourse and be enshrined in article 1 of the agreement: "parity of esteem" (Guelke 2003, 70). As a whole, the commission was instrumental in creating an atmosphere of inclusiveness that would underpin the peace negotiations.

Civil society groups abroad also performed a positive advocacy function. Diasporas are often politically hard-line, and Irish expatriates are no exception. In 1970, Irish Americans formed the Irish Northern Aid Committee (NORAID) to fund the IRA's armed struggle and were able to channel significant resources to their cause. However, at the same time, Irish Americans succeeded in lobbying support to promote equality of opportunity between Catholics and Protestants. Since the mid-1980s, a campaign attempted to encourage employers to engage in affirmative action by promoting the so-called MacBride principles, which required US investment in Northern Ireland to be conditional on a balanced workforce. Partly in response, the UK government passed the Fair Employment Act in 1989, requiring limited affirmative action and compulsory monitoring (McCrudden 2001, 87). More important, Irish Americans played an overall moderating role, which assisted the development of the peace process. In the early 1990s, new lobby groups of influential Irish Americans, including lawyers, journalists, and labor and business leaders, were able to sideline NORAID to support Sinn Féin's move toward political dialogue. This group persuaded US president Bill Clinton that progress was possible, leading him to upgrade the Northern Ireland peace process among his foreign policy priorities and to became personally involved in peace talks (Cochrane 2007). While the Irish diaspora worked to facilitate the condition for a peace settlement, civil society groups in the province similarly advocated for an end to the Troubles. In particular, the local business sector effectively set out the economic rationale for peace, successfully including the idea of a peace dividend among key issues to be considered in negotiations (International Alert 2006).

Perhaps the most immediate and far-reaching contribution to the peace process came in spring 1998, when the nonpartisan "Yes" campaign helped pass the referendum that sealed the deal between Protestants and Catholics. Although Sinn Féin and the UUP were key participants in negotiating the agreement, neither party was ready to put its full weight behind it. Nationalist as well as unionist politicians were keenly aware of the potential costs of running a cross-party referendum campaign shortly before they would compete in an election campaign. Sections of both the nationalist and unionist electorates were unconvinced by the agreement, either in whole or in part. Not only were nationalists uneasy about the prospect of IRA decommissioning; some also feared that any settlement of the Northern Ireland problem could undermine the prospect for a united Ireland. Unionists, however, had the most reservations about the agreement. Many lamented the nationalists' entry into government without prior decommissioning, the likelihood of police reform, and the early release of paramilitary prisoners. The skeptical camp also included the families of the victims of violence, whether inflicted by republicans, loyalists, or the state (Mac Ginty and Darby 2002, 159).

In this context, civil society played a crucial role. Less than three weeks after the Good Friday Agreement was signed, a group of Northern Ireland citizens, with members of Initiative '92 at its core, and representing a cross-section of society, launched the "Yes" campaign. In the following weeks resources were mobilized, the media was courted, and an information campaign was launched. A giant marketing firm, Saatchi and Saatchi, helped devise an effective logo that would identify the proagreement camp. This logo was used on street signs to convey the clear choice offered to the electorate: "yes" was equated with "move forward," whereas "no" meant "dead end." The campaign targeted moderate unionist voters in and around Belfast—those most likely to tip the balance between success and failure—and focused in particular on seeking out first-time voters (Oliver 1998, 33). To this end, the handshake between David Trimble (UUP) and John Hume (SDLP) at a U2 rock concert proved effective. Despite their initial insistence on maintaining balance in reporting, the media eventually came around to play a positive role in supporting the peace deal (Oliver 1998, 51–58). The use of public opinion polls, conducted by academics based at Queens University Belfast, further contributed to explore problems and solutions, to reassure political leaders of the presence of a population in support of the peace process, to guarantee transparency to the negotiations, and to sustain dialogue between the parties (Irwin 2002).

Overall, the "Yes" campaign was able to present the agreement as a fair political accommodation between unionists and nationalists. In the process, it performed an important intermediation function between political leaders and their respective communities and facilitated the citizens' endorsement of the Good Friday Agreement (Cochrane and Dunn 2002, 182). Notably, however, the majority of leaders in the civil society sector remained on the fence throughout the period preceding the key referendum. Many feared that taking a political stand might have negative repercussions among their constituencies, clients, or funders. The main civil society umbrella organization, the Northern Ireland Council for Voluntary Action (NICVA), was supportive but avoided recommending a "Yes" vote to members (Oliver 1998, 48). The business sector and trade unions were also cautious, and the churches were "the dogs that didn't bark" (Oliver 1998, 95) during the campaign. Despite these limits, the advocacy work of civil society provided an important positive contribution to the peace process: it involved society at large in an elite-led negotiation, offered significant inputs at key times, and lobbied effectively to adopt the agreement that would put an end to twenty-five years of conflict.

In-Group Socialization

In-group social cohesion is very strong in Northern Ireland. Informal networks in deprived areas provide social and economic support and day-to-day safety nets to the most vulnerable. At the same time, memberships in support networks often depend on excluding others, contributing to distrust of wider institutions and hindering the development of intergroup ties (Leonard 2004). Similarly, church attendance is a major indicator of communal separation (C. Mitchell 2006). Not only do informal groups re-create existing communal divisions; the majority of formal organizations are also structured along ethnoreligious lines. Three-quarters of all organizations have management committees or boards of directors that are either entirely or mainly from one community. In this context, all organizations tend to avoid addressing issues of divisions directly through their programs, with Protestant organizations even less likely to do so than Catholic ones (Acheson et al. 2006, 56).

For the most part, in-group socialization tends to reinforce differences and perpetuate suspicion about the other's intentions (Farrington 2008). This is true for both sides on the communal divide, where the most popular organizations have a clear political affiliation. The Orange Order is the most important representative of cultural/political Protestantism. It proclaims itself "primarily a religious organization," which is "Christ-centered, Bible-based, and Church-grounded." It officially stands for civil and religious liberty yet remains firmly sectarian. Its members must sign a declaration before joining that both their parents are Protestants, and they must leave if they marry a Catholic. The Orange Order's very existence and activities are a continuing source of tension and, occasionally, violent conflict. Among these activities, the Orange Order each year celebrates the military triumph in 1690 of the Protestant king William III of Orange over the Catholics. Throughout the 1990s, at the time when open confrontation and violence between Catholics and Protestants was declining and a peace agreement was being negotiated, the organization's parades and marches through Catholic neighborhoods heightened tensions between parts of the Protestant and Catholic communities. Although the Orange Order's overall influence on Northern Ireland's politics and society has declined considerably since the late 1980s, it remains the most popular Protestant organization in the province, with an estimated membership of more than 40,000.

On the Catholic side, it is difficult to find a similarly contentious organization; but the broader reality of a society divided along exclusivist and sectarian lines remains. Indeed, Catholic civil society often reflects the same political preferences of the Catholic/nationalist political class. The most popular Catholic organization—the Gaelic Athletic Association (GAA)—is firmly nationalist. It hopes for the end of British control over Northern Ireland and the reunification of the island under the government in Dublin. The most controversial among GAA's rules was a ban prohibiting members of the British Army and the RUC from playing Gaelic Games (Rule 21). In practice this rule had limited impact, as it was unlikely that very many RUC and army personnel would have joined the organization anyway. However, for the Orange Parades, Rule 21 constituted an important symbolic statement. The ban provoked considerable controversy and was lifted only on November 17, 2001, after the creation of the new Police Service of Northern Ireland (Belloni 2009).

The Orange Order and the GAA are more representative of civil society than any other organization in Northern Ireland—not least for their considerable memberships. While NGOs often embody the values of the liberal elite of society, both the Orange Order and the GAA reflect the popular sentiment. Such a sentiment may include a deep-seated skepticism about the possibility and usefulness of engaging in cross-community contacts. Political suspicion, fear of negative reactions from within one's own community, and apprehension about hostility from the other side all combine to limit intergroup cooperation. Furthermore, most sites of socialization, particularly for the working class, and including work, education, recreation, as well as housing, are effectively divided between the two communities, allowing most individuals to conduct their lives with very limited interaction with members of the other group.

In this context, "single-identity work" is sometimes touted as a necessary prerequisite and as an avenue to engage working-class individuals who would not have become involved. At its best, this work increases a group's self-confidence and creates the preconditions for successful intergroup cooperation. Organizations such as Cunamh, Hard Gospel, the Centre for Contemporary Christianity in Northern Ireland, and the Clonnard Monastery have worked tirelessly within their own communities to ease tensions and to build bridges (see below). Former political prisoners have often relied on their strong identity to engage with former enemies (Shirlow and McEvoy 2008). At its worst, single-identity work may increase segregation and reinforce the negative views of the "other side." Since single-identity projects rarely incorporate systematic monitoring and evaluation, their impact remains speculative (Church, Visser, and Johnson 2004). It should be noted, however, that to the extent that single-identity work has no vision of eventually moving to cross-community work or of mitigating the conflict, it reflects an essentialist view of the conflict, perpetuating divisions within society. On balance, strong in-group solidarity in Northern Ireland has proved to be a hindrance to intergroup social cohesion. Particularly in working-class areas, most individuals have deep ties to their communities but maintain a suspicion of and reluctance to engage with the "other side."

Intergroup Social Cohesion

Civil society has been least effective in performing the social cohesion function, despite the obvious need for such work. In late 1969, the Northern Ireland Community Relations Commission was established to address the problem of relationships between Protestants and Catholics. The commission's policy was focused on community development and tried to foster self-confidence and solidarity among disaffected sections of the population. Its support of groups carrying out community relations programs was indirect and secondary to community development. With a poor record of achievement, the commission was dissolved in 1975 (Bloomfield 1997, 51–58). In 1990, the Community Relations Council (CRC) was created as a government-sponsored but independent organization tasked with improving relationships between the two communities and with assisting any groups engaged in promoting dialogue. Reconciliation figures prominently among CRC's interest areas. CRC's main innovation is represented by their goal of making community relations the task of all social groups in the community, not just the job of reconciliation groups with this specific mission. To this end, CRC provides funding and extensive training on a range of issues, including prejudice reduction, nonviolent action, human rights education, and others. In addition to formalizing the status of practitioners, this training provided extensive networking opportunities to participants (Bloomfield 1997, 162–168).

According to NICVA (2005), 129 organizations currently describe themselves as primarily cross-community, committed to improving bridging social capital between Catholics and Protestants. Many organizations provide occasions for intergroup mixing in a controlled safe space. Such mixing is skillfully directed toward constructed interaction in cooperative endeavors, whereby participants learn conflict management and transformation skills, question divisive stereotypes, "deal with the past," and discuss ways forward along with the related organizational and political skills for getting there. However, although many organizations provide such opportunities, several problems complicate the work of civil society in this area. First, the segregated nature of living, which has increased since the signing of the Good Friday Agreement, and the fact that many organizations were created as single-identity groups, limit occasions for contact.[6] Second, donors have sometimes failed to effectively support cross-community work. For example, the first European Union Programme for Peace and Reconciliation, which channeled 350 million ECUs into Northern Ireland between 1994 and 2000, without emphasizing cross-community work, has been described as a "failed opportunity" (Acheson et al. 2006, 32). Only with Peace II, and even more so with Peace III, did the European Union emphasize the importance of cross-community aspects.

Third, and most important, the "community relations" agenda remains controversial. Parts of the unionist and nationalist communities fear that this agenda hides an unspoken and ominous strategy. Unionists are worried it is a first step toward a "United Ireland," while some nationalists interpret it as a way to convince them to "buy into the state" (Hall 2001, 4–5). Many activists, particularly in the most deprived and violent neighborhoods, are also skeptical and raise two issues. To begin with, couching the problem as poor "community relations" between Catholics and Protestants conceals the deprivation and marginalization that are typical in the most sectarian and violent areas. As mentioned, particularly during the Troubles, the most deprived districts in Belfast were the most violent. In addition, skeptics point out that the community relations agenda assumes the state is an honest broker trying to mediate between hostile local communities. This approach neglects the state's role in bringing about the problem in the first place, and unfairly places the burden of managing legitimate political differences in the hands of local communities (Hall 2001, 7–9; McVeigh 2002).

Civil society activists often identify community development as the alternative to community relations. Even when they receive external funding for community relations work, they focus on community development, referred to as "single-identity work." The complacent attitude of funders permits this move (Hall 2001, 17). A survey of the voluntary sector found that a striking 80 percent of all organizations experience "no external pressure to work in a more cross-community way" (Acheson et al. 2006, 39–40). As noted above, working with only one community can in fact preserve hostile and conflictual relationships. Perhaps unsurprisingly, despite substantial economic investments, and although sectarian violence has decreased, community divisions have deepened since the signing of the Good Friday Agreement (Acheson et al. 2006, 16).

In March 2005, the government published an important policy document, *A Shared Future,* recognizing the problems posed by sectarianism and racism and outlining the vision for "good community relations"—the Northern Ireland variation of bridging social capital. The government's overall goal was to establish "a shared society defined by a culture of tolerance: a normal, civic society, in which all individuals are considered as equals, where differences are resolved through dialogue in the public sphere, and where all individuals are treated impartially. A society where there is equity, respect for diversity and recognition of our interdependence" (Office of the Prime Minister and Deputy Prime Minister 2005, 10). All civil society projects, whether single-identity or cross-community, are required to contribute to improving community relations. Similarly, the EU-funded Peace III program requires all projects to contribute to good relations and understanding (EUPTC 2007, 42).

Given the persisting divisions, such requirements seem appropriate. So far, civil society has been at its weakest in developing intergroup bridging ties—despite an apparent interest in community relations among civil society groups and activists. However, the nature of the Belfast Agreement, based on consociational principles, emphasizes the top-down management of divisions over civil society's potential role in overcoming sectarianism. Within this institutional context, the almost complete lack of interest at the executive level for cross-community work risks making policy statements about a "shared future" sound hollow. Without the elites' political commitment, limited trust and suspicion between two main communities are unlikely to be softened and overcome.

Intermediation

Several NGOs and the clergy have been involved in mediation, as well as in engaging politicians, paramilitaries, and local communities. Mediation often progresses from talks with one side, which build a trusting relationship with the mediating NGO or individual, to shuttle diplomacy between opposing sides, to face-to-face talks in neutral space provided by an NGO. A number of Catholic monks at the Clonnard Monastery and some Protestant clergymen were instrumental in the late 1980s to early 1990s in facilitating secret talks between Sinn Féin's Gerry Adams and SDLP's John Hume, as well as with unionist politicians. This eventually led to the all-party peace talks that produced the Good Friday Agreement (McCartney 1999). The Centre for Contemporary Christianity in Ireland (CCCI, previously known as the Evangelical Contribution on Northern Ireland, or ECONI) has quietly brought together groups of politicians, sometimes of different persuasions within a community, and sometimes across communities, to build understanding and relationships in private settings. Although it is a Protestant organization, CCCI's mission involves calling Protestants' attention to the message of peace in the Gospel. This internal criticism and CCCI's early willingness to meet with Sinn Féin have given it credibility with nationalists and republicans. Some other groups that have provided skilled mediation or facilitation in neutral space include Quaker House (Cox 2003) and the Corrymeela Community (McCreary 2007). Notably, the Corrymeela Community was established in 1965, before the outbreak of the Troubles, as an ecumenical community to promote dialogue and reconciliation, including (but not only) between Protestants and Catholics in Northern Ireland. It has been involved in facilitating dialogue between political parties and between paramilitaries. The community has also provided training in mediation and reconciliation to many individuals and groups and has spun off specialized groups such as Mediation Northern Ireland and the Northern Ireland Mixed Marriage Association.

In addition, several groups worked directly with paramilitaries to prevent violence and draw them into the peace process. This work included helping feuding loyalist paramilitary groups to halt intracommunity violence in the wake of the peace agreement. Peacebuilding activists also facilitated communication between communities to reduce violence. One innovative form, which has spread since it was first used in 1997, has been the development of cellphone networks between Protestant and Catholic activists, so that rumors of threatening developments can be investigated and quelled (Jarman 2006). This is especially important during the summertime parade season, when tensions are high.

The most visible intermediation function was performed by the Northern Ireland Women Coalition during the negotiation of the Good Friday Agreement (Fearon 1999). In order to promote women's representation and participation in the peace process, a group of women primarily from the voluntary and community sector, but also including teachers, other professionals, and home workers, formed a political party to contest the elections (the only civil society activists to do so). The Women Coalition's electoral result was modest, obtaining only two seats, but its influence extended beyond mere parliamentary representation. By focusing on process rather than outcome (the coalition took no official position on constitutional issues), it worked to promote an inclusive ethos based on cooperation and a readiness to share ideas. Substantively, it proposed the creation of the Civic Forum as part of the Northern Ireland Assembly—a proposal that was incorporated in the peace deal. Furthermore, in the run-up to the May 1998 referendums, the coalition supported the "Yes" campaign. Overall, the often confidential and sensitive nature of mediation work, which becomes momentous to politicians and even dangerous for paramilitaries, usually results in vague public reports. Thus, it is often underanalyzed and, perhaps, has more impact than generally acknowledged. On balance, however, this kind of low-key, behind-the-scenes effort has made a significant contribution to the peace process.

Service Delivery

Civil society in Northern Ireland has always been heavily engaged in service delivery. In the vacuum created by the imposition of direct rule from London in 1972, civil society organizations stepped up work to replace local institutions in the field. Primarily in Catholic areas, where the legitimacy of Protestant- and UK-dominated institutions has always been questioned, civil society developed an extensive network of groups. Since the late 1990s, the government's strategy further augmented civil society's role in this respect. New Labour has seen the voluntary sector as instrumental in carrying out government policy through the delivery of core social services (Acheson 2001). Professionalization, training, coordination, and standardization of goals and activities have been promoted to improve the sector's efficiency in the delivery of services. Currently, welfare organizations providing specialist services represent the largest share among the voluntary and community sectors in Northern Ireland (NICVA 2005).

In the vast majority of cases, service delivery organizations engage in avoidance, a strategy that ignores issues of community relations and provides assistance, in principle, to all in need. Typically, community divisions are not considered in planning and providing services (Glendinning 1999). This approach is justified by a work ethos focused on addressing needs without discrimination and by the fear of compromising the organization's work by entering the political field. Fairness in service provision is a practical matter aimed at avoiding political sensitivities while helping citizens meet basic needs, rather than the expression of an antagonistic ideology. Despite its technical mold—or perhaps because of it—this approach sometimes allows individuals from different backgrounds to share a social setting in the pursuit of common goals. For example, women's and senior citizens' groups often reach across communal divisions and are able to build a lasting sense of solidarity among members (Acheson et al. 2006).

However, at the same time, service delivery is blind to communal divisions and has its shortcomings. There remains a reluctance to enter territory perceived to belong to the "other community." Thus, existing spatial divisions limit opportunities for contact between members of the two main groups. Moreover, even when bridges are built, they might not have an effect on political life. Notably, women's organizations have developed a strong cross-community network to address common needs, but they failed to capitalize politically on this experience. The fate of the Women Coalition, which contested the 1998 elections and was able to win only two seats, illustrates the difficulty of turning intergroup ties into political power (Acheson et al. 2006, 58–77). Women's groups have been more effective when lobbying the political system. For example, Women into Politics, an organization not associated with the Women Coalition, runs widespread and ambitious programs to promote the political participation of women as a bloc of citizens concerned with women's issues, including peace.

On balance, the impact of service delivery on community relations and peacebuilding remains hard to gauge, but it is likely to be limited (Acheson et al. 2006, 27). Service delivery promotes primarily economic and social, not political, purposes. Moreover, the government's view of civil society as a tool of policy has undermined the advocacy/monitoring role of voluntary groups.

Conclusion

The impact of civil society on peacebuilding has been positive, but primarily by operating in the background and for the long term. Throughout the Troubles, public opinion polls showed consistent cross-community support for ending the violence, yet it was not the existence of a propeace constituency that spurred on the peace process (Mac Ginty and Darby 2002, 171). Most political analysts and activists would agree that the main impulse came from political violence, not from the activities of the civil society sector—although the third sector played an important role in supporting a cultural change toward nonviolent and inclusive approaches to intergroup relationships (Cochrane and Dunn 2002, 152–155). Bombings and shootings in October and November 1993 raised the specter of an unending spiral of violence and motivated the main political/military elites to undertake a credible peace process. At the same time, republicans reached the conclusion that the armed struggle they had waged throughout the Troubles would not achieve its objectives of reuniting the island, and thus they sought a new political route.

Moreover, since the mid-1970s, Catholic grievances have been gradually addressed, thus undermining one of the key reasons for violent confrontation. Electoral reforms allowed a more equitable representation of Catholics in political life; education reform both ensured that schools offer a broad and balanced curriculum and made Catholics more employable; the percentage of Catholics in the total workforce increased; and the housing stock was upgraded and allocated more fairly between the two groups (Fitzduff 2002, 21–29, 158). From a constitutional point of view, the British government's dual strategy—of searching for an acceptable power-sharing formula and of recognizing the role of the Republic of Ireland in the peacemaking process—proved successful.

Although violence, power politics, and political, social, and economic reforms shaped the development of the peace process, civil society still performed useful functions. During the Troubles, civil society revealed a dark side (epitomized by paramilitary violence) and a prepolitical, amateurish impulse "to do something" (exemplified by Peace People). Between the two, the voluntary sector eventually was able to assert itself to protect thousands of individuals threatened by paramilitary violence. Furthermore, it monitored state, and increasingly paramilitary, human rights abuses. Although these activities may have had a limited direct impact, they were useful in raising the public profile of the problem of violence in the province. Monitoring merged with advocacy, as civil society's public denunciations resulted in calls to devise and implement a human rights strategy to address the conflict.

It is in the negotiation phase that civil society played its most visible (although not necessarily most important) role. When, in the mid-1990s, the peace process tentatively began moving forward with the aid of civil society, the voluntary sector provided an important intermediation function between politicians and between estranged communities, becoming a crucial link between formal negotiations and the public at large. The sector involved the grassroots in the debate over the future of the province, was instrumental in facilitating the dialogue between the parties, and mainstreamed the equality agenda by favoring its inclusion in the peace negotiations. Furthermore, civil society contributed several key proposals, most notably by advocating for the creation of the Civic Forum. Perhaps the "Yes" campaign represents civil society's most noticeable and lasting contribution. The campaign helped secure an agreement that was only reluctantly negotiated by the parties under heavy British, Irish, and US pressure.

In the postagreement period, pressed by the government's priorities, civil society focused on service delivery, with only limited political impact on the peace process. Yet, even in this period the voluntary sector has been providing a positive contribution. Most notably, politically motivated groups of former prisoners have been playing an important part in reintegrating paramilitaries into communities. The relatively successful transformation of paramilitaries, from obstacles to a resource for peacebuilding, is a far-reaching achievement that could serve as a model for other countries torn apart by civil strife. Likewise, restorative justice programs have provided a viable alternative to informal justice delivered by self-appointed community vigilantes.

Although the level of civil society activity remains enormously high, the reduction in political urgency following the signing of the Good Friday Agreement, as well as a decline in violence and a booming economy, contributed to political disengagement. In addition, the establishment of new institutions created an avenue for the expression of nonviolent and legitimate political interests, undermining the rationale for civil society's unofficial role. More important, the consociational nature of devolved institutions, focused on elites' collusion and the entrenchment of societal divisions, has served as the main disabling factor for civil society's contribution to easing cross-community divisions. Intergroup cooperation at the political level has effectively sidelined the community relations agenda. Political elites in both communities appear satisfied with managing their respective groups exclusively—a predictable product of consociational politics. The education system, with only a small minority of children attending integrated schools, constitutes a further obstacle vis-à-vis the development of cross-community ties. Today, more than a decade after the signing of the Belfast Agreement, Protestant and Catholic communities continue to be as divided and suspicious of each other as ever.

In sum, civil society fulfilled important functions throughout all phases of the peace process. During the Troubles, civil society contributed to the development of a human rights culture, protecting individuals threatened by violence, monitoring state abuses, and lobbying to raise the profile of human rights issues. The most effective function was the difficult and patient intermediation work, conducted largely behind the scenes, which set the stage for subsequent peace negotiations. With the signing of the Belfast Agreement, civil society campaigned in favor of its adoption, undertaking a clever advocacy strategy, which effectively linked the political process to the population at large.

Since then, civil society's most notable contribution has been the reintegration of former paramilitaries into civilian life—a task related to the protection function. Currently, civil society remains at its weakest in the crucial area of developing intergroup bridging ties. Much of civil society's efforts are focused on service delivery or on single-identity work, with unclear effects on building bridging ties. The fact that the vast majority of voluntary organizations report experiencing little external pressure to employ more cross-community methods suggests that the responsibility cannot be assigned entirely to the civil society sector; this also calls into question the broader political/institutional context that is inhospitable to social cohesion efforts. The development of a culture of tolerance and mutual acceptance between estranged communities remains the most difficult challenge for civil society actors.

Notes

Many thanks to John Darby, Mari Fitzduff, and Bruce Hemmer for their helpful comments on an earlier draft of this chapter. I am particularly grateful to John Darby who, in addition to commenting on a written version of this chapter, discussed several points with me during a number of insightful conversations. Needless to say, I am solely responsible for any remaining errors of fact or interpretation.

1. Some nationalists and many republicans eschew references to "Northern Ireland," created at the time of the partition, which they reject, in favor of the "North" or the "six counties," which emphasizes a connection to the other counties of the united Ireland, which they envision.

2. Civil society groups, however, are skeptical of this method, which they consider too formal and ineffective in involving stakeholders (NICVA 2006, 11 and 25).

3. By contrast, the leading human rights organization in Northern Ireland (the Committee on the Administration of Justice) has maintained its policy of focusing on state abuses (and thus is seen as biased by many unionists). As stated on its website, "The Committee seeks to secure the highest standards in the administration of justice in Northern Ireland by ensuring that the government complies with its responsibilities in international human rights law" (CAJ 2008).

4. Not all of the trade union movement was subjected to uncompromising political pressures. From the early 1990s onward, the Irish Congress of Trade Unions committed itself to eradicating sectarianism in the workplace. In 1990, it established COUNTERACT, an antisectarian unit that has intervened in disputes in the workplace and has engaged a range of organizations, including the police, the community and voluntary sectors, and former prisoners. On the problems and prospects of the trade union movement, see Gormally (2008).

7

Bosnia-Herzegovina: Civil Society in a Semiprotectorate

Roberto Belloni and Bruce Hemmer

Civil society in Bosnia-Herzegovina (henceforth Bosnia or BiH) is weak and divided but slowly rising to the political role that it must play if it is to make peace and democracy sustainable. Bosnia is recovering, simultaneously, from the legacy of communism and from more than three years of the most brutal conflict seen in Europe since World War II. Massive human dislocation resulted in ethnically homogeneous areas being controlled by the same political parties responsible for the carnage. Unemployment is almost 40 percent (Labour and Employment Agency of Bosnia and Herzegovina 2008), and corruption is widespread. In this context, Bosnian citizens are often more concerned with issues of economic survival than with participation in the public sphere. Yet, despite this difficult environment, Bosnian civil society has provided important contributions to the peacebuilding process. Many groups have been engaged in rebuilding relationships and in mediating between ethnic communities to facilitate the postwar return of refugees and displaced persons. An increasing number are involved in building the civic attitudes and practices necessary for democracy, and a few civic initiatives have resulted in legal changes helpful to cementing peace.

Being a European country, Bosnia experienced a gigantic post–civil war international intervention, including the North Atlantic Treaty Organization (NATO), the European Union (EU), and the Organization for Security and Cooperation in Europe (OSCE), along with the United Nations (UN), many other IGOs, bilateral development agencies, and myriad INGOs. But this situation was not entirely beneficial. The international community was overeager to develop civil society as "local partners" and as a vehicle for restoring social cohesion and instilling a culture of participatory democracy. It had unrealistic expectations of how quickly this could or should happen in a society with no consolidated democratic tradition and virtually no local sources of funding. In this chapter we explain how international intervention had harmful effects on the effectiveness, legitimacy, cooperation, and networking of the emergent civil society. Moreover, we highlight how the strong role that the international community has played, often necessarily, in guaranteeing security and in pushing democratic and economic reforms has paradoxically inhibited the development of civil society's protection, monitoring, and advocacy roles. As a result, civil society has fulfilled important peacebuilding functions, especially at the grassroots level, but has struggled to become a vehicle for broad social and political change.

Context

The three main ethnic groups in Bosnia are all Slavic and speak variants of the same Serbo-Croatian language.[1] They are distinguished principally by religious heritage, though many were secularized by communism and socioeconomic development. The largest group, the Bosniaks, are of Muslim heritage, having converted when Bosnia was occupied by the Ottoman Empire. According to the 1991 census, Bosniaks form a 43 percent plurality. Serbs, of Orthodox Christian tradition, are the next largest ethnicity, at 31 percent of prewar Bosnia. Croats, of Catholic tradition, were 17 percent of prewar Bosnia.[2]

Yugoslavia and Its Demise

Throughout most of the twentieth century, Bosnia was part of Yugoslavia. Formed in the wake of World War I in 1918, Yugoslavia united the southern Slavs under a constitutional monarchy. Yugoslavia's experiment was extinguished by the outbreak of World War II and the collapse of the country under the Nazi war machine. Axis occupation and the establishment of a fascist Croatian puppet state created the context for extreme ethnic violence in both Croatia and Bosnia, often involving atrocities in which hundreds of thousands died, principally Serbs (Paris 1961). After World War II, Yugoslavia was reformed as a communist state a second time, this time under Josip Broz Tito, with a federal structure of six republics: Bosnia, Serbia, Croatia, Slovenia, Montenegro, and Macedonia. Yugoslavia adopted a milder form of communism compared to countries in the Soviet bloc, famously taking a "third way" between East and West. The system was decentralized under the concept of "self-management," giving citizens more freedom and control over their own affairs, even allowing limited private ownership of property and businesses and travel abroad, especially to work and remit wages back home. But the system was still totalitarian, and freedom did not extend to politics. All media were controlled by party organs, unions served the party more than workers, any formal associations required approval by the party apparatus, and only apolitical or communist associations were permitted. Counterrevolutionary speech (including jokes) was considered a "verbal attack" on government and was punishable by law (Bokovoy, Irvine, and Lilly 1997).

Tito died in 1980, and communism weakened in the ensuing decade of economic decline. In the late 1980s, as the disoriented Communist Party was losing its grip, independent and politically vocal civil society organizations began to develop. The number of workers' strikes increased; some politically relevant professions (e.g., journalists) began to enjoy some autonomy; citizens' initiatives presented petitions to the authorities; new countercultures, such as the punk rock movement, emerged; and a growing number of intellectuals problematized the relationship between state and society and demanded creation of a public sphere free from pervasive state influence (Krizan 1989). In Bosnia, this opening began with student organizations in Sarajevo, following the lead of students in Slovenia a few years prior. But nascent liberal civil society was quickly overshadowed by the rise of ethnonationalist parties—in Bosnia as well as in all the other republics.

Multiparty free elections were held in 1990 in each republic. Slobodan Milosevic, president of Serbia, sought to dominate the Yugoslav Federation, driving Slovenia and Croatia toward declaring independence in June 1991. The Serb-dominated federal army intervened, focusing on Croatia, where a large Serb minority was concentrated along the borders with Serbia and Bosnia. Bosniak parties in Bosnia were struggling to maintain peace but did not wish to remain in a rump Yugoslavia heavily dominated by Serbs. The international recognition of independence for Croatia and Slovenia in January 1992 finally forced the Bosniaks to act, and a referendum on independence was held in April 1992. It overwhelmingly passed among Bosniaks and Croats, but virtually all the Serbs boycotted it.

An incipient civil society attempted to prevent the escalation to war. The first peace organization, the Centre for Peace, was created in Sarajevo in early 1991, followed by the Bosnian branch of the Helsinki Citizens' Assembly. Although these and similar organizations (particularly youth organizations) were able to introduce liberal ideas into urban society, they were unable to gain significant popular support in the short time left. Their activities were localized and did not reach outside major cities into the segregated and undereducated rural areas. In this context, opportunistic nationalist politicians used their control of the media to drum up support via the politics of fear. A last-ditch effort to avoid war came on April 5, 1992, when thousands of citizens occupied the parliament building in Sarajevo and formed the All Peoples' Parliament, demanding peace, the resignation of nationalist politicians, the banning of ethnic parties, and new elections. Serb paramilitary units fired on marching peace demonstrators, marking the beginning of the Bosnian war (Andjelic 1998).

The warring ethnic groups were intermingled, which led to a particularly brutal civil war. In all, 97,207 people died or are missing and presumed dead (2.2 percent of the population), and 41 percent of the dead and missing are civilians.[3] Half the population of 4.4 million was displaced. The dead and missing are 66 percent Bosniaks, 26 percent Serbs, and 8 percent Croats. And among *civilian* dead and missing, 83 percent are Bosniaks, the result of the Serb nationalist strategy of "ethnic cleansing" to create a purely Serb area called the Republika Srpska (RS). There was widespread rape of females, especially by Serb paramilitaries and soldiers, for whom this was part of the ethnic cleansing strategy.

The violence against civilians was especially strong in the eastern half of the RS, along the Serbian border, where many Bosniaks lived before the war. The most infamous location is Srebrenica in eastern RS, where a UN-protected area was overrun in July 1995; some 7,000 or more Bosniak men and boys were massacred after being taken prisoner by Serb troops. The primary site of nonbattle deaths in western RS is Prijedor, where 5,209 people died over the course of the war. In the Mostar region, a conflict between Croats and Bosniaks broke out in March 1993, with Croats attempting to annex portions of Bosnia to Croatia. This conflict was ended through heavy US diplomatic intervention, which led to the Washington Agreement of March 1994. The agreement (accord) created the Federation of BiH, which allied the Croats and Bosniaks in fighting the Serbs. NATO bombardment of Serb positions, with a coordinated push by Bosniak and Croat forces in September 1995, proved decisive, leading to a peace settlement reached in Dayton, Ohio, in November. Bosnian civil society played no role in the official peacemaking process.

Postwar Bosnia

Within a week of signing the agreement, a very robust NATO-led Implementation Force, including Russian forces, began to deploy throughout Bosnia (a role later taken over by the European Union). Whether because of this massive peacekeeping force, or the peace agreement, or simply exhaustion with war, there was no significant further violence. Along with the troops came a tremendous contingent of IGOs, foreign government aid agencies, and international NGOs to help with every aspect of implementing the peace agreement. Several large IGOs were given important responsibilities under the peace agreement, including police monitoring by the United Nations (later handed to the European Union) and political implementation, including running elections and monitoring human rights, by the OSCE.

The Dayton Agreement established a complex federal structure consisting of weak state structures arching over two "entities" within the state: the RS in the north and east, dominated by Serbs; and the Federation of BiH, consisting of ten cantons, some mostly Croat and some mostly Bosniak. The entity and canton governments hold most of the power. The 2002 constitutional reform required, among other issues, that the ethnic distribution of ministry posts reflect the relevant population at each level of government throughout Bosnia, and established two vice presidencies within each entity, reserved for the two ethnicities not holding the entity presidency. Notably there are no reserved seats at any level for citizens who do not identify with any of the main ethnic groups, or for those who reject ethnic identity altogether. Since the early post-Dayton years, these complex structures have created difficulties for effective governance and complicated civil society's monitoring and advocacy's functions. Given all of the posts to be filled, roughly 40 percent of GDP is spent in the public sector (Belloni 2007, 43–72).

The agreement also established the Office of the High Representative (OHR) of the international community to oversee implementation. At the December 1997 meeting of the Peace Implementation Council in Bonn, the High Representative was further empowered to remove officials acting against the peace agreement, to bar obstructionist parties from running for office, and to impose laws as necessary to move the peace process forward. All of these powers have been used, albeit reluctantly. This has created a paradox. The use of such powers to promote peace and democratization encourages local politicians to play to their ethnonationalistic bases and remain obstinate, as the High Representative will eventually fix the problem for them. If the High Representative does not act, little progress is made. According to critics, this protectorate role reinforces the bad habits of the old Yugoslav political culture, in particular the keenness for a "strong hand" acting outside the political process, as with Tito before the High Representative (ESI 2004).

Bosnia is thus only partially democratic and free, partially an international protectorate. As Freedom House's scores confirm, the environment of democratic liberties that civic activists experience has steadily improved after the war, with Bosnia crossing into the top half of the world on this scale in 2006 (Freedom House 2007; Dizdarevic et al. 2006). Unlike in the communist days, currently there is no appreciable government intimidation or repression. However, Bosnia is still not deemed ready to stand on its own. The last three High Representatives have claimed they will be the last, only to see a replacement being appointed. In addition to the so-called Bonn powers, the desire of most Bosnians to join the European Union is a very useful lever for requiring reforms, and the High Representative is transitioning into the Special Representative of the European Union, which will not enjoy Bonn powers but will be able to withhold integration until reforms are made.

The key problem is that nationalist parties continue to dominate elections, although their hold has been slipping over time. The nationalist parties generally do not have well-developed programs for socioeconomic and democratic progress, because their focus is on holding power through the politics of fear. Fear of how the other sides will vote drives voters to choose the party of security for their own ethnicity. This is combined with corrupt, ethnic-based patronage systems to win voter loyalty. The only large, significantly multiethnic party is the Social Democratic Party (SDP), the reformed successor of the Communist Party. A coalition led by this party won power at many levels, including the state, in 2000, but the coalition was unable to make significant progress on Bosnia's deep problems of economic and governmental reform before it fell apart and nationalist parties retook office. Milder nationalist parties now dominate elections, so there has been some progress. But other than SDP, nonnationalist votes are diluted across a myriad of small parties that have so far been unable to coalesce into a reasonable number of choices across the usual spectrum of nonnationalist socioeconomic positions.

Postwar peacebuilding in Bosnia is about making the new democratic system take root, as this is the prerequisite for the international occupation to withdraw and leave behind a sustainable peace. Peacebuilding is also about reversing lingering effects of the war, such as the return of millions of displaced persons, strengthening state institutions at the expense of ethnically divisive entities, and prosecuting war criminals. International organizations took a heavily top-down approach (especially since 1998, with the Bonn powers) but also attempted to support development of civil society organizations that interact with governmental institutions as advocates, monitors, and partners in solving social problems. With a few exceptions as detailed below, these efforts tended to produce short-term activities that lasted only as long as internationals were heavily involved, because politicians were not responsive and citizens lacked faith in the process. Internationals generally have had unrealistic expectations of how quickly civil society could be effective in such roles given the political and cultural context, and they underestimated the importance and difficulty of changing interethnic and democratic attitudes at the grassroots level.

As explained below, most peacebuilding by civil society could be described as "bottom-out," as it involves no ambition to interact with political structures but aims instead at rebuilding peaceful attitudes and relationships at the grassroots level, through socialization, social cohesion, intermediation, and service delivery. Many peacebuilding NGO leaders see this work as a prerequisite to political engagement. Increasingly, some groups do engage in fully "bottom-up" work, aimed at creating democratic citizens capable of making the new institutional system work for them and connecting them to political leaders. Advocacy and intermediation between citizens and politicians by NGOs are slowly growing in frequency, ambition, and sophistication. When combined with rebuilding positive interethnic attitudes and relationships, the democratic empowerment of citizens constitutes peacebuilding in this context, because it has the long-term potential to break the nationalist stranglehold and to compel the political system to begin solving socioeconomic problems effectively, without ethnic discrimination.

A key area for international organizations and local civil society—cutting across several peacebuilding functions—is seen in the attempts to reverse ethnic cleansing through "minority return" (i.e., returning displaced persons and refugees to areas under the control of another ethnic group). Minority return peaked in 2002 and then sharply dropped, totaling approximately 44 percent of the potential minority return.[4] Much of this was temporary return to repair homes for sale, but a significant portion was permanent. Nowhere in the RS did non-Serbs regain plurality or majority status. Serbs did regain majority status, however, in several municipalities of the Federation. The international community was active in pressuring local officials to support return (notably in implementing municipal election results and property restitution), as well as in monitoring the human rights of returnees. Local civil society was very active in supporting minority return at the grassroots level, as detailed below, often in partnership with the UN High Commissioner for Refugees (UNHCR).

Status of Civil Society

Until the last few years of the regime, the only voluntary civic organizations allowed to exist were either communist in orientation or apolitical, and they were closely monitored to prevent any from taking on political roles (Andjelic 2003, 81–97). Unions served the party more so than members, and in the post-Dayton era they continue to lack transparency and are often mistrusted by the general population (Fischer 2007a). Churches, mosques, and faith-based charities were allowed to function and remain highly regarded in the wake of their work during and after the war. Additionally, some other nonpolitical "citizens' associations" were allowed, for veterans, pensioners, women, and youths, and for cultural and leisure activities, such as team sports, hunting, fishing, and mountaineering—many of which have survived in the post-Dayton era.

Rebirth and International Support

During Yugoslav times, the contact point between citizens and the government was the *mjesna zajednica* (MZ), roughly translated as "local community" (Pusic 1975). These were submunicipal units akin to large neighborhood associations, but with the power to raise revenue, commission local infrastructure projects, and issue permits and other government documents. MZ presidents would also be involved in resolving local disputes. During the war, MZs were often important centers of localized support activities for those in need, but since then it is more difficult to find such community spirit. Many MZs have disappeared, but some have continued to function as voluntary community organizations, which advocate before the municipality for development and services to the locality and also organize voluntary community service by citizens. A few MZs, frustrated with being ignored or poorly funded by municipal governments, reorganized as NGOs and sought funding from international donors. But the majority of surviving MZs remain dependent on municipal governments and thus are likely to be controlled by political parties. Interestingly, however, Bosnian citizens still contribute to the work of MZ boards where they remain and are more likely to volunteer and provide funds to MZs than to other organizations (World Bank 2002, 69–80). MZs remain deeply rooted in Bosnian society and represent an effective—although waning—participation mechanism (Bajrovic 2005).

While MZs are locally rooted bodies inherited from the old system, Western-style NGOs are a post-Dayton creation stimulated by the availability of international funding. It is estimated that between 1995 and 2000, when international aid was at its peak, international donors spent about US$5–6 billion on various forms of assistance to local communities, including support for the development of civil society, democratization, and media (Papic 2001, 30). In this period, donors seemed to equate the number of NGOs with the strength of civil society. Unsurprisingly, this approach resulted in the development of donor-driven, Western-style NGOs (Sali-Terzic 2001). New organizations mushroomed in a rich international funding environment, many beginning as the local partners of international actors. Most of these new NGOs continued to focus on issues allowed before the war, such as sports and folk culture, while others were new types of equally apolitical self-help or service delivery organizations. A significant minority, however, had a more politically sensitive quality, addressing topics such as human rights, democratization, legal aid, and peacebuilding. International donors targeted in particular women and youths, both considered to provide fertile ground for peacebuilding and Western values.

The initial availability of considerable international resources created several problems (Belloni 2001). First, aid dependency skewed the priorities of local organizations away from local needs. In order to be funded, NGOs operated according to the changing preferences of donors, rather than the needs of communities they were supposed to serve. Instead of favoring forms of partnership between international and domestic actors and the gradual local ownership of the peace process, civil society building reinforced a form of foreign colonization and patronage (Stubbs 2000). Second, competition for funding discouraged cooperation and long-term planning among local organizations, weakening the sector's advocacy role. Forced by donors' short-term deadlines, NGOs adopted a pragmatic approach aimed at securing contracts for discrete projects, rather than focusing on structural goals requiring long-term strategies and slow and patient work. Finally, many of the early NGOs were not motivated by ideals but simply wished to take advantage of the money available. Thus a profit motive, shoddy work, donor-driven projects, and even outright fraud led to widespread suspicions: all NGOs were being characterized as "foreign mercenaries." The legitimate NGOs had to defend themselves from acquiring such a reputation and had to be very careful about which NGOs they cooperated with, causing a lasting negative impact on collaboration among local civil society groups (Hemmer 2008, ch. 5).

As the money began to dry up after four years or so, the blossoming of new local NGOs slowed; many organizations disappeared. The survivors are generally driven more by ideals than money, as evidenced in a propensity to be both self-critical and critical of donors for not being sensitive enough to local needs. The overall number of associations of citizens, including NGOs, active in Bosnia is a matter of dispute (ICVA 2005; DemNet Hungary 2004; USAID/BiH 2004). There are about 6,500 associations registered, but estimates for active groups range from 500 to 1,500. In total, the NGO sector has a considerable impact on the economy, contributing about 4.5 percent of Bosnian GDP

(Dizdarevic et al. 2006, 319). At least sixty-nine Bosnian NGOs have a significant peacebuilding component (Hemmer 2008, ch. 3), and their work will be the focus of the analysis of the social cohesion function (see below). Very few organizations are involved in policy analysis per se, strongly limiting the sector's ability to perform monitoring and advocacy functions. Furthermore, very few organizations operate across the country or can genuinely claim to represent their stakeholder at the state level.[5]

In this context—in which international funding is increasingly scarce and most mercenary NGOs have disappeared—donors have placed more emphasis on the sustainability of the sector and on improving consultation between government officials and local organizations (Sterland 2006). As a result, they concentrate on large NGOs at the expenses of smaller, newer, and often rural ones. Furthermore, the EU Commission delegation, currently the main funding agency in Bosnia, requires an application process that is far too complex for most local organizations. This further favors the larger and older NGOs with the staff, time, and capacity to meet all requirements (Fagan 2006). In practice, donors' choices reinforce an already existing rural-urban divide, as larger NGOs are found in the more populated Bosnian cities (Sterland 2003). At the same time, however, many of the large urban NGOs do have rural programs, and some of these, such as Mozaik, use their funds to support NGO development in rural areas with secondary grants and mentoring.

Near-total dependency on foreign funds continues to influence program choices and implementation, although nearly all NGOs now claim to plan projects based on needs before seeking funding. Many of these surviving NGOs benefit from long-term relationships with individual foreign NGOs, rather than broader networks. Womens' organizations abroad have developed close partnerships with organizations in Bosnia, channeling funds and supporting the implementation of projects. In some cases, Bosnian organizations are local offshoots of organizations based abroad (such as Stope Nade, which springs from the British based Marie Stopes International, and PRONI, formerly under the PRONI Institute for Social Education in Sweden).

Civil Society's Participants and Standing

It is difficult to assess the membership base of Bosnian civil society. Many organizations do not have formally defined memberships, so it often makes more sense to speak in terms of beneficiaries or participants (World Bank 2002, 88–89). Furthermore, some NGOs have an antiethnic, individualistic philosophy, which causes them to reject collecting or providing information on membership by ethnicity.

What is clear is the presence of several organizations focusing on women, such as handicraft NGOs and organizations providing microcredit; many women's groups are involved in peacebuilding (Helms 2003; Kvinna till Kvinna 2006). Many such groups are involved in war trauma therapy, in part due to the mass rapes that occurred during the war, and also because survivors are disproportionately female. Moreover, the most likely minority returnees are women, particularly older women. This situation has led a number of women's groups to become involved in supporting minority return, in helping reintegrate returnees, and in solving conflicts associated with their return (described below). One particularly vocal monoethnic organization, Mothers of Srebrenica, is formed of women who lost relatives in the Srebrenica massacre and stridently campaigns for justice on this issue.

Civil society has also been heavily involved with young people. Some peacebuilding NGO leaders claim today's youths are "more nationalistic than their parents," having grown up in a polarized and more segregated society, and educated mostly in segregated classrooms with ethnonationalist texts (Milosevic 2004). This is more likely in rural areas, which are more segregated, and among youths old enough to have been schooled. More often, peacebuilders claim that youths, especially children, are less burdened with ethnic hatred and more easily adopt cosmopolitan attitudes and develop interethnic bonds.[6] Many peacebuilding NGOs are focused on youths for this reason, and some have been started and managed by youths, such as the Youth Communication Centre and the Democratic Youth Movement. Yet, youths participate in youth wings of ethnonationalist political parties, as well. Moreover, many young people suffer disproportionately from lack of economic opportunities.[7] In 2000, a striking 62 percent of young people expressed a desire to leave the country (IBHI/UNDP 2000), and many were able to do so (about 100,000 since the end of the war). The most educated and cosmopolitan youths are best able to obtain travel visas, leaving behind the most parochial and intolerant.

Bosnians were initially skeptical of and aloof from new local NGOs, and they still display some distrust. Particularly in the first few postwar years, "nongovernmental" was understood as "against the government" (Hemmer 2008, ch. 5). As mentioned above, the mercenary and donor-driven nature of many NGOs only confirmed suspicions of this new form of organization. Over time, however, Bosnian citizens and some politicians (especially at the municipal level) came to see that at least some NGOs were doing useful work that was not adequately done, or done at all, by governmental agencies (Grødeland 2006). Politicians have been slower to change their minds, and even now many see civil society organizations as competitors for power; they disparage inconvenient ones as "agents of foreign influence," a term of intimidation in the communist past (Pearson and Robertson 2008; World Movement for Democracy 2007).

In a context dominated by a generally low level of trust (Häkansson and Sjöholm 2007; World Bank 2002), civil society groups tend to be better regarded than political institutions. The World Values Survey[8] asked how confidence in several types of civil society groups compares to confidence in political institutions. The environmental movement ranks highest, followed closely by religious organizations and the women's movement, averaging about halfway between "not very much" confidence and "quite a lot." But this ranks much better than political parties and parliament, which average between "not very much" confidence and "none at all." Labor unions, discredited by their historical domination by the Communist Party, are rated low along with Bosnian political institutions such as parliament and government. The overall picture is that civil society, in the distrustful culture of Bosnia, is at least less distrusted than political society.

Peacebuilding Functions

The following section compares the seven different functions: protection, monitoring, advocacy, socialization, social cohesion, intermediation and facilitation, and service delivery.

Protection

During the war, civil society did not perform any visible protection function, other than lifesaving relief aid, chiefly by religious charities. Some individuals protected people of other ethnicities during the war (Broz 2004), but these stories remain mostly untold, according to NGOs organizing the "dealing with the past" activities (described below in the section on intermediation). The violence was so intense that even armed UN peacekeepers had difficulty providing protection. In Srebrenica, UN peacekeepers were forced to allow some 7,000 men and boys under their "protection" to be taken to their deaths. In other instances, they were robbed of guns, vehicles, and uniforms. Given this lack of respect for the UN peacekeeping force, it is understandable that unarmed civil society groups could not fare better than they did.

Civil society's potential to protect against ethnic violence after the war was preempted by the deployment of robust international military and police forces. However, this large influx of men with money and legal immunity also created a new threat to human security, leading to a significant increase in the trafficking of women for prostitution. Bosnia turned into a source, transit, and destination country for the sex industry. Weak border control, corruption, and the presence of organized criminal gangs further exacerbated the problem.

Local civil society organizations did visibly protect victims of trafficking, which is a safer issue than openly protecting ethnic minorities. They provided educational and support programs for potential victims, as well as shelters where trafficked women could receive assistance and support. For example, Zena BiH in Mostar, La Strada in Mostar and Sarajevo, the International Forum of Solidarity in Tuzla and Doboj, Lara in Bijeljina, and Buducnost in Doboj and Modrica have provided a range of services to actual and potential victims; services provided include health care, counseling, legal aid, and other forms of support (Limanowska 2005). The NGOs' work, combined with the creation of a specialized antitrafficking unit within the United Nations in 2001 and the adoption of the National Action Plan in 2002, contributed to a significant improvement of the situation. Ironically, however, the decline in the number of trafficked women has more to do with the gradual withdrawal of international personnel from Bosnia than with antitrafficking and prevention policies (Vandenberg 2007).

Domestic violence, which often increases in postwar societies, is another area in which Bosnian NGOs provide protection. In the immediate post-Dayton period, the problem was aggravated by a legal framework that characterized men's violence as "disturbance of public order" and not as a criminal act. Typically, women had the opportunity to press charges only in cases of very serious injuries. Women's organizations offered legal assistance and shelter to victims and, simultaneously, campaigned to raise awareness and create the conditions for legislative change (Kvinna till Kvinna 2006, 44–51). Thus, protection activities merged with advocacy and contributed to the drafting of a new criminal law in 2000 in the Federation and in 2003 in the RS classifying domestic violence as a criminal act. Women's advocacy also contributed to the 2003 Gender Equality Law—regulating, among other issues, ownership rights within the family; it is regarded as one of the best gender equality laws in the world (Kvinna till Kvinna 2006, 39).

Despite these successes, protection by civil society actors has not generally been a strong factor at any point of the conflict. Civil society lacked sufficient presence and standing to have been effective in this role against the powerful nationalist forces during and immediately after the war (OSCE 1999), though now this may be changing. Instead, an assortment of IGOs, including NATO, OSCE, EU, UN agencies, and the OHR, have provided protection by keeping up the pressure on local authorities—particularly in the case of refugees and displaced persons returning to areas controlled by other ethnic groups. The slowly evolving departure of the international community may give local civil society more opportunities to take over additional responsibilities in performing the protection role. However, other than a handful of human rights organizations, which might be prepared to step up their work, local NGOs have not paid much attention to protection. They are too comfortable in the international security blanket that they currently enjoy.

Monitoring

Monitoring, like protection, is not widely or efficiently performed by Bosnian civil society. During the war the Za-Mir ("For Peace") Internet network, which began in Croatia before the war, grew to share information among civic groups and individuals across the former Yugoslavia, including Bosnia, but its reach was limited by the number of activists and access to the technology. After the war ended, monitoring has been done primarily by the international community.

Furthermore, early efforts to create NGO networks—important instruments for both monitoring and advocacy—were not very successful. Much of these donor-driven efforts went into trying to build NGO forums that were defined geographically rather than topically. While some survived, many NGOs saw these as a waste of time and resources. Topically focused networks have tended to function for one internationally supported campaign, such as domestic election monitoring (see below) or the creation of a civil service for conscientious objectors to military service, only to disappoint their supporters by collapsing afterward, even if the campaign was successful. Other networks, such as the Igman Initiative and the Nansen Network (discussed below), have carried out useful work, but they do not have broad memberships. An important initiative led by a local NGO, the Center for Promotion of Civil Society, beginning in 2001, is "To Work and Succeed Together," a coalition of more than 300 NGOs organized into fifteen regional "reference groups" and aimed at increasing domestic leadership and ownership of civil society (KRUZ 2002). None of these groups is strongly engaged in monitoring, but the GROZD network (the Citizens' Organization for Democracy, described in the section on advocacy) aims to be.

In this context, Bosnian NGOs have usually performed the monitoring function individually and not as part of a larger effort. Human rights NGOs release reports documenting abuses and try to use the media to "shame" responsible individuals, thus combining fact-finding and reporting with public advocacy programs, but initially only on the relatively safe topics of rights for women, children, and the disabled. The Helsinki Committee for Human Rights, with regional offices in both the Federation and the RS, is perhaps the most active and well-known organization in this area. Other local NGOs have joined forces with international organizations (OSCE 1999). The influential International Crisis Group, an international think tank, has released reports researched by an anonymous group of Bosnian human rights organizations, which are more challenging to the ruling parties. Some local human rights NGOs became bolder, such as the Helsinki Citizens' Assembly in Banja Luka, which now issues public reports monitoring the implementation of the law on the protection of national minorities in the RS.

In addition, some organizations have merged monitoring with the promotion of democratic attitudes and advocacy. The Center for Civic Initiatives (CCI—currently known as the Centers for Civic Initiatives), a protégé of the US-based National Democratic Institute, acted as the hub of a massive domestic election monitoring effort involving nearly all Bosnian NGOs for the 1998 elections. CCI continued its work during later electoral rounds (national, entity-level, cantonal, and municipal), involving thousands of volunteers in monitoring the preelection, election-day, and postelection processes, thus contributing to the transparency, regularity, and fairness of the elections. The Sarajevo chapter of the International Council on Voluntary Agencies, a global association of NGOs focused on human rights advocacy, has been coordinating monitoring efforts since 2005, addressing issues such as the implementation of the International Covenant on Economic, Social, and Cultural Rights as well as measures on social protection, education, and the environment (ICVA/CRS 2007).

Overall, however, the situation with monitoring is very similar to that with protection. Because of the robust international monitoring presence after the war, this function has not been very relevant for local civil society. Furthermore, monitoring by civil society appears futile when political structures are unresponsive. Instead, peace-oriented civil society focused on psychosocial service delivery, socialization, and social cohesion. As the international community gradually winds down its presence, local civil society might find itself more involved in monitoring. However, little preparation for taking over this role is visible. The strong and focused domestic networks that would be necessary for effectively coordinated nationwide monitoring of, communication about, and subsequent advocacy against human rights abuses or threats to peace have not fully developed. Instead, as Bosnia slowly moves toward increasing integration into European political, economic, and legal institutions, it subjects itself to growing scrutiny by European bodies rather than by domestic actors.

Advocacy

Despite the emphasis of donors and civil society development programs on supporting public advocacy, the overall extent and quality of advocacy by Bosnian civil society remain behind those of other states in the region, though advocacy by a few organizations is becoming increasingly ambitious and effective (DemNet Hungary 2004; Pearson and Robertson 2008). Civil society organizations are caught between two massive impediments that have only slowly been improving: the grip of unresponsive politicians, especially nationalists, on political institutions, and the distracted and disempowered mind-set of the citizens they would need to mobilize for stronger political influence. Because of the paralyzation of Bosnian political institutions by nationalist gridlock, and the disdain and suspicion most politicians initially had (and many still harbor) for civil society in general, civil society long tended to gravitate toward lobbying OHR or other IGOs instead and was initially effective only with their assistance in pressuring Bosnian politicians. Thus, the international community, much to its own exasperation, became a middleman that interfered with the orientation of civil society and politicians toward one another.

Several organizations have campaigned on specific issues, especially women's NGOs. Alternative, a women's NGO based in Kakanj, helped initiate the 1998 law on property repossession, which greatly accelerated the return of refugees and displaced persons. The Citizens' Association for Truth and Reconciliation was formed in 2000 for the sole purpose of lobbying the BiH Parliament for a state law to create a truth and reconciliation commission. This organization was established by a group of multiethnic NGO leaders rather than as a mass-membership organization. Despite "overwhelming support" (USIP 1998) expressed by top religious and political leaders of all three ethnicities—

including leading nationalist parties that hoped to score political points through this initiative—positive Bosnian media coverage, and support from the US Institute of Peace, the law did not pass. The idea was resisted by some international actors, such as the International Criminal Tribunal for the Former Yugoslavia in The Hague, which thought it would interfere with its own work; as well, some victims' organizations felt that they have not been involved enough in the initiative. Eventually, a law establishing a trimmed-down version for Sarajevo was passed only in 2006, but it has yet to start working (Belloni 2007, 120–121).

The most consequential advocacy effort is the work of the Serb Civic Council (SCC). This organization was created on March 27, 1994, to represent, in the words of its founder, "that part of the Bosnian Serb nation which had never accepted the policy of ethnic cleansing and ethnic division of Bosnia" (Pejanovic 2002, 194). In April 1997, it began lobbying international agencies on human rights grounds to terminate the legal discrimination of nationalities by extending the "constitutive people" status, which grants a privileged status to Croats and Bosniaks in the Federation and to Serbs in the RS, to all three ethnicities throughout Bosnia. Prominent international officials, most notably the High Representative, publicly supported it. Yet, no concrete steps were taken until the SCC called upon the Bosniak member of the presidency, Aljia Izetbegovic, to submit the issue to the Constitutional Court (Pejanovic 2002, 235–236). The court's 2000 decision to guarantee legal equality to Serbs, Croats, and Bosniaks throughout the Bosnian territory led to reforms that increased the multiethnic character of entity institutions (Belloni 2007, 58–70).

One of the most sophisticated NGOs in advocacy work is the Centers for Civic Initiatives. After debuting with the 1998 domestic election monitoring effort, it undertook a mission to organize an impressive array of campaigns resulting in legislative changes. While the main focus is democratization rather than peacebuilding per se, several campaigns helped reduce nationalist influence and re-create a multiethnic society, through minimizing political interference in school management and requiring direct election of municipal mayors in the Federation (USAID/BiH 2004, 47–50). The campaigns often include other civil society organizations.

The Center for Promotion of Civil Society is another sophisticated advocacy NGO. It advocates for the entire NGO sector and negotiated an agreement with the Bosnian Council of Ministers on governmental relations with civil society as the organizer of the "To Work and Succeed Together" network. It also leads GROZD, a newer network of about sixty NGOs that has become one of the most well-known groups in Bosnia. GROZD produced, based on civic input, the "Civic Platform for 2006 Elections" with twelve demands for politicians to implement by 2010. These include the peace-related demands of completing education reform and completing reforms required for EU candidate status.[9] GROZD took the unprecedented step of gathering a half-million signatures in support of this platform and got political parties to sign on. It is currently monitoring whether politicians implement these demands. This cooperative, sustained campaign with mass support and follow-through is a breakthrough for civil society development in Bosnia (Pearson and Robertson 2008, World Movement for Democracy 2007). The Dosta! ("Enough!") movement has also become a well-known civic effort, urging citizens to participate in pressuring politicians to actually solve problems.

Overall, NGOs' attempts to influence political leaders have steadily increased over time. By 2002, a majority of the peacebuilding NGOs were politically engaged, meaning at least one activity per year designed to influence political leaders.[10] Although the trend is positive, the overall level and quality of advocacy are inadequate. Many activities take on noncontentious issues, mostly at the municipal level. For the majority of local organizations, "advocacy" is equated with complaints against the government or the international community—without sustained constructive engagement. Rarely do NGOs engage in coordinated and strategic approaches and follow-through, from initial events to passing laws to monitoring their implementation. Large networks dedicated to advocacy on specific topics have proven fleeting (at least until the growth of GROZD). Mass participation in campaigns is even more rare. Unsurprisingly, implementation of reforms remains patchy. For instance, the Gender Equality Law has been largely ignored, and women remain subject to discrimination. Moreover, international actors have played an important role in most advocacy campaigns, especially by providing funding and, often, policy analysis and technical assistance.

In-Group Socialization

Before the outbreak of war, ethnonationalists were active in emphasizing ethnic identity, making minorities afraid, and discouraging attempts to build bridging ties. Given the significantly increased segregation after the war, it is likely that most organizations today are ethnically homogenous, or nearly so, especially outside the larger cities such as Sarajevo and Tuzla, which tend to be more mixed and tolerant.

The largest civil society groups are religious humanitarian organizations with strong in-group identity: the Catholic group Caritas, the Muslim Merhamet, and the Serb Orthodox Dobrotvor provide a sense of common belonging in addition to various services to their communities. These organizations are motivated by religious values and are clearly tied to one ethnic group. Although their contribution to peacebuilding is difficult to assess, it is likely to be positive—at least for the normalcy, security, and trust they have been rebuilding inside broken communities (USIP 2003). Some single-identity groups have also been active in promoting minority return, such as the Democratic Initiative of Sarajevo Serbs, which promotes reintegration of Serbs in Sarajevo. More often, however, single-identity associations for displaced persons are promoting return to homogenous villages.

In some cases, single-identity groups have contributed directly to confidence-building efforts. Several peacebuilding NGOs have partnered with single-identity folk culture groups to put on multiethnic folk festivals (e.g., Nansen Dialogue Centre in Banja Luka, Alternative in Kakanj, and Firefly in Brcko). These activities blurred the in-group/intergroup categories, providing individual ethnicities with security in expressing their cultures, all in a setting of mutual tolerance and even appreciation by other ethnicities. Such activities demonstrate that ethnic identity can be safely expressed and preserved within an overarching civic identity.

Despite these positive examples, civil society groups often socialize their members to exclusionary, confrontational values and norms. In particular, war veterans' associations are homogeneous and nationalist and have frequently acted as spoilers in the peace process by obstructing refugee return, war-crime prosecution, and institution-building (Bojicic-Dzelilovic 2006). In the RS, the Serb Movement of Independent Associations (SPONA), composed of eleven hard-line NGOs, including war veterans, has been particularly vocal in opposing various internationally imposed reforms and even threatened to call a referendum on the RS's secession from Bosnia. Although the relationship between SPONA and RS authorities is difficult to establish conclusively, it is likely to be close, with prominent RS politicians frequently attending the association's initiatives.

In the Federation, the radical Wahhabi form of Islam, unknown in Bosnia until the outbreak of the war, has been slowly spreading via Islamic charities. During the war, Muslim humanitarian groups developed ties to Islamic terrorist groups in Algeria, Saudi Arabia, Chechnya, and particularly Afghanistan. They helped infiltrate mujahidin into Bosnia and provided arms, funds, and logistical support to Islamic fighters. The most involved NGO was the Benevolence International Foundation (BIF), currently recognized by the US government as an Al-Qaida terrorist front group (Kohlmann 2004, ch. 3). Although BIF's premises in Sarajevo have been raided and its manager detained, the US government claims that at least seven NGOs with offices in Bosnia are still involved in terrorist-related activities. The local Muslim community appears not to be directly involved in these activities, with the exception of Active Islamic Youth, which was formed in 1995 with the goal of transforming Bosnia into an Islamic state. Some of its members have been involved in violent episodes, but its membership remains small (Latin 2003). In general, only a small fraction of Bosnian Muslims, estimated between 3 percent and 13 percent, support the Wahhabi movement to any degree. Among other political and religious leaders, the chief Muslim cleric, Mustafa Ceric, has repeatedly rejected Wahhabism as a form of Islam culturally inappropriate for Bosnia, while also underlining the Western and European heritage of Bosnian Muslims.

Intergroup Social Cohesion

Even during the war, when activities to foster some degree of social cohesion were most difficult, a few groups attempted to build bridges across the ethnic divides. Mladi Most was engaged in this effort in Mostar between Bosniak and Croat youths, beginning in June 1994, just after active fighting ended with the signing of the Washington Agreement. They maintained a youth center on the front lines running through the city and accessible to both sides. The Tuzla Citizens' Forum kept multiethnicity alive during the war in a city known for its tolerance, with cooperative efforts to oppose ethnonationalism and to solve practical problems.

Social cohesion efforts increased after the war, spurred by the support of international actors. Many donors require multiethnic membership or cross-ethnic projects (or both) as conditions for funding. NGOs often vocally support multiethnicity, but it is unclear the extent to which this support is genuine or carries the same meaning as it does for international actors, especially in the RS (Dizdarevic et al. 2006, 320; Katana 1999). Some civil society organizations with the support of nationalist parties have been vociferously opposed to ethnic reintegration, such as Ostanak ("Remain"), which encourages displaced Serbs to stay in the RS.

Of course, a great deal of genuine effort has also gone toward improving relationships among Serbs, Croats, and Bosniaks. A number of organizations, especially women's NGOs, have targeted social cohesion programs that support the reintegration of minorities in communities resentful of returnees. These programs often involved intermediation (discussed below). Several organizations teach conflict-resolution skills (see the section on intermediation) or conduct general peace culture activities, such as art that promotes tolerance, usually targeted at youths and educators. Sezam in Zenica, for instance, began peace education training for teachers and youths in 1997. Most of these social cohesion activities have been disguised as more generally recreational, educational, or practical initiatives, especially in the early postwar years. As one peacebuilder put it, "If you call it reconciliation, they will not come." For instance, a project to clean a local park might involve multiethnic participants and end with a joint picnic and a multiethnic folk music festival. This approach removed the social pressures surrounding reconciliation with the "enemy" and facilitated viewing other participants as individuals. Similarly, English classes could provide some interethnic contact, create a sense of "normality," and allow tolerance to develop naturally through common experiences. All this could set the stage for peace education and social cohesion work.

The ideology of many peacebuilding groups is to deemphasize ethnicity and instead view everyone as "humans." This ethnicity-blind approach is peace-oriented, but it risks ignoring the very real need for securing ethnic expression, as well as the need to discuss the past sources of ethnic violence. However, peacebuilding NGOs have become more comfortable addressing such topics, as in multiethnic folk festivals and the "Dealing with the Past" programs (described below). Overall, these civil society activities have had an undeniable positive influence on reestablishing various degrees of social cohesion. However, in most cases Bosnians seem to have accepted the inevitability of coexistence following the postwar return of hundreds of thousands of displaced persons and refugees, but they have rejected intimate interethnic relations and, more broadly, multiculturalism (Pickering 2007). Social cohesion has not returned to prewar levels, even in urban areas.[11]

Intermediation

Since the war began, and even more so since the signing of the Dayton Agreement, international agencies have been heavily engaged in mediating between estranged communities, principally at the political level, and in providing occasions for contact among them. Hundreds of seminars, workshops, and conferences for politicians, professionals, and civic leaders have been useful means to create a line of communication, especially in the first years after the war, when traveling across the country could be difficult and dangerous. Bosnian civil society has progressively developed intermediation roles at the grassroots level and, eventually, between citizens and politicians.

In particular, civil society combined intermediation with social cohesion activities in support of minority return. Returnees entering towns dominated by another ethnic group initially faced harassment, government discrimination, neglect, and even violence. Returning minorities were assisted in reintegrating into schools and accessing other government services, reestablishing utilities services, and building or rebuilding relations with neighbors. Women-to-women contacts and relationships have been especially instrumental in supporting the process of return (Kvinna till Kvinna 2006). In the Srebrenica-Bratunac area, where many men were killed and returnees were primarily women, at least four women's organizations support return: Srebrenica 99, SARA, Priroda, and the Women's Forum Bratunac. More broadly, starting in 1998, the women's organization Zena Zenama began educating mediators in villages around Bosnia to help smooth the return process.

As the return process began to accelerate in 1999–2000, conflict-resolution training expanded, especially peer mediation programs within schools. These are presented as general-purpose, but with an underlying goal of aiding reintegration of minority returnee pupils. (Examples include programs by Omladinski Komunikativni Centar, or "Youth Communication Center," throughout eastern RS and Diakom in the Prijedor–Sanski Most region.) There is no pressure for the students to "reconcile" in mediation training; they can focus on skills and maybe develop better interethnic relationships along the way. *Reconciliation* is a word that does not resonate well with the Bosnian public, but a more accepted phrase has been found. Several NGOs were by 2003 engaged in public discussions on "dealing with the past"—that is, publicly talking about the sources and conduct of the war and how to prevent its recurrence. A particularly brave version was organized by the Center for Nonviolent Action, in partnership with Sezam, the Youth Center in Gornji Vakuf–Uskoplje, and the Nansen Dialogue Center in Banja Luka. This initiative involved televised discussions by former soldiers of low rank from each army concerning war crimes orchestrated by their leaders, as well as difference between group and individual responsibility (Fischer 2007b). Notably, this is one of very few peacebuilding programs that deal explicitly with men, most being focused on women and youths. Quaker Peace and Social Witness (QPSW)[12] also consulted a large number of peacebuilding NGOs on ideas for a series of public discussions on dealing with the past. Many groups have been jointly developing such projects with QPSW. These discussions cumulatively could be considered as an outcome-oriented social cohesion effort, as they are attempting to finally end the cycle of violence by putting the ghosts of the past to rest.

In addition, the Nansen Dialogue Centers regularly hold facilitated public dialogues that could be considered intermediation, blended with aspects of socialization, social cohesion, and advocacy. These were founded in 2000 as a network of nine centers throughout the Balkans, three of which are in Bosnia (Sarajevo, Banja Luka, and Mostar). The central idea is to "promote dialogue, particularly interethnic dialogue, as a tool for democratization and reconciliation in the region" (Savija-Valha 2004). These centers operate as independent local NGOs, developing unique local programs but also cooperating as a network on some national or regional programs. They benefit from steady funding and common training and mentoring from the Nansen Academy in Norway and the Norwegian Foreign Ministry. These centers are more politically engaged than most Bosnian peacebuilding NGOs, regularly holding public dialogues involving political leaders conversing with ordinary citizens, often on politically sensitive topics, usually with media coverage. They also provide joint democratic training to young political leaders from diverse parties. However, like most Bosnian NGOs, they are better at holding events than in following through to produce concrete policy changes. For example, they held a conference of peacebuilding NGOs in 2004, which produced an impressive list of recommendations that was sent to political leaders. But there was no continuing effort to exert pressure for their implementation.

Civil society's contribution to minority return has also been positive, although the presence and work of international agencies at the political level and in security were at least as important. International organizations imposed a set of laws harmonizing property repossession and ensured the safety of returnees with monitoring of police and human rights and, ultimately, with peacekeeping forces. As the return process wound down after 2002, so did the need for this type of intermediation; about the same time, however, public dialogues facilitated by local NGOs on sensitive topics were becoming more common. It seems likely that such dialogues are not only helping to bring particular issues to resolution; they are also teaching citizens and politicians how to constructively manage conflict within a democracy. Despite some helpful television coverage, these dialogues need to continue to expand in location and frequency, especially outside the main cities, before a broad societal effect can emerge.

Service Delivery

The vast majority of Bosnian civil society groups are involved in various forms of service delivery. During the war, at least three NGOs in Sarajevo, Tuzla, and Zenica provided war trauma therapy, a service that directly aids peacebuilding. Humanitarian relief was given by others, especially by religious charities, notably including the Jewish group La Benevolencia in Sarajevo, which was seen as impartial. The Franciscans in central Bosnia also developed a reputation for caring for all, regardless of faith. The relief functions of religious groups may help explain the relatively high regard for them.

In the post-Dayton period, war trauma therapy became a widespread service delivered by NGOs; it tapered off in later years but remains a central activity of a few NGOs such as Corridor in Sarajevo and Vive Zene in Tuzla. Because many women had been raped or lost husbands and other male relatives, women's groups were particularly likely to develop such services. As mentioned above, a number of women's groups, in the course of supporting women generally, started supporting women returnees of other ethnicities, which led to peacebuilding activities. This was a case of an overarching gender identity trumping ethnic identity to turn service delivery into peacebuilding.

Service delivery can create standing for an organization in a community, which facilitates parallel or subsequent peacebuilding. As described above, educational and recreational activities often served as vehicles for covert social cohesion aims. Plenty of organizations adopted peacebuilding as one of several equally prioritized purposes. In particular, women's centers and youth centers often sponsor educational and recreational activities alongside explicit peacebuilding activities, such as peace education (the Youth Center in Gornji Vakuf–Uskoplje is a leading example). Peacebuilding activities may then recruit participants who come to the center for some other purpose, and the center can diversify its funding sources to keep afloat when funds for one type of activity are scarce.

In most cases, however, service delivery has no peacebuilding component. When service delivery NGOs operate as servants of international agencies or donors with little or no civic participation in decisionmaking, they also provide no democratic empowerment and may discredit civil society through donor-driven waste. For this reason, service delivery organizations can actually have negative long-term consequences for local civil society and the development of social capital (World Bank 2002, 94).

Conclusion

Bosnian civil society's engagement in peacebuilding has steadily increased over time. There was little activity to prevent the war because, in the wake of communism, little civil society existed. The war itself was too violent, and the period between the final cease-fire and the peace agreement was too brief, to permit much civil society development. Intergroup activities were extremely constrained during the war, and any type of advocacy was likely to fall on deaf ears. Service delivery, especially war trauma therapy, was the primary civil society function that was feasible at this time, although the special environments in Tuzla and Mostar did allow some social cohesion activities to occur.

In the postwar period, the overbearing presence of the international community, although providing some space for civil society to develop, impeded the development of a democratic relationship between civil society and politicians. On the positive side, the semiprotectorate allowed the fledgling civil society time to prepare for a politically engaged role through building organizational legitimacy, fostering democratic attitudes, and reconstructing interethnic relationships at the grassroots level. On the negative side, the use of the Bonn powers and other international influences on Bosnian politicians as a substitute for democratic pressure preempted the need for civil society to engage in protection, monitoring, and advocacy. Arguably, this cut short Bosnian efforts to create solutions that might have succeeded if given more time. As a result, politicians and civil society developed the habit of viewing the international community as their primary interlocutor, rather than each other.

Ironically, the overconfidence of the international community in the ability of civil society to quickly develop and mount ambitious grassroots advocacy campaigns damaged the development of both civil society and advocacy. The initial flood of international funding, often targeted toward advocacy, that accompanied the international semiprotectorate produced an explosion of opportunistic NGOs that misused funds. This inhibited the growth of civil society legitimacy, cooperation, and networks, which in turn are critical to developing efficient monitoring and advocacy. The subsequent disillusionment with local civil society may have led to the Bonn powers being used more heavy-handedly than necessary, as civil society developed its potential for effective and increasingly ambitious political engagement over the next decade. The central paradox of postwar Bosnia is that the semiprotectorate was simultaneously necessary and disempowering. It has not been easy for the international community to achieve the right balance of intervention and patience for each stage of development.

Throughout the postwar period, service delivery, understood as delivering services that are not clearly or primarily peace-oriented, was by far the most common function performed by civil society. War trauma therapy was most common in the early years after the peace agreement, and some of it continues. In cases, service delivery was a useful mask for peacebuilding, a source of participants or funds for peacebuilding, or a purposeful entrée to later peacebuilding. However, the majority of service delivery today is not notably related to peacebuilding.

Peace-oriented civil society engaged in social cohesion activities and socialization for peace and democratic culture and skills (though, for citizens, not in-groups per se). It also engaged in some intermediation/facilitation, first in supporting minority return, and then in public dialogues on politically sensitive topics. Advocacy became more common over time, when civil society and political institutions were more established, but it was modestly effective. Politicians are still not very responsive, and most citizens have not been ready to join a politically engaged peace movement—although the GROZD movement demonstrates how ready they are to join a movement advocating more productive politics. Furthermore, most Bosnian civil society groups have had other priorities. Many see improving interethnic and democratic attitudes as a prerequisite to effective political action to deepen peace and build equitable prosperity.

Some civil society groups, particularly in the RS, socialize members to exclusionary norms and lobby against certain aspects of the peace process, especially minority returns and strengthening the central state institutions. Most groups avoid or ignore controversial issues such as peacebuilding and politics. On balance, however, the net contribution of civil society to peacebuilding has been positive, and peace-oriented groups have been able to build visibility, legitimacy, and momentum even in the face of resistance, skepticism, and dwindling funding. Civil society has slowly increased its effectiveness thanks to relaxing security concerns, a slowly recovering economy, slightly more functional political institutions, and the increased legitimacy and sophistication of its activities over time. The international community has provided helpful support for civil society to develop (with some missteps), but it also stands in the way of the complete maturation of civil society; it needs to continue stepping back while improving the quality of assistance. Key to this improvement is an increased reliance on local initiatives, not international ones, and the development of a more effective partnership between international and domestic actors. Developing local sources of philanthropy as the economy improves will further support the development of truly local civil society by reducing dependency on international donors. From a civil society perspective, it is time for local organizations to take on more responsibilities in the three political roles of monitoring, protection, and advocacy. They need to do more to mobilize citizens desiring peace and prosperity instead of turning to the international community for political clout. This political role is essential to accelerate the transformation of political parties into responsive parties that compete to address socioeconomic issues for all citizens, rather than competing in nationalist rhetoric, the politics of fear, and ethnically selective benefits. The decisive steps have to come from civil society, because peace through democracy, in the long run, cannot rely on waning international interest.

Notes

Many thanks to Florian Bieber and Martina Fischer for their insightful comments on an earlier draft of this chapter. Needless to say, we are solely responsible for any remaining errors.

1. Nationalists have exaggerated regional differences to invent separate Serbian and Croatian "languages," but these are closer to dialects, which present no significant difficulty in communication.

2. For a good history of Bosnia and its peoples, see Malcolm (1996).

3. All data used in this chapter on the dead and missing of the war come from the Research and Documentation Center (2007).

4. All return data were provided to the authors by the United Nations High Commissioner for Refugees (UNHCR) Mission to BiH. Potential minority returns are estimated from figures contained in UNHCR (2003).

5. Prominent among these are the Center for the Promotion of Civil Society and the Center for Civic Initiatives (promoting citizens' democratic participation and involvement); the Youth Information Agency (supporting youth initiatives, including political engagement); Zene Zenama (addressing gender issues); Mozaik (providing a range of services to community groups); and the Independent Bureau for Humanitarian Issues (working in the area of social policy).

6. Such views have been conveyed to the authors during several conversations with NGO leaders in Bosnia.

7. Unemployment among 19- to 24-year-olds is 2.6 times higher than among 29- to 49-year-olds and 3.6 times higher than among 50- to 60-year-olds (UNDP 2003). Juvenile delinquency is also on the rise (Subasic and Bulja 2008).

8. World Values Survey 2000 wave, n = 1100+ (Inglehart et al. 2005). All differences in means are significant at $p < .05$ or better, except between the women's movement and the European Union, and between religious organizations and the environmental movement.

9. Education is dominated by the "two schools under one roof" phenomenon, which, though encouraging return by families with school-aged children to areas in which they constitute a minority, also effectively legitimized and institutionalized a form of segregation. The teaching of the so-called national subjects (history, religion, literature, geography, language, art, and music) is often done to promote stereotypes and questionable historical interpretations and cultural myths (Perry 2003).

10. Based on interviews of twenty-five peacebuilding NGO leaders during 2006–2007, selected to be roughly geographically and topically representative of a population of sixty-nine known, currently existing, peacebuilding NGOs. Sampling error increases slightly in earlier years, as some organizations no longer exist (Hemmer 2008, ch. 3).

11. See the UNDP's annual reports, which track, among other issues, interethnic relations trends (UNDP Bosnia and Herzegovina).

12. This recently reregistered as a local NGO called TERCA. As QPSW, it was officially an international NGO, but with completely local staff operating with great autonomy, and was thus closer to a well-supported local NGO.

8

Turkey: The Kurdish Question and the Coercive State

Ayşe Betül Çelik

In 1999, Turkey's long-lasting Kurdish question[1] took a new turn after the capture of Abdullah Öcalan, the leader of the Kurdistan Workers' Party (Partiya Karkerên Kurdistan—PKK[2]), and the acceptance of Turkey's candidacy for membership in the European Union. The negative peace that began with the capture of Öcalan and the PKK's decision of cease-fire in 1999 saw an increase in the number of civil society organizations (CSOs) concerned with and working in areas related to the Kurdish conflict. However, since mid-2004, sporadic violence in conflict-affected areas, as well as the spread of violence in western Turkish cities, has hampered attempts to bring about peace and affected the functioning of CSOs. In this chapter, I analyze peacebuilding issues and the degree to which CSOs fulfill peacebuilding functions within the framework of the Kurdish conflict. The data derive largely from fieldwork conducted in the cities of eastern and southeastern Anatolia, where there are high concentrations of Kurds, as well as cities where most CSOs working on the issue are located, such as Istanbul and Ankara.

Context

It can be argued that the roots of the so-called Kurdish question date to the Ottoman Empire and national uprisings at the end of the nineteenth century. In the early years of the Turkish Republic (1924–1938), there were eighteen Kurdish rebellions. However, the conflict became distinctly "Kurdish" after 1984 with the emergence of the PKK as a separatist group within Turkey, when it first attacked Turkey's state apparatus. Ever since, the conflict has unfolded with several stages. In 1987, the government declared emergency rule in thirteen Kurdish-populated provinces.[3] The conflict peaked from 1991 to 1999, when the highest number of deaths and human rights violations occurred. This period was followed by a negative peace period, which ended with the reescalation of conflict in mid-2004. The conflict became internationalized yet again[4] in late 2007 with the Turkish Army's bombings of PKK camps within the territory of northern Iraq. Between 30,000 and 40,000 people are estimated to have died during the conflict.

The Kurdish Question in a Broader Context

Kurds have never existed as an independent political community[5] and thus have been under the rule of others throughout history—the Sassanian, Safavid, and Ottoman Empires in addition to the Turkish Republic, to name but a few. There are no official statistics identifying the number of Kurds in Turkey. However, studies estimate that Kurds constitute 15–20 percent of the total population in Turkey (Andrews 1992; McDowall 1997; Gunter 1997). In the absence of verifiable statistics, some scholars claim that Kurds are the largest "stateless" group of people in the world (McKeirnan 1999; Council of Europe 2006). Such studies argue there are 20–30 million Kurds living in the region where the borders of Turkey, Iran, Syria, and Iraq meet. There are, in addition, some 1 million Kurds living in Western Europe (Council of Europe 2006), most of whom migrated there after the 1970s.

It is important to note that Kurds do not make up a homogenous group in terms of religious affiliation. Although most Kurds (70 percent) adhere to the Sunni sect of Islam, there are considerable Alevis[6] and a few Yezidis (together, 30 percent; Barkey and Fuller 1998, 67; Andrews 1992). This heterogeneity in demographic characteristics is also represented in the Kurds' political and social organizations. For example, Kurdish votes in eastern and southeastern Anatolia are usually divided among the government's Justice and Development Party (Adalet ve Kalkınma Partisi—AKP), the pro-Kurdish Democratic Society Party (Demokratik Toplum Partisi—DTP), and lesser center-right parties.

Also, there exists no specific region in Turkey where the population is exclusively made up of Kurds; in most parts of eastern and southeastern Anatolia, however, they constitute the majority. Kurdish populations in the western cities started to increase with economic migration in the 1950s, intensifying especially after the forced displacement of many Kurds in the 1990s.[7] Today Kurds live throughout every region of Turkey, with Istanbul, Ankara, Mersin, and Izmir having the largest populations of displaced Kurds.

Conflict Parties

The primary parties to the conflict are the organs of the Turkish state and society, the PKK, the pro-Kurdish DTP,[8] and, more generally, the Turkish and Kurdish citizens of Turkey. Within those categories, the most important actors are the ruling AKP government, under Prime Minister Recep Tayyip Erdoğan, and the state security forces, including the military, police, Village Guards,[9] and Gendarmerie.[10] Important secondary actors are the European Union and the United States.

Kurdistan Workers' Party. Even though the conflict is rooted in an earlier period of imperial rule, the Kurdish question crystallized after the emergence of the PKK as an armed group within the Republic of Turkey. The Kurdistan Workers' Party was founded in 1978 by Abdullah Öcalan to "set up a democratic and united Kurdistan in southeastern Turkey to be governed along Marxist-Leninist lines" and sought to "monopolize the Kurdish nationalist struggle" (Çağaptay 2007, 2). The Turkish state declared the PKK to be an illegal organization whose cadres are fed by indigenous and expatriate Kurd_. Due to the lack of scholarly works and reliable sources on the structure and functioning of the PKK, except for its political cadres, we know little about the PKK' membership profile. According to Orhan Doğan, a Kurdish former member of parliament who was released in June 2004 after thirteen years in prison,[11] there are 3,000 PKK combatants in Turkey (*Radikal* 2005a).[12] In addition, several PKK subgroups perform nonviolent political, social, and community functions. As in other cases where illegal groups fight against the state, some countries support the PKK as a "stick" in their negotiations with Turkey. Syria long gave refuge to Öcalan because it gave the Syrians a bargaining chip in the negotiations for water from the Tigris-Euphrates river basins. Iran, in opposition to Turkey's secular system, "long saw the PKK as a useful tool to use against Turkey. Tehran allowed the PKK to maintain about 1,200 of its members,"[13] which later formed the basis for the PJAK [Partîya Jîyane Azadîya Kurdistan—Kurdistan Free Life Party], in around fifty locations in Iran (Çağaptay 2007, 3). The PKK is allegedly financed through criminal rings (mostly drug traffickers), propaganda, and fund-raising auxiliaries in Europe. It also sponsors TV stations (e.g., Roj TV) that actively promote PKK ideology and mobilize supporters (Çağaptay 2007, 3–4).

Over the years, the PKK's positions have changed. There is no clear analysis of what the PKK sought in the past and what it seeks today. According to some, the PKK never demanded an independent state (SORAR 2008); others argue such was the case in the 1980s (Kocher 2002; Çağaptay 2007). However, after the capture of Öcalan, the PKK started to emphasize the notion of a "democratic republic,"[14] as argued by its leader (Öcalan 1999). However, this position might be considered the result of his capture rather than an actual position of the organization.

Peacebuilding means different things within the heterogeneous Kurdish society, but one can summarize the dominant options for the PKK, DTP, and Kurdish intellectuals. Although the conflict has increased in intensity since late December 2007, an interview conducted with higher-ranking PKK officers shows that the first option is no longer armed conflict, even though it continues.

These officers claim that peace can be achieved only by "freeing" the Kurdish language in public, by making education in Kurdish available in Turkey, and by "securing" the Kurdish identity through constitutional guarantees and democratic autonomy to Kurds, meaning federalism or decentralization (Çongar 2008). A committee of wise men (*akil adamlar*), they believe, can achieve these through mediation.[15] Even though these officers declined to elaborate a specific position, the PKK and its followers also demand the release of Öcalan as a precondition for "peace." DTP,[16] the alleged follower of the PKK[17] (Çağaptay 2007), seems to be in agreement and does not denounce the PKK's use of violence as a means to achieve peacebuilding goals. Finally, the Kurdish intelligentsia's descriptions of peace and peacebuilding include the same cultural and political goals but also include general amnesty. However, Kurdish intellectuals condemn any use of force and violence, emphasizing instead the necessity to recognize the PKK as a social and political phenomenon among Kurds (Radikal 2008). This means public discussion of the underlying reasons for people joining the PKK, as well as exploring ways in which the members of the PKK can return to society.

The Turkish state. When the Kurdish question became prominent in Turkish politics through PKK activities, many state officers perceived the conflict as a "terrorist act" whose aim was to carve out an independent Kurdistan within Turkish territories. The Turkish state refused to consider the PKK as the legitimate "other" in the conflict and treated the Kurdish population as part of the citizen population. That is why the Kurdish question was never pronounced as such, but rather denounced as "terrorism" or, in the best case, as the "southeast underdevelopment problem." In contrast, most Kurds and the international community perceived the issue as an identity conflict and a problem of representation. One of the difficulties is the fact that conflict parties define the nature of conflict differently. Especially given rising violence, the state's emphases have been security and territorial integrity, whereas Kurds chafe at the slow and unwilling moves of the state in the EU integration process to grant more rights to Kurds.

Although there is no clear, stable, and well-constructed government policy, the government perspective on peacebuilding involves the military, given its definition of peace as state security and territorial integrity. Moreover, there are different perceptions of the state as an actor. Over the years, its understanding of peace has changed. As Kemal Kirişçi argues, it is easier to discuss what is not included in the state's understanding of peace and peacebuilding than what it means. Although the state's emphasis on "dialogue and economic interdependence with the Kurdish administration in northern Iraq" can "foresee an important effort to improve governance at the local level and relations between ordinary Kurds and the Turkish state" and allow "education in the Kurdish-language and media broadcasting in Kurdish languages," its understanding of peace does not include any "transformation from unitary state to a federal one," "territorial autonomy," or acceptance of Kurdish as an official language (Kirişçi 2008, 7).

Since it assumed power in 2002, the AKP has taken several different positions. According to M. Hakan Yavuz and Nihat Ali Özcan (2006), the AKP treats the Kurdish question as part of forced secularism and Turkish nationalism, of the type enforced by Kemalist ideology, and argues that if Turkey stresses common Islamic ties and brotherhood, then the conflict would eventually end.

Another reason for the preeminent role of the military in the conflict is the legacy of the coups d'état and quasi–coups d'état that have occurred in Turkey once every decade since 1960. These events not only hampered democratic governance; they also solidified the strong role that the military still plays in Turkish politics. The legacies of coups and state coercion on certain civil rights diminish Turkey's democracy score despite a vigorous multiparty system. The European Union, in its progress reports, criticizes the military's intervention in democratic governance from time to time, arguing it is a threat to democratization. During the period of negative peace (1999–2004), the military's public visibility decreased. Since the upsurge in violence, beginning in March 2006, the military and the other security forces reemerged and are again taking a more active role.[18]

Secondary parties. The most important secondary parties are the European Union and the United States. Although both recognize the PKK as a "terrorist organization," their positions have differed. Since the acceptance of Turkey's EU candidacy, the union has become an important actor with respect to Kurdish issues, through pressure to implement democratic reforms and to improve the human rights record.

Especially through Turkey's EU application, the Turkish government has taken steps to recognize the conflict.[19] However, the EU's eagerness to solve the issue through democratization, as opposed to referring to it as a Kurdish question per se, from time to time has failed to bring about effective mechanisms. Although EU membership has served as a carrot for the Turkish state to introduce reforms (e.g., broadcast in Kurdish), it has not produced mechanisms to change perceptions and attitudes. Such macro-mechanisms seem to work to a certain degree, at least during the negative peace. However, many CSOs representing the dissident Kurdish population find such attempts to be insincere and temporary (Çelik and Rumelili 2006).

The United States became another important actor after the creation of the autonomous Kurdish region in northern Iraq, which harbors PKK camps. After the Turkish military operations in northern Iraq, the United States became the focus of bilateral communications on the issue. It is also important to note that while the EU position remains somewhat stable, given its emphasis on democratic governance and cultural rights for Kurds, the US position shifts according to developments in the Middle East. Especially after the state's refusal to open air bases to the US Army prior to the attack on Iraq in 2003, Turkish-American relations soured. Moreover, the worsening of Turkish-American relations helped the PKK grow its bases in Iraq and attack targets inside Turkey. There are claims that the United States has allowed Iraqi Kurds access to Iraqi armaments, some of which ended up in PKK hands (Yavuz and Özcan 2006). However, the sharing of US intelligence with the Turkish state during its attack on the PKK in northern Iraq softened relations, even though anti-Americanism has remained high among the Turkish public (PEW 2008, 3).[20]

Reasons for the Conflict

Understanding the Kurdish question today requires a summary of the Turkish Republic and Kemalist ideology. Established in 1923 after the dissolution of the Ottoman Empire, the Turkish Republic was founded by Mustafa Kemal Ataturk. The new republic rested on six arrows (tenets) of the Republican People's Party (Cumhuriyeti Halk Partisi—CHP), the oldest party of the republic: republicanism (an emphasis on the rule of law, popular sovereignty, and civic virtue and liberty practiced by citizens), nationalism, étatism (state regulation of economy and investment in areas where there is lack of private enterprise), secularism, populism, and revolutionism (replacing the traditional institutions and concepts with modern institutions). Although Kemalist doctrine, established upon these six tenets and emphasizing civic nationalism, did not make a differentiation based on ethnicity (Kramer 2000), the republic registered only Armenians, Greeks, and Jews as minorities under the terms of the Lausanne Treaty signed between Turkey and the Allied and Associated Powers after the War of Independence in 1923. Moreover, Kemalist ideology registered all citizens of Turkey as "Turkish" without differentiating on the basis of ethnicity. It was partly in response to this aspect of Kemalist ideology that the Kurdish national identity developed later in the century. Mesut Yeğen argues that Kurdish nationalist aspirations flourished as a response to the "transformation of an a-national political community to a national one in the first quarter of the twentieth century" (Yeğen 2007, 121).

This Kemalist ideology explains the failure of the AKP to solve the Kurdish question; since the 1920s, no government was able to address the issue effectively. Yavuz and Özcan (2006) explain the AKP's failure to solve the issue based on the following arguments:

- Prime Minister Recep Tayyip Erdogan's definition of the Kurdish question is very different from that of the Kurdish actors, especially PKK-led political parties.
- There is a major conflict between the state institutions and the AKP over the conceptualization of the Kurdish issue and the foundations of the Turkish Republic.

- The AKP fears that the Kurdish issue could split the party and undermine its support in Turkish-Muslim provinces in central and eastern Anatolia.
- The Kurdish issue has the potential to lead to a major confrontation.

Even though Erdogan's 2005 speech in Diyarbakır stressed the existence of the Kurdish question and offered citizenship rather than "Turkish identity" as a supra-identity for both the Kurds and Turks, and thereby set up Kurdish hopes for democratic resolution, his emphasis on state security in later speeches, and the resort to military means since 2007, dampened any optimism.

Today, the Kurdish question cannot be explained only as a reaction to state ideology. Heinz Kramer (2000), for example, argues that economic and social underdevelopment, political resistance, and the political fallout of the continuous warfare in the southeast are other dimensions. Similarly, Yeğen (2007) argues that while Turkish nationalists viewed the Kurdish question in the first half of the twentieth century as a fatal rivalry between the backward, premodern, and tribal past and a prosperous present, it was perceived in the 1950s and 1960s in terms of tensions between the peripheral economy and national market. In the 1970s, Kurdish unrest was believed to be a product of communist incitement. Starting in the late 1980s and early 1990s, the Kurdish question was largely shaped by global forces as well as domestic developments. The increasing significance of human rights discourse in the language of Kurdish resistance, the rising publicity of the Kurdish question after the Gulf War, the growing impact of the European diaspora on Kurdish mobilization, and the formation of an autonomous Kurdish authority in northern Iraq are all the immediate outcomes of globalization. Their impacts on the state of unrest are of major importance (Yeğen 2007, 121).

Despite progress since the 2001 economic crisis, economic disparity among regions is stark. Turkey is often classified as a newly industrialized country by economists and political scientists and is a founding member of the Organization for Economic Cooperation and Development (OECD) and the G20 group of industrial nations. Based on per capita GDP, Turkey is among the upper-middle-income countries. Turkey has a strong and rapidly growing private sector, yet the state still plays major roles within industry, banking, transportation, and communications. Its economy is still largely agriculture based. Despite relatively moderate economic measures, the greatest flaw of Turkish economy is the disparity among its regions. According to the United Nations Development Program (UNDP 2007), "human development levels in the southeastern Anatolia region lag behind national levels, while the incidence of human poverty is much higher and there is continued migration out of the region. The region faces development challenges in terms of income level, educational opportunities, gender equality and socio-economic opportunities and facilities."

Another important issue marginalizing the Kurds' position is the national election quota. The Turkish political structure allows pluralist representation by different political interests. However, the extreme polarization of the political system in the 1970s, leading to the 1980 coup d'état, pushed legislators to impose a national quota on the electoral system, which prevents any political party from being represented in parliament if it fails to garner more than 10 percent of the national vote, even though it might enjoy higher support within specific districts. Even though this was put in effect to prevent chaos, it disadvantages pro-Kurdish political parties, which can receive 65–80 percent of the vote in the southeast but cannot gain more than 10 percent nationally.

In terms of press freedoms, one can argue that new regulations curbing the freedom of the press[21] escalated the conflict. And whereas many Kurds follow the national media, and thus are aware of public opinion and state policies, the Kurdish media,[22] which from time to time is subject to legal bans, is not followed by the average Turkish citizen. Within this context, the lack of peace journalism (Boğa 2006) contributes to the existing conflict and hampers the democratization process initiated by the EU accession negotiations. Except for a few academic studies showing that the media use escalating rhetoric in times of crisis (Boğa 2006), there is almost no research studying the role the media plays in the Kurdish question.

Status of Civil Society

Turkish political life has been marked by a "strong state" tradition (Mardin 1969; Mardin 1991; Mardin 1992; Heper 1985), partly due to the Ottoman heritage of absolute power of patrimonial rulers, "whose comprehensive political authority accepted no legitimate rivals" (Kalaycıoğlu 2006, 2). This tradition, however, does not mean that the state is strong in its extractive, regulative, and distributive powers, but rather is coercive and arbitrary (Kalaycıoğlu 2002a). It is this coercion and arbitrariness that one needs to take into account in the study of state-civil society relations in Turkey. Related to this, some general observation about civil society in Turkey can be made.

A study has argued that the state is indifferent toward voluntary associations as long as civic activism avoids regime-contesting activism, considered to be against the republican order in Turkey. Other solidarity and self-help, patronage, economic, professional, charity, and recreational groups and associations are neither harassed nor supported by the state (Kalaycıoğlu 2006, 13). What Ersin Kalaycıoğlu describes as civil society actors questioning the raison d'être of the Republican order, and what Elise Massicard calls the "enemies of unity" (Massicard 2006), are those that, by their acts and ideas, challenge the territorial integrity of the state and its secular foundation, principles strongly emphasized by Kemalist ideology. All those who do not refer to the "obligatory consensus," established within such frameworks as the Turkish flag and the figure of the Ataturk, are not recognized by the state as legitimate and are subject to accusations of separatism (Copeaux 2000; cf. Massicard 2006, 79).

An interesting example is business groups, which, due to close affiliations with the state, have more impact than other civil society actors. One of the most important efforts was undertaken by the Turkish Industrialists' and Businessmen's Association (Türk Sanayici ve Işadamlari Derneği—TÜSIAD). In 1997, TÜSIAD published a report recommending a number of constitutional and political reforms, a solution for the Kurdish question by political means, and more freedom to civil society (CS). It is still the case that voices such as TÜSIAD, and others that are ideologically close to the state, are heard to a greater extent by the state. This is because state-CS relations, when it comes to business groups, "seem to be evolving toward a policy of co-optation, which may be best defined as active-inclusive"[23] (Kalaycıoğlu 2006, 13).

In addition to enmity between the state and some CSOs, CS in Turkey lacks the fundamental values of associability. Turkey does not have a CS rich in what Robert Putnam refers to as "social capital" (Kalaycıoğlu 2002a, 71), and primordial relations penetrate most CSOs. Clientelistic relations that exist in society are reflected in civil society membership, where some CSOs (especially hometown associations[24]) become sources of political support for candidates running for political office rather than fulfilling peacebuilding functions, let alone any civic role (Çelik 2002). "The associational life of Turkey is still influenced by blood ties (*akrabalık*), marital relations (*hısımlık*), local and regional solidarity (*hemşehrilik*), bonds created in military service between men (*askerlik*), and through religious orders (*tarikat*)" (Kalaycıoğlu 2002b, 267).

The results of another project show that the impact of CS on socioeconomic and political developments is low, "partly as a result of limitations on civil society advocacy initiatives (due to state interference), as well as lack of civil society activities in holding the state and private sector accountable and responding to social interests. These limitations, however, are balanced by a particularly strong role in meeting societal needs, empowering citizens and increasing level of engagement around policy issue" (Bikmen and Kalaycıoğlu 2006, 13–14; CIVICUS 2006). Civil society is often perceived by the state and some citizens as an arena in which CSOs should fulfill the functions that the state cannot. The most important are founding schools, dormitories, rescue missions and relief efforts for natural disasters, and poverty reduction. The CIVICUS study also reveals that even as a strong and highly capable group of CSOs is emerging, the majority of Turkish citizens remain detached. The report recommends that attention be paid to creating mechanisms to facilitate the flow of resources to civil society, increasing training opportunities around basic skills of fundraising, program delivery, and other areas, and investing in capacity (human and technical infrastructure) (CIVICUS 2006, 13–14).

The CIVICUS report rates the "environmental factors" for the development and nourishment of civil society as 1.4 (on a scale of 3), indicating that the social, economic, and political context, though improving, still impedes the growth and prosperity of civil society (CIVICUS 2006, 59). Political context, state–civil society relations, and private–civil society relations seem to be in the worst state.[25] In terms of socioeconomic conditions, the presence of armed conflict, severe ethnic and/or religious conflict, dense rural population, rapid urbanization, and unemployment are also barriers to the effective functioning of civil society (CIVICUS 2006, 66). The violence in eastern and southeastern Turkey also affects the functioning of CSOs. For example, "the post-conflict condition in the southeast has led to an increase of CSOs" (CIVICUS 2006, 49), whereas an increase in violence has paralleled increasing restrictions on freedom of association and expression, having the greatest effect on CSOs working for the Kurdish question and human rights.

Civil Society Activities and the Kurdish Question

CS actors dealing with the Kurdish question range from trade unions to bar associations to NGOs to informal gatherings. Historically, it has been easier to address the issue through informal gatherings and platforms than through formal organizations due to the state's legal restrictions and repressive and discriminatory approach.

The first steps in mobilizing Kurdish associations began in the late 1950s and 1960s; these organizations almost exclusively had separated from leftist organizations. The formation of the Eastern Revolutionary Cultural Hearths (Devrimci Doğu Kültür Ocakları—ERCHs) in May 1969 stands as the first important legal Kurdish mobilization.[26] The influence of the ERCHs quickly spread to all types of associations. During the polarized political environment in the 1970s until the 1980 coup d'état, it was common to observe all types of CSOs polarized along the leftist ideologies. After the 1980 coup d'état, the activities of leftist syndicates, trade unions, and professional groups, along with almost all CSOs, have been hampered. Only in the 1990s was there a revival in Turkish civic life (Çelik 2002); however, the tradition of state repression was triggered again by the polarized civil society, mostly on the issues of political Islam and the Kurdish question. Today, along with associations working on human rights issues, syndicates, labor unions, bar associations, academia, and some media exist as CSOs trying to make their voices heard. However, it is mostly the associations in the Kurdish-dominated regions that directly identify issues relevant to the Kurdish question.

After 1999, and increasingly since then, "Kurdish society, especially in major urban centers, has become much more plural and assertive"; compared to the late 1980s and 1990s, it has started to overcome its position of being "squeezed between the repression of the state on the one hand and the PKK on the other hand" (Kirişçi 2008, 5). However, in the late 1990s there emerged an "uncivil" civil society on the Kurdish question. NGOs with an emphasis on Kemalist principles—government-operated nongovernmental organizations

(GONGOs),[27] which are founded by the state—and uncivil social movements led by ultranationalists hamper democratization and the peace process and marginalize Kurdish CSOs. These actors can be considered "uncivil" because their ideas and engagement with democracy (in most cases attacking members of ideologically different CSOs) exclude different opinions and are antagonistic to democratic norms.

Over the years, polarization in the Turkish political system (e.g., left-wing ideologies versus right-wing ones, Islamicism versus laicism, Kurdish nationalism versus Turkish nationalism) has been reflected in civil society. This is also the case for women's CSOs. As in other conflicts, the Kurdish question spawned mothers' movements on each side of the spectrum. Especially toward the end of the 1990s, women mobilized and started to voice their "pain." Whereas mothers of Turkish soldiers joined the Association for the Families of the Martyrs (Şehit Aileleri Derneği), mothers who lost sons and daughters fighting in the PKK mobilized a well-known movement, the Mothers of Peace (Barış Anneleri).

CSOs working on the Kurdish question include those that concentrate on the economic and social dimensions of the issue (especially poverty), and those that link the issue to legal and political issues (human rights) within the democratization process; those that focus on regional issues, and those that focus on overall cultural and human rights in the country; and those close to the state's position, and those close to the Kurdish nationalist movement. There is also an urban-rural divide. Although CSOs in underdeveloped southeastern and eastern cities provide information (e.g., on human rights abuses, killings in the conflict), data are used mostly in the reports of the CSOs whose headquarters are in the urban west. Urban CSOs and those working on the democratization and human rights issues seem to have more effect and "voice" due to more moderate positions. Kirişçi (2008) notes that some CSOs in urban centers in the southeast (namely Diyarbakır) were able to distance themselves from the PKK (in contrast to the PKK's dominant public presence in the 1990s) and denounce violence. These organizations were also able to call for democratic dialogue and expressed moderate views.

We can also point to an increase in the number of NGOs[28] and informal gatherings that address the conflict from a rights-based perspective and frame the issue differently from the state. For example, for a long time these CSOs have asked the state to provide compensation to Kurdish internally displaced people (IDPs), the right of return, economic guarantees (i.e., regional investment, solving unemployment), protection of cultural rights (i.e., the right to teach and broadcast in Kurdish), removal of barriers for political representation of Kurds as a group, and demilitarization of the region (especially abolition of the Village Guard system and the system of emergency rule). We also see an increase in the number of Kurdish women's associations addressing the problems of women IDPs. CSOs in this cluster argue that the state disregards the problem and purges stakeholders.

After 2000 some informal attempts produced effective outcomes. The Initiative of the Intellectuals (Aydın Girişimi), the Initiative of the Citizens (Yurttaş Girişimi), and Peace Group (Barış Grubu) are endeavors to pressure policymakers in Ankara to place greater emphasis on carrying out political/legal reforms and to acknowledge the Kurdish question. These informal gatherings of intellectuals and human rights activists are important not only for their impact on policymakers but also because of the coalescence of Turkish and Kurdish intellectuals under the same banner for the first time.[29] In fact, these initiatives were transformed into the Peace Assembly, composed of academicians, Kurdish NGOs, human rights NGOs, and unions, which proposed solutions to the conflict in September 2007. In May 2008, the Peace Assembly organized a protest in Istanbul against the Turkish military attack on northern Iraq.

INGO branches in Turkey have also started paying attention to the issue despite strong opposition from ultranationalists, who argue that "foreign powers" are trying to divide the country.[30] These claims are directed at the European-based NGOs in Turkey and local NGOs like TESEV, which are partly funded by US sources like the SOROS Foundation. The Heinrich Böll Foundation of Germany (HBF), for example, started a project on "confronting the past," with the aims of preparing a civic movement to request social forms of truth-seeking and of confronting painful memories in history, including but not limited to the Kurdish question. A small group also claimed that the EU was trying to partition the country through the HBF and protested the NGO's conference in Diyarbakır.

Moreover, in the late 1990s, universities emerged as important actors for easing restrictions on academicians working on controversial issues such as the Kurdish question, the Armenian issue, and political Islam. Academicians who addressed the Kurdish question, and liberal universities like Boğaziçi, Bilgi and Sabanci, which hosted conferences on the issue, created a different perspective for analyzing the conflict.[31]

CSOs working on the issue are connected mostly to CSOs in Europe. Kurdish NGOs in Germany, Holland, Belgium, France, and Great Britain try to affect the issue directly through political mobilization or indirectly by acting as pressure groups within EU organizations to compel the Turkish state to grant more rights to Kurds. Within the EU, there are some institutions, such as the EU-Turkey Civic Commission, that are trying to foster international public advocacy. Human rights NGOs report to the international human rights networks minority rights violations, as well as deaths, disappearances, and homicides. The EU has also been influential in areas that affect CSO functioning. For example, the CIVICUS report points out that, according to CSOs, the most significant and positive effects of EU involvement were "related to the enabling environment (reform of CSO laws) and increased ability of CSOs to promote democratic values. Among the least significant yet still positive effects was promoting capacity for collective action and CSO dialogue with the state" (CIVICUS 2006, 19). Globally, Kurdish local and international civil society is also connected to organizations such as Amnesty International and Human Rights Watch (mostly through reporting and advocacy). The women's and human rights movements especially have become networked. "A comparable increase is observed in the number of meetings and conferences organized with international CSOs—likely a result of EU related initiatives that encourage collaboration. However, [the CIVICUS report] reveals that CSOs continue to remain concerned about cooperation and communication among their fellow organizations—both within and between sub-sectors and internationally" (CIVICUS 2006, 16). The same results can be observed in Euro-Kurdish CS actors (Eccarius-Kelly 2007). European actors have become important players, affecting the Turkish state's stance on the issue indirectly (by lobbying in EU institutions) or directly (by vocalizing "Kurdish voices" in Europe).

The diaspora's influence is also visible in the media. For example, in March 2007, Roj TV, publicizing the PKK ideology, was the main cause of tension between Denmark and Turkey. Roj TV, permitted to broadcast in Denmark despite demands for its closure by the Turkish state, called for a demonstration by Kurds in the southeast, which created a significant uprising.

It is important to note as well that the negotiation process for EU accession enabled most CSOs (especially those based in conflict regions) to receive funding through the EU Commission, which helped inform citizens about rights and mobilized them for democratic participation. Nevertheless, a discourse against EU funding (the so-called pollution of the CS) also emerged. Those who were against EU-funded projects, somewhat reasonably, argued that getting money from the EU was an end in itself and did not carry a civic function. There is also the argument that CSOs can plan good projects yet may not be funded, as applying for EU funds is a complex process, requiring skills and training to satisfy bureaucratic procedures.

Peacebuilding Functions

The following section compares the seven different functions: protection, monitoring, advocacy, socialization, social cohesion, intermediation and facilitation, and service delivery.

Protection

Protection has different meanings in different regions. The western cities from time to time are the target of PKK bombings.[32] Rural people in the southeast have also experienced conflict, including homicides, human rights abuses, displacement, economic disparity, and psychological terror. Accordingly, protection means protecting citizens from PKK violence and violence by state security forces, as well as providing relief to those caught between the conflict parties.

This function in rural areas was crucial during the peak period of violence and the reescalation, but it could not be provided by CSOs due to limitations on mobility imposed by the state. Most places where conflict takes place are considered to be military zones, and access is prohibited to civilians, including journalists; in mountainous areas any contact is difficult. Protection in the cities is still needed in terms of increased security measures against any possible violent attacks on the public; this function is defined by law as belonging to the police force.

Protection of citizens against the arbitrary use of state power is one of the most important functions of civil society, but CSOs have not had much success. Especially at the peak of conflict (mid-1990s), apart from a few independent media journalists there was almost no CSO fulfilling this task. This can be attributed to several factors:

1. The state of emergency (OHAL regime of 1984–2004) totally controlled and suppressed civil society.
2. The civil society tradition against coercive state power does not have a long history in Turkey.
3. The state assumes that the protection function should be under its control as part of its "internal affairs"; thus protection was considered too sensitive a matter to be monitored. The failure to protect is perceived as the failure of the military, one of the most trusted, almost "sacred," institutions in Turkey.
4. Protection also requires effective reporting and monitoring. Especially during the peak period of conflict, such information was not made public due to strong state control in conflict areas.

Since 2004, due to the reescalation of conflict, the protection function became relevant particularly for Kurdish IDPs who returned to villages and those close to the Iraqi border, where many PKK camps are located. Due to the increasing role of the military and the reemphasis on the state security and territorial integrity, CSOs cannot perform the protection function. However, NGOs having an organic link to the pro-Kurdish parties maintain a discourse on the demobilization and reintegration of PKK militants. Yet again, there was a demand to the state for general amnesty, rather than the creation of an environment for dialogue. The failure of the protection function even during the negative peace can be explained by the security measures taken by the state even after the state of emergency. Consequently, rather than actively protecting civilians from violence, CSOs focused on monitoring and reporting.

The protection function in the form of human shields was tested by the DTP and CSOs in the southeast, close to the DTP, to generate domestic and international publicity. However, due to military control in the region, it remained an experiment. Moreover, because DTP's aim was to protest the Turkish military's operations in northern Iraq (Türkiye'de Vicdani Retlerini Açıklayanlar 2008), the test served the advocacy function (perceived by many Turks as advocacy for the PKK, not for peace) rather than the protection function.

It is important to mention the protection of culture as the most important function of CSOs. Although strict state regulations limit public use of the Kurdish language, many Kurdish NGOs formed in the late 1990s worked to protect the culture by teaching the language (illegally, before the law on teaching Kurdish was passed, and legally afterward) and publishing in Kurdish.

Monitoring

The monitoring function means the creation of a human rights monitoring system and forcing the state to accept its responsibility in addressing human rights abuses. Almost exclusively, monitoring is aimed at the state's actions. The state is already keeping a record of PKK violations ("terrorism") and making them public. Moreover, for many CSOs "accountability" rests only with the state because it is considered the legitimate actor; therefore it is the state's responsibility to protect citizens not only from PKK violence but also from any situation where citizens feel threatened. It is also important to note that most CSOs considered that civilians need to be protected only from the state and did not address PKK violence.

Among the main activities under this function are watchdog activities undertaken by human rights organizations (such as Human Rights Associations, TESEV, Human Rights Foundation, Mazlum-Der) and the newly emerging civic initiatives (e.g., on the abolition of landmines). Human rights organizations, bar associations, and international NGOs issue annual reports in cooperation with international partners (such as Human Rights Watch and Amnesty International) and check on relevant local laws. Before the 1990s, this function was mainly performed by INGOs with the help of media based in Kurdish-populated regions.

Although monitoring seemed to be the most important function during the peak of the conflict (1991–1994), it was hampered by the coercive state presence in the region. Today, civil society is fulfilling this function without necessarily developing a system for early warning. It would require an analysis of conflict indicators and well-trained CSO personnel to evaluate the conflict and produce effective measures.

The monitoring function is relevant because the state perceives itself as the single most powerful actor in the conflict; only CSOs can publicize issues pertaining to monitoring and accountability. The 1980 coup d'état silenced civil society so strongly that any attempt to monitor the state became a threat to its existence; the reaction was the closure of informal associations, syndicates, and other organizations. However, the impact and effectiveness of monitoring became more influential when the EU emerged as an important actor and during Turkey's period of democratization, in which CSO capacities increased.

Advocacy and Public Communication

The CIVICUS report "reveals an increase in the number of CSOs which wish to take a more active role in the policy-making process, which will be of great value to society given the immense amount of legislative reform awaiting Turkey in the EU accession process" (2006, 18). The emergence of the EU as an important actor, overseeing Turkey's democratic practices, caused CSOs to pay more attention to the advocacy function. The reports prepared by some CSOs tackled issues such as Kurdish IDPs, human rights abuses in southeast Anatolia, broadcasting in Kurdish, and allowing private courses in the Kurdish language. It can also be argued that by drawing international attention to such issues CSOs also protected citizens.

Advocacy for CS usually meant informing the public about state abuses and the "democratic rights of the Kurds." Demands for political, cultural, and economic rights of Kurds as a group and the cessation of violence are made in public via demonstrations, press releases, and other statements. Interestingly, most public demonstrations for the "rights of the Kurds" are perceived by the state as pro-PKK (which is true for some) and become violent as a result of the security forces' overreaction to protesters. However, starting with the period of negative peace, public advocacy in the form of printed declarations by influential Turkish and Kurdish intellectuals was much more successful.

The advocacy and public communications function is the strongest function. However, this is undertaken without receiving feedback from, or establishing communication with, the state. There is also little coordination among CSOs for advocacy. Leftist-oriented and human rights CSOs are more successful in coordinating advocacy activities at the local level than at the macro level. In the cities of southeastern Anatolia, especially in Diyarbakır, the most populous city among Kurdish-dominated regions, platforms are created by labor unions, human rights associations, professional groups (especially bar associations), and sometimes political parties. These so-called Democracy and Labor Platforms address important issues in democratization, including those pertaining to the Kurdish question. Raising themes through public campaigns (e.g., on landmines and Village Guards) and awareness workshops is the most common activity.

This function challenges the state discourse in crucial areas. For example, there exists a conflict over the terminology used to define internal displacement. The Ankara branch of the UNDP translated the official Guiding Principles into Turkish. This official translation adopted the active phrase *yerinden olma*—giving no indication that displacement was done by someone—despite opposition from NGOs. NGOs claimed that the correct translation should be passive—*yerinden edilme*—indicating that displacement was done by some agency.[33] Most CSOs adopted the latter, which has become public usage. This opposition to discursive hegemony of the state delegitimizes CSOs in the state's eyes and implicitly makes them "enemies of the state."

The conflict was internationalized with establishment of the Kurdish autonomous region in northern Iraq and attacks by the Turkish Army in the northern Iraqi territories. Advocacy thus became yet another tool for CSOs and the DTP. On controversial issues such as the status of Kirkuk, in which different ethnic groups in Iraq and Turkey claim rights, and whether the Turkish Army should enter northern Iraq, Kurds in Turkey and northern Iraqi authorities, on one hand, and the Turkish government, on the other, have clashing views. Kurdish political parties and some CSOs close to them echoed the views of northern Iraqi authorities. Massoud Barzani, president of the Autonomous Kurdish government in northern Iraq, for example, argued Kurdish forces would intervene in Diyarbakır if Turkey intervened in Kirkuk (Radikal 2007). This is why advocacy by CSOs and pro-Kurdish political parties triggered a harsh response by the state and the general anger of Turkish citizens.

In-Group Socialization

Socialization means building or consolidating Kurdish identity. Along with increased violence in the 1990s and subsequent democratization in the early 2000s, many "Kurdish" institutions emerged.[34] While some worked to protect culture, especially language, most performed a political function (similar to that of the political parties) rather than a civic one (Çelik 2002). In the 1990s, two women's associations doing similar work emerged in Istanbul, reaching out to Kurdish women in the city; but they were not in touch with, or perhaps were even hostile to, each other because they were direct extensions of pro-Kurdish political parties. Although most Kurdish CSOs helped Kurds learn legal mobilization, most NGOs maintain organic links to political parties and follow in their footsteps, rather than teaching members civic attitudes (Çelik 2002) or skills for peacefully handling conflicts.

Hometown associations in the western parts of the country still provide necessary social capital (e.g., trust, finding housing and jobs, making the transition to urban life easier for the IDPs). However, they also challenge social cohesion by keeping the identity boundaries exclusive to place of origin and by reproducing the traditional life in the city (Çelik 2002).

Social Cohesion

Social cohesion is one of the hardest functions to assess. The Kurdish question is perceived by many as one between the state and the PKK (with Kurds providing human capital for the PKK). Through this perception, the social cohesion function can be interpreted as bridging the gap between the state and Kurdish citizens. Although this might have the most significant impact on the conflict, any peace attempt would be likely to fail unless tensions were lessened between ultranationalist Turks and Kurdish nationalists. Thus, building *trust* between the state and Kurds, and creating *empathy* and *collaboration* between different groups in Turkey, are the most important elements for social cohesion (Çelik and Blum 2007).

The CIVICUS report indicates that civil society is an arena where many groups remain divided by ideology, geography, and in some cases ethnicity. Although CSOs express concern about such divides, and attribute an important role to civil society, they remain vague and uncertain when addressing the root causes and building greater social cohesion (CIVICUS 2006, 17). Turkish society is not tolerant of diverse views. Regional differences are problematic. For example, in Diyarbakır and Ankara, CSOs report low tolerance for diversity, and in Istanbul and Izmir (the Aegean region), participants express that formerly high levels of tolerance are deteriorating rapidly (CIVICUS 2006, 67).[35] It is hard to bring people together with different opinions to discuss issues surrounding the Kurdish question. One positive exception was a conference ("Turkey Is Searching for Its Peace"), a dialogue project of the Peace Assembly, composed of Kurdish opinion leaders, politicians, and academicians, along with many Turkish, Armenian, and Arab academicians and activists.[36]

Intermediation

The intermediation function means enabling a dialogue between Kurdish actors and the state. However, since the state does not consider the PKK as a legitimate actor, and treats the DTP as its political representative, it refuses to engage in a dialogue with these actors. So far, only the AKP government has taken the initiative and held a dialogue with Kurdish intellectuals and civil society representatives. This changed in the wake of increasing violence. Nevertheless, most Kurds believe that the PKK should be accepted as a "party" in any dialogue or negotiation.

When intermediation is performed, politicians rather than CSOs usually undertake this function. Such was the case in the PKK's hostage-taking incident in October 2007. After a sudden ambush of the Turkish military in Hakkari, the PKK took hostage eight Turkish soldiers; it returned them after the DTP members of parliament (MPs) acted as intermediary. However, these MPs later were accused of being traitors.

Despite these shortcomings, the intermediation function is one of the most important functions for CSOs. Any attempt by CSOs to fulfill this function, however, is perceived by the state as a demand to accept the PKK as a legitimate actor; the state outright rejects such efforts. Due to restrictions on access to information, one can never be certain whether negotiations on any issue in the conflict are taking place.[37]

Service Delivery

Service delivery usually means relief, rehabilitation, and sociopsychological help provided to conflict-affected populations; this function is defined by the state as the only role for civil society in the Kurdish question.

During the peak of conflict, service delivery meant assistance in finding housing and jobs for Kurdish IDPs in big cities, as well as trauma-healing and legal services for conflict-affected populations. Hometown associations in eastern and southeastern Anatolia promote social capital via services provided to members in an urban setting, forming a "decadent environment"—a community based on the principles of social cohesion, solidarity, and moral support. These networks also promote vertical relations, such as political patronage and/or clientelism, among members. This is a source of deterioration of social capital (Çelik 2002).

Such activities are still among the largest functions (both in quantitative and qualitative terms). However, it is important to note that CSOs have recognized the crucial importance of this function and have become more professional in reaching a wider population in need.

Service delivery creates entry points for other functions, such as advocacy and public communication, monitoring, and socialization. Through service delivery, CSOs collect data and mobilize members to insist on rights vis-à-vis the state.

Although the demand by Kurdish civil society for delivery of services in Kurdish is unacceptable to the state, the latter is not unaware that the CSOs in the southeast deliver services in Kurdish, especially to women who cannot speak Turkish. Therefore, through service delivery, the protection of culture is also provided. However, there is a difference of opinion between the state and CSOs not only on the scope but also on the nature of service delivery. For example, the state's understanding of humanitarian service delivery to Kurdish IDPs means assistance to them as citizens of Turkey, without discussing the root causes of the problem, whereas many CSOs claim that undertaking humanitarian action requires accepting the issue as one related to identity rights, returning dignity to these people, and healing their pain via understanding and sharing. Almost all NGOs emphasize the need to use the Kurdish language in reaching out to IDPs, some of whom (especially women) cannot speak Turkish.

Conclusion

The Kurdish question reinforces the basic notion that CSOs can be important actors in peacebuilding. Because they work with people on the ground, they provide a holistic picture of the problem. However, conflict parties can instrumentalize CSOs and they can become restricted by those in power. In most cases, CS is a training ground for the political arena; especially in asymmetric relations, it is an opportunity to speak up for the diverse needs of society. However, there is a tipping point at which CSOs become "political." In cases like the Kurdish question, a hard task awaits: to reach out to Kurds and represent their demands and needs, but also not to antagonize the state and those with different opinions in society. Failure might result in CSOs remaining weak, too isolated from recipients, and unable to develop skills to work with diverse populations. That is why the most important functions of CS are advocacy, along with social cohesion and intermediation, although all other functions are also relevant given the different phases of the conflict. Intermediation and social cohesion (along with protection) have been the weakest functions performed by the CSOs in Turkey.

CSOs that are engaged in peacebuilding provide advocacy and service delivery (see Table 8.1). These functions peaked during the armed conflict and reescalation, due to the asymmetric relationship and state limitations on CS. Such findings are not surprising given the conclusion of the CIVICUS report. It argues that challenging context factors, such as weak state-CS relations and problems in democracy, prevent nourishment of CS in Turkey. In a political environment where political parties are closed and precluded from the arena, political parties can instrumentalize CSOs. In this context, CS becomes the only game in town; CSOs focus mostly on advocacy and mobilization for political causes. Moreover, the presence of "uncivil" CSOs leads to the hardening of this position.

Because service delivery is recognized by the state as the only legitimate function for CS, it is not surprising that most activities fall under this category. CS has only just realized this crucial need and that it can serve as a channel to collect data and publicize the "other side of the story."[38] Therefore, service delivery becomes an important entry point for other functions seen as more critical by the Turkish state.

The general conclusions are that for CS to fully serve its peacebuilding functions the state's perceptions of CSOs should be altered; third parties should pressure the Turkish state to stick to its democratization process. Therefore, the EU's direct role in pressuring the state to comply with the Copenhagen Criteria (as part of the EU accession negotiation process)[39] and democratize the country can be the most important enabling factor for CS to perform peacebuilding functions. However, a word of caution is also needed when evaluating the EU's role in fostering the role of CS in Turkey. Depending on the timing of EU intervention in funding CSOs, the EU could produce positive or negative outcomes. Especially during the negative peace, EU funds fostered the advocacy and social cohesion functions by allocating money to CSOs. But during the reescalation of violence and the increase in nationalism on both sides, EU funding was perceived as a threat to national unity. In fact, regardless of the conflict stage, the EU can educate CS personnel, providing skills to analyze the conflict context and produce effective projects. It can also provide money for peace education to CS. However, there is a strong emerging need to fund projects that foster social cohesion as well as advocacy. The EU is funding projects to deliver services where such service can provide a basis for advocacy and monitoring.[40] However, there is a greater need to carry out projects bridging different actors in the conflict.

Table 8.1 Relevance and Effectiveness of the Peacebuilding Functions in the Kurdish Question

Civil society functions in peacebuilding	Relevance of functions in context	Effectiveness of implementation with reference to phases of conflict
1. Protection	1984–1987: Relevant 1987–1999: Most needed 1999–2004: Protection of culture becomes important 2004–?: Important	• Effectiveness depends on state limitations on CS. • Lack of analysis by CSOs prevents effective conflict prevention mechanisms.
2. Monitoring and early warning	1984–1987: Relevant 1987–1999: Relevant 1999–2004: Relevant 2004–?: Relevant	• Impact differs based on the environment (level of democratization) and coordination between local and international CSOs. • Always linked to public communication. • Impact is stronger if all parties are addressed.
3. Advocacy and public communication	1984–1987: Relevant but limited due to state's power 1987–1999: Relevant and most performed function in this stage 1999–2004: Relevant 2004–?: Relevant	• Most commonly exercised function but also sometimes counterproductive. • Most effective role through agenda-setting and mass mobilization.
4. Socialization	1984–1987: Not very relevant 1987–1999: Somewhat relevant 1999–2004: Not very relevant 2004–?: Not very relevant	• It leads to politicization rather than producing social capital. To be effective, it needs to be linked to intragroup social cohesion.
5. Social cohesion	1984–1987: Not very relevant 1987–1999: Relevant but necessity not recognized 1999–2004: Relevant 2004–?: Relevant	• Effectiveness depends on the parties' willingness, capacity, and leverage. • More effective when groups address smaller issues (e.g., internal displacement, human rights issues) rather than macro conflict (the Kurdish question). • More relevant in negative peace period but could affect peace attempts more if addressed in reescalation as well.
6. Intermediation/ facilitation	1984–1987: Relevant but necessity not recognized 1987–1999: Relevant 1999–2004: Relevant 2004–?: Relevant (peak)	• Not existent at all due to the fact that state does not recognize "the other party," but this is perhaps the most important function, especially in peak and deescalation.

(continues)

Table 8.1 continued

Civil society functions in peacebuilding	Relevance of functions in context	Effectiveness of implementation with reference to phases of conflict
7. Service delivery	1984–1987: Relevant 1987–1999: Relevant 1999–2004: Relevant 2004–?: Relevant	• Most exercised function without necessarily addressing the conflict per se. • Depends on the messages sent to the receivers and parties to the conflict. • Becomes a source for advocacy and monitoring functions. • Efficiency requires reaching the wider population in need and professionalism in service delivery.

There is also a pressing need to study whether projects funded by the EU with the aim of bridging Kurdish citizens with state officials succeeded in their objectives. If and when the EU provides such data, this can also be used to analyze the barriers to social cohesion. Evaluation of project success can provide crucial insights into CS's role in peacebuilding.

Notes

A word of gratitude goes to Hamit Bozarslan, Neclâ Tschirgi, and Jordi Tejel for their comments and criticism on an earlier draft of this chapter. Any remaining errors are the responsibility of the author.

1. The "Kurdish question" is the academic phrase used to refer to the conflict. It has been argued by Ayata and Yükseker (2005) that its use was an attempt to escape state repression by academics in the 1980s and 1990s when the state refused to acknowledge the existence of the conflict.

2. The PKK has also used such names as KADEK (Kongreya Azadî û Demokrasiya Kurdistanê, or Kurdistan Freedom and Democracy Congress) and Kongra-Gel (People's Congress).

3. The state of emergency rule known as OHAL (Olağanüstü Hal) has been defined by the 1982 Constitution and Extraordinary Governing Law No. 2935, and later by laws 424, 425, and 430. Under the OHAL regime, governors of the cities gained the right to pass regulations functioning like laws. Among several rights the governors enjoyed, one can list the right to expel citizens from the region, restrict ownership and freedom rights and liberties, and restrict freedom of the press and expression.

4. The first internationalization of the Kurdish question can be considered to be the mass influx of Iraqi Kurds into Turkey in the early 1990s. World attention focused on the Kurds at the end of the Persian Gulf War in 1991 and continued throughout the 1990s with increasing levels of forced migration from the Kurdish-populated regions of eastern and southeastern Anatolia. Although this event was a spillover effect of what happened in Iraq, the "Kurds" as a group became known in the international arena after this.

5. The only exception is the short-lived Mahabad Republic in present-day Iran in December 1945. That republic ceased to exist when Soviet forces and support, which helped found the republic, were withdrawn in December 1946.

6. Alevism is a sect in Islam. There are significant differences in the beliefs and worship practiced by Sunnis and Alevis in Turkey, which has created long-lasting animosity. Alevi Kurds are large in number, especially in the cities of Bingöl, Tunceli, Erzincan, Sivas, Yozgat, Elazığ, Malatya, Kahramanmaraş, Kayseri, and Çorum. Although there are no accurate statistics on the number of Alevis in Turkey, estimates indicate that there are 8–9 million Alevis, of which 2–3 million are Alevi Kurds (Shankland 1999, 136).

7. Internal displacement, or forced displacement, is one of the most important subcategories impacting the Kurdish question. The conflict-induced internal displacement of the Kurds in the 1990s was the result of the evacuation of villages by the military, allowed by the 1987 emergency rule; the PKK's intimidation of villagers who did not support the PKK to leave their villages; and insecurity resulting from being caught between the PKK and Turkish security forces. Many Kurds left their villages and moved to the nearest urban centers (Kirişçi 1998). A significant proportion of the population has moved from the region since the early 1990s, mostly to the periphery of nearby cities, as well as to shantytowns surrounding the big cities, such as Istanbul, Ankara, Izmir, and Adana. Although the state claims that there are around 350,000 internally displaced people (IDPs), local and international organizations argue that their number ranges from 1 million to 3 million and that they are Kurdish citizens. A recent report prepared by a Turkish university, commissioned by the Turkish government following the recommendations of the Representative to the Secretary-General on Internally Displaced Persons, the size of the population migrating from the fourteen provinces due to security-related reasons is around 1 million (HÜNEE 2006).

8. There are other pro-Kurdish political parties and groupings, such as Hak-Par (Hak ve Özgürlükler Partisi—Party of Rights and Freedoms) and KADEP (Katılımcı Demokrasi Partisi—Participatory Democracy Party). However, DTP stands as the only political party that can garner a significant amount of votes in the southeast.

9. Village Guards are locally recruited civilians armed and paid by the state to oppose the PKK. According to Abdülkadir Aksu, the former minister of the interior, there were 12,279 voluntary Village Guards in the region as of November 2003. Also according to Aksu, 5,139 provisional Village Guards "committed crimes" between 1985 and mid-2006. The national media have carried various stories about Village Guards' criminal activities, such as the abduction of women, aggravated assault, and forming armed gangs (Kurban et al. 2006).

10. The Gendarmerie is a military law-enforcement organization, which carries out security and safety services in rural areas. It is also responsible for ensuring internal security and general border control.

11. Doğan is one of the four Kurdish deputies who were stripped of parliamentary immunity in 1994. These deputies were given thirteen-year sentences based on the claim that they were members of an armed group (the PKK).

12. With recent operations under the Turkish Army against PKK camps in northern Iraq, it is not clear whether the number has changed. During the recent northern Iraqi operation that took place between February 22 and 29, 2008, the military claimed that 240 PKK rebels were killed and that twenty-seven Turkish soldiers died (CNN 2008). However, it is also a known fact that PKK has great human potential to mobilize for its cause.

13. According to Köknar (2006, 2), the PKK used the period from 1999 to 2003 to reorganize its command structure, recruit new members, and, especially after Saddam's

quick defeat in April 2003, acquire former Iraqi Army weapons and explosives. This is also the period when the PJAK was founded.

14. By "democratic republic," Öcalan meant the use of democratic means to resolve the Kurdish question without changing the territorial integrity of the state. "As long as it adheres to the democratic system and its state structure, every party can offer a solution without resorting to violence. There is no question here of either imposing a religion by force or breaking and shattering the structure of the state" (Öcalan's testimony at the 1999 trial).

15. *Akil adamlar* refers to those who are experienced in ombudsmanship on the issue, such as opinion-makers (intellectuals, academicians, etc.) and international mediators.

16. DTP is the fifth party whose political ideology can be considered pro-Kurdish. The first pro-Kurdish party HEP (Halkın Emek Partisi—People's Labor Party) was founded in June 1990 by Kurdish MPs, who were expelled from the Social Democratic Party (SHP) after their participation in an international conference held on the Kurdish question in Paris. After HEP's closure by the Constitutional Court, the three consecutive pro-Kurdish parties, namely DEP (Demokrasi Partisi—Democracy Party) and ÖZDEP (Özgürlük ve Demokrasi Partisi—Freedom and Democracy Party), DEHAP (Demokratik Halk Partisi—Democratic Society Party) shared the same destiny.

17. According to Çağaptay, for example, Öcalan was intimately involved in the movement, and Turkish intelligence officers have traced communications between Öcalan and the deputies. Öcalan acknowledged his role in shaping DTP's policies in remarks published in the Kurdish nationalist daily *Özgür Politika.*

18. Although Turkish security forces have always been a central actor in this conflict, their significance has varied over time depending on the context within which the Kurdish question was perceived by the Turkish public. Recently, their role has become more pivotal, mainly as a result of the PKK rescinding its promise of "inaction."

19. For example, in a speech delivered in Diyarbakır, the most important city for Kurds in southeast Anatolia, on August 12, 2005, Prime Minister Erdoğan stated that "the Kurdish Question is a problem of everyone, especially of mine. Disregarding the mistakes made in the past is not an attribute of the big states. The solution lies in providing more democracy, citizen law, and welfare" (Radikal 2005b).

20. According to the latest results of the PEW's Global Attitudes Project, the percentage of the Turkish population who expressed positive opinions of the United States increased from 9 percent in 2007 to 12 percent in 2008, but the percentage has remained much lower than that in the rest of the countries who participated in the survey. According to the survey, a large majority in Turkey say they think of the United States as "more of an enemy" rather than as "more of a friend" (70 percent in Turkey).

21. For example, a recent amendment to the Turkish penal code (Law No. 301), adopted on June 1, 2005, made it a crime to "insult Turkishness." The law mostly affected journalists, activists, and academicians. Since passage of this law, charges have been brought in more than sixty cases, some of which are high-profile. The law makes the Armenian issue and the Kurdish conflict hard to discuss openly in public and punishes any statement contradictory to the founding principles of the Turkish Republic.

22. There are a few Kurdish daily newspapers, among which *Özgür Gündem* is the most popular among the Kurds. The publication of *Özgür Gündem* has been suspended several times, most recently in November 2007 following the capture of Turkish soldiers by the PKK. Many Kurdish websites are used by Kurds in Turkey and abroad.

23. Kalaycıoglu borrows the term from Dryzek, who argues that "oppositional groupings can only be included in the state in benign fashion when the defining interest of the grouping can be related quite directly to a state imperative" (Dryzek 1996, 479–480), and when there is active inclusion, states co-opt certain economic, social, cultural, or environmental groups (Dryzek 1996, 482).

24. Hometown associations are formal voluntary associations founded on the spirit of *hemşehrilik*—solidarity based on sharing geographical origin. They are born out of the conditions following rapid urbanization that Turkey began to experience in the late 1950s to the 1970s. The main objective for the foundation of such associations was to provide a "comfort zone" for recent migrants to cities by providing them with the necessary adaptation skills as well as by preserving the traditional norms of their places of origin.

25. The remaining four are basic freedoms, socioeconomic context, sociocultural context, and legal environment.

26. However, note that even the title of the organization indicates that it brings together the people of the "East," not necessarily mentioning an ethnic group, the Kurds. The founding objectives of the ERCHs are: (1) to attract Kurdish university students to some cultural activities and mobilize solidarity among them; and (2) to destroy all the racist-chauvinist ideologies of Turkey and mobilize Kurds through the democratic and revolutionary institutions, which struggle for the brotherhood and equality of the nations (*Sosyalizm ve Toplumsal Mücadeleler Ansiklopedisi* 1988, 2119).

The Hearths were first established in Istanbul, Ankara, and Diyarbakır and later in Ergani, Silvan, Kozluk, and Batman. The founders of the ERCHs were usually Kurds who split first from the WPT along with their "fellow Turkish leftist friends" and later from this leftist movement. Although the members of the ERCH supported the WPT in elections, it became a movement by itself. What is important to note about the ERCH is that it mobilized a significant number of Kurds, especially among the youth. Some scholars argue that this young generation replaced the old one, "whose traditional ties limited its rebellious temptations," with "one raised with all the symbols of nation and state" (Barkey and Fuller 1998, 15).

27. Especially in the southeastern cities there are NGOs founded directly by the state governors or their wives. In most cases, these are the only CSOs besides bar associations and syndicates.

28. Due to the state regulations on associations and the enormous numbers of CSOs that exist in the country, it is not possible to get statistics on the number of associations in Turkey. The arguments made here come from the author's fieldwork. Most of the CSOs, whose leaders the author interviewed, were founded in the post-1990 period.

29. In the 1970s, there were similar attempts, but mostly under socialist/communist causes and are referred to as an "underdevelopment" problem rather than the "Kurdish question."

30. These claims are widely known as "Sèvres paranoia," which refers to fears that there are external powers who are trying to challenge the territorial integrity of the Turkish state and implement the provisions of the Sèvres Treaty of 1920 signed between the Allied and the Associated Powers. Article 62 of the treaty in particular calls for local autonomy for the predominantly Kurdish areas lying east of the Euphrates, south of the southern boundary of Armenia, and north of the frontier of Turkey with Syria and Mesopotamia. Even though this treaty was replaced by the Treaty of Lausanne, signed between Turkey and the Allied Powers on July 24, 1923, the fear that Turkey's borders are under the threat of such reconfigurations still exists among many Turkish citizens and officials.

31. These universities also engaged in bringing about new perspectives and opening up a channel for a dialogue on the Armenian issue. These three universities held a national conference on the Armenian issue in 2005.

32. In early 2008, the biggest city of southeast Anatolia witnessed a bombing by the PKK. Otherwise, this type of PKK attack would be seen in the West.

33. TESEV, for example, insistently uses *yerinden edilme,* arguing that based on Principle 6, Para. 1, of the Annotations to Guiding Principles on Internal Displacement,

such actions done arbitrarily for security reasons are *"ülke içinde yerinden edilme"* (Kurban et al. 2007).

34. It should be remembered that the recognition of Kurdish people is the product of the late 1990s, when the state discourse shifted from the claim that Kurds are Turks who lost their language because they were isolated from the general population. Although the constitution prohibits forming political parties along racial, ethnic, and religious lines, associations can be established on a cultural basis. However, there are a few associations that work on Kurdish culture. Yet again, there also exist some NGOs that concentrate on the needs of the Kurdish people without referring to Kurdish culture.

35. Also note that Istanbul and Izmir are the cities that have the highest level of Kurdish IDPs.

36. However, this attempt, while unable to attract the attendance of those close to the mainstream and far-right ideologies, was successful in having a former member of MIT (Turkish intelligence) participate.

37. In fact, in summer 2006 a Turkish journalist argued that the Turkish government was negotiating with the PKK to demobilize and dismantle it by granting a general amnesty to its lower-ranking militants and enabling EU countries to provide residence to higher-ranking PKK members (Sabah 2006). However, this was quickly denounced by the government and military.

38. For example, after the Law on Compensation for Losses Resulting from Terrorism and the Fight Against Terrorism was passed in late 2004, many CSOs reached the Kurdish IDPs to collect data about their stories and losses to be submitted to the compensation committees formed at the district level. Unfortunately, by June 2008 there has been only one recent attempt to publicize these human stories.

39. The conditions for starting the EU accession negotiation process *(acquis communautaire)* with candidate states are set forth in the Copenhagen Criteria, adopted in the Copenhagen European Council Meeting of June 1993. According to the Copenhagen Criteria, candidate states must fulfill several standards: (1) political standards: stable institutions governing democracy, the rule of law, and respect for human rights; (2) economic standards: the existence of a functioning market economy and the capacity to cope with competitive pressure; (3) compatibility standards: the ability to take on the obligations of membership, including adherence to the principles of political, economic, and monetary union.

40. A close look at EU funding trends in its European Instrument for Democracy and Human Rights Turkey Program (EIDHR) can provide us a better understanding of the EU role in promoting different functions. According to data collected from the European Commission's delegate in Turkey, there have been sixty-five micro and macro projects funded by the commission since 2000 (EIDHR 2008). It is obvious that EU funding over the years has focused on fostering advocacy and monitoring functions. This is no surprise given the objectives laid out in the program's objectives: promoting freedom of expression and independent journalism; safeguarding freedom of assembly and association; enhancing the role of civil society organizations in monitoring and advocacy for nondiscrimination based on race or ethnic origin, religion or belief, disability, age, and sexual orientation; enhancing human rights education, as well as respect for human rights in education and the media; and fighting the occurrence of torture and ill-treatment, restricted to the fight against impunity and advocacy for independent monitoring of detention facilities. Out of sixty-five projects funded, nineteen deal with some aspect of the Kurdish question or include Kurds as part of their target group. Although in these projects advocacy and monitoring are also prevalent, the service delivery function seems to be a bit more dominant (seven projects for advocacy, seven for monitoring, and ten for service delivery). More interestingly, when it comes to dealing

with the Kurdish question, the social cohesion function has become important (six projects). However, we have to note that both service delivery and social cohesion functions usually occur in tandem with advocacy and monitoring functions. Also, the program funds projects to protect the minority culture's rights and the cultures of other groups (e.g., Alevis, Assyrians, Armenians, Lazs, etc.), but no specific project includes "Kurds" in its title.

9

Cyprus: A Divided Civil Society in Stalemate

Esra Çuhadar and Andreas Kotelis

The conflict on the island of Cyprus is long-standing, intractable, and currently at a stalemate. In this chapter we explore the functions of civil society in the Cypriot conflict, tracing its historical background, providing an overview of the status of civil society on Cyprus, and presenting findings about peacebuilding-oriented civil society. Then, following the theoretical framework developed by Thania Paffenholz and Christoph Spurk (see Chapter 4), we elaborate on the peacebuilding functions that are performed by Cypriot civil society.

Context

Located in the eastern Mediterranean, Cyprus is the third largest island in that sea; it lies south of Turkey and is strategically positioned near the Middle East. Its population is currently slightly more than 1 million, mainly Greek (748,217 concentrated in the South) and Turkish (265,100 concentrated in the North),[1] with minorities of Armenians, Maronites, and Latins. The Greek Cypriot and Turkish Cypriot communities are the main adversaries in the conflict, although the conflict cannot be separated from the broader conflict between the countries of Greece and Turkey.

It is difficult to summarize the conflict in a few paragraphs, especially when considering the historical narratives adopted by the parties (Dodd 1998; Hannay 2005; Müftüler Baç 1999; O'Malley and Craig 1999; Bölükbaşı 2001; Arım 2002; Chrysostomides 2000; Papadakis 1998; and Volkan 1979). Below we describe the conflict in the context of peacebuilding and civil society.

Even though intercommunal violence became rampant in the 1960s, for some scholars the conflict dates to British colonialism, when the seeds of ethnocentric nationalism were sown (Anastasiou 2006; Hasgüler 2000). At one level, the conflict is the result of competing Greek and Turkish nationalism, relying on the historic claims of *enosis* (integrating the island with mainland Greece) and *taksim* (partitioning the island into respective Greek and Turkish political entities). At another level, the conflict is about power-sharing between two ethnic identity groups, as well as statehood. After 1974, other issues arose, such as the property of Greek Cypriot refugees and the presence of the Turkish military on the island.

The state of Cyprus was established in 1960 after the British withdrew, ending colonial rule. The new state was founded with the Zurich and London Treaties under the guarantorship of Greece, Turkey, and Britain.[2] The new constitution and the political system adopted proportionality for all ethnic groups: political offices were arranged on the basis of a 7:3 ratio (of Greeks to Turks), with the president being a Greek Cypriot and the vice president a Turkish Cypriot. The state soon became dysfunctional because of disagreements over its functioning and the constitution. Civil war broke out in 1963. For the Turkish side, the situation was an attempt at *enosis* perpetuated by attacks from the Greek guerrilla organization Ethniki Organosi Kiprion Agoniston (EOKA). In 1967, the legitimacy of the state was in danger of collapsing, with many Turks being pushed into enclaves; even the Greek Cypriot community divided between those who were in favor of *enosis* and those who wanted to maintain independence from Greece.

In 1974, a colonels' junta in Greece undertook a coup that toppled the Greek Cypriot president, Makarios, and replaced him with a former EOKA militant. The coup led to the military "intervention"[3] of Turkey in 1974. The northern part of the island was occupied by the Turkish military and was left to the Turkish Cypriot community, which in 1983 resulted in the founding of the internationally unrecognized Turkish Republic of Northern Cyprus (TRNC). Many Greek Cypriots became refugees after 1974 and fled to the South, leaving their property behind. The troubles created many displaced peoples who formerly lived in mixed cities and villages. In addition to displacement due to violence, a population exchange was initiated soon after 1974, allowing Greek Cypriots in the North to go South and Turkish Cypriots in the South to go North.

The events following the watershed years of 1963 and 1974 created the major issues of contention during ongoing negotiation and mediation efforts led by the United Nations. The Turkish side sees the division of the island, with the establishment of an independent Turkish state in the North, as the logical way to end the violence; the presence of Turkish troops is a safeguard. For the Greek Cypriot side, the situation is perceived as a violation of sovereignty and victimization of Greek Cypriots, who suffered displacement and property loss after 1974.

Status of the State and Economy

Before detailing the political and economic conditions of both Greek and Turkish Cypriots, we must stress Cyprus's complicated and unique status. In the international arena, the Republic of Cyprus (RoC) in the South is the formal legal successor under the founding treaties: the Treaty of Guarantee, the Treaty of Alliance, and the Treaty of Establishment. It is recognized by the international community, but not by Turkish Cypriots or by Turkey. Since 1974 the presence of the Turkish Army and the declaration of the TRNC have created a de facto situation in the North, which has the full characteristics of a state but is dependent on Turkey for its administration and finances. In this chapter, we examine the status of the state based on the de facto situation; thus there is an overlapping assessment of both societies in regard to the status of civil society on Cyprus.

According to the RoC constitution, Cyprus is an independent democracy with a presidential system. The executive power is vested in the president, elected by universal suffrage to a five-year term of office (Cyprus Government Web Portal 2006). The RoC's is a liberal constitution in which the basic liberties and rights of citizens are described. The constitution, however, has not changed since 1960, to manifest that the RoC is the only legal state on the island and the only one recognized by international treaties. According to the Greek-Cypriot Ministry of Foreign Affairs, the RoC has consistently pursued policies promoting human rights, the rights of women and children, and others (Greek-Cypriot Ministry of Foreign Affairs 2008).

As far as economic status, estimates for the Greek Cypriot state show a GDP of US$18 billion, or US$23,000 per capita. According to EUROSTAT data, Cyprus's per capita gross domestic product–purchasing power standards (GDP-PPS) for 2006 was 21,900 euros, reaching 93 percent of the GDP-PPS average for the twenty-seven members of the European Union (EU-27) (Eurostat Yearbook 2006–2007). The RoC also rates "excellent" on combined averages under the Freedom House Index for 2006, being rated as having the highest degree of freedom (Freedom House 2006).

On the Turkish Cypriot side, the TRNC constitution is a newer document, prepared after the TRNC declared independence on November 15, 1983. The TRNC constitution guarantees human rights and liberties and includes detailed provisions on protecting basic human rights and freedoms as compared to the 1975 Constitution of the Turkish Federated Republic of Cyprus (Turkish Republic of Northern Cyprus Presidency 2008). The Turkish Cypriot side has a president and a multiparty political system.

Economic conditions in the North show important differences, despite improvement. The per capita income had a ratio of 2:1 in 2006 (Greek Cypriots to Turkish Cypriots), which improved from 4:1 in 2001 (Nami 2006). Overall, GDP for the Turkish Cyprus is US$1.865 billion, or $11,800 per capita, for 2006 (World Factbook CIA 2009). The growth rate in the North is a fast 11 percent annually from 2001 to 2006. During the same period, the economic growth rate in the South was reported at 3 percent (Platis 2006). The Turkish Cypriot economy is highly dependent on support from Turkey.

Stages of the Conflict

Historically, the Cypriot conflict reached a climax in terms of destruction during the 1960s and 1970s, when violent armed conflict was waged between the two parties. The two communities are currently segregated, but hostility continues absent the daily violence on the ground. Today the conflict is waged in legal and political arenas, such as the European Court of Human Rights (ECHR), and within various international institutions such as the European Union and the United Nations.

There are three important features. First, this is an intercommunal conflict characterized by low levels of violence and an interminable stalemate. The violence subsided after 1974, except for a few instances at the UN-controlled Green Line. Second, Cyprus hosts one of the longest-lasting UN peacekeeping missions, even though the effectiveness of the mission is debatable. Third, although the conflict is intercommunal, it is dependent on and influenced by the internal situations in Greece and Turkey. The conflict is in fact closely linked to Turkey's negotiations for EU accession.

The latest developments include a round of UN-led negotiations over the Annan Plan in 2004, just before the Republic of Cyprus joined the EU. These negotiations failed to result in an agreement. In a referendum on April 24, 2004, the Turkish Cypriots accepted the plan by 65 percent, but the Greek Cypriots rejected it by 76 percent (Alexandrou 2006, 25). The change in the Turkish Cypriot leadership just before the referendum, with the replacement of the pro–status quo Rauf Denktaş and the support of the Justice and Development Party (Adalet ve Kalkinma Partisi—AKP) government in Turkey for the Annan Plan, were important factors in the Turkish Cypriot community. The hard-line nationalist Greek Cypriot president, Tassos Papadopoulos, did not support passage.

Since the 2003 opening of checkpoints along the Green Line, for the first time since 1974 there have been increasing exchanges and crossings between the two sides. On February 24, 2008, during research for this chapter, the Republic of Cyprus elected Dimitris Christofias, the leader of the Communist Party (AKEL), as president. The 2008 election results were a surprise, and many interpreted Christofias's victory as a strong indication that Greek Cypriots were willing to find a solution. At the same time, the loss by the hard-line Papadopoulos was interpreted as a turn toward moderation and conciliation.

Regardless of the reasons behind the Greek Cypriot vote, for the first time since 1974 there are two leaders on the island who simultaneously express an interest in solving the impasse, coming from similar ideological backgrounds. Only weeks after the change of leadership in the South, Christofias and the new Turkish Cypriot president, Mehmet Ali Talat, met and agreed to open the Ledra Street crossing in Nicosia, closed since 1963. They also agreed to restart the stalled negotiations. The technical preparations for negotiations are completed and talks between the two Cypriot leaders are under way.

Peacebuilding in the Context of Cypriot Conflict

Although there has been an ongoing peace process for decades under UN sponsorship, different stakeholders and actors have different interpretations as to peace, peace agreements, and the process that achieves peace.

Political parties interpret peace and peacebuilding differently. All mention the need for negotiations, but they differ in expectations. In both communities, there is a division along a moderate-to-hard-line continuum. In the North, the National Unity Party (Ulusal Birlik Partisi—UBP) and the Democrat Party (Demokrat Parti—DP) traditionally support a confederation or else maintenance of the status quo (Tocci 2002, 111). The Communal Liberation Party (Toplumcu Kurtuluş Partisi—TKP) and the Republican Turkish Party (Cumhuriyetçi Türk Partisi—CTP) have been more open to a federal solution based on a bizonal and bicommunal state (Tocci 2002, 112). Overall, it can be argued that regardless of differences, the baseline in the Turkish Cypriot community is that a solution needs to recognize Turkish Cypriots as equals, not as a minority, and needs to introduce a centrally weak federal state that is bizonal and bicommunal.

On the Greek Cypriot side, moderates are traditionally represented by the Reformist Workers Party (Aristera Nees Dynameis—AKEL) and the United Democrats (Enomenoi Democrates—EDI), which have been supportive of a federal solution. The Socialists (Kinima Socialdemocraton—KISOS) and Tassos Papadopoulos's Democrat Party (Democratiko Komma—DIKO) traditionally opt for hard-line positions and are more skeptical of federal solutions that recognize Turkish Cypriots as a nonminority (Tocci 2002, 115). A survey among Greek Cypriot teenagers investigating the "most preferred" and "most feasible" solutions to the conflict found the most frequently mentioned preferred solution to be the creation of a federal state dominated by Greek Cypriots; the least preferred solution was the creation of a federal state with two equal communities. The latter was also considered to be feasible least often; for the majority of the sample, maintaining the status quo was perceived as a feasible way forward (Pahis and Lyons 2008). Thus, it can be argued that the baseline within Greek Cypriot society is a federal state; however, contrary to Turkish Cypriots, Greek Cypriots are inclined toward a centrally strong federal state in which Turkish Cypriots are assigned minority status.

Greece and Turkey are important, as both countries have leverage over their kin communities; policy preferences have changed over time (Loizides 2002; Çarkoğlu and Kirişçi 2004). Greece in the 1990s shifted toward a cooperative model; the Greek government (Nea Democratia, or ND) and the main opposition party (Panellinio Sosialistiko Kinima, or PASOK) supported the Annan Plan, which adopted a federal solution (Evin 2004; Loizides 2002, 438; Anastasiou 2007, 199). It should be pointed out, however, that the support of ND was not as clear as the support of PASOK. Turkey, after 2002 and the ascension to power of AKP, changed its pro–status quo position on Cyprus and made concessions on confederation-oriented solutions (Çarkoğlu and Rubin 2005; Stavrinides 2005, 83).

International actors also see the peace process from different angles. The UN and EU perspectives on peacebuilding differ especially in their approach to the peace process (Çuhadar-Gürkaynak and Memişoğlu 2005). The UN understanding of peacebuilding in Cyprus is summarized in the Annan Plan: a federal government with two equal constituent states and a single Cypriot citizenship (Alexiou et al. 2003). The UN has been careful about taking an impartial role. EU impartiality is dubious. The EU position evolved from uninterested third party in early 1990s to a secondary party at the end of the accession talks with Cyprus (Eralp and Beriker 2005; Yeşilada and Sözen 2002). Although the EU does not have a specific plan for an agreement, the membership process has been used as a tool to facilitate reconciliation between the two communities (Eralp and Beriker 2005, 180–181; Tocci 2004).

This suggests that most actors in Cyprus are hoping, or could "live with," a federal solution, more or less confined by the principles in the Annan Plan. However, disagreements arise over structure, power-sharing, and organization within a federal state, as well as procedures to reach the final goal. One could argue that civil society functions to prepare Cypriots for a federal state, such as confidence-building and citizenship-building initiatives, are relevant to the conflict.

Status of Civil Society

Civil society in Cyprus, in both the North and the South, is weak, not quite independent from the state, politicized, and a recent development. An independent civil society, albeit an ineffective one, began to emerge in the Turkish and Greek communities only after 1974. Historically, civil society was dominated by the political society in both communities and, in particular, by the Greek Orthodox Church in the South (Kızılyürek 2004). In both communities after 1974, civil society tried to thrive within a patronage system; independence from the state remained very limited (Kızılyürek 2004, 50–51). In the South, civil society has been tied organically to political parties, in which almost all civil society formulations, including sports and youth associations, have functioned as party extensions. In the North, the part of the civil society that rejected the idea of *taksim* was excluded by the pro–status quo governments (Kızılyürek 2004, 51).

The patrimonial and nonindependent characteristics of civil society in both Cypriot communities are also reflected in the CIVICUS report of 2005, which shows that the status of civil society in Cyprus is weak: although civil society is considered developed in Cyprus overall, it is still far from levels seen throughout Western Europe. The CIVICUS study assessed Cypriot civil society on four dimensions: structure, the environment in which civil society is located, the extent to which civil society promotes positive social values, and the impact of civil society at large.

The exact number of civil society organizations (CSOs) in the South is difficult to configure exactly, but based on the information from the *Civil Society Organizations Directory* as well as civil society leaders interviewed for this study, it is estimated to be around 2,000 total. However, among registered CSOs, only a fraction are active or include a significant membership. The main civil society actors in the South are trade unions, charity organizations, the Greek Orthodox Church, and sports clubs. According to the *Civil Society Organizations Directory,* about 60 percent of organizations are based in Nicosia; the rest are scattered mostly in other big cities, indicating urban concentration. The opportunities for citizen participation are limited in rural areas partly because CSOs are not actively organized in local communities.

In the South part, the CIVICUS report suggests, civil society structure is ranked "slightly weak." This means that the level of public participation, through volunteer work, is low (CIVICUS 2005, 4–5). The report also suggests that prejudice and discrimination are widespread in regard to certain ethnic or linguistic minorities and foreign workers. Rural dwellers are also largely excluded from membership and leadership in CSOs (CIVICUS 2005, 4–5). Furthermore, according to the report, cooperation and communication among different sectors of civil society are limited. The majority of the organizations operate at the local or national level, but it is more common for trade unions and employers' organizations to be linked to international organizations (CIVICUS 2005, 5). Overall, data from the CIVICUS report show that only 43 percent of the population in the South belong to a CSO, and only 17 percent belong to more than one. Moreover, data reveal that 60 percent have taken some form of nonpartisan political action, such as signing a petition (CIVICUS 2005, 53).

In the North, the number of Turkish Cypriot CSOs is about 1,200. However, as in the South, only a fraction are active. According to the *Civil Society Organizations Directory* and interviews, the number of active CSOs in the North is around 200. The key actors are trade unions and sports clubs. Roughly 70 percent of CSOs are based in Nicosia (Lefkoşa); Famagusta (Gazimağusa) is another active community. Thus, as in the South, civil society in the North is also in urban areas.

The structure of civil society on each side is similar. The CIVICUS report suggests that it has been relatively weak, except for the period of mass demonstrations for and against the Annan Plan in 2004 (CIVICUS 2005, 9). The findings from the CIVICUS study suggest that the proportion of Turkish Cypriots belonging to a CSO, or who may have undertaken some form of nonpartisan political action and volunteerism, is fairly low. Participation in bicommunal events together with Greek Cypriots is also low. On the Turkish Cypriot side, there is prejudice and discrimination toward certain minorities, poor people, workers, and settlers from Turkey (CIVICUS 2005, 132). The extent to which civil society promotes positive social values, and the impacts of civil society at large, in the Turkish Cypriot community are akin to the Greek Cypriot side.

Overall, the problems faced by civil societies in both communities (i.e., the rural-urban gap, the dominance of family ties as opposed to individualism, prejudice and discrimination toward certain social groups) are similar. One major difference is that the Greek Cypriot civil society has more resources (human, financial, infrastructure, availability of external funds) and better access to international umbrella organizations that support local civil society compared to Turkish Cypriot civil society.

Peacebuilding-Oriented Civil Society

These general characteristics—that is, civil society is not independent of the state and political society, reflects a low level of volunteerism and civic participation, as well as dominance of Greek and Turkish nationalisms—also shape peacebuilding-oriented activities on the island. Participation in bicommunal meetings is common among moderates or those who are predisposed to dialogue. Often, people who engage in dialogue are alienated in society by mainstream nationalist actors, such as the Greek Orthodox Church on the Greek side or pro-*taksim* groups on the Turkish side. Political parties and their preferences still determine people's actions in the Greek Cypriot community. Such was the case during the referendum for the Annan Plan, in which people followed party lines when voting. We elaborate on these characteristics below.

During the history of peacebuilding in Cyprus, we see three types of actors. The first one is formal CSOs, which function in various issue areas, from the environment to women's issues to mediation. The second type of CS actor is citizens (local and international) who are involved with various bicommunal activities. The third type, social movements and ad hoc public campaigns, sometimes galvanize support for or against negotiation processes and usually operate around social networks. Therefore, in discussing the functions of civil society in peacebuilding we focus on CSOs (not limited to those that define only peacebuilding in their mandate), citizens (foreign and local), and networks that organize social movements and campaigns. Religious organizations are important CS actors, especially in the Greek Cypriot community, but their peace-support activities are limited or nonexistent. Historically, the Greek Orthodox Church has been associated closely with nationalist struggles for *enosis* and Hellenism and disregarded the fears and needs of the Turkish Cypriot community (Hadjipavlou 2007, 354). Recently a few Greek Orthodox bishops recognized the suffering of Turkish Cypriots, challenging the close association between the Church and the Greek nationalist movement (Hadjipavlou 2007, 355). In the next section we provide a general picture of CSOs in Cyprus before discussing their functions in detail.

In order to provide an overall picture of the status of CSOs in Cyprus, we gathered a list based on the *Civil Society Organizations Directory,* a two-volume work published in 2007. This is to our knowledge the most comprehensive and up-to-date civil society directory published in both the North and the South. It provides information on all CSOs in Cyprus—peacebuilding and otherwise, a total of 418 active CSOs (271 Greek Cypriot and 147 Turkish Cypriot). We then coded CSOs according to their interests (sports, charity, professional associations, etc.), gender and youth focus, year of establishment, level of operation, and whether they have a special interest in peacebuilding or not.[4] We present the findings from this analysis below.

Among CSOs in Cyprus, 65 percent are Greek Cypriot and 35 percent are Turkish Cypriot.[5] On the Greek Cypriot side, 21 percent of these work on issues related to peacebuilding; on the Turkish Cypriot side 45 percent work on such issues, more than double that of the Greek Cypriot side. The number of Greek Cypriot CSOs interested in peacebuilding (fifty-seven) is less than Turkish Cypriot CSOs (sixty-six). This is significant given the fact that the total number of Turkish Cypriot CSOs is much smaller. Thus, we can say that CSOs that work toward peacebuilding form a significant proportion of the Turkish civil society as opposed to the Greek Cypriot civil society.

Another difference in peace-oriented civil society emerges when we look at dates of establishment. Figure 9.1 shows dates of establishment for Turkish Cypriot CSOs, comparing trends for all CSOs (total), and trends for peacebuilding-related CSOs and general-interest CSOs. Figure 9.2 shows the same trends for both general-interest and peacebuilding CSOs for the Greek Cypriot side.

Figure 9.1 Turkish Cypriot CSOs According to Dates of Establishment

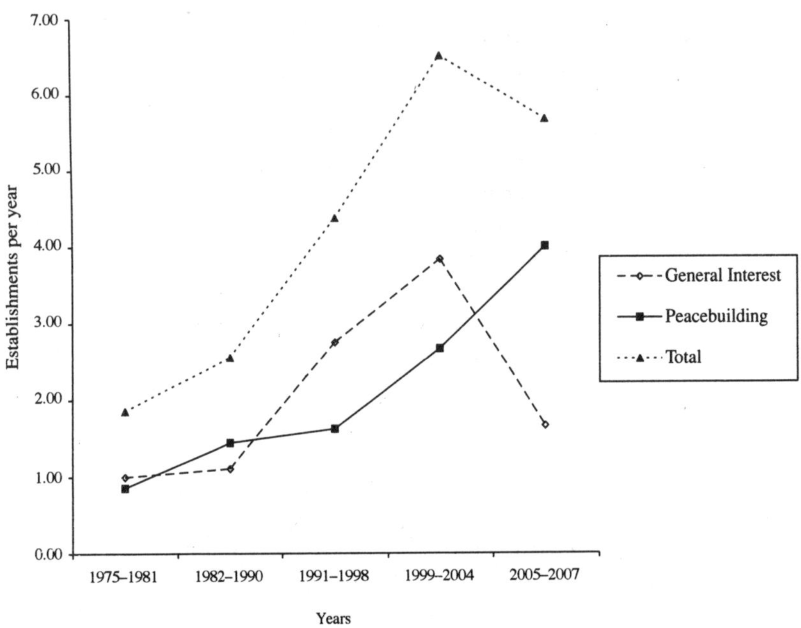

Figure 9.2 Greek Cypriot CSOs According to Dates of Establishment

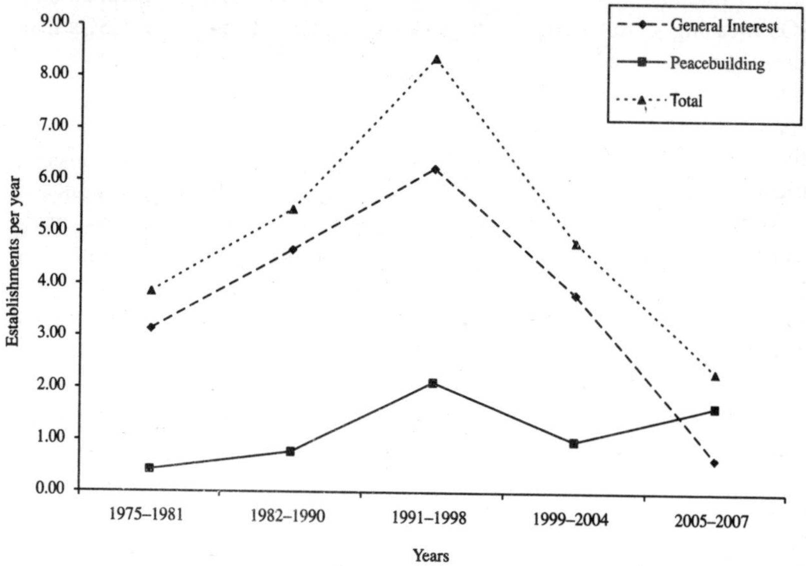

The time periods reflected in Figures 9.1 and 9.2 follow the major turning points in the conflict. The y-axis indicates the number of CSOs established during that period, divided by the number of years within that period.[6] A comparison reveals patterns in the evolution of CSOs in general and the evolution of peacebuilding CS in particular. Beginning in 1975, the Turkish Cypriot community saw a steady increase in the number of peacebuilding CSOs. A similar but less significant increase in peacebuilding CSOs is also observed on the Greek Cypriot side after 1975. A decline in the number of new CSOs is observed in both communities beginning in the late 1990s. Another striking similarity is that the 1990s were boom years for peacebuilding CSOs in both communities; the numbers increase during these years compared to previous periods. Overall, the data suggest that peacebuilding CSOs are young in Cyprus; on the Greek Cypriot side there is a decline after 1998 in the number of new peacebuilding CSOs, while the upward trend continues on the Turkish Cypriot side.

As for any focus on women and youth, we see that women's associations show differences between the Greek CS and Turkish CS. Turkish Cypriot women's organizations are common and widespread, accounting for slightly more than the 25 percent of all CSOs. This includes prominent associations such as Hands Across the Divide and the Turkish Cypriot Women Association. In contrast, the Greek Cypriot CS performs poorly on gender issues. The percentage of women's associations, or associations dealing with gender issues, is only 9.59 percent. Numerically, there are thirty-seven Turkish Cypriot women's organizations compared to twenty-six on the Greek Cypriot side. A common finding with regard to gender is that the number of peacebuilding CSOs focusing simultaneously on gender is higher than for other CSOs that address gender issues exclusively. This indicates that in both communities gender issues are incorporated into the peacebuilding agenda, but tilting in favor of the Turkish side. Finally, this is an indicator that women take an active role in peacebuilding work on both sides, again tilting in favor of the Turkish Cypriot side.

Maria Hadjipavlou and Cynthia Cockburn (2006) provide information about women's involvement in civil society and argue that early peacebuilding initiatives failed to address gender aspects of the conflict and lacked training and discussion on issues of gender. Thus, Cypriot women themselves had to take the first steps in organizing women's groups to address gender issues that resulted from the conflict. This led to the creation of a small group of Greek and Turkish Cypriot women who became leading figures in civil society.

As for youths, in both communities the percentage of youths' and youth-related organizations exceeds 50 percent (52.3 percent for Turkish Cypriots and 53.1 percent for Greek Cypriots). The picture is positive when we take into account CSOs that specialize in peacebuilding but simultaneously work with youths and their issues. This indicates that youths are an important part of peacebuilding activities in both communities.

Peacebuilding Functions

In the following sections we examine the functions performed by civil society in peacebuilding, following the framework in Chapter 4. We discuss the types of actors, their activities, and the relevance and effectiveness of each function.

Protection

In conflicts where violence is a daily phenomenon, protection is an urgent and important function and means providing safety and security to the victims of conflict. In Cyprus, where daily violence is nonexistent, the protection function in this classic sense is not applicable. Thus, any protection function provided by civil society in Cyprus is virtually absent. The conflict is a long-lasting stalemate, in which interaction between the two communities and violence are minimal.

Any protection function has come from non-CS actors, such as the United Nations Peacekeeping Force in Cyprus (UNFICYP), deployed before 1974 to maintain the cease-fire between the parties and to surveil the Green Line buffer zone (UNFICYP 2008). For Turkish Cypriots, the Turkish Army in the North is the main protector, but Greek Cypriots do not perceive it as such.

Therefore, any protection function means protecting the interests of individuals whose well-being may have suffered during the violent period of conflict.

This includes protecting abandoned private property and the cultural heritage in combination with advocacy and monitoring.

Some CS actors protect people in danger, unrelated to the conflict. The Turkish-Cypriot Human Rights Foundation in the North and the Association for the Prevention and Handling of Violence in the Family deal with human trafficking, domestic violence, child abuse, and refugees from other countries. Even though these activities do not directly address peacebuilding, it is not uncommon for Turkish Cypriot and Greek Cypriot CSOs to cooperate on such general protection matters. Such cooperative protection of human beings generates contact between individuals from the two communities and thus serves as an entry point to social cohesion.

Monitoring

Monitoring is also a lower priority in the violence-free context of Cyprus, focusing mainly, if not exclusively, on specific issues emanating from the conflict rather than on violence and how violence affects citizens.

Our research has shown that CS actors providing monitoring are not very common and can be assigned to two categories: monitoring of institutions' properties (especially religious institutions) and monitoring of private property for the purpose of protection or compensation.

The Greek Orthodox Church actively monitors its property in the North, some 500 Christian churches. The Church of Cyprus has also published a booklet titled "The Occupied Churches of Cyprus" (2000). Citizen groups organizing through the Internet also monitor churches in the North (Kypros-Net—The World of Cyprus 2008). Turkish Cypriots monitor mosques in the South, a function assigned to a formal state actor, the Religious Affairs Directorate (Diyanet İşleri Başkanlığı). These actors have easier access to monitoring than nonstate actors. CSOs often have to confront the state actors to do monitoring. Organizations that are known as credible, representative, and neutral in the eyes of the public can perform this role more effectively.

Monitoring private properties focuses on claims to lands left behind in the South and the North after the population exchange. The issue was highlighted after 2002 when the ECHR, in *Loizidou v. Turkey,* found Turkey to be in breach of the Human Rights Convention and granted the Greek Cypriot applicant (Loizidou) the right to her property (Gürel and Özersay 2006, 363; Necatigil 1999; Loizidou vs. Turkey Overview 2000). Since then a number of Greek Cypriots have followed the same course, claiming compensation from Turkey. Soon after, Turkish Cypriots followed, claiming their rights to properties in the South through international legal channels. The Human Rights Foundation provided limited assistance to individuals who filed two pilot cases at the ECHR. The issue of private property has become a legal issue, where the role of civil society did not go beyond providing legal counseling. This service hardly serves a peacebuilding goal but instead escalates the conflict into an international legal battle.

Ancient cultural heritage is an important issue that receives monitoring. Greek Cypriots claim a need to protect the many antiquities in the North. However, monitoring is done by the Department of Antiquities of the RoC rather than CS actors (Republic of Cyprus Department of Antiquities 2008).

A unique monitoring activity by civil society is the Landmine Monitor, an international NGO that monitors the demining process following the implementation of the Land Mine Ban Treaty signed by the RoC in 1997. Landmine Monitor has produced several reports describing the progress of the demining processes undertaken by the RoC and the Turkish Army in the buffer zone (International Campaign to Ban Landmines 2009).

Advocacy and Public Communication

Civil society actors carry out advocacy functions to promote resolution of the conflict and to advance peace efforts. In addition, advocacy is pursued to advance the rights of those victimized by conflict. In this sense, advocacy is prevalent, as various CS groups understand how negotiations should proceed.

Advocacy as a CS function can be divided into two categories: advocating for ideas and proposals at the policymaking and decisionmaking levels to influence the negotiation agenda in peace talks, and public advocacy, which focuses on the public sphere through demonstrations, public campaigns, and media.

Many CS actors perform public advocacy and communications on both sides of the island. Every CS actor may have its own system of beliefs (ranging from moderate to extreme nationalist) that it communicates, consciously or not, to the public. Below we identify some CS actors that see advocacy as their main function and that are propeace; they carry out activities that facilitate the peace process and protect universal human rights.

One of the most important is the Peace Research Institute Oslo (PRIO) Cyprus Center. PRIO is one of the main international CSOs with a significant field presence in Cyprus, engaging in advocacy during the turning points of the conflict. PRIO "contribute[s] to an informed public debate on key issues relevant to an eventual settlement of the problem . . . through the establishment and dissemination of information and by offering new analysis . . . and through facilitating dialogue." Its research should always be of public interest and be disseminated in understandable language, alongside academic publications. PRIO does not advocate for a specific solution to the Cyprus conflict but rather facilitates dialogue and cooperation.

Public advocacy campaigns, and some of the first examples of bicommunal cooperation, have been organized by left-wing sectors such as labor unions. The left wings in both communities shared a common ideological agenda for the Cypriot state, and their involvement and interests went beyond labor issues to include the peace process as well. Important examples of advocacy work were undertaken by the Cyprus Turkish Secondary Education Teachers' Union (Kıbrıs Türk Orta Eğitim Öğretmenler Sendikası—KTOEOS) and the Cyprus

Turkish Teachers' Union (Kibris Türk Öğretmenler Sendikası—KTOS). Although these are labor unions, they also worked toward a peaceful solution to the Cyprus conflict. KTOEOS activities range from national issues, to human rights issues, to EU-related issues.

Several social movement campaigns galvanized by civil society have been important, beginning in the 1980s. One of the first examples formed after a meeting in Berlin, the Movement for Peace and Federation in Cyprus (Kızılyürek 2004, 52).

Other public campaigns were organized to mobilize people for the Annan Plan, especially on the Turkish Cypriot side. One of these, called Bu Memleket Bizim ("This Country Is Ours"), organized nearly ninety organizations to rally in support of the referendum. A public demonstration was held on January 14, 2003, when thousands of people gathered in İnönü Square in Nicosia to demonstrate in support of the Annan Plan and to voice dissatisfaction with the attitude of the Turkish leader, Rauf Denktaş, toward negotiations. Similar rallies were organized before and after this event. The organization of the rallies in the North was a result of cooperation among different civil society actors (e.g., trade unions, bus drivers) whose participation was crucial.

Public advocacy efforts were also organized by those who opposed the Annan Plan, eventually leading to a confrontation between the two blocs and deepening the polarization in each community. The "yes" platform, especially for the Turkish Cypriot side, included a wide variety of CS actors. After the change of political leadership in the TRNC, the new leadership campaigned for the Annan Plan and managed to unite business, academia, and NGOs within a coalition (Akçakoca 2005). The Greek Cypriot mobilization for approval was not very effective. The opposition platform was formed mainly by right-wing civil society, as well as actors close to political authorities in the South. For example, a demonstration opposing the Annan Plan was organized by Democratic Rally (Demokratikos Sinagermos—DISI) on April 21, 2004, a few days before the referendum. The Greek Orthodox Church was also active during the referendum process and advocated against passage. One of the leaders of the opposition was the bishop of Pafos, Chrisostomos (who later became archbishop of Cyprus). The bishop even claimed that people voting "yes" would go to hell; other members of the clergy denounced the plan as a "US-Zionist" plot (Gorvett 2004). The only bishop who supported the plan was the bishop of Morfou, Neophytos (Alexandrou 2006, 37).

Public advocacy work is also undertaken by human rights organizations to protect individuals whose rights were violated because of the conflict or because of conditions the conflict created. For example, the newly established Pancyprian Steering Committee Claiming the Rights of Refugees and Sufferers (Pankipria Sintonistiki Epitropi Diekdikisis Dikaiomaton Prosfygon kai Pathonton) acts on behalf of Greek Cypriots. The organization argues that Greek Cypriots who fled the North after 1974 are at a disadvantage compared to the nonrefugee Greek Cypriots and that the government should protect and assist them because of these disadvantages. Other organizations are the Pancyprian Refugee Union (Pankipria Enosi Prosfygon—PEP), the Pancyprian Organization for the Rehabilitation of Sufferers (Pankipria Organosh Apokatastashs Pathonton), and the Greek Pancyprian Refugee Union—Cyprus 1974 (Pankipria Enosi Prosfygon Elladas—Kipros 1974), established by Greek Cypriot refugees who fled to Greece after 1974. The International Association of Human Rights in Cyprus is another CSO doing advocacy work in the human rights tradition. The association is concerned with protecting Greek Cypriots whose human rights were violated after 1974 (International Association of Human Rights in Cyprus 2009).

On the Turkish Cypriot side, advocacy work for human rights is not as well organized as in the South. A few civil society actors struggle for the rights of Turkish Cypriots victimized due to conflict. The Human Rights Foundation protects and defends the human rights of the individuals living in the North (Turkish Cypriot Human Rights Foundation 2009). It has also addressed issues concerning the property rights of Turkish Cypriots who fled the South before 1974. The foundation works through legal channels to demonstrate that the RoC's policies do not meet acceptable human rights norms.

The CIVICUS report mentions that 62 percent of the Greek Cypriot population believes that civil society is "active" or "somewhat active" in influencing public policy. In the South, 64 percent of survey respondents said that civil society has an impact on the Cyprus problem and related policies (CIVICUS 2005). Nonetheless, the report does not mention the direction and intensity of this impact, such as whether or not the impact is propeace.

Other advocacy efforts aim directly and exclusively at decisionmaking. These initiatives are organized in a Track 2 setting (discussed in the section on social cohesion), where key individuals from both sides come together to discuss possible solutions and then advocate for solutions at the decisionmaking level. Advocacy is one of the major strategies used by the Track 2 participants and by organizers to influence decisionmakers and negotiations.

In-Group Socialization

In-group socialization as a civil society function supports the practice of democratic attitudes and values within society, realized through active participation in associations, networks, and democratic movements. In Cyprus, two factors make this function essential and important. The first one is various rounds of negotiations that advocate for a bizonal and bicommunal federal state. When the end goal is defined as a federal state with citizenship for Greek and Turkish Cypriots, one expects civil society to work hard toward socializing each community in democratic and civic values to facilitate a transition. For many years youths in each community have been educated along nationalist lines, in a way that disregarded the needs and fears of the other side. Greek

Cypriot children were socialized with the idea that the island was and "will always be Greek"; Turkish Cypriots learned that "the island is Turkish and should go back to Turkey" (Hadjipavlou-Trigeorgis 1987; Papadakis 1998).

The second factor is the low level of volunteerism and civic participation. Despite its relevance and importance in the successful transition to a federal state, in-group socialization does not receive the attention it deserves. Still, some civil society initiatives are undertaken to this end.

In Cyprus, CS actors contribute to the development of a democratic attitude, meaning the socialization required to participate in a democratic political life. Examples are the youth organizations of political parties, such as the DISI Youth (Neolaia Democratikou Sinagermou—Ne.Di.Si.) and the AKEL Youth (Eniaia Democratiki Organosi Neolaias—EDON). However, these organizations do not always aim to lay the groundwork for a functional bicommunal federal state; some also serve as schools for political parties' future recruits and voters.

Besides democratic attitudes, in-group socialization includes learning about the peaceful management of conflicts and strengthening an in-group identity that facilitates peacebuilding. Many initiatives provide conflict resolution training and peace education exclusively to one community or both simultaneously. The Media Symposium organized by Hasna brought to Washington, D.C., a group of ten journalists working in the Greek-Cypriot media to learn and practice conflict resolution skills (HasNa 2009). The Fulbright Foundation also supported conflict resolution training for each community separately. During 1994–1995, Benjamin Broome met for several months with Greek Cypriot and Turkish Cypriot groups separately. Later, Marco Turk, another Fulbright scholar, offered workshops for each community, which included exercises, discussions, role-playing, and the like to teach problem-solving and conflict resolution skills. The groups that received training included youths, a Turkish-Cypriot women's group, the Cypriot Police Academy, and others (Broome 2005a, 278). Another example is the Cyprus Mediation Association (CYMEDA), which apart from professional mediation aims at educating the public on issues of peaceful conflict resolution via mediation (CYMEDA 2009).

In regard to strengthening in-group identity to facilitate peace, to our knowledge there are no CS actors that deal with this. "Cypriotism" never existed as a concept of shared common identity before or after 1974 (Asmussen 2003). Even before 1974, when the RoC was an independent state and the two ethnic groups coexisted in mixed villages, each ethnic group showed more loyalty to the "motherland" than to the state of Cyprus; a culture of independence and power-sharing never developed (Hadjipavlou 2007, 357–358). Yet, this highlights the importance of strengthening in-group identity in the Cypriot context. Establishing a federal state will be impossible to implement without it.

Intergroup Social Cohesion

Intergroup social cohesion is about building ties between conflicting parties. In Cyprus this means organizing various bicommunal activities across the Green Line. Such initiatives are significant for eliminating distrust and for maintaining communication and contact. In a 2002 survey conducted by Maria Hadjipavlou (2007, 13), 70 percent of Greek and Turkish Cypriots alike thought that lack of communication contributed to the conflict. Therefore, bicommunal contact and communication are seen as the best mechanism to overcome the problem.

In Cyprus, the intergroup social cohesion function has been overwhelmingly performed by CS actors and has been the most frequent civil society function performed (at least until the Green Line opened in 2003 and the referendum of 2004). There are dozens of initiatives organized by citizens, CSOs, scholars, and practitioners, all aimed at bringing together various groups from the two communities.

Cooperation among CSOs across the divide. During the preparation of the *CSO Directory,* CSOs were asked whether or not they cooperate with organizations from the other side. The findings are important because they indicate cooperation between Greek Cypriot and Turkish Cypriot CSOs and, thus, peacebuilding activity. Cooperation occurs in areas such as the environment and charity work, as in the case of the Laona Foundation for the Conservation and Regeneration of the Cyprus Countryside. The data are positive, especially for the Greek Cypriot side. The percentage of Greek Cypriot organizations that cooperate across the Green Line is 54.6 percent; it is higher for peacebuilding CSOs (59.6 percent). Approximately 40 percent of all Turkish Cypriot CSOs have some type of cooperation with Greek Cypriot CSOs. For Turkish Cypriot peacebuilding organizations, the percentage is 54.5 percent.

In the same survey, CSOs were also asked whether or not they intended to cooperate with the other side in the future. The results are encouraging. Among Greek Cypriots, 179 of 271 organizations (66 percent) said they would be interested in cooperating with CSOs in the North, such as the Cyprus Consumers Association and the environmental NGO Green Shield. Among peacebuilding CSOs, the percentage is 77 percent. For Turkish Cypriots, the respective percentages are 64 percent and 86.3 percent. The results suggest further cooperation is likely between Turkish Cypriot and Greek Cypriot CSOs in general and for peacebuilding.

Bicommunal activities. Bicommunal meetings and initiatives, rare during the 1970s and 1980s, became common after the mid-1990s; by late 1997 at least one bicommunal group was meeting every day of the week (Broome 2005a, 268). Beginning in the 1980s and throughout the 1990s, a group of Fulbright and international scholars initiated a series of bicommunal activities, including conflict resolution training, dialogue groups, and problem-solving workshops. From the mid-1990s onward, there was a boom in peacebuilding activities on Cyprus. Eventually some 2,000 individuals became involved in these initiatives (Broome 2005b, 14). According to Hadjipavlou, between 1993 and 2001 more than sixty different interethnic groups were formed, and the participants received, among other things, formal training in conflict resolution, intercultural education, mediation, and negotiation (Hadjipavlou 2004, 202).

Bicommunal contacts can be grouped into six categories: political contacts, business and professional projects, citizen gatherings and exchanges, conflict resolution activities, ongoing bicommunal groups, and special projects (Broome 2005b, 15). These activities prevailed until the referendum for the Annan Plan in 2004. However, after the plan was rejected, the number of bicommunal activities dropped significantly. Therefore, 2004 constituted a turning point for bicommunal meetings and projects. After the referendum, there was a shift in the approach toward peacebuilding and types of activities. Most CS actors seem disenfranchised, and it is not clear if a new orientation has been adopted. Thus, after 2004, civil society moved toward internal strengthening and coalition-building; intergroup social cohesion activities reduced in number overall.[7]

Challenges to bicommunal peace activities included the closure of the Green Line by the Turkish Cypriot leader Rauf Denktaş following the rejection of Turkey's membership application at the EU Luxembourg Summit in 1997. Individuals who had been participating in those early meetings, especially before the early 1990s, claim that to some extent bicommunal meetings engaged only the intelligentsia and other limited groups to overcome the obstacle of a common language. Only individuals with good command of English participated.

We gathered a comprehensive list of bicommunal initiatives organized by citizens, CSOs, and scholar-practitioners, ranging from the grassroots to the elite level. The list includes sixty-two initiatives that were organized in a bicommunal setting, mainly after 1990, but also includes some important activities prior to that. The initiatives were then coded along two dimensions: first, to see whether they were relationship-oriented or outcome-oriented, and second, whether they were undertaken at the grassroots or elite level. Relationship-oriented initiatives aim at bringing people together and focus on the process of communication, with the hope that relations among individuals will improve; outcome-oriented initiatives also aim at generating an outcome such as a proposal, negotiation framework, and so on (Çuhadar and Dayton 2008).

The analysis, as seen in Figure 9.3, shows that the grassroots initiatives (e.g., village meetings, youth festivals n=40) were predominantly relationship-oriented (87.5 percent), whereas the initiatives including elite and influential individuals (e.g., academics, policy people n=22) were mostly outcome-oriented (81.8 percent).

Figure 9.3 Types of Intergroup Social Cohesion Initiatives (in percentages)

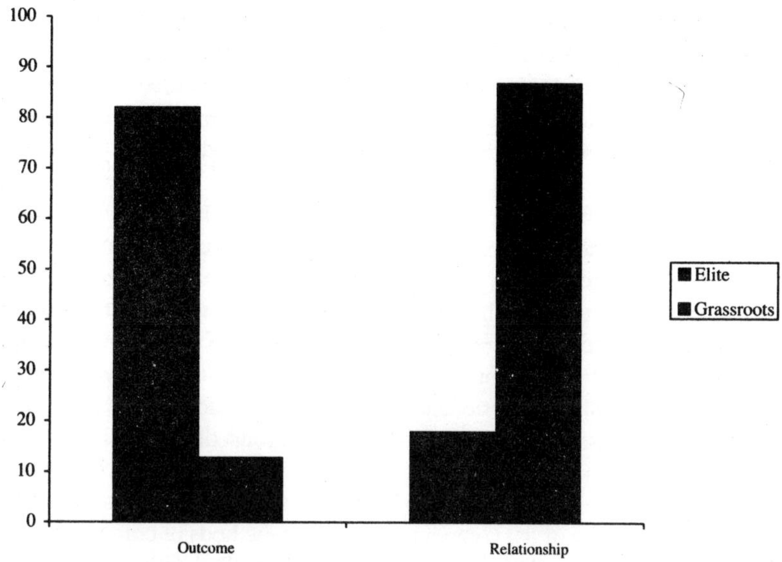

Source: Çuhadar and Kotelis files, 2008.

The relationship-oriented initiatives have been organized by various local and international CS actors: citizens, CSOs, and international scholars. Most of the time, these projects were held at a Green Line checkpoint, either at the Ledra Palace or the mixed village of Pyla. The initiatives ranged from bicommunal workshops and youth camps to joint celebrations and music festivals. For instance, several bicommunal youth festivals and workshops were organized by youth organizations such as Youth Encounters for Peace. Youth Promoting Peace organized workshops with Turkish Cypriots and Greek Cypriots in which participants could talk about the future of the conflict. Another prominent example is the project titled "The Civil Society Dialogue on Intercultural Cooperation in Cyprus," organized by the European Academy of Bolzano/Bozen and the German Cypriot Forum.

Sometimes these grassroots initiatives were organized by political parties. An example was the Festival of Mutual Understanding, organized in 2002 by political parties like AKEL, KISOS, PUM, CTP, and TKP; 7,000 Cypriots from both sides attended.

Similar activities were also organized and funded by international organizations such as AMIDEAST, UNDP, and USAID. UNFICYP organizes an annual bicommunal meeting on the Global Day of the United Nations (Broome 2005b, 21).

There have been many outcome-focused initiatives, distinguished by two categories: those that included influential people, and others that included citizens from the grassroots such as women. In the first group are several Track 2 groups that have met over the years. For instance, the Harvard Study Group that started in 1999 in Cambridge, Massachusetts, included former ministers, key international actors, and university professors. The group met six times to generate ideas that would contribute to the peaceful solution of the Cyprus problem. Other outcome-oriented elite-level groups are the Westminster Educational Group, which met in 1995; the FOSBO workshop in August 1997 (Broome 2005a); and the Cyprus chapter of the Greek Turkish Forum.

The Greek Turkish Forum (GTF) is a Track 2 initiative formulated in the late 1990s to discuss Greek-Turkish relations. However, after the political rapprochement between Turkey and Greece, the forum shifted to the Cyprus problem (Kotelis 2006). GTF is currently meeting two or three times per year and includes prominent Turkish Cypriot and Greek Cypriot academics and politicians.

The US Embassy in Cyprus also invited a group of Greek and Turkish Cypriots, including journalists, low-ranking politicians, and university professors, as a "decisionmakers' group." It tackled different perceptions of conflict resolution, the history of the Cyprus problem, and methods of communication.

The so-called Oslo Group put together by Marco Turk is well-known. Although the initial plan was for mediation training, participants became interested in tackling specific issues such as property rights, human rights, and missing persons.

It should be emphasized that most of the outcome-focused elite-level Track 2 meetings were organized by international CSOs and scholar-practitioners like PRIO, Fulbright, the Fondation Suisse de Bons Offices, and Benjamin Broome, Ronald Fisher, and Louise Diamond. Local CSOs and scholars were more involved in organizing at the grassroots level and relationship-focused social-cohesion activities.

The final category of intergroup social cohesion initiatives meets to achieve social cohesion with objectives other than peace per se. For example, representatives of sixteen trade unions gathered two times (once on each side of the buffer zone) to discuss internal issues and to hold debates on issues such as Cyprus's entry into the European Union (Broome 2005a, 271). Likewise, the Pancyprian Public Employees Trade Union (PASYDY) has organized a series of meetings since 1995, the All Cyprus Trade Union Forum, attended by representatives of PASYDY, SEK, PEO, TURK-SEN, DEV-IS, and KTAMS (PASYDY 2008). Greek Cypriot and Turkish Cypriot business leaders have also met as the Brussels Business Group, coorganized by Richard Holbrooke and PRIO.

We observe a reduction in the number of bicommunal activities after the opening of the Green Line in 2003 and after the referendum in 2004. Opening the Green Line made it possible for every Greek Cypriot and Turkish Cypriot to visit the other community. Thus, organizing grassroots-level meetings via third parties became less relevant, as communications between Greek Cypriots and Turkish Cypriots became easier, no longer monopolized by those who participated in bicommunal meetings. Dissatisfaction with the defeat of the referendum among Turkish Cypriot CS activists especially (but also among Greek Cypriots) also led to fewer bicommunal meetings.

Intermediation/Facilitation

In Cyprus, the intermediation/facilitation function is connected to the issue of mutual nonrecognition of state bodies. Thus, any attempt to mediate is characterized as conspiracy or treason. Furthermore, intermediation and facilitation between key decisionmakers have usually been carried out by official UN, US, and EU bodies. Even when direct negotiations were not under way, UN special envoy Alvaro de Soto merely listened to the parties like a "fly on the wall." Therefore, most intermediation between political actors is led by international organizations.

However, some intergroup social cohesion initiatives (especially the outcome-oriented ones) are related to this function. As participants tried to get proposals and ideas accepted by the decisionmakers, they consulted and communicated with Track 1 people. Furthermore, some participants assumed key policymaking positions inside government and in working groups. Participants in Track 2 initiatives also play an intermediation role. Scholar-practitioner Benjamin Broome communicated conciliatory messages between the two sides when intercommunal violence broke out in August 1996 (Wolleh 2001, 16). Broome facilitated communication between the participants of the bicommunal Conflict Resolution Trainer Group when all direct communication between the two communities halted due to the events (Wolleh 2001, 16–17).

Service Delivery

In Cyprus, a number of CS actors deliver services to people, especially when the state cannot meet social needs. These services include charities for disadvantaged groups, such as the work of St. Spyridonas Special School in the South, which promotes donations and charities for children with special needs. In addition, medical services and psychological counseling are offered by some CS actors, such as the I Live with Diabetes association in the North.

But service delivery is almost nonexistent otherwise. One notable example is the Cypress Tree Project: An Initiative for the Rehabilitation of Cemeteries, which allows Greek Cypriots and Turkish Cypriots to rehabilitate cemeteries that have become inaccessible due to the division (UNDP/UNOPS Bi-Communal Development Programme 2005). The initiative is funded by UNDP and USAID and also performs monitoring of cemeteries.

Assessment

CS actors in Cyprus have performed some civil society functions more than others. To sum up, advocacy and intergroup social cohesion functions are widespread, whereas protection, monitoring, in-group socialization, facilitation, and service delivery are generally ignored. Below we explain why some functions have been preferred over others and which variables determine the relevance of functions in the case of Cyprus. These variables are grouped as structural and actor related.

The first structural explanation includes the low level of violence and the long-standing stalemate. The separation of the communities since 1974, coupled with the presence of a UN peacekeeping force for more than forty years, created a peculiar situation. Even at its worst, Cyprus's was not a very violent conflict. Individual well-being is not in danger, thus the irrelevance of the protection function.

Human rights violations are a part of the history, and basic security needs of citizens are being met. Therefore, no monitoring of armed conflict is necessary at the moment. The conversion of the conflict from an armed one to a legal and political one in the last decades led to limited relevance for protection, monitoring, and service delivery.

The second structural variable—the strong and functioning state structures—explains why some functions are irrelevant in Cyprus. Monitoring of the past violations of human rights is provided by political authorities that each party considers legal. Hence, civil society has little to offer by providing monitoring tasks, apart from the status of property and cultural and religious sites. As part of their remit, political authorities address past human rights violations. The absence of violence and the presence of a functioning state also have an impact on the service delivery function. The state not only has the capacity to offer these services, but also there is reduced need compared to a conflict that is waged in a failed state.

Actor-related variables can be attributed to individual and institutional actors rather than to the structural characteristics of conflict. The most important is the attitude of one party toward the "other." The RoC claims to be the legal successor of the state that was founded by the 1960 treaties, while it considers the North part as illegally occupied by the Turkish Army. Furthermore, many Greek Cypriots believe that bicommunal activities would give the impression that the Cyprus conflict is "only" an interethnic conflict, while the official line has been that this is an international problem. This attitude has an impact on the functions of civil society, particularly on facilitation and intermediation. It is difficult for Cypriot CS actors (mostly for Greek Cypriots) to organize activities, for fear of being accused of treason (Wolleh 2001, 9). This is not uncommon in other conflicts.

The tradition of peace-building is another actor-related variable that has vastly influenced the civil society functions in Cyprus. It is common to hear from a civil society actor that it does things the way it does "because this is what the Americans brought to us," when asked why bicommunal meetings dominated the peace-building activities. Indeed, the history of bicommunal meetings shows that the number of meetings and civil society actors organizing them increased in the 1990s, most likely emulating the practices introduced by international scholar-practitioners. This period chronologically coincides with the presence of scholar-practitioners like Benjamin Broome and Louise Diamond on the island and with funding from AMIDEAST and USAID.

Apart from these variables, funding is a secondary factor that influences CS functions. (It is secondary because the main funders of civil society working in Cyprus [USAID, UNDP, and the EU] do not undertake their own initiatives but fund proposals that are submitted by third parties.) Not all initiatives are funded; bicommunal projects were more likely to get funding than in-group socialization projects. Between 1998 and 2005 over US$50 million was allocated by USAID and UNDP to intergroup social cohesion initiatives under the bicommunal development program.[8]

The case of Cyprus supports most of the propositions put forth by the Paffenholz and Spurk framework in Chapter 4. The relevance of the protection function is reduced in cases of nonviolent conflict. The relevance of monitoring, too, is reduced during the stalemate stage of the conflict and when the level of violence is low. The function is limited to specific issues only, such as property. Thus, the proposition that monitoring is not equally relevant during all stages of the conflict seems true.

Advocacy is not only relevant but also one of the most frequently performed functions in Cyprus. In times of agenda setting and political turning points, advocacy becomes more relevant and intense. It was effective during the referendum when all the bodies politic on the Turkish Cypriot side were in convergence toward the same goal. The AKP government in Turkey and the new Turkish Cypriot leadership by President Talat supported the passage. There was more overlap between the goals of the new Turkish Cypriot leadership and the goals of the peace activists.

On the contrary, during the referendum campaign, the actors of bodies politic were in disarray on the Greek Cypriot side. The propeace civil society could not effectively organize a campaign. Civil society activists we interviewed from the Greek Cypriot side argued that the time they had to prepare for a "yes" campaign was not enough. At the same time the opposition had already been working when the first Annan Plan was declared. Furthermore, the Greek Cypriot government under the presidency of hard-liner Tassos Papadopoulos used all instruments, including the media, to oppose the plan. On the Greek Cypriot side, people who had been key activists in peacebuilding were identified, legally pursued, or brought in front of a parliamentary ethics committee. They had to bear accusations such as improper use of UNDP funds in order to advocate in favor of the Annan Plan. Finally, unlike the previous

PASOK government that supported the Annan Plan, the Greek government of the time did not state a clear preference. Therefore, those in the civil society and government that were against the passage managed to garner a more effective coalition and had a bigger impact than the propeace camp. Nonetheless, advocacy has become especially important and relevant as a function during this crucial juncture more than at any other time in the conflict.

In-group socialization has been somehow neglected by civil society in Cyprus, often at the expense of intergroup social cohesion, even though it is extremely relevant and important. Without it a transition to a federal state and a common citizenry will be deemed to fail again. Recently, there were some important projects, such as one aimed at eliminating derogatory terms about the other group from history textbooks (Papadakis 1998). Yet, it still remains too early to comment on their overall effectiveness. It takes many years of work for the propeace camp to replace the negative attitudes people acquire through traditional means of political socialization.

Intergroup social cohesion is still relevant, however, after the disappointment following the referendum and the opening of the Green Line in 2003; motivation to continue these activities has diminished. The effectiveness of intergroup social cohesion meetings is difficult to assess, but there are points to be made for and against their success. Before these points for success and failure, we find it useful to talk about some criteria for the evaluation of such initiatives. Cuhadar (2004, 2009) identifies three directions of "transfer" to assess the impact of Track 2 initiatives at the macro level. These are upward, downward, and lateral. While upward transfer is concerned with impact on negotiations and policymaking, downward transfer is the impact on public opinion. Lateral transfer is the impact on other Track 2 and peacebuilding initiatives. In upward transfer, the impact can be on the process or on the outcome. In the former, the initiatives have input on the process of negotiations even though they do not impact the outcome of the negotiations. Input on the process can take various forms. One example is input of human capital, as in the case of the transfer of people with improved negotiation skills to negotiation teams. Another is input of ideas into the negotiation process even if they are not adopted.

In the Cyprus case, intergroup social cohesion workshops were successful in having input on the process in the upward direction. Ideas from Track 2 workshops were successfully transferred to the policymaking level, which was possible mainly due to the capacity of the participants. Influential individuals used their personal networks to transfer knowledge and ideas generated in these meetings. Participants who were active in the bicommunal activities became mayors and took roles in the government and in the current negotiation working groups preparing for the upcoming Track 1 negotiations.[9]

Bicommunal activities managed to achieve downward transfer as well. Participants from intergroup social cohesion activities took on active roles in the civil society campaigns, especially during the events leading to the 2004 referendum. The Turkish Cypriot participants played an important role in triggering a change in the Turkish Cypriot leadership. They organized demonstrations against the Denktaş regime and policies. Finally, these people served in leadership positions in civil society organizations. For instance, the executive director of the Management Centre of the Mediterranean was part of Benjamin Broome's group. The president of the Human Rights Foundation was a participant of the Oslo Group. All of these efforts resulted in creating a group of Cypriot activists who would later become community leaders in civil society both in the South and in the North.

However, in the upward direction, these activities have not managed to impact the outcome of negotiations. In the downward direction, they were not very successful in generating islandwide support for a peace plan. Without a common strategy jointly envisioned by civil society activists across the Green Line, the isolated activities of community leaders in their own societies were not very effective in changing the outcome. In addition, reduction in the number of initiatives seeking to enhance the intergroup social cohesion function was not followed by other peacebuilding functions.

The function of intermediation and facilitation is relevant especially because the conflict is managed by negotiations and third-party assistance. However, international governmental actors dominate this function rather than civil society.

Finally, service delivery in the context of Cyprus cannot be considered a function on its own as far as peacebuilding is concerned. This function has, however, offered an entry point to civil society related to monitoring in a non-peacebuilding dimension.

Conclusion

The Cypriot civil society has assumed a more active role in peacebuilding beginning in early 1990s. The most important actors who took part in peacebuilding activities have been citizens, CSOs, citizen networks, scholar-practitioners, and labor unions. Although different actors perceive peacebuilding in different ways, the bottom line is a peaceful solution through dialogue that eventually leads to a negotiated agreement with an arrangement for a bicommunal and bizonal federal state.

The advocacy and intergroup social cohesion functions are prominent and receive the bulk of funding. Among the more neglected functions, in-group socialization and intermediation/facilitation are most relevant. Therefore, in-group socialization should become a priority for future funding. This function lays the groundwork for values (e.g., pluralism, democratic citizenship) necessary to implement a negotiated peace agreement. Intergroup social cohesion initiatives are relevant at the elite level in negotiation processes. However, because of the opening of the Green Line in 2003 and increasing exchanges at the grassroots, certain types of intergroup social cohesion initiatives have been put aside. Advocacy has been and continues to be an important function after the defeat of the Annan Plan and the regime change in the North. Funders and CS actors need to pay more attention to developing a joint advocacy strategy for both communities.

Structural and agency-related variables influence functions performed by civil society: low violence, stalemate, the separated nature of the communities, strong state structures, the predominance of other actors, the tradition of peacebuilding, and funding preferences. All of these can lead to a more or less vibrant civil society on the island of Cyprus.

Another obstacle is declining interest in establishing new civil society organizations. There is some cause for optimism, however, especially after the last round of Greek Cypriot elections, along with the prospect of restarting negotiations.

Civil society in Cyprus has the potential to continue growing positively into the future, especially because civil society capacity-building has become more frequent and accepted by the conflict parties.

Notes

We would like to thank Benjamin Broome, Harry Anastasiou, and Thania Paffenholz for detailed comments on drafts of this chapter. We also would like to thank Jaco Cilliers, Sabine Kurtenbach, and other project participants for their very helpful comments during the Antalya workshop in November 2007.

1. The populations of the South and the North are based on the RoC Statistical Service estimate for 2007 and the TRNC general population census of 2004.

2. These 1960 treaties are the founding treaties and are also known as the Treaty of Alliance, the Treaty of Guarantee, and the Treaty of Establishment.

3. While most of the international community defines this military intervention as an "invasion," Turkish authorities use the phrase *peace operation.* Here, we simply use *intervention* as a neutral term.

4. Note that we defined *peacebuilding* broadly in our coding in a way that includes any activity that would contribute to peacebuilding, even though the organization did not define itself as a peacebuilding organization. Thus, activities listed, such as building of a democratic citizenship, promoting universal human rights, and cultural diversity, were some examples that were coded under "peacebuilding interest."

5. The analysis does not take into account the size or strength of these organizations, as data were not available.

6. The six time intervals chosen are the period before 1974, between 1975 and 1981, 1982 (declaration of the TRNC) to 1990 (the arrival of scholar-practitioners), 1991 to 1998 (closing of the Green Line in 1997), 1999 to 2004 (referendum), and the postreferendum era.

7. This was done to make comparisons between periods possible, as the number of years in each interval is different.

8. This is a conclusion that was derived after interviews with key civil society activists.

9. See http://mirror.undp.org/cyprus/projects/sectorsubsector.pdf, accessed September 10, 2008.

10

Israel and Palestine: Civil Societies in Despair

Esra Çuhadar and Sari Hanafi

In the history of armed warfare, the Israeli-Palestinian conflict is one of the longest-lasting, as well as one of the most analyzed and discussed. It is highly significant because it is seen at the heart of all conflicts in the Middle East.

The Israeli-Palestinian conflict is characterized by some as an intractable identity conflict between two social-identity groups, enduring for generations and resistant to resolution (Crocker et al. 2005). For others, it is a colonial conflict involving a minority that expelled the indigenous people with the help of the colonial powers and established a regime of occupation (Pappe 2006; Rouhana forthcoming; Hanafi 2005). In any case, efforts to resolve the conflict, whether by traditional means, such as negotiation and mediation, or by military means, have failed time and again over many decades.

In this chapter, we focus on the role of civil society (CS) in peacebuilding in the Israeli-Palestinian conflict since the 1993 signing of the Oslo Accords. Although much has been written on this topic, especially since Israeli statehood, most studies discuss specific actors; few examine the functions fulfilled by CS actors. To bridge this gap, we concentrate on how CS actors perform peacebuilding functions according to the framework outlined in Chapter 4. In our analysis we focus on the period from the 1993 signing of the Oslo Accords through the present, since the attention to peacebuilding came about after 1993. Before 1993, peacebuilding was mostly composed of individual contacts (Salem and Kaufman 2006). In addition, before 1993, Palestinian CS had boycotted Israeli institutions, and Israeli authorities had for a long time repressed civil society activism. After presenting an overview of the Israeli-Palestinian conflict, we discuss its context. We then focus on civil society's relevance to peacebuilding. Finally, we discuss and assess CS peacebuilding functions.[1]

Context

The conflict dates to the turn of the twentieth century, with the Jewish immigration to Palestine after 1898 and Zionist Jews' search for an independent state. In 1948, the British Mandate in Palestine, established in 1917, ended with a UN partition plan and the establishment of the state of Israel. Initially, this was an Arab-Israeli conflict, as the Arab states opposed the partition and fighting commenced in earnest over territory. The Arab states refused to accept the terms of the partition because, they argued, the United Nations, under the influence of the colonial powers in the region, gave the Jewish population 55 percent of the best land, yet Jews constituted only 31 percent of the total population at the time, and most were immigrants (UNSCOP 1946, 143). The building of the Israeli state resulted in the destruction of many Arab localities and the deportation of the Palestinian population. Some 750,000 Palestinian refugees would be thrown out, representing perhaps 70 percent of Palestine's Arab population at the time (Gidron et al. 2002, 56). For Palestinians, this event was known as Al Nakba, a disaster that forced many people to leave their homes and flee to neighboring countries. Few remained behind in Israel to become the Arab citizens of Israel; many remained internally displaced.

The Arab-Israeli wars continued off and on during the following decades: the 1956 Suez War, the 1967 Six-Day War (the June War), the 1973 October War (the Yom Kippur War), and the 1982 Israeli invasion of Lebanon. The 1967 Six-Day War drastically changed the nature of the conflict: it resulted in Israel's occupation of the West Bank, Gaza Strip, and other territories belonging to Egypt, Syria, and Jordan.[2] These became known as the Occupied Palestinian Territories (hereby Occupied Territories) and lay at the heart of the conflict even today.

Palestinian resistance to the occupation, as well as pressures from international community and developments within the Israeli society, changed the focus of the conflict. What had been a regional Arab-Israeli conflict became an interminable period of enmity and violence between Israelis and Palestinians. Egypt and Jordan signed peace treaties with Israel (in 1979 and 1994, respectively), the only other Middle East conflict was between Syria and Israel over the occupied Golan Heights. The Palestinian component of the Arab-Israeli wars took center stage after 1967 because of Israel's occupation of the West Bank and Gaza and its direct administration of Palestinians living there. After 1967, local Palestinian resistance against occupation culminated in the first intifada (uprising) in 1987. The Oslo peace process, which began in 1993, made Palestinians a direct party to peace talks with Israel.

The 1993 Oslo Accords were an important step toward recognizing a two-state solution. Following the recognition of Israel by the Palestine Liberation Organization (PLO), the Palestinian National Authority (PNA) was founded under Oslo II in 1995. Oslo adopted a gradualist approach and left final-status issues to later negotiation. However, neither party completely fulfilled its promises, even after signing the accords. The area of Israeli settlements increased threefold, and the number of settlers doubled, during the negotiations.[3] Suicide bombings by Palestinians took place inside Israel during the same period. And the entire process began to teeter after the assassination of Israeli prime minister Yitzhak Rabin in 1995 by a Jewish fanatic and the subsequent election of the hard-line Benjamin Netanyahu in 1996. The collapse of the Oslo process with the outbreak of the second intifada (the Al-Aqsa intifada) in 2001 was a turning point. Until then, none of the efforts to end the occupation and violence proved successful, and the conflict devolved into a series of unilateral actions by both parties that complicated any path to peace: Israel withdrew from Gaza in 2005; Hamas won democratic Palestinian elections and took over Gaza in 2007.

Considering the interests of the mainstream and moderate political actors, it can be said that for Palestinians peacebuilding means ending the Israeli occupation and building a Palestinian state in the West Bank and Gaza Strip with East Jerusalem as a capital. For mainstream and moderate Israelis, the goal is to sustain the Zionist state with Jerusalem as the capital recognized by its Arab neighbors and to maintain its security. The hard-line actors on both sides are not satisfied with such goals. Right-wing parties in Israel oppose the establishment of a Palestinian state and ending settlement activity. Religious right-wing Palestinian groups, such as Hamas, seek resistance while negotiating. Historically, Hamas claimed to "liberate" the whole of Palestine and rejected the recognition of an Israeli state. Recently, Hamas leaders have made statements about accepting a Palestinian state within the 1967 boundaries, provided that the right of return for refugees to Israel is ensured.

Besides the establishment of a Palestinian state, the character of its borders, and an assurance of security for Israel, other major issues include sovereignty over Jerusalem, water resources, the return of Palestinian refugees, Jewish settlements built after 1967 on Palestinian lands, and the economic regime between the two countries.

The Israeli-Palestinian conflict has been waged mostly as an armed conflict since the earliest violence in the 1920s. The latest round of fighting (the Al-Aqsa intifada) started in September 2000 after Ariel Sharon's visit to the Haram al-Sharif, among the holiest places in Islam (and known to Israelis as Temple Mount, which is holy for Judaism). Violence further grew with the excessive retaliation from Israeli security forces. The Al-Aqsa intifada turned out to be more violent than the first intifada. The psychological impact of the second intifada was massive on both parties (Halperin and Bar-Tal 2007; Shikaki 2004).

Following the failed negotiations, the second intifada led to hardened positions: a decline of public support for the peace process, and an increase in support for military and armed groups, coupled with fear and hopelessness. Several joint Israeli-Palestinian public opinion polls, conducted after 2000 on a regular basis by the Palestinian Center for Policy and Survey Research (2006–2008) and the Tami Steinmetz Center for Peace Research at Tel Aviv University (2003–2005), indicate that after the collapse of the final-status negotiations, more Israelis and Palestinians—including those in the center—lost faith in peace negotiations in the short term and began to support military solutions. This shift in opinion also led to the weakening and shattering of the part of the society—also known as the peace camp—mobilized to support a peace process throughout the years (Halperin and Bar-Tal 2007 for Israel; Shikaki 2004).

Since Israel's withdrawal from Gaza in 2005, unilateral moves have dominated the conflict. Attempts to move the parties from unilateralism to cooperation, such as within the Annapolis process initiated in 2007, have not been fruitful.

The political systems in Israel and the Occupied Territories show significant differences. There is a functioning parliamentary democracy in Israel, with formal democratic institutions and processes in place since its establishment. The Israeli state ensures free and fair elections, the distribution of power, and the existence of democratic political institutions, according to the Israel Democracy Institute (Arian et al. 2003; cf. Halperin and Bar-Tal 2006). However, problems persist regarding the internalization of basic democratic values and norms, such as lack of respect for the rule of law, institutional discrimination against minorities (especially Palestinian citizens of Israel and foreign laborers), breaches of freedom of the press, military involvement in government affairs, the existence of influential antidemocratic, ultrareligious groups, and human rights violations (Halperin and Bar-Tal 2006).

The Israeli political system has also been criticized by some scholars (e.g., Yiftachel 2006) for being an ethnocracy, referring to an ethno-class stratification and polarization. This stratification and polarization go beyond the Arab-Jew distinction. When the Israeli state was founded, it claimed to be a melting pot for any Jewish immigrant coming from any part of the world. However, in time the divide among Jews of different ethnic and religious backgrounds (i.e., Ashkenazim, Sephardim, Russian, secular versus Orthodox) grew and has become a major fault line within Israeli politics (Peled and Navot 2005; Kop and Litan 2002). Such divisions within Israeli politics and society have major implications for CS and its support of the peace process.

Palestinian society within the Occupied Territories is in the process of state- and democracy-building, a major political influence on the Israeli-Palestinian conflict and CS. An important characteristic is external involvement, as Palestinian political institutions rely heavily upon foreign aid. The involvement of the donor community has negative and positive consequences for the development of Palestinian CS and democratization.

Western governments have incorporated a concern for good governance and postconflict reconstruction into funding and aid programs, in which they emphasize development of multiparty elections, the rule of law, protection of civil and human rights, and various sorts of development and infrastructure projects (Brynen 2000). However, these programs pressured mostly PNA, the main aid recipient, and did not sufficiently address Israeli policies and Israel's military. Furthermore, donors conditioned aid on the development of an enabling environment for some civic groups, mainly secular peacebuilding NGOs, and excluded other types of CS actors. Another program for which donors have allocated funds is People-to-People projects. This program funds joint projects that bring together groups from Israeli-Palestinian civil societies to promote dialogue and cooperation.

The effect of the conflict on the economic situation is asymmetrical. While the Israeli economy managed to maintain its vitality during the Al-Aqsa intifada despite some initial difficulties, the Palestinian economy experienced severe structural shocks and readjustments.

At the moment, the Palestinian economy is in deep stress, characterized by a chronic trade deficit, 40 percent unemployment, and dismal economic growth, with almost half the population living below the poverty line (Merriman 2006). The most severely affected are those living in Gaza and those living in the West Bank close to the newly built Wall, which is often situated inside the Palestinian area and separates different Palestinian localities (UN 2003; Daoudy and Khalidi 2008).

Overall, three main factors emanating from the Israeli-Palestinian conflict detrimentally affect the Palestinian economy: (1) closures that increase transaction costs; (2) the Revenue Clearance System, according to which Israel is required to transfer money to the PNA but withholds payments frequently; and (3) the reduction in the Palestinian labor flow to Israel after the two intifadas.

Status of Civil Society

There is considerable asymmetry between the Palestinian and Israeli civil societies. Palestinian CS is "stateless" in that the state structure is not fully formed and has different institutions compared to Israel. The level of CS development in the Occupied Territories differs from one area to another. Jerusalem and Ramallah in the West Bank are the most developed areas; refugee camps and Gaza are the least developed (Hanafi and Tabar 2005, 50).

Palestinian Civil Society

The history of CS in Palestine is rich (Hanafi and Tabar 2005, 46–55). A long tradition of Islamic and secular charitable societies, as well as local and missionary Christian organizations, has been observed in Palestinian society. In contrast to the labor unions in the Occupied Territories, professional associations (especially engineers) have been active politically and socially. With the donor policy favoring the new form of professionalized NGOs, some organizations changed to meet donor requirements while others collapsed.

Despite a succession of encounters with foreign rule, Palestinian social institutions and political factions have arisen to advance Palestinian national and social agendas. Local development was constrained in the absence of structures for local populations to determine social and developmental options outside Israeli military authority. Events in the 1970s, in particular the Camp David Accord between Egypt and Israel and the recognition of the PLO as the only representative of Palestinians, led to an awareness of the need for greater Palestinian self-reliance as well as a new strategy of resistance (Barghouthi 1999, 76). Within this context, a new generation of activists emerged. These newcomers created an infrastructure of mass organizations through the national movement, thereby expanding the existing roster of social organizations, including voluntary charitable societies, the oldest type of NGO in Palestine. Popular organizations were also formed, including women's committees, labor unions, student organizations, and volunteer initiatives. This was followed by the creation of developmental NGOs and Islamic organizations providing services in areas like health and agriculture (Barghouthi 1994).

Thus, NGOs established the basis for a system for providing services in the Occupied Territories. They also took a role within the broader national movement, forming an institutional network that enabled resistance against Israeli rule and sustained the first intifada for the first two years (Usher 1995, 18). Palestinian NGOs (PNGOs) were linked to the Palestinian political factions; the parties Popular Front of Liberation of Palestine (PFLP), Democratic Front of Liberation of Palestine (DFLP), Palestinian Communist Party (PCP), and Fatah each set up their own women's, students', labor, medical, and agricultural committees (Hilterman 1990, 47); in this regard the PLO, as an umbrella organization, played a major role (Giacaman 1998). Organizational forms reflected the broader effort to organize the grassroots: organizational structures were informal, and emphasis was put on volunteer work. Also, many organizations reflected a popular character, and attempts to incorporate the masses into these new structures were evident in the way that committees and organizations became grounded in diverse social groups and regions (Taraki 1997). To this end, organizational practices were shaped by a combination of nationalist and developmental goals. This meant that organizations extended services to marginalized social groups to empower them and to mobilize them politically (Giacaman 1998, 14). Independent NGOs also proliferated: professionalized centers, such as research institutes and media groups, were set up—a trend that accelerated after the decline of the national movement in the 1990s.

In 2002, after the first two years of the first intifada, the popular-based NGOs underwent rapid changes. Rima Hammami describes the transformation of PNGOs over time in three phases. First, the initial drive to mobilize the grassroots in the 1970s was organized across factions. Second, this was quickly succeeded by the rise of factionalized committees in the mid-1980s that operated their own popular and development organizations. And third, party-affiliated NGOs became institutionalized over time and by 1991 were run by professionalized staff, with activists identifying themselves as professional development practitioners seeking to empower the population through development rather than through mobilization (Hammami 1995, 54–55). The shifts in donor characteristics contributed to these turning points, as suggested by Hammami. According to Benois Challand (2008b, 408), until the late 1980s and early 1990s most of the funding for CS came from regional Arab contributors. After the 1990s, contributions from regional Arab donors dried up and were replaced by Western governments.

Therefore, many Palestinian activists, intellectuals, and community leaders were embedded in the popular struggle and bound up in a mass-based national movement in late the 1980s and early 1990s, also with the help of many international organizations (IOs) (Hanafi and Tabar 2005, 14). This flourishing of CS intensified during the Oslo peace process. However, it did not necessarily mean that space created for CS has become more autonomous. The relationship between the PNGOs and the IOs and donors has gone through a transition from solidarity forms of support to politically driven aid to bolster the peace process with Israel (Hanafi and Tabar 2005, 39; Challand 2008b).

In short, after 2000 several factors have threatened the existence of a vibrant and autonomous Palestinian CS. The first threatening factors were related to the limitations imposed by the ongoing Israeli occupation. The second threat was imposed by the PNA and various armed Palestinian groups. The third was the result of policies followed by international donors.

Within the first category, threats to CS include the Israeli financial embargo and Israeli control over daily life. Such restrictions prevent free participation and mobility in CS. In the second category, one example of a PNA activity undermining the autonomy of the CS is the conflict between the PNGOs and the PNA over drafting the NGO law. In the third category was the dependence of PNGOs on Western donors and the choices made by donors about whom to fund and how much to limit the autonomy of CS (Challand 2008b). The capacity of local NGOs to make their own decisions about priorities in communities became severely hampered (Challand 2008b, 411), and this outcome altered the nature of NGOs' relationship to the grassroots.

A similar threat to CS from increasing professionalization was also observed in Israel during this time. Increased professionalization of CS organizations led to a decrease in grassroots support, mainly because volunteerism decreased (Hermann 2002, 114). Also as a result of professionalization, collaboration between the peace groups decreased, and a division between more and less professionalized CSOs emerged (Hermann 2002, 115).

In sum, the Oslo peace process, which allowed for the creation of the PNA and the commencement of statebuilding with the assistance of donor countries, carved a space for the growth of NGOs and civic institutions in the Occupied Territories and in Israel. However, the creation of this space was also accompanied by a detachment of local organizations from society and their grassroots base.

Israeli Civil Society

In Israel, historically there have been two camps in civil society: the active peace camp, mostly including politically left, Ashkenazi, middle-class, educated, and secular Jews; and the "national" camp, mostly composed of the religious and nationalist right.[4] Although there are some examples of peacebuilding by religious actors (e.g., Oz Ve'Shalom, Rabbis for Human Rights) or by those traditionally opposed to dialogue (e.g., the few dialogue attempts between settlers and Palestinian refugees), the peace camp has historically supported the establishment of a Palestinian state in return for security and recognition of Israel. The peace camp has also been active in CS since 1967, organizing activities within Israel, such as antigovernment rallies, and in cooperation with Palestinians across the divide.

The Israeli peace camp began to be more active after 1978 with the emergence of the Peace Now movement in response to the obstructionist policies of the Likud-led government during the Israel-Egypt peace talks (Hermann 2002, 101). Tamar Hermann suggests that the peace camp has become mostly elitist and outside the political mainstream; thus it had limited influence despite the fact that it was successful in creating a cognitive change and an eventual attitude change in society (Hermann 2002, 118–119).

In contrast, an antipeace CS also existed in Israel, and its influence in politics and society has grown over time (Sprinzak 1991). These were right-wing religious groups such as Gush Emunim, the Haredi camp, as well as the extreme Zionist nationalists seeking a Greater Israel. This second group claims that all the land belongs to the Jews, and some even argued for the ethnic cleansing of Palestinians. The Kach movement is one of the most notorious examples (Sprinzak 1991).

On the Palestinian side, defining the boundaries of the peace constituency of civil society is more difficult. Because of the occupation and lack of a proper state structure, the peace constituency in Palestinian civil society was primarily involved with service delivery and human rights activism. NGOs, human rights activists, trade unions, and voluntary associations became the main actors. CS was also mostly limited to the middle and upper classes in urban areas (Hassassian 2006, 61). Historically, few individuals or notable families shared a common social space, including both Jews and Palestinians (especially in Jerusalem), or were willing to reach out to the other side (Dockser Marcus 2007). However, the sharing of common social space decreased with the ascendance of nationalist movements and armed conflict. Furthermore, Palestinian civil society found it more appropriate to resist occupation through armed resistance and boycotts rather than through participation in CSOs (Hassassian 2006, 64). As mentioned above, it was only after the flow of Western funding after 1993 to peacebuilding NGOs that a Palestinian professional class emerged, working mostly with peacebuilding NGOs. However, for the most part these were elites who remained disconnected from the mass political movements engaged in national struggle.

In the Israeli-Palestinian conflict, CS actors working toward peacebuilding can be grouped as follows: local NGOs (mostly secular but also a few religious ones), social networks and constituencies, campaigns and rallies, voluntary associations, international NGOs (INGOs), and initiatives by private citizens. NGOs became the most common type of CS actor in peacebuilding for several reasons: (1) other CS actors, like Islamic charities in the Occupied Territories, are mostly involved with service delivery, and some are affiliated with Hamas (Levitt 2006; Tamimi 2007); (2) the Israeli law that encourages civil society to organize as formal organizations (Hermann 2002, 111); and (3) the preferences of Western donors toward NGOs.

Before discussing the functions of peacebuilding and the CS actors involved, we need to look more closely at the peacebuilding-related NGOs in Israel and the Occupied Territories. The data used for this overview (from the *Directory of Israeli and Palestinian NGOs*) were coded according to the peacebuilding functions following the framework in Chapter 4.

By looking at the establishment years of the NGOs in the *Directory*, we can determine that 62 percent of Israeli peace NGOs were founded before the signing of the 1993 Oslo Accords. The Israeli organizations founded during the peace process years is 33 percent. By contrast, there is a sharp decrease in the peace NGOs founded after the outbreak of the second intifada (only 5 percent).

When we look at the establishment years of the Palestinian peace NGOs, there are important differences. PNGOs working in peacebuilding are much younger. Unlike Israeli NGOs, the majority of Palestinian peace NGOs were founded after the signing of the Oslo Accords in 1993. This is understandable, because until 1993 there were few Palestinian institutions in the Occupied Territories. Also, the sharp increase in peace NGOs after 1993 coincides with the increase of Western funding to Palestinian CS and the decrease in Arab funding. In addition, the number of PNGOs founded after the collapse of the Oslo peace process is higher than that of Israeli NGOs.

As for the focus on gender, 20.6 percent of Israeli NGOs and 29.7 percent of Palestinian NGOs involved in peacebuilding also work on women's issues. Gender played an important role in shaping the peace camp, especially in Israel. During the 1980s, women led the Israeli peace movement by establishing movements such as Mothers Against Silence, Bat Shalom, Four Mothers, and Women and Mothers for Peace (Hermann 2002, 117).

Before we turn to an in-depth discussion of each function performed by CS, it is useful to look at the overall functions performed by NGOs. Figures 10.1 and 10.2 show the distribution of Israeli and Palestinian NGOs according to the functions identified in Chapter 4.[5]

Figure 10.1 Israeli Peace NGOs' Focus of Activities (n = 63)

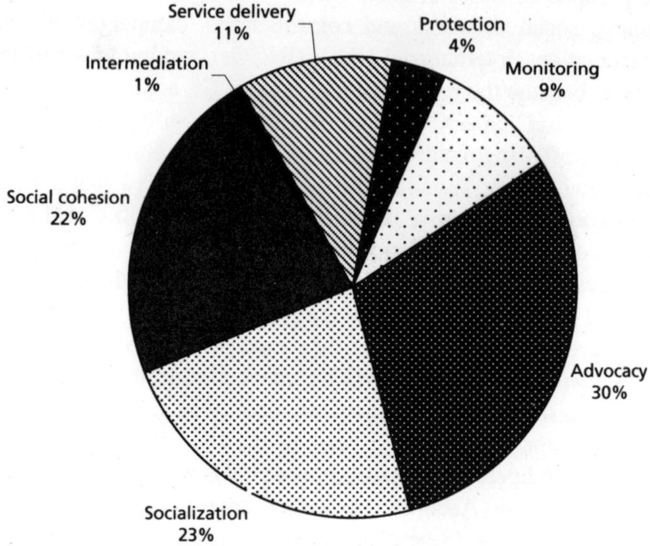

Figure 10.2 Palestinian Peace NGOs' Focus of Activities (n = 37)

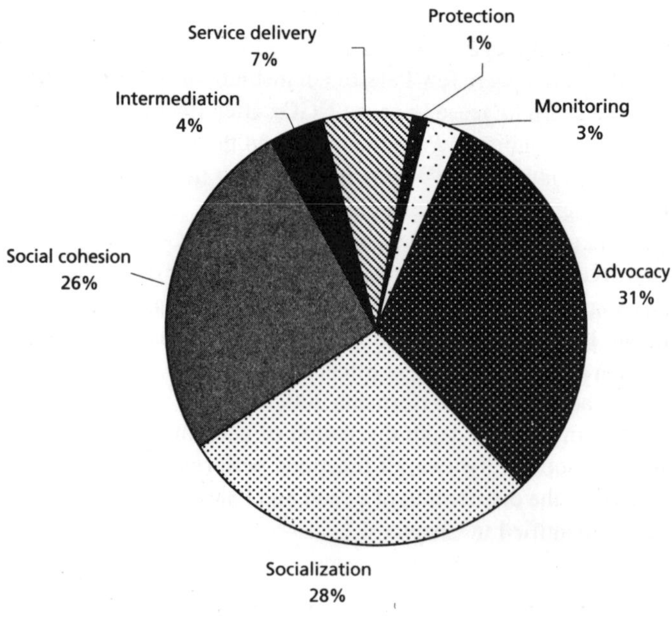

A survey of activities carried out by sixty-three NGOs in Israel indicates that they are mostly involved with the functions of advocacy, in-group socialization, and intergroup social cohesion. Furthermore, many organizations carry out activities of socialization and social cohesion at the same time. The other four functions are not very frequent. Protection and intermediation are especially rare. Interestingly, 11 percent of Israeli NGOs are engaged in service delivery. The nature of these functions is detailed in the next section.

The survey of thirty-seven Palestinian NGOs (PNGOs) reveals similar results in the functions performed most frequently. Again, advocacy, intergroup social cohesion, and in-group socialization are the most common functions performed by the PNGOs. The remaining four functions are less common. Israeli organizations are slightly more involved in protection, monitoring, and service delivery than PNGOs.

Peacebuilding Functions

The following section compares the seven different functions: protection, monitoring, advocacy, socialization, social cohesion, intermediation and facilitation, and service delivery.

Protection

In the Israeli-Palestinian context, Israeli, Palestinian, and international CS actors carry out protection of civilians, not only from the insecurity created by occupation but also from the armed groups engaged in intra-Palestinian fighting. Protection is performed by NGOs, INGOs, and some local militias. Any protection provided by local militias is often directed at kinship relations, but it has gained more importance in the climate of Gaza.

In addition to this classical sense of security, we can identify other important aspects of security and protection. One is the need for security against criminal activity in the Occupied Territories, especially in areas where there is Palestinian civil control but no police force. This function is performed by local notables (*mukhtars*), neighborhood-level local administrators, rather than CS per se.

The other aspect is economic and environmental security for Palestinians. Such functions often are not addressed by CS, although a few organizations, such as Bustan L'Shalom and Friends of the Earth Middle East, fight the degradation of resources and other damage resulting from the ongoing armed conflict.

Even though armed conflict marks the Israeli-Palestinian conflict (since 2000), the protection function is performed by a few CS actors, mostly through intervention in specific crises and support for disadvantaged groups, such as women and children. Several Israeli human rights organizations (HROs), such as Kol Halsha, protect battered women—both Palestinian and Jewish—and some, such as the Defense for Children International (DCI, which includes the Israel and Palestine sections), focus only on protecting children. These organizations monitor the conditions affecting children and intervene in prison situations on behalf of juveniles. DCI-Palestine additionally provides support to prisoners and for watchdog activities.

Another example includes solidarity activities undertaken by private citizens and organizations. The Ta'Ayush—Arab-Jewish Partnership—is an Israeli movement of Palestinians and Jews fighting for full civil equality in Israel and against the occupation (Ta'Ayush 2008). This movement has new forms of activism for protecting populations under occupation. It has been active since the beginning of the second intifada and is known for directly protecting Palestinian peasants harvesting crops and demonstrating against the Wall.

A second example of solidarity is civil missions. There is a growing number of individuals arriving in the Occupied Territories from European and North American countries to demonstrate solidarity and to call for the protection of Palestinian people. By April 2005, about 4,000 individuals had arrived. Some have been denied entry into Israel, and some were detained (Hanafi forthcoming).

Another important example is in the health sector. There have been initiatives to protect Palestinian ambulances and paramedics to help them to perform medical duties. We also see some activities for the protection of Palestinian civilians at checkpoints. The International Committee of the Red Cross (ICRC), the Danish NGO Dan Church Aid, and the Israeli Physicians for Human Rights conducted several protection missions to smooth the passage of Palestinian Red Crescent ambulances through checkpoints. Doctors Without Borders, Amnesty International, Human Rights Watch (HRW), and the ICRC are IOs that carried out a series of protection missions in the Occupied Territories.

In sum, the protection function is highly relevant, as there is daily violence on the ground; civilian security is a daily need. The role of CS in this context is vital because on the Palestinian side there is no efficiently functioning state mechanism to provide security to its own civilians. It is also vital because there is no international peacekeeping force situated on the ground to perform this function.

Protection is closely linked with risk assessment and early warning. Given the limited resources of CS actors, such supplementary functions are crucial to increasing the overall effectiveness of protection. Even though CS alone cannot undertake protection, it can bear witness and mobilize international public opinion for organizing protection campaigns.

The effectiveness of protection varies from one incident to another. Although there are successes in protecting individuals and villages, it is hard to say whether CS actors make an important impact at the macro level by changing the protection policies of the occupying Israeli forces or of the armed Palestinian groups.

Monitoring

Monitoring is directed at all sorts of issues: civil and human rights, implementation of peace agreements, building of facts on the ground (e.g., water usage, settlement activity), and violation of international legal documents, including the relevant UN Security Council resolutions. The monitoring function is performed by a number of Israeli, Palestinian, and international CS actors. Most combine monitoring with advocacy (as in the case of B'Tselem and al-Haq), with protection, and with service delivery (mostly in the form of pro bono legal representation).

CS actors that undertake monitoring are mostly human and civil rights activists and organizations. They usually have a mission to make the state adhere to the law, for example by accompanying monitoring with public advocacy and free service delivery to victims in the form of legal counsel. And even though CS monitors many issues that are linked to the peace process (settlements, prisoners, etc.), monitoring the implementation of a peace agreement is largely missing. An exception is Bringing Peace Together, a joint Israeli-Palestinian local CS committee consisting of intellectuals and activists formed to monitor the Annapolis Peace Initiative.

While some of the monitoring organizations, such as Arab Association for Human Rights or B'tselem, have a broader scope and monitor various issues, others focus on very specific issues within the conflict, such as the status of children (DCI–Palestine section), budget distribution (Adva), demolitions of Palestinian houses inside Israel (the Association of Forty), security checkpoints (Machsom Watch), and water use (Applied Research Institute of Jerusalem—ARIJ). Some add a monitoring function to their advocacy initiatives. Some organizations (e.g., ARIJ and Palestinian International Peace and Cooperation Center, or IPCC) engage in research and collect data, especially facts on the ground. Data collection and dissemination are especially relevant during peace negotiations.

Although most CS actors involved in monitoring are either Israeli or Palestinian, a third category includes Israeli CSOs founded by Palestinian citizens. Some try to achieve civic equality between Jewish and Palestinian citizens in the state and to correct discriminatory policies against Palestinian citizens of Israel.

Overall, monitoring is highly relevant in the Israeli-Palestinian conflict, although it is not often a stand-alone activity. Monitoring campaigns succeed because they effectively use monitoring reports for advocacy in the international community. Campaigns, such as the one against the torture of Palestinian prisoners in Israel, fail due to their lack of international leverage.

Advocacy

Advocacy is one of the most frequently performed functions and refers to advocacy to improve civil and human rights, and legal representation, as well as advocacy to influence agendas present in the peace process and other negotiations.

CS actors engage in both public and nonpublic forms of advocacy. Most perform other functions as well, like monitoring, protection, in-group socialization, service delivery, and intergroup social cohesion. Very few focus solely on advocacy. Among these are social movements that bring people around a cause, such as "refusenik" organizations like Courage to Refuse, Shministism, Youth Refusal Movement, and Kvisa Shchora (an antioccupation gay and lesbian movement). Another group that performs advocacy primarily includes think tanks and research centers that combine research and advocacy, such as the Israeli Council for Israeli-Palestinian Peace.

As for the nature of CS actors doing advocacy work, we see that human rights organizations create awareness in the international and domestic political arenas. These include local organizations (B'Tselem, Ir Shalem, Palestinian Human Rights Monitoring Group) and IOs (HRW).

Human and civil rights advocacy is also performed by individual lawyers and law firms. This is categorized separately because legal representation and related activities have become important in the Israeli-Palestinian context, bridging advocacy, service delivery, and protection. Lawyering became a privileged and widespread means of collective action since the beginning of the 1990s in the wake of the "judicialization of politics" (Tate and Vallinder 1995). The transfer of political questions to the courtroom has transformed legal skill into a form of political capital and legal professionals into experts of cause-building. From the defense of disadvantaged and minority groups to sectarian sociopolitical interests, so-called cause lawyers are now believed to play a role in the democratic game; their actions are no longer viewed as a transgressive activity.

Peace and conflict resolution organizations also perform advocacy, usually in combination with in-group socialization and intergroup social cohesion. Some (such as the Israel/Palestine Center for Research and Information, or IPCRI) also perform research in conjunction. They include local actors (the Coalition of Women for a Just Peace, IPCRI, Economic Cooperation Foundation, or ECF) and international actors (Search for Common Ground).

Social movement networks are the third group of CS actors that perform advocacy. Most are local, but there are several international networks as well. One example, an important social movement network engaged in both advocacy and intergroup social cohesion, is the People's Voice initiative led by Sari Nusseibeh and former Shin Bet chief Ami Ayalon. It aims at gathering public support for a two-state solution on both sides of the conflict (People's Voice 2002).

Advocacy work can be distinguished according to the *strategies* and *tactics* that are pursued. While some of the strategies used by CS favor "insiders," meaning they try to influence decisionmakers and elites, other strategies favor the "outsiders," focusing on motivating the masses (Fitzduff and Church 2004, 2–6).

Looking at strategies employed by the Israeli peace camp, we see that in the 1970s and 1980s most peace activities focused on mass protests to raise consciousness and to mobilize the grassroots (Hermann 2002, 112). However, in the 1980s the popularity of mass protests in Israel declined, and there was a shift toward "insider strategies"; peace activities shifted from grassroots mobilization and public communication to nonpublic advocacy (Hermann 2002). The professionalization and domination of NGOs in general also contributed to this trend, which resulted in the disconnection of peacebuilding activities from the grassroots.

In addition to insider and outsider strategies, international advocacy is a distinct strategy. For example, Palestinian CS has long attempted to lobby the PNA against torture, but the PNA began to take measures only after it was criticized by Amnesty International and HRW in 2000. As a result, local CS actors prefer helping international HROs to monitor human rights violations at the local level but publicize their findings mainly in Europe and North America in order to make a policy impact on their own governments.

Agenda-setting was an important aspect of CS advocacy during the peace negotiations. CS actors advocated and lobbied for greater CS involvement in the peace negotiations, as well as for the inclusion of certain proposals developed jointly in problem-solving meetings and/or for the inclusion of certain people in peace negotiations. Several problem-solving groups working on final-status issues (e.g., Jerusalem, refugees) constitute examples of this type of advocacy. For example, the Panorama Center in Ramallah and an Israeli consultancy group conducted a survey of Palestinian refugee real estate holdings. The result of such cooperation can be crucial to the compensation of refugees once negotiations begin. A three-day workshop (titled "Right of Return and Resolving Palestinian Refugees Issue") was organized in 2003, gathering many prominent Israeli and Palestinian scholars as well as international experts. The meeting generated new knowledge and ideas that could be essential to negotiations once they are revised (see Benvenisti, Hanafi, and Gans 2006).

In the case of Jerusalem, the Arab Studies Society, the Palestinian Academic Society for the Study of International Affairs (PASSIA), the Israel/Palestine Center for Research and Information (IPCRI), the Jerusalem Institute for Israel Studies, and the Economic Cooperation Foundation (ECF) have attempted to influence final-status negotiations (Abdul Hadi 2005; Hassasian 2002; Çuhadar 2009).

When advocating behind closed doors (nonpublicly), CS actors used various tactics. Contacting negotiators, decisionmakers, and official third parties led to the inclusion of certain people and ideas in the peace negotiations (Çuhadar 2009). For example, some Palestinian participants in these problem-solving groups were part of Palestinian political circles, and others participated in problem-solving meetings and final-status negotiations, including some scholars from the Palestinian Center for Refugees and Diaspora (Shaml) and the Panorama Center. These two organizations provided valuable information to the Negotiation Unit of the PLO.

A study conducted by Esra Çuhadar and Bruce Dayton (2008) on problem-solving workshops between 1989 and 2004 found that after the Camp David failure and the outbreak of intifada, more of the problem-solving groups directed advocacy openly at public opinion, instead of nonpublic advocacy directed at elites and decisionmakers. The Geneva Initiative is a good example of this shift in strategy. While the same group used an elite-oriented advocacy strategy before Camp David, it shifted to public opinion–oriented advocacy after the Camp David negotiations failed. The Geneva Initiative's proposal was disseminated through public mailings, and campaigns were initiated to garner public support for the proposal (Beilin 2004). Furthermore, public opinion polls were conducted to measure support for the initiative, and the results were used for additional advocacy work on the initiative (Palestinian Center for Policy and Survey Research 2003). In sum, advocacy for the masses, rather than for elites (People's Voice, the Geneva Initiative), became more popular after the failure at Camp David, although any success or effectiveness is debatable.

In general, advocacy efforts contributed insights to the process of negotiation, but they hardly impacted the outcome of the negotiations themselves (Çuhadar 2009). In addition to the effective formulation of an advocacy strategy, the organizational capabilities of the advocacy actor, the openness of the decisionmaking and negotiation system to outside information, and the type and flow of information to and the receptiveness of the decisionmaking unit (whether symmetrical or not) are among the variables that determine the effectiveness of nonpublic advocacy (Çuhadar 2009).

There has been an important barrier to effective public advocacy since the 1990s: NGOs have become disconnected from their grassroots bases. This mostly affected the advocacy function, especially in the Palestinian context. At the beginning of the intifada, NGOs were generally absent from the popular demonstrations in the Occupied Territories. Instead of propeace CS, radical elements of CS—such as some Islamic organizations and paramilitary groups—took over this role in popular demonstrations.

Besides the NGOs' disconnect from the grassroots, timing also limited the effectiveness of advocacy. Especially before the Camp David negotiations, certain issues were taboo and many feared being cast as traitors; CS actors thus refrained from openly advocating for certain ideas and solutions. One example was the Israeli position on Jerusalem. It was well-known by elites that excluding Jerusalem from the negotiation agenda was a political nonstarter, and opinionmakers and CS actors started talking about Jerusalem very late in the process. Therefore, by the time negotiations began it was too late to generate public support to rally around a mutually acceptable solution. The mirror image of this debate in Palestinian society concerns the different modalities of resolving the Palestinian refugee issue.

In-Group Socialization

Socialization is one of the three most frequently performed functions. In this context it means socialization for democratic attitudes and values, for handling conflicts peacefully, and for consolidating an in-group identity supportive of peace.

The following data about the Israeli society indicate how socialization for democracy and peace values is necessary in the Israeli-Palestinian context. Reconciling the Jewish nature of the state with democratic values has always created tension in Israeli politics (Cohen and Rynhold 2005; Kop and Litan 2002). Consider the following two pieces of evidence.

According to a survey by the Israeli Institute for Democracy, 53 percent of Jews in Israel oppose equal rights for Jewish and Arab citizens, and only 4 percent support CSOs that cut across the ethnic divisions and challenge the discriminatory system (Dichter and Abu Asba 2006, 175).

Several studies regarding democratic education in Israel (e.g., Halperin and Bar-Tal 2006) also reveal the shortcomings in the Israeli education system for socializing youths in the values of a liberal democratic state. They argue that education for a Jewish and Zionist identity has historically been prioritized over education in liberal democratic values and that democratic education in Israel is largely dependent on the ideological views of the government.

In sum, considering the need for socialization in democratic values, the importance of CS should be highlighted. CS has to play a complementary role to government, regardless of the latter's ideological position, in order to provide sustainability to socialization in democratic values. Activities may include fighting institutional discrimination against Palestinian citizens of Israel, leveraging against influential antidemocratic groups, educating youths and children in human rights and democracy, and revealing violations of human rights.

In Israel, there is a major gap between the socialization of secular and that of religious citizens. Compared to secular Jews, religious Jews are socialized in a way that makes them more hawkish toward the establishment of a Palestinian state and the recognition of Palestinian rights (Rynhold 2005). Jonathan Rynhold explains this by pointing to the ethnocentric character of religious socialization. Religious and secular citizens are socialized in their own institutions and live in distinct neighborhoods. Furthermore, they do not mingle within the ranks and officer corps of the army, which is a powerful socialization agent that all Israelis must pass through.

Another historically powerful socialization agent in Israel has been the kibbutzim, especially during the early days of the Israeli state; in 1948, 7–8 percent of the population lived among 177 kibbutzim (Livni 2004). This communal movement was especially important to elites. The movement declined in popularity after the 1970s, and perhaps 2 percent of the population lives in a kibbutz today (Livni 2004). Most kibbutzim have been secular, and some engage in and encourage joint activities with Arab Bedouins in Israel (especially in agriculture; see Livni, Naveh, and Cicelsky 2006). However, the effect of liberal economic policies in Israel is not the only reason that kibbutzim have dwindled in number; secular values now compete with those in the Orthodox kibbutz movement, which are often directed against the establishment of a Palestinian state (Livni 2004).

Other important actors in socialization are Israeli-Palestinian academics and NGOs (the Adam Institute for Democracy and Peace, the Israel Democracy Institute, the Bethlehem Peace Center, Panorama) that teach people democratic and civic attitudes. The target populations of such initiatives vary from children to adults, depending on the activity. Some carry out systematic democracy education in coordination with the school systems, curricula, and the Ministry of Education; others engage in single events and are not necessarily coordinated with the authorities. In addition to NGOs, youth clubs teach democracy and citizenship to their constituencies. These grassroots clubs touch base with larger segments of society.

The second type of in-group socialization is training in conflict resolution skills. The goal often is to teach people to resolve conflicts peacefully and thereby contribute to a nonviolent and peaceful society. NGOs and individual scholar-practitioners carry out such training, in which they use teaching methods ranging from the use of media, soap operas, and psychodrama (Middle East Non-Violence and Democracy) to traditional peacemaking methods like *sulha* and the politics of persuasion (Wiam-Palestinian Conflict Resolution Center).

Concerning *sulha,* the major actors are leaders of tribal units and extended families. By browsing the Palestinian newspapers, one can realize announcements of *sulhas* almost daily, concerning any dispute between members of the same community. *Sulha* is used more to resolve disputes among feuding Palestinian families and communities.[6]

Finally, a number of CS actors work toward the consolidation of an in-group identity while teaching democratic attitudes. Several Israeli CSOs (Givat Haviva) and some scholar-practitioners teach citizens about the Holocaust and Jewish history and raise awareness of and resistance against racism. Dan Bar-On's (1989) work with Holocaust survivors and perpetrators, using the storytelling approach, is an excellent example.

However, not all CS actors consolidate in-group identity through democratic and peaceful means. There are examples of radicalization within civil society, such as some religious Jewish organizations that consolidate the in-group identity at the expense of the "other group" instead of using it as a means to resist racism and discrimination.

Overall, CS's role in socialization has implications beyond the Palestinian-Israeli relationship, influenced by several factors. One is the tension between religion and democracy in Israel. Defining the Israeli state mainly as Jewish has been an obstacle to creating a truly pluralist Israeli democracy. Demands from Orthodox religious groups have become a major hindrance to creating liberal democratic and pluralist values. A similar argument can be made for Palestinian society, which is currently experiencing a tension between religious and democratic values, especially in Gaza. However, this debate is just beginning to emerge within Palestinian society after the takeover of Hamas; its effects are yet to be seen.

A second factor that influences this function is the ongoing armed conflict. Regardless of conflict-resolution training that focuses on replacing enemy images, the ongoing armed conflict and occupation make it difficult to sustain these efforts (Rosen 2006). Children on both sides are reported to be psychologically affected by violence, to the extent that some 33 percent of Israeli youths and 70 percent of Palestinian youths experience symptoms of posttraumatic stress disorder, including anxiety, depression, and sadistic and aggressive tendencies (Jewish News 2004). These constitute a severe threat to any normal political socialization that emphasizes democratic values, respect for the other, and coexistence.

Intergroup Social Cohesion

Social cohesion refers to bridging ties between Israelis and Palestinians (both within Israel and in the Occupied Territories), between different ethnic groups and secular and religious Jews in Israel, and between Fatah and Hamas.

For Israeli CS and Palestinian CS, the peace process and the Oslo Accords ushered in new funding. Programs of cooperation increased significantly due to the interest of the donor community (especially the United States, Norway, and the European Union) to revive contacts between Palestinians and Israelis. Of the channeled funding, human rights and democracy absorbed an increasing proportion. In 1998, this sector represented 9.5 percent of all funding (US$5 million), whereas during the preceding four years (1994–1997) this area averaged only 4.4 percent of total funding (about US$11 million). A significant percentage of funding was also provided for people-to-people projects. Such funding went to all types of activities, including grassroots-level people-to-people and dialogue and problem-solving efforts targeting elites and professionals.

In 2005, Çuhadar and Dayton (2008) conducted a study on the Israeli-Palestinian Track 2 initiatives and compiled a list of eighty initiatives undertaken between 1989 and 2004 (excluding those carried out inside Israel between Palestinian and Jewish citizens). The study indicates that the number of outcome- and relationship-oriented initiatives (see Chapters 4 and 9 in this volume) are about the same. However, more Track 2 initiatives were undertaken with elites and professionals than with the grassroots. This is not surprising given that many of the Track 2 initiatives in the Israeli-Palestinian context were undertaken in preparation for the final-status negotiations. Furthermore, the study shows that grassroots-relationship and elite-outcome combinations dominate the others (see Figure 10.3, adapted from Çuhadar and Dayton 2008). Most of the relationship-focused initiatives tend to take place with grassroots populations, such as youths. In contrast, initiatives geared toward achieving an outcome for peace negotiations or toward a specific product are carried out mostly with professionals and elites. Less common are other combinations that create relationship-focused activities with elites and outcome-oriented activities with the grassroots.

Social cohesion initiatives between Israelis and Palestinians were organized by various Israeli, Palestinian, and international CS actors, including NGOs, academic institutions (e.g., American Academy of Arts and Sciences meetings in the early 1990s), business associations (e.g., Turkish Chambers of Industries and Commerce), and scholar-practitioners (e.g., Herbert Kelman of Harvard University). They were also organized on almost any issue (trade, refugees, Jerusalem, water, borders) related to the conflict and with all types of participants (see Figure 10.3) from all levels of society, ranging from youths to high-level policymakers.

Figure 10.3 Distribution of Track 2: Goals and Levels of the Initiatives

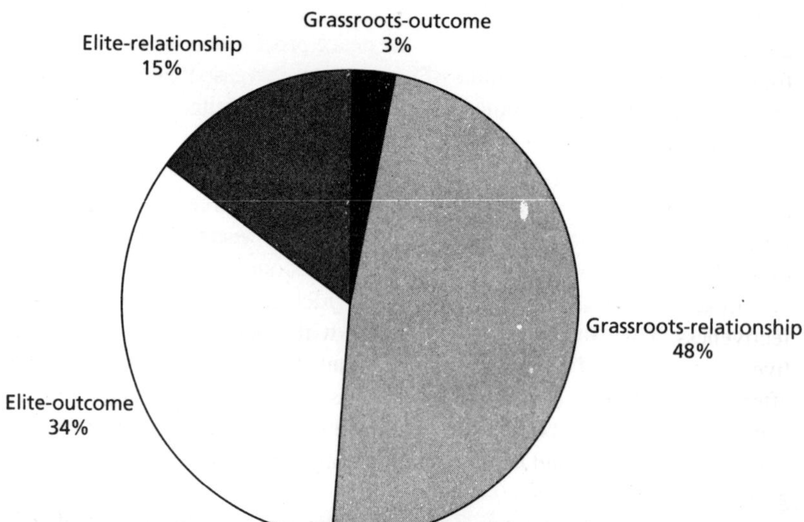

The presence of a third-party mediator in these projects has often expedited cooperation. The EU-sponsored Barcelona Process and neighborhood policies, for example, have been occasions to create networks in many sectors (human rights, environment, media, etc.). In the academic field, joint projects between Israeli and Palestinian universities and research centers are prominent. In his inventory of these projects, Paul Scham (2000) counted 217 projects that were held in the 1990s between Israel and some of the Arab countries, of which about 62 percent (133 projects) were conducted directly with Palestinian partners.

Comparing the grassroots and relationship-building projects and the high-level Track 2 talks with elites and other influential people, some criticisms are common to both. However, in terms of effectiveness, initiatives that focus on a common task and are held with influential people of equal status are considered to be more useful than those that bring people together for the sake of dialogue and focus on relationships only.

Given the political nature of task-focused activities, they have been found especially effective as a complementary prenegotiation strategy (e.g., Agha et al. 2003; Kelman 2005; Çuhadar 2009; Kaye 2005). These meetings become avenues of new learning for Palestinians and Israelis and contribute to the *process* of negotiations by helping build Palestinian human capital, by developing ideas and strategic insights relevant to the negotiation process, and by making politically relevant contacts.

The effectiveness of intergroup social cohesion has been assessed and discussed by various scholars and practitioners.[7] Several studies (Maoz 2000; Endresen 2001; Mu'allem 1999) have assessed the grassroots level, people-to-people workshops. Ifat Maoz (2000) looked at the degree of attitude change among Israeli-Palestinian youths attending a peace education seminar and found that the Palestinian attitude changed in a positive direction but did not reach a significant level, whereas the Israeli change in attitude did (Maoz 2000, 731). Maoz also suggested that the workshops, despite this Israeli-Palestinian asymmetry, helped the empowerment of Palestinians. The results of this study and that of Lena Endresen (2001) encourage further research on the accomplishments of initiatives that are purely oriented toward relationship-building, especially when there is power asymmetry.

In addition to asymmetry, sustainability is another issue important to effectiveness. Yigal Rosen's (2006) research with youths showed that the positive achievements of workshops among Israeli and Palestinian youths declined after two months. Rosen argued that this was because workshops influence peripheral attitudes and beliefs (i.e., negative emotions and stereotypes) rather than central attitudes and beliefs (i.e., those arising from the beliefs about each group's conflict narrative).

People-to people projects were also criticized on political grounds (Kuttab 1998; Rouhana 1997). First, Palestinian intellectuals criticized them for not acknowledging Palestinians' rights and called for a boycott on joint projects with Israeli organizations unless the latter "supports the Palestinian right to freedom and statehood and a comprehensive, just and durable peace that meets Palestinian national rights" (PNGOs 2000). Second, they were criticized for poor "transfer" of the effects and outcomes of the workshops to a larger level (Mu'allem 1999). Third, they were criticized for gathering people who lacked representativeness, such as the "usual suspects" and "convenient" participants (Agha et al. 2003, 174–178). Finally, activities that avoided tackling the hard political issues were criticized by Palestinians for separating the political domain from the academic, economic, and cultural domains. It was argued that cultural cooperation between two civil societies hides the power imbalance and that it is impossible to separate the cultural from the political domain.

Furthermore, the efficacy of peacebuilding is related not only to the workshop approach itself but also to achievement in the ongoing peace process. Such projects suffer if the Track 1 negotiation does not succeed, if it does not allow freedom of movement for Palestinians, if extensive settlement activities continue, and if there is no prospect for economic development. Moreover, the social cohesion initiatives became less relevant after the peace process collapsed, with the further radicalization of the conflict. Still, some projects are a real success despite a lack of funding. This success can be attributed to the fact that participants addressed the root causes of conflict, criticized Israeli occupation practices publicly and through advocacy campaigns, and contributed to strengthening human capital and the knowledge base relevant to negotiations. Therefore, it is important to follow a more systematic research to identify the conditions and people-to-people projects that lead to greater success.

A type of bridging activity by CS takes place between religious and secular Jews in Israel. As the secular and religious divide grows within Israeli society and the religious Zionist movement gains more influence in politics, bridging this divide is crucial for the future of the peace process. There are few attempts in this regard.

The most important is the "covenantalist" movement. This movement brought together religious and secular Jews to build consensus over religion-state relations (Cohen and Rynhold 2005, 726). The Gavison-Meidan and Chuka BeHaskama (Constitution by Consensus) initiatives were the most comprehensive attempts to reconcile differences between secular and religious Jews (Cohen and Rynhold 2005). These initiatives included different sections of society. So far the content of social covenants has been limited to issues related to tensions in the daily lives of Israelis, such as Shabbat rules and the definition of Jewishness. According to Asher Cohen and Jonathan Rynhold (2005), who comparatively studied these social covenants, they are vague as to details and are difficult to translate into practical solutions. For instance, the Kinneret covenant, which stated that "Israel is willing to recognize the legitimate rights of the neighboring Palestinian people," was vague as to whether or not this meant the far right's idea of endorsing a Palestinian state extending to the eastern bank of the Jordan River (Cohen and Rynhold 2005, 738). Despite the fact that issues related to the Palestinian state and peace are not addressed directly in these covenants, Israelis find them useful because they are taking a step toward building trust between two parts of society that dislike one another.

Concerning Palestinian society, there has been little effort to initiate dialogue between secular and religious groups. One example is the Palestinian Model Parliament. Launched in 1997–1998, a series of activities involving secular and religious groups and organizations was organized around the theme of women's rights, culminating in national debates in March and April 1998 on the status of Palestinian women under law. Since the split of the PNA between Fatah and Hamas, there is a rupture not only in polity level but also in the level of supporters in civil society.

Facilitation

Facilitation refers to the efforts of third-party CS actors to settle disputes between the main parties and between Palestinian factions. There are few of these CS activities that wc can point to, because in the Israeli-Palestinian context most facilitation work is carried out in the form of social cohesion.

A couple of Israeli and Palestinian organizations trained youths and some professionals as mediators and then assigned them to mediate specific issues related to the conflict. One example is the Joint Environmental Mediations Team—a network of Israeli and Palestinian environmental mediators that IPCRI helped establish to address environmental disputes. Another example is the Jerusalem Mediation and Arbitration Center (1996), established jointly by the Israeli think tank Jerusalem Institute for Israel Studies and the IPCC. The center trains mediators to work on small disputes between Palestinians and Israelis in the Jerusalem area. It was created due to the refusal of Palestinians to deal with the Israeli court system and a need to create a dispute-resolution mechanism in the Jerusalem area that was more sensitive to cultural backgrounds.

Although there have been many people and organizations around the world trying to mediate between the Israelis and Palestinians over many decades, including Norwegian, European, and various Middle Eastern envoys, they have not been very effective in mediating intra-Palestinian disputes so far. Thus, the divide between the West Bank and Gaza continues to be a major obstacle to an effective peace process. This is one area that will most likely become more important to the agendas of facilitators in coming years.

Service Delivery

Service delivery as an entry point for peacebuilding also exists, though not as commonly as some other functions. More Israeli NGOs provide service delivery than do PNGOs. The motivation of Israeli NGOs for service delivery may be a result of expressing solidarity, the availability of resources, freedom of movement, and fundraising.

Services provide an entry point to other peacebuilding functions; through the provision of services, solidarity with a population under occupation is expressed (e.g., Ta'Ayush and the Israeli Physicians for Human Rights—PHR). Some may provide services simply because they have resources that Palestinian society lacks. Finally, service delivery among Israeli NGOs may be more common because it helps to maintain the survival of NGOs and to raise funds for other activities that are not preferred by donors (Hermann 2002, 113). NGOs are concerned not only with solidarity; they are also concerned with raising funds, as service delivery is one area that may be prioritized by donors. In this way, some Israeli NGOs raise money and channel funds to other areas of peacebuilding that have not previously been funded by donors.

Service delivery is performed by CS in several innovative ways. These include legal counsel and services to victims, especially in combination with advocacy work (Adalah); infrastructure services for demolished Palestinian villages (Association of Forty); sports, library, and recreational facilities for disadvantaged youths affected by conflict; free health services in the Occupied Territories (PHR); psychological counseling (Gaza Community Mental Health Program); and water services to Palestinian villages (Friends of the Earth Middle East).

In most cases, service delivery is provided in tandem with other functions, especially protection and advocacy. One example, mentioned above, combined protection and service delivery: NGOs sent drivers for Palestinian ambulances to safeguard passage through Israeli checkpoints. Most service delivery is in the areas of health, agricultural cooperation, and the environment.

Conclusion

In the Israeli-Palestinian context, advocacy, in-group socialization, and intergroup social cohesion have been the most frequently performed functions by CS. However, these functions are not by definition more relevant or urgent than the other functions. Protection, monitoring, facilitation, and service delivery are at least as relevant, if not more necessary.

The relevance of functions differs between the Israeli and Palestinian societies, as each has different needs. The two societies are at different social, political, and economic development stages. Because Palestinian society is stateless, suffers from severe economic hardships, and is fighting against the occupation and the creation of daily facts on the ground (e.g., settlements and the separation wall), protection, monitoring, service delivery, and advocacy are more relevant as CS functions. Furthermore, a peacebuilding strategy focusing on the advancement of and struggle for "rights" is more pronounced on the Palestinian side. This has made human rights monitoring and advocacy the preferred functions of Palestinian CS.

And because one of the major obstacles to peace has been religious ideology and the rift between the secular and religious Israelis, socialization for democratic values and pluralism is currently more relevant for Israeli society. Contrary to the rights-based peacebuilding approach of Palestinians, Israeli CS has often adopted a more pragmatic approach to peacebuilding that emphasizes dialogue and negotiation. This has made social cohesion and facilitation the preferred functions within Israeli CS. However, donors have paid little attention to the priority of different needs within each society and have instead promoted a one-size-fits-all strategy to peacebuilding.

Several factors affect one or more of the peacebuilding functions of civil society:

1. The effects of the ongoing armed conflict and lack of peacekeeping forces
2. Donor policies and a dependence on donors and their peacebuilding agenda
3. Restrictions arising from the Israeli occupation, such as closures and human rights violations
4. The weak nature of the Palestinian state, the authoritarian tendencies of the PNA, and infighting among factions
5. Leverage wielded by international powers
6. The strategies and tactics used and their timing

The effects of the ongoing armed conflict and the lack of international peacekeeping forces on the ground affect almost all the peacebuilding functions. While protection and monitoring have become more relevant, the effectiveness and relevance of social cohesion have been diminished.

Donor policies affect almost all peacebuilding functions. The clear preference among Western donors to fund people-to-people programs (i.e., social cohesion activities), especially after the Oslo Accords in 1993, has made this function among the most frequent. At the same time, less funding is channeled to monitoring, protection, and socialization.

Furthermore, the channeling of Western funding has led to the professionalization of CS and has resulted in the establishment of organizationally more complex NGOs. Although this increases efficiency and operability, it also leads to a weakening of ties between NGOs and their grassroots bases. Unlike the trend in the 1970s and 1980s, which made grassroots activism an important CS action, in the 1990s such activities decreased in number and took a backseat to elite-based and middle class–oriented dialogues. Such activities remained limited in scope, could not become part of the political mainstream, and could not incorporate the religious groups. This trend weakened the effectiveness of advocacy. One could go farther and argue that the donor community contributed to, directly or indirectly, a process of "dedemocratization" at several levels of the Palestinian body politic (i.e., weakening the PLO versus strengthening the PNA; weakening unions and political factions).

Finally, by disconnecting civil society from politics, especially on the Palestinian side, donors' policies diminished the effectiveness of political advocacy. The inefficiency created by aid systems and their "conceptual maps," which envision the social field as neatly divided into political and civil societies, diminished the advocacy capability of PNGOs; rather than present their own conceptual map, they internalized the donors' vision.

The ongoing Israeli occupation and the human rights violations (especially at checkpoints and prisons) make it harder for CS actors to perform certain functions like protection, monitoring, service delivery, and advocacy while increasing their relevance. Restrictions by Israeli authorities especially discourage small or less formal CS to undertake such functions. Instead, large INGOs gain important advantages on the ground.

The weak nature of the Palestinian state structure and the authoritarian tendencies of the PNA also have implications for protection, service delivery, advocacy, and monitoring. Due to the lack of security forces and state agencies that provide services, CS for years has assumed the functions of protection and service delivery. Furthermore, some of the authoritarian policies of the PNA in the past have made monitoring, advocacy, and socialization functions especially relevant.

The leverage wielded by international powers has become an important variable, affecting especially the protection, monitoring, facilitation, and advocacy functions. CS actors have often used international leverage vis-à-vis governments to garner support for their own agendas. So far, such leverage has become more influential on the Palestinian side than the Israeli side.

Finally, CS's strategies and tactics, as well as their timing, have influenced the advocacy and social cohesion functions. For instance, while nonpublic advocacy became more relevant and effective before and during peace negotiations, public advocacy was preferred after they failed. Furthermore, social cohesion activities focusing on a common task and outcome with professional people became more relevant and effective during the prenegotiation phase, and relationship-building social cohesion activities became more relevant after the end of the armed conflict.

In conclusion, we argue that social cohesion programs need to encourage cooperation between the Israeli and Palestinian civil societies in a way that promotes responsible action, such as taking a joint position against the occupation and facilitating a mutually agreed-upon peace agreement. A joint Israeli-Palestinian position to end the occupation is an essential step for ending conflict. Failure to do so manipulates reality and presents a false image of the conflict itself.

Notes

We would like to thank Amjad Zeid, Yasemin Ipek Can, and Deniz Ugur for their research assistance. We are also grateful to Thania Paffenholz, Christoph Spurk, John Darby, Ricardo Bocco, Benoît Challand, and other reviewers in the project for their valuable comments.

1. We draw on a variety of data sources. Information taken from an NGO directory was coded in line with the theoretical framework to provide an overview of NGO activities in the Israeli-Palestinian context and to present a quantifiable description. Data also were collected through field study and secondary analysis; different types of CS actors were taken into account, such as private citizens, social networks and movements, academic and research institutions, and think tanks. Data regarding the assessment of advocacy, social cohesion, and facilitation functions were gathered by Çuhadar throughout her fieldwork between 2002 and 2005 and by Çuhadar and Dayton during a USIP-funded research project that involved surveying peace practitioners.

2. For further reading on the history of the conflict from various perspectives, see Lustick (1994); Morris (1999); Kimmerling (2003); Gilbert (2008); Lesch and Tschirgi (1998); Nazzal and Nazzal (1997); Shipler (1986); Nusseibeh (2007); Khalidi (2007); and Avnery (1975).

3. See statistics at B'Tselem (2008) and the Applied Research Institute Jerusalem (2008).

4. For Israeli public support for the peace process by the left and right wings, see Hermann (2002, 96 and 115; 2006, 43).

5. It should be noted that most of the organizations perform more than one function. For such cases, each function is coded separately. The activities were coded from the mission statements and by looking at the NGO activities listed in the directory or mentioned in other sources, such as websites published by the organizations.

6. *Sulha* refers to a formal public ceremony that marks the culmination of the peacemaking negotiations through mediation. *Sulha* entails reconciliation, cooperation, and forgiveness. For more details about the importance of the *sulha* in Palestinian society, see Lang (2002).

7. The effectiveness of this function should be treated separately for grassroots-oriented people-to-people and peace education projects, as well as elite-level Track 2 workshops. Although they have common characteristics, these activities have different goals that should be taken into consideration in any assessment.

11

Afghanistan: Civil Society Between Modernity and Tradition

Kaja Borchgrevink and Kristian Berg Harpviken

Since the fall of the Taliban in late 2001, the massive attention given to civil society in Afghanistan stands in sharp contrast to the period of de facto Taliban rule (1996–2001), a period during which the regime was hostile to, and the international community unwilling to invest in, civil society. Civil society is primarily seen as a provider of services, yet it plays increasingly important roles in other areas, especially advocacy (with government and international actors), socialization (on peaceful coexistence, democracy, and human rights), and mediation (at the local level). Dominant conceptions of civil society in Afghanistan emphasize types of organizations such as NGOs, which, emerging in the 1980s, are a recent phenomenon, at the cost of more traditional forms, such as religious networks and local councils. Nonetheless, what we see on the ground, particularly after 2001, is that many initiatives are based on close interaction between modern and traditional CS actors. Furthermore, we witness that such synergy is effective in overcoming the weaknesses of each type of actor.

Afghanistan has been the scene of armed conflict since 1978. Regimes have been authoritarian, as in the case of the People's Democratic Party of Afghanistan (PDPA) during the 1980s, or have lacked capacity for anything but engaging in war, as with the so-called mujahidin government (1992–1996). Alternatively, in the case of the Taliban, they have been both authoritarian and had weak administrative capacity. While the authoritarians have tried to form civil society for their purposes, the weaker regimes have been deeply suspicious of it. The Taliban regime co-opted the religious parts of civil society and sought to constrain the modern parts to service delivery. Following the 2001 intervention, Afghanistan's regime is democratically elected. Despite a good measure of skepticism, the Afghan regime works closely with civil society in a number of areas. The conflictual nature of the Afghan peace process, including the exclusion of the Taliban from the 2001 peace agreement, has gradually brought the country back to full-scale war. This situation seriously constrains the space for CS actors.

Applying the framework developed by Thania Paffenholz and Christoph Spurk (2006; see Chapter 4), we concentrate on two phases of conflict: the reign of the Taliban (1996–2001) and the post-2001 period.[1] The analysis is based on a review of the existing literature, complemented by interviews with well-informed observers. Additionally, we draw upon previous work by the authors (Borchgrevink 2007; Harpviken, Strand, and Ask 2002). The existing literature has limitations. First, it is overly focused on policy and the role of NGOs; second, there is scarce reporting from the Taliban years; and third, assessments of impacts are rare. We attempt to corroborate evidence from various sources, and we consulted regularly with well-informed observers to fill in the gaps and resolve contradictory evidence. Nonetheless, determining the impact of civil society on each of the seven functions in the Paffenholz and Spurk framework has been a challenge. Largely, what we present is a qualitative assessment of the contributions of Afghan civil society to various peacebuilding functions, emphasizing the constraints on CS action. First, however, we provide some background on the conflict, followed by a discussion of the form of civil society in Afghanistan.

Context

Afghanistan is a landlocked country situated at the intersection of South Asia, Central Asia, and the Middle East. The country was—unlike its neighbors—never colonized. Its boundaries were established in the late 1800s, when the country came to serve as a buffer between two imperial powers, Russia and British India. A century later, Afghanistan's neighborly relations remain troubled. Its neighbors are deeply entwined in regional security complexes in which Afghanistan is not a central concern. Such is the case for Pakistan, whose relationship with India is an existential issue that informs all foreign and security policy, including the relationship with Afghanistan (Harpviken forthcoming b). In addition, serious bilateral conflict issues, such as the status of the Afghan-Pakistani border, must be understood in light of regional dynamics. The end result is that Afghanistan, a weak state in a conflictual neighborhood, has seen its own internal conflicts complicated by a number of geopolitical conflicts in which it is only a marginal stakeholder.

On the domestic front, Afghan political history has been characterized by an unstable relationship among tribes, religious actors, and the ruler (Olesen 1995). Attempts by the central government to instill modernization in the form of extending its presence, claiming revenue, dismantling patron-client relationships, and building a strong army under its control have historically triggered strong resistance (Suhrke 2007a). Rights of women and legal reform have been particularly contentious issues. By the early 1960s, expanded access to higher education went in parallel with exposure to new international political thinking. The king, Zaher Shah, launched a "new democracy" initiative. In the expectation of party-based elections, new political parties were established, including various breeds of socialists, Islamists, and ethnonationalists (Dupree 1980, 649). The new groups were closely linked to the universities, had limited popular support, and were perceived as irrelevant by much of the rural population. When the king hesitated to ratify the political parties act, massive frustration among the new activists was triggered.

In 1973, the king was deposed, as his own cousin, the former prime minister Daud Khan, took power in a bloodless coup. Daud allied with the PDPA, which was already well placed within the army, to conduct the coup, but soon turned against the party. He was an impatient reformer with visions of infrastructural and industrial development, but he alienated the new radical groups bred by modernization and failed to build an alternative constituency among the tradition-oriented (Saikal 2005). Opposition to Daud was dominated by the new radical parties—socialist and Islamist—which were also entangled in mutual conflict (Roy 1986). In April 1978, the Soviet-oriented PDPA took power in a coup and killed Daud and his family, unleashing the use of organized violence on an unprecedented scale.

PDPA dominated government throughout the 1980s, with heavy backing from the Soviet Union, who intervened militarily on Christmas Eve 1979. The PDPA was a party of impatient modernizers who were not hesitant to use violence (Shahrani 1984). Spontaneous localized resistance, led mainly by religious and traditional leaders, gained increasing force. Many fled to Iran and Pakistan, and support started coming in from both Islamic and Western countries. Pakistan handpicked Afghan political parties to represent the resistance; a refugee passport was contingent on membership in one of the parties, which were all of a radical Islamist or Islamic-traditional breed.[2] The resistance parties became known as the mujahidin, the "holy warriors." For them, resistance to the Soviet intervention rested on religious grounds. What was, for the West, a fight against communism became, both locally and for the Muslim world, jihad—or "holy struggle"—against infidels. New groups—and new types of leaders—gained power at the cost of traditional ones (Centlivres and Centlivres-Demont 1988). The international refugee regime, and humanitarian assistance, became instruments for mobilizing resistance (Baitenmann 1990; Fielden 1998).

The Soviet Union withdrew its forces in early 1989. Soon after the dissolution of the Soviet Union, the PDPA regime imploded in April 1992. Its various parts allied with different groups in the resistance, largely along ethnic lines. This signaled a new era in the Afghan war: the reign of the mujahidin. Kabul was demolished in fighting between former resistance groups, while the rest of the country was carved up in unstable fiefdoms where insecurity, repression, and continued fighting characterized most areas.

The emergence of the Taliban in 1994 and their capture of Kabul in 1996 initiated a new phase in the civil war. In reaction to chaos and lawlessness, the Taliban was rooted in networks of Afghan religious leaders and in the religious schools (*madrasas*) of the Afghan-Pakistani borderlands. In one perspective, the Taliban was a social revolution, whereby representatives of the dispossessed rural population took revenge on urban-based modernizers (Atmar and Goodhand 2002). Over time, the Taliban also came to enjoy generous support from Pakistan (Rashid 1998). Although the Taliban's ascendance was initially welcomed by many Afghans, this was soon reversed as the Taliban enforced restrictive policies, punishing violations brutally. The Taliban recruited primarily in the Pashtun rural south, and resistance soared once they started to expand into areas where other ethnicities were in the majority (Harpviken 1997).

The Taliban state apparatus placed its own people in all major positions yet was institutionally weak, despite maintaining whatever remained of the old bureaucracy. Compensating for its institutional weakness, the Taliban coopted the religious networks in areas under its control, using mullahs to gather information and collect taxes. In this fashion the Taliban demonstrated an unprecedented level of penetration at the local level. For the Taliban, the state was to provide security and uphold Islamic principles, but there was minimal concern with the economic and social welfare of the populace. The Taliban was increasingly isolated by the international community as the Taliban's relationship with Al-Qaida grew more important.

Just as the conflict has had many forms, so have the attempts at bringing peace. As elsewhere, "peace" means different things to different actors. Broadly, the peacemaking initiatives can be divided between a number of high-level peace negotiations in the 1980s and the 1990s—mainly top-down approaches led by the international community—on one side, and local-level initiatives attempting to create an environment for peace among Afghans on the other. At the international level, there were the UN-led Track 1 negotiations, its major achievement being the 1988 Geneva Accord that prepared the way for Soviet withdrawal (Rubin 1995).[3] Numerous agreements brokered in the early 1990s failed. Domestically, the Taliban and their counterparts, the so-called Northern Alliance, set up a joint commission of religious scholars in 1998, tasked to come up with a framework for negotiations, based on their knowledge of Islamic law (*sharia*) and norms of warfare. This initiative also failed, probably because the status held by religious leaders differed so greatly between the two sides.

Beginning in the first half of the 1990s, some Afghan NGO employees established organizations with an explicit peacebuilding mandate (Strand 1999).[4] These organizations have assiduously avoided high-level politics, focusing on what they refer to as "social peacebuilding," a pretext for apolitical, bottom-up, community-level initiatives. This is in contrast to "political peacebuilding" processes that aim at impacting the national and international situations. Conveniently, the social peacebuilding mandate is to shield against accusations of being political. Interestingly, the Afghan peacebuilding NGOs emerged in a climate where there was little international interest in Afghanistan and where—in a halfhearted effort to use conditionality to rein in the Taliban—only life-saving, humanitarian assistance was given.

After the terror attacks in the United States in September 2001, the world's attention again turned to Afghanistan. The US-backed intervention resulted in the rapid collapse of the Taliban regime. The Afghan parties and their various international supporters met in Bonn to negotiate a deal. Hamid Karzai was inaugurated as head of the transitional administration in early December. The ensuing process has been described as a "conflictual peace," referring to the gaps or "built-in elements of conflict that were either ignored or deliberately set aside" in the Bonn process (Suhrke, Harpviken, and Strand 2004, 3). Most obvious is the noninclusive nature of the peace agreement, which included only the winning party; yet it is clear that the failure to accommodate the traditional rural Pashtun constituency of the south has been key in strengthening the new Taliban (Giustozzi 2007). Further, the US-led military effort (labeled the "War on Terror" by the administration of George W. Bush) made the hunt for Osama bin Laden and the Al-Qaida leadership its prime objective. At times this undermined the secondary objective: reconstituting a functioning Afghan state. Importantly, as Oliver Roy (2004) has pointed out, in contrast to its undertaking in Iraq, the United States never aimed at a radical modernization of Afghanistan. The ambition was to deprive Al-Qaida of its sanctuary at the time and in the future.

The spine of the 2001 Bonn treaty was an ambitious political timetable; a new constitution was drafted in 2003, presidential elections were held in 2004, and parliamentary elections—the first in thirty-five years—were held in September 2005. Regardless of modest US ambitions, the transition to liberal democracy is an integral part of the international peacebuilding project in Afghanistan. These tall ambitions, the timetable associated with it, and the fact that the main driving forces for political modernization are external have, as Shahrbanou Tadjbaksh and Michael Schöiswohl (2008) argue, contributed to a process that has little resonance in Afghan society. The ambitious political reform program moved ahead, but there has been limited interest in genuine input from civil society at large. The NGO-led consultations in the run-up to the adoption of the constitution in 2004, for example, took place in the absence of a draft document (Schmeidl 2007).[5]

Although the state is weak at the center, it is even weaker outside the capital. As Barnett Rubin (2007, 62) has pointed out, it is ironic that Afghanistan, probably the country in the world that needs decentralization the most, has adopted one of the world's most centralized templates for governance. This centralization translates into a major legitimacy problem. Common Afghans find that the state, at best, has little to offer and, at worst, that it is penetrated by corruption and power abuse. For civil society this means that local entities—such as community councils—do not have much of a government to interact with.

An ambitious economic reform program has yielded an average annual growth, since 2001, exceeding 11 percent (IMF 2008). A major challenge is that the absolute bulk of economic activity is informal—some 80–90 percent by World Bank (2004) estimates—with drugs and other illicit business playing a major role. Furthermore, the Afghan state is highly dependent on foreign funding, most of which is not channeled through the government but instead contracted to businesses and NGOs. Furthermore, the new parliament has very limited control over the national budget (Suhrke 2007b, 13). The net result is a state that is more easily held accountable by external actors than by its own citizenry.[6]

Security remains the overriding concern, particularly from 2005, when the Taliban and other insurgents became increasingly able to inflict harm on the Afghan government and its foreign backers. At the same time, the Taliban are expanding the areas where political influence can be exerted (Giustozzi 2007). There is growing resentment among the local population with heavy-handed warfare by international forces. A poll conducted in December 2007 found that 29 percent of respondents thought the foreign forces did a bad job; when asked why they thought so, 39 percent would refer to the increasing number of civilian casualties (ABC News Polling Unit 2007).

Classical distinctions between civil and military efforts are challenged in Afghanistan. Humanitarian and development aid has increasingly been seen as instrumental for swaying public opinion in favor of the international military effort. This has generated strong critique from parts of civil society, primarily from NGOs, concerned about their safety and security, their ability to operate independently, the short time horizon that often applies, and ultimately that aid priorities in Afghanistan are set by domestic concerns in troop-contributing countries (Waldman 2008). Military personnel also play important roles related to reform of the state apparatus, particularly through the Provincial Reconstruction Teams (PRTs). There is a concern that security imperatives and frequent staff rotation are at odds with the need for local capacity-building and broader accountability.

Status of Civil Society

Afghan civil society is diverse—it comprises both modern and traditional institutions—informal and formal. There are vast variations from one region to another, between the countryside and the cities. Masoud Kamali (2001) draws a distinction between modern and indigenous civil society in contemporary Muslim societies, which finds resonance in an examination of civil society in Afghanistan.[7] Specifically, Kamali distinguishes between indigenous civil society based on a core of quasitraditional and quasimodern influential groups, and modern civil society constructed on a core of Westernized intellectuals and modern social groups. Inherent in Kamali's conceptualization of indigenous or, what we will here refer to as "traditional," civil society lies the realization that they are also exposed to the pressures of modernization. In Afghanistan, war, mobility, and economic transformation have had deep impacts on traditional institutions. Following this notion, we focus on what we view to be the dominant forms of civil society in Afghanistan. As for the various components of modern civil society, we focus on the NGO sector, in addition to voluntary associations and interest groups. Within traditional civil society, we examine community councils and religious networks.

The modern CS sector in Afghanistan spans sports clubs and youth organizations, women's groups, cultural foundations and associations of traders (*bazaris*), professional associations, and NGOs. Diaspora groups, also highly significant, will be addressed only in passing.[8] Since the early 1990s a number of community-based organizations (CBOs) have been established with assistance from development agencies to deal with specific issues (such as water-user organizations and parent-teacher groups).[9] NGOs hardly existed before the war but started emerging in the 1980s, particularly in the exile environment in Pakistan. External actors, international NGOs in particular, have been instrumental in establishing the Afghan NGO sector, with close links between Afghan entities and NGO coordination bodies and networks across the globe.[10] With difficult working conditions under both the mujahidin and the Taliban, most of these agencies maintained a foothold in exile until after 2001, when they shifted fully to Afghanistan. The first generation of Afghan NGOs were mainly engaged in aid and, to a large extent, driven by funding opportunities. After 2001 several new entities have been set up, many of which have a more explicit focus on their principled role as civil society, underscoring their work for human rights or advocacy in general.[11] Examples are the Afghan Civil Society Forum (ACSF), set up in the wake of the CS meeting that ran in parallel with the Bonn conference, as well as the Foundation for Culture and Civil Society (FCCS).

Among traditional forms of civil society, the main focus has been on community councils and assemblies, or *shuras*.[12] Such councils exist throughout Afghanistan, with considerable variation between areas and between rural and urban settings. Traditional *shuras* are open to all members of the community; age, religious authority, and family position are decisive for influence. Their "modus operandi" is largely reactive, solving problems or conflicts as they emerge (Harpviken, Strand, and Ask 2002). During the 1980s, *shuras* were set up both by communities (to organize local security) and by military commanders (to coordinate the fight). Simultaneously, aid agencies began to see *shuras* as their principal partners in implementing assistance, without necessarily realizing the large contrast between a traditional *shura* and what we may term a "community development association" (Canfield 1989; Carter and Connor 1989).

The preference for *shuras* as implementing partners at the local level has been institutionalized after 2001, with the so-called National Solidarity Program

(NSP), a hallmark of the reconstruction program.[13] Executed by the Ministry of Rehabilitation and Rural Development (MRRD), the facilitating partners of the NSP are national and international NGOs throughout the country. NSP has facilitated the formation of democratically elected Community Development Councils throughout the country, tasked to plan, implement, and maintain small-scale projects, based on their own prioritized use of a cash block grant. The program, funded by a consortium of donors through the World Bank, takes the *shura* as its starting point, then modifies its composition and mandate, creating a traditional-modern hybrid. In effect, NSP is not only a development channel; it is also a massive exercise in building democratic and accountable local institutions (Boesen 2004; Carlin 2004). As important, in working with this age-old local CS entity, the government uses the archetype of modern civil society—the NGOs—as its intermediary. Still, the new *shuras,* with their focus remaining on local affairs, coupled with the absence of an effective mechanism for expressing a concerted voice at higher levels, may also have negative effects on statebuilding.[14]

Religious civil society in Afghanistan is made up of informal networks of religious actors and institutions. These actors and institutions provide both theological and spiritual guidance and a framework for daily life in moral, social, and political terms. In times of crisis, religious networks have taken on key functions either in the form of legitimizing resistance or by forming the backbone of resistance (Edwards 1986). Among Sunnis, which constitute some 90 percent of the Afghan population, there is no clear hierarchy but rather networks based on personal loyalty and allegiance.[15] Religious networks were at the heart of the Taliban movement. They were built around loyalties and competence developed during training at one of the many *madrasas* (religious seminaries) in Pakistan or Afghanistan. It is possible to view the initial Taliban mobilization—an overwhelmingly spontaneous reaction against misrule—as civil society at its most powerful.[16]

An insistence on the role of religious actors in civil society is not uncontroversial.[17] In one respect, there exists the idea of civil society as intrinsically linked to a civility norm and democratization rooted in individualization, in contrast to Islamic collectivism (Gellner 1994). An alternative argument is that the *ulama*—the "higher clergy"—see themselves as custodians of the law, which places them above the law. Relatedly, the *ulama*—being on the state payroll—lack independence. There is an institutionalized system of *ulama* councils in Afghanistan, paid by the government, but not all religious leaders are part of that system. Further, other CS actors are not discounted because their lines with government are blurred. More important, although it is true that Islam is a law religion, and that many *ulama* see themselves as its guardians, there are other interpretations and possible roles. There is every reason to be careful not to place everything religious under the rubric of civil society, yet it would be a mistake to exclude the civil society functions of actors that have considerable influence in their own societies, not only to wreck but also to enhance a peace process.

Excluding actors that have malign objectives from the definition of civil society is problematic, as many analysts have cautioned (Carothers and Barndt 1999; Paffenholz and Spurk 2006). In Afghanistan, the concept of civil society is often given a normative quality; it entails something "civilized." Modern civil society organizations promoting peace and reconciliation are "civil," whereas antigovernment groups are described as "uncivil." However, when people come together for "collective actions around shared interests," these interests represent values and ideas over which there is no universal consent. Parts of civil society promote values that may be undemocratic, repressive, and intolerant. The labeling of actors as "civil" or "uncivil," as "good" or "bad"—as in the case of religious networks—is also fundamentally political (Borchgrevink 2007).[18] More concretely, NGOs, widely perceived as the genuine civil society, may also serve political-cum-military purposes, as was the case with many of the party-affiliated entities set up in Pakistan in the 1980s. Relatedly, aid agencies may serve as perfect platforms for individuals with a political agenda.[19]

The experience with formal democratic governance is limited in Afghanistan. The best Afghan NGOs, and some international ones, have held a high standard; they have contributed to training individuals and are committed to setting an example for political parties and the government.[20] And even though many of the modern CS organizations seemingly have a formal structure, they may also display weak internal governance structures. New legislation stipulates clear organizational standards, but the government's oversight capacity is limited.[21] Traditional Afghan civil society, largely informal by nature, is neither democratically organized nor fully subject to state oversight. Leaders are often strong, powerful, and well-resourced personalities, which leads to organizational vulnerability. Civil society leadership is a masculine privilege, as one informant pointed out: men head any organization; women head (most) women's organizations.[22]

Thus the critical question: To whom are civil society actors accountable? The NGO sector owes much of its prominence to donor funds. External assistance has been heavily politicized in the Afghan context (Johnson and Leslie 2002). Throughout the 1980s and 1990s, a large part of NGOs and voluntary associations were closely associated with a political group; those that were intent on maintaining neutrality had to cultivate political contacts for their own protection (Ludin 2002). The PDPA regime inspired its own set of entities, preferably one entity for any given purpose. NGOs have taken on a number of roles in the implementation of aid programs, as well as in government contracts (as with NSP), predictably leading to accusations that they are agents of the government or foreign interests (Borchgrevink 2007). Yet, the independence of religious civil society institutions—such as the national *shura-e-ulama* (the national council of religious leaders) and *madrasas*—from the government inevitably varies. In Taliban-controlled areas many of these institutions are still under strong pressure to adhere to Taliban ideology and rules. The national *shura-e-ulama* are, in contrast, criticized by other members of the *ulama* for being loyal servants of the government (Borchgrevink 2007).[23] Thus, poor accountability is the combined result of political pressures, reliance of external funding, and a lack of mechanisms by which constituents can hold organizations responsible.

NGOs are often identified as the main CS actors in Afghanistan. Popular perceptions of NGOs—and therefore of civil society—have not all been positive. Rather, common allegations by the government and the media are that NGOs are profit-seeking, corrupt, and not reaching those in need, a view also shared by traditional religious actors (Wardak, Zaman, and Nawabi 2007). Because NGO-bashing has a certain popular resonance, it is also an effective way to take focus away from the government's failings. Government attitudes and regulation since 2001—including the new NGO law—have not contributed to creating an appropriate enabling environment for civil society (Irish and Simon 2007).[24]

Understandably, many in government see the capacity of CS entities, often directly financed by foreign actors, as undermining the state's need to strengthen institutions. In the post-2001 structure, however, the state is reliant on modern CS actors to reach out. The same is the case for its communication with local councils, where NGOs serve as interlocutors, a setup that favors neither concerted efforts based in the *shura* system nor its direct exposure to representatives of the state. The engagement of religious actors, despite their considerable potential, remains controversial among scholars, other civil society actors, and analysts. Understandably, the definition of, and the state's interaction with, civil society are deeply political.

Peacebuilding Functions

What functions does civil society in Afghanistan fulfill? How does it contribute? In the following section, we compare the post-Taliban period with the period under Taliban rule, looking at seven different functions: protection, monitoring, advocacy, socialization, social cohesion, intermediation and facilitation, and service delivery.

Protection

The importance of protection seems self-evident in a country where three decades of war have caused the deaths of more than 1 million people, displaced more than half of the population once or several times, and caused immeasurable levels of suffering. "Protection"—both physical protection against violence and social protection of vulnerable groups—has traditionally been provided by solidarity networks and local community institutions (Shahrani 1998). The localized nature of Taliban rule made protection provided by the communities possible (e.g., Suleman and Williams 2003). An example is when a community brokered a deal with local Taliban representatives to avoid conscription, instead paying compensation.[25] Local councils contributed to settling disputes and reducing violent conflict, and community committees were established to guard local communities and neighborhoods against attacks and intruders. Escapes were assisted by kin and other personal networks (Harpviken forthcoming a). Beyond the local level, traditional entities have had little ability to offer protection.

Under the restrictive Taliban regime, modern Afghan civil society was largely incapable of providing protection to civilians. One exception is the Afghan Red Crescent (ARC), which had backing from the International Committee of the Red Cross (ICRC) and the United Nations. ARC focused on treatment of war injuries and humanitarian relief, information about international humanitarian law, as well as facilitating contact between prisoners of war and their families. More proactive measures, such as the declaration of peace zones and the establishment of safe houses, were virtually nonexistent, although there are examples of institutions giving protection to women and children. Afghan NGOs also played an important role in Humanitarian Mine Action, seeking to ameliorate the impacts of landmines and unexploded ordnance. Ultimately, Afghan organizations that were capable of offering protection under the Taliban, few as they were, almost always had international allies.

Even though the space for modern civil society to take on protection roles expanded after 2001, there are few organizations that directly address this. Civilian casualties in international warfare, however, have been a key concern for both the Afghan Independent Human Rights Commission (AIHRC) and the United Nations Assistance Mission in Afghanistan (UNAMA), calling on civil society to step up their activities (Thier and Ranjbar 2008). The security situation in the south, however, impedes on Afghan civil society's ability to protect the population from violence committed by the Taliban, Afghan forces, and international military forces. Mine-action agencies, for example, which have operated successfully under shifting regimes since the late 1980s, were severely affected during the 2001 intervention and have since become a target for the armed opposition.[26] In sum, the intervention and the statebuilding project have not improved the capacity of existing entities to offer protection but have inspired the establishment of certain specialized institutions, such as AIHRC.

Monitoring

As the Taliban regime put severe restrictions on public space, monitoring and reporting on the regime were punished brutally. While atrocities committed by both parties in the conflict intensified with the Taliban's expansion, there was a dearth of information about what actually happened inside the country. A few

Afghan NGOs did, however, work to monitor and report on the conflict during the Taliban reign. The Cooperation Center for Afghanistan (CCA), for example, had seven reporters working clandestinely, sending coded reports to international human rights organizations. The virtual absence of independent media in Afghanistan during the Taliban regime meant that foreign media were a critical link for reporting events on the ground.

The BBC's Dari and Pashtu service, with a long-standing reputation for reliability, was especially critical in delivering news about Afghanistan to Afghans in and outside of the country. The documentation of atrocities—such as the images of female executions at Kabul stadium[27]—was instrumental in stimulating international pressure on the Taliban, including the UN Security Council resolutions in 1999 and 2000, which imposed sanctions on the regime.

Since 2001, there has been an explosive growth of Afghan media. Print and broadcasting media have mushroomed with new radio stations, TV stations, and publications. The media, like most sectors in Afghanistan, are highly dependent on external funders. The post-2001 influx of funding led to the establishment of some 300 new print publications (BBC 2005). Although the number of printed publications has increased dramatically since 2001, the main media outlet remains the radio. Only 2 percent of the population regularly read printed media (BBC 2006). Lack of journalistic competence is a bottleneck, and generally there is little analytical and critical journalism.

After the fall of the Taliban, the number of new Afghan advocacy organizations has grown considerably. Afghan civil society has taken a greater role in documenting human rights violations (human rights monitoring) and developments that might escalate into violence (early warning). The AIHRC was established as the main Afghan monitor of human rights violations in Afghanistan in 2001.[28] A number of advocacy networks have been established, such as the Foundation for Culture and Civil Society (FCCS), Afghan Civil Society Forum (ACSF), Afghan Women's Network (AWN), Human Rights Research and Advocacy Consortium (HRRAC), and Civil Society Human Rights Network (CSHRN). In the more secure areas, modern civil society groups have taken a rather proactive role in reporting and early warning; elsewhere, insecurity remains a key impediment.

Community *shuras* and tribal and religious institutions have traditionally been representing their communities to the authorities (Roy 1986). During the Taliban reign, many religious leaders were co-opted by the regime and had limited ability to fulfill any independent monitoring role. In general terms, traditional institutions lack formal organization like NGOs and rarely have links to modern Afghan civil society organizations or international outlets, which are critical players in disseminating their reports. After 2001, representatives of local *shuras* and other religious actors have reported on violence and human rights abuses to the AIHRC, to the government, and to NGOs. President Karzai regularly meets with tribal and religious leaders, providing them the opportunity to voice concerns over situations in their areas. However, while the *shura-e-ulama* is criticized for being co-opted by the government, where the Taliban is in control it exerts heavy pressure on religious leaders to cooperate. Independent religious leaders find that they have minimal access to the government (Wardak, Zaman, and Nawabi 2007). Religious civil society, therefore, is squeezed between two spheres and has little opportunity to fill independent CS functions.

According to an AIHRC commissioner in 2007, the number of complaints about violence and human rights abuses fell. This is explained not by a reduction in violence and abuses (quite the contrary: it has increased) but by people being disillusioned with reporting abuses to no effect. A feeling of powerlessness is expressed by many CS actors. Security issues, capacity constraints, and co-optation by the various groups stand out as the most important reasons for the lack of monitoring and early warning, both during the Taliban reign and after 2001.

Advocacy

The advocacy and public communication functions performed by Afghan civil society have focused in part on influencing governments directly, in part on stimulating public debate. Under the Taliban regime Afghan CS advocacy was severely constrained and the opportunities to influence the regime were limited. There are exceptions, however, such as the NGO anti-landmine campaign that convinced the Taliban leader Mullah Omar to issue a religious decree, or fatwa, banning the use of landmines in 1998 (ICBL 2002). A number of Afghan human rights groups operated with headquarters in Pakistan, reporting on violations inside Afghanistan. The links between Afghan NGOs operating inside Afghanistan and Afghan and international organizations abroad were essential for keeping the Afghan conflict on the international agenda.

After 2001, with new opportunities to access government, as well as international actors in some cases, modern Afghan civil society has expanded its advocacy and public communication roles. A number of advocacy-oriented organizations have emerged promoting peace, democracy, and human rights. After 2001, modern CS actors have been drawn upon as resources in several processes at the international level, with a parallel civil society forum during the 2001 Bonn conference as well as subsequent high-level events. Access to international funding, in the wake of the 2001 intervention, undoubtedly encouraged the foundation of new entities. Yet, it is also clear that the new momentum is spearheaded by a core of highly committed CS activists. However, the institutional capacity of Afghan entities remains weak. As one well-informed observer noted in the aftermath of the Paris support conference in June 2008, without internationals taking the lead there would have been no CS event. Civil society has arranged a number of demonstrations since 2001, with 3,000 people turning up for the 2007 Peace Day.[29] Nonetheless, Afghan civil society has not been able to generate broad-based mobilization for peace since 2001.

Religious CS actors and institutions have only partially been engaged, and seldom are they given an independent voice in the post-2001 statebuilding process. Yet, religious institutions remain important, with the political role of religious leaders—particularly through the Friday prayers—being used to mobilize against national and international political actors, as well as to spread messages of reconciliation and to promote development and collaboration (Borchgrevink 2007). There are, however, examples where traditional *shuras* work in collaboration with modern CS organizations that facilitate the production and dissemination of communication material, enabling local voices to reach new audiences.[30]

Although civil society has started to place issues on the agenda post-2001, the impact is uncertain. Susanne Schmeidl (2007), who was deeply involved in facilitating the civil society forum at Bonn and subsequent international events, doubts that they had any direct impact on the process, but she also emphasizes the longer-term symbolic value. Many CS actors are critical of the government. They believe the government is merely paying lip service to civil society, not taking their concerns seriously. As is common in weak-capacity governments, CS actors are easily seen not as complements but as competitors (Schmeidl 2007). The security situation is also impeding civil society public advocacy and communication activities, and public campaigns and mobilization remain high-risk activities within the major conflict zones.

In-Group Socialization

Afghanistan has experienced three decades of armed conflict along shifting lines that reflect religious, ethnic, and political divides. Trust—both between various groups and in state institutions—is low. Rebuilding trust and creating an environment for coexistence are crucial to lasting peace. Afghan civil society has been segregated, with divisions following tribal, kin, and religious identities. Thus, in-group socialization has been strong, at the cost of ties that cut across identity differences.

Some of the modern CS organizations dealing explicitly with local-level peacebuilding continued their work during the Taliban reign.[31] However, they kept a low profile, with a limited presence within Afghanistan, focusing primarily on training and capacity-building among local NGOs' staff. For these organizations, peacebuilding was in essence about socialization: in order to affect others, one had to start with oneself and one's immediate environment, setting a credible example. Some of these organizations have also worked to mainstream peace education, developing curricula that could be included in the nationwide educational system.[32] Conflict-sensitive development practices, in line with "do no harm" principles, also had a central role (Atmar and Goodhand 2002).

After 2001, myriad of development-oriented groups and *shuras* have emerged; a number of organizations are promoting peace and reconciliation through arts, culture, research, and advocacy; and there has been an increase in CS organizations that are explicitly focusing on "social peacebuilding." Initiatives to work with traditional organizations are mainly led by the modern CS organizations (such as Tribal Liaison Office, Sanayee Development Organization, Cooperation for Peace and Unity in Afghanistan, Foundation for Culture and Civil Society, Afghan Civil Society Forum, and others), bridging divides between customary structures and the government or other external actors.

Afghan civil society has played an instrumental role in some of the major socialization initiatives linked to the post-Bonn statebuilding process. Most notable is the work of ACSF in civic education around the constitution-making process and in preparation for both the parliamentary and presidential elections, when the United Nations outsourced its entire civic education effort to the ACSF with support from the International Foundation for Election Systems (IFES; Schmeidl 2007).

The government's National Solidarity Program, aimed at introducing democratic structures and values through elected Community Development Councils across Afghanistan's villages, represents the biggest socialization initiative post-2001. The program is implemented by international and Afghan NGOs, a handful of which have integrated conflict sensitivity into their general approaches. The general design, however, makes scant reference to peacebuilding, and the NSP can be seen as performing a more traditional function of socialization for democratization (Paffenholz and Spurk 2006, 30).

The conversion of the traditional *shuras* to development councils may substantially strengthen representation at the local level; this also serves to educate people about fundamental social and political rights and democratic processes. The objectives and the basic functioning of new *shuras,* however, are very different from those of old ones. The new councils are expected to be involved in the planning, implementation, and long-term administration of a variety of development projects in the community. Critics argue that the peacebuilding impact of NSP is marginal and that its impact may in fact be negative where local solidarity is weak or local tensions are prevalent (Zakhilwal and Thomas 2005). Yet, by 2009 it remained too early to judge how effective this program would be for peacebuilding in the long term and to what extent the NSP *shuras* will impact earlier power relations, values, and practices and promote a "culture of peace." Despite the introduction of the new development associations, many communities still maintain traditional types of *shuras* in which elders and religious authorities remain the most influential players. The reference to traditions, custom, and the sacred also means that socialization through traditional institutions is particularly strong. Religious CS actors and institutions retain considerable influence on moral values, social practices, and political opinions. Such influence may support peacebuilding, but it may at other times undermine it. In a conflict with divisions drawn along ethnic, religious, and political lines, in-group socialization—unless explicitly seeking to promote peaceful attitudes toward the "other"—can enhance rather than reduce differences.

Social Cohesion

Civil society can, of course, also contribute to create bridging social capital—or "good social capital," in Robert Putnam's (2002) terms. In the case of Afghan civil society, this implies strengthening links across tribal, ethnic, and regional divides, or between different religious schools and doctrines. In a country where adherence to the immediate solidarity group—often referred to as the *qaum*—remains of primary importance to most citizens, one of the effects of modernization and war has been the increasing relevance of larger-scale identity (Roy 1995). Within such a context, there has been limited room—particularly during active conflict phases—for modern civil society to contribute to social cohesion.

Under Taliban rule, Afghan peace-oriented NGOs worked on a local level but also concentrated on enhancing awareness in the aid community through training in "social peacebuilding" (i.e., awareness of conflict sensitivity, nonviolent conflict resolution, coexistence). The co-optation of religious civil society by the Taliban, widely perceived as a Pashtun movement, did little to enhance bridging ties between ethnic, political, and religious communities. *Shuras* and *jirgas* (consultative councils), however, are age-old mechanisms for conflict resolution and frequently address conflicts both within the community and at higher levels. In some cases, as in Jaghori district during the Taliban reign, trusted neutral mediators were used to create bridges between different local groups and between the local population and the Taliban (Suleman and Williams 2003).

After the Taliban, the climate for confidence-building initiatives changed considerably, and Afghan NGOs initiated a number of relationship-building activities.[33] Examples include peace education with a focus on coexistence, the establishment of peace committees and "peace *shuras,*" reconciliation initiatives between former enemies, and exchange visits between people from different identity groups. These initiatives are small in scale and impact. Moreover, there has been no mainstreaming of social cohesion measures in any of the main national development programs. Many modern CS actors promote a concept of "Afghanness" as a national identity, and several organizations focus on cultural activities, sports, and commerce that draw people together across erstwhile conflict lines. Yet, even within modern civil society, organizational patterns to a large extent are still drawn along ethnic, religious, and political lines.

Intermediation/Facilitation

The main role of traditional civil society lies in conflict resolution, particularly at the local level. The traditional *shuras* are primarily reactive bodies that address conflicts after they have erupted, seeking to limit their impacts in both time and space. During the Taliban reign, facilitation and mediation by Afghan civil society were particularly important, as room for official negotiations was constrained by the political standoff between the regime and much of the international community. Yet, as Hanif Atmar and Jonathan Goodhand (2002, 125) have pointed out, the effectiveness of both traditional and modern civil society entities was limited due to the absence of any coherent initiative at the central (or international) level. Local impacts may be important enough, but the idea that they may somehow self-aggregate to impact high politics is overly optimistic.

Neither the Taliban nor the mujahidin regimes were unitary entities, and access to the civilian population could be negotiated locally. Both modern and traditional CS organizations have functioned as mediators and facilitators, finding peaceful solutions to local conflicts. The *Afghanistan Human Development Report* (CPHD 2007, 9), devoted to the role of traditional actors in justice, states that more than 80 percent of all local conflicts are settled by traditional councils. CS entities also negotiate access to civilians with humanitarian assistance. The situation is not very different after 2001, when local civil society organizations demonstrated their ability to gain access to groups in which government or international actors are unwelcome. Afghan civil society has, however, had limited access to high-level international political forums and has very little influence on diplomatic Track 1 peace processes. This pattern still prevails after 2001, when both the government and international actors underline their willingness to engage in civil society even though their role in high politics remains largely symbolic.

The Afghanistan-Pakistan Peace Jirga held in Kabul in October 2007 was initially conceived to bring together the traditional civil society on both sides of the border as a step toward finding peaceful solutions to cross-border violent mobilization and conflict (Weitz 2007). By the time the 700-participant *jirga* took place, however, state-driven definitions of security had taken over; CS actors played only a secondary role.

A number of Afghan CS organizations are working to create new space for dialogue at the local level. One notable example is the Tribal Liaison Office (TLO), which conducts peace *jirgas* in the southeastern region, whereby religious and tribal leaders are brought together to discuss how local actors can contribute to end the conflict (TLO 2007). CS actors complain—perhaps not surprisingly—that their work is undermined by the government's unwillingness to heed agreements reached in these forums, which may ultimately compromise the credibility of the mediating organizations. The government, for its part, is skeptical of NGOs working in this field, in part because they are relating to antistate elements, and in part because they are subcontracted by other governments and their military contingents. TLO's work, for example, has been controversial, and the organization's permit was revoked by a government decree in early August 2008, on the grounds that it was engaged in suspicious activities contrary to government policy.[34] A different problem in this field is security, and with so many actors on the ground, obtaining the necessary security guarantees may be virtually impossible.

Service Delivery

In Afghanistan, "service delivery" is associated with the aid industry and the establishment of modern NGOs.[35] Under the Taliban, international actors were unwilling to channel relief through the regime. As a consequence, after the Taliban, the implementing capacity of the government has been an additional constraint. Throughout the Taliban's rule, Afghan NGOs played an important function in service delivery, mainly providing humanitarian assistance and, in some areas, basic services in health, education, and agriculture as well. The Taliban leadership had only marginal interest in providing welfare to citizens; its priorities were security, Islamic justice, and religious purification. Locally, many Taliban administrators recognized the population's need for humanitarian aid and thus allowed access to humanitarian aid agencies. This effort was fraught with tension. The Taliban wanted to steer aid to their own political purposes, donors introduced various conditions, and aid agencies both responded to and reported on Taliban excesses.

Although traditional CS actors are not commonly seen as "service providers," they have for a long time played an important part in local resource distribution and in providing social security and religious education. During the Taliban, religious educational institutions were supported in this function by foreign Islamic NGOs and charities. After 2001, religious civil society still plays a role in providing religious schooling and in redistributing resources. Redistribution of resources occurs through various Islamic practices for charity, such as *zakat* ("alms"), *ushr* ("tithe," or one-tenth of one's agricultural produce), and *wazifa* ("food donation").

At the time of writing, almost eight years after Bonn, NGOs continue to dominate service delivery. After years of neglecting state capacities, the NGO sector is seen by many international actors as the only efficient system in place and, moreover, as the best way to access local communities. In principle, service delivery may help form the foundations for other types of engagement, particularly when all other forms of intervention are likely to be unwelcome. Nevertheless, the limitations are severe. The insertion of external resources into a conflictual context always carries the potential of escalating tensions. In post-Bonn Afghanistan, many actors—not in charge of military operations—see aid as a political tool that can be used to sway the population. Under such circumstances it is very demanding to leverage service delivery as an entry point. Not only does it presuppose a certain political restraint on the part of other actors; it also requires of CS actors an extraordinary ability to act strategically and consistently.

The government, as well as international actors, commonly view NGOs as service providers operating in a private market, on a par with other private contractors, rather than as humanitarian actors who promote specific values and work according to defined codes of conduct rooted in popular participation and social mobilization. The demand on CS actors to engage in service delivery also diverts capacity and attention from core peacebuilding activities. The temptation is powerful, as service delivery is generously funded, and politically less challenging, than many other types of peacebuilding. Even programs designed specifically to enhance peace, including those where aid is only a means of entry, are often overtaken by the challenges of delivering services using the most effective means possible.

Conclusion

Afghan civil society has contributed significantly to peacebuilding in a number of domains, both during the Taliban reign and in the postintervention era. Modern and traditional civil society have filled different and often complementary functions. At the same time, a number of constraining factors stand out.

Under the Taliban, the space for CS engagement was limited. The regime was generally hostile to modern CS entities; traditional entities were to a large extent co-opted. Institutionally, the Taliban regime lacked the capacity to engage systematically in any dialogue with civil society. The repressive character of the regime—including threats, arbitrary arrests, and infiltration—meant severe restrictions.

Nevertheless, civil society performed important functions, especially advocacy and monitoring. During the reign of the Taliban, the monitoring and advocacy functions were mutually reinforcing, and collaboration with international CS groups was critical for reaching out. These have become some of the most common and most effective peacebuilding functions performed by modern Afghan civil society. Service delivery was also a key function under the Taliban, particularly for NGOs, which—despite the Taliban's limited enthusiasm for welfare policy—found this to be a legitimate niche. Intermediation was important at the local level given the localized nature of the conflict. Yet, in the absence of a comprehensive process, intermediation had minimal impact at the macro level. Protection was, on a limited scale, provided by traditional civil society, but it was largely seen by modern actors as too risky. The effectiveness of socialization was limited given the repressive political climate. Similarly, efforts at fostering social cohesion, few in number, also had limited impact in a political climate where ethnic, religious, and regional fault lines were deepening.

In the post-2001 context, the space for CS engagement has widened considerably, not least as a result of international support. The consecutive administrations led by Hamid Karzai have taken an ambiguous position on civil society, relying on it to reach out to citizens while seeking to constrain its political role. Service delivery has become the key function, with NGOs—at times in synergy with *shuras*—used as implementers of key government programs. Counting on service delivery as the ideal starting point for broader engagement proved overly optimistic; the heavy engagement that service delivery requires diverts scarce personnel resources from more direct peacebuilding activities. Parts of modern civil society have also played a significant role in socialization, particularly in education programs prior to the elections and the adoption of the new constitution. Similarly, some CS actors pursue monitoring and advocacy objectives, greatly helped by new media, yet continue to find that their actual impact on high-level politics is limited. The same is the case for attempts at intermediation, where civil society initiatives are seen with increasing skepticism by a government that tries to assert political control. The protection role—for example, on the issue of civilian casualties in the war—has been challenging. The actors involved find that their interventions, although welcomed, have but little effect. Fostering social cohesion has proven difficult for all parts of civil society, which is itself affected by the divisions that characterize Afghan society at large. Escalating warfare, political tensions, and a weak government administration—all are factors that contribute to constraining the peacebuilding impacts of civil society.

We have argued for an inclusive definition of Afghan civil society, one that encompasses not only modern forms of association but also traditional forms. This enables us to see a civil society that has proven its resilience and adaptability under rapidly shifting conditions. On the traditional side, the limited engagement of religious actors represents a large untapped potential; it is also possibly detrimental given that these actors have considerable legitimacy as well as a capacity for concerted action beyond the local level. *Shuras,* in contrast, are engaged as conduits for services, becoming semimodernized in the process. Although *shuras* are effective at the local level, they depend on a coordinating mechanism to be effective at a national level. Modern entities—such as the NGOs emerging in the 1980s—often lack resonance at the local level; this lack of a real constituency is a threat to both their accountability and their survival. Currently, *shura*-NGO collaborations are commonplace for service delivery, with some playing a role for other functions as well. Such synergies across the traditional-modern divide seem particularly effective in overcoming the challenges that each faces alone and possibly suggest a model that can be refined and adapted, not only for a more expansive role in Afghanistan but also in other contexts. This would require a comprehensive concept of civil society, in addition to a critical examination of how power is distributed in synergistic relationships that span traditional-modern divides.

Notes

We are grateful for the financial support of the Norwegian Ministry of Foreign Affairs to conduct this work. We are also deeply grateful to all those who volunteered their time to be interviewed for this study, who will remain anonymous. We have received comments on earlier drafts of this chapter from John Darby, Jérôme Gouzou, Jolyon Leslie, Alessandro Monsutti, Thania Paffenholz, Barnett R. Rubin, and Susanne Schmeidl. The full responsibility for the contents of the chapter, of course, remains with the authors.

1. A total of twenty-three interviews were conducted specifically for this study, with Afghan and international observers of Afghan civil society, in Kabul and London during October 2007.

2. Other political groups, such as the Maoist-oriented Shula-e Jawed and the secular social-democratic Afghan Millat, were not granted recognition by the authorities in Pakistan, on whom the resistance depended for sanctuary, and were therefore also cut off from international support.

3. According to some scholars (Atmar and Goodhand 2001), "the primary peacemaking role has been assumed by the UN, which operates in Afghanistan without either major collaboration or competition from other inter-governmental organizations."

4. The main ones are Cooperation for Peace and Unity (CPAU), the Sanayee Development Organization (SDO), and the Afghan Development Foundation (ADA)—all still working in Afghanistan. A series of workshops and training sessions was held by international entities: Responding to Conflict (RTC), Birmingham; the Post-War Development and Reconstruction Unit (PRDU) at the University of York; and the Collaborative for Development Action (CDA), Cambridge, Massachusetts. Norwegian Church Aid, operating as a locally based donor agency in partnership with Afghan NGOs, was instrumental in promoting and funding these initiatives.

5. According to the International Crisis Group, "The UN has justified the absence of a fuller public process with three concerns—security for members of the Constitutional Commission and the public, the risk that the process might be hijacked by extremist groups, and the danger of public confusion" (ICG 2003, i).

6. Also, the lack of implementation capacity has been a major constraint, as have security problems in parts of the country. The internal inequalities are great both from one region to another, and between, on the one hand, the predominantly rural majority that is poor, largely illiterate, and often traditionalist in outlook and, on the other hand, a small, urban, educated, and modernized elite.

7. On the conceptualization of civil society in Afghanistan, see Atmar and Goodhand (2002); Harpviken, Strand, and Ask (2002); and Ludin (2002).

8. For more on diasporas, see Brinkerhoff (2004); Braakman and Schlenkhoff (2007); and Monsutti (2008).

9. These are registering with the Ministry of Justice as "social organizations" and can be seen as an "indigenized" type of modern civil society organization.

10. There are several coordinating bodies for NGOs, most of them set up in the aid environment of Pakistan in the 1980s and 1990s, such as the Agency Coordinating Body for Afghan Relief (ACBAR), the Afghan National Coordination Bureau (ANCB), and the Afghan Women's Network (AWN). Other coordination bodies active in Pakistan in the 1980s, such as the Islamic Coordination Council (ICC), have closed down.

11. In terms of size, scope, and organizational development, modern Afghan civil society has grown considerably since 2001. A total of 1,119 civil society organizations (registered and unregistered) were identified by a civil society baseline survey carried out by the Foundation for Culture and Civil Society (FCCS) from 2004 to 2006. In the same period, 190 NGOs were registered with the Ministry of Planning (FCCS 2007). In comparison, there were 206 Afghan NGOs (defined as "an NGO established by Afghans and working in Afghanistan or with Afghan refugees in Pakistan and/or Iran") registered as members of coordination bodies in 1999 (Strand et al. 1999).

12. Used interchangeably with *jirga,* the traditional Pashtu term for consultative councils and assemblies in Afghanistan. *Shura* is the Arabic term, which has increasingly become the one in common usage for "community councils."

13. NSP designs draw heavily on the World Bank's experience with community-driven development.

14. Based on the local councils, the template includes *shuras* at district and province levels, but they have been slow to evolve, and their mandate in relation to other institutions at the same levels remains unclear. The NGOs are not well positioned to serve as a "scaling-up" mechanism for local development councils, both because various NGOs are responsible for implementing the program in different parts of the country and because the government structure—with which they should work closely—is incoherent and institutionally weak.

15. In contrast to neighboring Pakistan and Iran, which both have well-established religious charity sectors, there are few formalized Islamic charity organizations in Afghanistan.

16. Undoubtedly, the Taliban leadership was quickly corrupted by the power it had, and external backers—particularly various Pakistani actors—quickly got involved in supporting the movement and affecting its agenda. Related to this was the fact that the Taliban was from day one a movement willing to threaten with, and use, violence, which by many definitions excludes it from civil society.

17. Post-2001 Afghanistan is marked by new experiences and ideas challenging traditional ways of life. Tensions between modern-liberal values and more conservative-religious ones are at the root of many political confrontations. The 2005 case of an Afghan convert to Christianity—first sentenced to death—who was saved by an Afghan president under heavy international pressure is widely referred to as an example of undue external interference (Wardak, Zaman, and Nawabi 2007, 42). The Taliban leadership also plays on what they frame as a Western-inspired treason of Islamic values in their efforts to gain political support.

18. Another example of "uncivil" elements might be the National Rifle Association in the United States, which may think it is speaking for the "common good" but, on the contrary, may represent highly contested values (Carothers and Barndt 2000).

19. We are grateful to Alessandro Monsutti for raising this point.

20. According to some scholars (Atmar and Goodhand 2002, 127), "One of the primary sources of Afghan leadership has been held in 'cold storage' during the war years, within the NGO sector." Haneef Atmar (previously with Norwegian Church Aid and the International Rescue Committee) is a key minister in Karzai's cabinet.

21. The two main laws are the Islamic Republic of Afghanistan's Law on Non-Governmental Organizations Law (Official Gazette 2005) and the Islamic Republic of Afghanistan's Social Organizations Law (Official Gazette 2002).

22. There are exceptions, of course. Many of the new youth organizations, particularly those in urban areas, have good gender representation (ASCF/AYCA 2005).

23. This is nothing new in the history of Afghanistan; the PDPA government in Afghanistan (1978–1992) pursued both the strategies of co-opting existing organizations and creating new ones that were loyal to the state (Ludin 2002). The *ulama* have regularly been paid to be the "eyes and ears" of the government since the late 1800s. Amir Abdur Rahman (1880–1901) introduced a religious police force to check that religious leaders preached the official version of Islam (Ghani 1978). The PDPA's intelligence services, KHAD, covertly distributed instructions for Friday prayers (Dorronsoro 2005, 179).

24. To counter the criticism and to demonstrate the commitment of NGOs, an NGO "code of conduct" was launched by the NGO coordination body ACBAR in Kabul in 2005.

25. The compensation for equipping soldiers—the *basij*—was also a financial burden on the community and its families, but it did not have to send its young men to war. The payment of *basij* was also practiced in areas, mainly those inhabited by non-Pashtuns, where the regime had little trust in the locals.

26. Earlier successful demining operations were already brought to a halt due to the military action in 2001–2002. The mine-action infrastructure suffered greatly during the subsequent military conflict, as some warring factions looted offices, seized vehicles and equipment, and assaulted local staff (ICBL 2002).

27. The Revolutionary Association of the Women of Afghanistan (RAWA), with its clandestine networks, shot films, smuggled them out of the country, and made them available to global TV networks. The film *Beneath the Veil,* including the British-Iranian reporter Saira Shah, documents this.

28. AIHRC was established by presidential decree in 2001. Being semigovernmental, however, its structural independence is questioned.

29. In 2008 the official UN International Day of Peace was marked by a cease-fire between the national and international military and the Taliban and celebrated across Afghanistan. This, however, was a UN-led affair with civil society participation.

30. Examples of work with traditional *shuras* include the Tribal Liaisons Office and the Foundation for Culture and Civil Society (FCCS).

31. Cooperation for Peace and Unity and the Sanayee Development Organization, for example, have been engaging long-term with local communities, setting up local peace *shuras* and working with them to strengthen their capacity for peaceful conflict resolution.

32. The government's Action Plan on Peace, Reconciliation, and Justice (Islamic Republic of Afghanistan 2006a) states the intention to include peace and reconciliation messages in the national curriculum, but the Ministry of Education's four-year strategy (Islamic Republic of Afghanistan 2006b) makes no direct reference to this.

33. The main protagonists were the Afghan Civil Society Forum, Cooperation for Peace and Unity, the Foundation for Culture and Civil Society, the Sanayee Development Organization, and the Tribal Liaison Office.

34. This decision was taken in the cabinet meeting on August 11, 2008.

35. Prominent examples are the Afghanistan Development Association, the Agency for Rehabilitation and Energy Conservation in Afghanistan, the Afghan Women's Education Center, the Afghan Women's Resource Center, and Co-ordination of Humanitarian Assistance.

12

Nepal: From Conflict to Consolidating a Fragile Peace

Rhoderick Chalmers

Nepal is emerging from a decade-long armed conflict that killed more than 13,000 of its citizens. The Maoist rebels who launched an insurgency in 1996 entered a peace process ten years later and, in an April 2008 election, won the seats in the constituent assembly that they had long demanded.[1] The transition from nationwide armed conflict to a negotiated settlement, managed largely by domestic actors and without formal outside mediation or peacekeeping, is justly claimed as a significant achievement.[2] Civil society organizations and leaders played a number of roles in the process, from maintaining pressure on both warring parties to restore democracy and protect human rights to assisting, through public advocacy and private facilitation, the delicate negotiations that achieved a settlement. However, the peace is not yet stable, and the longer-term project of peacebuilding is entering a new phase with its own new risks. Central issues of the Maoist-state conflict remain to be resolved, even though the Maoists now lead the government. Not least, there has been no progress on deciding the future of the two armed forces, which have abided by a bilateral cease-fire but remain at loggerheads over the question of whether they can or should be integrated. Meanwhile, new conflicts have arisen as smaller armed groups—criminal outfits and freshly invigorated identity-based movements—have made the most of the weaknesses of the transitional state. With contributions from civil society, the mainstream parties have reconciled themselves to accommodating identity-based political aspirations, but they have yet to translate this recognition into programmatic form.

In this chapter I assess the role of Nepali civil society at various stages of the conflict, as well as its response to the challenges of the transition following the cease-fire. I argue that four major factors have affected civil society's peacebuilding role: the nature and shape of the conflict, the structure of civil society itself, the relationship between the civil and political spheres, and the relationship with international donors and their agendas.

CS actors occupied an occasionally critical, but often fraught, position in national political space during the conflict. Hit hard by restrictions and intimidation from armed actors on both sides (on the state side, particularly under states of emergency), CS society activists nevertheless acted as a fulcrum in the transition from intense conflict to a negotiated settlement. When political parties struggled to respond to the royal coup of February 2005—and the Maoists suffered a debilitating internal split—it was civil society pressure that paved the way for talks that hammered out a roadmap for conflict settlement. Still, CS actors were always constrained by the character of the Nepali state, which under successive governments remained centralist, unaccountable, and unwilling to respond to public pressure. Similarly, it was only during the post-royal coup political upheaval that civil society voices had a significant impact on the powerful external players, most notably India, which exerted significant influence on all sides. Perhaps most important, political parties that were keen to accept civil society support in the campaign for restoring democracy have proved extremely reluctant to take on board the messages about greater inclusiveness and transparency that activists had repeatedly underlined in constructive criticism.

Although this chapter draws on a range of published sources, the data and observations, which underpin its analysis, are based primarily on several years of continuous field research in Nepal. Resident in Nepal for most of the conflict period, from the start of 2004 the author was engaged full-time in conflict research and analysis. Both in the capital and in the course of travel across most of Nepal's seventy-five districts, he has had the opportunity to conduct hundreds of interviews with actors in all sectors of Nepal's civil society, as well as with political leaders, donors, and academic experts.

Context

Sandwiched between China and India, Nepal has a population of some 28 million spread along the central belt of the Himalayas from the high mountains to the Tarai Plains on the Indian border. The country's people are diverse—speaking more than 100 languages and encompassing different religions, ethnicities, and Hindu caste communities—and, on the whole, extremely poor. Nepal ranks near the bottom of the human development indexes.[3]

The country was unified in the late eighteenth century, when King Prithvinarayan Shah used military force and diplomacy to consolidate dozens of small principalities in the face of the British East India Company's advance. A war with the British in 1814–1816 cut Nepal's borders back to more or less their current extent but left it nominally independent, albeit subject to significant indirect control from British India.

The nineteenth century saw the development of many enduring characteristics of the state, first under Prithvinarayan's heirs and, from 1846, under a dynasty of hereditary prime ministers—the Ranas—who usurped power from the Shahs while retaining them as titular figureheads. Both Shahs and Ranas considered the land that they governed primarily as personal property to be valued for what an extractive state could earn from it.

By the 1940s, Nepalis were edging toward the start of a democracy movement. In the wake of Indian independence, the Nepali Congress (NC) and the Communist Party of Nepal (Maoists), known by the acronym CPN(M), were founded with the aim of overthrowing Rana rule. With the cooperation of the Shahs, who had a shared interest in freeing themselves from a century-old subjugation, an NC-led movement achieved this in the winter of 1950–1951. However, a tripartite Shah-Rana-NC deal put together by the Indian government in Delhi delivered almost a decade of instability. When the first general election delivered an NC landslide, King Tribhuvan's successor, King Mahendra, decided that he was not so keen on democracy after all. In December 1960, eighteen months into the first parliament's tenure, he ordered a military coup to return power to the palace. With a new 1962 constitution, he instituted a form of partyless autocracy branded "Panchayat," after the name of traditional village councils that offered a form of democracy "suited to Nepal's soil."

Under Panchayat rule, the state modernized itself in some respects, in particular by embracing a developmentalist agenda and drawing in foreign aid. However, its stunted political growth built up pressure, which in 1990 erupted in the form of a people's movement that restored multiparty democracy and forced the king into a relatively tight constitutional straitjacket. Relatively effective authoritarian rule had also successfully kept a lid on ethnic and caste tensions, while ensuring that the nature of national identity and political representation was never open to serious public questioning. Yet, the refusal to acknowledge social and cultural diversity was storing up problems for what one prominent academic and activist has termed the "predatory unitary Hindu state" (Bhattachan 2000).

State and Conflict

The NC found itself back in power following a convincing win in the 1991 general election. It pursued the development agenda with some success but also embedded features of governance and politics that kept the ground fertile for further conflict.[4] Political parties and state institutions remained in the hands of a small, largely male and high-caste, elite.[5] The political system was marked by patronage and clientelism, nepotism and corruption—as were the bureaucracy, judiciary, and security forces and, indeed, much of the private sector.[6] Politics as such flourished: for most ordinary citizens, parties and members of parliament are the first resort for assistance in the absence of basic government services; some party affiliation, even if not active participation, is a necessary form of social insurance. With a rapid expansion in communications and the birth of a lively free press, Nepal developed a vibrant, if flawed, political culture. Basic human rights were constitutionally guaranteed, even if the state's long habit of exercising power without transparency or accountability made their safeguarding in practice less certain. Despite progress in some areas such as local governance and infrastructure, the major indicators of development did not rise dramatically above their traditionally low levels. A period of instability after the 1994 fall of the NC government (brought down by an internal split) left plenty of space for opponents of the system to operate. Inequality had grown, and large sections of the population still felt marginalized by Kathmandu and its ruling classes.

The Maoists launched their "people's war" in February 1996, ostensibly because of the government's failure to respond to a set of forty demands, but in fact it was a premeditated strategy.[7] The Maoist agenda was to overthrow what they characterized as a semifeudal, semicolonial regime and to institute in its place a socialist state.[8] The rebel heartlands were neglected rural districts, particularly in the midwestern part of the country, heavily populated by ethnic groups that had traditionally been non-Nepali-speaking and non-Hindu. These were not Nepal's poorest districts (one of the clearest reminders that underdevelopment alone is an inadequate causal explanation for the insurgency), but they were areas where there was enough education, exposure to the outside world, and political activism for there to be no dearth of recruits. The Maoists' target was the state: they aimed to weaken it, roll back the bounds of its control, and supplant it—first in rural areas and then in the center. The state itself was disunited. The major parties in power were divided; they were also constrained by their unresolved power struggle with an assertive palace that retained command of the army. At its simplest, the conflict was triangular, but there were further complexities, from quiet tensions between the palace and army to the disruptive capacity of new armed groups in the Tarai Plains. Ever present—though rarely discussed in direct terms—were the immense influence and sometimes direct intervention of powerful external players, in particular India.

In comparison to the shifting and highly populated political scenario, Maoist strategy was simple. First they networked, recruited, trained, and planned: the launch of a viable war would not have been possible without years—decades for most of the leaders—of quiet mobilizing and preparation. Then they attacked the soft parts of the state in rural areas, picking off isolated police posts one by one, threatening and influencing village and district officials, stealing cash and weapons, and extorting donations. But not neglecting politics: their violence was almost never random, and their efforts to move among the people and win their support were in most respects genuine—though undercut by the casual brutality with which they sometimes sought to create shortcuts. As they picked up organizational strength, political momentum, and military capacity, they expanded rapidly out of their far-flung hill hideouts until they held sway over much of the country.

The Maoists sought control of people, not territory, so the battle for them was to supplant the state's authority and legitimacy, not to defend front lines drawn on a map. Resources and commodities did not lie at the heart of the conflict, although economic factors were relevant, including the inequalities that helped fuel it; the basic self-interest that encouraged businesspeople to do deals with the warring parties; the growth of the remittance economy as a safety valve; and India's huge interest in natural resources as, ultimately, an incentive for enough stability to deliver a functional central government able to sign deals.

Formal attempts at peace negotiations took place in 2001 and 2003, with neither reaching agreement. It was the royal coup of February 2005, in which the king dismissed a multiparty government to seize complete power, that acted as the main catalyst for peace by reconfiguring the triangular deadlock. King Gyanendra's intransigence encouraged the mainstream parties (and, crucially, India) to explore the possibility of an alliance with the Maoists to restore democracy and end the conflict. Months of off-and-on dialogue in Delhi resulted in a twelve-point agreement between the grouping of seven mainstream parties and the Communist Party of Nepal (Maoists), CPN(M). This agreement committed both sides to collaborating to end the autocratic monarchy, enter a cease-fire, and elect a constituent assembly to write a new constitution reshaping the state. The twelve-point agreement was the basis for a mass popular uprising against royal rule that lasted for nineteen days in April 2006 until the capitulation of the king. It then took a further seven months for the parties to negotiate the Comprehensive Peace Agreement (CPA), which was signed that November.

A full year after the people's movement, the Maoists finally joined the interim government that the twelve-point agreement had envisaged. By this stage, a United Nations mission had been established, at the request of the government and Maoists, to oversee the two armies (the Maoists' People's Liberation Army [PLA] had entered cantonments), to assist in preparations for the constituent assembly elections, and to monitor the progress of the peace process. After many false starts, elections went ahead successfully in April 2008, delivering a surprise Maoist victory: the CPN(M) did not achieve an absolute majority but won 40 percent of the seats, twice as many as its nearest rival, the NC (International Crisis Group 2008). In August 2008, Maoist chairman Pushpa Kamal Dahal ("Prachanda") was elected by the assembly to lead a coalition government. The NC refused to join; the CPN(M)'s major partners were the moderate communist UML and the Madhesi Janadhikar Forum (MJF), the Tarai regional party. The latter owed its strength to the most distinctive feature of the post–cease-fire phase—the emergence of vigorous identity politics that changed the balance of party power and gave birth to new armed outfits and conflict risk.

Phases of Armed Conflict

Periodization is not a straightforward task. Nevertheless, the following phases offer a useful guide for analyzing the different functions of civil society through the conflict.

The preconflict phase. Many features of the conflict were conditioned by events in the immediately preceding years. The weaknesses of the 1990 constitution, which shared power between the monarchy and the parliamentary parties, were seized upon by the Maoists and became a central negotiating platform as they demanded a new constitution (International Crisis Group 2005). The generally weak respect for the rule of law and obstacles to checking, or seeking redress for, state abuses were a natural continuation of the history of the Nepali state. With very few exceptions, since its inception it had been unaccountable to citizens and barely limited by constitutional or other legal provisions.[9]

1996–2001. Most Kathmandu-based political leaders and opinionmakers were slow to acknowledge the potential for nationwide conflict and treated the insurgency as a relatively minor irritant. The formation of a high-level government panel of inquiry in 1999 was the first recognition that resolving it would require much more thinking. The 1999–2001 period saw an intensification of conflict on both sides. The Maoists organized their small guerrilla forces into a more systematic military outfit, the PLA. The government, unable to deploy the army in the face of palace reluctance, formed the counterinsurgency Armed Police Force (APF). Although the first rounds of negotiations in early 2001 enabled both sides to consider the options for dialogue, they did not come close to a deal. Finally, the June 2001 royal massacre (in which King Birendra and his entire branch of the Shah dynasty were killed) brought Gyanendra to the throne.

2001–2005. November 2001 marked the start of full civil war. The Maoists attacked an army barracks in the midwest, bringing the Royal Nepalese Army (RNA) into the conflict. The first national state of emergency marked the militarization of the state response and severely undermined basic human rights. These events were natural precursors to the palace assuming a more active political role. With the army ascendant and, in May 2002, parliament dissolved, the stage was set for democracy to be sidelined. The king's dismissal of the prime minister in October 2002 was the start of a slow march toward direct royal rule; despite initially encouraging signals, a further attempt at talks in 2003 was almost certainly doomed to failure. Apart from the growing militarization on both sides, the changed post-9/11 international environment encouraged outside powers to categorize the Maoists as terrorists and prompted coordinated military aid to the state. This led to a doubling in size of the RNA and further marginalization of the democratic parties. However, there was increasing evidence of a military stalemate: the RNA could not uproot the Maoists or significantly weaken their sway over the countryside, yet the rebels could not permanently control territory or launch a decisive assault on the well-defended capital.

February 2005–April 2006. The single most productive shift in the political landscape came with King Gyanendra's ill-advised coup of February 2005. Although already in de facto control of state affairs, in particular through his exclusive control of the army, Gyanendra wanted overt power. In this he was probably encouraged by RNA assurances that sidelining the weak-willed democrats would enable it to force the Maoists to sue for peace on the palace's terms. However, such plans were overoptimistic: the army had no strategy to win hearts and minds and managed little on the military front beyond digging in behind effective defenses in urban areas.[10] At the same time, the king's move pushed the alienated parties into talks with the Maoists. The international community was largely unimpressed by the return to royal autocracy; India quietly supported the framing of a November 2005 twelve-point agreement between the parties and the Maoists. Slow-burning popular resentment (which had been brewing ever since the 2001 royal massacre, in which most people suspected Gyanendra had a hand) soon translated into street protests. Nineteen days of nationwide mass demonstrations in April 2006 forced the king to return power to the parties and accept their roadmap for peace—a roadmap that by now included joining hands with the Maoists to rewrite the constitution.

April 2006 onward. The end of royal rule paved the way for a prompt bilateral cease-fire and lengthy negotiations leading to the CPA in November 2006. After some months' delay, an interim legislature-parliament and, later, an interim government incorporating significant CPN(M) representation were formed. Following two postponements, constituent assembly elections took place in April 2008. The new assembly abolished the monarchy at its first sitting and declared Nepal a federal democratic republic; the Maoists, who had emerged as the largest party, with more than one-third of the seats, eventually formed a coalition government in August 2008. The 2007–2008 period was, however, characterized by the emergence of new forms of conflict and instability, particularly in the Tarai Plains. Madhesi communities on the plains bordering India had historically been marginalized in national life and seized the opportunity to demand that the peace and constitutional processes address their long-standing grievances. Small armed outfits mushroomed, some claiming political agendas (largely regionalist or ethnic-based) and some simply exploiting the state's inability to provide basic services and maintain law and order. Nonviolent protest movements and campaigns for political representation also burgeoned, with members of other marginalized communities determined to ensure their voices were heard. The settlement of the Maoist conflict had exposed the wider rifts in society, and it remains unclear how successfully national political leaders, and the constituent assembly, can address them.

Phases of Peacebuilding

Building a sustainable peace called for not only the cessation of armed conflict but also structural changes to the state and governance as well as deeper reform of inequitable socioeconomic relations. Short-term mitigation efforts, such as pressing for better protection of civilians, could not be entirely separated from longer-term measures to address the root causes of the conflict. And whereas the CPN(M) had a vision for what such measures might look like, the mainstream parties had shaped themselves around the status quo and representing the interests of those who profited from it: a change of course would have required more boldness than they could summon.[11] Initially, a negotiated peace process was implausible. The Maoists were not strong enough to come to the table with realistic hopes of securing gains; the state was ill-prepared to tackle political issues underlying the conflict. Civil society helped facilitate two attempts at formal talks, in 2001 and 2003. Although neither came close to a successful conclusion, they demonstrated that dialogue was possible and enabled both sides to refine their negotiating stances.

The critical peacebuilding phase came when prominent CS players entered the political realm. Following King Gyanendra's February 2005 coup, it was civil society that led resistance to royal autocracy. While mobilizing popular pressure on the streets, CS figures quietly helped pave the way for the twelve-point agreement. In the more complex post–peace agreement environment, the political aspects of peacebuilding are likely to remain fraught. Contributing to democratization and trying to eliminate some of the original causes of the conflict will necessarily involve civil society remaining active in "political" areas. Peacebuilding will mean helping state and society to move forward in a difficult atmosphere conditioned by multiple small rebellions, heightened identity politics, and unresolved elements of the main peace deal.

Status of Civil Society

Civil society is relatively new terminology in Nepal and has come to be associated almost exclusively with new forms of individual activity and organizations, in particular NGOs.[12] Some observers argue that civil society itself, not just the nomenclature, only recently came into being.[13]

Early History

However, early forms of civil society include associations such as *guthis* (social and religious voluntary associations, which maintain temples and communal facilities or provide mutual assistance), as well as more distinctly modern undertakings such as local *pathshalas* ("basic schools") and library associations. Such activities started even under the Ranas but differed in some important ways from later understandings of civil society association.[14] As one leading political scientist suggests (Khanal 2004, 73), Nepal's historically weak central governance meant that community-based associations such as *guthis* assumed de facto governance roles: "The practice of an open assembly of village people . . . and deliberation on various issues concerning the members of the community and the village has a long tradition. In fact, these traditions have provided grounds and the basis for shaping up the local leadership in Nepal."[15] Language- and culture-related efforts were also suspect; a few were grudgingly offered government backing, but none were the result of deliberate state policy. Some organizations focused on uplifting individual groups, such as the Tharu Welfare Society (founded in 1949, near the end of Rana rule), but these were few and far between.[16] As with party politics, and to a far greater degree, much initial development happened among Nepalis resident in India.[17]

Within Nepal, the changing nature of state power and the stuttering progress toward democracy naturally shaped the development of civil society movements. The chaotic, but relatively open, 1950s interlude showed how much suppressed desire for civil organization and engagement there was. This was not only in terms of political parties (although they gained strength and support remarkably quickly), but also in areas such as cultural and regional rights: in the Tarai Plains a vigorous campaign for the recognition of Hindi as an official language emerged (Gaige 1975), and in the eastern hills Limbus also pressed for language rights and better educational facilities (Chemjong 2003). The fact that such movements sprang up almost immediately on the collapse of Rana control strongly suggests that they were already present in embryonic form.[18] The 1950s also showed that there was an urge and capacity to develop a free press and broader public debate. Most of these moves were, not surprisingly, halted by the strictures of Panchayat rule, which sought instead to impose its own unitary narrative of national identity. Nevertheless, the spread of formal education and direct and indirect exposure to the outside world molded the building blocks of post-1990 civil society.

The Composition of Nepali Civil Society

Although the conflict brought significant challenges, the context within which contemporary civil society started to operate has been generally positive. A young independent media sector has rapidly developed and contributed to fostering an informed public debate. The state has great regulatory powers over NGOs but tends to be either too liberal or too weak to use them restrictively.[19] The pioneers of human rights advocacy have established a solid sense of the rights and space that should be accorded to NGO/CS actors and have been vocal in reminding authorities of their limits. In this, the media has generally been a positive additional influence; its shared interests in protecting its own freedoms overlap with broader civil society goals. The conflict did, however, threaten civic action. The Maoists were often suspicious of independent social activists, viewing them as political opponents or potential agents for other parties or the security forces. Successive governments had similar suspicions, and the post–February 2005 royal regime made a point of detaining CS activists at the least sign of trouble (a habit that even post–April 2006 governments did not shake off entirely).

Civil society reflects the positive and negative aspects of society at large—including its vertical and horizontal divisions and the sometimes productive, sometimes challenging interaction of traditional and modern values and forms of social organization and civic behavior.[20] In general, "civil society" is seen to encompass influential individuals and associations, primarily NGOs but also organizations such as unions and professional associations. If civil society exists independently, it does so in complex, sometimes controversial relationships to the political sphere and donor agendas.[21] Participation is hard to gauge. Although large networks, such as those of community forest user groups, involve millions of individuals, active involvement in other organizations may be much lower.[22]

Individuals. Prominent individual activists are, for most people, the public face of civil society. They come from diverse backgrounds, including politics, media, the bureaucracy, the arts, and various professions. Some have built organizations, single-handedly or in coalition, but others maintain a public profile by dint of their own background. The latter include such diverse figures as popular film actors, singers, and poets to dedicated single-issue campaigners, intellectuals, and writers.

NGOs. Many thousands of NGOs are active in various fields.[23] The majority cite "development" as their main objective; those focused on human rights, social development, and other rights-based approaches are often seen as forming part of civil society, especially if they concentrate on advocacy alongside, or to the exclusion of, operational activities. The debate over the extent to which NGOs embody civil society and how their performance affects public perceptions remains lively (see, e.g., Ghimire 2008). Major donors often use *civil society* and *NGOs* as near-synonyms, with the added complication of a further category of associations, community-based organizations (CBOs), which may or may not include registered NGOs.[24]

Professional associations. Some formal associations are consistently active and vocal (such as journalists' and lawyers' groups), and other professional groups have occasionally played a high-profile social/political role—for example, doctors in the 1990 democracy movement (Maskey 1998). Conversely, some of the most powerful professional classes have been notable for their near-invisibility. This is particularly the case, ironically, for the very development professionals who have done the most to institutionalize the terminology of civil society and its NGO/project-driven formations. Development professionals were even slower than government bureaucrats to join the April 2006 people's movement. Some actors who fall under the CS umbrella have a track record of using uncivil methods, including violence. This has sometimes been the case with trade unions (which are also party-affiliated). Under the Panchayat system, state sports institutions were used to train and remunerate thugs, known as *mandales,* who were deployed to harass prodemocracy activists; some sports clubs are still alleged to provide hired muscle for political purposes.[25]

Religious and traditional associations. Civil society includes religious organizations, from traditional Newar *guthis* and those overlapping with the state given their formal registration by the Guthi Sansthan to entirely new outfits representing minority religions. These, like other local initiatives, often draw on the strong tradition of contributing labor and in-kind support to community projects. Indeed, the social institutions of many Nepali communities have a redistributive and mutually supportive nature. The better-off are expected to fund public religious celebrations, feasts, and local infrastructure efforts. A complex network of social obligations underlies much intra- and intercommunity organization.

Community/special interest. There are a multitude of ethnic/regional/caste–based cultural and rights-based organizations. Trade unions have also proliferated, although (as mentioned above) they are hard to class as civil society given their affiliation with political parties. A more productive area of growth has been the various self-help and support groups, working in fields such as HIV/AIDS; disability rights; and lesbian, gay, and transgender issues.

User groups. On the borderline of civil society stand mass-membership national community networks, in particular the community forest user groups, which manage large tracts of forest and have a membership numbering in the millions.[26] Such groups are not purely CS organizations. However, they occupy an interesting position—state-sanctioned and regulated but standing formally outside the state—and certainly have encouraged systematic civic engagement outside the political sphere. Forest user groups not only maintained functional resource management structures during the conflict but also preserved one form of participatory local governance at a time when other forms of authority had largely collapsed. The development of handing state schools to community management, partly inspired by the success of forest user groups, also raises questions over the boundaries between government and community control.

Academia. Organized academia was traditionally under exclusive state control: there were a few early private schools but no nonstate universities until the 1990s. Academics were naturally restricted in the scope of their civic engagement by the political discipline that governments imposed on their institutions and work. Nevertheless, their role should not be overlooked, if only because academics form the backbone of media commentators and analysts and therefore contribute to the development of ideas and debates within civil society, as well as acting as a critical watchdog to the political process. Meanwhile, the post-1990 period saw the emergence of active intellectual/academic/discussion–based organizations such as Martin Chautari and the Social Science Baha. These have fed into broader public culture, fostering debate on social and political issues. Last, many people, including journalists, see the non-state-owned media (including both for-profit commercial media and community-run radio stations) as one wing of civil society.

Organizations and networks. Many NGOs and other associations are still led by traditionally dominant groups; many are also justifiably accused of being family businesses, with boards packed with relatives. There has not been a good balance of gender and youth representation, except in organizations specifically devoted to women's or youth issues.[27] NGOs are subject to legal requirements to hold regular board meetings, audit accounts, elect officeholders, and so on, but this does not appear in practice to have made them as democratic as intended. Many organizations, especially NGOs, depend on external financial support, but there remains a strong tradition of local fund-raising for community projects. Membership across social cleavages is not a notable feature of most CS organizations.[28] Instead, separate organizations have emerged to represent marginalized groups and serve their interests, both practically and with advocacy. The divide between the Madhesis of the plains and the hill-origin *pahadis* became particularly apparent when the Madhesi movement took off in early 2007: none of the major NGOs involved in human rights and peacebuilding had significant Madhesi representation. Indeed, some had no Madhesi district or regional head even in their Tarai district offices.[29]

Nepali civil society draws on a variety of existing domestic and international networks. The nature of such networks inherently privileges people in certain positions, both geographically (as no significant network fails to run through the capital, which is inevitably the most important nodal point), in terms of access (to political or donor power centers and, thereby, to funding, etc.), and in relation to other forms of hierarchy, such as class and caste. CS networks reflect most of the inequalities of wider society: they are not flat and egalitarian; they tend to be dominated by a few individuals who are keen to secure their own positions of influence and exercise power through patronage; and they have tended to exclude women and members of caste/ethnic, religious, or regional communities as a matter of fact.[30] Donor NGO funding and agenda-shaping can exacerbate such exclusivity, further privileging a small number of English-speaking intermediaries and reinforcing their position as gatekeepers.

CS networks tend toward the informal, depending more on interpersonal relations between a handful of key players than on written rules or policy agendas. Grassroots activists perhaps enjoy a stronger solidarity: at least during the conflict, individuals working in different ways had to share similar risks and hardships, often alongside one another. The strongest flows between network members are the most tangible ones: project funding, employment opportunities, and hierarchical authority at different levels. Such networks are flexible in both day-to-day functioning and goals; critical decisions are more likely to be taken in individual or small-group face-to-face meetings than in large, formal contexts or through written communications. Maintaining international connections and relations with important donors is essential for organizations that depend on outside funding. Donors sometimes shape national networks. Some projects demand that different organizations collaborate under one umbrella; others may favor particular individuals or NGOs at the expense of broader solidarity.

General Status and Public Perceptions

Civil society has performed important functions but has also attracted much criticism. Individuals and organizations are often accused of being foreign-funded and motivated solely by donor dollars, family business–oriented, and politically partisan.[31] Some prominent CS leaders and NGOs are linked to political parties; some are accused of allowing personal ambition to obstruct collective action. The mushrooming of CS organizations took place in the wake of the 1990 transition to multiparty democracy, under the first NC administration. While NC workers were being accommodated in government positions, the main opposition (UML) concentrated on establishing NGOs and turning them into a rival power base. UML still appears to hold significant sway over the NGO world, and NC activists complain that leftist organizations have been favored by donors.[32] Some of the most well-known CS members do indeed come from an openly political background.[33] However, the harshest critics tend to be too sweeping in their judgments: many individuals have successfully retained an independent stance.

State influence is harder to avoid. The heavy legal framework means the state retains the potential to interfere, even if in general it appears to manage a light regulatory hand. Organizations' political leanings sometimes define how they will relate to the state depending on which party is in power. Furthermore, almost all are in some way working alongside or in collaboration with statal or parastatal organizations. This is most obvious in the case of those that deliver services (in collaboration with the state, under government contract, or filling a gap left by state weakness), but there are other types of civic associations (such as the community forest user groups mentioned above) that exist by definition in the liminal area between state-sponsored and purely voluntary associations.

Civil society inevitably has multiple relations to other spheres of public life such as business and the media. Apart from certain basic common interests, there are occasionally direct overlaps in areas of engagement. For example, the business community has demonstrated only a faint interest in peacebuilding but has a growing appetite for corporate social responsibility undertakings, which often perform civil society–type functions such as supporting youth groups, self-help initiatives, and local civil works. More debilitating in terms of public perception is the major rural-urban divide, in particular the capital-centrism that some CS activity exhibits. This is partly inevitable—the influence and attraction of Kathmandu is vastly greater compared to any other urban center—and there are countervailing trends, such as the many locally registered NGOs and nationwide outreach by CS leaders. Nevertheless, even admirers of CS leaders tend to assume that they will be well-intentioned, educated Kathmandu residents rather than grassroots activists.

Peacebuilding Functions

The following section compares the seven different functions: protection, monitoring, advocacy, socialization, social cohesion, intermediation and facilitation, and service delivery.

Protection

From the outset of the conflict, most actors saw civil society's protection function as dual: guarding against abuses from both the state and the Maoists.

1996–2001. In the early stages, the general lack of a clear picture of the shape of the conflict, coupled with the fact that its most immediate victims were almost voiceless residents of rural areas remote from the capital, meant that practical protection measures were severely limited. Nevertheless, committed CS actors woke up to the seriousness of the conflict, and the associated protection risks, well before the government was willing to acknowledge the scale of the challenge. At the same time, international concern had grown: for example, the International Committee of the Red Cross (ICRC), which had sent India-based staff for an initial assessment mission in 1998, established a Nepal office in 2000. Such steps depended on pressure and practical assistance from national observers able to relay their concerns over protection issues.

2001–2005. The question of using protection activities to preserve space for democracy, civic functions, and development gained greater relevance with the presence of multiple domestic and international development agencies, whose programs were threatened by the constriction of operational space.[34] The formulation and dissemination of the Basic Operating Guidelines by a broad coalition of the major international donors both drew on and fed into domestic CS actors' efforts. In particular, it stemmed from a recognition that national development staff and human rights defenders had long had to negotiate the most difficult and dangerous frontline relations, attempting to maintain their projects' viability on the basis of fundamental principles while frequently having to make minor compromises in the face of demands that could otherwise have led to the closing of programs that were directly benefiting local communities. This period also saw the launch of a new coalition-building effort: the Children as Zone of Peace campaign was funded by Save the Children (Norway) and brought together leading NGOs, gradually drawing support from politicians, educationists, and international agencies.[35]

2005–2006. The royal coup brought two significant changes in the perception and practicalities of protection work. First, it rapidly led to a widely shared sense that the state had become the prime source of abuses and should be the major, though not exclusive, focus of protection activities. This stemmed partly from immediate developments (such as the mass detentions of democratic politicians and activists on February 1, 2005, and iconic images of armed soldiers deployed in media newsrooms) and partly from the long-growing trend toward state impunity for extralegal measures against suspected Maoists and democracy activists (such as the 2004 arrests of mainstream student leaders supporting republicanism to the growing lists of citizens suspected to have been disappeared by the state security forces). Second, the royal coup proved to be the tipping point for international involvement in efforts to resolve the conflict. Apart from the broader ramifications for international policy, the most significant change to protection was the establishment of a substantial presence of the UN Office of the High Commissioner for Human Rights (OHCHR) in Nepal. This had long been an aim of national human rights organizations, and the push to have it established depended on a well-coordinated campaign undertaken jointly by national and international outfits—as well as on the surprising decision by India to tacitly support the move at the Commission on Human Rights in Geneva, a step conditioned more by its desire to put pressure on Gyanendra than by any love for UN human rights monitoring. The OHCHR presence provided a major boost to protection efforts and opened up additional space for broader conflict-resolution and settlement initiatives, although the synergy between it and existing domestic organizations was at times disappointing.[36]

2006 onward. With the advent of a substantive peace process, the headline concerns of protection underwent a further shift. The successful maintenance of the military cease-fire meant that violations of international humanitarian laws were no longer the main problem. Instead, protection started to revolve around addressing the many unresolved injustices of the conflict period (in particular the pending cases of more than 1,000 disappearances); pushing for legal changes to address impunity (such as reforming the Army Act and trying to ensure that a proposed Truth and Reconciliation Commission did not become a provider of blanket amnesties); and, the greatest challenge, coping with the new threats posed by the upsurge in local and regional conflict. This last came to the fore with the 2007 Madhesi movement, which not only brought renewed direct confrontation between armed police and demonstrators but also involved a plethora of new, shadowy armed groups and the background difficulties of providing protection in a context where state capacity and respect for the rule of law reached an even lower ebb than during the Maoist insurgency.

Monitoring

1996–2001. Extant human rights NGOs performed some monitoring functions; their pressure also helped persuade the government to establish the National Human Rights Commission (NHRC; authorizing legislation was passed in 1999, and the commission was established in 2000). There was some monitoring of the conflict areas, but for most organizations and individuals it was still very distant from Kathmandu. The first serious mainstream press coverage can probably be dated to mid-2000 (Sudheer Sharma's *Himal Khabarpatrika* cover story); from this point onward there was more leverage for monitoring. Local human rights defenders' reports played an important role in generating international attention and providing warnings that, if not early, at least added to the impetus to develop serious monitoring mechanisms at a point when for most outsiders the conflict was well off the radar.[37]

2001–2005. The first emergency was a challenging period for monitoring, with human rights defenders coming under more direct pressure from both sides, in particular from the government. The free media, which had started developing a capacity to assist, by fulfilling its normal reporting duties more professionally, in protection and advocacy, came under tight restrictions. During this period national human rights organizations not only maintained their own activities but also played a crucial role in providing the information that enabled major international research and advocacy groups to monitor the deteriorating situation in Nepal. It was during this period that major reports by Amnesty International, Human Rights Watch, and the International Commission of Jurists added to global advocacy efforts. None of them would have been possible without the experience developed by national human rights defenders over the preceding years. This was also a fertile period for new organizations, most notably Advocacy Forum, which was established in 2001.[38]

2005–2006. The February 2005 royal coup raised the stakes for monitoring of abuses and placed monitors in a very difficult, polarized political situation. National efforts in the preceding years were not entirely free of political bias, with each of the more established human rights organizations known to have some party leanings. Nevertheless, the basic collection of information was not entirely compromised, and there was broad agreement across party lines on the definition of fundamental rights and the responsibility of the state to protect them. In the postcoup period this provided a basis for more unified action. In parallel, the significant international presence (especially following the May 2005 agreement to establish an OHCHR office) offered a degree of protection against more blatant abuses.

2006 onward. The bilateral cease-fire that immediately followed the king's relinquishment of power changed the priorities for monitoring. Although some abuses continued, the major new task was to monitor the observation of the cease-fire and its associated code of conduct. From November 2006, the CPA brought additional commitments from the seven-party government and CPN(M), as well as an explicit provision for CS monitoring. However, the proposed national cease-fire monitoring committee never developed into an effective body.[39] When regional conflict emerged, most national CS organizations were caught off-guard. In this they were not alone, but their structures and outlooks had left them ill-prepared to anticipate or respond to new forms of civil conflict.

Advocacy

Nonpublic and public advocacy have both been a near-constant characteristic of the many efforts to end the conflict and to consolidate longer-term peacebuilding measures in the confused postagreement period. In the case of Nepal, nonpublic advocacy efforts focused on encouraging parties to prepare for dialogue. As these often included concrete efforts to support private talks, it is hard to separate this from facilitation: the two functions were frequently two sides of the same coin. This section therefore considers only public advocacy; nonpublic efforts are examined under the section on facilitation below. Public campaigns were, by their nature, more visible and therefore perhaps more easy to assess in terms of impact. They ranged from awareness and agenda-setting initiatives to a critical role in mobilizing mass protests against royal rule and in favor of peace and democracy.

1996–2001. Public advocacy was not a major feature of the initial response to the conflict. The lack of coordinated positions within civil society was natural, given the time it took for society at large to appreciate the gravity of the situation. Nevertheless, the intensification of police action prompted some advocacy messages from established human rights activists. Although the 1999 election campaign could have provided some focus for public advocacy dealing with the insurgency, it was not then seen as a major electoral issue. Instead, it was the first formal negotiations of 2001 that encouraged broader public endorsement of dialogue and more serious discussion of political means to address manageable Maoist demands.

2001–2005. By the later stages of the conflict, there was more overlap between national and international public communications. More important, national CS organizations gained much more expertise and field research–based information about the nature of the conflict and the key priorities for public advocacy. In the post-2001 period, the army was drawn into the escalating military conflict, and the international community showed greater concern. This changed the dynamics of peacebuilding efforts. There was greater traction for lobbying and advocacy, domestically and overseas, but also a greater resistance to dialogue from a resurgent royal government and major international powers who started to view the Maoists through the lens of the so-called Global War on Terror (the label used by the George W. Bush administration to characterize its military action against Islamist extremism).[40] Civil society embraced a range of different approaches and techniques. For example, many individuals and organizations mobilized to seek redress for individual injustices, such as the army's murder of a teenage girl, Maina Sunuwar, in 2004 and the Maoist bombing of a bus in 2005. While some organizations focused on detailed research and quiet advocacy, others used different media, from street protests to popular music concerts and radio broadcasts, to reach the public. New coalitions were built, such as the Children as Zone of Peace initiative, which brought together the United Nations, donors, government, civil society, and owners of private schools. Some undertakings were direct donor creations, for example the Nepal Business Initiative, which attempted to mobilize the business community for peace, as well as newly established "local" NGOs, such as Friends for Peace, which were funded and directed by international organizations.

2005–2006. The months following the royal coup formed the most critical period for public advocacy. Civil society sustained a campaign for peace and democracy that should perhaps more naturally have been led by the mainstream parties. This role was inherently controversial: political parties had been unable to come up with a coherent agenda of their own yet resented the sudden prominence of alternative actors, whereas supporters of the royal regime argued that civil society had no right to raise political issues. However, the momentum was with the activists, who had tapped into a deep well of popular frustration with the conflict and the desire to push for a negotiated settlement. Public pressure was an important factor in paving the way for the twelve-point agreement and building national and international consensus; this represented a viable way forward. Civil society maintained critical pressure on the Maoists to sign up to democratic and human rights norms while also making a bridge for them to legitimize themselves and enter a peace process with some sense of security. Organizations such as the Citizens' Movement for Democracy and Peace (CMDP), as well as individuals, took their message well beyond Kathmandu, with public meetings and debates across the country.[41] In this there was a synergy with individuals from within the political parties. For example, although the NC leadership was quiet, individual leaders such as Narahari Acharya, Gagan Thapa, and (from outside the party structure) Professor Krishna Khanal became vocal and committed public activists alongside nonparty political figures.

2006 onward. This was the most difficult period for civil society in general, reflected in the challenge of finding common messages for public advocacy. On the grand issues of the peace process there was little unity—some more vocal advocates were criticized for pushing too hard on republicanism and the formation of the interim parliament and government (this was seen as being "pro-Maoist"), whereas others appeared to pull their punches out of a desire to give the newly reestablished mainstream parties' government an easy ride. Public messages on the Tarai were not always easily agreed on but were still there, and civil society visits and statements on events such as mass killings in Gaur and Kapilbastu showed a willingness to engage. More advocacy was focused on specific issues, such as the shape of a proposed Truth and Reconciliation Commission, perhaps reflecting the fact that most organizations found it more comfortable to stick to their areas of expertise and their own mandates rather than building wider political platforms.

Socialization

The complex composition of Nepali society has produced many social and interest-based groups, with differentiation along ethnic, caste, economic, and professional or class, regional, and urban-rural lines. However, unlike group identity–based conflicts such as in Sri Lanka and Northern Ireland, Nepal's conflict was not built solely on clearly defined group cleavages. Only the more recent phase of postinsurgency instability has brought significant intergroup tensions to the fore and created a real need for intragroup cohesion to prepare for peace. Socialization in the case of Nepal therefore has two main features: first, strengthening the in-group identity of marginalized ethnic, geographical, or caste groups; and second, more programmatic efforts to inculcate democratic and peace values into society at large as well as specific interest groups.

1996–2001. The most notable trend was the emergence and consolidation of new ethnic-, caste-, and regional-based associations, as well as growth in issue-based organizations, such as various elements of an increasingly confident women's movement. Much as these developments related to causes that the

Maoists were championing, it is important to note that these trends predated the launch of the Maoist insurgency. Socialization aimed at working toward a negotiated peace was only a minority interest until the advent of the first formal Maoist government negotiations in 2001. There was little attention paid by civil society to conflict-resolution measures or preparatory training. Internal democratic practices within civic associations closely mirrored those of the political parties. Many associations' internal politics are directly related to national politics (e.g., elections within the Nepal Bar Association and the Federation of Nepalese Journalists are conducted along party lines); even for those that are at some remove from party politics (such as business federations), internal politics reflected national patterns. In the early phase of the conflict, there were few steps within civil society to move beyond such well-established models.

2001--2005. In this period there was further consolidation of a politics of diversity, marginalization, and inclusion. The multiple cleavages across Nepali society were increasingly acknowledged by political leaders and public commentators; in parallel, activists took more concrete steps to organize, network, and advocate on behalf of marginalized communities. Within organized civil society, the experience of failed peace talks, coupled with a surge in international interest in funding new efforts, led to a mushrooming of conflict-resolution and negotiation training projects. Many of these initiatives were externally driven; civic discussion—in the media and in academic and activist forums—that laid the foundations of an internal coalition for peace was of much greater significance in solidifying a social coalition for peace. At the same time, the escalation of the conflict prompted a more profound rethinking of in-group democratic practices and of the exclusive character of Nepali society, polity, and much civic organization. These years saw a fitful, occasionally superficial, but ultimately productive effort to grapple with the need to reshape the state on more inclusive lines. Although the CPN(M) in particular forced this topic onto the agenda, much credit goes to civil society for taking it up and carving out the space for it to be discussed meaningfully. However, this function remained confined primarily to advocacy rather than to concrete progress in socialization.

2005–2006. In the postcoup tumult, consolidation of in-group identity was not a major question. Indeed, the success of the April 2006 people's movement suggested that multiple in-group identities were strong enough in themselves and compatible enough alongside each other to form an impressively broad street solidarity—one that easily eclipsed the state's power to ignore it. By this stage, civil society was well placed to perform twin functions in pushing for peace. First, the years of learning about peace processes meant that organizations were more confident in asserting alternative narratives to those proposed by an increasingly bellicose government—and promoting such alternatives boldly in public forums. Second, individuals were well placed to persuade key players in the parties to take some risks for peace. These processes did not deliver any instant change in the internal attitudes of civil society organizations but made it much easier for them to adopt cohesive agendas and to recognize the primacy of democracy as a rallying point.

2006 onward. The apparent settlement of the civil war, however, gave birth to new forms of conflict. The political solidarity generated by the struggle to bring the Maoists into peace negotiations and to overthrow royal autocracy had not taken into account the very different perspectives of numerous marginalized communities who felt their sidelining all the more intensely as peace agreements appeared to sidestep their concerns. This new situation highlighted severe shortcomings in the type of identity politics that had, unseen to most, underpinned group activities. Despite rhetorical commitments to building a "new Nepal," there was no noteworthy effort within CS associations to make their internal structures more inclusive or consultative. On the contrary, party loyalties and partisan interests that had been suppressed in the pursuit of a common objective rapidly reasserted themselves and led to some debilitating public splits between former CS collaborators. Although some individuals have remained active, many observers fear that the promise of 2005 and 2006 has been betrayed as civil society has largely accepted a return to politics as usual and failed to transcend party politics. As one commentator complains, "After the fall of the king [civil society] seems to have gone to sleep. It has lain moribund while problems in creating a new Nepal rage all around" (Sharma 2008).

Social Cohesion

The fact that the Maoist conflict was not a simple intergroup conflict makes many of the questions about social cohesion and bridging hard to map onto a more complex picture. One clear trend was that most conflict-related CS activism was more concerned with the warring parties, and other established political actors, than with broader questions of social cohesion. In this respect, many steps that appear to involve cohesion are in fact better seen as support to facilitation. Many divides that contributed to the escalation of conflict were not seriously addressed by CS action. The gulf between urban elites and the rural population affected civil society as much as any other institution, often leaving elite opinionmakers in the capital out of touch with realities on the ground. The early years of the conflict saw little effort to bridge caste, ethnic, and regional cleavages. Ironically, this lack of attention to social cohesion beyond the principal political actors became starkly apparent once the peace deal had been signed. The upsurge of unrest in the Tarai Plains and the surge of popular resentment that fueled the Madhesi movement illustrated that the focus on resolving the insurgency had encouraged a neglect of other tensions—

and had perhaps even reinforced them. The successful progress toward resolving the triangular political parties/Maoist/palace conflict had of necessity been an elite affair at the leadership level. Civil society's awareness of the narrow base of this power game could have translated into greater pressure to broaden the scope of the peace process and to ensure that it embraced marginalized groups. The fact that it did not was primarily ascribed to the priorities of political leaders. Nevertheless, the shortcomings of less than fully inclusive efforts directed toward social cohesion were illuminated.

Intermediation/Facilitation

It was in the latter stages of the conflict that civil society became a prominent vehicle for bringing issues to the negotiation table and for helping the principal actors to address them. However, CS actors had been involved in intermediation and facilitation from the earliest days of the conflict. Much of this took place at the local level, involving efforts to mitigate the impact of the conflict on local communities and to peacefully resolve some political disputes by bypassing higher authorities. Inevitably, such functions became increasingly important in safeguarding development activities; local CS actors thus became essential mediators to enable government and international donor programs to continue operating. At the same time, well-placed individuals made use of personal connections to facilitate quiet dialogue between powerful leaders on all sides, both in coordination with formal negotiations and during periods when official talks would have been impossible.

1996–2001. Mediation between citizens and the state became essential as violence intensified and concerns grew over the militarization of the state response. Civil society carried out much local-level mediation with both sides, much of it unreported and uncelebrated. Such intermediation ranged from negotiating the release of individuals from state or Maoist custody to brokering agreements that would enable local development work to proceed unhindered. CS actors had also facilitated discreet informal contacts between the conflict parties at a higher level long before the start of formal talks, as well as in parallel to open negotiations. Such facilitation provided an important basis for contributing to the first international efforts to explore openings for dialogue. For example, the Center for Humanitarian Dialogue started establishing contacts and a regular engagement from 2000 onward. Subsequently, the United Nations (whose Department of Political Affairs started engaging closely with Nepal from mid-2003) drew on CS intermediaries to establish critical contacts, which slowly allowed it to play an important role in preparing all sides for a negotiated solution.[42] CS actors had a role in advocating for, and facilitating, the first round of peace negotiations in early 2001. The talks were not successful (not surprising, given the wide gap between firmly held positions), but the fact that they took place at all established a precedent for future attempts to reach a negotiated settlement and established facilitation as a necessary component.

2001–2005. As development agencies woke up to the need to reorient themselves to the conflict environment and the new risks it brought, the role of civil society in mediating the provision of services and continuation of development projects gained ground. By the time of the 2003 peace talks, the space for a CS role in facilitating dialogue had grown. Contacts with the Maoists had increased, and members of royal appointee Lokendra Bahadur Chand's government were aware that facilitators would help both sides engage more effectively. Unfortunately, however, most analysts agree that the 2003 facilitation was poorly handled. Although it is unlikely that this in itself was a major contributor to the resumption of conflict (when Prime Minister Chand was replaced midterm by Surya Bahadur Thapa, it appears that Gyanendra had already been persuaded to drop dialogue in favor of an intensified military offensive; the Maoists were similarly prepared to return to war), it damaged the credibility of civil society as a neutral third party. Meanwhile, even as successive royal regimes adopted a more aggressive approach to dealing with the Maoists, their own backchannels to the rebels meant they did not need to rely on other contacts and could afford to ignore nonpublic advocacy messages.

2005–2006. This was the most critical period, as civil society helped ensure that negotiations between the Maoists and the political parties stayed on track and reached a settlement. Actors were involved not only in smoothing the way for interparty talks but also in pressing for the resolution of intraparty disputes that were blocking progress. This happened most notably in the case of a serious split between the Maoist leaders Prachanda and Baburam Bhattarai in early 2005. This rift raised the risk of the Maoists refusing, or losing the capacity, to engage in a meaningful dialogue for peace.[43] Similar informal mediation within and among the seven mainstream parties whose alliance was the driving force on the other side of the table was also important. For example, when the NC was driving toward a rapid deal with the Maoists, CS representatives urged its leaders to pause and bring other parties on board, in particular UML. Although carried out against a backdrop of organized CS activism in Nepal, such interventions were largely the preserve of trusted individuals with the necessary personal access to party negotiators. The talks could have taken place without CS involvement: the parties had functional channels of communication and were capable of sitting down together without third parties to break the ice. But it is very unlikely they would have seen their secret negotiations through to conclusion without the constructively critical support of CS figures, who encouraged all parties to approach talks with seriousness and helped to ensure that topics such as human rights remained firmly on the agenda.

2006 onward. With a bilateral cease-fire in place, formal and informal steps helped bring the CPN(M) into open politics. High-level peace talks were the most obvious driver of this process, but CS pressure for all sides to come together, coupled with quiet private contacts, facilitated much bridging of remaining divides. However, there was not such an obvious facilitation/mediation role in Madhesi issues, although Kathmandu woke up to the realization that trustworthy Madhesi CS figures had a much better understanding of Tarai politics and personalities and could manage contacts with armed groups. Capital-based Madhesi activists and development professionals helped to maintain channels of communication between the governing parties and newly significant rebel groups; they were also called upon by development agencies to serve as go-betweens.

Service Delivery

1996–2001. Nepal has historically had weak government-based service delivery; in this context, CS organizations have often played roles to supplement, or even supplant, state responsibilities. In the early years of the conflict, however, efforts were under way to strengthen local democratic structures and to redress the overreliance on nongovernmental services. The 1999 Local Self-Governance Act devolved significant budgetary powers to elected local bodies—in rural areas, the village development committees.[44] This measure appeared popular, and the initial results of its partial implementation were encouraging. However, this took place as the Maoists intensified their assault on all wings of the government. They attempted, with much success, to drive the state out of the large areas over which they held sway. This opened a new and more intense need for other organizations to fill the gap. By 2000, civil society had come to be seen as an integral player even in state-led development efforts. In a paper prepared for a conference with major donors, the government stressed that "it recognizes that civil society organizations have the potential to contribute not only to the development efforts of the country but also dialogue and awareness of development issues. . . . The participation of civil society organizations in development activities will be stressed" (His Majesty's Government of Nepal 2000).

2001–2005. Elected local bodies were dissolved by the government in 2002, just as the Maoist insurgency was gaining critical mass and the palace was moving to take over central power. Development donors, many of whom had been trying to channel funds through line ministries in order to strengthen state capacity, increasingly turned to alternative channels to deliver direct, quick-impact assistance to local communities. Against this backdrop, NGOs functioned partly as service-delivery contractors but also as an interface between development actors and Maoist parallel governance structures. This was a difficult and dangerous relationship for them to manage and one that did not develop out of any conscious desire to explore new avenues for peace talks. Nevertheless, it prompted the major donors' development of the Basic Operating Guidelines; these were arguably prompted by the first systematic attempt to engage the Maoist senior and local leadership in negotiations about abiding by external norms of behavior. Such regular engagement formed an important entry point for peacebuilding. It maintained channels of communication and built a degree of trust and comfort in discussions relating to practical issues affecting local communities. However strained the circumstances of some service-delivery organizations interactions' with the Maoists may have been, they constituted a form of dialogue that linked high-level leadership commitments to the daily concerns of local Maoist commanders and state authorities. In this way, service-delivery activities enhanced the prospects of meaningful dialogue when the broader political conditions became more propitious.

2005–2006. The postcoup period complicated the question of service delivery. Relations between donors and the government deteriorated—not only because donors found a royal autocracy uncomfortable to deal with but also because the king's government was reluctant and inept in its handling of relations with international partners.[45] Even as this increased the need for NGOs to step in, the renewed state of emergency and intensified military clashes made the task more dangerous. During this period, civil society's inability to deliver services effectively probably contributed as much to the push for peace as its previous ability, by indicating the unsustainability of the situation and increasing pressure on all sides to find a way out. Still, a certain synergy developed between development agencies and local CS actors. For the former, community-based organizations became increasingly essential channels for local development projects: even under difficult circumstances they managed to keep many programs alive. For the latter, the sheer presence of international actors afforded a degree of protection and moral support.

2006 onward. Service delivery during the government-Maoist negotiations had little impact on the shape of the peace process. Of more significance was the nongovernmental response to the unrest in the Tarai Plains. Although national CS organizations were active in some relief efforts, heightened communal tensions placed them in an awkward position: because their own staffing was in general deeply unrepresentative of local communities, they were in a weak position to engage with those who needed services and to deal with the new armed and nonviolent political actors whose cooperation was essential. Looking toward postconflict development that could address long-standing inequalities, Bhaskar Gautam (2003, 151) called for "special incentives" to involve CS organizations and "new modes of social mobilization" to boost local development initiatives. Whether this is even possible will depend on the state's approach to reestablishing local government and the willingness of dominant political parties to encourage alternative forms of civic engagement. The Maoist-led government has shown some interest in involving civil society in areas such as local peace committees and the monitoring of service-delivery and anticorruption efforts.[46]

Assessing Civil Society in Context

Effectiveness and Impact: Linked to the Nature of the Conflict

As the preceding sections demonstrate, Nepal's civil society was active across all peacebuilding functions during most periods of the conflict. In the initial stages it was strong in providing an early warning on the deteriorating human rights situation but slow to urge that the developmental thrust of most NGO work had to be revised in light of the conflict. Most CS actors were for some years either too suspicious or dismissive of the CPN(M) to make much progress in dealing with it as a serious stakeholder. However, it would be unfair to blame civil society for failing in its peacebuilding duties. Once the insurgency had taken hold, there was little chance that the leadership on either side would see conditions as ripe for a negotiated solution until the cycle of military escalation was complete. Also, the state was weakened by severe internal rifts (primarily between the palace/army and the democratic parties), which in themselves made any determined effort to peace unlikely—whatever the pressure from civil society.

The areas in which civil society was able to make a demonstrable impact were largely determined by the nature of the conflict itself. The most consistent engagement, throughout all phases, was in the three related functions of protection, monitoring, and advocacy, particularly on questions of human rights and democratic values. The strength of the warring parties and their reluctance to play by the rules meant that civil society alone could not counter the threats to civilian protection, but it did manage to work effectively in concert with international organizations. Monitoring increased in scope and depth as the conflict intensified and provided the basis for persuasive and consistent advocacy. This exerted a degree of influence over the main political players and—no small achievement—ensured that human rights was always on the agenda, however much political leaders on all sides would have been happy to let it slip. None of these three functions could have been carried out in isolation, although it appears the importance of advocacy grew in the latter stages of the conflict and depended on the long-term investment in protection and monitoring that gave civil society the access, information, and legitimacy to push public and private messages.

Service delivery was also a constant feature of NGO work and became more predominant as the state's capacity weakened and left more gaps to be filled by international and domestic nongovernmental initiatives. The question of whether this function had an impact on peacebuilding efforts cannot be answered easily. However, to the extent that it necessarily entailed negotiating with Maoist and state authorities and working with local communities, service delivery helped to ensure some common understandings and prevent greater damage to the social fabric. Given that Nepal's conflict was not between distinct ethnic or other groups (although this is one aspect of the post-2006 tensions in the Tarai Plains), in-group socialization and intergroup social cohesion were not seen as critical functions. This has now changed, but it is too early to assess how civil society will cope with the new challenges of identity politics. One important trend is already clear: many of the groups that have turned to political action on identity issues had their roots directly in CS movements and associations.[47]

The final areas where civil society did play a critical part are mediation and facilitation. The fact that the 2001 and 2003 talks reached no conclusion encourages most analysts to see them as failures. However, they and the other constant contacts between the warring parties were probably essential precursors to the process for talks that took shape in 2005–2006. Civil society was never the exclusive channel for peace proposals, but the constant presence of secure, independent backchannels and other contacts undoubtedly contributed to the parties' willingness to engage in negotiations. Keeping dialogue channels open and keeping up pressure on all sides to talk were an achievement deserving credit. Nevertheless, CS leaders themselves are only too aware that the final deals are cut by politicians behind closed doors. Thus, they had little or no influence on critical parts of the peace deal, such as the future of the security sector and measures to address impunity.[48]

The Nature of Civil Society

The second determining factor in peacebuilding functions is the nature of Nepali civil society itself. Two aspects stand out as restricting the scope of engagement: exclusionary practices and the dominance of NGO models. CS organizations have found it hard to avoid echoing the patterns of social, caste, and ethnic exclusion in the wider society.[49] Women have been sidelined and are tacitly expected to concentrate on "women's issues" rather than broader questions. (Although here, too, there are notable exceptions, such as Human Rights Watch prizewinner Mandira Sharma, of Advocacy Forum, and Gruber International Women's Rights prizewinner Sapana Pradhan Malla, of the Women's Forum for Law and Development.) With the exception of a handful of dedicated associations, such as the Collective Campaign for Peace–Nepal (COCAP) and the Alliance for Peace, Nepal's youths have not been effectively mobilized in CS initiatives despite their evident appetite for activity, which is clear enough in student politics and from street agitations such as the April 2006 people's movement. The dominance of the NGO as the form of organization also brings limitations. It has encouraged a limited sense of institutional ownership and interests and a focus on project-driven approaches to social and political problems. Such efforts are not necessarily without value but had at best a tangential relationship to the critical achievement of civil society in mobilizing public pressure for peace and democracy.

At the same time, Nepali civil society has displayed remarkable strengths. While sometimes seen as an elite sphere, it demonstrated in 2005–2006 that it could tap into public sentiment and represent broad swathes of society. The most memorable turning points in the people's movement were almost exclusively driven by civil society rather than political parties. Protestors tend to remember the peaceful sit-ins addressed by poets, musicians, and professors more than any of the belated politicians' speeches. Although the narrowness of CS leadership networks can be a constraint, the positive benefits of close contacts with the bureaucracy, parties, media, and other parts of the state offered extra leverage at critical moments. Last, the fact that the people's movement and peace process resulted from broad social and political trends should not obscure the contribution of tireless CS leaders and activists, whose collective energies helped shape the peace process.

The Political Sphere

The ever-present third factor is the ambiguous relationship between civil society and mainstream politics. There is no clear line between the civil and political spheres, nor was civil society ever entirely removed from the armed parties. At times, much of civil society swung behind the state in its response to the Maoist "threat"—not least because the prospect of Maoist rule did threaten some of the freedoms and comfort enjoyed by CS organizations. In such cases, civil society's response was not only purely that of a neutral intermediary but also, in part, that of an interest group in its own right. For example, Maoist totalitarian tendencies raised major questions over the possibility of independent civic networks' survival, not only in the areas where they held sway but also in the hypothetical case of their seizing state power; at the same time, Maoist critiques of corruption and patronage in networks embracing government, donors, and NGOs made many uneasy—and with some justification, as such critiques were not always unfounded. Relations with the state were similarly mixed: government action often threatened civic autonomy, but many individuals and organizations also depended on constructive relations with the state.

There is a tendency, particularly among international donors, to idealize civil society's democratizing urge. One offered a one-dimensional picture of universal prodemocracy leanings: "Political parties and civil society organisations have likewise, over a long and sustained period of many years, clearly stated and demonstrated their desire for continued democracy" (DANIDA 2005, 1). However, as S. Tamang (2002, 317) rightly comments, "not all organisations falling under the rubric of civil society are necessarily working towards the promotion of democratisation. In Nepal, for example, the World Hindu Federation is as much a part of civil society as ABC Nepal, an anti-trafficking organisation."

Against this backdrop, the overtly political role embraced by a broad coalition of CS actors following the royal coup was bound to be controversial. Palace supporters argued that using street protests to call for peace was a political rather than civil act, and that the ringleaders were being financed by outsiders and encouraged to step beyond their legitimate sphere. Political parties were similarly skeptical, and they were alarmed at seeing the duties they had studiously neglected being picked up by actors beyond their direct control. Nevertheless, it was only after this apparent transgression—stepping into the political arena and mobilizing on the streets—that civil society finally fulfilled a pivotal role in creating the environment for peace.

Donors: A Double-Edged Sword?

The great influence of international players on Nepal's politics and development efforts naturally affects the space for civil society and the scope of CS activities.[50] The many impacts include both positive and negative aspects. This colored the many peacebuilding efforts in Nepal and requires some detailed assessment.

Few, if any, of the most effective CS organizations could survive without external support. Donors enabled the creation and sustenance of NGOs that have performed vital work; without their training and funding this would not have been possible on a large enough scale to have an impact. International partners' moral support for the campaign for peace and democracy was important, both in boosting civil society efforts and in adding to leverage over the conflict parties. At the same time, donors offered invaluable practical assistance in mitigating the worst impacts of the conflict, providing relief to victims, and working alongside domestic governmental and nongovernmental efforts. In the field of protection, the ICRC and OHCHR, as well as operational and advocacy-oriented INGOs, made a big difference, as did the lobbying of diplomats in Kathmandu and in their own capitals to ensure they were able to operate. International observation and monitoring—and, indeed, the sheer presence on the ground—had a deterrent effect on both warring parties, who were conscious of the need not to alienate themselves permanently from international opinion. Last, some exposure to outside models and experience has been useful in adding depth to national expertise.

However, donor funding brings with it donor-driven agendas that tend to take priority even if they are not necessarily the most appropriate responses to the situation.[51] Budgetary dependence contributes to a general dependence by limiting the autonomy of domestic actors and cementing restrictive patron-client relations. Development agency–led initiatives channeled political energy into project-oriented approaches that may not have been as effective as straightforward street protests and mass mobilization.[52] And many of these steps were in any case belated: the weight of development culture and institutions was a major obstacle to recognizing the seriousness of the conflict and the need to adopt new thinking to address it. National and international development professionals were loath to accept that conflict resolution would require changes to their established ways of working.

Beyond these practical obstacles, Nepal's aid dependence has had a long-term corrosive effect on society. Donor co-option of academia and a wide tranche of middle-class professionals has debilitated Nepal's natural civic resources. Capable Nepali constitutional and political experts have often felt that their existing capacity has been undermined and devalued as donors have set up nominally independent client "peacebuilding" organizations driven by their own, rather than local, agendas. Meanwhile, the contribution of internationally funded and trained "conflict experts" has been marginal at best. Nepali go-betweens have been used in overselling a multitude of international "models" without much consideration paid to local particularities and the practical applicability of outside experiences.[53] Western donors have a major blind spot in accepting and understanding the dominant role played by India; Indian development funding, in contrast, has often been deployed as a tool for political leverage without involving Nepal's government or civil society. As peace negotiations intensified through 2006 and beyond, national resentment at the opaque role played by some international facilitators became evident.

None of these negative factors has been critically disabling or damaging. However, in combination they have a debilitating effect on autonomous civil action—something that became most starkly apparent when the political role needed to push for peace came to the fore. Such factors urgently deserve serious analysis, yet donor interests make various topics almost taboo. It became fashionable to understand the origins of the conflict as lying solely in underdevelopment, popular grievances, and the multiple failings of Nepali state and political institutions. But there was no space in this conventional wisdom to question how much the decades of aid programs might have contributed to creating the conditions for conflict. Donors are not likely to commission such research; if they were to do so, it would probably remain in private hands. International actors appear to have little interest in contributing to a Nepali public sphere that, for all its vigor and capacity, hardly impinges on their consciousness. Yet, they still hold the purse strings. Such unequal relationships are hard to avoid, but their detrimental effect needs to be recognized.

Conclusion

Nepal stands as a rare example of a country that has, so far, managed to emerge from a brutal civil war through nationally owned negotiations with relatively little external intervention or assistance. The major credit for this must go to the political leaders who have negotiated a difficult transition while maintaining enough basic unity to avoid a reversion to conflict. The role of civil society in the halting progress toward conflict settlement has at some times been hard to discern but at others very visible. This chapter has argued that the nature of the conflict and the composition of Nepali civil society were the first factors that determined the peacebuilding role that civil actors could play. The delicate balance between civic and political engagement was one that, at the crucial moment, CS leaders managed with boldness and conviction—even as the main parties were languishing in indecision. At this point, donor support was important, and circumstances enabled its restrictions to be overcome. However, the delivery of a peace accord to end the Maoist insurgency has opened up new forms of instability and conflict. Whatever the established strengths of Nepali civil society—and they are many—the test will now lie in its adaptability, responsiveness, and inclusiveness.

Notes

The author would like to thank all reviewers of this chapter for their valid comments.

1. The Maoists described their armed campaign against the state as a "people's war" *(janayuddha)* and also, more generally, as a "revolution." The concept of a protracted people's war has a specific significance within Maoist military strategy. On this and the Maoist movement in general, see Thapa (2003); Karki and Seddon (2003); Sudheer Sharma (2004); Parajuli (2004); and Communist Party of Nepal (Maoist) (2004a and 2004b).

2. In the wake of the November 2006 peace agreement, United Nations Security Council Resolution 1740 established the United Nations Mission in Nepal (UNMIN). This was a political mission that also included nonuniformed military arms monitors (to supervise the storage of weapons in Maoist cantonments and army barracks); it was not a peacekeeping mission.

3. Nepal currently ranks 142 out of the 177 countries in the Human Development Index (HDI) report of the United Nations Development Program (UNDP 2008).

4. One leading political scientist (Kumar 2000, 50) has argued that post-1990 governments' inability to reform antagonistic state-society relations undermined the democratic exercise: "State-society relationships in Nepal, despite the imposed national harmony, have quite often been antagonistic. . . . The long and arduous struggle for democracy is testimony to the nature of state-society interactions in Nepal. A decade of democratic experience, however, has not been able to make any dent in the process."

5. Indeed, by many measures, the state became even more exclusive in the multiparty period than it had been under palace rule, when royal advisers were careful to maintain at least a token impression of ethnic and caste diversity. See DFID/World Bank (2006).

6. On the weaknesses of the post-1990 polity, see Kumar (2000).

7. This chapter uses "CPN(M)" and "Maoists" as near-synonyms, although in fact the Maoist movement is broader than just the party, as it encompasses the Maoist military and a range of "united front" organizations, from trade unions and youth groups to ethnic and regional liberation fronts. See Sudheer Sharma (2004).

8. Their model of a protracted people's war drew heavily on classical Maoist strategy, and their membership in the Maoist Revolutionary Internationalist Movement

made plain where they stood on the ideological spectrum. But at the same time, their revolution was always colored by Nepali particularities. Many of their original demands had nothing to do with Marxist theory but were drawn more from a long vein of Nepali nationalism—for example, the demand to restrict the inflow of Hindi films and music and revoke "unequal" treaties with India.

9. The immediate precursor of the conflict in its midwestern cradle of Rolpa was a brutal police crackdown, Operation Romeo, launched by the NC-led government in 1995. As with earlier state atrocities dating to the Panchayat period, it probably did much to breed the general resentment and suspicion of the Kathmandu-led administration and police that fueled Maoist recruitment. The pattern of repressive action against the Maoists had been well practiced, albeit on a smaller scale, in the Panchayat years when the government responded to both peaceful and armed challenges to its rule with some brutality. Similarly, the Maoists were far from the first rebels to take up arms against the state. The Nepali Congress had led a "liberation army" in military attacks on the Rana regime in late 1950 and again adopted paramilitary tactics, including small-scale armed assaults and plane hijackings, in the 1970s. Leftist extremists, modeling themselves on the Maoist "Naxalites" of India's West Bengal (a movement that was launched from the village of Naxalbari, only a few miles from Nepal's border), ran a short-lived campaign of assassination of landlords and other terror tactics in the early 1970s in the eastern district of Jhapa. The NC's guerrillas and hijackers went on to assume respectable positions in the party hierarchy; many of the communist "Jhapali" leaders ended up as prominent leaders of the UML—and one, R. K. Mainali, was selected to join Gyanendra's postcoup royal cabinet.

10. On the then–Royal Nepalese Army and its counterinsurgency capabilities, see Mehta (2006) and Cowan (2008).

11. This was perhaps most critical when it came to the call for a constituent assembly (CA) to write a new constitution. While the Maoists had always demanded constitutional change, the CA (originally an NC proposal, which King Tribhuvan had verbally promised to fulfill after the overthrow of Rana rule in 1951) only became an explicit part of their negotiating platform in 2001. Once the CA came to be seen as a "Maoist" demand, it was very hard for other parties to sign up for it, although it became increasingly clear that no other mechanism for constitutional change was likely to be viable.

12. The author of one of the earliest studies of Nepali NGOs describes the NGO movement as "a core element of civil society" (Maskay 1998, preface), offering "a departure from both state maximalism and the supremacy of market materialism to people-centered development with key elements of creating choices for the people to participate [through] self-help organizations, indigenous institutions and communities, citizens' groups, voluntary non-government organizations and civil society." The two most incisive assessments of the emergence of "civil society" as a central plank of donor policy in Nepal and as a new brand for NGOs (Shah 2002 and Tamang 2002) are sharply critical of the way in which the term has been used to justify unhelpful development interventions under a new guise.

13. One prominent anthropologist of Nepal has argued that caste and ethnicity were the sole organizing principles of Nepali society and that civic institutions were in effect nonexistent (Macfarlane 2001). Others have taken issue with this stance; Liechty (2002), for example, argues that such an interpretation is too narrow and that other factors, such as class, have conditioned a far more complex web of social interactions.

14. S. Shah (2002, 145), for example, notes that such early efforts were "motivated by a sense of community, self-help or the transcendental values of *dharma.* In the NGO-sponsored din of civil society, these sustainable roots of social engagement have

largely been eclipsed in the public consciousness." D. Gyawali (2001, 13) cautions that the term *NGO* in Nepal "is not quite the age-old Nepali tradition of *guthi, kipat, parma* or the like, which are community-based organizations. It also does not capture the centuries-old institutions of resource management in our midst such as farmer-managed irrigation systems and their very complex, multi-hued social organizations."

15. The nature of Rana rule meant that almost all such associations were viewed with suspicion and seen as inherently subversive. Just land title naturally resided with the state, so public culture and social behavior were seen as necessarily under state control. Organizations such as Charkha Sansthan (a 1930s Gandhi-modeled spinning collective that urged self-reliance) therefore always carried some political significance and an implicit challenge to the state's denial of civil space. Religious movements were seen as dangerous unless under tight state control. Thus the government saw both Newar Theravada Buddhist revivalism and popular Hindu sects as threats.

16. On the Tharu Welfare Society and later Tharu-based NGO and civil society associations, see Krauskopff (2003).

17. Voluntary associations founded in Darjeeling, such as Nepali Sahitya Sammelan (1924) and Gorkha Dukha Nivarak Sammelan (1932), showed a great capacity for civic organization. Other social movements took on a more political flavor, such as the campaign for rights by the Tezpur Graziers Association (1933, in Assam).

18. Many leaders from these communities played a role in bringing down the Rana regime; some were accommodated in the emerging multiparty polity, but others either rebelled or were left out.

19. NGOs were first formally defined in the Social Work Act of 1977 (Maskay 1998, 69); various efforts were undertaken to revise and streamline legal regulation during the 1990s (NESAC 2002, 142). However, the civil society sector is subject to a confused regulatory framework: more than fourteen acts contain provisions related to CSOs (e.g., the Forestry Act for forest user groups); all associations must register with district authorities, but affiliation with the Social Welfare Council is optional (DANIDA 2005, 25). In the wake of the 2005 royal coup, efforts to review legislation led to fears that "revisions may be more restrictive in respect of rights based NGOs in an attempt to stifle criticism of the Government by such organizations. In particular, the proposed Code of Conduct for NGOs/INGOs, drawn up without consultation with civil society and other stakeholders, has caused widespread concern as, among others things, it goes against the fundamental principles of the freedom of association" (DANIDA 2005).

20. Civil society is not as dominant a theme in academic literature on Nepal as it is in development discourse; it receives only passing mention in an important collection of essays on resistance and the state (Gellner 2003) and does not feature in the most comprehensive history of Nepal's later twentieth-century politics (Hoftun et al. 1999). Of the studies that do exist, S. Tamang (2002, 314) comments that "academic analyses of civil society in Nepal—many of which have been sponsored or co-sponsored by donors—are . . . conceptually troubled, and quite deceptive in their presentations." Theoretical and practical analyses of civil society have been a topic of concern for South Asian political scientists. See, e.g., Chandhoke (1995 and 2003) and Kaviraj and Khilnani (2002).

21. H. Ghimire (2003, 138–140) comments on the growing role of CSOs in influencing public policy debates, citing examples such as the successful campaign against a proposed high dam project led by the Arun Concern Group, but also notes the increasing co-option of NGOs by donors as service-delivery agents rather than policy advocates.

22. Participation in CSOs may not be as high as is sometimes assumed. In one survey (Hachhethu 2004, 29), 61 percent of respondents reported that they never participated in community organizations, and 84 percent reported that they never participated

in NGOs. Those who did take part were disproportionately male, better educated, and urban-based. And whereas 44 percent of respondents said they participated in "solving local problems," only 15 percent said they took part in protests (Hachhethu 2004, 30). (It is, however, worth noting that the tense conflict atmosphere may have affected respondents' answers; the same survey found that 65 percent of people never discussed politics, a figure that other evidence, such as consistently high turnout in national and local elections, as well as the vast participation in the 2006 people's movement, suggests is implausible.) One study carried out for the UK Department for International Development also reported low participation (Bhattarai 2003, 12): "Only 16 (6 percent) of the 250 respondents said they were members of NGOs, CBOs, or other civil society organizations. Of these only three held decision-making posts. The poor respondents said that the VDCs, DDCs, government line agencies, and civil society institutions in their area were dominated by rich upper caste Hindu men. They also said that they had little or no access to the government line agencies but comparatively good access to local government and civil society institutions."

23. By July 2006, 19,944 NGOs were registered with the Social Welfare Council (SWC); it is estimated that perhaps double that number exist but are only registered at the district level or are unregistered. A majority of those registered with the SWC (11,526) work in the field of community and rural development services. (Statistics provided by the Social Welfare Council, Kathmandu.)

24. The UNDP (2007, 4) cites cooperation with civil society as one of its priorities and notes that support to civil society initiatives was particularly significant in HIV/AIDS programs (2007, 36), where more than half of total expenditures was channeled through fifty-nine NGOs and sixty-one CBOs in forty-four districts. The conceptual differentiation of civil society and service delivery NGOs/CBOs is unclear. The Asian Development Bank (2007, 14) likewise looks to "enhanced institutional capacity of public bodies and civil society institutions" and the "increased role of private sector and civil society in service delivery" in terms more suggestive of operational NGOs than of other civil society functions.

25. Several candidates in the April 2008 CA elections alleged that their opponents had brought in hired thugs; some even named the martial arts clubs and teachers who had allegedly sent them. Interviews, Dhading, Tanahun, Nuwakot, and Dolakha districts, March–April 2008.

26. By 2007, 39 percent of households across the country were members of Forestry User Groups (Chapman et al. 2007, 14).

27. Of the 19,944 NGOs registered with the SWC, there are 3,223 and 1,674 working in the youth and women sectors, respectively. (Statistics provided by the Social Welfare Council, Kathmandu.)

28. Some organizations have started making special efforts to become more inclusive. For example, the Collective Campaign for Peace (COCAP) has reserved seats on its executive committee for regional directors, women, and one representative each from Dalits, *janajatis,* Madhesis, and the far western Karnali region. COCAP press release, August 18, 2008.

29. Interviews, regional and district office heads of human rights NGOs, Biratnagar, Inaruwa, Janakpur, Nepalgunj, and Dhangadhi, January–April 2008.

30. One study on midwestern Nepal criticized the narrow caste, gender, and social base of almost all civil society organizations but had some positive observations on networking (Bhattarai 2003, 23): "They have formed networks and coalitions with seven district networks and coalitions formed in Banke. These are the NGO Mobilization Committee, NGO Federation, NGO Co-ordination Committee, Development Forum, Dalit NGO Network, Liberated Kamaiya Support Committee, and National Federation

of Nationalities. The NGOs are more or less acting as intermediaries, either advocating on behalf of poor people or developing the capacity of the poor to exercise their political rights and to represent their own interest in the democratic processes."

31. On the perception of NGOs being channels for foreign funds, see Bhattachan (2001, 67) and Sharma (2004, 170–171).

32. For example, one NC district official criticized donors for their lack of support to "democratic" NGOs (as opposed to "communist" ones), although he admitted that very few "democratic" NGOs existed in his district and that none had the experience and capacity of their longer-established rivals. Interview, Kailali district, January 2008.

33. For example, the prominent talks facilitators Daman Nath Dhungana and Padma Ratna Tuladhar are both former members of parliament (NC and independent leftist, respectively).

34. Peace Brigades International introduced the concept of protective accompaniment; although it did not become a significant feature of domestic human rights defenders' activities, it underlined the threats that they had faced and the constriction of democratic space that they indicated.

35. The Children as Zone of Peace campaign was launched in January 2003 by four NGOs: Child Workers in Nepal (CWIN), the Institute of Human Rights and Communication Nepal (IHRICON), the Center for Victims of Torture (CVICT), and Save the Children (Norway).

36. Although all welcomed OHCHR's presence, in the period following the people's movement, many established national human rights activists criticized OHCHR for a perceived lack of action on its mandate to collaborate with and build the capacity of domestic organizations. Interviews, human rights activists, Kathmandu, 2006.

37. International attention did start growing as the conflict spread. Amnesty International highlighted the seriousness of the situation in a March 1999 report ("Nepal: Human Rights at a Turning Point?"); Human Rights Watch's first report on the armed conflict was published in October 2004 ("Between a Rock and a Hard Place: Civilians Struggle to Survive in Nepal's Civil War").

38. Advocacy Forum's lawyers made major contributions to research reports published by international organizations; Advocacy Forum's director, Mandira Sharma, received Human Rights Watch's highest award in 2006 and 2007.

39. Before the peace agreement, a twenty-one-member parliamentary cease-fire monitoring committee had been formed (on May 30 under Speaker Subash Nembang) but was never active. A cease-fire code of conduct national monitoring committee was established in the wake of the bilateral cease-fire but did not assume an active role. The November 2006 Comprehensive Peace Agreement (art. 3.4) called in general terms for "monitoring by civil society" within the future political system but did not set up any specific mechanisms.

40. The government of India first categorized the Maoists as terrorists in November 2001; the US government followed suit in October 2003.

41. On the CMDP campaign and the emergence of the republican political agenda as part of the civil society platform, see Panday (2008).

42. On the role of the Center for Humanitarian Dialogue, the United Nations, and other international peacebuilding actors, see Whitfield (2008).

43. Following a major dispute over strategy, Baburam Bhattarai was expelled from party positions. Civil society intermediaries played an important role in persuading Prachanda and other leaders that Bhattarai's role as a key interlocutor with other parties and international actors as well as the architect of a revised policy that embraced dialogue made it essential for him to be reinstated. Interviews, New Delhi, April–May 2005.

44. Hari Sharma (2004) argues that the growing role of civil society organizations in Nepal was assisted by decentralization efforts. This is a claim that the government itself was happy to make (His Majesty's Government of Nepal 2000, 2): "In a sense what Nepal has achieved on decentralization during the past decade is a matter for pride. Despite political instability the landmark LSGA was approved and there has been intimate collaboration between HMGN, donors and civil society in supporting a common framework."

45. The challenges of the conflict situation, as well as poor relations between the postcoup royal government and the donor community, contributed to greater donor–civil society engagement. As an evaluation of DFID's program noted (Chapman et al. 2007, 61), "Work with civil society and NGOs has been a major feature of DFID's programme, and these channels have received the bulk of DFID's overall funding during the evaluation period."

46. The 2008–2009 budget calls for "representatives of civil society" to join local peace committees alongside the security forces, local administration, and political parties "to ensure public participation in maintaining peace and security at the local level" (art. 29). It also identifies roles for civil society in the areas of good governance, improvement in service delivery, and public accountability, both in a regulatory capacity (art. 245) and to support anticorruption measures (art. 251). The National Planning Commission (Government of Nepal/UNDP 2006, 50) had noted that "the role of civil societies is critically important in fostering people's participation" in achieving Millennium Development Goals. The interim government (National Planning Commission 2007, 1) had also recognized the "many changes in the mutual relationship between the government, civil society and the people." It called for steps "to make NGOs, communities and the civil society active in the empowerment and development of the target groups" (2007, 58), and specifically calls for an NGO and civil society role in peace and reconciliation as well as in development monitoring (2007, 69–70), including "special monitoring . . . for reconstruction, rehabilitation, reintegration and social inclusion" (2007, 74).

47. For example, the Madhesi Janadhikar Forum, which emerged as the fourth largest party in the CA elections, was originally established as a civil society discussion forum; it registered as a political party only immediately before the election. Similarly, the major *janajati* pressure group, the Nepal Federation of Indigenous Nationalities, originated as a civil society group, developed more service-delivery-oriented NGO functions as it received large donor grants for capacity-building, and ended up negotiating with the interim government for political concessions in the same way as overtly political groups. It secured a twenty-point agreement with the government on August 7, 2007, guaranteeing greater representation for ethnic communities in state bodies and the electoral system, as well as steps to recognize minority languages and other cultural practices.

48. For all the solid advocacy and arguments, civil society leaders had great trouble stopping the TRC plans—but have been successful in holding the line so far.

49. One district-level study confirms some negative aspects (Bhattarai 2003, 23): "The poor respondents were asked about the makeup and performance of Banke's NGOs. A large majority of the 250 respondents said that the civil society institutions were dominated by well-off high caste Hindu men. They also believed that only a few of these institutions had been successful in raising issues and acting for change. They also said that they tended to be politically partisan and not very active."

50. The most sophisticated—and damning—critique of donor-driven efforts to promote "civil society" in Nepal is offered by S. Tamang (2002). Shah (2002) also takes a critical stance, while others (Bhattarai et al. 2002) offer a mixed critique based

on individual case studies from their own experiences. For an analysis of international involvement in conflict resolution and peacebuilding efforts, see Whitfield (2008).

51. One detailed report (NESAC 2002, 150–151) observes that this dependency has driven a wedge between donor-funded NGOs and the rest of civil society: "In financial terms, almost all of the operational NGOs derive their funding from the INGOs. The NGOs also remain extremely dependent on the INGO regime on the policy, programming and implementation-strategy domains as well. The dependence that this generates among the NGOs—together with its implications on the future prospects of an autonomous NGO regime, as elsewhere in the developing countries, has been the subject of considerable criticism. This dependence has also generated a powerful divide between the 'NGO sector' and the civil society. There has been increasing emphasis on 'partnership' relationships between the NGO and INGO. In most of the cases, however, this concept has been more of rhetoric than the actual change in practices. As most of the programs still are dictated by INGOs, the partnerships in large measure remain illusive. Excepting a few cases, in the large measure the program contents of the NGOs reflect that of the INGOs and patron donor agencies."

52. As R. Jenkins cautions (2002, 259), there is little empirical justification for donors' tendencies to separate political parties from civil society, especially during periods of democratic transition: "To assert that political parties can and ought to remain distinct from the social groups it is their function to reconcile is to assign them a role as dispassionate interest aggregators, shorn of ideology and immune to the pressures of power."

53. For example, one leading civil society figure complained about an international effort to involve local figures in a peacebuilding project: "I wrote back saying that peace building can not be a project or a profession. It is among us, Nepalese, to build the peace. They never came back with reply to me." Another international NGO brought national figures on board: "The whole idea was to use us for getting a foot hold in Nepal, to bring experts . . . the money allocated to peace building in Nepal by foreign tax payers is being spent on foreign professionals' travel and production of junk, collecting what we say and putting simple things into unreadable high sounding papers and books." E-mail communication, August 2008. Skepticism about the utility of outside-driven efforts has a long pedigree. As one commentator observed: "Numerous civil society and NGO based groups have also formed numerous forums for peace. At last count there were at least two dozen government and non-government outfits with the word 'peace' on them like the Peace Secretariat, High-Level Peace Committee, Civic Solidarity for Peace and Citizen's Peace Commission . . . the process of peace has become a multi-million dollar industry" (The Peace Industry in Nepal 2004).

13

Sri Lanka: Peace Activists and Nationalists

Camilla Orjuela

The peace rally organized by the National Anti-War Front (NAWF) in Sri Lanka's capital, Colombo, in August 2006 made headlines around the world. The rally gained attention not because this civil society initiative was a turning point toward peace in the war-ravaged South Asian country, but rather because it ended in a scuffle between the peace activists and Buddhist monks who disagreed with NAWF's peace message. NAWF called for a return to peace negotiations and for a political solution to the almost quarter-century-long civil war between the Sri Lankan government and the separatist Liberation Tigers of Tamil Eelam (LTTE). The Buddhist monks were members of the National Bhikku Front, an organization that viewed the attempts to broker peace with the LTTE as a sellout and a threat to the Sinhala Buddhist nation (Amarasinghe 2006).

This confrontation between representatives of the peace movement and the Sinhala nationalist movement was in no way an isolated event. On the contrary, it underscored the contradictory views and struggles within Sri Lanka's civil society. The armed conflict in Sri Lanka, raging from 1983 to 2009, claimed an estimated 100,000 lives and contributed to a polarization of society along ethnic lines, most noticeably between the majority Sinhalese, who dominate the government, and the minority Tamils. The space for independent CS engagement shrunk along with the militarization, and civil society came to reflect the divides in society at large. Thus, in civil society, and in Sri Lanka in general, there has been no consensus as to what peace is and how to achieve it. Sinhala nationalists, like the National Bhikku Front, advocated for a peace defined as an end to the armed conflict in which the LTTE is defeated and the unitary Buddhist state is preserved. Tamil nationalists (including the LTTE), by contrast, believed that peace is possible only when the Tamil people have achieved self-determination. Military means may be necessary to achieve peace, according to both Sinhalese and Tamil nationalists. Cutting against these views, there was an array of CS groups that were committed to interethnic understanding and a nonviolent political solution to the conflict. This chapter looks at the contradictions within civil society in Sri Lanka, maps out the different roles CS actors have played in relation to building peace (in both positive and negative terms), and analyzes the possibilities and obstacles for civil society to contribute to finding an end to the ongoing war/armed conflict. The first section of the chapter analyzes the context of armed conflict and peacebuilding, as well as the composition of civil society in Sri Lanka. Thereafter, seven peacebuilding functions of civil society are examined. The last section draws conclusions about CS roles and civil society's impact in this country.[1]

Context

The armed conflict in Sri Lanka was rooted in the failure of the centralized state to respond effectively to the grievances of marginalized groups. Uneven development and a general lack of access to power not only triggered the Tamil nationalist struggle for self-determination in the northeast but also gave rise to a violent socialist insurrection in the marginal areas of the south. In both insurgencies, it is noticeable that youths were the main players due to their frustration with the lack of opportunities available to them. In Sri Lanka, grievances have been politicized along both ethnonationalist and class lines. Ethnicity was brought into politics during British colonial rule, when Tamils were disproportionately represented in the administration and higher education. After independence in 1948, the political elite in the new democracy had to satisfy their most important constituency: the Sinhalese majority. The result was a "Sinhalesation" of the state. Language policy, university admission reform, unfair access to public service employment, state-run settler programs for Sinhalese farmers in traditional Tamil areas, and clientelism all contributed to a sense among minorities that they were second-class citizens. These grievances laid the foundation for the Tamil struggle for self-determination (Spencer 1990; De Silva 1998; Wilson 2000).

Years of violence increased the polarization between ethnic groups—most clearly between Sinhalese and Tamils—who often held incompatible views about the roots of the conflict and the method by which it could be resolved.[2] However, the conflict in Sri Lanka involved more than the polarization between the government and the LTTE and between Sinhalese and Tamils. Intragroup tensions were important in terms of both the dynamics of the conflict and the possibilities for conflict resolution (Bush 2003). In regional terms, the southern polity has been characterized by a rivalry between political parties and the mobilization of Sinhala nationalism. In the northeast, the LTTE's claimed status as the "sole representative of the Tamil people" was challenged by political/military groups critical of the LTTE, including a breakaway faction in the east.

The economically and politically important Muslim minority, which makes up a substantial part of the population in the contested east, has been squeezed between conflict lines. The Indian Tamils in the tea-estate areas similarly have long-standing grievances that may yet result in future political radicalization (Goodhand and Klem 2005, 53).

The phases of the conflict can be described as an oscillation between full-scale armed conflict and attempts at making peace. The Tamil nationalist struggle turned violent on a smaller scale in the 1970s, with the formation of the LTTE and several other militant groups in northern Sri Lanka. After widespread violence against Tamils in 1983, civil war broke out, fueled by India's support of Tamil militants. Various cease-fires and peace attempts have since interrupted the armed conflict. In 1987, an agreement between India and Sri Lanka brought most Tamil militants into the political mainstream, but it failed to demobilize the LTTE, which took up the fight against the Indian peacekeeping forces. In 1994–1995, a 100-day cease-fire, with talks occurring between the Sri Lankan government and the LTTE, failed to lead to any substantial conflict resolution. In the latest peace process, Norway took on the role of facilitator. The most noteworthy achievement at this time was the signing of a cease-fire agreement in February 2002, which significantly decreased the level of violence. Six rounds of negotiations were held between the government of Sri Lanka and the LTTE until the latter withdrew in 2003. The peace process was criticized for being too elite-centered, as it included only representatives of the Sri Lankan government and the LTTE; it marginalized other voices, including the political opposition, non-LTTE Tamil groups, Muslims, and CS actors (Rupesinghe 2006; ICG 2006b). During 2006, violence escalated and the country was thrown back into a situation of humanitarian crisis and ongoing war. In 2009, the war was brought to an end as the Sri Lankan government managed to defeat the LTTE and kill its leadership. The victory was won with a high cost in civilian lives. Efforts toward reconstruction and reconciliation thereafter have been carried out in a context of continued polarization and asymmetric power relations between those who celebrate the military success and those who mourn their dead.

This chapter focuses mainly on events between 1995 and 2001, the peace process that started in 2002 (then afterward gradually deteriorated), and the new phase of full-scale war from 2006 to 2009.

The war in Sri Lanka was waged on several fronts. In the Tamil-dominated north, where the LTTE controlled a considerable area and ran a statelike administration, a conventional war for control over territory was undertaken. In the multiethnic east, guerrilla warfare dominated; terrorist tactics such as suicide bombings were used by the LTTE in the Sinhalese-dominated south region. Although all ethnic groups suffered from the violence, the Tamils were disproportionably affected, being targeted by government attempts to wipe out the LTTE as well as by LTTE violence against some Tamils whom they viewed as "traitors."

Most individuals and groups in Sri Lanka—even those demonstrating against peace negotiations—have claimed that they are in fact working to build peace in the country. But the definition of "peace" and the ideas put forward to achieve it vary considerably. Nonetheless, one unquestionably important aspect of peacebuilding has been the need to stop the violence itself: between the government and the LTTE, between the LTTE and government-supported paramilitary groups, as well as the violence directed toward citizens by the government, the LTTE, and paramilitaries. As such, sustainable peace necessitates more measures to reduce and ultimately end the violence. Uneven economic development and the frustration felt by groups who experience exclusion from the development efforts of the centralized state (specifically the ethnic minorities as well as sections of the Sinhalese) are at the root of violent conflict in Sri Lanka. Long-term peacebuilding will have to address these development-related grievances. Moreover, in order to resolve the problems at the root of the conflict, inequality and discrimination (along ethnic, class, and other lines) need to be addressed in order to avoid the feeling among large portions of Sri Lanka's population that they are treated as second-class citizens. The inability of the centralized state to cater to the needs of minorities and the long-standing Tamil demand for self-determination suggest that a restructuring of the state toward regional power-sharing is necessary. Apart from the initial grievances at the root of the conflict, other problems caused by conflict also need to be addressed before building a sustainable peace. These include the suffering and trauma caused by the conflict, the possible impunity given to the perpetrators of violence, the enemy images and social divides created during the armed conflict, and the dependency of Sri Lanka in general on a war economy (e.g., for employment of rural youths). Peacebuilding thus has to take place at several levels simultaneously—international, national, local—and involve many different stakeholders. Although the leaders of the government and the LTTE have been the most important actors for peacemaking, it is also important to recognize the role of international actors, such as states and diaspora groups, in giving economic and/or military support to the warring parties—and thereby facilitating the continuation of conflict. The business community in Sri Lanka, with its interest in stability, is one potential actor for peace. Additionally, people at the grassroots level play an important role—as voters (supporting military strategies or peace initiatives), as potential participants in violent acts, and as possible activists campaigning for or against peace initiatives.

Status of Civil Society

On the surface, Sri Lanka possesses a vibrant civil society, with tens of thousands of community-based organizations, NGOs, and other CS groups (Fernando 2003, 12); a strong trade union movement; and a democratic system that once earned the island a reputation for being a successful third world democracy. However, a closer look at contemporary civil society in Sri Lanka reveals that most organizations are created or sustained with outside assistance—either by political actors or foreign NGOs and other donors. Community-based organizations tend to be monoethnic and maintain few horizontal links to other CS organizations (Forut 2001). Political divides along party lines cut through society down to the village level, and political parties have been far more efficient mobilizers of mass protest than CS groups. The bulk of Sri Lanka's trade unions (more than 1,600) are strongly tied to political parties, functioning largely as "industrial wings" of those parties (Biyanwila 2006, 19).

During precolonial times, grassroots communities organized around the need for collective work in temples and for irrigation. Colonialism brought modern organizations, many of which sprang from Christian missionary activity and carried out educational and social work to benefit disadvantaged groups. Christian organizations were soon mirrored by a similar set of Buddhist, Hindu, and Muslim organizations (Wickramasinghe 2001, 76). During the nineteenth century, Sri Lanka experienced large-scale social mobilization in the labor, temperance, and religious (Buddhist and Hindu) revivalist movements (Fernando and de Mel 1991, 3). Civic mobilization and organization in Sri Lanka have been carried out around several different lines: temperance, rural, caste, democratic, religious, anticolonial, and socialist. Although the labor movement contributed to the secularization of civil society politics along class lines, religious and/or nationalist divisions soon came to dominate CS activity. Much of the anticolonial struggle pursued a greater recognition of Sinhalese as well as Tamil languages and cultures; following independence, however, the Sinhalese came to dominate the state. This eventually resulted in Tamil nationalist protests and LTTE's separatist struggle. The Sinhalese and Tamil nationalist struggles were fought by actors from political parties and from civil society. The large-scale nonviolent Tamil protests of the 1950s and 1960s were often led by political leaders, with the involvement of CS groups. With the rise of militancy, there was a decline in earlier movements in the Tamil-majority northeast, such as those of the oppressed castes, teachers' associations, trade unions, and the leftist movement.

After Sri Lanka moved from a socialist economy to an open-market economy in 1977, foreign NGOs and donors began to enter in larger numbers. The growth of the NGO sector can be described as a "taming of protest movements"—what started as popular protest movements were professionalized and formalized into NGOs dependent on foreign funding (Kaldor 2003, 13; Uyangoda 2001). Some CS organizations had also been co-opted by the state; already in the 1950s and 1960s, cooperatives, rural development societies, and school development societies became increasingly used by the government to implement more general development policies and to influence and mobilize the grassroots on political issues (Fernando and de Mel 1991, 4). The most self-sufficient and independent organizations at the village level tended to be funeral assistance societies, where villagers pay a small membership fee and, in case of a family death, receive help with almsgiving and the funeral. Villages also have youth and sports clubs, rural development societies, and temple, church, and mosque associations. Furthermore, Sri Lanka has almost 15,000 cooperative societies, with some 7 million members (Department of Cooperative Development 2007).

The relationship between the Sri Lankan state and CS actors has at times been tense. The state has a history of repressing popular protests, for example in its brutal counterviolence against socialist uprisings in the south, as well as its violent responses to Tamil nonviolent protests in the 1960s and 1970s and the public-sector strike in 1980. NGOs have been viewed suspiciously by the state as well as the general population and have often been perceived as corrupt entities serving foreign interests that need to be controlled by the state (Uyangoda 2001, 192). The natural disaster of December 2004, when a tsunami devastated large parts of the coast, brought a dramatic inflow of foreign funds to international and local NGOs. NGOs were accused of corruption through fierce campaigns undertaken by Sinhalese nationalist parties and organizations, and cries were raised for greater control over NGO activities. The large influx of aid strengthened international NGOs, yet many indigenous CS groups were simultaneously weakened as committed people took up better-paying jobs within international organizations.

The media sector, highly politicized and polarized, has reflected and contributed to the ethnic and political polarization within Sri Lankan society (Kandiah 2001). Sinhala- and Tamil-language media have perpetuated fundamentally different pictures of the armed conflict. During periods of full-scale war as well as after the war, freedom of the press has shrunk considerably; independent reporting has been hampered by unofficial and official censorship, restrictions on travel to war zones, and violence against journalists.

The Sinhala Nationalist Movement

Sri Lanka is often characterized as a country with an "uncivil society." In a country that is ethnically and politically divided, popular mobilization has repeatedly taken place along nationalist and even racist lines. Anti-Christian agitation during British rule and violent anti-Tamil riots in 1958, 1977, and 1983 are examples, as is the Sinhalese nationalist mobilization against attempts to negotiate peace with the LTTE. Political leaders (including government ministers) played key roles in close connection with (un)civil society. An array of Sinhalese nationalist and Buddhist organizations grew out of the preindependence movement for Buddhist revival, independence, and temperance. The Buddhist clergy has been involved in voluntary associations to stage political protests (Frydenlund 2005). Examples in the late 1990s and early 2000s are the National Movement Against Terrorism (NMAT), established with the support of a Sinhala business network; the National Bhikku Front, consisting of

Buddhist monks; and political parties such as Janatha Vimukthi Peramuna (JVP) and Jathika Hela Urumaya (JHU). The parties have been important in terms of providing support and coalition possibilities for the major ruling parties.

The common thread that ties together this range of organizations is mobilization, centered on a commitment to preserving the unity and sovereignty of what they consider to be a holy Buddhist country. This has resulted in protests against giving any concessions to minorities and the view that any negotiation with Tamil militants is "a betrayal of the country" that will lead to a division of the island nation. The notion that the Buddhist religion and Sinhalese race are under threat—a threat perceived as coming mainly from Christianity, the West, and Tamil terrorism—is also central to this discourse (DeVotta 2007). Sinhala nationalist forces have been used to challenge state power, but to a large extent they have also become part of state policy. Organizations promoting nonviolent conflict resolution and democratic values work in the shadow of and challenge the often dominant discourse of Sinhala nationalism.

Civil Society in the Northeast

In the northeast, more than two decades of armed conflict resulted in the brutalization of society as violence, emergency legislation, and limits on the freedoms of association and expression became part of everyday life. This clearly impinged on the development of civil society. While some village-level CS organizations perished, others were formed or strengthened to carry out relief and social services with support from international donors. CS organizations in the war zone have often been monoethnic and lacked contact with civil society in the rest of the country, as well as with organizations in other villages, due to the insecurity, fear, and obstacles to mobility imposed by the war (Forut 2001). Large numbers of educated and economically better-off individuals and youths—the traditional recruitment bases for CS organizations—fled the war zone. Fear and violence have discouraged the northeastern population from taking up leadership roles in civic organizations, as no one wants to take unnecessary risks (Goodhand et al. 1999, 21).

The main impediment to CS activity in the war zone has been military control and repression by the armed forces of the Sri Lankan government, the LTTE, and paramilitary groups. The LTTE claimed to be the "sole representative of the Tamil people" and was unwilling to accept Tamil political engagement outside the guerrilla organization. The guerrilla-controlled area had a number of so-called local NGOs, which were controlled or heavily influenced by the LTTE. Also, CS organizations in government-controlled parts of the northeast were strongly influenced by the LTTE, something that was facilitated and expanded by the 2002 cease-fire. Nevertheless, one CS actor that had a certain degree of integrity and freedom to function in the war zone (including in LTTE areas) was the Catholic Church, with its long-term commitment to working with war-affected people. Under the protection of the Church, priests were able to raise human rights concerns with the warring parties. However, the strong divide between Tamils and Sinhalese within the Church has prevented it from taking a more effective stand against the war.

After 2001 and until the reescalation of war, the environment in Tamil areas was somewhat less oppressive, making nonviolent popular mobilization more common in the Tamil areas, enabling popular protests against the government and its forces. Numerous demonstrations, sit-ins, and *hartals* (during which shops close down in protest) were staged to pressure the government to negotiate with the LTTE in 2001 and to protest the army's occupation of so-called high-security zones, the failure to implement the cease-fire agreement in 2002, killings of LTTE leaders in the east in 2005, and various other issues—all of which converged with LTTE security interests. Although not explicitly stated, it was generally understood that the LTTE, or groups linked to it, were behind the protests. These mobilizations, which often involved students and schoolchildren, sometimes resulted in positive responses from the government administration. In other instances, provocative protests led to violence (Tamilnet 2002). As the war restarted in 2006, there was explicit targeting of CS leaders and people who had engaged in nonviolent protests. Killings and abductions, mainly of Tamils, became common, and the space for freedom of expression and association shrunk drastically (ICG 2007).

Civil Society Peace Work

A number of CS organizations concerned with peace, human rights, and democratic reform were established in Sri Lanka during the 1970s in response to ethnic riots and government repression. After the 1983 anti-Tamil violence, international attention generated an influx of foreign relief funds, much of which was handled by NGOs. Although CS actors had been working for peace and interethnic harmony for decades, a more vibrant peace movement gained momentum in connection with the election campaign and subsequent peace process between the government and the LTTE in 1994–1995. At that time, an opportunity for political change opened up after seventeen years of repression. This, together with the peace attempt, inspired the development of a more active civil society. A number of peace demonstrations and civil society visits to the north were organized. New organizations were formed, and old ones intensified their peace work. The new government brought some CS activists into its structures, but when the peace process failed after only 100 days of cease-fire, many peace activists, like the government itself, lost hope in finding a nonviolent resolution. The peace movement weakened due to its close association with the government, as well as the lack of political opportunities for peace. Civil society largely failed to mobilize protests against the government's increasingly brutal "war for peace" strategy. It was several years before CS actors began again to raise strong voices against the war (Orjuela 2008a, 113–118).

The availability of foreign funding has been an important factor in enabling the growth of CS peace work in Sri Lanka. Donor interest in promoting peace, as well as their channeling of funds through CS organizations, started in the mid-1990s. With the signing of the cease-fire agreement in 2002 and the optimism that prevailed at the time, a number of new donors entered, and older donors intensified their programs in a quest to become part of the Sri Lankan peacebuilding success story and to lay the ground for sustainable peace by promoting reconciliation and popular support for negotiations. The escalated violence thereafter increased the difficulty for peace organizations to advocate for nonviolent conflict resolution. During the peak of the violence and after the defeat of the LTTE, CS organizations that had promoted a negotiated solution to the conflict were pointed to as "traitors," while organizations from within the Sinhala nationalist movement gained wide recognition as "peace organizations" displaying both support for the military solution and solidarity with Tamil war victims.

The CS organizations that have worked to build peace in Sri Lanka have been of many types, with activities at the national as well as the local level. Among the older organizations are the Movement for Interracial Justice and Equality (MIRJE), Devasarana, and the Sarvodaya movement with its Gandhian and Buddhist ideology and large village-level outreach efforts. New professional peace NGOs were formed later, including the National Peace Council (1995) and the Foundation for Co-Existence (2002). A number of research institutes, such as the International Center for Ethnic Studies and the Center for Policy Alternatives, engaged in critical research about potential political solutions to the conflict. Cultural groups like the Center for Performing Arts, several women's organizations, and faith-based organizations, such as the Center for Society and Religion, the Social Economic Development Center (SEDEC), the Young Men's Christian Association (YMCA), and the Inter-religious Peace Foundation, became involved in peace education, dialogue projects, peace demonstrations, and other peace work. In addition, organizations working with development, women's issues, culture, and victims of war (e.g., displaced Muslims, disabled soldiers, and relatives of soldiers missing in action) took part in campaigns and activities explicitly aimed at peacebuilding. Other organizations and individuals engaged in the monitoring of and campaigning against human rights violations, also providing legal assistance to conflict victims. Examples of organizations reporting on human rights violations are University Teachers for Human Rights (Jaffna) and the Law and Society Trust. Additionally, the Civil Monitoring Commission, formed in 2006, organized families of persons disappeared since the new outbreak of war.

A central message has been conveyed by many CS peace groups: a negotiated solution to the conflict (in which the LTTE, being a main actor, would be present at the negotiation table) is essential; moreover, that solution should involve a restructuring of the state toward some type of power-sharing arrangement. CS organizations have also campaigned for human rights issues and the protection of civilians. During and after the 2002 peace process, CS groups advocated for a UN-led human rights monitoring role in Sri Lanka. Some organizations have been more vague about their goals and talked only generally about the need for interethnic tolerance and dialogue. Peace organizations have engaged in a range of activities, including research and advocacy, mobilization of people for rallies and marches, the formation of peace committees to address local conflicts, exchange and dialogue programs, artistic expressions with peace messages, peace education, and raising awareness about the roots of and possible solutions to the violent conflict.

Although an impressive number of organizations, groups, and committed individuals have been involved in peace work,[3] it is not realistic to characterize this as a mass movement for peace in Sri Lanka. Mobilization of protests against the armed conflict to a large degree has proved difficult in the context of ethnic polarization, deep-rooted nationalism on both sides, and the general population's primary interest in securing their livelihoods and safety. The inflow of funds from foreign donors enabled peace organizations to professionalize, to expand, and to staff offices, but accepting funding also obliged them to adjust to the donor's bureaucracy and to focus attention on convincing donors—rather than locals—that they are doing a good job. Foreign funding contributed to transforming peace work from something carried out by enthusiasts in their spare time to more of a business and a source of full-time employment.

The structure and size of peace organizations vary. Some have a large membership base (e.g., the Sarvodaya movement and its youth peace brigade, as well as various associations for disabled soldiers and relatives of soldiers missing in action). But others have limited memberships or are not membership-based at all. Most organizations maintain formal democratic structures, but in practice it is not uncommon to grant decisionmaking power to a charismatic leader who may be the founder and leading figurehead. Trade unions have only by way of exception taken public stands for peace, meaning that the mass-based trade union and labor movements largely operate outside the peace movement. Peace activists have often expressed concern over the lack of cooperation among different peace organizations. The peace movement has thus been fragmented, and attempts to build coalitions or to form umbrella organizations have often not been sustained.

Although most peace organizations aspire to be inclusive, to be nonpartisan, and to bridge ethnic and other divides, the peace movement is itself divided. The definition of *peace* can vary considerably, as expressed by one peace activist during a personal interview (2000): "Peace for Tamils is that the army should get out [from the Tamil areas in the northeast]. Peace in the south might be the LTTE surrendering." The divergent understandings about the character of the conflict and how it should be resolved are present in Sri Lanka's society at large and are thus reflected in the peace movement itself. However, joint actions and meeting points offer a space for people with differing views to negotiate their definitions of and strategies for "peace," however defined. Another crucial divide exists along urban-rural and class lines. The most visible peace organizations have been based in Colombo, and their leading figures are often from the well-educated, English-speaking, urban middle class. Some Colombo-based organizations have been accused of "trying to build peace in English" and of having closer contact with international diplomats than with the grassroots. The gap between the transnational Colombo-based elites (who intermingle with Westerners) and the rest of the population that marks society at large (Hettige 1998, 91) is thus mirrored in, and perhaps even reinforced by, civil society. The urban-rural divide has been widened by the fact that donor agencies are based in Colombo and often limit their contacts to English-speaking elites. Although many peace NGOs have maintained links across geographical divides, some civic leaders in remote areas (e.g., in the war-torn northeast) observe a greater need for reconstruction and reconciliation yet see few prospects for obtaining funding. The gap between the educated elites and the lower classes has to some extent been maintained by the ways in which they engage in CS organizations; Colombo elites interact with diplomats, whereas the poor on the periphery are mobilized for mass demonstrations. The gendered nature of CS peace organizations must also be noted: men tend to dominate the leading positions in peace NGOs and in "peace politics," whereas women are more active at the local level and in less political peace work.

The space within which civil society can work for peace has also had its ebbs and flows. Peace attempts in 1995 and in 2002 generated optimism that spurred peace activism. Intensified war, by contrast, drastically shrunk the space to speak out for peace and to promote interethnic reconciliation. When war escalated, the patriotic discourses (both Sinhalese and Tamil) dominated, characterizing any peace negotiations and attempts to understand the "other" as traitorous. Peace work has been harshly criticized by Sinhala nationalist groups, and examples of attacks against organizers and participants in peace events (e.g., meetings about federalism, cultural events) are numerous. Some of these attacks are suspected to be encouraged by high political offices (Interview with CS leader 2006).

Peacebuilding Functions

The following section discusses the seven different functions: protection, monitoring, advocacy, socialization, social cohesion, intermediation and facilitation, and service delivery.

Protection

Civilians have been the indirect and direct targets of aerial bombings by the government, LTTE suicide attacks, and murders and abductions carried out by all sides. Protection of civilians is an obvious priority: this includes safeguarding civilians against direct attacks, as well as displacement and poverty as a result of war. Both the state and the LTTE have claimed to be the primary protector of civilians, yet it is clear that the main interest for each side (at least during times of ongoing war) was military victory, even at the expense of civilian life.

Local civil society in this context has been painfully powerless. The lack of security has limited their activities. The belief that peace work should contribute to civilian protection remained largely an idealistic and unfulfilled notion. Nevertheless, there are examples where civil society initiatives have contributed, at least indirectly, to protecting civilians against violence and human rights abuses. First, local CS actors have played an important role as partners with international players. The presence of UN agencies and international NGOs involved in humanitarian assistance, as well as organizations with a specific mandate to provide protection, such as the International Committee of the Red Cross (in Sri Lanka since 1989) and the Non-Violent Peace Force (since 2003), has meant that the world closely watches events unfold in the war zone. This has had a certain (albeit not easily verifiable) protective effect. International organizations have often worked closely with individuals and groups from local civil society, which thus has had an indirect protective function by facilitating the very presence of internationals. During the peace process initiated in 2002, local committees created to assist the Nordic Sri Lankan Monitoring Mission (SLMM), designed to monitor the implementation of the cease-fire agreement, included respected CS leaders. These CS representatives thus supported the protection function of the SLMM (even though its actual ability to protect civilians was de minimus).

Second, advocacy work and campaigns carried out by CS organizations could indirectly compel the conflict parties to increase security for civilians. For instance, the families of victims of disappearances organized and voiced concerns publicly and thereby may have contributed to some extent to preventing further kidnappings. In connection with disappearance and other human rights violations, organizations of affected families, such as the northern and southern Mothers' Fronts and the Civil Monitoring Commission, played a role in publicizing atrocities and shaming the government, which was largely believed to be behind the disappearances (De Alwis 1998; Interview with leader of human rights group 2007).

Third, CS actors have engaged in conflict resolution between civilians and armed actors, which can help prevent violence. In many instances, networks of religious and other CS leaders have been spontaneously mobilized to respond to local disputes. But there have also been a large number of more or less formalized peace committees (many established on the initiative of NGOs).

Such committees can include religious leaders and other leading figures; some are committees working for women's issues. The functioning of these committees varies, and it is difficult to prove the extent to which their engagement in conflict resolution has contributed to the deescalation or prevention of violence. One study finds that religious and peace committees are important conflict resolution mechanisms in some cases, such as harassment, interethnic violence, and disputes involving the LTTE and the Sri Lankan armed forces; these are in addition to other mechanisms for conflict resolution that may be available locally. Externally created committees, which may be more representative of the population, often have less legitimacy and authority than those run by established local leaders, but that may exclude women and persons from the lower classes and castes (Center for Policy Alternatives 2003).

Although it is clear that the protection function of civil society is of special relevance during the most violent phases of the conflict, protection is also the hardest function to fulfill. During the peace process starting in 2002 and from 2009, CS groups have engaged in another protection function: demining. Most demining has been carried out by international NGOs, but a local organization, the Milinda Moragoda Foundation, has also been active. Other CS groups have engaged with the landmine issue by raising public awareness about the risks, an activity with great relevance during ongoing war and otherwise.

Monitoring

Human rights abuses have been rampant in Sri Lanka in conflict and nonconflict areas. War-related and antiterrorism legislation has paved the way for further human rights violations. The government's Human Rights Commission has lacked independence and has largely been defunct. The LTTE created the Northeast Secretariat for Human Rights, also with highly questionable independence and effectiveness. CS actors have been crucial to collecting information about human rights violations and developments that might escalate into violence, as well as to conveying this information to national and international audiences. The network created by the Foundation for Co-Existence in some volatile areas (mainly the east) has provided important information to detect risks for escalation. Similarly, human rights organizations—although not always coordinated and comprehensive in their approaches—have published informative reports about human rights abuses, an indispensable counterbalance to the biased and partial reports provided by the state, the LTTE, and the media. Such information has been used by international donors, diplomats, and opinionmakers and indirectly influenced how they act, especially when putting pressure on the warring parties or granting funds for development cooperation. There is little evidence, however, that such early-warning information actually has generated action to prevent violence.

The peace process initiated in 2002 is an interesting example of how "human rights" and "peace" can (at least to some extent) be posed against each other. The initial optimism about the peace process and the unwillingness to focus on negative developments caused international actors and local peace organizations to generally avoid discussions about human rights and, most important, discussions about the LTTE's political murders and its recruitment of children. Even as CS peace organizations enjoyed increased funding opportunities during the peace process, human rights groups found that their funds were drying up.

Human rights groups such as University Teachers for Human Rights were sometimes seen as "spoilers" for pointing out flaws in the peace process (Liyanage 2006, 295). The squelching of discussion about human rights issues contributed to the failure of the peace process by providing arguments to critics. Sinhala nationalist groups pointed to human rights abuses to gain support for claims that the LTTE was not serious about peacemaking and to accuse the international community of turning a blind eye to violence in order to gain peace at any price. As full-scale war broke out in 2006, donors again saw the need for human rights monitoring, but by that point they could turn only to an emasculated group of human rights organizations.

As with the protection function, monitoring is most relevant during large-scale violence. However, during these same periods the space for civil society to undertake protection and monitoring shrinks. Although they are less urgent during times of formal peace, these functions are necessary, as violence most likely has not completely stopped. The impact of civil society's monitoring function can be understood mainly as a support function to protection and advocacy.

Advocacy and Public Communication

Putting pressure on and convincing key actors to engage in conflict resolution, and mobilizing popular support for peace, are necessary steps to end conflict nonviolently. Here, international actors (donors, diplomats, and UN agencies), the business community, and political leaders are likely to have more leverage than CS peace groups. For instance, pressure from business leaders was an important motivation for the government to enter the 2002 peace process. Most of the lobbying efforts by CS peace organizations have been directed at government representatives and other politicians; it has been much more difficult for CS actors to access and influence the LTTE. Advocacy efforts have also been directed toward the international community—diplomats and donors—to convince them to become actively involved in peace efforts and to pressure the belligerent parties to deescalate violence and take steps toward peace.

Research carried out or commissioned by CS organizations has been used to highlight the immense economic and human costs of armed conflict; such information has been used by politicians in parliament speeches. Through publications and seminars, research institutes and NGOs have contributed knowledge, or a larger vision, regarding potential political solutions to the conflict (e.g., federal setups, experiences from peace processes elsewhere). Moreover, media campaigns and the collection of signatures have highlighted the need to end violence, protect civilians, negotiate peace, and find a political solution, at times placing these issues on political agendas. The mobilization of people for rallies and demonstrations has been another way to convey to key actors that "people want peace." Numerous demonstrations have been organized in various parts of the country, but compared to the popular prowar mobilizations carried out by political parties and Sinhala nationalist groups, these have been relatively small in scale. The large-scale peace mediations organized by the Sarvodaya movement avoided explicit political messages. Generally, CS mobilization has exacerbated conflict rather than resulting in a peacebuilding effect. Historically, some attempts to forge deals between Sinhala and Tamil leaders were aborted in the wake of Sinhala nationalist protests. During the 2002 peace process, the demonstrations against peace negotiations and the Nordic mediation—often carried out by Buddhist monks—were more frequent and louder than were the demonstrations in support of the peace process. The end of the war through military means in 2009 is a clear indication of the failure of the peace movement to contribute to peaceful conflict resolution.

It is also important to underscore the role that civil society has played in enabling marginalized and/or frustrated groups to articulate their interests in a nonviolent way. This function is important to prevent violent conflict, but it is more difficult to carry out when ongoing armed conflict shrinks the space for civil society to speak up. It is, as noted above, difficult to define which types of interest advocacy can be understood as "peacebuilding." The lack of space in the political system to facilitate the articulation of grievances was behind the violence of the Sinhalese youth movement in the south in the early 1970s and late 1980s, as well as the violent Tamil nationalist struggle. Ultimately, the state needs to provide channels to articulate and come to terms with such grievances, but civil society (religious organizations, farmers' associations, trade unions, student organizations, and the women's movement) has played a role in articulating the grievances of different constituencies toward the state. CS groups have also campaigned for political reforms that would allow increased access to power for marginalized groups.

The interest of the government and the LTTE in expanding the peace process, conveying information to the grassroots, and building popular support for the process was limited during the peace attempt in 2002. Peace education was instead mostly carried out by CS actors (with donor funding). Some activities explicitly aimed to "take the peace process to the people" (e.g., the People's Forums held in different parts of the country, organized by Sarvodaya, and the National Peace Council). The One Text initiative provided a platform for representatives from political parties and civil society to discuss problem-solving. Opinion polls carried out regularly (although excluding parts of the northeast) by the Center for Policy Alternatives made key actors in the peace process more aware of popular views of peace efforts and current events.

One attempt to make the Track 1 peace process more inclusive was the creation of the Sub-Committee on Gender Issues in 2002, which was to submit proposals on women's issues to the main negotiators and subcommittees formed under the negotiating teams. The committee included nominees from the Sri Lankan government (academics and activists from the women's movement) and the LTTE (former combatants within existing LTTE structures). As the peace process came to a stalemate in 2003, this limited window for CS involvement closed. The lack of separate representation for Muslims was also a concern. The creation of the Muslim Peace Secretariat (parallel to the government and LTTE peace secretariats, which played an important role in administrating the peace efforts) was an attempt to strengthen the Muslim voice. The secretariat was strongly influenced by Muslim politicians, although persons from civil society also played an important role.

The advocacy and public communication function is relevant during all phases of conflict but addresses different issues depending on the situation. During ongoing conflict, advocacy for peace negotiations and for protection of civilians is most relevant; during peace talks, suggestions to broaden the peace process and its agenda are more relevant. It remains difficult to prove the direct impact of CS work on the dynamics of war and peace. However, it is possible to identify CS-promoted ideas that have been picked up by key actors. One example is the language of "facilitation," introduced during a CS meeting with politicians and thereafter used to characterize the Nordic involvement; this was seen as an alternative to the politically unacceptable language of "mediation" (Interview with leader of peace NGO 2001). Many of the suggestions for a political solution raised by the government and the LTTE have been discussed within civil society. International actors supporting peace initiatives have stressed the importance of local CS public advocacy and mobilization for peace, as these provided legitimacy to international and national actors willing to engage in peacemaking.

Socialization

After almost a quarter-century of armed conflict, outright war, peace negotiations, and postwar reconstruction, Sri Lankan society is characterized as living in a "culture of war." Violent acts have led to fear and suspicion, and immobility, general insecurity, and ethnic cleansing have led to the separation of people along ethnic lines. The education system, divided into Sinhala and Tamil schools, along with the one-sided and restricted media coverage, served to reinforce divisions. Reversing the fear, prejudices, and enemy images that characterize this culture of war is critical to making peaceful coexistence possible—but also to building the trust necessary for key actors to engage in peacemaking and for ordinary people to accept a peace deal. Attitude changes can influence the way people vote in elections, whether they choose to support armed actors, and whether they are willing to be mobilized to take part in violence or to protest peace initiatives.

A range of CS organizations have aimed to change popular attitudes and to generate support for peace efforts through peace education, public seminars, information dissemination (media campaigns, books, pamphlets), and training in conflict resolution and negotiation. Such efforts have often been relatively small in scale, and one-off events. Attempts by peace organizations to change people's attitudes have been criticized by forces that do not support peace initiatives and have been described as foreign-funded attempts to "brainwash" the population. Many believed that the best way to promote peace is to lend support to either the government forces or the Tamil struggle. It is clear, not least after the military end to the war, that a critical discussion is needed to decide which attitudes count as "good," and who is to determine what is necessary, when one assesses CS roles in promoting a culture of peace.

When it comes to fostering a democratic culture, it should be clear that being a "civil society organization" does not automatically mean being an organization with a democratic culture. The cultures within CS groups reflect the authoritarian and hierarchical culture of Sri Lanka's society at large. CS groups are often centered on one personality, and decisionmaking is hierarchical (even though many organizations have democratic structures in place). CS organizations at the village and national levels tend to be run and dominated by adults rather than youths, men rather than women, and those of higher class rather than lower. Yet, there are many examples of how civil society provides a space within which marginal and suppressed groups can organize and voice concerns (despite being led by elder men of a higher class). These groups are thereby empowered, and there is broader participation in discussions about peace and human rights.

In Sri Lanka, monoethnic CS organizations are common, and engagement in civil society has tended to strengthen the shared identity of members and participants. Thus, civil society has more often strengthened ethnic identities rather than built identities that bridge ethnicity. Many CS groups have aimed to strengthen their own culture and ethnicity. For example, CS organizations have provided a rare space to express and celebrate the Tamil culture in a context where Tamils otherwise avoid emphasizing their ethnicity for fear of being singled out as suspected "terrorists." The LTTE has also encouraged cultural activities as a way to express and generate support for the Tamil suffering and struggle. Similarly, Sinhala nationalist CS organizations and politicians have promoted the preservation of Sinhalese culture and religion while celebrating the heroism of the Sinhalese armed forces. Such in-group socialization in civil society forms part of the structures of war and heightens the polarization of society; it cannot be seen as peacebuilding. However, there is a fine line between in-group socialization, which supports enemy images and war propaganda, and fostering a shared identity necessary for suppressed and frustrated groups to mobilize and voice concerns.

The socialization function is most visibly relevant during elections. However, attitude change is a long process; this function cannot be limited to certain strategic times. In times of escalated war the media has been dominated by patriotic discourse and the space to publicly talk about peace negotiations and power-sharing has been limited. CS activities aimed at attitude change have been too fragmented, sporadic, and small in scale to achieve any real impact on popular attitudes. Participants in workshops may claim to have gained insights that changed their attitudes, but little long-term attitude change results from a short workshop or peace camp; even fewer change behavior (e.g., in voting patterns). Often, the participants in peace events have come from groups who already support the peace message. The fact that people in 1994 and 2001 voted for a political party that promised peace negotiations but in 2004 voted for a party critical of the peace process cannot be attributed to attitude change facilitated by CS initiatives but rather to dissatisfaction with sitting governments. The lack of functional democratic structures and a democratic culture inside many CS organizations also limits their positive impact on democratic attitudes.

CS actors have been relatively powerless when it comes to instigating change in structures that foster popular attitudes (e.g., the education system and media), although CS groups to some extent have addressed this through advocacy. Nonetheless, small-scale CS initiatives have been important locally and may also have served as positive examples for the state that could spread under conducive conditions. When the government decided in 1996–1997 to undertake an awareness-raising campaign for the devolution of power, it "borrowed" CS methods, ideas, and players for outreach. However, it should be noted that CS "peacebuilding initiatives" aimed at attitude change can backfire with negative effects.

Social Cohesion

Segregation between ethnic groups and strong enemy images have been part of the structures of war in Sri Lanka; they represent obstacles to conflict resolution. The ethnic divides have fed into the conflict; party politics and class divides have also created deep-seated problems. Although civil society is structured along ethnic lines, there are many organizations that bridge divides (e.g., the Lions and Rotary Clubs and the Boy Scout and Girl Guide associations). Most peace organizations have included people from different ethnic groups, who in their day-to-day work have interacted and negotiated definitions of and strategies for peace work. The Kantale Rural Women's Network, which consists of Sinhala, Muslim, and Tamil women in the east, is a powerful example of how joint efforts around shared development concerns can contribute to trauma-healing and building friendly relations with the "other." Joint meetings and visits between district-level chambers of commerce are another example of how people from the war zone and the south have come together around a shared interest (business). The Center for Performing Arts has brought together youths and artists from different parts of the country for joint performances; other peace organizations have initiated dialogue and meetings among local politicians, journalists, and teachers. Youth camps organized by Sarvodaya and other initiatives have regularly brought people together. CS organizations thus have contributed to social cohesion by fostering interethnic relations and organizing people of different ethnic backgrounds around shared interests.

In what ways do such links matter for peace? First, links across ethnic divides can help prevent and deescalate violence (protection). Second, the meeting spaces and friendships created can help change people's attitudes toward the "other" and Track 1 peace attempts. Third, they provide space for facilitation initiatives. Social cohesion is undoubtedly a relevant function, yet people from different ethnic groups interact on a daily basis in most parts of Sri Lanka. In the war zone, there was ethnic segregation and lack of contact; whether CS groups can provide meeting points depends on their ability to protect people who participate. In the war zone and outside, the space for interethnic dialogue shrunk during periods of escalated war or repression.

Like the attitude-change initiatives discussed above, attempts by peace organizations to build bridges across ethnic divides have been small in scale, fragmented, and short-term. The focus has been on carrying out time-limited projects rather than on changing structures. Outcome-oriented activities have been likely to be more sustainable than those carried out "only" to foster interethnic links. Another problem is that peace programs have often concentrated on Sinhalese-Tamil dialogue, ignoring the importance of intracommunity divides and (perhaps more important) the division between moderates and extremists. The impact of civil society's social cohesion activities has been limited as well by the inability to change structures that segregate ethnic groups, particularly the perpetuation of policies of division in segregated schools and media. Poorly organized activities that reproduce discriminatory structures—and a nonconducive environment of insecurity, militarization, and polarization—merely have cemented nationalist and exclusionist attitudes and confirmed prejudices.

Intermediation/Facilitation

Deep mistrust and lack of communication make mediation crucial for nonviolent conflict resolution between key actors and in local conflicts. When Norway took on the role of facilitator at the invitation of the Sri Lankan government and the LTTE in 2000, an official channel for communication opened up. Before that, contact had been more ad hoc, and key persons from civil society—particularly two bishops from the Catholic Church—had played a crucial role in conveying messages between the parties. During times of war, CS delegations in the north provided rare opportunities for southerners to listen to the views of the otherwise isolated LTTE. Even as Norway provided a communication link, CS actors maintained contact at high levels in the government and LTTE and were thus able to expand points of contact. Although CS actors lacked an official role in the Track 1 process, they kept in contact with the main belligerents as well as the facilitators and could provide firsthand information about events unfolding on the ground. Norwegian NGOs, which maintain close links with Sri Lankan civil society, became central as suppliers of information and as contacts for the Norwegian facilitators (Kelleher and Taulbee 2005, 78). The elimination of one of the key actors in the conflict, the LTTE, in 2009, and the imposition of a "solution" by the Sri Lankan government rendered top-level mediation irrelevant.

Facilitation between key actors is most important when official channels of communication are lacking, most often during violent phases, and may actually serve to lay the groundwork for peace initiatives. However, escalated violence narrows the space for civil society to perform facilitation. Restrictions on travel to LTTE-controlled areas, and the general lack of safety, prevented the involvement of many CS groups. During the 2002 peace process, however, the opening of the border and the main road to the north enabled a range of CS actors to visit and contact LTTE and CS groups in the region.

Local civil society has provided mediation assistance at the local level between civilians and between civilians and armed actors. Local peace committees, NGOs, and other CS actors have been important in solving day-to-day problems and improving local relations in the war zone. CS organizations have also facilitated contact and instigated cooperation across other divides, including political divides. The National Peace Council has worked with politicians locally and nationally in a bid to forge links across political party lines, as a crossparty consensus is deemed necessary to sustainable peace.

The facilitation function is relevant when civil society is the sole channel for information exchange between key actors and when CS contacts support and complement official actors. However, the effectiveness of CS actors in facilitating dialogue is limited. Although respected CS leaders can at times have greater access than official actors, the ability to convince the parties to engage in dialogue is restricted. In contrast, foreign governments have the power to threaten the actors with sanctions or offer financial aid to encourage dialogue. At the local level, CS leaders can facilitate the solving of local conflicts, although other conflict resolution mechanisms exist.

Service Delivery

CS actors have been involved in a range of service-delivery activities, including poverty alleviation, microfinancing, the empowerment of women, education and training, and humanitarian work. In many ways civil society steps in where the state fails to provide welfare to citizens. Since the 1970s, CS groups have been engaged by international donors to deliver a variety of services. The tsunami disaster of December 2004 accelerated the inflow of foreign funds through CS channels and increasingly made local CS groups subcontractors for international NGOs.

CS involvement in development and humanitarian service delivery has the potential for peacebuilding and for exacerbating conflict. The peacebuilding potential lies in civil society's relative independence from the state, with its centralized tendencies and history of marginalizing minorities in its development efforts. Civil society can provide services and uplift people in marginal areas ignored by the state and thereby contribute to preventing grievances. Grievances among the Tamil population in central Sri Lanka, which has traditionally worked on the tea estates under appalling conditions, can lead to radicalization. From this angle, CS groups working to improve conditions there can indirectly prevent violence. Trauma-healing is another area where state resources are inadequate, but CS groups have been able to step in. Dealing with the traumas of war may have an effect on the ability of victims to overcome enemy images and to reconcile with the "other."

However, CS service delivery can also increase the divides in society. Ethnic and religious divides within CS groups are reproduced by way of service delivery, and most development and humanitarian activities have not contributed to social cohesion and interethnic cooperation. Some CS service-delivery groups have been explicitly linked to political machinations that lie behind the armed conflict. A number of humanitarian and development organizations active in northeastern Sri Lanka identified themselves as part of "civil society" but were in reality very closely linked with the LTTE and have been accused of channeling resources to the LTTE war effort. Sinhalese CS organizations, meanwhile, have worked closely with the armed forces while using service delivery to "win the hearts and minds" of people in areas captured from the LTTE. Some Sinhalese development organizations have encouraged Sinhalese villagers to stay in or return to contested areas.

During the 2002 peace process, the government, the LTTE, and international players believed that the physical reconstruction of war-torn areas was central to fostering popular support for the peace efforts. Although less important than the state and foreign donors, CS actors also took part in reconstruction efforts. However, there is little evidence of any link between efforts to improve living conditions and popular support for peace (Orjuela 2008b). Eventually, attempts to use reconstruction as a road to peace failed, as the parties could not solve the larger problems of political structure and security (Shanmugaratnam and Stokke 2006).

CS service delivery has played an indirect role in peacebuilding. In some cases it has supported social cohesion (but in fact merely reinforced divides in others) and addressed the grievances of marginalized groups. The impact of CS service delivery has, however, been limited; it pales in comparison to service delivery by the state and international development and humanitarian actors.

Conclusion

In Sri Lanka, the patterns of CS peacebuilding activities have to a large extent been determined by the availability of resources (i.e., funding from foreign donors). Since the mid-1990s, donors have had an interest in supporting "peace activities." This gave civil society an incentive to organize activities that explicitly addressed peace. Workshops and seminars about peace, conflict resolution, exchange programs, and dialogue events (socialization and social cohesion) are relatively easy activities to carry out. Organizations engaged in monitoring and protection experienced financial problems during the peace process, during which they received less donor interest. Since the new outbreak of war, these activities became more important—and also received more financial support. The advocacy function remained important during ongoing war and the cease-fire, but became less feasible after the government victory. Advocacy directed at key actors has been dependent on the initiative of respected, highly educated, and well-connected persons. During periods of escalated violence and after the end of the war, peace advocates have been accused of being unpatriotic. Some activists have also been threatened, and public events have been attacked. This has limited the ability of civil society to engage in advocacy and public communication. The generally weak peace movement has limited the ability of civil society to carry out public advocacy. It has been difficult to mobilize mass support against armed conflict in a polarized society where nationalist mobilization dominates. While the Sinhalese and Tamil nationalist movements have mobilized the masses in what they frame as a "righteous struggle" against a clear enemy (LTTE "terrorists" and the Sri Lankan "terror state," respectively), the peace movement has lacked any such clear-cut enemy. Human rights abuses and the repression of popular protests, past and present, have discouraged and even prevented many people from engaging in public demonstrations.

CS peace organizations have been reactive rather than proactive, both during times when peace seemed possible and when full-scale war diminished their space to act. Vasuki Nesiah (2002) argues that civil society during the peace process was given a role as a "variable that can be strategically plugged-in to legitimate the peace process rather than challenge or re-negotiate its terms." The dependence on foreign funds also implies that peace activism has to some extent been governed by donor priorities. Donors, of course, have not dictated the activities that CS groups undertake, but funding opportunities certainly have guided the planning and priorities of larger CS organizations.

Generally, CS groups that have wanted to support and build peace have focused on relevant problems caused by armed conflict or that maintain it, such as violence against civilians, local conflicts, mistrust, negative attitudes about peace efforts and the ethnic "other," and a lack of interest by top leaders in solving the problem. The relevance of these efforts to producing a sustainable solution are questionable when we look at how the conflict in fact came to an end in 2009. It turned out that the "solution" propagated by the Sinhala nationalist movement in the end produced "peace"—however, a peace that has not solved underlying conflicts and is not owned by large parts of the

Tamil population. It is not easy to categorize CS activities and groups under labels such as "peacebuilding" and "war-mongering." The popular mobilization in the northeast could be seen as support for LTTE military interests, as part of a righteous struggle for a solution (self-determination for the Tamils), and as a way to channel Tamil grievances and to protest in nonviolent rather than violent way. Similarly, Sinhala nationalist protests can be seen as promoting military strategies and polarization—but also as a means to nonviolently articulate Sinhalese grievances and fears. Likewise, we cannot take for granted that an activity carried out by a peace organization actually contributes positively to peace.

There are serious questions as to the effectiveness and impact of CS peace initiatives in Sri Lanka. Part of the problem is, of course, the difficulty in accurately measuring impacts. This is due to problems of attribution, the differences between short-term and long-term effects, and the impracticality of knowing what would have happened in the absence of any CS activities. CS activity did not appear to be central in enabling the peace process in 2002 and in the factors that caused it to fail. In 2002, a "mutually hurting stalemate" between the parties, a change in government, economic incentives, and international pressure were key factors enabling the peace process. Its collapse can be attributed to a dwindling interest by the main parties in continuing, a shift in the power balance between the government and the LTTE, continued violations of the cease-fire, the LTTE's feeling of international marginalization, party politics in the south, a split within the LTTE, and deteriorated trust between the parties. Although propeace attitudes among the general population facilitated the start of the peace process by voting a pronegotiations government into power, the general elections in 2004 brought in political leaders who had less rapport with the LTTE and less willingness to compromise for peace. It is unlikely that CS initiatives to change attitudes had much impact on voting patterns.

Before, during, and after the peace process, CS actors more often protested against peace initiatives. A massive movement for peace in the south and the northeast could have provided an incentive to leaders on both sides to stick to the peace process and the cease-fire. As it was, the propeace CS actors were too weak to counterbalance the Sinhala nationalist movement and to place meaningful pressure on the parties. Sri Lankan experience thus shows that CS actors should be understood as a potential complement to other peacemakers. Peace organizations and activists have been important players in the struggle to promote alternative discourses and practical alternatives to ethnic segregation and prejudices. Although attempts to change popular attitudes and bridge ethnic divides have been fragmented and small in scale, and thus cannot have wide-reaching effects, the networks that peace organizations uphold could potentially be used for larger-scale popular mobilization during more conducive times. The escalation of war and the one-sided victory instead weakened the peace movement and encouraged an upsurge of "peace" activities within the Sinhalese nationalist movement. The Sri Lankan case hence illustrates the difficulty of mobilizing social movements for peace in identity-based conflicts. Popular mobilization and collective action tend to require a shared enemy. In Sri Lanka, the dominant nationalist discourses and enemy images have made it far easier to mobilize Tamils against the "Sri Lankan terror state" and the Sinhalese against "LTTE terrorism" than to mobilize both groups against the destructive war itself. Donor funding can facilitate popular mobilization for peace only to a limited extent (e.g., by funding transportation and other costs in connection with demonstrations).

In spite of the existence of a vibrant civil society in Sri Lanka—and a number of organizations working for nonviolent conflict resolution—the importance of CS peace work is dwarfed by other forces that influence the violent conflict. The main obstacle to CS peacebuilding has been the war itself: the state's and the LTTE's domination over and suppression of civil society, the fear and violence that circumscribe independent mobilization and peace activism, and the deep polarization of society along nationalist lines. As the armed conflict has ended, it remains to be seen if civil society can become strengthened to work for solutions to the many problems that remain in Sri Lankan society.

Notes

The author wishes to thank John Darby, Esra Çuhadar, Neil DeVotta, and Udan Fernando for their useful comments on earlier drafts of this chapter.

1. The chapter is based on research carried out during numerous field visits to Sri Lanka from 1999 to 2009, including more than 140 interviews with leaders of civil society organizations and participants in peace activities, as well as with key actors such as politicians, LTTE representatives, religious leaders, academics, and media representatives (Orjuela 2008a).

2. The Sinhalese make up about three-fourths of the population of Sri Lanka, whereas the Tamils represent 18 percent (including Indian Tamils, 5 percent) and the Muslims 7 percent (according to the last all-island census from 1981).

3. On its website, CHA's "Peacebuilding Directory" listed 214 civil society organizations across the island in 2005.

14

Somalia: Civil Society in a Collapsed State

Ken Menkhaus with Hassan Sheikh, Shane Quinn, and Ibrahim Farah

Somalia is unique as a case study of civil society and its role in peacebuilding.[1] Somalia has been without a functioning central government since January 1991, constituting the longest-running instance of complete state collapse in the postcolonial era. No other citizenry in the world has had to organize itself in such a context. This poses enormous challenges, especially since the explosion of violence following the Ethiopian military occupation of Mogadishu from 2007 to 2008. Somalia arguably has become the most dangerous place in the world to be a civic leader of any sort. The result is that Somali civil society is under extraordinary pressure to provide basic public goods normally associated with a state and to manage and resolve multiple layers of communal disputes and armed conflict—all in an environment that is as "nonpermissive" as anywhere on the planet.

The analysis in this chapter supports the claim that Somali civil society's capacity to engage successfully in peacebuilding has been determined largely by its capacity to assess and manage security risks. That capacity has been impressive in periods of limited armed conflict, producing a robust, adaptive civic peacebuilding in 1995–2006. During periods of war, however, high levels of displacement, social polarization, and targeting of civic leaders for assassination have made it very difficult for civil society to function at all.

Context

Any attempt to organize Somalia's history of state collapse into neat and mutually exclusively categories of war and peace invariably oversimplifies the country's complicated realities. Nonetheless, we can break down Somalia's past into five periods:

1. The period 1988–1992, defined by war
2. The 1993–1994 UN intervention, which constituted a window of opportunity for peacebuilding
3. The period 1995–2006, characterized by localized armed conflict and insecurity but not outright civil war
4. The very brief window of opportunity over several months in 2006 when the Islamic Courts Union came to control most of south-central Somalia
5. The period of renewed war (insurgency and counterinsurgency) since the Ethiopian military occupation of Mogadishu in late December 2006

This timeline, however, is not without imperfections. For instance, there have been brief windows of opportunity for peacebuilding; the Arta peace process in 2000, and the Kenyan peace talks that culminated in the establishment of the Transitional Federal Government (TFG) in 2004, are two such cases.[2] For purposes of this study, however, we need a classification of the time periods in the Somali crisis that respects both precision and parsimony.

War of 1988–1992

The war that began in May 1988 had its roots in decades of oppressive misrule. For twenty-one years (1969–1990), the regime of President Siad Barre governed his poor, mainly pastoral East African country with an increasingly heavy hand. After coming to power in a military coup, Barre consolidated his control of the government by arresting political rivals, recasting the coup as a socialist revolution, and establishing a one-party state. Some notable early accomplishments of the regime were overshadowed by its horrific human rights record, corruption, and manipulation of clannism (Laitin and Samatar 1986). By the early 1980s, the regime faced several liberation movements, and in 1988 one armed group, the Somali National Movement (SNM), launched a major offensive into northwest Somalia. The civil war that ensued produced more than 50,000 mainly civilian casualties, enormous refugee flows, the destruction of Somalia's second largest city, Hargeisa, and a campaign of violence by government forces (Africa Watch 1990). By 1989 other clan-based liberation movements formed, and by 1990, government forces were in retreat.

When the government was overthrown in January 1991, a critical opportunity to forge a transitional unity government was missed. Instead, the various armed factions began fighting among themselves. Mogadishu, like most of the rest of the country, was thrown into turmoil during an extended period of ethnic cleansing (which was clan-driven) by warring militias, resulting in massive displacement, a refugee crisis, and looting of civilians. What began as grievance-based insurgencies degenerated almost immediately into a war economy in which warfare and violent criminality became indistinguishable. A major famine followed in which an estimated 240,000 Somalis died, in addition to the estimated 80,000 killed by fighting in the civil war (Refugee Policy Group 1994, 19–24). This was a period of such grave dislocation and violence that CS movements were not in any position to play a peacebuilding role except in very localized settings.

UNOSOM Intervention, 1993–1994

An unprecedented, US-led peace enforcement mission under the United Nations in December 1992 broke the back of the famine and forced armed militias to keep their weapons and battlewagons off the streets. In May 1993, the peace operation was formally handed over to UN leadership, which was assigned the much more expansive and challenging tasks of promoting national reconciliation and reviving the central government. The two-year period of the United Nations Mission in Somalia (UNOSOM) constituted a critical window of opportunity for Somali political and civic leaders to broker a peace and to revive the collapsed state. But UNOSOM became embroiled in a four-month battle with a local militia, which derailed the mission, leaving Somalia in March 1995 with neither national reconciliation nor a functioning government. Interpretations of the failure vary. Some blame the United Nations for seeking to marginalize the "warlords," thereby provoking the armed confrontation; others blame the United Nations for legitimizing the warlords at the expense of CS leaders; still others place responsibility on the shoulders of Somali leadership that failed to take advantage of the opportunity that the UN operation afforded them to negotiate an end to the war.[3] Whatever the interpretation, nascent Somali civil society was not at that pivotal point in history able to play a significant role in peacebuilding.

Governance Without Government, 1995–2006

When UNOSOM departed Somalia in March 1995, most observers feared that the country would descend into a renewed period of war and anarchy. Instead, south-central Somalia settled into a complex state of "not peace not war" featuring more localized and less lethal armed conflicts, improved local capacity to constrain criminality, and rapid expansion of commerce. In several locations—most notably the secessionist state of Somaliland in the northwest, as well as the autonomous regional state of Puntland in the northeast—formal administrations gained a modest capacity to govern. Throughout most of the country, however, the more common trajectory was the rise of "governance without government," in which informal governance arrangements, involving various combinations of customary law, *sharia* courts, municipalities, business leaders, neighborhood watch groups, and civic movements, worked to provide a modicum of law and order and services to communities. Islamic charities and movements grew in importance during this period as well, playing a central role in expanding basic social services such as education and health care. During this period a more robust Somali civil society began to take shape.

The Islamic Courts Union, June–December 2006

Seismic political changes occurred in Somalia after 2006, transforming the environment in which civil society operated. In June 2006, the Islamic Courts Union (ICU) won a three-month battle with US-backed militias in Mogadishu. The ICU quickly assumed control over the capital and most of south-central Somalia. Though unprepared to take on such an enormous task on short notice, the ICU provided a level of administration and public order that southern Somalia had not seen in sixteen years, earning "performance legitimacy" from the Somali public in the process.

The ICU was a loose umbrella movement, consisting of moderate Sufi clerics, Salafists, and hard-line Islamists. Once in power, the movement gained even wider support from businesspeople, the diaspora, and many Somali nationalists who saw in the ICU's victory an opportunity to reunite the Somali people and to revive the central state.

For CS associations in south-central Somalia, the sudden ascent of the ICU was a mixed blessing. On the one hand, the ICU's defeat of the warlords, its impressive delivery of public order, and the promise of restoring the state won over most civic leaders and groups. Civic groups actively sought to provide policy advice to the ICU and even devised a training program to help ICU commanders create an interim administration, although this had the unwanted effect of aggravating some hard-liners. CS leaders were also supportive of diplomatic efforts to promote dialogue toward a power-sharing accord between the ICU and the weak Transitional Federal Government (TFG), and some urged the ICU to pursue diplomatic rather than military means with the TFG. Those talks constituted the "window of opportunity" in 2006 that, had it succeeded, could have consolidated peace in Somalia.

But the relationship between civic groups and the ICU grew tense as hard-line Islamists came to dominate the movement and began shutting civic leaders out of policy discussions. Women's groups found themselves immediately relegated to second-class status. Even nonprofit groups with Islamist credentials were at odds with hard-liners in the ICU. Civic leaders were also very worried about the ascent of the *shabaab* militia; it was feared in Mogadishu and had earned a reputation for engaging in political assassinations, including the targeting of several of the city's most visible CS leaders. This was particularly a concern for CS organizations with financial and organizational ties to Western donors.

The most troubling aspect of the ICU for CS groups, however, was the bellicose rhetoric voiced against Ethiopia by the hard-line Islamist leadership, a tactic that eventually provoked an Ethiopian military offensive and occupation of the capital in December 2006 (Menkhaus 2007). CS figures were among the voices warning about impending war with Ethiopia. But their influence with hard-line leaders within the ICU was very limited.

The Ethiopian Occupation and Renewed War, 2007 to the Present

When an Ethiopian military offensive routed the ICU militia in late December 2006, the ICU leadership was confronted by angry clan elders and business supporters who accused them of provoking a reckless war with Ethiopia and demanded that the ICU hand over arms and militiamen to their clans. This dramatic confrontation led to the dissolution of the ICU and appears to be the last time that civic leaders were able to wield such direct political power in Mogadishu. Ethiopian forces occupied the capital and were joined by the TFG. As was the case with the ICU, the TFG leadership was dominated by hard-liners. Whereas the ICU had merely marginalized civil society during its short reign, the TFG was much more hostile to any civic organization in the capital. Several of its top leaders insisted publicly that some local NGOs were terrorist fronts and invoked the TFG's declaration of a state of emergency to restrict, harass, and in some instances arrest civic leaders and close down local NGOs and media outlets.

The insurgency, which arose in opposition to the Ethiopian occupation and the TFG, as well as the brutal counterinsurgency that ensued, plunged Mogadishu into the worst levels of violence and displacement since 1991. A combination of indiscriminate shelling of neighborhoods, uncontrolled bouts of looting, and assaults by TFG security forces displaced more than 400,000 people in Mogadishu in 2007, nearly a third of the city's population. For civic groups choosing to remain in the shattered capital, dangers increased with the rise of an epidemic of political assassinations targeting community leaders—elders, clerics, journalists, professionals, and others. These attacks were emanating from both the *shabaab* and TFG paramilitaries. Insecurity worsened as unpaid TFG security forces became a law unto themselves, targeting civic leaders for "arrest" solely for the purpose of extorting payments from families to release the captives. Somali staff members of international and local NGOs were routinely "detained" and then released by insurgents while their activities were scrutinized. By summer 2008, most CS leaders had either fled the country or were keeping a very low profile. Though the Ethiopian forces pulled out of Somalia in January 2009, and a new, moderate Islamist leadership took control of the TFG, the insurgency and counterinsurgency violence has continued, as have the targeted killings of civil society figures. The level of war and political violence has essentially shut down social space within which civic groups operate, temporarily neutralizing any meaningful capacity to promote peacebuilding (Menkhaus 2008).

Status of Civil Society

Civil society has been especially difficult to define in Somalia because of the country's unique context of protracted state collapse, which has posed a series of problems for anyone attempting to locate civil society in the spaces between the state, the private sector, family (clan), and religion (Islam). Thus the very concept of Somali civil society has been subject to debate. Two sequential questions lie at the heart of the discussion. First, is there such a thing as Somali civil society? And second, which groupings in Somali communities can legitimately be considered as part of the definition of *civil society*?

Defining Somali Civil Society

To be sure, some local actors in Somalia are easily defined as part of civil society. Hundreds if not thousands of small community-based organizations exist across the country and provide essential support to their circle of members and to local residents, often in the form of informal neighborhood self-help groups. Likewise, the growing number of "modern" local NGOs devoted to social service delivery, advocacy, and training are incontestably members of Somali civil society. A third category includes professional associations and network groups of medical health professionals, businesspeople, educators, and others.

Beyond these groups, however, definitional problems abound. First, the protracted collapse of the central government since 1991 has meant that virtually every manifestation of social and civic organization in Somalia is, unavoidably, a "nonstate actor." Second, severe levels of poverty and underdevelopment, combined with a lack of government social services, have meant that most social and civic groups must devote considerable energy to generating revenue for themselves. Through no fault of their own, and given the imperatives to earn a livelihood and maintain financial flows to keep programs operating, many "nonprofit" groups take on the features of, and can become virtually indistinguishable from, for-profit businesses (NOVIB 2003b, 10–11). The absence of a government tax code that creates a legal differentiation between for-profits and nonprofits in Somalia compounds this problem.

A related problem is whether Somali businesses, especially large multi-clan partnerships, should be considered part of civil society. Businesspeople are unavoidably a part of civil movements, if for no other reason than they are inevitably approached with requests to provide financial support. In some cases, business figures take on leading civic roles as well. Earlier literature on Somali civil society tended to look past the private sector, but the business community has been accorded status as an important component of civil society (Saferworld 2008, 6–7).

Less easily resolved is the status of clans within civil society. The prominent role of clannism as a source of protection, a vehicle for claims on resources, and a form of identity complicates efforts to define Somali civil society. Historically, the combination of kinship and Islamic law, codified in customary law (*xeer*) and *sharia,* provided the basis of "folkways and habits of community" in precolonial Somalia, something that Ahmed Samatar describes as a "moral commonwealth," or *umma* (Samatar 1994, 111). In this sense, the reciprocal obligations of kin ties as well as the customary law binding lineage members could be seen as reflections of a vibrant civil society in a stateless context. Since 1988, gross insecurity and political manipulation of identity politics have led Somali communities to depend on clans as a source of protection and support. They have also led Somalis to often rely heavily on customary law as the only functioning source of dispute resolution. Because customary law is rooted in blood-payment compensation (*diya*) by lineage groups and is administered by clan elders, this, too, has had the effect of at least temporarily elevating the central role of clans in day-to-day life in Somalia.

Finally, the many Islamic actors in Somalia raise additional questions about who is and is not to be considered part of Somali civil society. Most Muslim clerics and Islamic organizations fall clearly within accepted definitions of civil society. Traditional Sufi clerics, for instance, have long played a central role in civic life as mediators and arbitrators in addition to other roles. Since the mid-1990s, mosques with access to either local or external funds have also played a valuable role as a safety net for destitute households, in addition to serving as the center of spiritual and social life for neighborhoods and villages. A wide range of Somali Islamic charities have sprung up since the mid-1990s across Somalia and are unquestionably part of Somali civil society as well. And the progressive Al-Islah movement, composed primarily of professionals and leaders in higher education and business, is considered by Somalis as an important CS actor (Le Sage 2005, 150–183). When Islamic movements take on overtly political and military roles, however, the consensus breaks down. Al-Ittihad Al-Islamiyya, the armed Islamist movement of the 1990s that aimed to create an Islamic state in all Somali-inhabited portions of the eastern Horn of Africa, is rarely considered part of civil society in Somalia, though some of its formers members are. Likewise, few Somalis would count the jihadist *shabaab* militia as part of civil society.

Confronted with these definitional difficulties, the majority of Somalis, aid agencies, and analysts following Somalia typically embrace a wide definition of civil society, including businesspeople, traditional clan elders, some aspects of lineage-based associational obligations, and most—but not all—Islamic movements in the country. For the analysis in this chapter we accept the broader conceptualization of Somali civil society while acknowledging that there are unresolved problems with extending such a wide definition to some actors.[4]

The nonstate actors that are typically left out of discussion of Somali civil society, or are subject to ongoing debate, fall into one of three camps. The first includes the civic movements that have developed into quasipolitical parties, factions, or aspiring governments focusing almost exclusively on national politics. The ICU, for instance, began as a civic umbrella movement of local *sharia* courts but eventually assumed the role of a de facto national government in 2006, at which point no one considered it to be a CS organization. The second camp includes groups with clearly negative social impacts, including warlord militias, mafioso protection and extortion rackets, and jihadists. Finally, in the third camp purely clannish manifestations of social organization are viewed by many Somalis as not part of civil society, although this in itself is contentious. On the one hand, conventional analyses of Somali civil society would not make the claim that precolonial Somalia was rich in civic associational life because all Somalis were members of lineage units and blood compensation groups. On the other hand, the deep levels of reciprocal obligation that are built into lineage ties, and the important role of clan elders as social leaders and custodians of customary law, are generally accorded a place within definitions of Somali civil society.

The Evolution of Somali Civil Society

In precolonial Somalia, Islamic associations and networks constituted the closest approximation of what would today be considered civic organization reaching beyond lineage ties. Islamic brotherhoods (*tariqa*) brought Somalis of different clans together in a common religious order, and in some instances those brotherhoods founded communal settlements and centers of learning, or *jamaaca,* which provided modest social outreach to the needy. Respected religious leaders of the *jamaaca* also played a vital role in mediating and arbitrating local disputes.

The development of civil society in Somalia in the twentieth century differed little from troubling patterns that existed in other colonial and postcolonial settings. Manifestations of formal civic associational life in colonial Somalia were very limited due to repressive colonial policies and the limited local capacity to organize in a highly rural, subsistence economy. Colonial authorities paid stipends to clan elders in order to maintain a modicum of control over them. In the 1950s, during the ten-year period of UN Trusteeship, the leading nationalist political movements, especially the Somali Youth League (SYL), absorbed nearly all civic energies.

Upon independence in 1960, a number of young CS organizations were formed—mainly student and trade groups. But opportunities to develop CS organizations were constricted by the recruitment of most of the educated and professional classes into the state civil service and by the concentration of much social organization around the dozens of clan-based political parties that emerged in that era (Laitin and Samatar 1986, 65–77).

When Siad Barre embarked on a twenty-one-year period of dictatorship loosely informed by the tenets of scientific socialism, legal space for almost any form of civic organization outside the purview of the state was severely restricted. The most successful civic mobilization of the era was government-led, including an ambitious national literacy campaign in 1974 that sent 30,000 students into the countryside to teach the nomadic populations (Lewis 2002,

216–217). The mosque remained beyond the direct control of the state, but in instances when Muslim clerics dared to openly preach against government policy, very harsh punishments were meted out. In 1975, ten clerics were publicly executed for criticizing a new law promoting equal rights for women (Samatar 1988, 109). In keeping with highly statist, authoritarian practices common to African politics in that era, the Barre regime sought to monopolize most social mobilization within government programs, or to manipulate and control forms of civil society as extensions of the Somali Revolutionary Socialist Party (SRSP). Predictably, the main type of autonomous nonstate organization came in the form of armed liberation movements aimed at deposing the government.

The simultaneous end of the Barre regime and the collapse of the state in 1991 did not initially produce new opportunities for civil society. On the contrary, the extraordinary levels of displacement and insecurity during the two-year civil war made it exceptionally difficult for older forms of civic life to operate and for new CS organizations to develop. Clan elders and the customary law they sought to enforce were entirely overwhelmed by the scale of the war. High levels of communal distrust, reinforced by the ethnic cleansing that polarized the country, made it very difficult for Somalis to forge cross-clan alliances. Most Somali professionals, who under normal circumstances would have provided an important component of civic organization, fled the country.

Even so, a handful of new civic groups were established in 1991–1992 and, despite the high level of insecurity, were able to function within areas their clans controlled. Interestingly, some of the most effective local NGOs at that time were launched, led, and managed by women, reflecting the importance of civil society as a platform for women's rights and organization in Somalia since 1988. For instance, Women Development Organization (IIDA), formed in 1991 by Somali civic activist Starlin Arush, became a major force in the politically contested area of Merka.[5] Another organization, Save Somali Women and Children (SSWC), was formed in 1992 by a group of women with the aim of providing relief and development assistance to women affected by the civil war. Both of these NGOs subsequently developed into leading peacebuilding movements; the director of SSWC, Asha Haji, was awarded the Right Livelihood Award, the "alternative Nobel Prize" for peacebuilding.[6]

The two-year (1993–1994) UN peace operation in Somalia created a dramatically different environment for Somali civil society, but it was not conducive to the development of authentic, sustainable civic groups. The intervention provided a somewhat safer climate for civil society, but Somalis who dared to organize against or threaten the interests of powerful factions still lived at considerable risk. As a result, the window of opportunity that UNOSOM thought it was creating elicited a weak response from Somali civil society, which understood correctly that UNOSOM was only in the country for a short period and was in no position to guarantee their security. CS figures had reason to be skeptical of the UN commitment to grassroots involvement in the peace process: UNOSOM convened only top factional leaders to broker the initial Addis Ababa Accord of March 1993, leaving civic groups out, and in the final year of the failing operation the United Nations sought only to broker a deal among the top three or four militia leaders in the country (Menkhaus 1997; Stork 1993).

Worse still, UNOSOM unintentionally distorted the entire concept of local NGOs. Sizable UN funding made available to promote development and economic recovery triggered a dramatic mushrooming of new "local NGOs" competing for contracts to implement those projects. World Food Program "food-for-work" projects required Somali community groups to apply for grants, in which they proposed to perform a community works project in return for food rations. Other relief and development agencies had similar programs. None of these involved local peacebuilding activities, and there was little if any thought given to how to infuse a peacebuilding component into local NGO projects.

The intent of these programs was well-meaning—to infuse food and funds into the economy and to create employment and alternative livelihoods for militiamen—but the unintended effect was to trigger the establishment of hundreds of local NGOs created solely to secure aid money and food. The port city of Kismayo alone had more than seventy registered local NGOs in 1993.[7] Across Somalia, these new "pocket NGOs" quickly gave themselves names, stationery, and a storefront sign, preferably on the road between the airport and town. Upon investigation, the vast majority of these local NGOs were created and controlled by local factions, militias, and businesspeople who sought to divert foreign aid flowing into the country. Others were merely charities formed by a single individual. Very few involved cross-clan partnerships; most local NGOs at that time were closely identified with a particular clan or subclan. Rumors also circulated of demands by some aid officials for various kickbacks and other favors from local NGOs in return for food-for-work contracts. Even legitimate local NGOs were hard to distinguish from small businesses seeking contracts from UNOSOM. The international aid agencies were largely responsible for this phenomenon, as they rewarded local institutions created in their own likeness. The level of cynicism this engendered in the relationship between external donors, international NGOs, and local NGOs is difficult to overstate.

The verdict on the UNOSOM period and its impact on civil society in Somalia has thus been surprisingly harsh. Far from creating space for civic groups to form and grow, UNOSOM unintentionally distorted the concept of the local NGO, produced an epidemic of hundreds of bogus NGOs, and contributed to a culture of corruption and lack of accountability that took years to reverse. In fairness to UNOSOM and the many development agencies operating in Somalia at the time, their principal objectives were to promote rapid economic recovery and to transition away from emergency relief, not to build a vibrant and sustainable local civil society. Revealingly, the vast majority of pocket NGOs disappeared as soon as UNOSOM departed (CRD 2006a, 8).

The period from 1995 to 2006, described above as a decade of "governance without government," witnessed an extraordinary blossoming of Somali civil society. Despite often severe problems, CS came to play central roles in social service delivery (especially education and health care), human rights advocacy, peacebuilding, and the provision of local governance.

This growth in the capacity and power of Somali civic groups in the post-UNOSOM period contributed to incremental improvements in local security and governance. At the same time, improvements in basic governance and public security during this period provided a more conducive environment for a range of civic groups to emerge or reassert themselves. The growth of civil society and improvements in public security thus constituted a virtuous cycle; each reinforced the other in mutually beneficial ways.

This period also saw clan elders reassert their authority. Elders served to contain lawlessness, mediate disputes, and broker local peace accords in much of south-central Somalia. In northeast Somalia—which in 1999 declared a nonsecessionist state of Puntland—clan elders were from the outset powerful actors in the maintenance of peace and served as the main brokers of the agreement creating the Puntland government. Elders were confronted with a new and extraordinarily complex political and security landscape. To cope with the challenges, clan elders forged working relationships with business leaders, other civic leaders, and professionals.

The well-documented rise of the Somali business class in the mid-1990s both created a whole new category of civic leaders and provided an important new source of financial support for some civic organizations. Local NGOs were quick to realize the potential of business leaders as supporters, and in some instances they brought in business leaders to serve as NGO board members. For their part, business leaders saw in many new civic organizations opportunities to advance their own interests, especially in the promotion of improved local security and public order. Business leaders became vital financial supporters of local *sharia* courts for this reason.

The large Somali diaspora—now estimated to number 1 million people—came to assume an important place in civic life in Somalia during the post-UNOSOM period as well. Its principal role has been and continues to be as an economic lifeline; the remittances it sends back to family members have been estimated to total about US$1 billion per year, dwarfing all other sources of revenue. By the late 1990s, wealthier diaspora members began to invest in businesses, helping to fuel the rapid expansion of private-sector activity; in some cases they funded or even established local NGOs and community projects. Today, many Somali civic associations rely to some degree on contributions from the diaspora. Not surprisingly, most of these civic projects targeted the clan home areas of the diaspora groups.

In a few instances, diaspora members have mobilized significant resources in support of a local nonprofit serving the broader community, not merely a particular clan territory. In Hargeisa, Somaliland, the Edna Aden Maternity Hospital is a high-quality medical center established in 2002 with generous contributions both from donor agencies and the Somali diaspora (Edna Aden Maternity Hospital 2008). A second example is Mogadishu University, a nonprofit institute of higher education created in 1997 by faculty from the prewar Somali National University and other civic leaders, including the Islamist society Al-Islah. It has drawn on extensive contributions from Gulf states and the Somali diaspora and by 2006 featured seven undergraduate programs and several thousand students (Mogadishu State University 2006). It has managed to stay partially operational despite massive violence and displacement since 2007.

The diaspora has also been a growing source of civic leadership in Somalia.[8] A small but increasing number of diaspora members are opting to return to Somalia—either for a fixed period of time or with the intention of remaining permanently—and assuming lead roles in civic associations. A similar process of "diasporization" has occurred in government, the private sector, and even the Islamist opposition movements, all of which feature a disproportionate number of diaspora members in influential positions. This trend is generally positive, in that it demonstrates an enduring commitment on the part of Somalis abroad to their home country, and because it is tapping into the main reservoir of professional expertise in Somali society, most of which is currently living abroad.

The ascent of Islam in Somalia's social and political life is probably the single most important trend shaping civil society since 1995. The rise of local *sharia* courts as a popular response to chronic insecurity and state collapse began as early as 1994 and quickly spread across much of south-central Somalia. The courts were one of the central pillars of the "governance without government" that defined the post-1995 period. Islamic charities also began to assume much greater prominence in this period, filling the vacuum left by the collapsed state and waning Western engagement. Islamic charities benefited from the growing flow of funds available from state and private Islamic benefactors in the Arab Gulf and Islamic states in South Asia, reflecting a shift in Somali civil society away from what had been in the past an exclusive orientation toward the West for ideas and support. By the late 1990s, Somali charities backed by external Islamic funders assumed a more important role, compared to Western-backed NGOs, in social service provision in Mogadishu.

Another factor contributing to the rise of Somali civil society in the post-UNOSOM period was a shift in policies on the part of the Nairobi-based donors and international NGOs working in and on Somalia. In contrast to the UNOSOM period, when local NGOs were viewed purely as instruments of project implementation, an effort was made to support sustainable Somali civic organizations and local, not foreign, ownership of agendas and priorities. A major study of donor policies in Somalia in 2002 concluded that a peacebuilding approach, one that "favors bottom-up development, with comprehensive civil society participation at all levels, as a means to local and national consensus and ultimately reconciliation, is increasingly supported by regional and international stakeholders, and by the Somalis themselves" (NOVIB 2002, 12). This approach translated into specific programs designed to build up CS capacity and promote peacebuilding. The European Commission, which in the post-UNOSOM period was the single largest donor for Somalia, created a program dedicated entirely to peacebuilding in the latter half of the 1990s and, later, recast it as a crosscutting objective. In 2000 the European Commission began funding the largest support initiative in Somali civil society, the Strengthening Somali Civil Society Organizations project administered by Oxfam-NOVIB. The US Agency for International Development (USAID) funded the Strengthening Civil Society program through CARE with the aim of fostering "strong civil society organizations that contribute to good governance and peace building with cooperative, productive linkages with civil authorities" (CARE/USAID 2002, 3).

In reality, some of this "subcontractor" relationship has remained intact, and relations among donors, international NGOs, and local civil society remain asymmetrical and strained. Donors vacillate between viewing local civic groups and NGOs as a useful means to an end (as implementers of foreign aid projects) and viewing them as a worthy end in and of themselves (as an essential foundation for good governance and economic recovery). It is also important not to overemphasize the impact of Western donors and aid agencies on Somali civil society. Donor policies impact only a subset of Somali civil society—namely, those local NGOs that rely heavily on Western funding.

In a number of instances local civic groups and organizations with a peacebuilding focus have been successfully spun off from international NGO projects and took on important roles in their regions. The Swedish international Life and Peace Institute (LPI) "midwived" a local successor in 2002, resulting in the creation of the Forum for Peace and Governance (FOPAG) (Tamm et al. 2004, 45–46). Interpeace (formerly the War-Torn Societies Project, or WSP) saw three of its national affiliates develop into research and peacebuilding centers of enduring importance in Mogadishu (the Center for Research and Dialogue, or CRD), Puntland (the Puntland Development Research Center, or PDRC), and Somaliland (the Academy for Peace and Development, or APD).[9]

One of the most important types of external support to Somali civil society includes efforts by international NGOs such as Saferworld, Interpeace, the Catholic Institute of International Relations (CIIR), and Oxfam-NOVIB to support national NGO networks to improve their abilities to coordinate with one another (Hutchison 2004; NOVIB 2002; Saferworld 2008).

Despite the blossoming of Somali civil society since 1995, and despite the wave of new networking opportunities and the expansion of training and support, Somali civic groups continue to face predictable, daunting challenges. Reports on the sector indicate that Somali CS groups are constrained by problems of low capacity, high turnover of personnel, basic management and accountability issues, and severe shortages of funding (NOVIB 2002; 2003a; 2003b). Most have had difficulties transcending clan or regional divides. They are generally viewed in the eyes of the Somali public as elitist. There remains a deep chasm between Islamist and non-Islamist local NGOs; with few exceptions, each operates largely in its own world, reflecting the weak collaboration between Islamic and Western donors. Relations with donors have at times been poor, reflecting donor uncertainty about the actual functioning of local NGOs in what aid officials call the "accountability-free zone" of southern Somalia. Some of the best local NGOs have been victims of their own success, as they have been inundated by demands on their time and expertise. Rivalries over scarce resources and leadership roles have hampered cooperation; the latter has in a few instances produced rival umbrella groups, defeating the very purpose of the concept. Some of the most effective local NGOs have been too dependent on charismatic personalities and have had difficulty creating deeper institutional capacity. And all Somali civic organizations have had to navigate the extraordinary security dangers associated with the Somali crisis. These security threats were generally manageable from 1995 to 2006, but since 2006 the levels of insecurity in south-central Somalia and Puntland have overwhelmed Somali CS activities.

Peacebuilding Functions

The following section considers the seven different CS functions: protection, monitoring, advocacy, socialization, social cohesion, intermediation and facilitation, and service delivery.

Protection

The notion of protection in the Somali setting is deeply rooted in clan and kinship ties. In the event of violence and threat of violence, individual protection is mainly ensured by the system of blood-payment compensation to the victim's clan or the clan's deterrence capacity (i.e., the certainty of a reprisal attack). In only a few instances have CS organizations outside the clan been in a position to afford protection to individuals against threat of physical attack from self-declared political authorities and violent nonstate actors. An obvious corollary to this rule is that membership in more powerful lineages, and in lineages with a strong presence in one's place of residency, affords greater personal protection than membership in a weak clan or one with a physical base far from one's domicile. A partial exception to this generalization has been the use of marriage, business partnerships, adoption (*shegad*) into a stronger clan, and other forms of strategic dependence in which individuals or groups enjoy a certain degree of protection courtesy of a patron clan.

The ability of clannism to serve as a source of protection has varied over the course of the past two decades. During the period of civil war in 1991–1992, membership in a strong clan could actually render Somalis more susceptible to attacks intended to kill, as the most powerful clans were at war with one another. Members of weak lineages and Somali social groups outside the Somali lineage system (Somalis with Bantu, Bajuni, Rer Hamar, and other "minority" identities) were much more vulnerable to looting, assault, and rape but were somewhat less likely to be killed outright. In the period of armed conflict between 1995 and 2006, the reassertion of customary law and *diya* payments afforded all Somalis a somewhat greater level of protection, with members of stronger clans enjoying greater freedom from threat of assassination and kidnapping. With the onset of renewed civil war since 2006, the protection of clans has partially broken down again, especially in contested areas where the TFG and jihadist insurgents are operating. The *shabaab* jihadists have in particular shown a willingness to assassinate members of their own clan—and have done so with impunity.

A few human rights groups provide protection to the Somalis at risk of attack due to ethnic identity or political affiliation, hiding individuals or providing accompaniment to their final destinations. The Mogadishu-based Dr. Ismael Jumale Human Rights Center (DIJHRO) and the Baidoa-based Isha Human Rights Organization (IHRO) are said to be engaged in such protection activities. This is a high-risk activity in the political environment, however, and remains almost exclusively an obligation shouldered by the clan of the individual under threat.

Monitoring

By contrast, the monitoring capacities of Somali CS groups have developed significantly since 1991. Virtually no local capacity existed in the civil war of 1991–1992 for monitoring and reporting on human rights abuses, war crimes, abuses of power by local government, and the activities of agents of armed violence and war. What little was known at that time was reported by Somali officials of international aid agencies and external media. During the UNOSOM period, Somalia witnessed the first explosion of private, locally owned media outlets. Most were initially linked to factional interests, but in the post-UNOSOM period, radio, newspaper, Internet, and even television stations in the country began to exercise greater independence and began to engage in investigative journalism. Radio Shabelle, Radio Galkayo, HornAfrik, *Somaliland Times*, Garowe On-line, and Hiraan On-line were among the more active media with the requisite levels of independence, resources, and commitment to investigative journalism to play a monitoring and watchdog role.

Beginning in the post-UNOSOM period, Somalia saw the rise of a number of civic groups dedicated to reporting on violations of human rights and civil liberties. Many local NGOs with operational activities have also played a formal or informal role in advocacy for human rights. This is especially true of women's NGOs and networks that have often been among the most forceful critics of warlordism, criminal violence, crackdowns by local authorities, and violence against women.

All Somali organizations playing a monitoring role have been vulnerable to pressure, threats, attacks, and even assassination, especially since 2006. The TFG has treated media outlets with great suspicion, periodically arresting journalists and closing down media operations. Assassinations of Somali journalists have reached epidemic proportions. In 2007, fourteen Somali journalists were killed, including the managing director of Horn Afrik Media, Ali Iman Sharmarke. Only one other country in the world, Iraq, had higher casualty levels among journalists that year (IFJ 2008). Likewise, Somali advocacy groups engaged in actual or perceived reporting of human rights abuses face extreme security threats. A number of prominent CS figures in Somalia, including the former director of CRD, Abdulkadir Yahya, have been assassinated. This has a chilling effect on the ability of civic groups to engage in even the most cautious reporting on abuses. NGOs that in the past cataloged abuses are now reluctant to disseminate their records and to mobilize campaigns on the basis of these findings for fear of reprisals from militia leaders, radical Islamists, freelance militias, and TFG security forces.

Advocacy and Public Communication

Somali civil society has a long history of effective advocacy toward political and militia leaders as well as external actors. Clans are in particular acutely sensitive to protection of their interests and aggressively lobby political figures and aid agencies to ensure they are accorded a fair share of resources and positions. In some cases, clans have effectively used affiliated CS groups to advance their claims.

Advocacy activities transcending narrow clan interests—such as women's rights, human rights, and business lobbies—have grown since the mid-1990s. The main targets of this advocacy continue to be the troika of Somali national and subnational governments, other nonstate political and military actors (militia leaders, politicians, elders), and external actors (both donor agencies and governments). Of these, the advocacy work directed at local authorities is of greatest interest.

Except perhaps for the *shabaab* and a handful of warlords, most aspiring political leaders and movements in Somalia are very attuned to public opinion. And Somali public opinion is shaped in large part by the local media, on which Somalis rely very heavily for news and opinion. In the post-UNOSOM period, Somali CS groups learned to use the media as an advocacy and pressure tool.

The more effective civic organizations cultivated close ties to major media outlets, helped to develop story lines, and provided interviews to raise public awareness and pressure political or military leaders. The three Interpeace affiliates—CRD, APD, and PDRC—developed impressive film documentary capacities used to promote awareness of peace and development issues across the country and to give voice to ordinary Somalis in powerful ways (CRD 2006b, 11–12). Those three local think tanks have also engaged in action research aimed at learning lessons from successful and failed peacebuilding efforts, resulting in a series of rich peacebuilding case studies.[10] Many of the "modern" local NGOs have established websites to communicate information, share written products, raise awareness, and fund-raise. Most Somali CS groups also learned to amplify their message via international partners, networks, and global media. The National Union of Somali Journalists (NUSOJ), for instance, garners far more attention to its appeals, and places local authorities under much greater pressure, by relaying its criticisms of attacks on the media through the International Federation of Journalists. This latter tactic has proven especially useful in the post-2006 context of repression and threat of physical attack; human rights groups are able to afford themselves a bit more protection by channeling sensitive accusations and information through international counterparts rather than saying it directly.

Communication outreach to the Somali public has also been successful through training workshops, which multiplied in the post-1995 period. Local NGOs are more often than not the conveners of training sessions funded by external donors yet are able to shape the agendas of these training sessions. CRD in particular has dedicated considerable time and energy to convening different sets of stakeholders in peacebuilding—elders, women, businesspeople, the diaspora—with the aim of strengthening their capacity to play a role in peacebuilding (CRD 2006b). There is no systematic means of measuring the longer-term impact of the hundreds of workshops convened on topics ranging from human rights to gender discrimination to peacebuilding, but anecdotal evidence suggests that the method has helped to raise awareness among the opinion-shapers of Somali society. For example, political and social awareness of the issue of protection, rights, and representation of minority groups in Somalia, a topic that in 1991 was nonexistent in Somali political discourse, is now institutionalized in the famous "4.5 formula" of proportional representation in Somali national assemblies (with minority groups constituting the "0.5" of seats in these assemblies).[11] Similarly, Somali women's NGOs have been very effective in raising awareness of the rights of women to direct representation in government and were instrumental in convincing the delegation at the 2000 Arta peace talks to accord women a share of representation in the talks as Somalia's "sixth clan." And Somali health NGOs have been crucial in raising awareness and promoting public policy on HIV/AIDS in Somalia. Likewise, women's NGOs have been forceful critics of the practice of female genital mutilation.

Networking among Somali NGOs has proven to be an important means of amplifying advocacy and public communication as well. Among the many consortia and NGO networks we can include the Coalition of Grassroots Women's Organizations (COGWO), in existence since 1996; Nagaad, an umbrella movement of thirty-two women's organizations, since 1997; the Consortium for Somaliland NGOs (COSONGO), an umbrella group of eighty-three local NGOs; the Peace and Human Rights Network, composed of twenty-one NGOs, since 1997; and the Somali South-Central Non-State Actors Association (SOSCENSA), a consortium established in 2007. Numerous professional associations, such as the NUSOJ, have also been created, in some cases with external support. External actors have also supported numerous national-level training programs to local NGOs and have underwritten the costs of major CS gatherings, such as the Somali Civil Society Meeting in Entebbe, Uganda, in March 2008, in which 150 CS leaders were able to meet, share information, and formulate common policies (Saferworld 2008); and the 2002 Somali Civil Society Project Symposium in 2002, at which CS leaders produced the "Hargeisa Consensus" on joint priorities and an NGO Code of Conduct (NOVIB 2003b). The Strengthening Somali Civil Society Organizations Project is the epicenter of national CS networking and coordination, as well as the repository for some of the most detailed studies on Somali civil society (SCS Project Website 2008). The Somalia NGO Consortium plays an important role in coordinating local and international NGOs. Established in 1999, it includes fifty-seven international and thirty-four local NGOs and serves as an important clearinghouse for information (Somalia NGO Consortium 2008).

External initiatives have also attempted, with mixed success, to organize the business community into more coherent interest groups. The UN Development Program has supported efforts to establish a number of business sectoral groups, such as a Somali Telecom Association and the Somali Airline Association, as well as the Somali Business Council based in Dubai. Local initiatives to build a more cohesive business community have also borne fruit. The nonprofit business university SIMAD (Somali Institute of Management and Administration Development) in Mogadishu began to publish a journal, *Somali Business Review,* with the objective of providing a forum for best practices for Somalia's businesspeople.

Since 2000, CS groups in the south have sought to establish a single Somali CS forum—a network of networks—in order to amplify the voice of civil society in dialogue with Somali political authorities and external actors. This local initiative is composed of four major networks, with the Center for Research and Dialogue serving as a facilitator.

Somali civil society has also resorted to the use of public rallies, demonstrations, and marches as a high-risk tactic to pressure political figures. The most dramatic example of this was the public mobilization surrounding the Mogadishu Stabilization and Security Program (MSSP) in the summer of 2005, which saw community-based women's groups single-handedly take responsibility for feeding demobilized militiamen, spontaneous public rallies at militia roadblocks to pressure gunmen to dismantle the checkpoints, and forceful public criticism of militia leaders on talk radio in Mogadishu (CRD 2006a, 22–24; Menkhaus 2007).

Finally, in a few instances Somali CS groups have moved beyond serving as advocates and interest groups and have actually become directly involved in shaping political processes in polities such as the Puntland administration and the Somaliland government. In Puntland, the WSP affiliate, which eventually took the name Puntland Development Research Center (PDRC), was deeply involved in the civic dialogue that eventually produced the decision to establish the Puntland government itself (WSP 2001). In Somaliland, local NGOs have played a variety of important political roles. Essential technical support was provided to the Somaliland National Electoral Commission by the Academy for Peace and Development to enable it to manage the many legal, procedural, and administrative tasks of overseeing the 2005 parliamentary elections (APD 2006, 8–9). NAGAAD successfully petitioned the Somaliland parliament to change laws to abolish the practice of female genital mutilation (Hutchison 2004, 13–14) and drafted proposed legislation on the legal status of NGOs. In national Somali politics, civil actors played a lead role in the Arta talks that produced the short-lived Transitional National Government in 2000; Al-Islah also had an influential role in the process (Le Sage 2005, 167; Marchal 2002, 15). In addition, several local NGOs have succeeded in negotiating the treacherous political terrain surrounding the Transitional Federal Government to provide assistance to several TFG capacity-building functions, including the Joint Needs Assessment exercise (a dialogue among the TFG, donors, and civil society about priority needs for development) and support to district councils.

A number of CS groups have also been instrumental as sources of information and analysis for external donors and governments involved in promoting Somali peace processes and peacebuilding. Because external actors are concentrated in Nairobi, Kenya—Somalia is far too dangerous to permit relocation of embassies and aid agency headquarters to Mogadishu—foreign actors face real limits on their ability to understand politics inside the country and are, as a result, especially dependent on local intermediaries to explain and interpret events. Local civic groups have at times enjoyed the position of having real impacts on the perceptions of key foreign actors involved in Somali peace processes. But this role has proven very risky, especially when Somali CS leaders and aid workers have been accused by *shabaab* jihadists of being "spies" for the West.

The capacity of Somali civil society to perform advocacy and public communication functions in the name of peacebuilding has proven more sensitive to conditions of violence than any other peacebuilding activity. Advocacy and public communication are typically a high-visibility exercise, and in periods of war—especially wars that are constrained by few rules regarding the targeting of civilians and that produce massive displacement—civic leaders engaging in public advocacy make themselves exceptionally vulnerable to threats and violent reprisals.

Socialization

As noted above, Somali CS groups undertook extensive efforts to socialize the public on a range of issues related to peace and good governance. What is difficult to measure with any degree of certainty is the actual impacts these efforts have had on public attitudes. Moreover, the ebb and flow of public opinion on matters of governance, conflict, and peacebuilding are shaped by hundreds of other factors besides the earnest work of a handful of civic groups in the community. This basic cautionary note about attribution of causality to peacebuilding projects has long bedeviled impact assessments of such CS work in Somalia and other postconflict settings (Menkhaus 2003).

Still, anecdotal evidence provides some reason to believe that Somali civil society has been influential in helping to reshape attitudes toward peace and peacebuilding, especially at the level of opinionmakers in society—the "second tier" of civic and business leaders whose own views can shape those of top leaders as well as the broader public.[12] Civic groups have had mixed success changing public attitudes about democratic values, good governance, and other political issues. And even though civic groups have certainly succeeded in placing new items on the political agenda (such as minority rights and HIV/AIDS), public attitudes toward the role of the state remain tightly linked to time-honored notions of patronage politics and a vision of the state as a "cake" to be carved up by clans. Perhaps because the country has been preoccupied by urgent matters of peace and reconciliation, public discussions of essential political questions—systems of representation, political devolution, clan identity and land rights, the role of Islam in future governance—have enjoyed less robust dialogue than peace and peacebuilding.

Some civic groups have unquestionably played a powerful in-group socializing role. The ascent of Islamic civic groups is especially important in this regard. The Islamic schools, charities, and networks that have rapidly expanded since the mid-1990s are playing a major role in creating a new form of in-group identity that stands apart from other forms of social organization in the country. Another set of CS groups, which are reinforcing a strong in-group mentality, includes some of the Somaliland-based NGOs that embrace and promote a separate Somaliland identity.

Social Cohesion

Given Somalia's protracted crisis of state collapse and armed conflict, it goes without saying that promotion of social cohesion is the most urgently needed function to be provided by civil society. Years of crisis have produced deep social cleavages; the dramatic upsurge in violence and displacement since 2007 has exacerbated these cleavages immeasurably.

Overall, Somali civil society has not been able to build adequate bridges across clan, regional, and ideological divides. On this score, Somali CS groups tend to fall into one of four camps. One group of civic actors actively reinforces social cleavages and works against national cohesion. Clan-based organizations are the most obvious example, running the spectrum from the relatively harmless (a Somali Bantu self-help group) to actively destructive (clan mobilization movements operating extremist websites demonizing rival clans). A second category includes civic groups that try to build broader social cohesion but simply face too many obstacles. Many of the local advocacy NGOs and networks in Somalia attempt to reach out to broader constituencies, but distrust, a history of association with a particular clan, and the realities of working in a particular region where outside clan members would be unwelcome and even unsafe limit the ability of NGOs to hire and collaborate with Somalis from other lineage groups. Practically speaking, every local NGO in the country knows that if it sought to open an office in an area of the country populated by one clan, and proceeded to hire on the basis of the 4.5 formula of clan proportionality, it would face serious objections from the local community. A third set of civic actors is those that have in fact succeeded in building genuine social cohesion at the national level. There are a number of examples. The Somali Olympic Committee brought Somali athletes and communities together to field national teams and to support local sports leagues. Business partnerships have been the most successful at building social cohesion. Businesses in Somalia typically involve multiple owners or shareholders—400 shareholders in the case of the Coca-Cola bottling factory—who are intentionally drawn from all social groups precisely because the business needs blanket buy-in across the country if it is to operate nationally.[13] One of the more remarkable aspects of the business community in Somalia is its ability to forge working trust relations across clan and ideological lines even in the midst of fighting. Although the political divide separating Somaliland supporters and Somali unionists is wide and deep, from an economic perspective the commercial sectors of Somaliland and Somalia are far more integrated than ever before thanks to the many business partnerships between Mogadishu and Hargeisa.

The final category consists of CS movements that succeed in building bridges that help overcome one social divide but that simultaneously contribute to the worsening of another social divide; the Islamist movements are an example. Islamist groups have had remarkable (though not complete) success transcending clannism and appealing to a particular form of Somali Islamic nationalism. No other ideology or civic movement has come anywhere close to matching the Islamists on this score. But their very success in creating a pan-Somali Islamic movement threatens to exacerbate new tensions—not only between Islamists and non-Islamists but also between rival interpretations of political Islam in Somalia.

More broadly, Islamic groups now play a central role in the realm of civic discourse. Some of the most important intellectual developments in Somalia have occurred in one of a number of Islamic circles, including Al-Islah and Al-Ittihad Al-Islamiyya (AIAI). The broad array of Islamist movements today constitute the most robust "party of ideas" in Somalia, in stark contrast to the vacuous platforms of factions and clan-based movements. Al-Islah was instrumental in setting up Mogadishu University, which at one point was described as the "brain trust" of that movement (though most faculty members today are not affiliated with any Islamist movement) (Bryden 2003, 19; Le Sage 2004, 171).

Intermediation/Facilitation

Somali civic groups have enjoyed growing success facilitating dialogue and reconciliation at the local level; success has been more elusive at the national level. Across Somalia, local-level reconciliation has consistently involved hybrid partnerships involving CS leaders, clan elders, businesspeople, and clerics. Importantly, local NGOs are important not only in promoting direct talks toward reconciliation; they also provide invaluable informal channels for "prenegotiation" dialogue in workshops and committees on social services. They can also be critical facilitators of actual peace talks, providing well-timed resources and good offices to help resolve conflicts. One of the most notable examples occurred in central Somalia in 2006 and 2007, where, with the assistance of the Center for Research and Dialogue, intensive mobilization by local women's groups, and the constructive engagement of local militia leaders, the elders of two Somali clans were able to negotiate an end to a prolonged and deadly period of communal clashes. The local NGOs were also able to support an innovative "peace caravan" in which elders from the warring clans traveled together across the region to discuss with local communities the terms of the initial peace accord before the final peace conference was held in Adado. This was important to ensure community acceptance and ownership of the final peace accord and is an excellent example of how civil society groups can leverage their ability to secure both external and locally generated funds to provide timely technical support to clan elders in peacebuilding.

At the national level, Somali civil society has made concerted efforts to facilitate dialogue and compromise between rival political factions but has had only limited success, as the long track record of failed national peace initiatives underscores. The leading role played by civic leaders, including clan elders and Al-Islah, at the 2000 national peace talks in Arta was the most significant instance. In the Mbagathi peace talks in Kenya in 2003–2004, faction leaders were given control over the process, thereby relegating civil society to a secondary role. CS figures were supposed to play a role in bringing the quarreling parties together in the second phase of the peace talks, wherein technical committees composed of Somali intellectuals were to meet to address key conflict issues. Political leaders expressed little interest in this aspect of the peace talks, however, rejoining only when the sponsors announced that the second phase of talks was completed and that the final phase—negotiations on power-sharing—was to begin.

However, some CS figures have quietly played an important role in facilitating dialogue between the TFG and an umbrella group composed of former ICU leaders and other opponents of the TFG known as the Alliance for the Re-Liberation of Somalia (ARS). This helped to produce the Djibouti Accord in the summer of 2008, which at that time represented the best hope for a mediated settlement of the war and power-sharing between moderate elements of the TFG and the opposition. It is precisely because most CS groups share common interests with moderate elements of the opposition and government that hard-liners in both the TFG and the insurgency view civil society with such hostility and seek to intimidate civic leaders with threats of violence. This points to the well-worn observation that groups taking a stand for peace and reconciliation are not seen as neutral parties by actors with vested interests in continued armed conflict and polarization. Promoting peace is, in Somalia and elsewhere, another way of taking sides.

Finally, it must be noted that CS efforts to facilitate dialogue among top political actors and to influence their thinking are only half the equation. More often than not, it is the Somali political leaders who are able to influence and manipulate civil society to their own ends. Clan elders, local NGOs, businesspeople, and clerics are used by factions and militias to legitimate their actions, advance their claims on resources and power, and vilify the opposition. Somalis know better than foreigners which of the local NGOs and associations among them have unwittingly or intentionally turned into mouthpieces for their clan's militia leader and which among them have been able to fight a rearguard battle with their own communities to maintain autonomy.

Service Delivery

The protracted collapse of the Somali state has meant that a host of for-profit and nonprofit organizations have come to fill the vacuum in the provision of key social services. Without question, the vast majority of the work done by Somali civil society today is in the field of social services—especially education and health care. In those sectors, local nonprofits compete with for-profit providers. Because some nonprofits charge fees for services, and some of the for-profits provide free or subsidized care to those in need, the line separating social service businesses and charities in Somalia is blurry.

The "golden era" of local NGO social service delivery was the period from 1995 to 2006, before renewed civil war, displacement, and insecurity badly disrupted the operations of virtually all Somali NGOs. During that period, Islamic charities were especially successful in service delivery. In his detailed 2004 study of Islamic charities in Somalia, Andre Le Sage concluded that Islamic NGOs have focused on education and health, "earning legitimacy by exploiting the failure of local government to provide these services" (Le Sage 2004, 185). He also found that while they rely heavily on foreign funding, they have had greater success than non-Islamist CS organizations in building a sense of local ownership of schools, through fee payments and local contributions, and have been better able to ensure transparency and accountability in their finances. They have also gradually succeeded in extending their networks across clan and regional lines, thereby contributing to peacebuilding. The majority of schools operated by Islamic charities reflect what Le Sage terms "mainstream" interpretations of Islam and society, but a minority of Islamic schools teach a more radical curriculum (Le Sage 2004, 185).

Whether Islamist or non-Islamist, education has been the most impressive success story in the civic response to the collapse of the state. In addition to dozens of for-profit institutes providing language and technical training throughout the country, as well as some public schools in Somaliland and Puntland (generally using mandatory school fees), nonprofit schools and universities have come to dominate the sector, especially in major urban centers. Virtually all of this investment in education was initiated either during or after the UNOSOM intervention. The Formal Private Education Network in Somalia (FPENS) is a consortium of thirty foreign and local Islamic NGOs that as of 2005 operated 124 schools, with 2,259 teachers, providing education to 81,168 students (FPENS 2008). FPENS was created only in 1999 yet was able to spark dramatic increases in both the quantity and quality of primary and secondary education offered in Somalia. In addition to creating a uniform curriculum and board exams, providing scholarships for poorer students, supporting education for girls, and ensuring its member schools' degrees were recognized by universities in several Islamic countries, FPENS has been instrumental in enabling member schools to become self-sufficient, relying on school fees to maintain operations.

Somali civic movements have been equally successful in creating institutions of higher education. Of the numerous nonprofit universities now operating in Somaliland, Puntland, and south-central Somalia, two are especially instructive. The Somali Institute of Management and Administration Development (SIMAD), created in 1999, now offers degrees in accounting, business administration, and information technology; boasts more than 1,300 graduates; and has secured grants from external donors for construction of new buildings on its campus (SIMAD 2006). Mogadishu University is another success story. It opened in 1997, and by 2006 it had 1,400 students enrolled in seven faculties, including nursing, education, humanities, *sharia* and law, and political science

(Mogadishu University 2006). SIMAD and Mogadishu University have been important centers of cross-clan dialogue and cooperation for both professors and students.

Islamic charities and networks involved in social services have generally been poorly integrated into broader networks. Some efforts have been made, most notably by NOVIB, to bring this important subset of civic actors into coordination mechanisms with other NGOs; in the case of FPENS and a few others, collaboration with Western-funded, Nairobi-backed sectoral committees has improved. But Somali Islamic charities have complained of being marginalized and poorly served in Nairobi-based networks and have found Western donors far too unresponsive and slow (Le Sage 2004, 216–217).

Islamic NGOs in social services have come under growing pressure since the onset of the US-led war on terror following the 9/11 terrorist attacks. Initially this pressure was manifested in close scrutiny by the US government and donors for possible linkages of charities to Al-Qaida. One prominent international Islamic charity, Al-Haramain, was listed as a Specially Designated Terrorist Entity by the US government; its offices in Somalia were shut down (Le Sage 2004, 187). Numerous others, even movements like Al-Islah that were explicitly progressive in orientation, came under suspicion. Fear of damaging charges of collusion with Islamic radicals has had a chilling effect on Islamic charities in Somalia. Those external pressures grew much greater in 2007 with the Ethiopian occupation of Mogadishu and the installment of the TFG in power in the capital. Both the Ethiopian government and the TFG leadership have a sharp antipathy toward any manifestation of political Islam and are not inclined to differentiate between moderate and hard-line Islamists.

Many of the local NGOs involved in social service delivery are also committed to peacebuilding and advocacy work and have sought to integrate peacebuilding into their other sectoral work. This "indirect peacebuilding" is a vital contribution to conflict management and prevention in Somalia. The many workshops and coordinating structures established in health, education, and other sectors have helped to create lines of cooperation on functional issues and established channels of communication that cut across conflict lines and that can be drawn on to defuse conflicts at any stage.

The post-2006 warfare in Somalia has been especially hard on local NGOs in service delivery. Relief and development workers have been targeted by jihadists, rogue TFG security forces, and criminal gangs in attacks that have made Somalia the most dangerous place in the world for aid workers. From August 2007 to July 2008, Somalia accounted for nearly one-third of the humanitarian casualties worldwide, with twenty Somali and four international aid workers killed during that period. Ten more went missing during that period and remain unaccounted for. This extraordinary level of insecurity has made it almost impossible for most local NGOs to operate at all.

Conclusion

The analysis in this chapter advances several general theses about Somali civil society and peacebuilding. First, it argues that Somali civil society has grown impressively since the early 1990s as a result of several drivers, including the prolonged collapse of the Somali state, the rise of a large and active diaspora, the rapid growth of the private sector, the ascendance of various Islamist movements, sustained external financial and other support, and strong local demand for basic services ranging from security to education that various civil society groups have come to fill. The very notion of a Somali civil society was a questionable concept altogether in 1991; today it is an important actor, even if it is difficult to define with precision in the unique Somali context. Second, Somali CS groups have had mixed success transcending clan, regional, and ideological divisions in the country, with certain types of social movements, networks, and organizations (such as business partnerships) better suited to bridging these divisions than others. Third, civic peacebuilding has been most successful when pursued as the result of hybrid partnerships among different civic actors, bringing together professionals, women's groups, clan elders, businesspeople, and clergy. Fourth, civic groups have enjoyed the greatest success in peacebuilding at the local and regional levels, engaging in direct peacebuilding as well as indirect promotion of peace through social service projects requiring cooperation across conflict lines. Although a number of impressive civic efforts to promote peace at the national level have been undertaken, to date they have been unable to overcome the sizable domestic and external impediments to consolidating peace accords; at times, civic groups have distanced themselves from national peace agreements, something they view as empowering warlords. Finally, CS groups have consistently been viewed by nascent governments as a rival or threat to be regulated, contained, co-opted, and disbanded rather than as partners in postconflict recovery and peacebuilding. This latter point is ironic, suggesting any success that civic groups enjoy in promoting reconciliation and revived government actually creates political conditions that threaten civil society's ability to continue to function.

The general conclusions above set the foundation for the more specific discussion of civic peacebuilding during war, armed conflict, and windows of opportunity. Evidence since 1988 suggests that civic peacebuilding in Somalia has proven capable of negotiating the dangerous complexities of armed conflict and the chronic insecurity linked to prolonged state collapse, yet has, with few exceptions, been overwhelmed during periods of outright war. This was made painfully clear by the period of war beginning in 2007. The epidemic of insecurity and targeted attacks on civic leaders by jihadist insurgents and violent paramilitaries linked to the dysfunctional Transitional Federal Government has essentially shut down the capacity of most CS groups to operate. Civic peacebuilding is stymied when war creates massive displacement and when civilians become the principal targets of attacks and political assassinations.

The capacity of some Somali CS groups to play a constructive role in facilitating peace talks at the national level as well as local levels in 2007–2008, despite the severe levels of insecurity in the country, may be explained in one of two ways. First, in contrast to some peacebuilding functions, facilitation and mediation roles are usually premised on neutrality. This arguably reduces the potential for any party engaged in conflict to view the civic facilitator as a threat—though spoilers outside the mediated peace process would still have reason to target the civic group. A second possible explanation relates only to national-level facilitation and focuses on the ability of CS mediators to travel and work outside the country. Because most of the national-level peace dialogue has occurred in neighboring countries, civic leaders with travel documents can play a mediating role while exposing themselves to far fewer security threats. As much of the civic peacebuilding work since 2006 has taken place in Djibouti, Dubai, and Nairobi, this explanation has some merit.

But the biggest single enabler of Somali civic groups to maintain some peacebuilding functions in times of war and armed conflict has been the capacity of individual groups and their leaders to protect themselves from threats of violence. Somali CS groups with links to powerful subclans usually enjoy some level of deterrent capacity against attacks, and those with leaders who are astute at managing risk, building networks, and anticipating and avoiding trouble have been better able to navigate the treacherous shoals of Somalia's wars and armed conflicts. It is not an exaggeration to say that much, if not most, of the typical workday of a civil leader in Mogadishu is devoted to tasks related to risk management.

This observation is important because it underscores a critical intervening variable in the capacity—or lack of capacity—of CS groups to operate in war and armed conflict in Somalia. It is not conditions of war per se that stymie civic peacebuilding efforts; it is a combination of the heightened violence and uncertainty surrounding periods of extreme armed violence among Somalis that has undermined civic peacebuilding. Some periods of war and armed conflict in Somalia have exhibited relatively predictable patterns of violence and thus have been more amenable to risk management by civic actors. Other periods, including the war since 2007, have produced extremely unpredictable violence, paralyzing most civic groups' ability to assess risk. The fact that the most productive peacebuilding work undertaken by Somali civic actors since 2007 has occurred outside the country speaks volumes about the capricious nature of armed violence following the Ethiopian occupation. If and when armed conflict again takes on more predictable patterns, Somali civil society will be able to gradually resume at least some of its work healing this latest, and most destructive, phase of the country's long crisis.

Notes

The authors would like to thank all the reviewers who commented on the different versions of the chapter.

1. This study makes occasional reference to the experience of civil society in the unrecognized secessionist state of Somaliland in northwestern Somalia, but it focuses mainly on the experience of civil society in south-central Somalia and Puntland. Somaliland's political, social, and economic trajectory differs so much from that of the rest of the country that it is increasingly difficult to generalize about both Somalia and Somaliland on certain topics. This approach does not in any way reflect a position by the authors on Somaliland's bid for recognition as an independent state.

2. We have opted not to treat the 2000 Arta talks as a distinct "window of opportunity" despite the fact that it was in many ways an innovative and promising approach to peacebuilding because only one of the two rival coalitions during that period was supportive of the process. Factions in the Ethiopian-backed Somali Reconciliation and Reconstruction Council (SRRC) never embraced the talks and rejected the government that was formed out of Arta.

3. See, e.g., Lyons and Samatar (1995); Hirsch and Oakley (1995); and Clarke and Herbst (1997).

4. This is generally the approach used in the most systematic inventory of Somali civil society, NOVIB's "Mapping Somali Civil Society" (2003). See page 9 of that study for a discussion of the criteria that NOVIB used to define civil society. See also the summary of discussions about what constitutes Somali civil society from a NOVIB-sponsored symposium (NOVIB 2003b).

5. Starlin Arush was killed in an armed attack in Nairobi in 2002.

6. Asha Haji is the second woman of Somali descent to win this prestigious peace award. Dekha Ibrahim, a Kenyan Somali, earned the award in 2005 for her pioneering peacework in Somali-inhabited northern Kenya.

7. One of the coauthors of this study, Ken Menkhaus, served as a political adviser in UNOSOM in 1993–1994. The information provided here draws on his field notes and direct experience from that period.

8. Recently, Somali civic leaders have expressed a preference for the term *expatriate Somali community* rather than *diaspora,* which they say has negative connotations (meaning "no home" in the Quran). For this study, the term *diaspora* is used because it remains the standard expression in the literature. For a Somali discussion of these terms, see Saferworld (2008, 8).

9. For more information about these three peacebuilding organizations, see the websites http://pdrcsomalia.org/index.php, www.crdsomalia.org, and www.apd-somaliland.org/index.html. Additional information is also available there on the WSP Puntland and Somaliland projects, which helped give birth to the PDRC and APD in WSP (2001) and WSP (2005).

10. This project, called "The Search for Peace," is managed by Interpeace and resulted in several publications by local research partner organizations, including APD, *Peace in Somaliland: An Indigenous Approach to State-Building* (2008); PDRC, *Community Based Peace Processes in South-Central Somalia* (2008); and Pat Johnson, ed., *A History of Mediation in Somalia Since 1988* (Nairobi: Interpeace, 2009) http://www.interpeace.org/pdfs/A_History_of_Mediation_in_Somalia_0609.pdf.

11. The 4.5 formula accords each of the main four clan-families equal numbers of seats in meetings and in governments, with the remaining 0.5 reserved for minority groups. The principle of rough clan proportionality has been in existence since the first government was formed in 1960 and is consistently used as one of a number of Somali

yardsticks to judge the legitimacy of a national-level meeting or government. The specific 4.5 formula was first put into practice at the Arta peace talks in 2000.

12. For an in-depth exploration of civic peacebuilding strategies explicitly targeting this group, see Lederach (1997).

13. This figure of shareholders was provided in a July 2008 interview in Dubai with a Somali major shareholder in the bottling company.

15

Nigeria: Dilemmas of Militarization and Co-optation in the Niger Delta

Darren Kew and Cyril Obi

Since the end of military rule in 1999, Nigeria has moved steadily, if fitfully, toward building democracy. The first post-1999 civilian administration undertook some economic reforms, yet it also attempted unsuccessfully to change the constitution to prolong its stay in office, and it held flawed elections in 2007 (EU EOM 2007; Obi 2008). At the same time, the nation's legislative and judicial branches have increasingly asserted their independence at the federal level and shown signs in some states of returning to life. Improved political freedoms along with greater openness in government, particularly an aggressive—albeit partisan—anticorruption drive, have also claimed some successes in bringing to justice some members of a rapacious political elite bent on looting public coffers. Nigeria's media, particularly the independent and privately owned ones, have flourished in this democratic opening by forcing several politicians from office and providing a venue for vigorous public debate and some measure of civic engagement.

Yet, the return of civilian rule has paradoxically coincided with the escalation of violent conflict in Nigeria's volatile oil-producing region of the Niger Delta. Between 1999 and the present day, there has been a remarkable proliferation of armed groups confronting government forces and oil companies, with far-reaching implications for national, regional, and international security (Lubeck, Watts, and Lipschutz 2007; Obi 2007). Instead of the return to democracy heralding a new dawn of "democratic dividends"—peace, stability, and prosperity for all—the Niger Delta region has grown increasingly ungovernable amid creeping anarchy and violence involving government actors, the armed forces, local politicians, and ever more powerful youth militias (ICG 2006a; Human Rights Watch 2005; Kash 2007; Ukiwo 2007).

From 1999 through 2009, but particularly during election periods, these players have utilized their access to oil wealth (often from illegal sources) and connections to highly placed local politicians to strengthen personal fortunes at the expense of the majority of the region's suffering peoples. As institutions continue to be undermined by narrow and exploitative interests and by the resort to violence rather than dialogue, local forces have resorted to building armed camps in order to compete with opponents and to secure their own positions. The proliferation of small arms and armed groups in a militarized Niger Delta poses a major challenge to peace in the oil region and to democracy in Africa's most populous country and leading oil exporter.

Peacebuilding in the Niger Delta, therefore, means addressing the conflict between the militants and the government. But more deeply, the roots of the festering conflict in the oil-rich region stem from the dysfunctional structure of Nigerian politics. The system is built upon clientelistic and increasingly predatory relationships among powerful politicians, multinational oil companies, and increasingly powerful local militias—at the expense of a desperately impoverished public. Consequently, sustained peace in the Niger Delta requires the transformation of these relationships into the more transparent and accountable patterns required for healthy democratic governance. Ultimately, such a transformation can be achieved only through increased community participation in the distribution of the region's lucrative oil wealth.

In the midst of the escalating crises in the Niger Delta, CS actors have shown a mix of responses designed to reach goals for peacebuilding. Some groups have sought to promote democracy and make peace among the feuding factions of the elite, within and between communities, and between the communities and oil companies, as well as exploring ways to address the governance gap left by the state at the local, regional, and federal levels. Other groups, meanwhile, have been co-opted by political elites or corporate oil interests.

Working at both the local and regional levels, different CS groups have undertaken initiatives that seek to bring together militants, the government, and the communities under a variety of circumstances and utilizing a variety of conflict resolution methods. Yet, success has been elusive for many reasons, first among them being the unstable political and economic environment of the Niger Delta. Other reasons include the weak resource base and structures of most CS organizations, the culture of violence and proliferation of armed groups, and the distrust and opportunism that have taken root in the region. Also relevant is the political agenda of the leadership of some CS groups, the activities of antidemocratic forces within certain sections of civil society that profit from escalating violence, and the near-absence of a unifying, grassroots-based, pan–Niger Delta democratic agenda.

Clearly, CS initiatives in the Niger Delta face an uphill climb. They suffer under a context in which massive oil revenues are siphoned by clientelistic (neopatrimonial) elites who manipulate their way into power over a deeply impoverished public, as well as a hegemonic state-oil alliance that defines political power as the prize of a zero-sum contest. Without genuine federal government and state-level leadership, there is very little space for dialogue on terms acceptable to all stakeholders as the interest in controlling power over oil continues to rise. CS groups are thus faced with the difficult task of seeking to build peace and advance democracy while simultaneously fighting a rearguard action to ensure that the few democratic gains are not erased by hegemonic extractive interests that define oil politics in Nigeria. While some groups have managed to gain the attention of the federal government or state governments for some time, such efforts have so far received feeble responses. Nonetheless, despite the odds against them, CS groups in the Niger Delta have had some modest positive impacts.

In this chapter, we examine the impact of the efforts of some CS groups in posttransition Nigeria to build peace amid complex crises and an incipient insurgency in the Niger Delta. Part of the analysis includes providing an analytical frame for understanding the role of civil society in peacebuilding in an ethnic minority region deeply immersed in the social contradictions connected to an oil-based political economy. We also explore the nature and roles that civil society can play in building peace and democracy in the Niger Delta. This is because democracy does two things: it provides a framework and space for civil society to operate, and it offers the most viable framework for conflict transformation and peacebuilding in Nigeria's troubled oil region. Today, however, these groups operate in a charged political atmosphere characterized by conflict between heavily armed militias, on the one hand, and predatory political elites and multinational oil companies, on the other. All this makes CS activity tremendously difficult.

Context

The roots of the ongoing conflicts are partly embedded in the history of the ethnic minority struggles for self-determination, local autonomy, and democracy. The creation of the Nigerian colony in 1914 by the British out of diverse precolonial social formations—city-states, kingdoms, and communities—consigned local peoples to the status of ethnic minorities in relation to the numerically preponderant neighboring ethnic groups, the Yoruba and Igbo, which dominated political life in what later became the western and eastern regions of Nigeria. Another majority group, the Hausa-Fulani, dominated the northern region of Nigeria's tripartite federation. Revenue-sharing and power distribution along regional lines reinforced the politicization of ethnic identity and its mobilization in the struggles for access to power and resources. On this basis, ethnic minorities tended to lose out while the dominant ethnic groups asserted power at the regional and national levels.

The initial reaction of ethnic minorities was to protest the perceived "majoritarian stranglehold of the three ethno-regional blocs" (Mustapha 2003, 8) over power and resources by seeking local autonomy through state or region creation in the context of emergent Nigerian federalism. When civil war erupted in 1967, the newly discovered oil of the Niger Delta became a central point of contention (Ikein and Briggs-Anigboh 1998, 128). As delta oil, produced mainly by foreign multinationals, became nearly the state's sole source of revenue, a new dimension of national interest in delta politics—beyond ethnicity—was added.

By the 1970s the delta had become the main source of oil and the new fiscal basis for the Nigerian state, replacing agriculture; oil accounted for more than 80 percent of national revenues and 90 percent of export earnings. Although military governments during this period added states (a total of thirty-six by 1996), ostensibly to give delta minorities their own states, the federal government—dominated by the three ethnic majorities—controlled oil revenues, reducing the share of oil profits given to oil-producing delta states from 50 percent in 1966 to 1.5 percent by the early 1990s. Several military decrees also transferred ownership of land from communities to government and gave the latter power to use land for development purposes, especially oil (Omeje 2005, 324). Consequently, the delta's ethnic minorities grew increasingly resentful of the neglect, marginalization, exploitation, and underdevelopment in their region by the ethnic majorities—who controlled not only the federal government (Saro-Wiwa 1995; Obi 2005, 187–204) but also the "political and economic exclusion of Niger Delta people from everything in Nigeria" (Ebiri 2006).

By the 1990s, these frustrations led to a growing campaign referred to, in Nigerian political language, as "resource control." This popular but sparsely organized movement is based on minority demands for self-determination to control resources within their territory of the Niger Delta; compensation for damage inflicted upon their communities by oil production (pollution, degradation, loss of livelihood); and access to an increased share of oil revenues needed to develop the region. The movement shares a common narrative of ethnic majoritarian tyranny that explains why the delta has suffered decades of neglect and why its people have been discriminated against in the federal distribution of political and socioeconomic opportunities, entitlements and welfare services, and development in general (Obi 2007, 101–104). Federal control of oil is thus seen as a conspiracy among the ethnic majorities to "colonize," exploit, and persecute the ethnic minorities as they purportedly "cannot pose any real threat to federal hegemony" (Okonta 2007, 7–8; 2008).

The other dimension of the campaign for resource control includes the grievances against foreign multinationals that actually undertake the oil production and share profits with the Nigerian state and its federal project, controlled by the three ethnic majorities. Across the oil-producing delta communities, there is a widespread belief that foreign oil companies exploit the natural wealth of the people, pollute the environment, which destroys local livelihoods, and discriminate against locals in terms of good-paying jobs as well as compensation for damage caused by oil spills. Also, the involvement of some oil companies in local politics—in the form of community relations and payments to youth groups for the protection of oil installations—has further complicated company-community relations.

Various ethnic minority organizations, such as the Movement for the Survival of Ogoni People (MOSOP) and the Ijaw Youth Council (IYC), led the agitation for resource control during the 1990s. Some environmental and human rights groups also protested the exploitation, neglect, and pollution of the region by successive governments and oil companies. Such demands were largely ignored by the military regimes, which typically repressed such protests—with one important exception. In the days before it handed power back to civilians in May 1999, the military promulgated a new constitution-by-decree that raised the percentage of oil revenues given directly to the oil-producing states of the Niger Delta (known as the derivation principle or formula) to 13 percent. The new democratic regime of President Olusegun Obasanjo, however, sought to co-opt some local elites and ethnic minority organizations through patronage, planning to neutralize them and thereby create more favorable conditions for oil industry operations. In fact, the strategy backfired, contributing to the emergence of ethnic minority militias, some with links to influential politicians, and to the proliferation of small arms (Ibeanu 2005, 36–56), the militarization of the region, and escalating violence.

At major political debates in recent years, and at the 2005 National Political and Reform Conference in particular, delegates from the Niger Delta demanded an increase in the derivation formula from 13 percent to 25 percent, with a progressive increase within five years to 50 percent (IRIN News 2005). The Obasanjo administration and its allies in the National Assembly rejected such demands, increasing frustrations in the Niger Delta and prompting further demands for restructuring the Nigerian federation to decentralize power and to emphasize local autonomy and resource control.

Consequently, the quest for democracy has been complicated by injecting the ethnic minority question into the acrimonious politics of sharing oil revenues. The high stakes over the spoils of oil, and the economic and strategic interests of oil multinationals and their home countries, have conspired with the depredations of self-serving politicians (mostly linked to the ruling People's Democratic Party, or PDP, in the region) to manipulate elections over the years. This pattern of politics based on patronage and corruption is known as neopatrimonialism, which has bedeviled political development across Nigeria, particularly in the Niger Delta. In neopatrimonial systems, political elites owe their loyalties upward to "godfathers" for access to state largesse and assistance in fixing election outcomes (Bratton and van de Walle 1994) and are dependent on (1) looting the state, (2) thugs and militias in order to retain power, and (3) connections to power centers and resources at the state and federal levels. In this fashion, political elites in the Niger Delta have developed growing interests in the corrupt and violent status quo and the continued disempowerment of the public writ large.

The governance dilemma in the Niger Delta has been inflamed by the rise of the new merchants of violence: armed groups and security forces, including the Federated Niger Delta Ijaw Communities (FNDIC), active in the Western Delta; the Niger Delta People's Volunteer Force (NDPVF), led by Asari Dokubo, and its rival, the Niger Delta Vigilantes (NDV), led by Ateke Tom (both initially linked to the Rivers State governor, a charge Ateke Tom denied), in 2004 and 2005; and since 2006, the Movement for the Emancipation of the Niger Delta (MEND).

This mix of ethnicity, violence, oil politics, and neopatrimonialism has played out over two phases of conflict in the Niger Delta.

Growing Patronage and Dissent: 1990–2002

The first phase began in November 1990, when protesters from Umuechem, a host community to Shell, were massacred by antiriot police that the company called in to disperse the protesters. This was soon followed by the Movement for the Survival of Ogoni People (MOSOP), which embarked on a campaign against the Nigerian military government and Shell, the largest onshore oil operator in the delta. MOSOP gained global attention when its leader, the charismatic writer and minority rights activist Ken Saro-Wiwa, was executed in 1995 despite pleas for clemency from Nelson Mandela and other world leaders.

MOSOP fragmented after the death of Saro-Wiwa but continued its nonviolent campaign for self-determination. Other movements among delta ethnic minority groups followed, prompting the Nigerian state to crush all protests against the state-oil partnership. By the mid-1990s, this sparked a disconnected militia-led insurgency in pockets of the delta, in part against military rule at the time, but more so against the lack of local control over oil reserves and the few returns on the oil that communities in the region enjoyed. Some of the conflict involved clashes between neighboring communities or ethnic groups over the ownership of oil-rich territory in order to collect surface rents and sundry payoffs from tenant oil companies. A notable case in point includes the violent clashes between the Ijaw and Itsekiri youth militias over the relocation of the Warri South West local government headquarters from Ijaw territory to Itsekiri territory in 1997 (Ukiwo 2007, 603). This insurgency was strong enough that militias even defeated the Nigerian military in several skirmishes, which shook the military's confidence enough to factor into their decision to leave power in 1999.[1]

A hiatus in regional conflicts held for several months after the 1999 election as delta communities waited to see if the new Obasanjo administration would undertake any new approaches. Hopes were dashed, however, when the president unveiled the centerpiece to his Niger Delta policy: a revamped regional development commission, perceived locally as an extension of the military government's corrupt commission. Moreover, in response to the November

1999 killing of two policemen in Odi, Bayelsa State, President Obasanjo ordered the army into the town to pursue the killers; military units destroyed the town and massacred some inhabitants. Soon after, the insurgency continued in earnest (Obi 2004, 24–25; Ukiwo 2007; Okonta 2007; Human Rights Watch 2002a; Ross 2007; Ebiri 2007).

The new constitution of 1999 did, however, raise the Niger Delta's priority share of oil revenues from 3 percent to 13 percent, which the six states of the region[2] receive before the oil revenues are shared among the states of the federation and the federal government. Obasanjo typically released these revenues as promised, which created a local bonanza for delta governors and strengthened their patronage networks. The boom in global oil prices from 2003 to 2008 raised the stakes in controlling power for the state governments in the delta, with Rivers State alone earning roughly US$1 billion annually by 2006 (see Table 15.1).

In the years after 1999, delta governors became fabulously wealthy and built massive patronage networks while freezing out political opponents, thereby exacerbating the neopatrimonial governance dilemma. The swelling public funds, however, did not actually result in properly functioning public services and development projects (Human Rights Watch 2005). Instead, most of these funds disappeared into private pockets. The Bayelsa governor, for instance, reportedly bought a yacht and several mansions in the United Kingdom and elsewhere, even when his state had only one paved highway.[3]

As the 2003 elections approached, however, governors put increasing funds toward buying the loyalty of the militias growing across the region, which were gaining access to the extensive arms trade in West Africa and beyond. Fearful of a public backlash over their poor performances, and intent on retaining power, the governors of Rivers, Bayelsa, and Delta states in particular channeled funds

Table 15.1 Monthly Federal Allocations for July 2006 for the Niger Delta

State	Statutory Allocation (in Naira)	Share of 13% Derivation	Total for July (in Naira)	US Dollar Value (N 130 = US$1)	Annual US$ Projection (July x 12) for 2006
Akwa Ibom	1.74 billion	4.43 billion	6.17 billion	$47.5 million	$569.5 million
Bayelsa	1.36 billion	6.13 billion	7.49 billion	$57.6 million	$691.2 million
Cross River	1.64 billion	402 million	2.04 billion	$15.7 million	$188.3 million
Delta	1.79 billion	4.89 billion	6.68 billion	$51.4 million	$616.6 million
Edo	1.75 billion	275 million	2.02 billion	$15.5 million	$186.5 million
Rivers	2.03 billion	7.66 billion	9.69 billion	$74.5 million	$894.0 million
Non–Niger Delta states:					
Lagos	2.82 billion	0	2.82 billion	$21.7 million	$260.4 million

Source: Kew and Phillips 2007.

and arms to youth gangs and militant bands, some of whose leaders had been CS youth activists in the 1990s. Lacking gainful employment, however, these leaders soon recognized that militancy was the quickest way to gain government attention and largesse. Prominent among them was Alhaji Dokubo Asari, a former leader in the Ijaw Youth Council, and Ateke Tom, a prominent gang leader in Okrika and Port Harcourt. These militias played pivotal roles in stifling political opposition and public participation in the 2003 elections.

Militancy, Predation, and Disarray: 2003–2008

When the 2003 elections produced predictable outcomes—near-total victories for ruling governors and their party (the PDP) across the Niger Delta, with widespread rigging (Kew 2004)—the governors moved to consolidate their positions and to enjoy the flood of oil revenues coming from surging global oil prices. Part of this consolidation meant reining in militias, which the governors soon neglected and sometimes even double-crossed, leading to rising hostility.

Capitalizing on growing arms caches, some militias were able to assert increasing independence from the governors, entering into a fluid bargaining relationship with political elites across the region. The militias' wealth grew from political patronage, security hires (including from oil companies), and tapping into transnational oil bunkering networks, which involves stealing oil from pipelines and selling it on the black market and the high seas. They used this wealth to tap into the global arms bazaar, gaining access to increasingly sophisticated weaponry.

Setting what would become the trend across the region, Dokubo Asari and his Niger Delta People's Volunteer Force attacked Port Harcourt, the capital of Rivers State, in late 2003. Asari thereafter signed a peace agreement, but he then threatened to expel all foreign oil companies from the region and rebranded himself as an advocate for resource control by calling for a Sovereign National Conference to renegotiate the basis of Nigeria's nationhood. He was arrested in September 2005 and released from custody in June 2007 as part of the peace initiative of the newly elected Umaru Musa Yar'Adua government. During Asari's detention, portions of his militia formed a loose alliance with other Ijaw militias under MEND, espousing a self-determination agenda, attacking oil platforms, and kidnapping industry workers for ransom (Okonta 2006).

Status of Civil Society

CS groups responding to this growing conflict were forced to navigate among the titanic forces of neopatrimonial leaders, impoverished and ethnically divided communities, increasingly violent militias, and a largely hostile and negligent government allied to powerful multinational oil companies. Consequently, CS activities can be placed into three general categories.

Collaboration and Co-optation

Individuals from some CS groups moved to work with the new state governments and federal government after 1999, often with initial good intentions of trying to make the new democracy work. Over time, however, some groups splintered, and some factions grew increasingly dependent upon government patronage and thus upon regional governors. Local chapters of major trade unions, local business and professional associations, community associations, traditional chieftaincies, and a range of NGOs, including some development, human rights, and conflict resolution NGOs, became wittingly or unwittingly ensnared in the neopatrimonial networks of state governors. The region's largest ethnic organizations, the Ijaw National Congress and the Ijaw Youth Council, retained some independence but were increasingly influenced by the Delta, Bayelsa, and Rivers state governors.

Opposition

A small number of CS groups sided with the pockets of opposition to regional governors, including some NGOs and community associations. Most notable during the 1999–2003 period, however, was the rise of women's movements, which occupied several oil platforms and company property on several occasions to protest the lack of community access to oil profits. These movements had informal organizational structures and benefited from advice from NGOs such as the local chapter of a women's legal assistance organization (known globally by its Spanish acronym, FIDA).

Professional Neutrality and Activism

Some CS groups remained focused on their goals and avoided either co-optation or direct confrontation. A growing number of conflict resolution groups, in part fueled by international donors like USAID, sprouted across the region after 1999, joined by established groups like Academic Associates Peace Works (AAPW). A number of human rights NGOs remained focused on promoting human rights in the region, and a number of development NGOs maintained efforts to improve public services in health, education, and other areas. Few of the other sectors of civil society avoided partisanship, although the powerful oil workers' unions retained their independence and remained largely focused on wages and other membership concerns.

The rising violence after 2003 forced many CS groups to restrict their activities for security reasons. The nascent women's movement in the region was one of the first major casualties. A number of the protests were already subject to violent reprisals from local police, but growing militia activity raised fears that women's protests could not occur without the approval of nearby militias and their politician backers. Development NGOs, environmental groups, community associations, trade unions, and other regional actors faced growing personal security concerns as the intermittent gun battles between the militias and the Nigerian military, or among the militias themselves over control of turf, raised the personal and material costs of doing work in the region. Work in the major towns and cities had to avoid potential conflict hotspots, while work in the countryside and creeks increasingly needed to gain the blessing—or at least avoid the wrath—of local militias and gangs.

Consequently, the scope of CS activity during the conflict saw an initial period of expansion in the 1990s and gained momentum until 2002, when growing violence forced civil society into an increasingly limited range of action. Opposition activities proved especially dangerous, and professional work was also viewed with suspicion by the government and militias.

Despite this restricted space for operations, civil society in the region, as in Nigeria at large, remains tremendously diverse. Groups that are active include trade unions; student and academic associations; professional associations (lawyers, accountants, nurses); religious institutions; traditional institutions (including chieftaincies, kingdoms, and other precolonial polities); ethnic community associations and ethnic town unions; and a host of NGOs that cover professional services and functions, including human rights, conflict resolution, development, and relief.

Consequently, many CS groups became engaged in peacebuilding activities, but they faced an increasingly difficult working environment after 2002. Increased violence forced many organizations into dormancy or limited performance; others saw no alternative but to collaborate with the governors and other neopatrimonial figures in the region in order to survive and have impact.

The role of civil society in conflict resolution and peacebuilding has its origins during the period of late military rule from 1990 to 1999, and from 1999 until the present day (Ibeanu 2006, 44). CS roles were often moderated by available skills, resources, and stated objectives. Many were involved in conflict management, peace education, training, conflict mediation, early-warning systems, and postconflict reconstruction (Ibeanu 2006).

Peacebuilding Functions

The following section compares the seven different functions: protection, monitoring, advocacy, socialization, social cohesion, intermediation and facilitation, and service delivery. Within this increasingly restricted scope of activity, civil society groups still managed to undertake a number of peacebuilding functions in the Niger Delta conflict. Table 15.2 lists these functions during the two phases of the conflict.[4]

Protection

Protection activities have primarily focused on securing basic human rights, often with a special focus on minority rights in light of the hegemony of the

Table 15.2 Civil Society Groups in the Niger Delta

	Type	Democratic Structure?	Protection	Monitoring	Advocacy	Socialization	Social Cohesion	Intermediation	Service Delivery
Movement for the Survival of Ogoni People (MOSOP)	Ethnic community association	Yes	x	x	x	x	x	x	
Egi Ethnic Coalition	Ethnic community association	Yes	x		x	x	x	x	
Community Rights Initiative (CORI)	NGO	Yes	x	x	x	x	x	x	
Chikoko	Ethnic community association	Yes			x	x	x	x	
Ijaw Youth Council (IYC)	Ethnic assoc./ youth assoc.	Yes	x		x	x	x	x	
International Women Lawyers Federation (FIDA)	NGO	Yes	x	x	x	x	x		x
Environmental Rights Action (ERA)	NGO	No		x	x				
Institute for Human	NGO	No	x	x	x				x
Rights and Humanitarian Law (IHRHL)									

(continues)

Table 15.2 continued

	Type	Democratic Structure?	Protection	Monitoring	Advocacy	Socialization	Social Cohesion	Intermediation	Service Delivery
Niger Delta Women for Justice (NDWJ)	NGO	No	x		x				
Our Niger Delta	NGO/ think tank	No		x	x			x	
Niger Delta Human Environment Rescue Organization (ND-HERO)	NGO	No	x	x	x				x
Ijaw Council for Human Rights (ICHR)	NGO	No	x	x	x				
Social Action Nigeria	NGO	No	x	x	x				
Center for Environment, Human Rights, and Development (CEHRD)	NGO	No	x	x	x				
Community Defence Law Foundation (CDLF)	NGO	No	x	x	x				x
Academic Associates Peace Works (AAPW)	NGO	No	x		x		x	x	
Coventry Cathedral International Center for Reconciliation (ICR)	Religious institution	No					x	x	

three majority ethnicities that control the federal government. Given the increasingly violent nature of the conflict, some CS groups have been less willing to play their usual protection roles between the public and the state. State and federal government and political actors became increasingly corrupt while arming militias for political muscle; these militias became increasingly independent over time, expanding the circle of violence and corruption. Politically well-connected organizations would in some instances try to lobby their powerful contacts to protect specific communities when they came under assault from gangs and militants, and at times these magnates would respond.

The most common form of protection performed by CS groups, however, included human rights assistance and legal activities. Growing discontent with the lack of government action in regard to economic development and social justice issues during the first phase of conflict led many activists to establish human rights NGOs, such as the Ijaw Council for Human Rights and the Community Defense Law Foundation; local affiliates of older organizations, such as FIDA, also increased their activities.

Inspired in part by MOSOP's success in drawing international attention to the massive degradation of the delta environment, several environmental NGOs, such as the Center for Environment, Human Rights, and Development (CEHRD), also sought to provide protection to communities through legal action to force oil companies and the government to clean up the region. CEHRD is emblematic of the protection activities performed by civil society in the Niger Delta. It was made up of human and environmental rights activists who, according to the CEHRD website, were "responding to government policies, oil and gas companies' activities, human rights violations, proliferation of Small Arms and Light Weapons (SALW) as they affect the rural people of the Niger Delta." According to CEHRD, part of its mission is to "forge a common link with the rural Niger Delta communities through campaigns, participatory education and enlightenment of the people on the problems confronting them" (CEHRD website).

CEHRD is supervised by a board of directors made up of Nigerians, as well as an international advisory board. Like many NGOs that undertake a protection function, it partners with CS organizations in Nigeria, West Africa, as well as the United States, Germany, United Kingdom, and the Netherlands. Notable international networks include the West African Human Rights Defenders Network (WAHRDN), People's Movement for Human Rights Education (PMHRE), the International Action Network on Small Arms (IANSA), the African Mangrove Network (AMN), Shell Corporate Accountability Coalition, and the Publish What You Pay (PWYP) network. Although CEHRD works in the areas of community health, development, and conservation, it also works for human rights, particularly the monitoring of small arms and light weapons, democratization, and peacebuilding.

Monitoring

Monitoring activities have typically involved data-gathering and reporting on issues of concern, such as human rights and elections, to at-risk communities. Monitoring functions are typically linked to protection and advocacy as well. A number of NGOs have engaged in monitoring human rights and environmental claims since 1999, increasing their activity since 2003. Most groups engaged in protection were also engaged in monitoring, but additional groups were engaged in monitoring without protection, as monitoring was generally deemed to be a less threatening function by the military and civilian authorities.

A number of monitoring groups managed to resist the co-optation pressures exerted by state governments during the second phase of conflict, particularly those based in Port Harcourt. Stakeholder Democracy Network (SDN), a prodemocracy and human rights organization, engages in extensive monitoring activities across the Niger Delta and in its assessment reports has been critical of regional governors (SDN 2007). Other human rights activists, however, chose to work with new governments in the region, which undermined monitoring activities. SDN collaborated with other groups and IDASA. IDASA, as a South African–based conflict resolution NGO administering a USAID grant to support Nigerian organizations, developed an early-warning and conflict analysis network among a number of NGOs in the delta, producing a "conflict barometer" for the region to help identify locales that are more prone to conflict. IDASA was also involved in election observation, working with the Niger Delta Civil Society Coalition, which reported on the subversion of the 2007 elections in the delta states (IDASA 2007).

CEHRD also conducted studies and peacebuilding interventions and issued several reports on the activities of armed cult groups, small arms proliferation, and the 2007 elections, which it noted were marked by a "high level of electoral violence in the region" (CEHRD 2007). In response to questions for this research, Patrick Naagbanton, the coordinator of CEHRD, made the point that conflict in the delta is rooted "in anger against the Nigerian state, Transnational Oil Corporations . . . and elites of the region that collude to under-develop the region." Noting that the "militarization of the region is creating much problems in terms of sustainable peace campaigns for civic groups working in the areas of peace building and conflict reduction," he underscored the problems within CS groups related "to the lack of skills and capacity to promote peace." However, he also notes that the lack of trust among delta society remains an enduring problem, even though "one cannot talk of peace without justice and equity."

Advocacy

Advocacy functions center on promoting the interests of ethnic groups, labor unions, women, and human rights victims. Nearly all CS groups mentioned here engaged in some form of public advocacy, lobbying state governments in the delta and/or the federal government. In fact, the only group that did not engage in advocacy was Coventry Cathedral's International Center for Reconciliation (ICR), which, as an international religious institution–based initiative, engaged in quiet mediation rather than public advocacy.

A growing number of advocacy organizations were co-opted, and others faced increasing difficulties in organizing advocacy efforts due to the worsening security situation after 2002. The nascent women's movement appears to have been a particular casualty, prevented from developing into a more permanent movement by the growing militarization after 2003. A number of trade unions remained active in advocating on issues related to wages and fuel prices, although many local affiliates succumbed to co-optation by state governments. Prior to the 1999 transition to democratic rule, opting for advocacy was simpler because groups confronted a military government and multinationals. Okechukwu Ibeanu (2006), however, sketches the dilemma confronting these groups under the civilian government as a difficult choice of supporting the "civilian governments on the grounds of preserving democratic experiments or confronting the excesses of government."

Most of the groups with conflict resolution initiatives that remained independent of state actors engaged in various forms of nonpublic advocacy. Other groups, however, drew inspiration and sought to replicate MOSOP's success in gaining international attention. Organizations such as the Environmental Rights Action (ERA), Institute for Human Rights and Humanitarian Law (IHRHL), Niger Delta Women for Justice (NDWJ), Egi Ethnic Coalition, Community Rights Initiative (CORI), Our Niger Delta, Niger Delta Human Environment Rescue Organization (ND-HERO), Ijaw Council for Human Rights (ICHR), Chikoko, and Ijaw Youth Council (IYC) came to the fore in campaigns for local autonomy, democratic rights, and resource control. Other groups are Social Action Nigeria, led by Isaac Osuoka, CEHRD, led by Patrick Naagbaton, and the Community Defence Law Foundation (CDLF), initially led by Oronto Douglas. Apart from these organizations, numerous community-based groups advocate for local causes as well.

Socialization

Socialization—often measured in terms of Robert Putnam's bonding social capital—can also be seen as part of civil society's long-standing Tocquevillean impact: building democratic political culture. In many ways, CS groups were nearly the *only* social actors promoting democratic cultural development and peacebuilding values both within their organizations and externally in the polity, as political elites grew increasingly corrupt and militarized.

Strikingly, the only organizations in our sampling that performed the socialization function were democratically structured groups (see Table 15.2). This finding underscores the importance of democratic structures in inculcating democratic political culture within CS groups (Kew 2008; Kew forthcoming).

FIDA, for instance, enjoys a strong democratic ethos and remained a strong proponent of peaceful, democratic social change throughout both periods of conflict. Community associations, development NGOs, ethnic associations, and other groups that resisted co-optation and featured democratic structures were able to provide democratic "safe havens" where individuals could still experience democratic processes and approach internal and external conflicts in a resolution-oriented fashion.

Just as notable in our sampling, however, is that many democratically structured organizations providing socialization were also ethnic community associations, like MOSOP and the Ijaw Youth Council. Given the ethnic polarization over control of resources, which the federal government sometimes encouraged to keep communities divided, ethnicity has proven an important motivation and vehicle for mobilization. In addition, these organizations actively seek to strengthen ethnic in-group bonds in order to strengthen their positions in bargaining with the federal and state governments. In some instances, the growing violence accelerated the consolidation (bonding) of in-group identities, but not typically targeted at a specific out-group, except perhaps the federal government.

Social Cohesion

Given such deep ethnic polarization, most social cohesion activities—"bridging capital" efforts that build networks across social categories—have been conducted across ethnic lines. For example, the Community Rights Initiative, a local NGO, in 1996 became involved in a negotiation and conflict resolution project in the Ogba-Egbema-Ndoni Local Government Area (LGA) and the Abuah-Oduah LGA of Rivers State, across ethnic lines (Ibeanu 2006). Important efforts have also been conducted between communities and government and between militias and government. An important finding is that the same organizations engaged in socialization were also engaged in social cohesion, suggesting similar roles for democratic structures and ethnicity. In addition, two nondemocratically structured groups in our sampling, AAPW and ICR, also engaged in these activities. Both are conflict resolution groups whose purposes are precisely to serve social cohesion functions.

Most groups focused on training local actors in conflict resolution skills, including student leaders, government officials, community leaders, and other NGOs. One of the more innovative efforts was led in 2006–2007 by Pastor James Wuye and Imam Mohammed Ashafa of the Interfaith Dialogue Center; they trained priests of the traditional Ijaw religion, called Egbesu, in peacebuilding skills. Many militants engage in Egbesu practices before their operations—some believed to make one impervious to bullets—and many priests who undertook the training pledged to utilize their influence over militants to push for peace.

Another important training effort was led by AAPW, and it trained former militants in peacebuilding techniques. With offices in Rivers, Bayelsa, and Delta states, AAPW spearheaded an even larger peace initiative during this period. The executive director, Judith Asuni, brought a particular kind of leverage that helped open doors with politicians and gave her some protection against militias: she was an old friend and peace adviser to President Obasanjo. This meshed well with Obasanjo's preference for informal networks of advisers—and his growing neopatrimonial system of supporters—to place her in a unique position to undertake conflict resolution efforts in the Niger Delta. Her regular contact with the president was well-known to regional politicians, and her ability to persuade the president to undertake policy actions in the delta gave her tremendous leverage, which she used to great effect.

After Dokubo Asari's attack on Port Harcourt in 2003, Asuni approached both Asari and his rival, Ateke Tom, to explore alternatives for peace. AAPW invited the assistance of Our Niger Delta, a local NGO that developed out of the 1990s Ijaw youth movements and had strong knowledge of the militia networks, and the UK-based International Center for Reconciliation (ICR) at Coventry Cathedral, which had advised Shell on how to build relationships with oil-producing communities in the region. Shuttling among Asari, Ateke Tom, President Obasanjo, and Rivers state governor Peter Odili, Asuni convinced militants to submit to a disarmament program while convincing the president to offer them amnesty and payments in exchange for guns, and convincing Odili to offer them a comprehensive employment and development package.

This initiative, brokered during 2004, became known as the Peace and Security Strategy (PaSS) for the Niger Delta (Asuni 2005, 1–2). PaSS soon expanded from a disarmament program into a comprehensive regional peace process, starting with Rivers State. Multinational oil companies, the Nigerian National Petroleum Corporation, the president's Niger Delta Development Commission, the military and State Security Services (SSS), and a host of NGOs and ethnic associations initially joined the effort, which produced a comprehensive blueprint for peace. Asari's NDPVF and Ateke Tom's militia handed in significant quantities of small arms in 2004. PaSS continued working through 2005, producing a comprehensive development plan for Rivers State to which Governor Odili promised US$20 million.

AAPW also embarked on field research in April 2006 on the identification, enumeration, and analysis of armed groups, militias, cults, and drugs in Delta. Rivers, Akwa Ibom, Bayelsa, and Ondo states (Akeni 2006, 5; Akeni 2007, 4). Apart from this, AAPW was involved in peacebuilding programs, such as nonviolent election activities, in twenty local government areas in Rivers, Bayelsa, and Delta states. These activities included "rallies, voter education, training of state monitors and 40 master trainers, training of election observers, a weekly television series entitled Solution Hour for Peace, and weekly meetings of Nonviolent Elections committees in the 20 LGAs" (Akeni 2007, 5). Lucky Dumaa (2007, 7) also explained that the committees acted as "a community think-tank in detecting and responding to early warning signs of election conflict, including those before, during and after the elections."

By 2005, however, federal attention toward the disarmament program lapsed, and some militants were not paid for their guns. Within months, most had returned to their previous activities and used lucrative oil-bunkering gains to purchase more modern weaponry, including shoulder-fired missile launchers. More ominously, signs increasingly indicated that Governor Odili and other powerful political actors, including national ones and some international criminal networks, reportedly had business interests in the bunkering networks and were sponsoring a wider array of militias as political muscle (Human Rights Watch 2005). As the 2007 elections approached, Odili and political elites across the region channeled more funds to militias in their bids to control localities and election returns. None of Governor Odili's promised US$20 million in government development funds materialized.

PaSS was also undermined as trust broke down among AAPW, Our Niger Delta, and Coventry's ICR. None of these three groups was democratically structured; thus there were no fundamental systemic checks to force their leaders to respond to the management conflicts that arose between AAPW and ICR's representative. AAPW and ICR also felt some propriety over the relationships with President Obasanjo and other government officials, and as their working partnership declined, anxiety over access to the president increased, accelerating the breakdown in trust.

Peacemaking efforts like PaSS were typically structured in a democratic fashion and showed some signs that participants may have come away with a measure of democratic learning and bridging capital. Even though PaSS eventually broke down and the participating governors pursued militia strategies with renewed vigor, most of the basic negotiating relationships forged during the PaSS process remained intact and provided the basic social network upon which President Yar'Adua's new Niger Delta initiative is based. Notably, PaSS and other civil society–led peace processes (see below) led many participants to raise greater demands for democratic reforms as well. These processes featured a range of commentary on the need for election reforms in order to produce more responsible politicians, as well as anticorruption measures to improve public service provision. In terms of PaSS, however, it is also notable that none of the facilitating groups are democratically structured, which not only allowed personality conflicts to undermine cooperation but also worked against the peace process.

Intermediation/Facilitation

Given the often hostile relationships between government at all levels (in partnership with the oil industry) and communities in the Niger Delta, much of the intermediation activities of civil society sought to transform relationships. A strong correlation appears to exist between groups performing social cohesion functions and those engaged in intermediation. All the groups in our sampling conducting social cohesion also engaged in intermediation, and only one additional group played an intermediation role but did not fulfill a social cohesion function. In light of the pervasive role of the state in the Niger Delta conflicts, the bridging efforts of social cohesion are likely to engage state actors, thus playing a state-society intermediation role. In addition, most mediation efforts in the region sought to build relationships across group divides.

Clearly, the CS groups participating in PaSS promoted dialogue among key conflict actors. Other NGOs sought to undertake similar efforts on a local basis, including training key local actors in conflict resolution skills. Some traditional chiefs and elders also sought to facilitate dialogue among government, oil companies, and militias, but their close association with political patronage networks undermined their role increasingly after 2002. Local religious leaders also sought to facilitate dialogue among local actors in some instances, and some hopes were raised after 2006 that traditional Egbesu practitioners and other religious figures might seek to undertake greater initiatives for peace.

One element of PaSS served an important intermediation function. ICR and AAPW approached Shell (in partnership with the government) and MOSOP (whose martyred leader, Ken Saro-Wiwa, had gained global attention for the Ogoni cause in the early 1990s) to explore possibilities for reconciliation and a return of Shell to the oil fields from which the Ogoni had barred it since 1993. ICR and AAPW prevailed upon President Obasanjo to name a presidential envoy to mediate between the Ogoni and Shell, and he picked a prominent human rights activist and Catholic priest from Kaduna State, Matthew Hassan Kukah.

After years of struggle against the government, however, the Ogoni leadership was itself divided among MOSOP, several prominent Ogoni families, and new Ogoni political leaders elected in 1999 and 2003, such that Kukah spent most of his time mediating among the Ogoni factions. Shell indicated that it was open to nearly any deal that the Ogoni were willing to offer if they could agree among themselves, but the Ogoni were unable to agree on a common bargaining position prior to the end of Kukah's mandate in May 2007. MOSOP insisted that it was the sole representative of the Ogoni in the negotiation and also insisted that it—and not the federal government, as indicated in the constitution of 1999—should be the licenser of oil rights in the Ogoni region. Kukah was, however, able to assist in reconciliation between MOSOP and the prominent Ogoni families and to gain agreement that the UN Environmental Program should come in to clean up the long-standing environmental damage from past oil exploitation.

Service Delivery

CS groups have been active in a host of service delivery activities across the Niger Delta since at least the early 1990s, as state services all but collapsed.

On the whole, service delivery appears to be dominated by the NGO sector. A large number of NGOs providing health, education, and economic development assistance have sprung up, as have human rights, environmental rights, and other social interest groups providing legal assistance. All of these activities, however, have been hindered by growing violence, and many have been permeated by patronage networks, as the need for scarce funds left them little alternative.

Nonetheless, many service activities have been utilized as opportunities for peacebuilding activities, and conflict resolution groups in particular have sought to piggyback conflict training onto basic services such as clean water drilling, youth sports and other youth activities, and community development projects. For instance, AAPW included job and employment skills training in the PaSS framework so that decommissioned fighters could improve their job prospects, but conflict resolution components were also included when these services were provided (Lewis and Davis 2005).

Peacebuilding Functions Compared

Overall, we see strong NGO roles in the protection, monitoring, advocacy, and service delivery functions. NGOs tend to bring specialized knowledge and skills, which gives them an orientation toward and strength in providing these functions. Moreover, NGOs, smaller in size than other civil society groups (such as trade unions and religious institutions), can sometimes perform these functions with greater focus and cultivate specialized expertise. Yet, this tends to hamper the scope of their advocacy impact, given the lack of broad constituencies and membership bases.

A striking aspect is the strong link between democratically structured organizations and the socialization and social cohesion functions. This connection points to the central importance of democratic structures in CS groups for the inculcation of democratic political culture—both bonding and bridging capital. Group members learn and enjoy democratic norms within these organizations, then engage other groups or society in a fashion that reflects these norms, thus creating bridging capital. In addition, all the democratically structured groups in our sampling also engaged in mediation, reinforcing the importance of such structures in promoting conflict resolution.

Just as striking, however, is that many democratically structured CS groups in our survey, and thus the groups engaged in the socialization and social cohesion functions, were also ethnic community associations. This may point to the importance of ethnicity within socialization roles, as well as to the motivation caused by ethnic marginalization. Moreover, in light of rigged elections in the Niger Delta over the past three election cycles (1999, 2003, and 2007), along with the massive failure of government at any level to deliver development, ethnic community associations seek to address the pressing need for community-level governance.

Conclusion

Overall, we see a modest impact for CS peacebuilding efforts in the Niger Delta, focused primarily on building democratic political culture through the socialization and social cohesion functions, in addition to salvaging a measure of political freedoms through the protection, monitoring, and advocacy functions. The growing violence across the region, especially since 2002, restricted the political space for public activities and increased the risks for efforts to reach across conflict divides. Part of the problem relates to the concentration of power and resources in the hands of elites in the federal, state, and local governments who control the patronage hubs for local political networks and exclude the long-suffering people from political participation and access to resources and opportunities in a paradoxically oil-rich but impoverished region.

Civil Society Functions and Their Impact on Peace

Consequently, an examination of CS peace efforts illuminates how such efforts can contribute to deepening democracy in fragile postmilitary transitional governments whose internal governance capacities have been undermined by contradictions linked to oil politics and the depredations of ruling elites. It underscores the magnitude of the challenges confronting CS groups as well as the potential for the federal government and the international community, which have strong interests in restoring some measure of stability to the crisis-ridden region, to engage these groups in the mutually rewarding quest for equity, human security, and democratic peace.

The challenges facing civil society can be summed up as follows:

The Neopatrimonial Governance Dilemma. Political elites are entrenched in "godfather" networks of patronage and corruption that require state largesse and military muscle to maintain. Consequently, elites have growing interests in the corrupt and violent status quo and the continued disempowerment of the public writ large.

The Public Action Dilemma. Gripping poverty, high levels of youth unemployment, and ethnic divisions, aggravated by elites and militant activities, make public organization and mobilization for the common good extremely elusive.

The Militia Dilemma. Growing cadres of youths socialized into violence as a "mode of production" by prolonged years of military repression and exclusion, and now enjoying access to sophisticated modern weapons, are making a living off the insurgency and criminal activities; they have an interest in perpetuating the violence-ridden status quo.

The Multinational Oil Dilemma. Global corporations face production losses (production is down 25 percent, with occasional spikes as high as 50 percent) and a hostile security climate for their staff (who are becoming regular ransom targets for some militias) from the growing insurgency

(Mufson 2008), yet their hegemonic alliance with the Nigerian government is virtually codependent to the point that the companies are paralyzed and complicit. That is, the alliance is still far too lucrative to risk undermining or severing it in order to bring sufficient pressure on the Nigerian government to resolve the crisis. Oil companies articulate that they see themselves as helpless, or with little leverage over the Nigerian government, as the government can always shift oil operations to another multinational or foreign state oil corporation.

Widespread Grassroots Anger, Alienation, and Anomie. There is an unhealthy mix of political apathy, opportunism, and hatred for the "other." This creates serious challenges for civic education and political mobilization for nonviolent politics, in a context where a culture of violence appears to be the norm. Continued indifference on the part of elites who control the federal government fuels this anger.

The public action dilemma, with its potent mix of poverty, unemployment, and politicized ethnicity, makes it far more difficult for CS groups to avoid co-optation by the elite-dominated state. CS groups were also in part constrained by their own limited resources and capacities. The potential resources and finances available to individuals willing to enter elites' patronage networks are vast in comparison to any other economic alternative in the Niger Delta, unless one is fortunate to tap the small amounts of donor funds available. This in turn feeds the neopatrimonial dilemma, as greater numbers of people come to depend on the patronage chain. When these dilemmas are combined with militias, the space for CS action is further diminished. Not only do the militias threaten the security of CS activities, exacerbating conflict in the region; they also create an attractive labor market for the burgeoning numbers of unemployed young men, giving them an economic interest in continuing the strife.

Together these dilemmas reinforce one another, fueling deep regional frustrations that are exacerbated by government indifference and multinationals' paralysis and complicity. They also pose another difficulty for CS groups: the question of competing alternatives. What can civil society offer to change people's lives that is *better* than what is being offered by the government patronage machine or the militias? Even if CS groups can avoid co-optation, their political and social room to build peace is whipsawed by the patronage of neopatrimonial elites and the tension and violence in the region, on the one hand, and the lure of militant action, on the other.

Moreover, the Niger Delta underscores the problem that a strong state—in this case, allied with multinationals and local elites—can be tremendously adept at co-opting civil society and crushing dissent. Given the localized nature of the conflict (at least 80 percent of the rest of the country is unaffected and focused on their own problems), the federal government in far-off Abuja can and has continued its business uninterrupted. Even the disruptions in oil production due to militant attacks have sometimes been offset by skyrocketing oil prices on the international market. Thus, the Nigerian government enjoys a far stronger position than its counterparts in nearby African states. Flush with billions of dollars in oil revenues and an 80,000-strong military force, the political and economic elites who control the Nigerian state can wield tremendous influence in the Niger Delta.

Together, these challenges undermine the effectiveness of CS functions. Pitched battles between militias and the Nigerian military, or among militias themselves, backed by leading politicians, restrict the scope and impact of CS groups, particularly after 2003. Some groups were able to continue advocacy roles with some positive impact, and others were able to mediate among the state, militias, and public interests. But the most effective were those with strong international contacts, like ICR (itself an international NGO) and AAPW, which had greater access to foreign funding and some ability to use their global leverage to protect themselves.

More important, perhaps, is that AAPW and ICR enjoyed unprecedented access to President Obasanjo, allowing them to prompt his intervention at key moments in the process. In essence, this allowed those groups to utilize the neopatrimonial structure of Nigerian politics to their own advantage, because "Baba" (the Yoruba word for "father," by which Obasanjo was called) could convince most of the political godfathers to engage in any CS-led process. This role for the president also proved to be a weakness for the AAPW/ICR effort, as it started to unravel after the president's enthusiasm waned.

The spiraling corruption of patronage politics also undermined civil society in performing its functions. Many groups, left with few local alternatives for funding, were forced to turn to patronage machines to cover expenses, forcing them to quiet any opposition they might have to ruling politicians and even to become active participants in the neopatrimonial network. In addition, the neopatrimonial structures of politics favored organizations like AAPW that had or built close relationships with the "Big Men" atop client pyramids, which also favored organizations with international contacts.

Yet, this apparent need to negotiate among the "Big Men" also seems to have caught civil society in a dilemma: negotiating with elites at the expense of public interests. PaSS sought CS involvement in the peace process, but the broader public was never consulted. The Ogoni mediation included opportunities for public input, but these were not systematic, and the main negotiation featured political leaders and a single CS group: MOSOP. The danger of PaSS's elitist orientation was clear: while brokering peace it also may have provided key political leaders with important standing, which they used as cover in their covert efforts to extend militia networks and avoid undertaking real development policies. The fragile peace soon collapsed, and many of the leading protagonists emerged with stronger militias and resources to promote their own agendas.

We can identify another problem facing CS groups engaged in peacebuilding: many were not democratically structured. Many NGOs were centered on strong executive directors, which limited the ability to spread democratic political culture. None of the nondemocratically structured CS groups in our survey provided socialization, and the only nondemocratic organizations engaged in social cohesion were conflict resolution groups (and thus created *precisely* to conduct social cohesion work). This shows a potentially deep failure in regard to nondemocratic NGOs' impact on peacebuilding. Despite undemocratic structures, however, several groups enjoyed democratic political cultures within their organizations; some were highly participatory, inclusive, and respectful of opposition.

Nonetheless, this raises the question whether democratic structure is an important component for CS groups if they are to promote socialization and social cohesion (i.e., *if* they are not explicitly conflict resolution organizations). In other words, unless an organization is created to enhance social cohesion, it is not likely to perform that function as an extension or consequence of other activities. Democratically structured groups, by contrast, spread democratic political culture and bonding and bridging capital *regardless* of their primary function. Consequently, democratic structures within civil society are an important element for any peacebuilding strategy that seeks a transformative approach by addressing the roots of the conflict.

The role of ethnicity in democratically structured groups raises two important possibilities. First, the democratic structure helped to moderate the exclusive aspects of ethnicity that can exacerbate conflict. The strong social bonding orientations of all the democratic CS groups examined suggest that any negative aspects of this are offset by a stronger inclination to bridge cultural divides, even though the organizations seek in part to foster ethnic in-group bonding. This reinforces Darren Kew's (forthcoming) finding in a separate study of sixty-six Nigerian CS groups in which members of democratically structured groups learn democratic political cultural norms that prefer dialogue to settle disputes, and the democratic structures of the organizations provide regular opportunities for such dialogues to occur. In this way, ethnic differences within democratic organizations are typically worked out before they create major divisions within the organization. Moreover, once these organizations have worked out their own internal pattern of ethnic compromise, they utilize it in dealings with other groups, thereby spreading bonding capital and democratic political culture. Even when they promote ethnic interests, ethnic community associations that are democratically structured tend to do so in terms of negotiable interests—such as MOSOP's preference for nonviolent strategies and principled negotiation—rather than zero-sum demands.

Some impact on cultural norms may be evident as well. In the case of PaSS, its efforts led to the development of a "replica" government program, the Rivers State Development Corporation, that was intended to undertake a comprehensive development effort in the state, but the governor's promised

US$20 million never arrived. As an enduring political cultural impact, PaSS appears to have at least showed government *how* to do conflict resolution programming in the region. PaSS thus left a valuable "blueprint" on government political culture that was picked up by the new administration that took office in May 2007 and informed its own peace efforts for the region, including a 2009 amnesty program with some components similar to the PaSS work.

PaSS's state government partners were, however, far less democratic in their functioning and clearly showed little change in neopatrimonial values. State and local government responses to CS initiatives have been tepid, preferring co-optation and repression. Oil company attitudes toward civil society have been ambivalent, working with some groups at times and in certain projects, like PaSS, but avoiding any systematic strategy for CS engagement. Chevron, to its credit, has created regional development councils in Delta and Bayelsa states through which community assistance funds will be channeled, and it plans to invite CS engagement in these councils.

Overall, however, the deck is so stacked against civil society that it has had great difficulty in building peace in the Niger Delta. The conflict continues to escalate, awaiting a serious peace process from the Yar'Adua administration. International donors can help ameliorate the massive barriers that civil society faces in the Niger Delta, and they have provided some assistance, but this has gone primarily to NGOs and their advocacy/protection/monitoring focus. Organizations addressing deeper needs, like socialization and social cohesion, have received less support, in part because of the large number of ethnic community associations already engaged in this work. Donors have been hesitant to deal with such groups in light of the conflict's ethnic dimensions. Yet, peace will have to be built from the grassroots upward if it is to be sustainable and whittle down the depredations of local, regional, and national elites who remain keen on retaining their positions of exclusive access to oil rents and reproducing their hegemonic power relations over the oil-rich region.

Clearly, peace can come only through genuine democratic participation and socially equitable development. Less clear, however, is how much of an impact CS groups are having on overall peace in the volatile context of the Niger Delta. Locally, at least, some groups do show that their peace and democracy promotion work has had some impact, despite the difficult challenges. Groups like CEHRD and others have creatively and constructively conducted peacebuilding despite daunting odds.

Confronting the Issues

Successful CS peacebuilding in the Niger Delta requires several issues to be addressed:

Genuine state interest in a comprehensive peace and the acceptance that a military solution is neither feasible nor sustainable. Given the near-monopoly over resources that the state can bring to bear, its indifference to a peace process leaves a gap that has proven too wide for civil society to bridge. State opposition to peace would surely prove far worse for civil society, as demonstrated during the occasional military operations the federal government conducted during the conflict. Conversely, if the state is genuinely engaged in peacebuilding, there is a strong likelihood that militias will follow. The Nigerian state is not monolithic, in that civil society can and has worked to interest some parts in lieu of a comprehensive effort, such as governors, the National Assembly, the judiciary, and oil companies; but a solution will require the leadership of the president. President Yar'Adua has promised a "Marshall Plan" and a comprehensive peace process for the region but has yet to initiate either in a substantive way, except to declare an amnesty for delta militants willing to lay down their arms in the context of a government-sponsored disarmament deal. CS groups have clamored for presidential leadership, but the resource disparity has so far left them at a disadvantage.

Militia demilitarization. CS groups have played roles in this regard, primarily in localities where militias are active. The most comprehensive demilitarization process to date occurred during PaSS, but it lapsed soon after the state lost interest, and a similar pattern is playing out in the 2009 amnesty program as well.

Democratize NGOs and other civil society groups. One of the most powerful findings of this study was the strong connection between democratic structures within CS groups and the conduct of socialization, social change, and intermediation functions. Internal restructuring of civil society provides an important vehicle for spreading democratic culture and peacebuilding orientations within these groups; it also promotes increased bridging activities across conflict divides. This may prove important in degenerating cases like the Niger Delta, where civil society can at least play a "safe haven" role, protecting democratic culture and building peace in the small pockets that it can preserve until state actors are ready to play positive roles.

Seek powerful friends—international and domestic political contacts. CS groups that proved most effective had strong international contacts and maintained relationships across the neopatrimonial patronage pyramids. Local NGOs also had some impact in the communities within which they worked. Working with neopatrimonial elites, however, runs the constant risk of co-optation.

Intercommunal dialogue and alliance-building versus the state-oil hegemonic complex. In order to provoke more positive state action, CS groups may have to take further action to bridge ethnic divides and thereby foster united public fronts against the overwhelming might of the state and multinationals. CS groups have made some progress in organizing communities and conducting empowerment activities, which may provide platforms for additional advocacy.

Election reform remains an important element that, if enacted, will enhance this and all the other CS roles. Free and fair elections would also facilitate the rise of a more credible political leadership and regional policies.

Working toward peace in the Niger Delta need not wait for all conflicts to end; they cannot all end at the same moment. The strategies for peace have to be multilevel, multilocation, and targeted but, more important, address the social, political, and economic conditions that fuel alienation, anger, and violence in the region. At the very least, the case of the Niger Delta demonstrates that violent phases see a lessening of CS functions and impacts. Advocacy efforts across all sectors of civil society appear to have suffered most as violence increased in the 2003–2009 period.

More hopeful, however, is the finding that democratically structured CS groups may be the only organizations able to provide the social cohesion and socialization functions outside conflict resolution groups. This finding stretched across all phases of conflict and indicates a strong role for democratically structured CS groups in providing social capital in war-torn societies.

Clearly, civil society has a crucial role to play but has to be supported, empowered, and retooled to challenge itself with more proactive roles in promoting peace in the region. Civil society can bring stakeholders together, work for a spirit of dialogue and trust, and conduct civic education, peace education, and policy advocacy work to open political space. National democratic deepening is also an important external factor that benefits CS peacebuilding functions. In the Niger Delta, election reform, economic redistribution, and anticorruption measures will do much to improve public representation, trust, and service provision, which would provide the context for civil society to flourish.

The fortunes of the Niger Delta and Nigeria are inextricably connected, and it is clear that peace in the oil-rich region will release great energies and resources that will add a boost to Nigerian state development. This in turn would enable this pivotal state to match its widely recognized potential with the achievement of greater prosperity, peace, and security for itself and West Africa.

Notes

1. Interview with a retired Nigerian general, July 1998.

2. Note that three additional states neighboring the Niger Delta also have small oil-producing locales and receive a modest additional revenue award under the 13 percent derivation principle.

3. The governor of Rivers State also reportedly bought two private jets and several properties overseas and built a lavish gubernatorial mansion, among other expenditures, including a power project that has yet to generate electricity (Human Rights Watch 2005).

4. Civil society groups for this study were chosen based on available data, as gathered in previous research projects (Kew 2007; Kew forthcoming; Obi 2004, 2005, and 2007) and by interviews conducted in 2007–2008. Most groups were then selected as leading representatives of particular subtypes of civil society organizations, such as human rights NGOs, community associations, and the like.

PART 3

What We Have Learned

16

What Civil Society Can Contribute to Peacebuilding

Thania Paffenholz

In order to set up the final discussions for the project *Civil Society and Peacebuilding,* the analysis in this chapter presents key findings on the seven civil society peacebuilding functions (presented in Chapter 4 as the "comprehensive analytical framework").

These findings are the result of applying the comprehensive framework to thirteen case studies, eleven of which are presented in this volume. The seven CS peacebuilding functions have been analyzed according to four general phases of conflict and peacebuilding: war, armed conflict (which is distinguished from war by its lower number of casualties),[1] windows of opportunity for peace negotiations, and the period following large-scale violence.[2] Findings were analyzed comparatively, through a combination of quantitative and qualitative analysis. The focus has been the relevance and effectiveness of the seven functions for peacebuilding. Relevance was assessed against goals, as defined by the four phases of conflict. Effectiveness was assessed against the ability of CS actors to contribute to peacebuilding goals in each of the four phases. Thus, the comparative analysis considered the contributions of CS initiatives to reducing violence, reaching a negotiated agreement, the medium- to long-term sustainability of a peace agreement, and/or the establishment of conditions for treating conflict constructively in society at large.

Protection

During armed conflict and war, the protection function was highly relevant in all cases but one: Cyprus (due to a UN mission that separated the conflict parties and led to a stalemate; in Cyprus the conflict was no longer executed by violent means). As for the protection function, the level of violence determines relevance. Guatemala reflects this. Usually the need for protection decreases after large-scale violence has ended, but after the peace agreement in Guatemala, a transformation of violence occurred from war/armed conflict violence between the main adversary groups to a situation of crime, selective political and social violence, and insecurity with extraordinarily high homicide rates. In some years this resulted in higher death figures than during the armed conflict. This made protection, again, very much needed.

Interestingly, the high relevance of protection did not correlate with the actual level of protection activities performed by CS organizations. Only in one-third of the cases was protection actually undertaken in a meaningful way. It could be argued that protection is not a function that should be performed by civil society. After all, it is usually the state, if it is a functioning state, that is responsible for protecting citizens. During war and armed conflict, however, the state is either one party to the conflict and/or unable to fulfill its protection function. Thus, strong outside actors take over this function (e.g., the United Nations or regional organizations), or civil society starts protecting itself and others. The longer a conflict endures, the more likely it is that people will revert to relying on clans, communities, families, or religious entities (see Chapter 1 in this volume). Such entities begin to take on the responsibility to protect their members. In Afghanistan and Somalia, clans played this role; in Guatemala, it was the Catholic Church; and in Northern Ireland, it was family groupings that tended to protect members from paramilitary violence. Next to these more "traditional" actors, professional organizations, such as specialized protection NGOs, were also active within this function. They were either involved in general protection measures (e.g., the National Committee of the Red Cross, Peace Brigades International) or addressed specific forms of violence, such as violence against minorities, children, and women.

One particular form of protection chosen by CS actors and others related to migration. The more the space for CS activities shrunk, the more activists and other people left the countries. Many of the CS activists continued to work from outside the country, often partnering with international NGOs and other organizations.

After large-scale violence comes to an end, the need for protection usually diminishes and shifts to specific needs (e.g., clearing landmines, reducing domestic violence). In some cases, however, violence prevailed or transformed into crime and general insecurity. Alternatively, other conflict lines manifested in violence after the signing of a peace agreement (e.g., Nepal, Democratic Republic of Congo [DRC], and Afghanistan). The more the international community ensured protection through monitoring or peacekeeping missions, the lower the level of violence became—and a larger space opened for civil society actors. This was equally true during armed conflict. The UN human rights monitoring missions in Nepal and Guatemala contributed not only to protection but also to ending the armed conflict itself.

Protection thus becomes a key precondition for civil society to act and perform other functions. The case of Somalia demonstrates this well: even under difficult circumstances during phases of armed conflict, CS actors could still fulfill many functions. However, when war broke out again after the Ethiopian intervention in December 2006, and the conflict parties became increasingly aggressive toward CS actors, the space to act for civil society almost vanished.

The effectiveness of protection—when performed—was mixed. Protection efforts by traditional and religious entities or families were often successful but confined to their immediate local contexts. The efforts of professional protection NGOs were effective in many cases when combined with monitoring and advocacy activities that attracted media attention. Moreover, the link to international actors also enhanced effectiveness. The cases of successful protection in Nepal and elsewhere confirm similar findings. In Afghanistan, the Afghan Red Crescent was able to perform effective protection work even under the Taliban rule as a result of the support it received from the International Committee of the Red Cross (ICRC) and the United Nations. The churches in Guatemala had the support of their respective international networks and also cooperated with UNMIN. International accompaniment from organizations such as Peace Brigades International and others also proved to be an effective mechanism for protecting civil society. The establishment of the Basic Operating Guidelines by a broad coalition of major international donors in times of armed conflict in Nepal also opened space for civil society.

Protection initiatives from traditional actors were not directly linked to external funds, but the work of NGOs was almost totally dependent on these funding sources. In consequence, the level of engagement—and thus the chance to have an effect—were influenced by the availability of donor funds. In Sri Lanka, for example, during the cease-fire after 2001, there was little funding available for protection, but in the DRC after 2006 the availability of funds increased protection initiatives.

An interesting case of preventative protection comes from Northern Ireland. After the Good Friday Agreement, former paramilitaries had a high potential for becoming an obstacle to peacebuilding and protection, and several groups turned into criminal groups. With the support of funds from the European Union, sixty-one groups of former political prisoners (i.e., former paramilitaries) from both sides of the conflict were formed and provided a range of services to their communities, including counseling, employment training, and dialogue. These groups became instrumental in reducing tensions and in persuading youths to engage in nonviolent conflict management. They were thus successfully transformed from a potential threat to a source for peacebuilding.

In sum, the main supporting factors for successful protection are sufficient space for civil society to act and the combination of protection, monitoring, and advocacy that can attract media attention and gain the support of international networks. The main limiting factors are a high level of violence, a lack of funding for professional initiatives, and a general lack of enabling conditions.

Monitoring

During armed conflict and war the relevance of monitoring by civil society actors was high in all cases, except those in which international monitoring missions were already fulfilling this task, as in Cyprus. The high relevance did not, however, correlate with the levels of activities. Monitoring was not performed in all cases or was performed only to a limited extent. This was mainly due to restrictions set up by a coercive state or an extreme level of violence. At the beginning of armed conflicts, the level of monitoring was low in all cases but tended to increase over time. Monitoring was perceived by the conflict parties (including the state) as a highly political task that was to be omitted, avoided, or co-opted. In consequence, volunteers and professional employees of monitoring organizations are subject to threats of violence and assassinations.

When monitoring was performed, activities focused on human rights violations and political developments. Also common was monitoring of specific groups like children, minorities, and prisoners, as well as conflict-specific issues (landmines, land access, elections, discrimination). The main actors involved were local and national professionals—mainly human rights organizations and research institutions, sometimes linked to international organizations such as Amnesty International. We also identified monitoring that was conducted by development organizations. The information collected was not, however, used systematically for protection or advocacy but mainly for the operational purposes of these organizations. In a few cases, monitoring was also performed by established organizations such as the Catholic Church.

After large-scale violence comes to an end, the relevance of monitoring remains generally high. However, the focus of activities shifts toward the monitoring of a peace or cease-fire agreement. For example, even in Israel and Palestine a monitoring initiative was never undertaken for the Oslo process during the 1990s. This would have been highly relevant, especially considering the fact that the process was criticized for parties not fulfilling their promises. In general, monitoring usually becomes less risky after an agreement. Interestingly, we could observe that monitoring activities were segregated during this period. Organizations tended to monitor a particular process or sector of the peace agreement (e.g., security sector reform, minority rights, women's issues), often not aiming to obtain the comprehensive picture. Monitoring by civil society was less relevant in those cases where strong—and effective—national or international bodies were mandated to do so (usually by the peace agreement). National institutions, such as human rights commissions, were strong when they were independent and had the necessary human and financial resources and legitimacy. However, many of them were co-opted or controlled by the state.

The effectiveness of monitoring—when performed—was fairly high in most cases; however, it was not performed as a stand-alone function. Monitoring often became the precondition for protection and advocacy in a mutually reinforcing way. As with protection, the effectiveness of monitoring was higher when the media picked up the information and included it in their normal reporting duties. Contrarily, when media freedom was restricted, monitoring activities were reported less often and thus were less effective. Still, once international attention was created, monitoring organizations already linked to international organizations could act more effectively. The successful monitoring of local and national human rights organizations in Nepal and Guatemala is discussed under the section on protection; in Sri Lanka, research institutions monitored the political situation and continued to create international attention. These activities thus led to an increase in protection initiatives. In Afghanistan under the Taliban, the Cooperation Center for Afghanistan managed to submit coded reports to international human rights organizations, and the country remained on the international agenda. In Nigeria, the ongoing human rights reports have also sustained international attention for human rights abuses in the Niger Delta.

The monitoring of specific issues was also successful in many cases. In Northern Ireland, the monitoring of war prisoners, combined with advocacy, brought their situation to the public's attention and, later, into the peace agreement. In the Israeli-Palestinian conflict, there were many monitoring initiatives related to specific issues such as checkpoints, children's rights, and prisoners, to name a few. Those initiatives, combined with advocacy and strong international attention, were often successful. Other initiatives without this attention often could not produce the envisaged results. For example, monitoring reports of torture in Palestinian prisons led to successful protection due to international pressure, but the monitoring of Palestinian prisoners in Israeli prisons did not contribute to a change in their conditions due to lack of attention. In Guatemala, discrimination and the exclusion of indigenous populations became important monitoring topics after the indigenous rights activist Rigoberta Menchú was awarded a Nobel Prize in 1992.

In sum, the main supporting factors for successful monitoring include the mutually reinforcing relationship between advocacy and protection, combined with media and international attention. Pressure by the international community often seems to have facilitated improved protection; in a few cases this was true at the broader national level. Mostly, however, protection took the form of many small successful initiatives that sustained lives or made life better for many people during times of armed conflict and war. The main limiting factor for monitoring—as with protection—is the massive restriction of the space for civil society and media by the state or other conflict parties, as well as the extremely high levels of violence. Many activists involved in monitoring come under direct threat, as sadly demonstrated by the long list of activists who were assassinated. Another limiting factor is the co-optation of monitoring institutions by the state. Moreover, lack of funding is an additional limiting factor, as organizations involved in monitoring are, with few exceptions, dependent on additional funds, even if many organizations work with volunteers. In some cases, as in Sri Lanka during the period of the cease-fire, when there was still hope for negotiations, human rights monitoring organizations were not supported by donors because they were perceived to be "spoilers" of the peace process when they accused the conflict parties (i.e., the negotiating parties) of gross human rights violations.

Advocacy

The research reveals that it is necessary to distinguish between different forms and foci of advocacy. We can distinguish informal as well as public forms of advocacy, the strongest form being mass mobilization, such as street agitation and mass demonstrations. *Advocacy was conducted in all cases throughout all phases of conflict/peacebuilding* with different foci, such as:

1. Advocacy with public agitation for massive change, mostly aimed at regime change (such as the end of authoritarian rule) or the end of war or armed conflict; it is mostly performed by a broad spectrum of civil society organizations and often organized by mass-based organizations
2. Agenda-setting for peace negotiations
3. Advocacy for conflict-specific themes or involved groups in light of the context and phase of a conflict. The main themes across cases were advocacy for:
   a. Protection from violence, mostly associated with general or specific human rights abuses (e.g., children and women, war prisoners or detainees, IDPs, disappeared people), taking place both locally and nationally and performed by local or traditional groups both informally and in public
   b. Legal issues around the recognition or implementation of rights for marginalized groups (e.g., lower castes in Nepal, the Maja in Guatemala, Kurdish minorities in Turkey, Muslims in Sri Lanka), mostly performed on the national level by specialized professional organizations, often NGOs
   c. Pertinent issues related to the underlying causes of conflict (e.g., land reform, political participation, minority rights)
   d. Specific issues around the implementation of peace agreements (e.g., refugee return in Bosnia-Herzegovina, truth and reconciliation commissions, impunity), also mainly performed nationally by professional specialized organizations

4. Advocacy for keeping the country on the international agenda; here national groups often worked hand-in-glove with diaspora groups

The effectiveness of the different forms and types of advocacy varied. We can, however, conclude that advocacy was the most effective function overall. Some success factors can be identified: when mass mobilization was performed, for instance, it made advocacy particularly effective in phases where windows of opportunity opened for peace negotiations and when the joint change-oriented forces for peace were stronger than counteracting forces. Another condition for success was the participation of large numbers of people who drew media and international attention. In Nepal, civil society groups were overwhelmingly united in the 2006 people's movement for accepting the peace agreement, as were the groups in Northern Ireland in the "Yes" campaign. In Cyprus, the propeace camp voted for the acceptance of the Annan plan in almost equal numbers to the counteracting forces and suffered a narrow defeat. In Sri Lanka, the propeace negotiation camp was by far outnumbered by strong counteracting forces.

Civil society organizations were in many cases also effective in bringing issues to negotiation or postagreement agendas. The most visible and successful case was the systematic advocacy of civil society groups organized in the Asamblea de la Sociedad Civil, which paralleled the two-year official peace negotiations in Guatemala. Here, civil society organizations successfully managed to put important topics onto the negotiation agenda; two-thirds of the proposals found their way into the peace agreement. A similar forum parallel to the official UN Afghanistan mediations in Bonn in December 2001 was far less effective in agenda-setting; however, it managed to put the issues of civil society, including women as actors in peacebuilding, on the postagreement agenda. The involvement of civil society at the negotiation table during the Inter-Congolese Dialogue in 2002 had practically no influence on the negotiations, as civil society participants were co-opted by political parties and did not manage to formulate an independent agenda. In Sri Lanka, civil society actors managed to successfully lobby for the representation of women within the peace negotiation's architecture; however, it was effectively too late to have an impact, as the negotiations had collapsed by then. In Northern Ireland, civil society groups managed to successfully lobby for the integration of human rights provisions into the peace agreement. In the Israel-Palestine case, many civil society initiatives have developed proposals for negotiations over the years and lobbed informally and publicly for their recognition.

Interestingly, after a peace agreement or system change was reached, civil society did not manage to maintain involvement. This was despite the fact that, in most cases, massive advocacy for the implementation of the peace agreement was still very much needed. Although advocacy continued, the form changed into small campaigns for specific issues—mostly reflecting the core interests of particular groups. Guatemala is a case in point: after successful agenda-setting during the negotiation period, civil society did not manage to properly monitor and advocate for the implementation of the very issues it had managed to bring into the agreement. When a referendum on the necessary constitutional reforms for implementation of the peace accord came up for vote, civil society groups failed to mobilize support. This led to the participation of less than 20 percent of the electorate. The "no" campaign won, and the peace process lost its momentum. The very issues that civil society had worked so hard to include in the peace treaty (indigenous rights, land reform, and others) were the ones that were not, or very insufficiently, implemented. The massive violence in the years after the agreement has never been the subject of huge civil society campaigns, as the common enemy became lost and civil society disintegrated into smaller, less effective entities.

As for informal advocacy, the effectiveness of civil society is more difficult to assess. In cases where sufficient data are available, we find that convincing the conflict parties to end war or armed conflict has to do with influence and perceived power. Thus, other actors, and not civil society, become involved—specifically politicians, businesspeople, and international actors. When civil society actors are successfully involved, it comes in the form of eminent leaders who are accepted by all groups. However, the line between civil leaders and politicians is often blurred in these cases. It is also important to note that informal advocacy for massive change is similar to informal facilitation (discussed in the section on facilitation). We also see that many public advocacy campaigns were further supported by behind-the-scenes informal advocacy vis-à-vis politicians, the conflict parties, and/or the international community, which certainly factored into their success even if it is difficult to measure.

Targeted advocacy campaigns for specific issues are in many cases effective when combined with monitoring. Especially in protection campaigns, civil society proved able to achieve positive results in reducing human rights violations in local and/or national contexts. Many local initiatives by community groups and leaders or local NGOs were effective and resulted in the release of prisoners, demining, and refugee return, to name a few examples. In Somalia, clan leaders are particularly sensitive to protecting their interests and aggressively lobby political figures and aid agencies to ensure that they are accorded a fair share of resources and positions. In some cases, clans effectively use affiliated civil society groups to advance claims. Women's groups in Nigeria played a successful advocacy role for the protection of women and ethnic minorities. In Afghanistan under the Taliban, an NGO antilandmine campaign convinced Mullah Omar to issue a fatwa banning the use of landmines. Specialized NGOs were in some cases also very effective in lobbying for legal issues. For example, in Bosnia-Herzegovina women's groups were instrumental in changing legislation on gender equality and domestic violence. A precondition for success was professional organizations' capacity to launch an effective campaign alongside their actual knowledge in the subject matter. Interestingly, external capacity-building tends not to focus much on supporting campaigning skills.

Civil society is, however, less effective when strong counteracting forces work against a given issue. In Bosnia-Herzegovina, advocacy for the establishment of a truth and reconciliation commission failed when the International Criminal Court lobbied strongly against it.

In many cases, civil society becomes an advocate for international engagement. Civil society groups inside the country—sometimes in cooperation with diaspora groups—have in many instances successfully managed to keep conflicts on the international agenda and thereby ensure ongoing support. Afghan NGOs linked up with Afghan and international organizations abroad, links that became essential to shaping the international agenda on Afghanistan. Kurdish civil society groups located outside Turkey in Europe successfully put the Kurdish question on the agenda of European governments and influenced the European Union to pressure Turkey to grant rights to Kurds. This enlarged the space for civil society.

In sum, the main supporting factor for successful mass mobilization was the existence of a common goal or issue (terminating violence or authoritarian rule, discontinuing forced recruitment, freeing political prisoners). In terms of agenda-setting during and after negotiations, we find that targeted civil society campaigns, combined with media attention and external pressure, are the most effective. Moreover, a precondition for an advocacy campaign addressing specific issues is a certain degree of professionalization, which enables the conduct of informed campaigns and international networking.

The main limiting conditions include a shrinking space for civil society. Conditions such as a coercive or co-optive state, high levels of violence, as well as a restricted media are examples. Moreover, for specific types of advocacy, the lack of capacities for both managing successful campaigns and specialized knowledge can become limitations. In conflicts with heavy international involvement (e.g., Bosnia-Herzegovina), the disempowered mindset of people also makes mobilization difficult.

Socialization

Our research reveals that the function of socialization in peacebuilding has to be understood as differentiated from that in democracy theory. In democracy theory, the impetus for this function is socialization of society at large toward democratic values in socialization institutions such as schools, clubs, associations, religious entities, workplaces, and others. For peacebuilding (see Chapter 4 in this volume), we see that this is applicable to general socialization toward a culture of peace within society. People can be socialized to deal with conflicts constructively. This function can be practiced as well in the above-mentioned socialization institutions. We also identify a second type of socialization in peacebuilding: the consolidation of in-group identity. This is relevant for oppressed and marginalized groups in asymmetric conflict situations. It serves as a means to strengthen their ability to formulate demands and to participate in processes as a meaningful partner or simply to preserve the culture and language of the groups in question.

We find in all cases that the existing socialization institutions in society (families, schools, religious, secular and cultural associations, clubs, workplaces) are *the key* influential factors in how people learn democratic and conflict behavior. In all cases, existing socialization institutions tend to reinforce existing divides, often fostering radicalization. This is the case in typical group-identity conflicts with at least two key adversary groups, as in Northern Ireland, Sri Lanka, and Israel-Palestine; the same holds true for conflicts with more differentiated divides, as in Guatemala, Nepal, Afghanistan, the DRC, and Nigeria. Schools and other educational institutions are also a major element of socialization. If segregated, they can reinforce conflicts and existing divides in society, and their hierarchical and competitive natures do not generally contribute to the practice of democratic attitudes and to addressing conflicts in a constructive way. In Israel, for example, the education in the Jewish and Zionist identity is historically prioritized over education in liberal democratic values and democratic education; Israel is largely dependent on the ideological views of its government. In Cyprus, youths have been educated along nationalist lines and in a way that disregards the needs and fears of the "other." Greek Cypriots are inculcated with the idea that the island was and "will always be Greek," whereas Turkish Cypriots learn that "the island is Turkish and should go back to Turkey." In Sri Lanka, Northern Ireland, Nepal, and Guatemala, schools also represent and reflect divides in society.

The military in many countries also serves as a space for socialization. In Israel, men who devote themselves to the study of religion are exempted from service and do not go through the same socialization process. More and more, Israeli society has become divided along the lines of secular versus orthodox.

We also find radical movements within civil society that openly foster an enemy image against the other group, such as the settler movement in Israel, veteran associations in Bosnia-Herzegovina, ethnic community associations in Nigeria, Sinhala nationalist organizations in Sri Lanka, and the Orange Order in Northern Ireland; members are being expelled when they marry a member of the other group. The *mutuelles,* an ethnically based community self-help group in the DRC, represent another example; they support and protect members in times of conflict and facilitate ethnically motivated recruitment for armed groups.

Aside from the roles these groups play in reinforcing existing divides through values and norms, they also perform important services for members.

Examples include Islamic schools, charities, and networks in Somalia, Afghanistan, and Bosnia-Herzegovina that have rapidly expanded since the mid-1990s. Such services play a major role in creating a new form of Muslim identity heretofore unknown in those countries. They can also develop opposition against a secular state and other organizations. Although they support members in daily life, the hometown associations of Kurdish people living in Western cities in Turkey can also make any attempt to integrate them into Turkish society more difficult while maintaining Kurdish identity.

Women's organizations are an interesting case in terms of socialization. They have been at the forefront of socializing women in their rights and thus creating preconditions for advocacy. However, this often happens at the expense of mainstreaming gender issues into broader civil society. Examples from the DRC and the Kurdish conflict show that when women are more actively engaged in civil society organizations, those organizations are more likely to put gender issues on their agendas.

The in-group education of the Maya in Guatemala by the Catholic Church helped to empower a generation of civic leaders. The experience of war and widespread violence allowed for the construction of a pan-Maya identity across the twenty-four separate language groups. The same holds true for Dalit (lower-caste groups) in Nepal, which have contributed a great deal to the empowerment of underprivileged groups. However, in both cases, empowerment often came at the expense of the ability to compromise with other groups. The case of the April 2006 people's movement in Nepal suggests that multiple in-group identities were sufficiently strong in themselves and compatible enough alongside each other to form a broader movement.

In addition, divides are often reinforced after peace agreements go into effect. We frequently find power-sharing mechanisms in these contexts. This may seem to be a good transitional mechanism, but there should be an understanding as to when such arrangements will end and in which cases society and politics can be based on values other than group identity.

It is astonishing that peace agreements were achieved at all in some cases, given the values and attitudes of strong counteracting forces deeply permeated within society. The main reason is found outside civil society. In all cases, the changing political environment, mostly originating from the conflict parties themselves, contributed in this respect. Thus, counteracting forces could be mitigated by the political process. Nevertheless, as is demonstrated by returns to violence and difficulties implementing peace agreements, these forces may continue to be obstacles to peacebuilding in the short, medium, and long terms.

These findings contrast with the performed activities by civil society organizations and the external funding flows intended to counteract negative trends. The striking finding here is that most activities happen outside the major socialization institutions.

The main activities we see are various kinds of peace education, including workshops, training, public seminars, peace media (e.g., soap operas and news features), and distribution of books and brochures. We also observe a mushrooming of such activities in conflicts that are framed as group-identity conflicts and are to be found at the top of the international agenda (e.g., Israel and Palestine, Cyprus, Northern Ireland). These activities were almost exclusively performed by specialized NGOs.

Moreover, the donor focus in conflict countries is directed toward conflict resolution and negotiation training, not toward the practice of democratic values and understanding. Our research, however, reveals that the strengthening of democratic values is equally important for peacebuilding. The lack of democratic procedures and understanding becomes a main obstacle to engage in a constructive way. In Nigeria, the only organizations that performed the socialization function were democratically structured groups. This finding underscores the importance of democratic structures for inculcating democratic political culture within civil society groups. Maya groups in Guatemala are a case in point: they fragmented and lost their ability to influence national politics due to specific leaders and clientelistic behavior.

Yet, activities that foster democratic values are rarely supported by civil society apart from general civic education campaigns, such as voter education for elections. Moreover, the nature of many civil society organizations is not democratic. The leadership is usually male-dominated (with the exception of women's groups); represents dominant and/or influential groups in society (upper classes, higher castes, whites, mestizo populations); often lacks democratic procedures; and thus contributes little to democratic socialization. Interestingly, this can have an influence on professional behaviors: in Nigeria, the more internally democratic civil society organizations were, the more they could contribute these values effectively through their work. In the same case, however, conflict resolution NGOs with weak internal conflict resolution mechanisms did not contribute effectively through their work. We find similar results in the Kurdish case. This is certainly a trend worth investigating, as we do not have sufficient data to identity this as a pattern throughout all the cases.

As for effectiveness, when looking at the nature of socialization initiatives, it is not astonishing that they have not been effective overall. There are many reasons why these initiatives tend to fail. However, the core reason is obvious: the deeply permeated notion of radical in-group socialization within existing socialization institutions cannot be counterbalanced by a few local or national NGO initiatives that take place outside these institutions. Rather, the focus should be on the slow—and difficult and long-term—change within socialization institutions. It would be helpful to include schools and associations that promote a climate of handling conflicts constructively and encourage members to practice democratic values through fair representation and the participation of all groups in decisionmaking. Of course, it could also be argued that socialization-oriented initiatives must be developed along a longer trajectory and that they do not have to have an effect on peacebuilding in the short and medium terms. Nevertheless, the cases demonstrate that socialization efforts are not fruitful during times of escalation and during high levels of violence. In such environments, people are occupied with other issues, such as survival; often the radicalization of society is too high during these periods.

In sum, the main positive effect of in-group socialization has been the empowerment of marginalized groups to make their voices heard. However, the initiatives of civil society organizations aimed at fostering a culture of peace through peace education and conflict resolution training have had little or no effect. Scattered initiatives that take place outside the main institutions for socialization generally cannot counterbalance a climate of radical group identity. During armed conflict, and shortly after large-scale violence has ended, the local impact was also limited, as it proved difficult to mobilize people for a long-term culture of peace while they lacked basic human needs (food and security). Media coverage often reinforces existing divides.

Social Cohesion

Regarding social cohesion—essentially, the bridging of divides between adversary groups—we find that the exact understanding of this function is not uniform. In many conflict situations, it is not always obvious who could eventually be bridged with whom. When looking at in-group identity conflicts in Northern Ireland, Sri Lanka, Bosnia-Herzegovina, Cyprus, and Israel-Palestine, it seems clear that social cohesion is about bridging divides between the main groups (e.g., Protestants/Catholics, Singhalese/Tamils). However, in societies with murkier divides, as in Guatemala and Afghanistan, there seems to be only a limited need for this function. A deeper analysis, however, reveals that societies often face deep divides among all sorts of groups. In Israel, there are deep divides between Orthodox and secular Israelis; in Sri Lanka, with its seemingly clear ethnic division, we also find class and regional cleavages within the respective groups. Bridging in the Kurdish question is needed not only between the PKK and the state, and Kurdish and Turkish citizens, but also between ultranationalists and their more moderate counterparts in both camps. In Guatemala, we find the population divided by indigenous and Latino identities as well as between rich/poor and urban/rural. In Afghanistan, cleavages exist between religious and secular groups, different religious schools and doctrines, tribal and modern parts of society, as well as various ethnic identities. In Nepal, there are persistently strong urban/rural, caste, regional, and ethnic cleavages. In Somalia, years of crisis reproduced deep social cleavages along clan, regional, and ideological divides. Besides the obvious ethnic tensions in the Niger Delta, other conflict lines exist between militias and the government and between various communities and the government. The same holds true for the DRC.

In all the case studies, societies at large and civil society groups were also divided along gender lines. However, the cases also show that all women within a society cannot be equalized. Women in society are naturally divided akin to society at large. Cleavages exist along class, caste, ethnic, religious, regional, and political lines. With the exception of women's organizations, civil society groups tend to be male-dominated. This is also reflected in the topics they choose (i.e., gender topics are mainly addressed by women's groups). In some cases, however, we found that the more that women participate in civil society organizations, the more that gender themes tend to enter the agenda.

As all sorts of cleavages exist in every society in the world, the question needs to be asked: Why do these cleavages matter for peacebuilding? If we start from the hypothesis that conflicts and tensions between people and groups are a necessary prerequisite for development of societies (conflicts in parliamentary democracies are a case in point), then a consequent assumption is that attention must be directed only at the main conflict lines expressed through violence. When analyzing conflict societies, we see that such an assumption is not enough. Once violent methods for dealing with conflict have entered a society, there is a high risk that other conflict lines will also turn violent. It thus becomes a matter of violence prevention. We find many examples in the case studies. The uprising of violence in the southern Nepali Tarai region immediately after the signature of the Comprehensive Peace Agreement in 2006 is a case in point. The focus on the main conflict line—between the Maoist movement and the government—has neglected other tensions and has possibly even reinforced ethnic divides. In Sri Lanka, growth rates in the economy have not been equally distributed, even in the Sinhala-dominated south; the greater Colombo area receives most of the wealth. Underprivileged and poor Singhalese have become a major political mobilization force for hard-line nationalist political parties. They contributed to a change from a negotiation-oriented government to a war-oriented government. This resulted in the resumption of war. The fights between Fatah and Hamas in Gaza are another example.

The relevance of bridging all sorts of divides seems obvious. Yet, these findings do not correspond to the activities performed by civil society groups in the social cohesion context. With a few exceptions, attention focuses exclusively on the main conflict lines, as well as on the known group-identity conflicts. Quantitatively, social cohesion initiatives are performed most often through civil society initiatives (aside from general service delivery). Most initiatives take place within group-identity conflicts, as in Israel-Palestine, Cyprus, Bosnia-Herzegovina, and Sri Lanka. Interestingly, there were no such activities in the Kurdish case in Turkey despite obvious divides. Activities reached their peak (i.e., there was a mushrooming of initiatives) in the above-mentioned cases during windows of opportunity or immediately after a peace or cease-fire agreement. Such was the case after the Oslo Accord between Israel and Palestine, during the cease-fire agreement in Sri Lanka, after the Dayton Accord for Bosnia-Herzegovina, and elsewhere. This was due to the high level of external funding for those activities.

The main activities and initiatives for social cohesion are:

1. Problem-solving workshops with civil society (and sometimes members of political parties as well) for developing a concrete common peace proposal
2. Work- or issue-oriented problem-solving workshops bringing professional groups together for common work objectives (e.g., urban planning in Jerusalem)
3. People-to-people projects bringing grassroots groups together
4. Community relations meetings (mainly in Cyprus, Northern Ireland, and Bosnia-Herzegovina)

In Bosnia-Herzegovina, many initiatives focused on deemphasizing ethnicity and finding alternative values. In Cyprus, bicommunal meetings and initiatives, even though rare during the 1970s and 1980s, were common after the mid-1990s, reaching a point in the late 1997 when at least one bicommunal group was meeting every day of the week. In Israel-Palestine, we find problem-solving workshops in preparation for negotiations (i.e., outcome-oriented initiatives aimed at the development of a concrete common proposal). There were also initiatives between professionals to solve a common problem, such as water management near the Jordan River, in addition to people-to-people initiatives bringing together youths, professional groups, and communities for dialogue with the objective of changing attitudes and enemy images. In Sri Lanka, the same patterns prevailed, but with more of a focus on elite meetings. In Northern Ireland, donors contributed huge amounts of funding toward community relations. However, most funds were actually used for community development in a single community.

In conflict settings that are not framed as group-identity conflicts, we see far fewer initiatives. However, some initiatives were undertaken to foster social cohesion. In Afghanistan, we see initiatives to support a national Afghan identity over tribal, religious, and other identities. In the DRC, Nigeria, and Nepal, mixed-community committees have become more popular for managing development initiatives. In Nepal, after the war escalated in 2001, many donor agencies started to introduce conflict-sensitive approaches to their development projects. Besides the political conflict between the main conflict parties, the underlying cause of conflict was identified as social, mainly the existence of inequalities between castes and genders. There was a real effort to include underprivileged groups in user groups and committees. A differentiation between the political and social conflicts is also seen in Afghanistan. However, no systematic interaction using an inclusive approach to any major national development program has been made to date.

In general, the main actors involved in problem-solving initiatives are international NGOs (with or without local partners), academic institutions, and individual scholar-practitioners. Initiatives with professionals are often run by professional associations, sometimes with international conflict resolution NGO partners. People-to-people programs are usually conducted by specialized conflict resolution NGOs (mostly international with local partners). Work on community relations is conducted by conflict resolution and development NGOs. Mixed-community and other development-oriented committees are, in general, initiated by development projects and supported by local NGOs with international partners.

As for effectiveness, we generally find that most peace- and relationship-oriented initiatives were largely ineffective for the reasons outlined below. As explained in the section on socialization (see above), there are many strong socialization institutions, including families, schools, professional associations, military groups, workplace groups, and religious organizations in divided societies. When these institutions preach hatred and formulate enemy images over a long period (usually generations), the existence of few social cohesion initiatives cannot be very effective. In Somalia, for example, clan-based organizations worked to reinforce social cleavages and worked against national cohesion. The spectrum runs from relatively harmless organizations (such as a Somali Bantu self-help group) to actively destructive types (such as clan mobilization movements that operate extremist websites demonizing rival clans). Moreover, divided communities by definition live segregated lives. In Northern Ireland, for example, the two communities live in different parts of towns, and any form of daily contact is limited. The same holds true for Bosnia-Herzegovina and Cyprus.

Interestingly, group divides are often strengthened after a peace agreement. Many peace agreements require management of divides at the political level. This management, which is often manifested in power-sharing arrangements, reinforces divides. The regulation of group conflict thus becomes a political-elite affair, as elites are chosen on the basis of group identity and thus may perpetuate divides. When such forces exist and work against social cohesion, most initiatives are too isolated and weak to be effective.

As a result, social cohesion initiatives may be effective only in the long term, although no definitive answer is possible from the analyzed case studies, as most of the peace agreements were signed within perhaps the past ten or fifteen years. Yet, with some plausibility we can argue that this does not hold, due to the nature of most initiatives. The lack of effectiveness can also be attributed to the scattered, short-term, and fragmented nature of most initiatives. In addition, problem-solving workshops tend to select English-speaking elites as representatives, people who are often already "converted" to the idea of positive images of the other group. As evidence, we can point to an evaluation of workshops in Cyprus that assessed attitudes of participants prior to and after the workshops. The evaluation revealed that most participants already had a positive attitude toward the other group; similar results were seen in a control group. That group was composed of people who wanted to participate in workshops but could not get a seat. Even though they never participated, those people showed a positive attitude toward the other group. A third control group, based on a representative sample of the population in the two communities, showed the existence of strong enemy images. In conclusion, people participating in these workshops seem to have already overcome strong enemy images, essentially indicating that such workshops may be "preaching to the converted."

Another critique is that social cohesion initiatives are externally driven; viewed as popular among donors and international NGOs, they often lack national ownership and a focus on changing attitudes instead of behaviors. In Bosnia-Herzegovina, there is resistance to any project labeled as a "bridging" project. Initiatives have therefore changed labels and tried to bring people together for reasons other than reconciliation and dialogue. Interestingly, these initiatives showed better results. People expressed positive experiences in working with the other group, often producing concrete outcomes and common work initiatives. Existing evidence from Cyprus and Israel-Palestine demonstrates that attitude change might not be necessary for behavior change.

The poor effectiveness of people-to-people workshops was also criticized for their limited ability to reach out to larger populations. While youth initiatives in the Israel-Palestine case show some change in enemy images, this could be achieved only on an individual level (essentially among workshop participants). However, the general enemy image vis-à-vis the other groups remained intact.

The poor effectiveness of social cohesion initiatives is also criticized on political grounds: by focusing only on group relationships, they tend to mask the underlying reasons for conflict. Framing a conflict or disadvantage solely as a relational problem can underplay the other reasons and divides. In Northern Ireland, critics of community relations initiatives argue that naming the problem "bad community relations" leaves out economic and other deprivations experienced by marginalized communities. Many Greek Cypriots believe that bicommunal activities give the impression that the Cyprus conflict is "only" an interethnic relation problem; in their view it is a deeply political issue with an international dimension. After the second intifada was launched, voices in Palestinian newspapers criticized Israeli peace activists for oppressing the political dimensions by focusing too much on relationship-building between Israelis and Palestinians. It was argued that too little attention was given to working with groups in Israel that were opposed to peacebuilding and to addressing the political nature of the conflict. The second criticism articulated by Palestinians was the separation of political and cultural issues in some meetings, with many avoiding political issues altogether. Thus, they argued that the reality inside the workshops often did not match the reality outside; cultural cooperation between two civil societies, it was argued, hides preexisting power imbalances. From this point of view, it is impossible to separate the cultural and political domains.

The same holds true for many outside initiatives. There is a danger that social cohesion initiatives are funded as a scapegoat for political inactivity. It is arguably easier for donors to fund such initiatives than it is to pressure the government and political actors. And even though social cohesion initiatives often cannot solve deeply political problems, the European Union's engagement in Turkey demonstrates that much can be done through political means to strengthen the environment in which civil society operates. When the European Union started pressuring the Turkish government, the space for civil society activities opened up substantially.

A positive sign is seen in the Israel-Palestine case. Although most workshops have not been effective in contributing agreed proposals to the official negotiation agenda, many workshops have been helpful. Many workshops invited professionals to build up Palestinian human capital by developing new ideas and strategic insights. Thus, many meetings became new avenues for learning and empowerment.

In sum, social cohesion is the most often performed civil society peacebuilding function, especially in group-identity conflicts that gain international attention. We see, however, that the main focus of most initiatives is almost exclusively on the dominant conflict lines; often, other divides in society are effectively ignored. The same holds true for non–group identity conflicts like Afghanistan, Nepal, and Guatemala, where societies are deeply divided; almost none of the divides in those countries are addressed through social cohesion initiatives. Even when social cohesion is the main focus of civil society work, its effectiveness is low due to the apolitical nature. Many other reasons for ineffectiveness can be found in the initiatives themselves, as well as in the contexts in which they operate.

Facilitation

When analyzing this function, it is important to distinguish between different levels of facilitation and to assess relevance and effectiveness separately. We find facilitation at the local level being performed by community leaders (e.g., traditional, religious, and others) and by local NGOs and associations. They facilitate between the conflict parties and the community, between aid agencies and the conflict parties (including the government in most cases), and between communities and returning refugees. We also find civil society organizations (usually leading civil society figures, however) involved in facilitation at the national level between the main conflict parties. Moreover, civil society groups facilitate between the international community and the population at large, a function closely linked to advocacy.

The main activities are:

1. Community mediation to reduce or prevent violence and tensions as a means to enhance protection and harmony in the community
2. Negotiation and conflict resolution training provided to elite and grassroots civil society leaders in preparation for an existing or potential facilitation role
3. Informal and formal facilitation or good offices between the major parties, mainly by eminent persons from established civil society institutions, such as churches and prominent society figures from other organizations

The relevance of facilitation by civil society actors at the local level is high; this is reflected by the high number of such initiatives.[3]

The effectiveness of local facilitation is mixed, but we do find many successful initiatives and events across the case studies. Some examples: in Afghanistan during Taliban rule, traditional mediation was the only resource for facilitating between the Taliban and the various Afghani communities. Local civil society groups also successfully negotiated between the Taliban and aid agencies. The Tribal Liaison Office helped organize local peace *jirgas* with religious and local leaders to explore options for peacebuilding. In Nepal during the armed conflict, local groups successfully facilitated the release of prisoners in many villages. In many cases, their efforts were helped by the monitoring and advocacy work of Nepali NGOs. In Somalia, civic groups have enjoyed growing success in facilitating dialogue and reconciliation at the local level; across Somalia, local-level reconciliation has consistently involved hybrid partnerships of civil society leaders, clan elders, businesspeople, and clerics. In central Somalia from 2006 to 2007, local elders were supported by the joint efforts of a research institute, as well as by local women's groups and militia leaders. These elders were able to negotiate an end to a prolonged and deadly period of communal clashes. In Bosnia-Herzegovina, a women's NGO trained local facilitators to act as mediators between the communities and returnees. Any success was, however, dependent on the protection of returnees by the international community. After the refugee return rate declined, civil society organizations continued their community mediation roles in many places and engaged in facilitating dialogues on important themes, such as democracy promotion.

The success of these initiatives is, nevertheless, context-specific and limited by violence, a coercive state, and conflict parties. Success factors include the legitimacy of community leaders, who often work in cooperation with more "modern" organizations and networks that can better connect on the national level through monitoring and advocacy. Mediation efforts in the Niger

Delta by traditional leaders thus have a low rate of success, as those leaders often lack legitimacy due to their co-optation by local governance and militia structures. As the case in Somalia demonstrates, local businesspeople can also be supportive, as they often have a keen interest in the reduction of violence.

The effectiveness of national civil society facilitation between the main conflict parties is largely contingent on the existence of eminent civil society leaders and their legitimacy vis-à-vis the conflict parties. As the Nepali case shows, these persons do not have to be perceived as neutral; on the contrary, they are often close to (and trusted by) the conflict parties. These civil society initiatives often pave the way for the involvement of other mediators. Church leaders have been successful in some cases and have been involved in the facilitation process in Guatemala, Northern Ireland, and Sri Lanka. Their involvement paved the way for an official negotiation process. These initiatives have been important during windows of opportunity for peace and after official negotiations broke down and no other channels were available. In the case of Nigeria, the government nominated a Catholic priest as chief mediator between Ogoni groups. The negotiations, however, have been less successful. Royal Dutch Shell was open to a deal, but the Ogoni groups could not agree among themselves to set up a joint negotiation agenda.

It must be noted that civil society efforts to facilitate dialogue among top political actors and to influence their thinking are only half the equation. More often than not, political actors and sometimes the business community are more prominent in this regard, alongside regional and international actors.

The effectiveness of negotiation and facilitation training is difficult to assess, and we do not have sufficient data to analyze patterns. It seems plausible, however, that targeted training for a clear purpose is more effective than random training. We can point to the successful training of community mediators in Bosnia-Herzegovina to negotiate refugees' return to their communities. Conflict resolution training without a specific purpose leaves participants with skills but no idea how to use them. High-level training of key civil society figures in negotiation and conflict resolution can expand their preexisting negotiation role, but often this does not lead to significant positive results. The four main civil society facilitators in the Nepali peace process stated during interviews that even though they appreciated the training, they could not use the techniques learned because their role within the process was often limited to good offices. Moreover, informal facilitation takes place within the rules of a specific cultural and political context that is very familiar to these types of inside facilitators. Their legitimacy and effectiveness derive from their position within and knowledge about their home context.

In sum, local facilitation by civil society groups is relevant during all phases of conflict and peacebuilding. Its effectiveness is contingent on the context, and we can point to many successful initiatives. A high level of violence and coercive conflict parties are the main limiting factors. Cooperation between traditional and "modern" forces supports the effectiveness of these initiatives. Facilitation at the national level between the main conflict parties is less of a civil society task. When eminent civil society persons are involved (i.e., religious and other leaders), they are effective in paving the way for official negotiations and supporting the official mediators during periods of stalemate.

Service Delivery as Entry Point for Peacebuilding

While we developed the theoretical framework for our project (see Chapter 4 in this volume), it was unclear whether service delivery is really a function within peacebuilding. We discovered three main threads in the literature, viewing service delivery as:

1. A separate function of civil society for peacebuilding, because it saves lives and thus creates the preconditions for civil society to exist
2. Not a civil society function, because it fulfills economic, social, and humanitarian objectives
3. A civil society function for peacebuilding, but only when it creates explicit entry points for other peacebuilding functions

We therefore decided to apply an exploratory approach to the case study research in order to better understand the nature of the service delivery function for peacebuilding—or else to remove it from the framework.

The results from the case studies strongly confirm the third line of argument: service delivery is in principle a civil society peacebuilding function, but only when it creates entry points for peacebuilding. The case studies demonstrate that service delivery projects can create entry points for protection, monitoring, and social cohesion. The relevance of the function is dependent on the number of entry points it can create for other functions, as well as on the state's ability to provide services to the population. The more entry points for peacebuilding created, the more relevant service delivery becomes during war and armed conflict, as well as immediately after large-scale violence has ended.

The cases of Cyprus and Somalia demonstrate this finding. In Cyprus, service delivery by civil society was virtually absent due to the presence of a functioning state and the lack of violence. Therefore, service delivery was not a function for peacebuilding. In Somalia, by contrast, the total absence of a state for almost two decades made service delivery *the main* activity performed by civil society; Islamic charities were especially successful. Although Islamic charities rely heavily on foreign funding, they have had greater success than non-Islamist civil society organizations. They have also been able to create entry points for peacebuilding by extending networks across clan and regional lines. Many Somali NGOs involved in social service delivery are also engaged in peacebuilding through workshops and coordination structures established for health, education, and other sectors. These structures have helped create channels of communication that cut across conflict lines.

The case of Somalia is a sad example of how extreme levels of violence become the biggest obstacle to civil society activities. The post-2006 warfare in Somalia, with its gross insecurity, has made it almost impossible for most local NGOs to operate at all. Somalia is today the most dangerous place in the world for aid workers. In general, the main actors involved in this function are local NGOs, such as community self-help groups, and religious actors, such as Islamic charities and church organizations.

Service delivery is quantitatively the most often performed function by civil society actors throughout all phases. However, when we account for projects that create entry points for peacebuilding, the number diminishes. This came as a small surprise, as conflict-sensitive approaches to development have become very popular among Western donors and NGOs. Even in Northern Ireland, where most development funding was explicitly geared toward community relations, most initiatives worked only with one group.

In the Kurdish case, service delivery was able to create entry points for peacebuilding. For a long time it was the only civil society function allowed by the government. It therefore created important entry points for monitoring the conflict area. In Nepal, we find that the presence of aid projects in many areas had an indirect protection effect, as the conflict parties felt that they were "being watched." Another example of combining protection and service delivery comes from Palestine, where the Israeli NGO Physicians for Human Rights (also supported by the ICRC and Dan Church Aid) conducted several protection missions for the smooth passage of Palestinian Red Crescent ambulances through Israeli army checkpoints. In Nepal, the establishment of the Basic Operating Guidelines by development donors and agencies during armed conflict also had a protection effect. Service delivery can additionally support peacebuilding by targeting aid systematically to marginalized groups and/or geographical areas, as in Guatemala, Sri Lanka, and Nepal.

Service delivery in general does not create entry points for advocacy due to the apolitical nature of aid NGOs and organizations. An exception is the Kurdish case, in which civil society organizations collected data and mobilized members to insist on their rights. This was most often the case with membership-based organizations.

The case studies also demonstrate that service delivery can have a conflict-escalating effect due to its apolitical nature, as well as a lack of contextual awareness. It is possible that an insufficient link exists between the context and its consequences for operations. This is often the case when aid delivery increases social cleavages: ethnic, caste, and class divides are reproduced through the act of distributing aid. Divides can be exacerbated due to the staff selection of organizations that privilege dominant groups in society (due to their levels of education) over marginalized groups. Aid delivery can also be subject to political co-optation by the conflict parties and political actors, as in Somalia, Afghanistan, and Sri Lanka.

The huge influx of aid resources also changes structures and relations within civil society and between civil society and other sectors. As service delivery is the function where most resources are available, it tends to divert energy from other civil society functions. Many organizations simply choose to engage in service delivery. Moreover, service delivery disconnects NGOs from constituencies, as accountability runs to the donor and not to the community (this also holds true for other NGO-dominated functions). The logic of fundraising makes it necessary to downplay local knowledge and resources, emphasizing instead local weaknesses and needs and thereby limiting the capacity to create domestic social capital.

In sum, service delivery can provide important entry points for other civil society peacebuilding functions, namely protection, monitoring, and social cohesion. However, the way in which service delivery is performed—mostly by NGOs—means that this potential remains largely untapped or underutilized. Service delivery is the civil society activity that receives the most resources. As a consequence, it diverts energy and resources from other civil society activities. Moreover, aid projects can also have a conflict-exacerbating effect by increasing social and geographical cleavages in society through unfair allocation of resources and recruitment of staff.

Conclusion

Overall, our research demonstrates that civil society can contribute in important ways to peacebuilding, but mostly it plays a supporting role. In systematically analyzing the different functions of civil society for peacebuilding, we also find patterns of supporting and limiting factors. Chapter 17 provides a deeper analysis of these factors, which can enable or limit the effectiveness of civil society peacebuilding.

Notes

I would like to thank Siegmar Schmidt, Christoph Spurk, Esra Çuhadar, Sabine Kurtenbach, Camilla Orjuela, and Darren Kew for their helpful comments.

1. The definitions *war* and *armed conflict* are as presented in the Uppsala Conflict Data Program (UCDP 2008). The objective is to differentiate intensity levels of violence. UCDP is making a distinction between armed conflict, i.e., *minor* (at least twenty-five but less than 1,000 battle-related deaths in a year; see www.pcr.uu.se/research/UCDP/data_and_publications/definitions_all.htm#brd); and *war* (at least 1,000 battle-related deaths in a year; UCDP 2008).

2. While all the case studies had a number of conflict and peacebuilding phases, for the purpose of comparison we managed to cluster them all into these four phases. It is also evident that the third phase (windows of opportunity for peace) usually overlaps with either war or armed conflict.

3. It seems that facilitation on the local level has been one of the functions most performed by civil society (even if we cannot fully support this judgment with adequate data, as it is difficult to gather data on this level and the availability of data across our case studies varied considerably for local facilitation).

17

Enabling and Disenabling Factors for Civil Society Peacebuilding

Thania Paffenholz, Christoph Spurk, Roberto Belloni, Sabine Kurtenbach, and Camilla Orjuela

The context in which civil society operates is crucial for its ability to act and play a constructive role in peacebuilding. The main influential factors that can support or reduce the space for civil society to act or to influence its effectiveness are listed below.

The behavior of the state: Several questions arise in any consideration of the state. Is it a source of or an active party in the armed conflict? Is it cooperative, co-optive, or coercive vis-à-vis civil society? Do different forms of governance affect this behavior? And how effective is the state in fulfilling its protection or service delivery functions? How do these factors influence the amount of space available for civil society to fulfill other functions?

The level of violence: What types and levels of violence and insecurity affect the space for civil society to act?

The freedom and role of the media: Is there sufficient freedom for the media to fulfill their professional reporting roles and to support civil society initiatives through adequate coverage and balanced reporting? Or are the media a conflict-exacerbating actor?

The diversity within civil society: How do divides in civil society along ethnic, religious, gender and power lines, including diaspora networks, affect their peacebuilding potential?

The influence of external political actors, regional actors in particular: To what extent does the behavior of external actors affect civil society peacebuilding?

The role of donor engagement: How does the involvement of donors and their resource flows influence civil society peacebuilding?

In this chapter we analyze these factors and provide some results from the case studies.

The Behavior of the State

The state plays a crucial role in all the case studies that we examined. First, the behavior of the state, in particular the government, can be a source of armed conflict. Second, when the state is repressive toward civil society actors, there is limited space for action. Third, democratic forms of governance enhance the space for civil society to act. And fourth, when state institutions fulfill their traditional functions, such as protection and service delivery, civil society is able to focus on other functions.

Underpinning the first argument, we find time and again that the state is at the heart of disputes pitting one group against another. Marginalized groups may choose to fight to obtain some degree of self-governing autonomy (and possibly even independence) from the state. Alternatively, they may demand recognition and inclusion in the state apparatus and a share in decisionmaking power and national wealth. In response, the state often wages a campaign of repression. Notwithstanding contextual differences, Guatemala, Turkey, Sri Lanka, Israel-Palestine, Nigeria, Northern Ireland, and Nepal are all instances where a militarily strong state used violence at certain points in history to crush dissent or prevent political and economic inclusion of marginalized groups. The evidence from the case studies suggests that these states may be militarily strong but are politically weak. They often lack legitimacy among the population, or sections of it, and are unable or unwilling to provide public goods such as security, political representation, and economic development.

In cases where the state is perceived as illegitimate by at least one significant section of the population, civil society is likely to fragment into opposing groups. To the extent that popular mobilization and collective action take place, it is along the major dividing lines in society. In this polarized context, civil society groups struggling to promote politics based on compromise, respect for human rights, and political accountability may even be denounced as sellouts—as in the case of Israel-Palestine. Moreover, real or perceived state discrimination combined with state repression may persuade some members of marginalized groups that armed confrontation is the only way to express grievances. Battles for political recognition and inclusion are often fought through violent, extralegal means. In Northern Ireland, Catholic/nationalist paramilitary groups (most notably the Irish Republican Army) have waged an armed struggle against the British state's claim to sovereignty over the province. In response, militant Protestant/unionist groups have emerged. Over time, most paramilitary organizations degenerated into mafia-like groups, enforcing tight control over their communities. They have come to control illegal businesses and resist the establishment of effective state institutions that would curtail their activities, especially a multiethnic police force. In Turkey, the state's perspective on peace has set the stage for continuing violence over Kurdish rights. The state considers security and territorial integrity as nonnegotiable and sees military victory as the path to peace. Its refusal to recognize Kurdish demands contributed to varying degrees of support among the Kurdish population for the PKK's violent acts. Similar observations about state violence and domestic insurgency could be made about Guatemala, Sri Lanka, Nigeria, and Nepal.

The form of governance also matters, as repressive governance limits the space for civil society activism. The presence of democratic institutions is often thought of as the most appropriate means to ensure access and participation. However, as the cases of Northern Ireland and Turkey suggest, this might not be enough. The state might formally be "democratic" but in actuality is clearly tied to a single group or ideology. Simultaneously, election laws might contribute to the exclusion of marginalized groups from democratic institutions. In Northern Ireland, the Protestant community always enjoyed a privileged position within the state administration while rejecting Catholics' demands for inclusion. Since the period 1921–1922, extensive gerrymandering contributed to the Protestant monopoly over the political process and the exclusion of the Catholic minority. In Turkey, the state has always been a bastion of Kemalist principles and rejected demands for territorial autonomy or recognition of the Kurdish language. A 10 percent threshold of the total national vote has prevented pro-Kurdish political parties from taking a seat at the national level, although they enjoy a high degree of support in the Kurdish region.

Despite the misuse of the democratic process, the presence of democratic institutions provides a crucial enabling condition for civil society groups to operate. Since the outbreak of the Troubles, Northern Ireland has enjoyed a lively and diverse civil society, even more so since the signing of the Belfast Agreement in 1998. In Turkey, the process of democratization, which started in 1999, opened the space for civil society groups to address various issues in the conflict. Similar considerations apply to Israel and Palestine, where the state has a clear religious identity. At the same time, democratic institutions and the rule of law favor civic engagement and activism. Guatemala is another case where even limited forms of democratization offer opportunities for different civil society organizations. A key lesson is that the democratic state plays an important role in setting the context to enable civil society to contribute positively to peacebuilding. In some cases, such as Cyprus, the presence of a functioning state can make some peacebuilding functions less relevant. Here civil society rarely performs service delivery and protection, as it is provided either by the state or by the UN mission.

Unfortunately from a civil society perspective, the predominant state form in conflict areas is neither functioning nor democratic in the Western liberal sense of the word. Rather, in the majority of cases included in this study, institutions function through a system of patronage and clan-based politics. These processes tend to be strongly demobilizing for civil society peacebuilding. The patrimonial system can be considered as a subset of the "state-in-society" approach (see Chapter 2 of this volume). Civil society and the state intertwine, and family relationships and networks are often essential for understanding this web of connections. This system is based on the patron's ability to deliver benefits in return for political support. The neopatrimonial states in Democratic Republic of Congo (DRC) and Nigeria are based on complex sets of loyalties that are used to gain access to state resources and wealth. In the Nigerian case, patronage politics is also partly instrumental to the extractive interests of international oil politics. In Guatemala, clientelism and personalism are part of the dominant political culture; sections of the state are even controlled by criminal interests. This prevents the onset of any structural reforms needed for successful peacebuilding. In Nepal, unequal social relations and the segmentation of civil society are reinforced by widespread cronyism. In Turkey, formally democratic institutions exist alongside an established tradition of patrimonial and clientelistic relations. In all of these cases, patronage politics is at odds with democratic norms and practices because it subordinates citizenship rights to patron-client relationships.

In the neopatrimonial state, the autonomy of civil society organizations and their ability to perform peacebuilding functions are undermined. Civil society groups are weakened by subordination to party politics in their independence and capacity to operate. Most civil society groups, including sports and youth associations, become a source of support for politicians running for office. From a civil society perspective, the problem with patronage politics is the possibility that civil society actors will quit any opposition to ruling politicians in exchange for access to state resources. There is also a risk that marginalized groups will consider armed struggle as a feasible alternative to democratic engagement, as in the Niger Delta. Patronage, clientelism, and co-optation are often effective in preventing regime-contesting civic activism. In some cases, as in Sri Lanka and Nepal, the state strictly regulates, or attempts to regulate, the legal establishment and existence of NGOs to further control civil society's activities.

Understanding the kinds of institutions that will favor the development of an independent and diverse civil society is difficult. One standard answer to demands for inclusion into political life by a particular group is the creation of consociational institutions that can serve as a guarantee of political representation for all major groups in society. However, consociationalism may hinder bottom-up civil society efforts aimed at overcoming the most virulent forms of communal divisions and at healing the societal gulf. The cases of Northern Ireland and Bosnia suggest that society remains fragmented when political institutions are structured according to consociational principles. Political elites continue to rule their own constituencies exclusively and prevent (or do not favor) the development of cross-ethnic ties at the societal level. Notwithstanding the immediate peacebuilding effects, these types of institutions may dangerously favor the reproduction of the very same cleavages that lead to violence over the long term.

A unique case is Somalia, where the state effectively collapsed in 1991 and was never revived. This presents threats as well as opportunities for civil society. The absence of a state paves the way for the development of strong kinship ties and power dynamics among groups, even allowing armed militia groups to disguise themselves as grassroots organizations. Furthermore, the absence of the state creates the context for high levels of insecurity and for the continuing influence of identity and clan politics. In the absence of any state services, Somalis rely on clans for protection and support. Perhaps understandably given the traditional dependence on lineage, all efforts to revive the state have occurred alongside the development of a neopatrimonial system of governance. At the same time, the absence of the state has favored various forms of civil society activism, in particular the delivery of basic services, such as ed ucation and health care. In addition, in 2005 a "people's power" movement emerged to pressure militia leaders to end violence. However, despite this activism, continuing political violence has essentially neutralized civil society's ability to engage in peacebuilding, and civil society leaders have even become targets for assassination.

Violence, Crime, and Insecurity

Next to the state's behavior, violence is the key dominant variable that limits civil society peacebuilding. The correlation is simple: the higher the level of violence, the more the space for civil society is reduced; violence destroys social networks and organizations. Additionally, civil society actors can themselves become targets of violence. At the same time, the high levels of violence in many cases were the main engine for peacebuilding.

War and armed conflict produce different forms and levels of violence. The direct confrontation of combatants is just one form—and not always the most dominant one. In many contemporary and past wars, other forms of violence have been systematically used. Rape, sexual violence, forced displacement, and selective violence against opponents have been used as instruments of intimidation against civilians. Even forms of criminal and economically motivated violence can be an instrument of war, as they force people either to adapt or to look for protection. In relation to civil society peacebuilding, all these forms and levels of violence limit the options for civil society to act. In all phases of armed conflict, however, there have been considerable civil society activities. During wars and other periods of extreme violence, the space becomes smaller and smaller.

Violence also destroys and disrupts existing forms of social organizations and social networks, replacing them with fear, distrust, and intimidation. It is important to note that violence-induced changes affect possibilities for civil society peacebuilding, and not just momentarily; they may also change the very structure of civil society. Violence increases polarization between groups, as seen in Sri Lanka, Northern Ireland, Israel-Palestine, and Bosnia. Moreover, armed actors have been limiting the scope of independent autonomous civil society action in Afghanistan, Turkey, Guatemala, Nepal, the DRC, and Nigeria.

A second limiting feature for civil society actors is the fact they become targets of selective as well as indiscriminate violence. Again, most of the case studies show common features: human rights defenders, journalists, peace activists, and other members advocating publicly for peace have become targets. An example of indiscriminate violence against civil society actors was the attack by paramilitary forces that fired on peace demonstrators in Bosnia. This episode sanctioned the end of mass-based mobilization in support for peace and led to the "outbreak of war."

Thus, protection of civil society actors is fundamental during all phases of conflict, because high levels of violence (as well as selective violence) directed against civil society undermine its ability to support peacebuilding. Most civil society organizations are not able to protect themselves or others. However, some established actors, such as churches, seem to have more room for maneuver than modern NGOs. Working in advocacy and monitoring to raise awareness inside and outside the war-affected countries has been an important first step for establishing alliances and networks between internal and external actors favoring peace. Cooperation between local human rights organizations and international NGOs and UN missions has, in some cases, served as a substitute for protection. In Cyprus and Bosnia, an external military or peacekeeping presence directly provided protection and limited or ended open violence.

At the same time, violence can be a central motive for civil society organizations to advocate for peace. In many armed conflicts and wars, the escalation and spillover of violence to everyday life stimulated the establishment of human rights groups, victims' organizations, and peace movements. The joint combat against violence has been a uniting factor for civil society groups in Guatemala, Northern Ireland, and Afghanistan (at least at the local level); it has also stimulated activism among women's organizations in the Kurdish conflict and in Bosnia.

The signing of formal peace accords raises hopes that violence will be reduced or even end, but there is rarely a clear-cut termination of violence. Even in cases where armed conflict ends, other forms of violence, such as selective political violence, social or criminal violence, and private violence, can prevail. These new manifestations of violence influence the implementation of accords, as well as civil society's peacebuilding capabilities. Violence by actors opposed to peacebuilding and reforms is closely related to armed conflict. These actors often attempt to prohibit or change the implementation of peace accords, as well as to obstruct the process of transformation toward peace and democracy. This has been the case in Guatemala, Sri Lanka, Afghanistan, the DRC, Israel-Palestine, and Somalia.

The Freedom and Role of the Media

Although mass media are not part of civil society as such, as discussed in Chapter 1 (with the exception of journalists' associations, free media movements, etc.), the media are an important enabling as well as disenabling factor for civil society peacebuilding. The case studies provide data on media freedoms and observations on media coverage of specific issues. Thus, we can deduce correlations and make some conclusions, although the case studies do not provide entire substudies of media effects on civil society peacebuilding.

The main point is that the media can influence the effectiveness of civil society protection, monitoring, and advocacy directly and in a positive manner during armed conflict, war, and the period immediately after long-term violence has ended. Civil society efforts are supported and strengthened by positive media coverage. For advocacy, this finding holds true even long after peace agreements and the end of major violence. Without positive media coverage, many civil society initiatives become far less effective. The media also play an important role in socialization and social cohesion as a vehicle for strengthening images and stereotypes in society.

Civil society protection can be directly enhanced by media coverage: in Northern Ireland, for example, an NGO campaign against paramilitaries attracted the attention of the media, which in turn presented the suffering of victims and helped protect future victims. But protection is enhanced mostly through the media's positive attention to civil society monitoring. In Nepal, some media outlets gave positive coverage to the human rights monitoring of the respective NGOs. This resulted in a much wider reception to the monitoring, both locally and internationally, which made it more difficult for human rights violators to continue their actions. Thus, civil society helped to protect potential victims, including media personnel. The same holds true for religious radio stations in the DRC covering the human rights monitoring of the churches, and in Afghanistan and Turkey, where local, sometimes newly founded media covered monitoring exercises by civil society. In other cases, international broadcasters like the BBC and Deutsche Welle conducted the monitoring coverage when local broadcasters weren't able to do so.

Sometimes civil society protection efforts address journalists directly. In Sri Lanka, for example, the Free Media Movement directly protects eminent journalists and their families by hiding them in safehouses or taking them out of country. An internationally funded safety fund enables this kind of work. Here again, the network of national and international efforts strengthens effectiveness when, for example, INGOs like Reporters sans Frontières and the International Committee to Protect Journalists raise international attention, use political contacts and get specific cases covered by international media, and thereby increase the pressure on government officials.

Media work also provides a space for civil society's advocacy activities. This was the case in the DRC, where talk-radio shows covered advocacy issues raised by civil society; in the Kurdish conflict the media published articles and press releases on civil society campaigns. The "Yes" campaign in Northern Ireland was covered positively by the media and was thereby strengthened. In Nepal, a vibrant and surprisingly free media enabled additional influence to civil society efforts, and in Somalia radio programs aired open debates about the conflict and even mobilized people for peace rallies and demonstrations.

This positive coverage of civil society peace efforts seems to be easier to create during "peace-oriented" times. In Sri Lanka during the peace process after 2002 until mid-2006, there was supportive coverage of civil society's peace campaigns. Yet, positive coverage of peace efforts has shrunk since the war resumed in 2006. In Bosnia, it was only after the war ended that civil society efforts were positively covered by the media.

The media's influence on social values (socialization) should also not be underestimated. Media can (even involuntarily) preserve long-existing images of the "others," which occurred in many cases, as in Sri Lanka. Comparative media content studies show that the majority of Sri Lanka's non-English media (i.e., Sinhala and Tamil) provide an ethnically divided picture of what is important and relevant for two different audiences. Stereotypes are preserved, and hardly any exchange of views between the "adversary population groups" is facilitated through the media. Moreover, there is little debate on causes of the war other than ethnicity. We find many examples for this in other case studies; websites, blogs, text messages, and entertainment radio (talk shows) easily spread "enemy" messages toward other clans in Somalia and toward other adversary groups in the DRC.

Generally, the performance of the media in supporting civil society is contingent upon the level of media freedom. During ongoing armed conflict, media freedoms are usually restricted; independent media become weak and victimized by threats and violence. This was the case for Sri Lanka during times of war, Bosnia before the war, the DRC during war, and Afghanistan under the Taliban regime. Nevertheless, the correlation among violence, media freedoms, and actual media performance is complex; courageous reporting is feasible even under harsh restrictions. In Nepal and Somalia, for example, media freedoms are limited, especially by the military during escalation phases, but a surprisingly vibrant media has raised sensitive issues and thereby supported civil society efforts. In Somalia, stations were shut down, and in Nepal editors were threatened.

This correlation needs to be analyzed carefully to discover media opportunities even during times of armed conflict. First, the case studies reveal that media and civil society are mutually dependent on each other. Evidence demonstrates that the more media freedom exists, the better the chance for civil society to effectively perform protection, monitoring, and advocacy roles. With restricted media freedoms and/or limited media performance, the probability of a discouraging effect on civil society becomes apparent. And the high performance of civil society—for example, in the protection of human rights—is also useful for protecting the media, as in Nepal. Second, media performance and civil society effectiveness are dependent on the comparative strength of other counteracting forces—of which peace-opposing media and civil society are part.

There are many examples of media and civil society being weak compared to proviolence factions. Having state media under its control, the state is already a counteracting factor and can increase its adverse effects, especially when state media reach large audiences. In Bosnia before the 1992 war, there were efforts by civil society actors to prevent the war, but they did not get their message across; prowar civil society, prowar parties, and their media allies were much stronger. In Guatemala, there are only a few "independent" media outlets, but they are weak compared to the leading mass media controlled by the elite and the status quo. In May 1999, leading mass media campaigned heavily against a change in the constitution necessary for implementing the peace accord. In Sri Lanka in times of war (until 2002, and from 2006 onward), the majority of media did not really question the war discourse despite a well-developed culture of debate in the country. This seems in part due to the fact that the media remain state-controlled. Additional factors include attacks against media personnel and institutions and the domination of the entire debate by the prowar political and civil society factions. This mixture of reasons resulted in a nonbalanced presentation of issues by the Sinhala and Tamil media, which strengthened existing divides and prevented debate on the underlying causes of conflict. Overall, the Somali media were too weak to promote a civic agenda in the peace processes against a myriad of factors favoring war.

In other cases, power relations were different and favored the propeace camp. In the DRC, Radio Okapi—set up after the war jointly by the UN Mission to DRC (Monuc) and the independent Swiss foundation, Fondation Hironelle—was able to counteract the partial media that were dominant before and during war. It opened some spaces for informed debate. In Nepal, the media managed to facilitate a civic discussion that helped to generate a "coalition for peace." And in Northern Ireland, the media were strong enough to give the "Yes" campaign more prominence.

These few insights on media and civil society support the need for a common analysis of the entire policy environment, including media and civil society and their contending currents. They also show that good media performance and media freedoms are decisive factors to be installed with a view to supporting civil society peacebuilding. Thus, the media can be seen as an important factor for civil society peacebuilding: supporting when media perform in a professional, balanced way covering both sides, and discouraging when media are more biased toward the war-supporting factions.

Diversity and Radicalization Within Civil Society

Civil society is part of society and reflects its characteristics. Consequently, it is not surprising that civil society organizations are also divided along lines of power, hierarchy, ethnicity, and gender and display moderate as well as radical images and behaviors. Civil society organizations are in general led by male leaders from dominant groups within society. Exceptions are women's and minority organizations. The following sections focus on the radicalization within civil society, as well as gender roles and diaspora networks.

Radical Socialization

Participation in civil society is an act of building social capital, as described by Robert Putnam (see Chapter 1). Thus, the norms and values transferred to members of civil society organizations determine to a large extent the behavior of those members. In some cases, civil society groups promote norms, values, and interests that are undemocratic, repressive, and intolerant as a response to a persisting situation of political, economic, and social crisis. The Settler Movement in Israel, veterans' associations in Bosnia, and the Orange Order in Northern Ireland are all examples of this phenomenon. In Sri Lanka, popular mobilization has often taken place along nationalist and even racist lines. Some Sinhalese organizations interpreted negotiations and/or concessions to Tamil militants as a way to undermine the unity and sovereignty of what they view as a holy Buddhist country. During the latest peace process, Buddhist monks staged frequent and vociferous demonstrations against peace negotiations. More generally, Sri Lankan civil society has protested more against peace initiatives than in support of such initiatives. An extreme example of a radical civil society actor can be seen in the emergence of the Taliban in Afghanistan. It developed from a civil society movement into a politically repressive, undemocratic, and violent regime.

In conflict areas, high emotional salience is attached to group identity. Civil society organizations that represent only one group are common. In most cases, in-group socialization reinforces members' shared identity at the expense of developing cross-ethnic ties. Membership in single-identity groups exacerbates differences between group insiders and outsiders while intensifying intergroup competition and conflict. Northern Ireland (especially the Orange Order), Israel (Jewish right-wing religious groups), Bosnia (the Serb Movement of Independent Associations), and the DRC (ethnic associations, or *mutuelles*) are the most gripping examples where civil society organizes along ethnic/national lines and thus fosters divisiveness and political and/or military recruitment.

Broadly speaking, two kinds of interests operate in conflict areas. First, some civil society groups may resist compromise and accommodation out of fear that they would lose political and economic influence. For example, membership in the Orange Order in Northern Ireland has been a tool for political, economic, and social advancement. Perhaps unsurprisingly, the Orange Order has not openly committed to the peace process, and in 1998 it even failed to express support for the Belfast Agreement. Although the motivations are multiple, they are in part based on a fear that the Protestant community (together with the Orange Order) would lose its privileged status it enjoyed since the partition of Ireland in 1920–1921. In Guatemala, the most effective civil society organization is the entrepreneurial CACIF, which has used its influence to prevent the reform of the existing political and socioeconomic structures.

Second, the radicalization of in-group identity may lead to violent behavior that can cause actors to leave civil society and join or transform into militant actors. In Nigeria, particularly in the Niger Delta, years of military repression and exclusion provided the background and motivation for an armed insurgency and criminal activities. In Sri Lanka, a similar marginalization motivated the Tamil Tigers to rebel. In Turkey, the government's focus on security and territorial integrity, combined with a Kemalist ideology insensitive to Kurdish identity needs, contributed greatly to the development of political extremism. Where institutions are undemocratic, exclusive, and unresponsive to political demands for recognition and inclusion, collective action is more likely to take militant, and even violent, forms. Although the lack of democratic remedies for exclusion and marginalization can motivate some groups to engage in armed confrontation, only in Nigeria did civil society groups turn to militias, when regional governors channeled funds and weapons to youth gangs, some of whose members had been activists during the 1990s. In general, the space for civil society's work and influence is reduced by political polarization and the rise of militancy.

The internal democratic structure of civil society organizations seems to play a supportive role in peacebuilding effectiveness. Although we do not have sufficient evidence from all the cases, there is some plausibility in the argument based on evidence from Nigeria and Turkey. In Nigeria, democratic decisionmaking is instrumental to inculcating a democratic and tolerant political culture among the organizations' members, not only in community associations and NGOs but also in ethnic-based groups. Likewise in Kurdistan, democratically structured CSOs promote positive socialization. In these and similar cases, democratic decisionmaking and participation in civil society groups produce positive social capital and promote collective action. In general, however, in situations of state repression and military uprising, civil society is more likely to split into opposing camps and to degenerate into a narrower set of special interests.

Gender Roles

The facts that violent conflicts affect men and women differently, and that gender roles and structures determine the ways in which individuals and groups can act during conflicts, have been recognized. Violent mobilization draws on gender stereotypes: man as protector, woman as protectee. In conflicts framed along identity lines, we see how gender roles become significant in insecure situations. The role of women to reproduce and protect tradition and culture (through their role as childbearers and child-care providers) becomes central, and gender identities become less negotiable (Stern and Nystrand 2006). The gendered nature of armed conflicts is perhaps most clearly illustrated in Afghanistan, where gender roles were the eye of the storm. For the Taliban, restricting women's participation in public life and making women adhere to tradition formed an important part of their political-religious ideology and identity. At the same time, women's liberation formed an essential part of the rhetoric that motivated the US-led war against the Taliban. Afghan women have been victims of the conflict through direct violence, as well as through social and economic exclusion. However, a focus on how women are victimized in armed conflict should not be allowed to obscure the fact that men (particularly young men) are often the prime targets of violence and that many men during wartime are pressured to become perpetrators of violence. With this caveat in mind, we can consider how gender roles affect the behavior and effectiveness of civil society groups.

In all our case studies, women's access to political power has been limited to varying degrees. Women who do reach high political positions often have to struggle against other, subtler forms of exclusion. The lack of political representation and voice has meant that women have had limited representation in peacemaking attempts, as well as in the implementation of peace agreements. In cases where women participate in peace processes, they may not necessarily be able to influence them. This was the case during the peace talks in the DRC.

The gendered nature of civil society is confirmed in all our cases. Women traditionally (to a larger or smaller extent in all societies) have been perceived as having the primary place in the domestic sphere; the public sphere—state, market, and civil society—has been male-dominated. There are, of course, numerous examples of female mobilization in civil society (women's movements, women's NGOs), and some have received international attention. However, the ways in which the production and reproduction of power within civil society are interlinked with gender structures of the family, the state, and the market are rarely analyzed. The possibilities to organize in civil society differ between men and women (as they differ between people from different classes or ethnic backgrounds). From our case studies, we see that men hold most of the leading positions in civil society organizations. The case study on the DRC notes that "the only organizations led by women are women's associations." A similar pattern is found in other cases. The strict policies of the Taliban in Afghanistan (i.e., forbidding women to go out unless accompanied) severely constrained women's opportunities to take part in civil society organizations. However, some women managed to find space to organize (e.g., to home-school girls). Post-Taliban Afghanistan opened up more engagement possibilities for women's civil society.

In all cases, civil society organizations formed by women and for women are common. Such organizations address the effects of violent conflict (displacement, violence against women) or engage in development activities. The upsurge has been enabled by donor funding and the general interest among donors to work with and for women. For instance, microcredit projects tend to target women as the primary beneficiaries. In Bosnia, we find that close partnerships had been formed between local organizations and women's organizations abroad. The foreign organizations supported various projects and encouraged local women's groups to become involved in peacebuilding. In Nigeria, women's groups occupied oil platforms and company property, protesting the lack of community access to oil profits. Women have therefore been subject to violent reprisals from local police.

Women in our case studies often mobilize and organize around explicit gender identities. There are several examples of organizations that formed around motherhood—women who lost sons or daughters in war or whose children serve in the armed forces. In Turkey and Sri Lanka, mothers on either side of the conflict divide mobilized protests against war atrocities.

Our case studies provide examples where civil society activism has been able to contribute to the inclusion of women in peace processes and to bringing greater attention to gender issues. In Guatemala, the peace accord called for gender equality and created the National Women's Forum. In Sri Lanka, pressure from civil society contributed to the creation of a gender committee to give input to peace negotiations. Some representatives on the committee came from civil society. In Northern Ireland, a coalition of women played an intermediary role in the negotiation of the Good Friday Agreement. Women, primarily from civil society, subsequently formed a political party that played an important role in the "Yes" campaign.

Although the subordinate position of women often is an obstacle to participation in civil society peacework, it can also provide opportunities for engagement. The fact that women are often perceived as "nonpolitical" and "domestic" may, in fact, make it less dangerous to criticize warring parties and to call for change. By using their identity as mothers, they may be seen as more legitimate critics of human rights abuses, freer to express alternative perspectives. In Somalia, women hold an important position as connectors between clans based on their involvement in trade and through interclan marriages. This positions them to push for more dialogue and understanding between clans, as we have seen with the creation of women's regional peace networks and women's demonstrations against violence.

The mobilization of women in civil society organizations working against poverty and for the empowerment of marginalized groups may also be important for addressing grievances that can lay the groundwork for violent conflict. In Bosnia, women were able to transcend ethnic divides by addressing shared problems of trauma and the return of refugees. Similarly, in Sri Lanka, cooperation among women from different ethnic groups around development needs provided space for local reconciliations.

Some cases point to the fact that engagement of women's organizations often happens at the expense of mainstreaming gender issues into broader civil society. Examples from the DRC and Turkey show that the more women are engaged actively in civil society organization, the more these organizations put gender issues on their agendas.

The Role of Diasporas

In today's increasingly interconnected world, we cannot fully understand civil society unless we look beyond state borders. We have seen how local civil society is weakened during armed conflict. The space for protest and civic engagement shrinks with violence and curtailed freedoms of movement, speech, and assembly. A war situation also encourages migration. It is often the key constituencies and leaders of civil society organizations—the educated, the middle-class, the young—who migrate. Many migrants continue activism from abroad and form civil society organizations. The contact between local civil society and the diaspora civil society can be close, and sometimes there is frequent movement of key members between the homeland and other countries. We find that this "globalization" of civil society is a reality in all the case studies.

Several of the conflicts we studied gave rise to large diasporas. Sizable Afghan, Israeli, Palestinian, Kurdish, Sri Lankan Tamil, and Somali diasporas reside in Western countries and established a multitude of diaspora organizations. We have also seen examples of the "near-diaspora"—migrants residing in neighboring countries who continue to be part of the conflict dynamics at home. The large group of Afghans in Pakistan is one example, as are the Nepalese who sought refuge in India and formed voluntary associations. Diaspora organizations both near and far engage in advocacy work and media production and support relief and development work in the homeland.

States have become increasingly aware of the importance of diaspora populations and their organizations—and the fact that they function beyond the control of the homeland state. The fact that diaspora civil society can become very powerful is partially explained by the education level and relative wealth of migrants to richer countries, as well as by their closeness and possible access to power in those countries.

The channeling of funds from the diaspora to the homeland is crucial for the survival and wealth of individuals and families, as well as for relief and development efforts carried out by local civil society. However, diaspora organizations have in several cases been accused of collecting money in support of terrorism—for instance, organizations of Somalis and Tamils.

Local civil society actors can make use of the near-diaspora to influence the homeland conflict through a "boomerang effect" (Keck and Sikkink 1998). When they cannot influence their own government and other power-holders nationally, they use their international network to influence other states and international organizations, which in turn influence the home government. NGOs inside Afghanistan are linked to Afghan and international organizations abroad—links that have been essential in shaping the international agenda. Kurdish civil society actors in Europe are important players in the Kurdish-Turkish conflict. Their activities ensure that Kurdish voices are heard in Europe, and they have been able to influence the European Union to pressure Turkey into granting rights to Kurds. The Kurdish case also illustrates how diaspora-based media can influence events in the homeland. Roj TV, a Kurdish TV network broadcasting from Denmark (and one cause of soured Danish-Turkish relations) in 2007 urged Kurds in Turkey to participate in demonstrations, something that contributed to an uprising. Key civil society persons in the diaspora may also provide input to peace processes. This was the case when experts from the Somali diaspora participated as advisers to the leaders of different factions during the Somali National Reconciliation Conference in 2002.

As in homelands, diasporas consist of civil society forces that support nonviolent conflict resolution and those that promote extreme nationalism and military confrontation. Polarization and enemy images created by the conflicts at home are reproduced—and sometimes reinforced—within the diaspora. Diaspora organizations may work closely with warring parties and function as extensions abroad, as in the Sri Lankan conflict. It is not rare that diaspora organizations take more hard-line positions than civil society in the homeland. Irish expatriates in the United States are one example. Through the Irish Northern Aid Committee, they channeled funds to the Irish Republican Army. Likewise, Tamil expatriates have been a key source of income for the Liberation Tigers of Tamil Eelam in Sri Lanka. Nevertheless, Northern Ireland illustrates that diasporas can also support peace initiatives. Since the mid-1980s, Irish Americans campaigned for equality of opportunity between Catholics and Protestants, promoting principles that required US investment in Northern Ireland to be conditional on a balanced workforce. By doing this, they addressed an underlying cause of conflict. In the early 1990s, influential Irish Americans formed lobbying groups that supported dialogue in Northern Ireland and managed to make the Northern Ireland peace process one of US president Bill Clinton's foreign policy priorities.

This demonstration of diaspora power shows a need to look at civil society as something that is not confined to one country but extends beyond its borders. However, gaps between civil society in the diaspora and civil society at home must also be noted. In some cases (Somalia and Sri Lanka), we note a tension between those who stay during war and struggle and those who left the homeland, and between the unskilled civil society activists who remained behind and the richer, more educated activists who spent time abroad. Diaspora civil society groups often have the advantage of access to education and resources. Being removed from the urgent threats and difficulties of a war-torn country, they have more space to engage in dialogue and to support peace initiatives from afar. However, even though being detached from the ground situation provides space for peacework, it also brings problems in legitimacy, specifically in cooperating with civil society back in the home country. A challenge remains for analysts and supporters of civil society peacebuilding: to lift the veil and see the complex ways in which civil society is extended to, and can perform peacebuilding functions in, the diaspora.

External Political Actors

Although there are many important external political actors that can influence war and peace, in our case studies we mostly find that strong regional political actors have the power to create suitable conditions for civil society peacebuilding: they can influence the peace process itself. In other words, they have powers to create (or limit) the space for civil society to act.

We find that regional powers play an overwhelmingly important role for peace and war. The peace process in Nepal demonstrates this: India is the key actor in the region. It has supported the king and the ruling government politically and militarily against the Maoist movement. This support hindered the opening of democratic space and reduced the chances for peacebuilding, the establishment of viable democratic structures, and the space for civil society to operate. When India changed its position, freezing military aid and political support to the government-king, a window of opportunity for peace opened and was embraced by civil society actors. This change facilitated the end of armed conflict and authoritarian rule. In Sri Lanka, India also played a key role in pressuring the parties to participate in peace processes, which in turn opened space for civil society peacework. In Central America, a regional escalation of the war was prevented by the shuttle diplomacy of the Contadora Group (Mexico, Colombia, Venezuela, and Panama), although the Costa Rican government formulated the final regional peace accord. Only when the US government finally withdrew support for the authoritarian regimes did peace processes at the national level become viable and civil society begin to play a major role in peacebuilding. In Bosnia, by contrast, constant meddling from Serbia and Croatia was partly responsible for the outbreak of war and the delay in reaching a negotiated solution.

The combination of political pressure and donor support for civil society is exemplified by EU politics. The European Union has become one of the major actors in the Mediterranean region and has, in most cases, produced a positive, enabling effect on peace processes, as well as on civil society peacebuilding.

Joining the European Union is in the major political and economic interests of eligible countries. The very foundation of the European Union was an act of peacebuilding, as was its enlargement to southward and eastward. The membership debate with Turkey has become a major variable for peacebuilding. The list of EU demands for opening negotiations emphasized democratic institutions and behaviors. Turkey's wish to be part of the European Union in turn fundamentally changed the behavior of the state vis-à-vis the civil society active in the Kurdish question. While civil society actors were only allowed to engage in service delivery, the space burst open after the EU dialogue started. The European Commission (EC), the EU donor institution, additionally supported this development through targeted civil society support. The European Commission opened funding channels to Turkish civil society organizations for advocacy, monitoring, and protection. Thus the combination of political pressure and targeted funding facilitated civil society peacebuilding. The European Union equally influenced the situation in Cyprus, albeit not in the same way. Even in Central America, the European Union played a strong supporting role for regional cooperation and for counterbalancing US policies toward the region during the 1980s.

Donor Engagement and Resource Flows

We see a variety of donors, mostly Western OECD donors alongside faith-based donors, such as Muslim and Christian organizations and networks. INGOs usually serve as intermediaries in funding between international donors and national and local NGOs. Donor resources enable many civil society activities to take place. Different civil society actors, however, depend very differently on donors.

Traditional entities like clans and religious groups or their leaders rarely depend on external funding. Church-based civil society organizations depend on external resources to a lesser extent for some functions, although they can profit from extensive national and international networks. Local Islamic charities that mainly operate in service delivery are dependent on donor money, which they usually get from international partners and governments in Muslim countries. Mass-based membership organizations and movements barely depend upon external funding. Nevertheless, their resources shrink in times of armed conflict, when members are less able to pay dues. Modern NGOs are the most dependent. Even though NGOs work with volunteers, many activities would simple not take place without donor money.

Not only has donor money enabled many initiatives; it also contributed positively to the professionalization of peacework. Traditional peacework was mostly a voluntary activity. Since 1990, a mushrooming of civil society peace initiatives has led to greater effectiveness. Many initiatives reach an impressive level of professionalism. Donor support enabled organizations to make efficient use of voluntary and professional staffs and to link local actors with international partners and donors.

These developments come at the expense of building social capital. Evidence confirms an ongoing trend described as a "taming of social movements" and the "NGOization of social protest" (Kaldor 2003). Activist networks and social movements increasingly become formalized and professionalized, looking more like NGOs. This process is linked to the presence of international donors, which enable professionalization through funding and demand professionalization as a prerequisite for aid. One consequence of professionalization has been a decline in voluntarism. In Guatemala, broader social movements formed into NGOs in order to access funds from international donors. This led to more professional ways of working—but also to increased competition among organizations and a weakening of social roots; the same trend of formalization can be seen in Sri Lanka. Thus, dependency on foreign donors is visible in all cases. In Bosnia, a large number of local NGOs lacking social roots were created to take advantage of the new economic opportunities after the war. Most of these disappeared after international support was scaled back. Also, the Israel-Palestine case indicates that professionalization of civil society led to a detachment from the grassroots.

The dependency on outside funds also shifted civil society's priorities toward international donors, as NGOs adopted international donors as their main constituency. In Bosnia, the competition for funding also had severe consequences for civil society's ability to play a peacebuilding role; rivalries between organizations discouraged cooperation and long-term planning and weakened the sector's advocacy role. In some cases (particularly in the DRC and Afghanistan), NGOs have been directly created by international NGOs and donors. Funding opportunities drive the NGO sector to an extent. The changes in organization and in the focus of local civil society engagements are also linked to a change in motivations for aid among international actors. In the case of Palestine, the relationship between Palestinian NGOs and international NGOs shifted, from solidarity to aid.

A consequence of the central role of international donors has been uneven participation in civil society peacework. The most active organizations (the ones donors are most likely to fund) are often run by persons from urban, middle-class, educated backgrounds. Activists are less likely to come from rural, lower-class backgrounds—or else their organizations will enjoy less access to donors. This has created a problem of legitimacy for many NGOs. In many cases (especially Afghanistan and Sri Lanka), NGOs face criticism from the state, media, and sometimes the population and have been accused of being profit-seeking, corrupt, and unable to reach those in need.

The very logic of donor resources has resulted in the disempowerment of local communities and civic disengagement from peace efforts, as in Sri Lanka, the DRC, and Bosnia. The logic of fundraising makes it necessary to downplay local knowledge and resources, emphasizing instead local weaknesses and needs. Donor-driven civil society initiatives have limited the capacity to create domestic social capital and ownership in the peace process. Thus, empowerment is undermined, leaving domestic groups in weak and subordinate positions.

The evolution of the NGO sector in peacebuilding has sometimes even led to the "colonization of space" by international and national NGOs. Many are seen as middle-class urban elites socialized to the language and expectations of international donors. Moreover, resources and opportunities gained in the NGO or international agency sector discourage talented and motivated citizens from joining civil society groups other than NGOs. We see here that the same negative effects of donor-driven support occur in peacebuilding, as was analyzed decades earlier in development research (e.g., in Mozambique; see Hanlon 1991).

Our cases confirm negative assessments about NGO peacebuilding (see also Chapter 16), most of which were known prior to our research. However, our research also shows that many important civil society activities for peacebuilding, such as monitoring and advocacy, have been carried out by NGOs successfully. Moreover, our findings reveal that there are successful civil society initiatives beyond the activities of NGOs; the NGO sector is not as dominant as we thought before starting our research.

Conclusion

In sum, we see that enabling and disenabling factors play central roles in enhancing or limiting space for civil society. The levels of violence and the behavior of the state—governments, in particular—are the two main factors that determine the space for civil society to act. Whereas democratic forms of governance generally enable civil society to act, the *formal* democratic structures or neopatrimonial characteristics inside many conflict countries can oppose or co-opt civil society and reduce its ability to act. Yet, high levels of violence and authoritarian rule are often the major reason why civil society begins mobilizing for change. The media also play a crucial role. Through professional reporting and coverage, the effectiveness of many civil society activities, especially protection, monitoring, and advocacy, is strengthened. Media personnel also suffer from violence and a repressive state; freedom of the press is often restricted in conflict situations. The media and civil society are thus interlinked. Press freedoms can even serve as an indicator of civil society space (i.e., the more freedom of the press is suppressed, the more space for civil society is reduced).

Finally, the composition and characteristics of civil society itself also influence its effectiveness. The more civil society is polarized and radical tendencies become dominant, the more difficult it is to act in a common cause for peacebuilding. External actors, including donors, can also have positive and negative influences on political situations and thus influence the conditions for civil society to act. Chapter 18 provides some general conclusions and highlights the major policy implications of our research results.

18

Conclusion

Thania Paffenholz

Until the end of the cold war, civil society was an almost invisible actor in the international peacebuilding arena. This changed in the early 1990s, with civil society peacebuilding becoming the common response to the failures of many international diplomatic and peacekeeping efforts. In consequence, there has been a tremendous rise in civil society peacebuilding initiatives; the policy, research, and NGO communities have almost undisputedly concluded that civil society is a key actor in peacebuilding.

In this volume we have critically assessed the relevance and effectiveness of a wide range of civil society peacebuilding activities, beyond and including NGOs. The results of our research (see Chapters 16 and 17) point to the conclusion that different kinds of civil society actors can play an important, and often effective, role in peacebuilding within all stages of conflict. Although this role is mainly supportive when compared to the contributions of political actors, such as the conflict parties themselves or strong regional actors, our research demonstrates that civil society's supportive role can make a difference when performed in an effective way at the right time of a conflict. Civil society groups have contributed successfully to reducing violence, negotiating settlements, and sustaining peace after large-scale violence has ended.

When examining the seven civil society peacebuilding functions, our research found that the relevance of the functions differs substantially according to the four analyzed phases of the conflict: (1) war, (2) armed conflict, (3) windows of opportunity for peace negotiations, and (4) after large-scale violence. Civil society's peacebuilding potential also varies significantly within these phases. During wars and armed conflicts, the functions of protection, monitoring, advocacy, and facilitation are of high relevance. In cases where there is a low level of violence over a longer period of time, the relevance of socialization and social cohesion increases slightly. During a window of opportunity for peace negotiations, taking place mostly parallel to the phases of war or armed conflict, advocacy is considerably more relevant. Mass mobilization to pressure for negotiations or a peace agreement is important as well, as is lobbying for the inclusion of pertinent issues into a negotiated settlement. After large-scale violence comes to an end, the need for protection generally decreases in relevance. However, violence can in some cases continue in other forms, such as crime and domestic violence. Monitoring, facilitation, and service delivery still remain relevant in this phase. Once the war is over, social cohesion and socialization become more relevant as people are able to focus on issues other than survival.

Even though the relevance of the seven functions ebbs and flows depending on the phases of conflict, service delivery is a special case. This function is not a genuine civil society peacebuilding function (unless it leads directly to entry points for peacebuilding; see Chapter 17). We found that when the state actively performs service delivery and the level of violence is extremely low, there is no need for civil society to engage in this function with a peacebuilding intention; the case study on Cyprus illustrates this finding (see Chapter 9). However, service delivery can become highly relevant if it serves as an entry point for the protection, monitoring, and social cohesion functions. Aid projects often provide even better opportunities to bring people together than purely dialogue-oriented projects; harnessing shared interests (such as water or other community resources) can facilitate greater communication and perhaps trust between former adversarial groups. Unfortunately, the bulk of aid activities largely ignores this potential; consequently, some organizations are unable to take advantage of service delivery.

Our research also demonstrates that the *effectiveness* of the seven different functions can vary tremendously.

Protection is effective in many instances, especially when performed by local (often traditional and religious) actors in local contexts. The work of professional protection NGOs shows high levels of effectiveness when combined with monitoring and advocacy campaigns that had been picked up by media and international networks. Many people also fled from the conflict situation and chose migration as a form of protection.

Monitoring during armed conflicts and wars focuses on human rights violations. The main actors are local and national professional organizations and research institutions, often linked to international human rights organizations. The effectiveness of monitoring is fairly high in most cases, but usually not as a stand-alone function. Rather, monitoring became a precondition for protection and advocacy.

Overall, *advocacy* is one of the most effective functions during all phases of conflict. In addition to advocating on protection-related issues, civil society groups advocate for the inclusion of relevant issues in peace agreements or for legal recognition and implementation of rights for marginalized groups. They also advocate for including important issues in the implementation of peace agreements (such as refugee return in Bosnia, or truth and reconciliation commissions). Women's groups are often successful in bringing minority and gender issues to the agenda. In general, if targeted advocacy campaigns are combined with monitoring, media attention, and support from international networks, their effectiveness is at its highest. Advocacy initiatives for protection can achieve positive results in local and national contexts.

Socialization of the population at large with generic democratic and peace values has little effect in times of armed conflict and war. We find in all cases that existing socialization institutions in society are the key factors influencing how people learn democratic and conflict behavior. Such institutions include schools, religious and secular associations, clubs, workplaces, and families. In all cases, those institutions tend to reinforce existing divides, often to an extent that fostered radicalization. Overall, the majority of NGO peace education and training work has not been effective. Deeply permeating radical in-group identities within existing institutions cannot be counterbalanced by a few local or national NGO initiatives that take place outside of these institutions.

In-group socialization of underprivileged groups in asymmetric conflict situations proves effective in many instances, as a generation of civic leaders has been empowered through training and capacity-building (e.g., Maya activists in Guatemala and Dalit organizations in Nepal). However, the strengthening of group identity can also have negative effects, such as the reinforcement, and sometimes even radicalization, of existing conflict lines, as demonstrated by some ethnic groups in the DRC.

Intergroup social cohesion depends on the effectiveness of conflict resolution workshops, dialogue projects, and exchange programs; overall effectiveness is relatively low for a number of reasons found within the initiatives themselves. This ineffectiveness is also impacted by the contexts in which initiatives operate. Influencing factors include radicalization within society that hinders counteracting peacework; the scattered, short-term, and fragmented nature of most NGO initiatives; the focus on attitude change as opposed to behavior change; and the apolitical nature of most initiatives, among others (see Chapter 17 in this volume). Moreover, these initiatives focus almost exclusively on well-known conflicts with obvious adversary groups, such as Northern Ireland (Protestants/Catholics), Bosnia (different group identities), and Sri Lanka (Singhalese/Tamils). This narrow focus can thus ignore other conflict lines within societies (e.g., radicals and moderates, or geographical regions). Deep cleavages in other societies with less clearly identifiable group conflicts (Guatemala and Afghanistan) are also often ignored. On the positive side, participation in such initiatives is, in most cases, an act of empowerment for marginalized groups. Moreover, activities that were not directly related to peacebuilding, such as initiatives that brought together people from different professional groups, were more successful than peace-related activities.

Facilitation by civil society at the local level seems to be one of the most commonly performed functions, although the availability of data on this point is limited across our case studies. Nevertheless, many facilitation initiatives are effective when they are undertaken. With effectiveness contingent upon context, however, it is difficult to pinpoint successful patterns. *National facilitation* by civil society between the main conflict parties is a lesser task; its importance depends on the existence of eminent persons within civil society, including religious, political, and other leaders, who can effectively pave the way for official negotiations and support official mediators during times of stalemate.

Service delivery was by far the most commonly performed activity, receiving most of the external funds. Still, projects specifically designed and implemented to create entry points for peacebuilding are limited in number. When aid initiatives are systematically used for peacebuilding, for instance, they often create entry points for protection, monitoring, and social cohesion.

In sum, our case studies show that the effectiveness of the seven functions differs according to the phases of conflict and context (see Figure 18.1). Protection, monitoring, advocacy, and facilitation—when performed—are oftentimes very effective, whereas social cohesion and socialization initiatives are, on the whole, less effective for achieving short-term and long-term goals. When systematically used as entry points for other functions, aid projects carry great potential for effective peacebuilding. The actual implementation of service delivery projects/entry points is very low; any in-depth assessment of this function is difficult due to data availability (demonstrated by the dotted line in Figure 18.1).

In addition, our research concludes that several influential factors (see Chapter 17) support or reduce the space for civil society to act. These factors include the behavior of the state, the level of violence, the role of the media, and the roles taken up by external political actors to support or limit the conditions for civil society peacebuilding. Donor resources have an enabling or limiting function, and it is important to use a sensitive approach when building social capital, rather than replace the efforts of social movements through the "NGOization" of peacework. Civil society is also subject to shifting power relations and responsibilities through funding flows, as well as to the behavior and composition of civil society itself. The more civil society organizations are divided along power, hierarchy, ethnic, and gender lines and display radical images and behaviors, the more difficult it becomes to mobilize them for a common peace cause.

Given the conclusions of our research, *three main policy implications* can be identified. First, all civil society functions that are relevant to peacebuilding need to be supported. Second, the effectiveness of relevant functions can be enhanced systematically. Third, the context variables need to be addressed equally.

Figure 18.1 Aggregated Effectiveness of Functions Across Cases and Phases

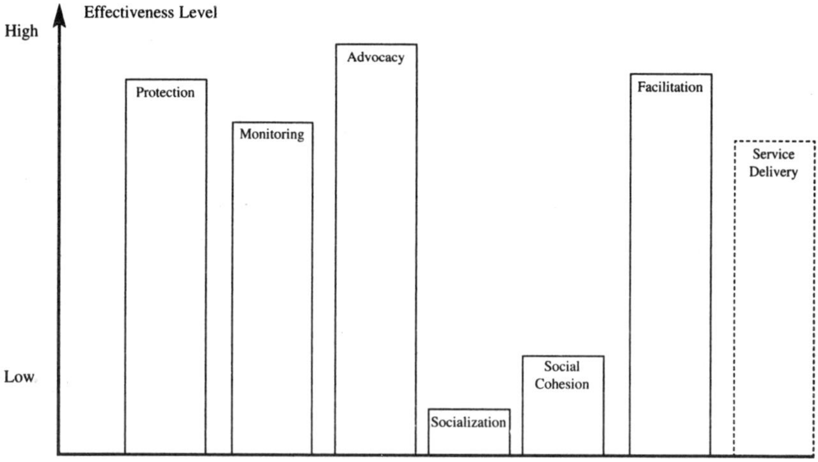

It is clear that an in-depth analysis is necessary prior to engaging in civil society peacebuilding initiatives, as well as for any engagement intended to improve the general enabling conditions for civil society peacebuilding. And any analysis of this nature should reach far beyond a standard conflict analysis. This includes analyzing civil society's composition, role, and potential, as well as the functions that are most needed during the changing phases of conflict. The advantage of this functional approach is clear: it provides the opportunity to identify *what* is needed prior to an analysis of *who* has the potential to fulfill these functions in the short, medium, and long terms. It also helps enhance cooperation with existing partners.

It is equally important to recognize that some civil society actors can be more effective than others in undertaking specific functions; on the whole, civil society consists of much more than NGOs. Although *NGOs* often can be effective in providing protection and in conducting targeted advocacy campaigns, traditional *mass-based organizations* (even though their record is spotty thus far) have far greater potential to promote socialization and social cohesion. *Traditional and local entities* are effective in facilitation and have shown positive results when providing protection, and *eminent civil society leaders* can be effective in preparing the ground for national negotiations. Leaders can also help parties break out of a stalemate in negotiations. *Women's groups* perform well in support of gender, women's, and minority issues and can be effective in bridging existing divides. It is also clear that broader change requires the uniting of all available change-oriented *mass movements. Aid organizations,* if they are aware of their peacebuilding potential and make systematic use of it, can support protection, monitoring, and social cohesion.

Other measures can enhance the effectiveness of civil society peacebuilding. These include the combined use of protection, monitoring, and advocacy, as well as the systematic strengthening of existing campaigns via political support and capacity-building. Funding for protection of activists can be helpful in tandem with active lobbying for human rights observation missions during times of war, in addition to continued monitoring of human rights violations after peace agreements are signed. As for socialization and social cohesion initiatives, our results suggest that a fundamental rethinking is needed to achieve objectives. This concerns not only the design of initiatives but also context and timing. Attention should be paid to all existing and potential social divides and to important socialization institutions, such as schools and professional associations.

Working with the media is also important. However, a general reassessment of existing media support strategies may also be needed. We have observed many peace journalism training sessions and peace "soap operas" that produce few results. Yet, when the media seriously undertake their professional reporting role, they can become an effective enabling partner for civil society. Consequently, media support could be focused much more on the professionalization of media outlets. If this is not possible, other media outlets (inside and outside the country) can provide accurate reporting and thereby contribute during periods of transition.

Finally, general support for civil society cannot replace political action. It is clear from the case studies that the major enabling and disenabling conditions arise from coercive states and high levels of violence. Thus, the engagement of the international community in any initiative that reduces violence, enhances protection, increases dialogue, and puts pressure on repressive governments facilitates the fundamental preconditions for civil society to fulfill a role in peacebuilding.

Acronyms

AAPW	Academic Associates Peace Works
ACBAR	Agency Coordinating Body for Afghan Relief
ACSF	Afghan Civil Society Forum
ADA	Afghan Development Foundation
AIAI	Al-Ittihad Al-Islamiyya
AIDPI	Acuerdo sobre Identidad y Derechos de los Pueblos Indígenas
AIHRC	Afghan Independent Human Rights Commission
AKEL	Aristera Nees Dynameis, Communist Party
AMAC	Assistance to Mine-Affected Communities
AMN	African Mangrove Network
ANCB	Afghan National Coordination Bureau
APF	Armed Police Force
ARC	Afghan Red Crescent
ARS	Alliance for the Re-Liberation of Somalia
ASC	Asamblea de la Sociedad Civil
ASCF	Afghan Civil Society Forum
ASS	Arab Studies Society
AWN	Afghan Women's Network
BIF	Benevolence International Foundation
BMZ	German Federal Ministry for Cooperation and Development
CA	constituent assembly
CAS	Consejo Asesor de Seguridad
CCA	Cooperation Center for Afghanistan
CCDP	Center on Conflict, Development and Peacebuilding
CDA	Collaborative for Development Action
CDLF	Community Defence Law Foundation
CEHRD	Center for Environment, Human Rights, and Development

CIIR	Catholic Institute of International Relations
COCAP	Collective Campaign for Peace–Nepal
COGWO	Coalition of Grassroots Women's Organizations
CORI	Community Rights Initiative
COSONGO	Consortium for Somaliland NGOs
CPA	Comprehensive Peace Agreement
CPAU	Cooperation for Peace and Unity
CRC	Community Relations Council
CRD	Center for Research and Dialogue
CS	civil society
CSCW	Centre for the Study of Civil War
CSHRN	Civil Society Human Rights Network
CSOs	civil society organizations
CVICT	Center for Victims of Torture
CWIN	Child Workers in Nepal
CYMEDA	Cyprus Mediation Association
DEHAP	Demokratik Halk Partisi, Democratic Society Party
DEP	Demokrasi Partisi, Democracy Party
DIJHRO	Dr. Ismael Jumale Human Rights Center
DRC	Democratic Republic of Congo
DUP	Democratic Unionist Party
EC	European Commission
ECHR	European Court of Human Rights
EIDHR	European Instrument for Democracy and Human Rights
ERA	Environmental Rights Action
EU	European Union
FAIT	Families Against Intimidation and Terror
FCCS	Foundation for Culture and Civil Society
FMS	Foro Multisectorial Social
FNDIC	Federated Niger Delta Ijaw Communities
FOPAG	Forum for Peace and Governance
FPENS	Formal Private Education Network in Somalia
GAA	Gaelic Athletic Association
GTF	Greek Turkish Forum
GTZ	German Technical Cooperation
Hak-Par	Hak ve Özgürlükler Partisi, Party of Rights and Freedoms
HBF	Heinrich Böll Foundation of Germany
HDI	Human Development Index
HEP	Halkın Emek Partisi, People's Labor Party
HRRAC	Human Rights Research and Advocacy Consortium
HRW	Human Rights Watch
IAM	Institute of Applied Media Studies
IANSA	International Action Network on Small Arms

ICC	Islamic Coordination Council
ICHR	Ijaw Council for Human Rights
ICR	International Center for Reconciliation
ICRC	International Committee of the Red Cross
ICU	Islamic Courts Union
IDPs	internally displaced people
IHEID	Graduate Institute of International and Development Studies
IHRHL	Institute for Human Rights and Humanitarian Law
IHRICON	Institute of Human Rights and Communication Nepal
IHRO	Isha Human Rights Organization
IIDA	Women Development Organization
INC	Instancia Nacional del Consenso
IP	Israeli-Palestinian
IR	international relations
IRA	Irish Republican Army
IYC	Ijaw Youth Council
JHU	Jathika Hela Urumaya
JVP	Janatha Vimukthi Peramuna
KADEK	Kongreya Azadî û Demokrasiya Kurdistanê, Kurdistan Freedom and Democracy Congress
KADEP	Katılımcı Demokrasi Partisi, Participatory Democracy Party
KOFF	Center for Peacebuilding
Kongra-Gel	People's Congress
KTOEOS	Kıbrıs Türk Orta Eğitim Öğ retmenler Sendikası
LGA	Local Government Area
LPI	Life and Peace Institute
LTTE	Liberation Tigers of Tamil Eelam
MEND	Movement for the Emancipation of the Niger Delta
MIC	Media in International Cooperation
MIRJE	Movement for Interracial Justice and Equality
MJF	Madhesi Janadhikar Forum
MOSOP	Movement for the Survival of Ogoni People
MRRD	Ministry of Rehabilitation and Rural Development
MSSP	Mogadishu Stabilization and Security Program
MZ	*mjesna zajednica*
NAI	Nordic Africa Institute
NATO	North Atlantic Treaty Organization
NAWF	National Anti-War Front
NC	Nepali Congress
NDPVF	Niger Delta People's Volunteer Force
NDV	Niger Delta Vigilantes
NDWJ	Niger Delta Women for Justice

NIACRO	Northern Ireland Association for the Care and Resettlement of Offenders
NICVA	Northern Ireland Council for Voluntary Action
NIIA	Nigerian Institute of International Affairs
NMAT	National Movement Against Terrorism
NORAD	Norwegian Agency for Development Cooperation
NORAID	Irish Northern Aid Committee
NUSOJ	National Union of Somali Journalists
ODHAG	Human Rights Office of the Archbishop of Guatemala
OECD	Organization for Economic Cooperation and Development
OECD-DAC	Development Assistance Committee of the Organization for Economic Cooperation and Development
OHCHR	UN Office of the High Commissioner for Human Rights
OSCE	Organization for Security and Cooperation in Europe
ÖZDEP	Özgürlük ve Demokrasi Partisi, Freedom and Democracy Party
PARC	Program on the Analysis and Resolution of Conflicts
PASYDY	Pancyprian Public Employees Trade Union
PDPA	People's Democratic Party of Afghanistan
PDRC	Puntland Development Research Center
PLO	Palestine Liberation Organization
PMHRE	People's Movement for Human Rights Education
PNA	Palestinian National Authority
PRDU	Post-War Development and Reconstruction Unit
PRIF	Peace Research Institute in Frankfurt
PRIO	International Peace Research Institute Oslo
PSNI	Police Service of Northern Ireland
PWYP	Publish What You Pay
QPSW	Quaker Peace and Social Witness
RNA	Royal Nepalese Army
RS	Republika Srpska
RTC	Responding to Conflict
RUC	Royal Ulster Constabulary
SALW	Small Arms and Light Weapons
SCC	Serb Civic Council
SDC	Swiss Agency for Development and Cooperation
SDLP	Catholic Social Democratic and Labour Party
SDN	Stakeholder Democracy Network
SDO	Sanayee Development Organization
SDP	Social Democratic Party
SEDEC	Social Economic Development Center
SEPAZ	Secretaría para la Paz
SHP	Social Democratic Party

SIMAD	Somali Institute of Management and Administration Development
SLMM	Nordic Sri Lankan Monitoring Mission
SNM	Somali National Movement
SOAS	School of Oriental and African Studies
SOSCENSA	Somali South-Central Non-State Actors Association
SPONA	Serb Movement of Independent Associations
SRSP	Somali Revolutionary Socialist Party
SSS	State Security Services
SSWC	Save Somali Women and Children
SYL	Somali Youth League
TFG	Transitional Federal Government
TLO	Tribal Liaison Office
TRNC	Turkish Republic of Northern Cyprus
TUBITAK	Scientific and Technological Research Council of Turkey
TÜSIAD	Turk Sanayici ve Işadamlari Derneği
UN	United Nations
UNAMA	United Nations Assistance Mission in Afghanistan
UNDP	United Nations Development Program
UNFICYP	United Nations Peacekeeping Force in Cyprus
UNHCR	UN High Commissioner for Refugees
UNMIN	United Nations Mission in Nepal
USAID	US Agency for International Development
UUP	Ulster Unionist Party
WAHRDN	West African Human Rights Defenders Network
YMCA	Young Men's Christian Association
ZHW	Applied Sciences Winterthur

Bibliography

Aall, P. 2001. "What Do NGOs Bring to Peacemaking?" In *Turbulent Peace: The Challenges of Managing International Conflict.* Ed. C. Crocker, F. O. Hampson, and P. Aall, 365–383. Washington, DC: United States Institute of Peace Press.

ABC News Polling Unit. 2007. "Where Things Stand in Afghanistan?" *ABC News, BBC, and ARD,* December 3.

Abdul Hadi, M., ed. 2005. *Palestinian-Israeli Impasse: Exploring Alternative Solutions to the Palestine-Israel Conflict.* Jerusalem: PASSIA.

Abdullahi, A. M. "Baadiyow." 2002. In *History of Modern Civil Society in Somalia.* Unpublished paper. Mogadishu, Somalia.

Abiew, F. K., and T. Keating. 2004. "Defining a Role for Civil Society." In *Building Sustainable Peace.* Ed. T. Keating and W. A. Knight, 93–117. Edmonton: University of Alberta Press.

Abootalebi, A. 1998. "Civil Society, Democracy, and the Middle East." *Middle East Review of International Affairs* 2(3): 46–59.

Academy for Peace and Development (APD). 2006. *A Vote for Peace: How Somaliland Hosted Its First Successful Parliamentary Elections in 35 Years.* Mogadishu and Nairobi: APD and Interpeace.

———. 2008. *Peace in Somaliland: An Indigenous Approach to State-Building.* Hargeisa: APD.

Acheson, N. 2001. "Service Delivery and Civic Engagement: Disability Organizations in Northern Ireland." *Voluntas: International Journal of Voluntary and Nonprofit Organizations* 12(3): 279–293.

Acheson, N., et al. 2006. *Voluntary Action and Community Relations in Northern Ireland.* Belfast: University of Ulster.

Adams, R., and S. Bastos. 2003. *Las Relaciones Étnicas en Guatemala, 1944–2000.* Antigua, Gua: Centro de Investigaciones Regionales de Mesoamerica (CIRMA).

Afghan Civil Society Forum (ACSF) and Afghan Youth Coordination Agency (AYCA). 2005. *Mapping Youth Organizations in Afghanistan.* Kabul: ACSF and AYCA.

Africa Watch. 1990. *Somalia: A Government at War with Its Own People.* New York: Africa Watch.

Agha, H. S. Feldman, A. Khalidi, and Z. Schiff. 2003. *Track II Diplomacy: Lessons Learned from the Middle East.* Cambridge, MA: MIT Press.

Aguilera Peralta, G. 1989. *El Fusil y el Olivo. La Cuestión Militar en Centroamérica.* San José, CR: FLACSO, DEI.

———. 1994. *Seguridad, Función Militar y Democracia.* Guatemala: FLACSO Sede Guatemala.

Akçakoca, A. 2005. *Cyprus—Looking to a Future Beyond Past.* Brussels: European Policy Center.

Akeni, L. 2006. "Demobilisation and Reintegration of Armed Groups in the Niger Delta." *PeaceWorks News* 7(1). Available at www.aapeaceworks.org (accessed February 12, 2008).

———. 2007. "Constructive Engagement of Niger Delta Youths." *PeaceWorks News* 7(1). Available at www.aapeaceworks.org (accessed February 12, 2008).

Alagappa, M., ed. 2004. *Civil Society and Political Change in Asia: Expanding and Contracting Democratic Space.* Palo Alto: Stanford University Press.

Alexandrou, C. 2006. *The Days That Shocked Cyprus: An Evaluation of the Campaigns on the Annan Plan.* Nicosia: Cypriot Students and Young Scientists Organization.

Alexiou, A., A. Gürel, M. Hatay, and Y. Taki. 2003. *The Annan Plan for Cyprus: A Citizen Guide.* Oslo: PRIO (International Peace Research Institute).

Alkire, S. 2003. "Concepts of Human Security." In *Human Security in a Global World.* Ed. L. Chen, S. Fukuda-Parr, and E. Seidensticker, 15–39. Cambridge: Harvard University Press.

Allen, C. 1997. "Who Needs Civil Society?" *Review of African Political Economy* 73: 329–337.

Altuntaş, B. 2003. *Mendile, Simite, Boyaya, Çöpe: Ankara Sokaklarında Çalışan Çocuklar.* Istanbul: Iletişim.

Amarasinghe, G. 2006. "Pro-War Monks Scuffle with Anti-War Demonstrators in Sri Lankan Capital." *Associated Press.* August 17.

Amnesty International. 1999. *Human Rights Defenders in Afghanistan: Civil Society Destroyed.* London: Amnesty International.

———. 2002a. *Guatemala: Guatemala's Lethal Legacy: Past Impunity and Renewed Human Rights Violations. AMR* 34/001. London: Amnesty International.

———. 2002b. *Guatemala: The Civil Defence Patrols Re-emerge. AMR* 34/053. London: Amnesty International.

Anastasiou, H. 2006. *The Broken Olive Branch: Nationalism, Ethnic Conflict, and the Quest for Peace in Cyprus.* Bloomington, IN: Author House.

———. 2007. "Nationalism as a Deterrent to Peace and Interethnic Democracy: The Failure of Nationalist Leadership from the Hague Talks to the Cyprus Referendum." *International Studies Perspectives* 8: 190–205.

Andersen, R. 2000. "How Multilateral Development Assistance Triggered the Conflict in Rwanda." *Third World Quarterly* 21(3): 441–456.

Anderson, K., and D. Rieff. 2004. "Global Civil Society: A Skeptical View." In *Global Civil Society 2004/5.* Ed. H. Anheier, M. Glasius, and M. Kaldor, 26–39. London: Sage.

Anderson, M. 1999. *Do No Harm: How Aid Can Support Peace—or War.* Boulder: Lynne Rienner Publishers.

Anderson, M., L. Olson, and K. Doughty. 2003. *Confronting War: Critical Lessons for Peace Practitioners.* Cambridge, MA: Collaborative for Development Action.

Andjelic, N. 1998. "The Evolution of Civil Society in a Pre-War Bosnia-Herzegovina." In *State Building in the Balkans: Dilemmas on the Eve of the 21st Century.* Ed. S. Bianchini and G. Schöpflin, 295–314. Ravenna: Longo.

———. 2003. *Bosnia-Herzegovina: The End of a Legacy.* London: Frank Cass.

Andrews, P. A. 1992. *Türkiye'de Etnik Gruplar* (Ethnic Groups in Turkey). Istanbul: Ant Yayınları.

Appiagyei-Atua, K. 2002. "Civil Society, Human Rights, and Development in Africa: A Critical Analysis." *Peace, Conflict, and Development: An Interdisciplinary Journal* 2 (December). Available at www.peacestudiesjournal.org.uk/dl/Civil.pdf (accessed March 1, 2008).

Appleby, R. S. 1996. "Religion as an Agent of Conflict Transformation and Peacebuilding." In *The Challenges of Managing International Conflict.* Ed. C. A. Crocker, F. O. Hampson, and P. Aall, 821–840. Washington, DC: United States Institute of Peace Press.

The Applied Research Institute—Jerusalem. 2008. Website available at http://www.arij.org.

Arévalo de León, B., J. B.Doña, and P. H. Fluri, eds. 2005. *Hacia una Política de Seguridad para la Democracia en Guatemala. Investigación Acción Participativa (IAP) y Reforma del Sector de Seguridad.* Münster: LIT Verlag.

Arias, A. 1985. "El Movimiento Indígena en Guatemala: 1970–1983." In *Movimientos Populares en Centroamérica.* Ed. Rafael Menjívar Camacho, 62–119. San José: Educa, FLACSO, United Nations University, Universidad Autónoma de México.

Arım, R. 2002. *Cyprus and the International Law.* Ankara: Dış Politika Enstitüsü.

Armon, J., R. Sieder, and R. Wilson. 1997. *Negotiating Rights: The Guatemalan Peace Process.* London: Conciliation Resources.

Arnson, C. J., ed. 1999. *Comparative Peace Processes in Latin America.* Washington, DC: Woodrow Wilson Center Press.

Asian Development Bank. 2007. *Country Operations Business Plan, Nepal 2008–2010.* Kathmandu: ADB Nepal Resident Mission.

Asmussen, J. 2003. "Patterns of Cypriot Identity or Why Cypriotism Doesn't Exist." In *Culture in Common—Living Cultures in the Cypriot Communities.* Proceedings of the German-Cypriot Forum Conference. May 22–24. Berlin. Available at http://dzforum.de/downloads/020101007.pdf.

Asuni, J. 2005. "Peace and Security Strategy for the Niger Delta." *PeaceWorks News* 5(1) (October). Available at www.aapeaceworks.org (accessed February 12, 2008).

Atieh, A., et al. 2005. *Peace in the Middle East: P2P and the Israeli-Palestinian Conflict.* Geneva: United Nations Publications (UNIDIR).

Atmar, H., and J. Goodhand. 2001. "Coherence or Cooption? Politics, Aid, and Peacebuilding in Afghanistan." *Journal of Humanitarian Assistance.* Available at http://jha.ac/articles/a069.htm.

———. 2002. "Afghanistan: The Challenge of 'Winning the Peace.'" In *Searching for Peace in Central and South Asia: An Overview of Peacebuilding and Conflict Resolution Activities.* Ed. M. Mekenkamp, P. van Tongeren, and H. Van De Veen, 109–140. Boulder: Lynne Rienner Publishers.

AVANSCO (Asociación para el Avance de las Ciencias Sociales en Guatemala) and M. González. 2002. *Se Cambió el Tiempo. Conflicto y Poder en Territorio K'iché, 1880–1996.* Cuadernos de Investigación No. 17. Guatemala: AVANSCO.

Avnery, U. 1975. *Israel and the Palestinians: A Different Israeli View.* New York: Breira.

Azar, E. E. 1990. *The Management of Protracted Social Conflict.* Hanover, NH: Dartmouth Publishing.

Babajanian B., S. Freizer, and D. Stevens 2005. "Civil Society in Central Asia and the Caucasus." *Central Asian Survey* 24(3): 209–234.

Badelt, C. 1997. *Handbuch der Nonprofit Organization: Strukturen und Management.* Stuttgart: Schäffer-Poeschel.

Bailey, S. 1985. "Non-official Mediation in Disputes: Reflections on Quaker Experience." *International Affairs* 61(2): 205–222.

Baitenmann, H. 1990. "NGOs and the Afghan War: The Politicisation of Humanitarian Aid." *Third World Quarterly* 12: 62–85.

Bajrovic, R. 2005. *BiH Municipalities and the EU: Direct Participation of Citizens in Policy-Making at the Local Level.* Sarajevo: Open Society Fund.

Baker, B., and E. Scheye. 2007. "Multi-layered Justice and Security Delivery in Post-Conflict and Fragile States." *Conflict, Security, and Development* 7(4): 503–528.

Barash, D. 2000. *Approaches to Peace: A Reader in Peace Studies.* Oxford: Oxford University Press.

Barash, D., and C. P. Webel. 2002. *Peace and Conflict Studies.* London and New Delhi: Sage.

Barghouthi, M. 1994. "Palestinian NGOs and Their Role in Building a Civil Society." Paper presented in Jerusalem. Union of Palestinian Medical Relief Committees.

———. 1999. "Palestinian NGOs and Their Contribution to Policy-Making." In *Dialogue on Palestinian State-Building and Identity: PASSIA Meetings and Lectures, 1995–1998.* Ed. A. M. Hadi. Jerusalem: PASSIA.

Barkey, H., and G. E. Fuller. 1998. *Turkey's Kurdish Question.* New York: Rowman and Littlefield.

Barkey, K., and S. Parikh. 1991. "Comparative Perspectives on the State." *Annual Review of Sociology* 17: 523–549.

Barnes, C., ed. 2002. "Owning the Process: Public Participation in Peacemaking." *Accord Series No. 13.* London: Conciliation Resources. Available at www.c-r.org/our-work/accord/public-participation/contents.php.

———. 2005. "Weaving the Web: Civil-Society Roles in Working with Conflict and Building Peace." In *People Building Peace II: Successful Stories of Civil Society.* Ed. P. van Tongeren et al., 7–24. Boulder: Lynne Rienner Publishers.

Barnett, M., et al. 2007. "Peacebuilding: What Is in a Name?" *Global Governance* 13: 35–58.

Bar-On, D. 1989. *Legacy of Silence: Encounters with Children of the Third Reich.* Cambridge: Harvard University Press.

Baskin, G. 2001. "Putting Money into Israeli-Palestinian Peace Projects Now? You Must Be Crazy." *Israel/Palestine Center for Research and Information.* Available at www.ipcri.org/files/peace-now.html.

———. 2008. "Encountering Peace: A City of Tolerance, Not a Museum of Tolerance." *Jerusalem Post.* November 4.

Bastos, S., and M. Camus. 2006. *Entre el Mecapal y el Cielo. Desarrollo del Movimiento Maya en Guatemala.* 2nd ed. Guatemala: FLACSO.

Bates, R. H. 2008. "State Failure." *Annual Review of Political Science* 11: 1–12.

Bayart, J. F. 1986. "Civil Society in Africa." In *Political Domination in Africa: Reflections on the Limit of Power.* Ed. P. Chabal, 109–125. Cambridge, UK: Cambridge University Press.

Beilin, Y. 2004. *The Path to Geneva: The Quest for a Permanent Agreement, 1996–2004.* New York: RDV Books.

Belloni, R. 2001. "Civil Society and Peacebuilding in Bosnia and Herzogovina." *Journal of Peace Research* 38(2): 163–180.

———. 2007. *State Building and International Intervention in Bosnia.* London/New York: Routledge.

———. 2008. "Civil Society in War-to-Democracy Transitions." *From War to Democracy: Dilemmas in Peacebuilding.* Ed. A. Jarstad and T. Sisk, 182–211. Cambridge, UK: Cambridge University Press.

———. 2009. "Shades of Orange and Green: Civil Society and the Peace Process in Northern Ireland." In *Social Capital and Peacebuilding: Creating and Resolving Conflict with Trust and Social Networks.* Ed. M. Cox, 5–21. New York: Routledge.

Bendaña, A. 2003. *What Kind of Peace Is Being Built? Critical Assessment from the South.* Discussion paper prepared on the occasion of the tenth anniversary of "An Agenda for Peace." Ottawa: IDRC.

Bendix, R. 1977. *Nation-Building and Citizenship.* 2nd ed. Berkeley: University of California Press.

Benvenisti, E., S. Hanafi, and C. Gans, eds. 2006. *Israel and the Palestinian Refugees.* Berlin: Springer and Max-Planck Institute.

Bercovitch, J. 1984. *Social Conflicts and Third Parties.* Boulder: Westview.

Bercovitch, J., and B. Rubin. 1992. *Mediation in International Relations: Multiple Approaches to Conflict Management.* London: St. Martin's.

Berger, G. 2002. "Theorizing the Media-democracy Relationship in Southern Africa." *Gazette: The International Journal for Communication Studies* (Sage Publications) 64(1): 21–45.

Berger, S. A. 2006. *Guatemaltecas: The Women's Movement 1986–2003.* Austin: University of Texas Press.

Berman, M., and J. Johnson. 1977. *Unofficial Diplomats.* New York: Columbia University Press.

Bhattachan, K. 2000. "Possible Ethnic Revolution or Insurgency in a Predatory Unitary Hindu State." In *Domestic Conflict and Crisis of Governability in Nepal.* Ed. D. Kumar, 135–162. Kathmandu: Center for Nepal and Asian Studies.

———. 2001. "(I)NGOs and Disadvantaged Groups in Nepal." In *NGO, Civil Society, and Government in Nepal.* Ed. K. Bhattachan et al., 67–99. Kathmandu: Tribhuvan University, Central Department of Sociology and Anthropology.

Bhattachan, K., et al., eds. 2001. *NGO, Civil Society, and Government in Nepal.* Kathmandu: Tribhuvan University, Central Department of Sociology and Anthropology, in cooperation with Friedrich Ebert Stiftung.

Bhattarai, A., A. Thapaliya, M. Thapa, and S. Ghimire. 2002. *Civil Society in Nepal: Some Self-Reflections.* Research report prepared as part of a research project carried out in collaboration with the Institute of Development Studies, University of Helsinki. Kathmandu: Nepal South Asia Center.

Bhattarai, H. P. 2003. *Voices of the Poor in Nepal.* Report submitted to Department of International Development (DFID). Kathmandu: DFID.

Bi-communal Development Program. 1998–2005. Available at http://mirror.undp.org/cyprus/projects/sectorsubsector.pdf.

Bieckart, K. 1999. *The Politics of Civil Society Building: European Private Aid Agencies and Democratic Transitions in Central America.* Amsterdam: International Books and Transnational Institute.

Bikmen, F., and Z. Meydanoğlu. 2006. *Civil Society in Turkey: An Era of Transition.* Istanbul: TUSEV.

Birle, P. 2000. "Zivilgesellschaft in Südamerika. Mythos und Realität." In *Systemwechsel 5. Zivilgesellschaft und Transformation.* Ed. W. Merkel, 231–271. Opladen: Leske and Budrich.

Birrell, D., and A. Williamson. 2001. "The Voluntary-Community Sector and Political Development in Northern Ireland, Since 1972." *Voluntas: International Journal of Voluntary and Nonprofit Organisations* 12(3): 205–220.

Bishara, A. 2002. "Beyond Belief." *Al-Ahram Weekly.* September 21 (no. 596).

Biyanwila, J. 2006. "Revitalizing Trade Unions: Global Social Movement Unionism." *Polity* 3(5–6): 19–24.

Black G., et al. 1984. *Garrison Guatemala.* New York: Monthly Review.

Bliss, F. 2003. "Was Ist Zivilgesellschaft?" *E + Z: Entwicklung und Zusammenarbeit* 5: 195–199.

Bloomfield, D. 1995. "Towards Complementarity in Conflict Management. Resolution and Settlement in Northern Ireland." *Journal of Peace Research* 32(2): 151–164.

———. 1997. *Peacemaking Strategies in Northern Ireland: Building Complementarity in Conflict Management Theory.* Houndsmills: Macmillan.

Bobbio, N. 1988. "Gramsci and the Concept of Civil Society." In *Civil Society and the State—New European Perspective.* Ed. J. Keane, 71–99. London and New York: Verso.

Bocco, R., and W. Mansouri. 2008. "Aide Internationale et Processus de Paix: Le Cas Palestinien, 1994–2006." *Contrario* 5(2): 6–22.

Boege, V. 2006. "Traditional Approaches to Conflict Transformation—Potentials and Limits." In *Berghof Handbook for Conflict Transformation.* Ed. M. Fischer, H. Gießman, and B. Schmelzle. Berlin: Berghof Research Center for Constructive Conflict Management.

Boesen, I. W. 2004. *From Subjects to Citizens: Local Participation in the National Solidarity Programme.* Working paper series. Kabul: Afghan Research and Evaluation Unit.

Boğa, G. 2006. *An Analysis of the Role of Media in Conflict Escalation: The Case of the "Armenian Conference" in Turkey.* Unpublished master's thesis. Istanbul: Sabancı University.

Bogner, A. 2004. "Ethnizität und die Soziale Organisation Physischer Gewalt. Ein Modell des Tribalismus in Postimperialen Kontexten." In *Anthropologie der Konflikte: Georg Elwerts Konflikt-theoretische Thesen in der Diskussion.* Ed. J. M. Eckert, 58–87. Bielefeld: Transcript Verlag.

Bojicic-Dzelilovic, V. 2006. "Peace on Whose Terms? War Veterans' Associations in Bosnia and Herzegovina." In *Challenges to Peacebuilding: Managing Spoilers During Conflict Resolution.* Ed. E. Newman and O. Richmond, 200–218. Tokyo: United Nations University Press.

Bokovoy, M. K., J. A. Irvine, and C. S. Lilly, eds. 1997. *State-Society Relations in Yugoslavia.* New York: St. Martin's.

Bölükbaşı, S. 2001. *Barışçı Çözümsüzlük: Ankara'nın ABD ve BM ile Kıbrıs Macerası.* Ankara: Imge Kitabevi.

Bongartz, H., and D. R. Dahal. 1996. *Development Studies: Self-Help Organizations, NGOs, and Civil Society.* Kathmandu: Nepal Foundation for Advanced Studies and Friedrich Ebert Stiftung.

Borchgrevink, K. 2007. *Religious Actors and Civil Society in Post-2001 Afghanistan.* Oslo: International Peace Research Institute (PRIO). Available at www.prio.no.

Botmeh, S. 2007 "The Israelis Cage Us, the Internationals Feed Us (Pauperization, Labour Market and [Food] Aid)." Paper presented at the international conference "The Economy and Economics of Palestine: Past, Present and Future." January 27–28, School of Oriental and African Studies, London.

Boulding, K. 1961. *Perspectives on the Economics of Peace.* New York: Institute for International Order.

Bozarslan, H. 1996. "Political Crisis and the Kurdish Issue in Turkey." In *The Kurdish Nationalist Movement in the 1990s: Its Impact on Turkey and the Middle East.* Ed. R. Olson. Lexington: University Press of Kentucky.

Braakman, M., and A. Schlenkhoff. 2007. "Between Two Worlds: Feelings of Belonging While in Exile and the Question of Return." *Asien* 104: 9–22.

Bratton, M. 1994. "Civil Society and Political Transitions in Africa." In *Civil Society and the State in Africa.* Ed. J. W. Harbeson, D. Rothchild, and N. Chazan, 51–81. Boulder: Lynne Rienner Publishers.

Brinkerhoff, J. M. 2004. "Digital Diasporas and International Development: Afghan-Americans and the Reconstruction of Afghanistan." *Public Administration and Development* 25(5): 397–413.

Brintall, D. E. 1979. *Revolt Against the Dead.* New York: CRS Press.

British Broadcasting Corporation. 2005. "Afghanistan's Post-Taliban Media." *British Broadcasting Corporation.* London. September 12.

———. 2006. "Afghanistan Performance at a Glance." PowerPoint presentation of survey made in December 2006. London: British Broadcasting Corporation, Communication and Audience.

Broome, B. 2005a. "The Role of Bi-communal Activities in Peace Building." In *Cyprus in the Modern World.* Ed. M. Michael and A. Tamis. Thessaloniki: Vanias.

———. 2005b. *Building Bridges Across the Green Line.* Lefkosa: UNDP.

Broz, S. 2004. *Good People in an Evil Time: Portraits of Complicity and Resistance in the Bosnian War.* Trans. Ellen Elias Bursac. New York: Other Press.

Bryden, A., and H. Hänggi, eds. 2005. *Security Governance in Post-Conflict Peacebuilding.* Geneva: Lit Verlag.

Bryden, M. 2003. "No Quick Fixes: Coming to Terms with Terrorism, Islam, and Statelessness in Somalia." *Journal of Conflict Studies* 22(2): 24–56.

———. 2005. *Rebuilding Somaliland: Issues and Possibilities.* Lawrenceville, NJ: Red Sea.

Brynen, R. 2000. *A Very Political Economy: Peacebuilding and Foreign Aid in the West Bank and Gaza.* Washington, DC: United States Institute of Peace Studies.

B'Tselem. 2008. The Israeli Information Center for Human Rights in the Occupied Territories. Available at www.btselem.org/index.asp.

Building Real Partnership. 1998. *Compact Between Government and the Voluntary Sector in Northern Ireland.* Belfast: Department of Health and Social Services.

Bundesministerium für wirtschaftliche Entwicklung und Zusammenarbeit (BMZ). 2005. *Förderung von Demokratie in der Deutschen Entwicklungspolitik.* Bonn: Ein Positionspapier des BMZ.

Burgermann, S. 2001 *Moral Victories: How Activists Provoke Multilateral Action.* Ithaca: Cornell University Press.

Burgess, J. P., and T. Owen, eds. 2004. "Special Section: What Is 'Human Security'?" *Security Dialogue* 35(3): 345–371.

Burton, J. 1969. *Conflict and Communication: The Use of Controlled Communication in International Relations.* London: Macmillan.

Bush, K. 1998. *A Measure of Peace: Peace and Conflict Impact Assessment of Development Projects in Conflict Zones.* The Peacebuilding and Reconstruction Program Initiative and the Evaluation Unit, Working Paper no. 1. Ottawa: IDRC.

———. 2003. *The Intra-group Dimensions of Ethnic Conflict in Sri Lanka: Learning to Read Between the Lines.* New York: Palgrave Macmillan.

———. 2005. *Fighting Commodification and Disempowerment in the Development Industry.* Available at www.berghof-handbook.net.

Buvollen, H. P. "2007: Sistematización de Experiencias y Lecciones Aprendida Programa Participación de la Sociedad Civil—PASOC." Guatemala: PNUD2004–2006 (GUA/04/001).

Çağaptay, S. 2007. "Can the PKK Renounce Violence." *Middle East Quarterly* 14(1): 45–52.

Cahn, S., ed. 2004. *Political Philosophy: The Essential Texts.* Oxford, UK: Oxford University Press.

Call, C., and E. Cousens. 2008. "Ending Wars and Building Peace: International Responses to War-Torn Societies." *International Studies Perspectives* 9: 1–21.

Cameron Report. 1969. *Disturbances in Northern Ireland: Report of a Commission Appointed by the Governor of Northern Ireland.* Belfast: Her Majesty's Stationery Office (HMSO).

Canfield, R. L. 1989. *On "Shuras" in Afghanistan Society.* Unpublished paper.

Caparini, M. 2005. "Enabling Civil Society in Security Sector Reconstruction." In *Security Governance in Post-Conflict Peacebuilding.* Ed. A. Bryden and H. Hänggi. Geneva: Lit Verlag.

Cardoso, H. F. 2003. "Civil Society and Global Governance." Unpublished paper for high-level panel on UN–civil society. New York.

CARE/USAID. 2002. *Civil Society Expansion Program: Mid-Term Review Report.* Nairobi: CARE-Somalia. Available at http://pdf.usaid.gov/pdf_docs/PDACA667.pdf.

Çarkoğlu, A., and K. Kirişçi. 2004. "The View from Turkey: Perceptions of Greeks and Greek-Turkish Rapprochement by the Turkish Public." *Turkish Studies* 5(1): 117–153.

Çarkoğlu, A., and B. Rubin. 2005. *Greek-Turkish Relations in the Era of Détente.* London and New York: Routledge.

Carlin, A. 2004. *Engaging the IFIs in Afghanistan—The Emergence of Afghan Civil Society.* Bank Information Center. Available at www.bicusa.org/en/index.aspxs.

Carmack, R. M., ed. 1988. *Harvest of Violence: The Maya Indians and the Guatemalan Crisis.* London: Norman.

Carothers, T., and W. Barndt. 2000. "Civil Society." *Foreign Policy* 117: 18–29.

Carter, L., and K. Connor. 1989. *A Preliminary Investigation of Contemporary Afghan Councils.* Peshawar: Agency Coordinating Body for Afghan Relief.

Casaús A., and M. Elena. 1992. *Guatemala: Linaje y Racismo.* Guatemala: F and G Editores.

Çelik, A. B. 2002. *Migrating onto Identity: Kurdish Mobilization Through Associations in Istanbul.* Unpublished Ph.D. thesis. Binghamton University, Binghamton.

———. 2005. "I Miss My Village! Forced Kurdish Migrants in Istanbul and Their Representation in Associations." *New Perspectives on Turkey* 32: 137–163.

Çelik, A. B., and A. Blum. 2007. "Track II Interventions and the Kurdish Question in Turkey: An Analysis Using a Theories of Change Approach." *The International Journal of Peace Studies* 12(2): 51–81.

Çelik, A. B., and B. Rumelili. 2006. "Necessary but Not Sufficient: The Role of EU in Resolving Turkey's Kurdish Question and Turkish-Greek Conflicts." *European Foreign Affairs Review* 11(2): 203–222.

Center for Environment, Human Rights, and Development (CEHRD). 2007. *Bi-Monthly Report on Incidence of Election Related Violence Monitored in the South-South Zone 1.* April 1–30, 2007. Available at www.cehrd.org (accessed February 12, 2008).

Center for Policy Alternatives (CPA). 2003. *Informal Dispute Resolution Mechanisms in the North East and Puttalam.* Colombo: CPA.

Center for Policy and Human Development (CPHD). 2007. *Afghanistan Human Development Report 2007.* Kabul: CPHD.

Center for Research and Dialogue (CRD). 2006a. *A Force for Change: Promoting the Roles of Civil Society and the Private Sector in Peacebuilding and Reconciliation in South-Central Somalia.* Mogadishu and Nairobi: CRD and Interpeace. Available at www.interpeace.org/pdfs/Publications_(Pdf)/Current_Reports/A_Force_for_Change.pdf.

———. 2006b. *Dialogue Not Guns: Promoting Security and Stabilisation Among the Communities of South-Central Somalia.* Mogadishu and Nairobi: CRD and Interpeace. Available at www.interpeace.org/pdfs/Publications_(Pdf)/Current_Reports/Dialogue_notGuns.pdf.

Centlivres, P., and M. Centlivres-Demont. 1988. "The Afghan Refugees in Pakistan: A Nation in Exile." *Current Sociology* 36(2): 71–92.

Centro de Estudios Económicos (CIEN). 2002. "La Magnitud y el Costo de la Violencia en Guatemala." Guatemala: CIEN.

Challand, B. 2005. "The Power to Promote and to Exclude: External Support to Palestinian Civil Society." Ph.D. diss. Florence: European University Institute.

———. 2008a. "A Nahdha of Charitable Organizations? Health Service Provision and the Politics of Aid in Palestine." *International Journal of Middle East Studies* 40: 227–247.

———. 2008b. "The Evolution of Western Aid for Palestinian Civil Society: The Bypassing of Local Knowledge and Resources." *Middle Eastern Studies* 44(3): 397–417.

Chan, S. 1997. "In Search of Democratic Peace: Problems and Promise." *Mershon International Studies Review* 41: 59–91.

Chandhoke, N. 1995. *State and Civil Society: Explorations in Political Theory.* New Delhi, Thousand Oaks, CA, and London: Sage.

———. 2001. "The Civil and the Political in Civil Society." *Democratization* 8(2): 1–24.

———. 2003. *The Conceits of Civil Society.* New Delhi: Oxford University Press.

———. 2007. *Interrogating the Concept of Civil Society: The Indian Context.* Center for Civil Society seminar paper. London: London School of Economics. Available at www.lse.ac.uk/collections/CCS/publications/seminarpapers.htm.

Chandler, D. 2006. "Back to the Future? The Limits of Neo-Wilsonian Ideals of Exporting Democracy." *Review of International Studies* 32: 475–494.

Chapman, N., et al. 2007. *Evaluation of DFID Country Programmes. Country Study: Nepal.* London: Department for International Development (DFID).

Chea Urruela, J. L. 1988. *Guatemala: La Cruz Fragmentada.* San José: Departamento Ecumenico de Investigaciones.

Chemjong, B. B. 2003. *Pallo Kirat Limbuvanka Magharu.* Kathmandu: Limbu Sahitya Vikas Sanstha.

Chesterman, S. 2007. "Ownership in Theory and in Practice: Transfer of Authority in UN Statebuilding Operations." *Journal of Intervention and Statebuilding* 1(1): 3–26.

Chetail, V., ed. 2009. *Post-Conflict Peacebuilding: A Lexicon.* Oxford, UK: Oxford University Press.

Chrysostomides, K. 2000. *The Republic of Cyprus: A Study in International Law.* The Hague and Boston: Nijhoff.

Church, C., and J. Shouldice. 2002. *Conflict Resolution Evaluation: Framing the State of Play.* Derry: Initiative on Conflict Resolution and Ethnicity.

Church, C., A. Visser, and L. Johnson. 2003. "The Evaluation of Conflict Resolution Evaluation, Part II: Emerging Theory and Practice." Derry: Initiative on Conflict Resolution and Ethnicity.

———. 2004. "A Path to Peace or Persistence? The 'Single Identity' Approach to Conflict Resolution in Northern Ireland." *Conflict Resolution Quarterly* 21: 273–293.

The Church of Cyprus. 2000. "The Occupied Churches of Cyprus." Available at www.churchofcyprus.org.cy/monastiria.shtml.

CIVICUS (World Alliance for Citizen Participation). 2005. *An Assessment of Civil Society in Cyprus: A Map for the Future.* Nicosia and Limassol: Intercollege and the Management Center of the Mediterranean.

———. 2006. *Civil Society in Northern Ireland: A New Beginning?* Civil Society Index Report for Northern Ireland. JJ McCarron: NICVA/CIVICUS. Available at www.civicus.org/new/media/CSI_Northern_Ireland_Executive_summary.pdf.

Clark, J. 2003. *Worlds Apart, Civil Society, and the Battle for Ethical Globalization.* Bloomfield, CT: Kumarian.

Clark, J., and B. Balaj. 1996. "NGOs in the West Bank and Gaza." Draft report. Washington, DC: World Bank.

Clarke, W., and J. Herbst, eds. 1997. *Learning from Somalia: The Lessons of Armed Humanitarian Intervention.* Boulder: Westview.

CNN. 2008. "Iraq Incursion Finished, Turkey Says." Available at http://edition.cnn.com/2008/WORLD/meast/02/29/iraq.main/index.html.

Coalition to Stop the Use of Child Soldiers. *Child Soldiers Global Report 2004.* Available at www.child-soldiers.org (accessed February 16, 2008).

Cochrane, F. 2007. "Irish-America: The End of the IRA's Armed Struggle and the Utility of 'Soft Power.'" *Journal of Peace Research* 44(2): 215–231.

Cochrane, F., and S. Dunn. 2002. *People Power? The Role of the Voluntary and Community Sector in the Northern Ireland Conflict.* Cork: Cork University Press.

Cohen, A., and J. Rynhold. 2005. "Social Covenants: The Solution to the Crisis of Religion and State in Israel?" *Journal of Church and State* (Autumn): 725–745.

Colás, A. 2002. *International Civil Society: Social Movements in World Politics.* Cambridge: Polity.

Coletta, N., and M. Cullen. 2000. *Violent Conflict and the Transformation of Social Capital: Lessons from Cambodia, Rwanda, Guatemala, and Somalia.* Washington, DC: World Bank.

Comisión de Esclarecimiento Histórico (CEH). 1999. *Guatemala: Memoria del Silencio.* Guatemala: CEH.

Commission of the European Communities. 2007. *Turkey 2007 Progress Report.* Brussels: European Union.

Committee on the Administration of Justice (CAJ). 2008. *About Us.* Available at www.caj.org.uk/about.html.

Communist Party of Nepal (Maoist). 2004a. *Some Important Documents of Communist Party of Nepal (Maoist).* Kathmandu: Janadisha.

———. 2004b. *Problems and Prospects of Revolution in Nepal.* Kathmandu: Janadisha.

Conflict Archive on the Internet (CAIN). 2008. *Internment.* Available at http://cain.ulst.ac.uk/events/intern/index.html.

Çongar, Y. 2008. "Bu Savaşın Galibi Yok." *Taraf.* February 3, 2008, 10.

Cooperation for Peace and Unity (CPAU). 2007. *The Role and Function of Religious Civil Society in Afghanistan: Case Studies from Sayedabad and Kunduz.* Kabul: CPAU.

Cortright, D. 2008. *Peace: A History of Movements and Ideas.* Cambridge, UK: Cambridge University Press.

Council of Europe (CoE). 2006. *The Cultural Situation of the Kurds.* Available at http://assembly.coe.int/Main.asp?link=/Documents/WorkingDocs/Doc06/EDOC11006.htm (accessed July 7, 2008).

Cowan, S. 2008. "The Lost Battles of Khara and Pili." *Himal Southasian* (September).

Coward, E., and G. Smith. 2004. *Religion and Peacebuilding.* Albany: State University of New York Press.

Cox, H. 2003. "Our Friends in the North: Twenty-one Years of Quaker House Belfast." Available at www.quakerhousebelfast.org/page4.html.

Crocker, C., F. O. Hampson, and P. Aall. 2001. *Turbulent Peace: The Challenges of Managing International Conflict.* Washington, DC: United States Institute of Peace Press.

———. 2005. *Grasping the Nettle: Analyzing Cases of Intractable Conflict.* Washington, DC: United States Institute of Peace Press.

Croissant, A. 2003. "Demokratie und Zivilgesellschaft in Ostasien." *Nord-Süd Aktuell* 2: 239–260.

Croissant, A., H. Lauth, and W. Merkel. 2000. "Zivilgesellschaft und Transformation. Ein internationaler Vergleich." In *Systemwechsel 5. Zivilgesellschaft und Transformation.* Ed. W. Merkel, 9–49. Opladen: Leske and Budrich.

Çuhadar E. 2004. "Evaluating Track Two Diplomacy in Pre-Negotiation: A Comparative Assessment of Track Two Initiatives on Water and Jerusalem in the Israeli-Palestinian Conflict." Ph.D. diss. Syracuse University.

———. 2009. "Assessing Transfer from Track Two Diplomacy: The Cases of Water and Jerusalem." *Journal of Peace Research* 46(5): 641–658.

Çuhadar E., and B. Dayton. 2008. "Oslo and Its Aftermath: Lessons Learned from Track Two Diplomacy." Paper presented at the International Society for Political Psychology's thirty-first annual meeting, Paris.

Çuhadar, E., B. Dayton, and T. Paffenholz. 2008. "Evaluation in Conflict Resolution and Peacebuilding." In *Conflict Resolution: A Multidisciplinary Approach.* Ed. D. Sandole et al., 383–395. London and New York: Routledge and Taylor and Francis.

Çuhadar-Gürkaynak, E., and O. Memişoğlu. 2005. "Varieties of Mediating Activities and Their Complementarity in the Cyprus Conflict." *Regional Development Dialogue* 26(1): 123–139.

Curle, A. 1971. *Making Peace.* London: Tavisstock.

CYMEDA (Cyprus Mediation Association). 2009. www.cymedas.com.

Cyprus Government Web Portal. www.cyprus.gov.cy.

Czempiel, E. 1972. *Schwerpunkte und Ziele der Friedensforschung.* München: Kaiser.

D'Estrée, T., et al. 2001. "Changing the Debate About 'Success' in Conflict Resolution Efforts." *Negotiation Journal* 17(2): 101–113.

Dahal, D. R. 2001a. *Civil Society in Nepal: Opening the Grounds for Questions.* Kathmandu: Center for Development and Governance.

———. 2001b. "Problems and Prospects of Relationship Between Government Organizations and NGOs/INGOs in Nepal." In *NGO, Civil Society. and Government in Nepal.* Ed. K. Bhattachan et al., 105–128. Kathmandu: Tribhuvan University, Central Department of Sociology and Anthropology.

Dahal, D. R., and T. Timilsina. 2006. *CIVICUS Report on Nepal.* Kathmandu: Institute of Cultural Affairs.

DANIDA. 2005. *Human Rights and Good Governance Programme in Nepal.* Program document. Kathmandu. October 2005.

Daoudy, H., and R. Khalidi. 2008. "The Palestinian War-Torn Economy: Aid, Development, and State Formation." *Contrario* 5(2): 23–36.

Davies, L. 2004. *Education and Conflict: Complexity and Chaos.* London and New York: Routledge.

Davis, S. H. 1983. "State Violence and Agrarian Crisis in Guatemala: The Roots of the Indian Peasant Rebellion." In *Trouble in Our Backyard: Central America and the United States in the Eighties.* Ed. Martin Diskin, 155–171. New York: Pantheon.

De Alwis, M. 1998. "Motherhood as a Space of Protest: Women's Political Participation in Contemporary Sri Lanka." In *Appropriating Gender: Women's Activism and Politicized Religion in South Asia.* Ed. P. Jeffery and A. Basu, 185–201. New York and London: Routledge.

De Silva, K. 1998. *Reaping the Whirlwind: Ethnic Conflict, Ethnic Politics in Sri Lanka.* New Delhi: Penguin.

De Soto, A., and G. Del Castillo. 1994. "Obstacles to Peacebuilding." *Foreign Policy* 24(2): 24.

Debiel, T., and M. Sticht. 2005. *Towards a New Profile? Development, Humanitarian, and Conflict-Resolution NGOs in the Age of Globalization.* Report no. 79. Duisburg: Institute for Development and Peace (INEF).

Debiel, T., et al. 2005. *Between Ignorance and Intervention: Strategies and Dilemmas of External Actors in Fragile States.* Bonn: Development and Peace Foundation.

DemNet Hungary. 2004. *Civil Society Mapping Mission in Bosnia and Herzegovina.* Budapest: DemNet. July.

Denitch, B. 1994. *Ethnic Nationalism: The Tragic Death of Yugoslavia.* Minneapolis: University of Minnesota Press.

Department for International Development (DFID). 2001a. *Civil Society Policy for DFID Nigeria.* London: DFID.

———. 2001b. *Making Government Work for Poor People: Building State Capability.* London: DFID.

———. 2005a. *Civil Society.* Available at www.dfid.gov.uk.

———. 2005b. *Why We Need to Work More Effectively in Fragile States.* London: DFID.

Department of Cooperative Development. 2007. *Statistical Abstract.* Chapter 12, "Cooperative Development." Available at www.statistics.gov.lk/Abstract_2006/Pages/chap12.

Development Assistance Committee (DAC). 2005. *Tip Sheet on Civil Society and Conflict.* Available at www.oecd.org/dac/conflict/tipsheets.

DeVotta, N. 2007. *Sinhalese Buddhist Nationalist Ideology: Implications for Politics and Conflict Resolution in Sri Lanka.* Policy Studies no. 40. Washington, DC: East-West Center.

DFID and World Bank. 2006. *Unequal Citizens: Gender, Caste, and Ethnic Exclusion in Nepal—Summary.* Kathmandu: DFID and World Bank.

Dhungana D. N., and B. R. Upreti. 2004. "Peace Process and Negotiation in Nepal: Revisiting the Past and Envisioning the Future." Paper prepared for the research study on the "Causes of Internal Conflicts and Means to Resolve Them. Nepal: A Case Study." Geneva and Kathmandu: Graduate Institute of International Studies.

Diamond, L., and J. McDonald. 1996. *Multi-Track Diplomacy: A Systems Approach to Peace.* West Hartford, CT: Kumarian.

Dichter, S., and K. Abu-Asba. 2006. "Two Peoples, One Civil Society." In *Bridging the Divide: Peacebuilding in the Israeli-Palestinian Conflict.* Ed. E. Kaufman, W. Salem, and J. Verhoeven. Boulder: Lynne Rienner Publishers.

Dizdarevic, S., et al. 2006. *Democracy Assessment in Bosnia and Herzegovina.* Sarajevo: Muller.

Dockser Marcus, A. 2007. *Jerusalem 1913: The Origins of Arab-Israeli Conflict.* New York: Viking Adult.

Dodd, C. H. 1998. *The Cyprus Imbroglio.* Huntingdon, UK: Eothen.

Dorronsoro, G. 2005. *Revolution Unending: Afghanistan, 1979 to the Present.* New York: Columbia University Press.

Doyle, M. 1983a. "Kant, Liberal Legacies, and Foreign Affairs." *Philosophy and Public Affairs* 12(3): 205–235.

———. 1983b. "Kant, Liberal Legacies, and Foreign Affairs Part 2." *Philosophy and Public Affairs* 12(4): 323–353.

Dryzek, J. S. 1996. "Political Inclusion and the Dynamics of Democratization." *American Science Review* 90(30): 745–748.

Dudouet, V. 2007. "Surviving the Peace." *Challenges of War-to-Peace Transitions for Civil Society Organisations.* Berghof Report no. 16. Berlin.

Duffield, M. 2001. *Global Governance and the New Wars: The Merging of Development and Security.* London: Zed Books.

Dumaa, L. 2007. "Peace Initiative Through Nonviolent Elections Committees (NEC's)." *PeaceWorks News* 7(1) (May). Available at www.aapeaceworks.org (accessed February 12, 2008).

Dunkerley, J. 1988. *Power in the Isthmus: A Political History of Modern Central America.* London and New York: Verso.

Dupree, L. 1980. *Afghanistan.* Princeton: Princeton University Press.

Ebiri, K. 2006. "How to Check Niger Delta Militants—by Ijaw Leader." *The Guardian* (Lagos). October 6. Available at www.guardianewsngr.com (accessed June 10, 2006).

———. 2007. "MEND Threatens Renewed Attacks on Oil Installations." *The Guardian* (Lagos). September 24. Available at www.guardiannewsngr.com (accessed September 24, 2007).

Eccarius-Kelly, V. 2007. *Kurdish Civil Society Activism in Europe.* Speech delivered at Sabanci University, Istanbul. November 6.

Edwards, D. B. 1986. "Charismatic Leadership and Political Process in Afghanistan." *Central Asian Survey* 5: 273–299.

Edwards, M. 2004. *Civil Society.* Cambridge, UK: Polity.

Eguren, L. E. 2001. "Who Should Go Where? Examples from Peace Brigades International." In *Peacebuilding: A Field Guide.* Ed. T. Paffenholz, 28–34. Boulder: Lynne Rienner Publishers.

Endresen, L. 2001. *Contact and Cooperation: The Israeli-Palestinian People-to-People Program.* Oslo, Norway: Norwegian Applied Social Research Center (FAFO).

Englebert, P., and D. M. Tull. 2008. "Postconflict Reconstruction in Africa: Flawed Ideas About Failed States." *International Security* 32(12): 106–139.

Eralp, D. U., and N. Beriker. 2005. "Assessing the Conflict Resolution Potential of the EU: The Cyprus Conflict and Accession Negotiations." *Security Dialogue* 36(2): 175–192.

Eriksson, A. 2006. "The Politicisation of Community Restorative Justice in Northern Ireland." *Restorative Justice Online—News 2006.* April. Available at http://restorativejustice.org/editions/2006/april06/erikssonarticle.

Ertman, T. 2005. "State Formation and State Building in Europe." In *The Handbook of Political Sociology: States, Civil Societies, and Globalization.* Ed. T. Janoski, R. Alford, A. Hicks, and M. A. Schwartz. Cambridge, UK: Cambridge University Press.

European Instrument for Democracy and Human Rights (EIDHR). 2008. *Turkey Programme.* Delegation of the European Commission to Turkey. Available at www.avrupa.info.tr/EUCSD,D.hag.html.

European Stability Initiative (ESI). 2004. *Governance and Democracy in Bosnia and Herzegovina: Post-industrial Society and the Authoritarian Temptation.* Berlin/Sarajevo: ESI.

European Union Election Observation Mission (EUEOM). 2003. *Nigeria Final Report, National Assembly Elections, 12 April 2003, Presidential and Gubernatorial Elections, 19 April 2003, State Houses of Assembly, 03 May 2003.* Brussels: European Union.

———. 2007. *Nigeria Final Report, Gubernatorial and State Houses of Assembly Elections, 14 April 2007, Presidential and National Assembly Elections, 21 April 2007.* Brussels: European Union.

European Union Program for Territorial Cooperation (EUPTC). 2007. *Peace III: EU Programme for Peace and Reconciliation, 2007–2013.* Belfast: EUPTC.

Eurostat Yearbook, 2006–2007. Available at http://epp.eurostat.ec.europa.eu/cache/ITY_OFFPUB/KS-CD-07-001-01/EN/KS-CD-07-001-01-EN.PDF.

Evans, P. B. 1995. "Government Action, Social Capital, and Development: Creating Synergy Across the Public-Private Divide." Paper presented at the conference of the Economic Development Working Group of Social Capital and Public Affairs Project of the American Academy of Arts and Sciences, Washington, DC.

Evans, P. B., D. Rueschemeyer, and T. Skocpol, eds. 1985. *Bringing the State Back In.* Cambridge, UK: Cambridge University Press.

Evin, A. 2004. "Changing Greek Perspectives of Turkey: An Assessment of the Post-earthquake Rapprochement." *Turkish Studies* 5(1): 4–20.

Eviota, D. 2005. "Grassroots and South-South Cooperation: Bantay Cease-Fire in the Philippines." In *People Building Peace II: Successful Stories of Civil Society.* Ed. P. van Tongeren et al., 388–393. Boulder: Lynne Rienner Publishers.

Fagan, A. 2006. "Civil Society in Bosnia Ten Years After Dayton." In *Peace Without Politics? Ten Years of International State-Building in Bosnia.* Ed. David Chandler, 100–113. London and New York: Routledge.

Farrington, C. 2008. "Models of Civil Society and Their Implications for the Northern Ireland Peace Process." In *Global Change, Civil Society, and the Northern Ireland Peace Process: Implementing the Political Settlement.* Ed. C. Farrington, 113–141. Houndmills, UK: Palgrave Macmillan.

Fast, L., and R. Neufeldt. 2005. "Envisioning Success: Building Blocks for Strategic and Comprehensive Peacebuilding Impact Evaluation." *Journal of Peacebuilding and Development* 2(2): 24–41.

Fearon, K. 1999. *Women's Work: The Story of the Northern Ireland Women's Coalition.* Belfast: Blackstaff Press.

———. 2000. "Civil Society and the Peace Process." Paper presented at "The Role of Citizen Peacebuilding in Conflict Transformation," June 1–4, Irvine, California.

Featherstone, A. 2000. "Peacekeeping, Conflict Resolution and Peacebuilding: A Reconsideration of Theoretical Frameworks." *International Peacekeeping* 7(1):190–218.

Fernando, U. 2003. *NGOs in Sri Lanka: Past and Present Trends.* Nugegoda: Wasala Publications.

Fernando, V., and J. H. de Mel. 1991. *Non-Governmental Organisations (NGOs) in Sri Lanka: An Introduction.* Colombo: NGO Water Supply and Sanitation Decade Service.

Fielden, M. B. 1998. "The Geopolitics of Aid: The Provision and Termination of Aid to Afghan Refugees in North-West Frontier Province, Pakistan." *Political Geography* 17: 459–487.

Fischer, M. 2007a. "Crossing Borders? Activities of the Trade Unions." In *Ten Years After Dayton: Peacebuilding and Civil Society in Bosnia-Herzegovina.* Ed. Martina Fischer, 141–156. Berlin: Lit.

———. 2007b. "Confronting the Past and Involving War Veterans for Peace: Activities by the Centre for Nonviolent Action, Sarajevo, Belgrade." In *Ten Years After Dayton: Peacebuilding and Civil Society in Bosnia-Herzegovina.* Ed. Martina Fischer, 387–416. Berlin: Lit.

Fisher, R. 1997. "Interactive Conflict Resolution." In *Peacemaking in International Conflict: Methods and Techniques.* Ed. W. Zartman and L. Rasmussen. Washington, DC: United States Institute of Peace Press.

Fisher, R., and L. Keashly. 1991. "The Potential Complementarity of Mediation and Consultation with a Contingency Model of Third-Party Intervention." *Journal of Peace Research* 28(1): 29–42.

Fitzduff, M. 2000. "First- and Second-Track Diplomacy in Northern Ireland." In *Peacebuilding: A Field Guide.* Ed. L. Reychler and T. Paffenholz, 110–120. Boulder: Lynne Rienner Publishers.

———. 2002. *Beyond Violence: Conflict Resolution Processes in Northern Ireland.* New York: Brookings Institute and United Nations University Press.

Fitzduff, M., and C. Church. 2004. *NGOs at the Table.* Lanham: Rowman and Littlefield.

FLACSO (Facultad Latinoamericana de Ciencias Sociales), WSP (War-torn Societies Project), and IGEDEP (Instituto Guatemalteco Desarrollo y Paz). 2002. *Hacia una Política de Seguridad para la Democracia.* Guatemala: FLACSO, WSP, and IGEDEP.

Florini, A. M. 2005. *The Coming Democracy: New Rules for Running a New World.* Washington, DC: Brookings Institution Press.

Flyvbjerg, B. 1998. "Habermas and Foucault: Thinkers for Civil Society?" *British Journal of Sociology* 49(2): 210–233.

Folley, M. 1996. "Laying the Groundwork: The Struggle of Civil Society in El Salvador." *Journal of Interamercian Studies and World Affairs* 38(1): 67–104.

Formal Private Education Network in Somalia (FPENS). 2008. *Factsheet: FPENS.* Somali Civil Society Network. Available at www.somalicivilsociety.org/index.php?option=com_content&task=view&id=57&Itemid=29.

Forut Sri Lanka. 2001. *Capacity Building of Civil Society in the Most Conflict Affected Areas of Sri Lanka.* Unpublished report. Colombo: Forut.

Foucault, M. 2004. *Sécurité, Territoire, Population: Cours au Collège de France, 1977–1978.* Ed. M. Senellart. Paris: Gallimard/Seuil.

Foundation for Culture and Civil Society (FCCS). 2007. *Afghan Civil Society Baseline Survey Provincial Analysis.* Kabul: FCCS.

Freedom House. 2006. *Freedom in the World* (annual publication). Washington, DC: Freedom House. Available at www.freedomhouse.org.

Frydenlund, I. 2005. *The Sangha and Its Relation to the Peace Process in Sri Lanka.* Oslo: International Peace Research Institute (PRIO).

Fundacion Myrna Mack. Available at www.myrnamack.org.gt.

Fundacion ProPay. Available at www.propaz.org.gt.

Gaige, F. H. 1975. *Regionalism and National Unity in Nepal.* Delhi: Vikas.

Galtung, J. 1969. "Violence, Peace, and Peace Research." *Journal of Peace Research* 6(3): 167–191.

———. 1971. "A Structural Theory of Imperialism." *Journal of Peace Research* 8: 81–117.

———. 1975. "Three Approaches to Peace: Peacekeeping, Peacemaking, and Peacebuilding." In *Peace, War, and Defense—Essays in Peace Research.* Ed. J. Galtung, 282–304. Copenhagen: Christian Ejlers.

Garbers, F. 2002. *Geschichte, Identität, und Gemeinschaft im Rückkehrprozeß Guatemaltekischer Kriegsflüchtlinge.* Hamburg, Münster: Lit.

Gautam, K. C. 2003. "Reconstruction and Reconciliation: A Way Forward for Nepal." In *Conflict, Human Rights, and Peace Challenges Before Nepal: Rishikesh Shaha Memorial Lectures, 2003.* Ed. Bipin Adhikari, 143–158. Kathmandu: National Human Rights Commission.

Gawerc, M. 2006. "Peace-Building: Theoretical and Concrete Perspectives." *Peace and Change* 31(4): 435–478.

Gellner, D. N., ed. 2003. *Resistance and the State.* New Delhi: Social Science.

Gellner, E. 1977. "Patrons and Clients." In *Patrons and Clients in Mediterranean Societies.* Ed. E. Gellner and J. Waterbury, 1–6. London: Gerald Duckworth.

———. 1994. *Civil Society and Its Rivals.* London and Toronto: Penguin Books.

Ghani, A. 1978. "Islam and State-building in a Tribal Society: Afghanistan 1880–1901." *Modern Asian Studies* 12(2): 269–284.

Ghani, A., and C. Lockhart. 2008. *Fixing Failed States: A Framework for Rebuilding a Fractured World.* Oxford, UK: Oxford University Press.

Ghimire, H. 2003. "Public Policy-making in Nepal." In *Conflict Resolution and Governance in Nepal*. Ed. A. P. Shrestha and H. Uprety. Kathmandu: Nepal Foundation for Advanced Studies in cooperation with Friedrich Ebert Stiftung.

Ghimire, S. 2008. "Nagarik Samaj Ra Gaisasa Ekai Ho?" *Samay* 5: 224.

Giacaman, G. 1998. "In the Throes of Oslo: Palestinian Society, Civil Society and the Future." In *After Oslo: New Realities, Old Problems*. Ed. G. Giacaman and D. J. Lonning. London: Pluto.

Giacaman, R. 1998. *Life and Health in Three Palestinian Villages*. London: Ithaca.

Gidron, G., S. Benjamin, N. Katz, and Y. Hasenfeld, eds. 2002. *Mobilizing for Peace: Conflict Resolution in Northern Ireland, Israel/Palestine, and South Africa*. Oxford: Oxford University Press.

Gilbert, M. 2008. *The Routledge Atlas of the Arab-Israeli Conflict*. New York: Routledge.

Giustozzi, A. 2005. "The Debate on Warlordism: The Importance of Military Legitimacy." Discussion paper. London: Crisis States Program, London School of Economics.

———. 2007. *Koran, Kalashnikov, and Laptop: The Neo-Taliban Insurgency in Afghanistan*. London: Hurst.

Glasius, M. 2004. *Civil Society*. Available at www.fathom.com (accessed January 10, 2006).

Glasl, F. 1982. "The Process of Conflict Escalation and Roles of Third Parties." In *Conflict Management and Industrial Relations*. Ed. B. Peteron. Boston: Kluwer-Nijhoff.

———. 1990. *Konfliktmanagement. Ein Handbuch für Führungskräfte und Berater*. Bern/Stuttgart: Verlag Freies Geistesleben.

Glendinning, W. 1999. "Providing a Service in a Divided Society." In *Service Delivery in a Divided Society*. Ed. S. Dunn and V. Morgan, 75–82. Belfast: Community Relations Council.

Global Security Website. Available at www.globalsecurity.org/military/world/para/pkk.htm (accessed June 1, 2008).

Goldman, F. 2007. *The Art of Political Murder: Who Killed the Bishop?* New York: Grove.

Goldstein, D. M., et al. 2005. *Classic Readings and Contemporary Debates in International Relations*. 3rd ed. Toronto: Wadsworth.

Göle, N. 1994. "Toward an Automization of Politics and Civil Society in Turkey." In *Politics in the Third Turkish Republic*. Ed. M. Heper and A. Evin, 213–222. Boulder: Westview.

Goodhand, J. 2006. *Aiding Peace: NGOs in Armed Conflict*. Boulder: Lynne Rienner Publishers.

Goodhand, J., and B. Klem. 2005. *Aid, Conflict, and Peacebuilding in Sri Lanka 2000–2005*. Colombo: Asia Foundation.

Goodhand, J., N. Lewer, and D. Hulme. 1999. *NGOs and Peace Building: Sri Lanka Study*. Bradford and Manchester, UK: Department of Peace Studies, University of Bradford, and the Institute for Development Policy and Management, University of Manchester.

Gormally, B. 2008. "Building a New Inclusive Society—An Action Plan for the Trade Union Movement." In *A Sustainable Peace? Research as a Contribution to Peace-Building in Northern Ireland*. Ed. Community Relations Council, 81–97. Belfast: Community Relations Council.

Gorvett, J. 2004. "Vote on Annan Plan Results in Reversal of Fortune for Turkish, Greek Cypriots." Washington Report on Middle East Affairs (June). Available at http://www.wrmea.com/archives/June_2004/0406040.html.

Greek Cypriot Civil Society Organizations Directory. 2007. Nicosia and Limassol: Management Center and Intercollege.

Greiter, M. 2003. "Möglichkeiten und Grenzen des Institutionalisierten Einbezugs Offiziell Mandatierter, Zivilgesellschaftlicher Prozesse (Track 2) in Offizielle Friedensprozesse (Track 1)." Bern: Erkenntnisse für Theorie und Praxis aus den Erfahrungen in Guatemala, Institut für Politikwissenschaft, Universität Bern.

Grødeland, Å. B. 2006. "Public Perceptions of Non-Governmental Organisations in Serbia, Bosnia and Herzegovina, and Macedonia." *Communist and Post-Communist Studies* 39: 221–246.

Guan, L. H. 2004. *Civil Society in Southeast Asia.* Singapore: Institute of Southeast Asian Studies.

Guatemaltekische Kirche im Exil 1991: Aufstandsbekämpfung in Guatemala. Stuttgart: Demokratisierung als Waffe der Militärs.

Guelke, A. 2003. "Civil Society and the Northern Irish Peace Process." *Voluntas: International Journal of Voluntary and Nonprofit Organisations* 14(1): 61–78.

Gunter, M. 1997. *The Kurds and the Future of Turkey.* New York: St. Martin's.

Gürel, A., and K. Özersay. 2006. "Cyprus and the Policies of Property." *Mediterranean Politics* 11(3): 349–369.

Gyawali, D. 2001. "Are NGOs in Nepal Old Wine or New Bottle? A Cultural Theory Perspective on Nepal's Contested Terrain." In *NGO, Civil Society, and Government in Nepal.* Ed. K. Bhattachan et al., 13–33. Kathmandu: Tribhuvan University, Central Department of Sociology and Anthropology. [Cited in *Civil Society and Political Participation,* K. Hachhethu, unpublished, 2004.]

Habermas, J. 1981. *Die Theorie des Kommunikativen Handelns, Zwei Bände* (Theory of Communicative Action). Frankfurt: Suhrkamp.

———. 1992. "Zur Rolle von Zivilgesellschaft und Politischer Öffentlichkeit." In *Faktizität und Geltung.* Ed. J. Habermas, 399–467. Frankfurt A. M.: Suhrkamp.

———. 1996. *Between Facts and Norms: Contributions to a Discourse Theory of Law and Democracy.* Cambridge, MA: MIT Press.

Hachhethu, K. 2004. *State of Democracy in Nepal: Survey Report.* Kathmandu: State of Democracy in South Asia/Nepal Chapter (in collaboration with International IDEA).

Hadjipavlou, M. 2004. "The Contribution of Bi-communal Contacts in Building a Civil Society in Cyprus." In *The Social Psychology of Group Identity and Social Conflict.* Ed. A. Eagly, R. Baron, and V. Hamilton. Washington, DC: American Psychological Association.

———. 2007. "The Cyprus Conflict: Root Causes and Implications for Peacebuilding." *Journal of Peace Research* 44(3): 349–365.

Hadjipavlou, M., and C. Cockburn. 2006. "Women in Projects of Cooperation for Peace: Methodologies of External Intervention in Cyprus." *Women Studies International Forum* 49: 521–533.

Hadjipavlou-Trigeorgis, M. 1987. "Identity Conflict in Divided Societies: The Case of Cyprus." Ph.D. diss. Boston: Boston University.

Håkansson, P., and S. Fredrik. 2007. "Who Do You Trust? Ethnicity and Trust in Bosnia and Herzegovina." *Europe-Asia Studies* 59(6): 961–976.

Hall, M. 2001. *Community Relations: An Elusive Concept. An Exploration by Community Activists from North Belfast.* Newtownabbey: Island.

Halperin, D. S., ed. 1997. *To Live Together: Shaping New Attitudes to Peace Through Education.* Geneva: International Bureau of Education, and Paris: UNESCO.

Halperin, E., and D. Bar-Tal. 2006. "Democratic Values and Education for Democracy in the State of Israel." *Democracy and Security* 2: 169–200. Available at www.eranhalperin.com/wp-content/uploads/2008/08/16-cco.pdf.

———. 2007. "The Fall of the Peace Camp in Israel." *Conflict and Communication Online* 6(2): 435–463.

Hamber, B., and G. Kelly. 2008. "The Challenge of Reconciliation: Translating Theory into Practice." In *A Sustainable Peace? Research as a Contribution to Peace-Building in Northern Ireland.* Ed. Community Relations Council, 3–26. Belfast: Community Relations Council.

Hammami, R. 1995. "Feminist Scholarship and the Literature on Palestinian Women." Working Papers Gender and Society. Birzeit: Birzeit University, Women's Studies Program.

Hampson, F. O. 1996. *Nurturing Peace: Why Peace Settlements Succeed or Fail.* Washington, DC: United States Institute of Peace Press.

Hampson, F. O., and J. Hay. 2002. *Human Security: A Review of Scholarly Literature.* Annual meeting of the Canadian Consortium on Human Security. Ottawa: Canadian Consortium on Human Security.

Hanafi, S. 1999. "Profile of Donors' Assistance to Palestinian NGOs: Survey and Database." Report submitted to the Welfare Association, Jerusalem.

———. 2005. "Spacio-cide and Bio-Politics: Israeli Colonial Project. From 1947 to the Wall." In *Against the Wall: Israel's Barrier to Peace.* Ed. M. Sorkin. New York: New Press.

———. Forthcoming. *International Civil Missions in Palestinian Territory.* (Arabic). Mustaqbal al-Arabi. Beirut: Center of Arab Unity Studies.

Hanafi, S., and L. Tabar. 2005. *Donors, International Organizations, Local NGOs: Emergence of the Palestinian Globalized Elite.* Washington, DC: Palestinian Studies Institute, and Ramallah: Muwatin.

Handy, J. 1984. *Gift of the Devil: A History of Guatemala.* Boston: South End.

Hänggi, H. 2005. "Approaching Peacebuilding from a Security Governance Perspective." In *Security Governance in Post-Conflict Peacebuilding.* Ed. A. Bryden and H. Hänggi. Geneva: Lit Verlag.

Hanlon, Josef. 1991. *Mozambique: Who Calls the Shots?* Bloomington: Indiana University Press.

Hannay, D. 2005. *Cyprus: The Search for a Solution.* London and New York: I. B. Tauris.

Hansson, U. 2005. *Troubled Youth? Young People, Violence, and Disorder in Northern Ireland.* Belfast: Institute for Conflict Research.

Harbom, L., and P. Wallensteen, 2007. "Armed Conflict, 1989–2006." *Journal of Peace Research* 44(5): 623–634.

Harneit-Sievers, A. 2005. *"Zivilgesellschaft" in Afrika: Anmerkungen aus Historischer Perspektive.* Lecture manuscript. December 2. Berlin: Humboldt-Universität.

Harpviken, K. B. 1997. "Transcending Traditionalism: The Emergence of Non-State Military Formations in Afghanistan." *Journal of Peace Research* 34(3): 271–287.

———. 2003. "Afghanistan: From Buffer State to Battleground—to Bridge Between Regions? In *Beyond the Nation State: New and Critical Security and Regionalism.* Ed. J. J. Hentz and M. Bøås, 152–176. Aldershot, UK: Ashgate.

———. 2009. *Social Networks and Migration in Wartime Afghanistan.* London: Palgrave Macmillan.

———. Forthcoming a. "Understanding Warlordism: The Trajectories of Three Afghan Warlords." In *Violence in the Post-Conflict State.* Ed. A. Suhrke.

———. Forthcoming b. "Afghanistan: Caught Between Security Complexes." *Comparative Social Research* 28.

Harpviken, K. B., and K. Kjellman. 2004. *Beyond Blueprints: Civil Society and Peacebuilding.* Concept paper prepared for the Norwegian Agency for Development Cooperation (NORAD).

Harpviken, K. B., A. Strand, and K. Ask. 2002. *Afghanistan and Civil Society.* Oslo: CMI/Norwegian Ministry of Foreign Affairs.

Harvey, P. 1998. "Rehabilitation in Complex Political Emergencies: Is Rebuilding Civil Society the Answer?" *Disasters* (2): 200–217.

Hasgüler, M. 2000. *Kıbrıs'ta Enosis ve Taksim Politikalarının Sonu.* Istanbul: Iletişim Yayınları.

HasNa Website. 2009. Available at www.hasna.org.

Hassassian, M. 2002. "NGOs in the Context of National Struggle." In *Mobilizing for Peace: Conflict Resolution in Northern Ireland, Israel/Palestine, and South Africa.* Ed. G. Gidron, S. Benjamin, N. Katz, and Y. Hasenfeld, 130–151. Oxford, UK: Oxford University Press.

———. 2006. "Civil Society and NGOs Building Peace in Palestine." In *Bridging the Divide: Peacebuilding in the Israeli-Palestinian Conflict.* Ed. E. Kaufman, W. Salem, and J. Verhoeven. Boulder: Lynne Rienner Publishers.

Haugerudbraaten, H. 1998. "Peacebuilding: Six Dimensions and Two Concepts." *African Security Review* 7(6). Available at http://www.iss.co.za/pubs/ASR/7No6/Peace building.html.

Heathershaw, J. 2008. "Unpacking the Liberal Peace: The Dividing and Merging of Peacebuilding Discourses." *Millennium: Journal of International Studies* 36(3): 597–621.

Hegre, H., et al. 2001. "Toward a Democratic Civil Peace? Democracy, Political Change, and Civil War, 1816–1992." *American Political Science Review* 95(1): 33–48.

Helms, E. 2003. "Women as Agents of Ethnic Reconciliation? Women's NGOs and International Intervention in Postwar Bosnia-Herzegovina." *Women Studies International Forum* 26(1): 15–33.

Hemmer, B. 2009. "The Democratization of Peacebuilding: The Political Engagement of Peacebuilding NGOs in Democratizing Societies." Ph.D. diss. University of California–Irvine.

Hengstenberg, P., K. Kohut, and G. Maihold, eds. 1999. "La Sociedad Civil en América Latina." Nueva Sociedad. Caracas: ADLAF, FES, and Nueva Sociedad.

Heper, M. 1985. *The State Tradition in Turkey.* Walkington, UK: Eothen.

Hermann, T. 2002. "The Sour Taste of Success: The Israeli Peace Movement, 1967–1998." In *Mobilizing for Peace: Conflict Resolution in Northern Ireland, Israel/Palestine, and South Africa.* Ed. B. Gidron, S. N. Katz, and Y. Hasenfeld, 94–129. New York: Oxford University Press.

———. 2006. "The Sour Taste of Success: The Israeli Peace Movement, 1967–1998." In *Mobilizing for Peace: Conflict Resolution in Northern Ireland, Israel/Palestine, and South Africa.* Ed. B. Gidron, S. Katz, and Y. Hasenfeld. Oxford: Oxford University Press.

Hettige, S. 1998. "Global Integration and the Disadvantaged Youth: From the Centre Stage to the Margins of Society." In *Globalization, Social Change, and Youth.* Ed. T. Hettige, 71–104. Colombo: German Cultural Institute and the Center for Anthropological and Sociological Studies.

Hilterman, J. 1990. "Trade Unions and Women's Committees: Sustaining Movement, Creating Space." *Middle East Report* 164/165 (May/August).

Hintze, O. 1970 [1906]. "Staatsverfassungs und Heeresverfassung." In Otto Hintze, *Staat und Verfassung.* Göttingen: Vandenhoeck und Ruprecht.

Hirsch, J., and R. Oakley. 1995. *Somalia and Operation Restore Hope.* Washington, DC: United States Institute for Peace.

His Majesty's Government of Nepal. 2000a. "Policy Paper on Decentralization." Nepal Development Forum, February.

———. 2000b. "The Role of Civil Society in Development and Poverty Reduction." Paper prepared for the Nepal Development Forum, April 17–19.

Hoffmann, M. 1995. "Konfliktlösung durch Gesellschaftliche Akteure. Möglichkeiten und Grenzen von Problemlösungs-Workshops." In *Friedliche Konfliktbearbeitung in der Staaten-und Gesellschaftswelt.* Ed. N. Ropers and T. Debiel, 284–303. Bonn: Dietz Verlag.

Hoftun, M., W. Raeper, and J. Whelpton. 1999. *People, Politics, and Ideology: Democracy and Social Change in Nepal.* Kathmandu: Mandala Book Point.

Howell, J. 2004. "Seizing Spaces, Challenging Marginalization, and Claiming Voice: New Trends in Civil Society in China." In *Exploring Civil Society.* Ed. G. Marlies, D. Lewis, and H. Seckinelgin. London: Routledge.

Howell, J., and J. Pearce. 2001. *Civil Society and Development: A Critical Exploration.* Boulder and London: Lynne Rienner Publishers.

Human Rights Watch. 2002a. *Niger Delta: No Democratic Dividend.* New York: Human Rights Watch.

———. 2002b. "Landmine Monitor Report 2002: Toward a Mine-Free World." New York: Human Rights Watch.

———. 2005. "Rivers of Blood, Guns, Oil, and Power in Nigeria's River's State." A Human Rights Watch briefing paper. New York: Human Rights Watch. February.

HÜNEE 2006. *Türkiye Göç ve Yerinden Olmuş Nüfus Araştırması.* Ankara: Hacettepe Üniversitesi. Available at www.hips.hacettepe.edu.tr/tgyona/TGYONA_rapor.pdf (accessed February 10, 2008).

Hutchison, G. 2004. *Evaluation of the Work of CIIR, 2001–2004.* London: Department for International Development. Available at www.dfid.gov.uk/aboutdfid/dfidwork/ppas/progress-eval-report.pdf.

Hutt, M., ed. 2004. *Himalayan "People's War."* London: Hurst.

Ibeanu, O. 2005. "The Proliferation of Small Arms and Light Weapons in the Niger Delta: An Introduction." In *Oiling Violence: The Proliferation of Small Arms and Light Weapons in the Niger Delta.* Ed. I. Okechukwu and F. Kyari Mohammed. Lagos and Abuja: Frankad Publishers for Friedrich Ebert Stiftung.

———. 2006. "Civil Society and Conflict Management in the Niger Delta: Scoping Gaps for Policy and Advocacy." CLEEN Foundation Monograph Series no. 2.

ICBL (International Campaign to Ban Landmines). 2002. *Landmine Monitor Report 2001: Toward a Mine-Free World.* New York: Human Rights Watch.

ICBL Website. 2009. Available at www.icbl.org.

IDASA (Institute for Democracy in Africa). 2007. "Nigerian Elections 2007 Election Report." Available at www.idasa.org.za/index.asp?page=output_details.asp%3FRID%3D1169%26PID%3D58 (accessed March 12, 2008).

IDMC (Internal Displacement Monitoring Centre). 2006. "The Engagement of Turkish NGOs: Recommendations on How to Improve the Dialogue and Develop Partnerships Between NGOs and Authorities on IDP Issues." Available at www.internal-displacement.org (accessed February 10, 2008).

Ikein, A., and C. Briggs-Anigboh. 1998. *Oil and Fiscal Federalism: The Political Economy of Resource Allocation in a Developing Country.* Aldershot, UK: Ashgate.

Independent Bureau of Humanitarian Issues (IBHI) and United Nations Development Program (UNDP). 2000. *Human Development Report Bosnia and Herzegovina, Youth.* Sarajevo: IBHI/UNDP.

Inglehart, R., et al. 2005. *European and World Values Surveys Integrated Data File, 1999–2002, Release I. Vol. 2005.* Cologne: Zentralarchiv fur Empirische Sozialforschung (ZA); Tilburg: Tilburg University; Amsterdam: Netherlands Institute for Scientific Information Services (NIWI); Madrid: Analisis Sociologicos Economicos y Politicos (ASEP); and Ann Arbor: JD Systems and Inter-university Consortium for Political and Social Research. Available at www.icpsr.umich.edu.

Inter-American Dialogue (IAD). 2004. *All in the Family. Latin America's Most Important Financial Flows.* Washington, DC: IAD.

International Alert. 2006. "Local Business, Local Peace: The Peacebuilding Potential of the Domestic Private Sector." Case Study Northern Ireland. London: International Alert.

International Association of Human Rights in Cyprus Website. 2009. Available at www.humanrightscyprus.org.

International Council on Voluntary Agencies (ICVA). 2002. "A Model of Cooperation Between the Government and NGOs: Development of the Poverty Reduction Strategy Programme." In *Perspectives on the NGO Sector in BiH: Research, Analysis, Laws.* Ed. ICVA, 40–43. Sarajevo: ICVA.

———. 2005. *ICVA Directory.* September. Sarajevo: ICVA.

International Council on Voluntary Agencies and Catholic Relief Services. 2007. *Independent NGO Report on the Implementation of Measures Within the Mid-Term Development Strategy BiH in Sectors: Social Protection, Education, Environment.* October. Sarejvo: ICVA/CRS.

International Crisis Group. 2003. "Afghanistan's Flawed Constitutional Process." *Asia Report* no. 56. Kabul and Brussels: International Crisis Group.

———. 2005. "Towards a Lasting Peace in Nepal: The Constitutional Issues." Asia Report no. 99. June 15. Kathmandu and Brussels: International Crisis Group.

———. 2006a. *The Swamps of Insurgency: Nigeria's Delta Unrest.* Africa Report no. 115–3. August. Dakar/Brussels: International Crisis Group.

———. 2006b. *Sri Lanka: The Failure of the Peace Process.* Asia Report no. 124. International Crisis Group. Available at www.crisisgroup.org/home/index.cfm?id=4523&l=1.

———. 2007. *Sri Lanka's Human Rights Crisis.* Asia Report no. 135. June. Columbo/Brussels: International Crisis Group.

———. 2008. *Nepal's Election: A Peaceful Revolution?* Asia Report no. 155. July 3. Kathmandu and Brussels: International Crisis Group.

International Federation of Journalists (IFJ). 2008. "Deadly Stories: Killings of Journalists Touch Record Level." Brussels: IFJ. Available at www.ifj.org/en/pages/ifj-annual-reports-on-journalists-and-media-staff-killed.

International Monetary Fund. 2008. "Islamic Republic of Afghanistan: Fourth Review Under the Three-Year Arrangement Under the Poverty Reduction and Growth Facility and Request for Waiver of Performance Criterion." Country Report 08/229. Washington, DC: International Monetary Fund.

Internet Haber. 2008. Available at www.internethaber.com/news_detail.php?id=128474 (accessed February 18, 2008).

Interpeace. 2008. "Community Based Peace Processes in South-Central Somalia." Garowe: Puntland Development Research Centre.

Iqbal, Z., and H. Starr. 2006. "Bad Neighbors: Failed States and Their Consequences." Paper presented at the fortieth North American Meeting of the Peace Science Society, November 10–12.

IRIN News (UN Office for the Coordination of Humanitarian Affairs) 2005. "Nigeria: Constitutional Change Conference Deadlocks over Oil Dispute." *IRIN News.* August 2. Available at www.irinnews.org/report.

Irish, L. E., and K. W. Simon. 2007. *Challenges Presented by the Legal, Regulatory, Administrative, and Fiscal Framework Governing Civil Society.* Background paper for the conference titled "The Enabling Environment." June. Kabul.

Irwin, C. 2002. *The People's Peace Process in Northern Ireland.* Houndmills, UK: Palgrave.

Islamic Republic of Afghanistan. 2006a. *Peace, Reconciliation, and Justice in Afghanistan: Action Plan.* Kabul: Government of Afghanistan.

———. 2006b. *National Education Strategic Plan for Afghanistan: 1385–1389.* Kabul: Ministry of Education.

———. 2007. *Joint Programme Document: National Youth Programme.* Kabul: Government of Afghanistan.

Jabri, V. 1996. "Discourses on Violence: Conflict Analysis Reconsidered." Manchester, UK, and New York: Manchester University Press.

Jácome, F., P. Millet, and A. Serbín. 2005. "Conflict Prevention, Civil Society, and International Organizations: The Difficult Path for Peace Building in Latin America and the Caribbean." FOCAL policy paper. Ottawa: Canadian Foundation for the Americas.

Jalali, R. 2002. "Civil Society and the State: Turkey After the Earthquake." *Disasters* 26(2): 120–139.

Janoski, T. 1998. *Citizenship and Civil Society.* New York: Cambridge University Press.

Jarman, Neil. 2006. *Working at the Interface: Good Practice in Reducing Tension and Violence.* Belfast: Institute for Conflict Research. Available at www.conflictresearch.org.uk.

Jenkins, R. 2002. "Mistaking 'Governance' for 'Politics': Foreign Aid, Democracy, and the Construction of Civil Society." In *Civil Society: History and Possibilities.* Ed. S. Kaviraj and S. Khilnani, 250–268. Cambridge, UK: Cambridge University Press.

Jeong, H. 2005. *Peacebuilding in Postconflict Societies: Strategy and Process.* Boulder and London: Lynne Rienner Publishers.

Jerusalem Mediation and Arbitration Center. 1996. "About the Center." Available at www.jiis.org.il/mediation/index.html.

Johnson, C., and J. Leslie. 2002. "Afghans Have Their Memories: A Reflection on the Recent Experience of Assistance in Afghanistan." *Third World Quarterly* 23(5): 861–874.

Jonas, S. 1991. *The Battle for Guatemala: Rebels, Death Squads, and U.S. Power.* Boulder: Westview.

———. 2000. *Of Centaurs and Doves: Guatemala's Peace Process.* Boulder: Westview.

Kalaycioglu, E. 2002a. "Civil Society in Turkey: Continuity or Change?" In *Turkish Transformation: New Century—New Challenges.* Ed. B. Beely. Huntingdon, UK: Eothen.

———. 2002b. "State and Civil Society in Turkey: Democracy, Development, and Protest." In *Civil Society in the Muslim World.* Ed. A. B. Sajoo. London and New York: I. B. Tauris.

———. 2006. "States and Civil Society in the Middle East: Coping with Democratization." Paper presented at the International Studies Association's annual convention, March 22–25, San Diego.

Kaldor, M. 2003. *Global Civil Society: An Answer to War.* Cambridge, UK: Polity.

Kamali, M. 2001. "Civil Society and Islam: A Sociological Perspective." *Archives Européenes de Sociologie* 42(3): 457–482.

Kandiah, T. 2001. *The Media and the Ethnic Conflict in Sri Lanka.* Marga monograph series on Ethnic Reconciliation no. 19. Colombo: Marga Institute.

Kant, I. 1995. *Zum Ewigen Frieden.* Berlin: Wiley-VCH Weinheim.

Karki, A., and D. Seddon, eds. 2003. *The People's War in Nepal: Left Perspectives.* Delhi: Adroit.

Karki, M. B. 2006. "Social Networking and the Recruitment Process Among Activists in Nepal." *Contributions to Nepalese Studies* 33(1): 33–72.

Karokhail, M., and S. Schmeidl. 2006. *Integration of Traditional Structures into the State-Building Process: Lessons from the Tribal Liaison Office in Loya Paktia.*

Publication series on Promoting Democracy Under Conditions of State Fragility. Issue no. 1: 59–79. Berlin: Heinrich Böll Foundation.

Kasfir, N. 1998. "Civil Society, the State, and Democracy in Africa." *Commonwealth and Comparative Politics* 36(2): 123–149.

Kash, E. 2007. "The Odili Years of . . . Blood, Tears, and Sorrow." *Post Harcourt Telegraph.* August 21. Available at www.thephctelegraph.com (accessed August 21, 2007).

Katana, G. 1999. "NGOs in Republika Srpska: Bashful Support of the Regime." *AIM Banja Luka.* September 20.

Kaufman, E., W. Salem, and J. Verhoeven, eds. 2006. *Bridging the Divide: Peacebuilding in the Israeli-Palestinian Conflict.* Boulder: Lynne Rienner Publishers.

Kaviraj, S., and S. Khilnani, eds. 2002. *Civil Society: History and Possibilities.* Delhi: Cambridge University Press.

Kaye, D. D. 2005. *Rethinking Track Two Diplomacy: The Middle East and South Asia.* Clingendael Diplomacy Papers no. 3. The Hague: Netherlands Institute of International Relations. Available at www.clingendael.nl/publications/2005/20050601_cdsp_paper_diplomacy_3_ky.

Keane, J. 1988. "Despotism and Democracy: The Origins and Development of the Distinction Between Civil Society and the State, 1750–1850." In *Civil Society and the State: New European Perspectives.* Ed. J. Keane, 35–71. London and New York: Verso.

Kelleher, A., and J. L. Taulbee. 2005. "Building Peace Norwegian Style: Studies in Track 1? Diplomacy." In *Subcontracting Peace: The Challenges of NGO Peacebuilding.* Ed. O. Richmond and H. Carey. Aldershot, UK: Ashgate.

Kelman, H. 1992. "Informal Mediation by the Scholar/Practitioner." In *Mediation in International Relations: Multiple Approaches to Conflict Management.* Ed. J. Bercovitch and J. Rubin. London: Macmillan.

———. 2005. "Interactive Problem-Solving in the Israeli-Palestinian Case: Past Contributions and Present Challenges." In *Paving the Way: Contributions of Interactive Conflict Resolution to Peacemaking.* Ed. R. Fisher. Lanham, MD: Lexington.

Kew, D., and D. Phillips. 2007. "Seeking Peace in the Niger Delta. Table 1: Monthly Federal Allocations for July 2006 for the Niger Delta." *New England Journal of Public Policy* 2 (Summer): 158.

Kew, Darren. 2004. "The 2003 Elections in Nigeria: Not Credible, but Acceptable?" In *Crafting the New Nigeria: Strengthening the Nation.* Ed. R. Rotberg. Boulder: Lynne Rienner Publishers.

———. 2008. "The Role of Civil Society Groups in Strengthening Governance and Capacity: Avenues for Support." In *Smart Aid.* Ed. R. Joseph. Boulder: Lynne Rienner Publishers.

———. Forthcoming. *Classrooms of Democracy? Civil Society, Conflict Resolution, and Building Democracy in Nigeria.* Syracuse, NY: Syracuse University Press.

Khalidi, R. 2007. *The Iron Cage: The Story of the Palestinian Struggle for Statehood.* Oxford, UK: Oneworld.

Khanal, K. P. 2004. "Village Leadership and Governance: A Case Study of Two VDCs of Kathmandu District." In *Nepal: Local Leadership and Governance.* Ed. L. R. Baral et al., 73–111. Delhi: Adroit.

Kieser, H. L., ed. 2006. *Turkey Beyond Nationalism: Towards Post-Nationalist Identities.* London and New York: I. B. Tauris.

Kimmerling, B. 2003. *The Palestinian People: A History.* Cambridge: Harvard University Press.

Kirişçi, K. 1998. "Turkey." In *Internally Displaced People: A Global Survey.* Ed. J. Hampton, 197–200. London: Earthscan.

———. 2008. *Revisiting Turkey's Kurdish Problem.* Discussion Paper series 2008/1, EDAM 5. Available at www.edam.org.tr (accesssed February 28, 2008).

Kirişçi, K., and G. Winrow. 1997. *A Translation of the Kurdish Question and Turkey: An Example of a Trans-State Ethnic Conflict.* London: Frank Cass.

Kızılyürek, N. 2004. "Kıbrıs'ta Sivil Toplum ve Sivil Toplum Kuruluşları Üzerine Düşünceler." In *Geleceğin Sesi: Türk-Yunan Yurttaş Diyaloğu.* Ed. T. U. Belge. Istanbul: Istanbul Bilgi University Press.

Knox, C., and R. Monaghan. 2002. *Informal Justice in Divided Societies: Northern Ireland and South Africa.* New York: Palgrave Macmillan.

Kocher, M. 2002. "The Decline of PKK and the Viability of a One-State Solution in Turkey." *International Journal on Multicultural Societies* 4(1): 1–20.

Kohlmann, E. F. 2004. *Al-Qaida's Jihad in Europe: The Afghan-Bosnian Network.* Oxford and New York: Berg.

Köknar, A. 2006. "Biting the Hand That Fed Them: Kurdish Insurgency Tests Iranian Conventional Military Power." Washington, DC: Terrorism Research Center.

Kolås, Å., and J. Miklian. 2008. *Rethinking Conflict Management: Are There Insights for India?* Oslo: International Peace Research Institute (PRIO).

Kop, Y., and R. Litan. 2002. *Sticking Together: The Israeli Experiment in Pluralism.* Washington, DC: Brookings Institution Press.

Kotelis, A. 2006. "Cognitive and Relational Outcomes of Track Two Initiatives and Transfer Strategies: The Cases of the Greek-Turkish Forum and the Greek-Turkish Journalists' Conference." Master's thesis. Istanbul: Sabanci University.

Kramer, H. 2000. *A Changing Turkey: The Challenge to Europe and the United States.* Washington, DC: Brookings Institute Press.

Krause, K. 2004. "The Key to a Powerful Agenda, If Properly Delimited." *Security Dialogue* 35(3): 367–368.

Krauskopff, G. 2003. "An 'Indigenous Minority' in a Border Area: Tharu Ethnic Associations, NGOs, and the Nepalese State." In *Resistance and the State: Nepalese Experiences.* Ed. D. N. Gellner, 199–243. Delhi: Social Sciences.

Krizan, M. 1989. "'Civil Society'—A New Paradigm in the Yugoslav Theoretical Discussion." *Praxis International* 9: 152–163.

KRUZ (To Work and Succeed Together). 2002. *A Strategy for the Development of a Viable Non-Government Sector in BiH.* Sarajevo: KRUZ.

Krznaric, R. 1999. "Civil and Uncivil Actors in the Guatemalan Peace Process." *Bulletin of Latin American Research* 18(1): 1–16.

Kumar, D. 2000. "What Ails Democracy?" In *Domestic Conflict and Crisis of Governability in Nepal.* Ed. D. Kumar, 14–57. Kathmandu: Center for Nepal and Asian Studies.

Kumar, K. 1993. "Civil Society: An Inquiry into the Usefulness of an Historical Term." *British Journal of Sociology* 44(3): 375–395.

Kurban, D., A. B. Çelik, and D. Yükseker. 2006. *Overcoming a Legacy of Mistrust: Towards Reconciliation Between the State and the Displaced.* Istanbul: Turkish Economic and Social Studies Foundation and Internal Displacement Monitoring Centre. Available at www.internal-displacement.org.

Kurban, D., et al. 2007. *Confronting Forced Migration: Post-Displacement Restitution of Citizenship Rights in Turkey.* Istanbul: TESEV.

Kurtenbach, S. 1994. "Die Suche nach Frieden in Zentralamerika. Analyse der Bisherigen Einflußversuche Einer Konfliktminderung von Außen in Guatemala und El Salvador." Bonn: Materialien zum Dialogprogramm.

———. 1998a. *Guatemala: Tradition und Moderne, Folklore und Gewalt.* München: Beck-Länderkunde.

———. 1998b. "La Sociedad Civil y la Regulación Civil de Conflictos—El Aporte de la Sociedad Civil a la Terminación de Conflictos Armados." In *La Sociedad Civil en América Latina.* Ed. FES (Friedrich Ebert Stiftung), 197–208. Caracas: Nueva Sociedad.

———. 2003. "Guatemala: Der Blockierte Friede." In *Den Frieden Gewinnen. Vergleichende Studien zur Konsolidierung von Friedensprozessen in Nachkriegsgesellschaften.* Ed. M. A. Ferdowsi and V. Matthies, 302–319. Bonn: Dietz.

———. 2006. "Guatemala—Das Überleben von Gewaltordnungen im Frieden." In *Gewaltordnungen Bewaffneter Gruppen. Ökonomie und Herrschaft Nichtstaatlicher Akteure in den Kriegen der Gegenwart.* Ed. J. Bakonyi, S. Hensell, and J. Siegelberg, 71–82. Baden-Baden: Nomos.

———. 2008a. "Die Rolle der Kirchen bei der Konfliktregulierung in Zentralamerika—Modell für Andere Regionen?" In *Friedensstiftende Religionen. Religion und die Deeskalation Politischer Konflikte.* Ed. M. Brocker, 269–283. Wiesbaden: VS Verlag für Sozialwissenschaft.

———. 2008b. "Case Study Guatemala of the Project 'Social and Political Fractures After Wars': The Role of Youth Violence in Cambodia and Guatemala." Working paper. Available at www.postwar-violence.de.

Kurtenbach, S., and T. Paffenholz. 1994. "Kirchen Können in Kriegen Vermitteln." *Der Überblick* 3(94): 16–119.

Kuttab, J. 1998. "An Exchange on Dialogue." *Journal of Palestine Studies* 17(2): 84–108.

Kvinna till Kvinna. 2006. *To Make Room for Changes: Peace Strategies from Women Organisations in Bosnia and Herzegovina.* Sarajevo: Kvinna till Kvinna.

Kypros-Net—The World of Cyprus. 2008. Available at www.kypros.org.

Labour and Employment Agency of Bosnia and Herzegovina. 2008. *Labour Market Statistics.* Available at www.agenrzbh.gov.ba/engleski/statistike.html.

Laitin, D., and S. Samatar. 1986. *Somalia: Nation in Search of a State.* Boulder: Westview.

Lang, S. 2002. "Sulha Peacemaking and the Politics of Persuasion." *Journal of Palestine Studies* 31(3): 52–66.

Larrabee, S. F. 2007. "A War of Nerves in Turkey." Available at www.rand.org/commentary/051207PS.html (accessed June 1, 2008).

Latin, E. 2003. "Suspicious Islamic Missionaries: Active Islamic Youth." *Southeast European Times.* Available at www.setimes.com.

Lauth, H. 2003. "Ambivalenzen der Zivilgesellschaft in Hinsicht auf Demokratie und Soziale Inklusion." *Nord-Süd Aktuell* 2/2003: 223–232.

Le Sage, A. 2004. "Somalia and the War on Terrorism: Political Islamic Movements and US Counter-Terrorism Efforts." Ph.D. diss. Cambridge, UK: University of Cambridge.

———. 2005. *Stateless Justice in Somalia: Formal and Informal Rule of Law Initiatives.* Geneva: Center for Humanitarian Dialogue.

Lederach, J. P. 1997. *Building Peace: Sustainable Reconciliation in Divided Societies.* Washington, DC: United States Institute of Peace Press.

———. 2005. *Moral Imagination: The Art and Soul of Building Peace.* Oxford, UK: Oxford University Press.

Leonard, M. 2004. "Bonding and Bridging Social Capital: Reflections from Belfast." *Sociology* 38(5): 927–944.

Lesch, A. M., and D. Tschirgi. 1998. *Origins and Development of the Arab-Israeli Conflict.* Westport, CT: Greenwood.

Levenson-Estrada, D. 1988. "Por Si Mismos: Un Estudio Preliminar de las "Maras" en la Ciudad de Guatemala." Cuadernos de Investigación AVANCSO No. 4. Guatemala: AVANCSO.

Levitt, M. 2006. *Hamas: Politics, Charity, and Terrorism in the Service of Jihad.* New Haven and London: Yale University Press.

Lewis, D. 2002. "Civil Society in African Contexts. Reflections on the Usefulness of a C ncept." *Development and Change* 33(4): 569–586.

Lewis, I. M. 2001. *Civil Society in Non-Western Contexts: Reflections on the "Usefulness" of a Concept.* Civil Society Working Paper no. 13. London: Center for Civil Society, London School of Economics.

———. 2002. *A Modern History of the Somali.* Oxford: James Currey.

Lewis, S., and S. Davis. 2005. *Disarmament in the Niger Delta.* Niger Delta Peace and Security Working Group background paper.

Liechty, M. 2002. *Suitably Modern: Making Middle-Class Culture in a New Consumer Society.* Princeton: Princeton University Press.

Limanowska, B. 2005. *Trafficking in Human Beings in South Eastern Europe: 2004—A Focus on Prevention.* Warsaw and Sarajevo: UNICEF (United Nations International Children's Emergency Fund), UNOHCHR (United Nations Office of the High Commissioner on Human Rights), OSCE/ODIHR (Organization for Security and Cooperation in Europe/Office for Democratic Institutions and Human Rights).

Livni, M. 2004. "The Kibbutz and Its Future: Historical Perspectives." Paper presented at the International Communal Studies Association's eighth international conference, June, Amana, Iowa.

Livni, M., M. Naveh, and A. Cicelsky. 2006. "Building Bridges of Clay, Mud, and Straw." *Communities* 131 (Summer): 42–45.

Liyanage, S. 2006. "Civil Society and the Peace Process." In *Negotiating Peace in Sri Lanka: Efforts, Failures, and Lessons.* Vol. 2. Ed. K. Rupesinghe, 279–302. Colombo: Foundation for Co-existence.

Loizides, N. G. 2002. "Greek-Turkish Dilemmas and the Cyprus EU Accession Process." *Security Dialogue* 33(4): 429–442.

Loizidou vs. Turkey Overview. 2000. Online information on *Loizidou vs. Turkey.* European Court on Human Rights. Available at www.cyprus.com.cy.

Lubeck, P., M. Watts, and R. Lipschutz. 2007. *Convergent Interests: U.S. Energy Security and the "Securing" of Nigerian Democracy.* International policy report. February. Washington, DC: Center for International Policy.

Ludin, J. 2002. "Civil Society in Afghanistan: Background Paper." Paper presented at the Second Afghan Civil Society Conference, May 15–19, Kabul.

Lund, M. 2003. *What Kind of Peace Is Being Built? Stock Taking of Post-Conflict Peacebuilding and Charting Future Directions.* Discussion paper prepared on the occasion of the tenth anniversary of "An Agenda for Peace." Ottawa: IDRC (International Development Research Centre).

Lustick, I. 1994. *From War Toward Peace in the Arab-Israeli Conflict, 1969–1993.* New York: Garland.

Lyons, T., and A. I. Samatar. 1995. *Somalia: State Collapse, Multilateral Intervention, and Strategies for Political Reconstruction.* Brookings occasional papers. Washington, DC: Brookings Institution.

Macfarlane, A. 2001 [1993]. "Fatalism and Development in Nepal." In *Nepal in the Nineties.* Ed. M. Hutt, 106–127. Delhi: Oxford University Press.

Mac Ginty, R. 2006. *No War, No Peace: The Rejuvenation of Stalled Peace Processes and Peace Accords.* Basingstoke, UK: Palgrave.

Mac Ginty, R., and J. Darby. 2002. *Guns and Government: The Management of the Northern Ireland Peace Process.* Houndmills, UK: Palgrave.

Mack, A. 2002. "Civil War: Academic Research and the Policy Community." *Journal of Peace Research* 39(5): 515–525.

Mageean, P. 1997. "Human Rights and the Peace Process in Northern Ireland." *Critical Criminology* 8(1): 31–48.

Mageean, P., and M. O'Brien. 1999. "From the Margins to the Mainstream: Human Rights and the Good Friday Agreement." *Fordham International Law Journal* 22: 1499–1538.

Maina, W. 1998. "Kenya: The State, Donors, and the Politics of Democratization." In *Civil Society and the Aid Industry.* Ed. A. van Rooy, 134–167. London and Sterling, VA: Earthscan.

Malcolm, N. 1996. *Bosnia: A Short History.* New York: New York University Press.

Maley, W., and A. Saikal. 2002. "Civil Society and Reconstruction: Some Reflections." *Afghanistan Info* 51: 7–8.

Maley, W., C. Sampford, and R. Thakur, eds. 2003. *From Civil Strife to Civil Society: Civil and Military Responsibilities in Disrupted States.* Tokyo: United Nations University Press.

Mamdani, M. 1995. "Introduction." In *African Studies in Social Movements and Democracy.* Ed. M. Mamdani and E. Wamba-dia-Wamba. Dakar: Codesria.

The Management Center—Managing Change for Sustainable Development. 2009. Available at http://www.mc-med.eu/index2.htm.

Manz, B. 1988. *Refugees of a Hidden War: The Aftermath of Counterinsurgency in Guatemala.* Albany: State University of New York Press.

Maoz, I. 2000. "An Experiment in Peace: Reconciliation Aimed Workshops of Jewish-Israeli and Palestinian Youth." *Journal of Peace Research* 37(6): 721–736.

Marchal, R. 2002. "Islamic Political Dynamics in the Somali Civil War." Paper presented at the conference "Islam in Africa: A Global, Cultural and Historical Perspective." Birmingham, UK: Institute of Global Cultural Studies, Birmingham University.

Mardin, Ş. 1969. "Power, Civil Society, and Culture in the Otoman Empire." *Comparative Studies in Society and History* 11(3): 258–281.

———. 1991. "Türkiye'de Muhalefet ve Kontrol." In *Türk Modernlesmesi: Makaleler 4.* Ed. M. Türköne. 176–193, Istanbul: Iletisim Yayincilik.

———. 1992. "Kontrol Felsefesi Ve Gelecegimiz." In *Siyaset ve Sosyal Bilimler: Makaleler 2.* Ed. Mümtazer Türköne and Tuncay Önder, 133–138. Istanbul: Iletisim Yayincilik.

Marks, G., and D. McAdam. 1999. "On the Relationship of Political Opportunities to the Form of Collective Action: The Case of the European Union." In *Social Movements in a Globalizing World.* Ed. D. della Porta, H. Kriesi, and D. Rucht. Basingstoke, UK: Macmillan.

Maskay, B. K. 1998. *Non-Governmental Organizations in Development: Search for a New Vision.* Kathmandu: Center for Development and Governance.

Maskey, M. 1998. "Janandolanma Chikitsakharu: Smritima Korieko Euta Andolankatha." *Studies in Nepali History and Society* 3(1): 127–180.

Massicard, E. 2006. "Claiming Difference in an Unitarist Frame: The Case of Alevism." In *Turkey Beyond Nationalism: Towards Post-Nationalist Identities.* Ed. H. L. Kieser, 74–82. London: I. B. Tauris.

McCall, C., and A. Williamson. 2001. "Governance and Democracy in Northern Ireland: The Role of the Voluntary and Community Sector After the Agreement." *Governance: An International Journal of Policy and Administration* 14: 363–383.

McCartney, C. 1999. "The Role of Civil Society." *Striking a Balance: The Northern Ireland Peace Process.* Accord Series. London: Conciliation Resources. Available at www.c-r.org/our-work/accord/northern-ireland/civil-society.php.

McCreary, A. 2007. *In War and Peace: The Story of Corrymeela.* Belfast: Brehon.

McCrudden, C. 2001. "Equality." In *Human Rights, Equality, and Democratic Renewal in Northern Ireland.* Ed. C. Harvey, 75–112. Oxford, UK, and Portland: Hart.

McDowall, D. 1997. *A Modern History of the Kurds.* London and New York: I. B. Tauris.

McEvoy, K. 2001. "Human Rights, Humanitarian Interventions, and Paramilitary Activities in Northern Ireland." In *Human Rights, Equality, and Democratic Renewal in Northern Ireland.* Ed. C. Harvey, 215–248. Oxford, UK, and Portland: Hart.

McEvoy, K., and H. Mika. 2002. "Restorative Justice and the Critique of Informalism in Northern Ireland." *British Journal of Criminology* 42: 534–562.

McKiernan, K. 1999. "Turkey's War on the Kurds." *Bulletin of the Atomic Scientists* 55(2) (March–April): 26–37.

McVeigh, R. 2002. "Between Reconciliation and Pacification: The British State and Community Relations in the North of Ireland." *Community Development Journal* 37(1): 47–59.

Mehta, A. K. 2006. *The Royal Nepal Army: Meeting the Maoist Challenge.* New Delhi: Rupa.

Melaugh, M. 2007. *Draft List of Deaths Related to the Conflict, 2002–.* CAIN (Conflict Archive on the Internet) Web Service. Available at http://cain.ulst.ac.uk/sutton/chron/index.html.

Menchú, R. (E. Burgos). 1984. *Leben in Guatemala.* Bornheim-Merten: Lamuv.

Menkhaus, K. 1997. "International Peacebuilding and the Dynamics of Local and National Peacebuilding in Somalia." In *Learning from Somalia: The Lessons of Armed Humanitarian Intervention.* Ed. W. Clarke and J. Herbst, 42–63. Boulder: Westview.

———. 1998. "Somalia: Political Order in a Stateless Society." *Current History* 97(619): 220–224.

———. 2003. "Measuring Impact: Issues and Dilemmas." Geneva: Interpeace Occasional Paper series.

———. 2007. "The Crisis in Somalia: Tragedy in Five Acts." *African Affairs* 106: 357–390.

———. 2008. "Desperate Exodus: Somali Civil Society in Peril." *Horn of Africa Bulletin* (August): 2–3.

Merkel, W. 1999. *Systemtransformation. Eine Einführung in die Theorie und Empirie der Transformationsforschung.* Opladen: Leske and Budrich.

———. 2000. *Systemwechsel 5. Zivilgesellschaft und Demokratische Transformation.* Opladen: Leske and Budrich.

Merkel, W., and H. Lauth. 1998. "Systemwechsel und Zivilgesellschaft. Welche Zivilgesellschaft Braucht die Demokratie?" *Aus Politik und Zeitgeschichte* 6(7): 3–12.

Merriman, R. 2006. "Speaking with the Enemy." The Electronic Intifada. Available at http://electronicintifada.net/v2/article4716.shtml (accessed November 22, 2006).

Miall, H., et al. 1999. *Contemporary Conflict Resolution.* Cambridge: Polity.

Migdal, J. S. 1988. *Strong Societies and Weak States: State-Society Relations and State Capabilities in the Third World.* Princeton: Princeton University Press.

———. 2001. *State in Society: Studying How States and Societies Transform and Constitute One Another.* Cambridge, UK: Cambridge University Press.

Milani, C., S. B. Nefissa, S. Hanafi, and N. A. al-Fattah, eds. 2005. *NGOs and Governance in the Arab World.* Cairo: American University in Cairo Press.

Milliken, J., ed. 2003. *State Failure, Collapse, and Reconstruction.* Oxford, UK: Blackwell.

Milliken, J., and K. Krause. 2003. "State Failure, State Collapse, and State Reconstruction: Concepts, Lessons, and Strategies." In *State Failure, Collapse, and Reconstruction.* Ed. J., Milliken, 1–24. Oxford, UK: Blackwell.

Milosevic, J. (President, Mirovna Akcija Humanista [Humanist's Peace Action]). 2004. Interview by B. Hemmer. May 5. Sarajevo.

Mishra, C. 2001. "New Predicaments of Humanitarian Organizations." In *NGO, Civil Society, and Government in Nepal.* Ed. K. B. Bhattachan et al., 1–12. Kathmandu: Tribhuvan University, Central Department of Sociology and Anthropology.

Misión de Naciones Unidas en Guatemala (MINUGUA). 2002a. "Situación de los Compromisos Relativos al Ejército en los Acuerdos de Paz." Guatemala: MINUGUA.

———. 2002b. "Los Linchamientos: Un Flagelo Que Persiste." Guatemala: MINUGUA.

Mitchell, A. 2009. "A Deeply Divided Society? Peace-Building Policy and NGOs in Northern Ireland, 1970–2006." In *NGOs in Contemporary Britain.* Ed. M. Hilton, N. Crowson, and J. McKay, 142–160. Basingstoke, UK: Palgrave.

Mitchell, C. 2006. *Religion, Identity, and Politics in Northern Ireland: Boundaries of Belonging and Belief.* Aldershot, UK: Ashgate.

Moghadam, V. M. 1992. "Patriarchy and the Politics of Gender in Modernising Societies: Iran, Pakistan, and Afghanistan." *International Sociology* 7: 35–53.

Molkentin, G. 2002. *Kriegsursachen und Friedensbedingungen in Guatemala.* Frankfurt A. M.: Vervuert.

Monsutti, A. 2008. "Afghan Migratory Strategies and the Three Solutions to the Refugee Problem." *Refugee Survey Quarterly* 27(1): 58–73.

Morris, B. 1999. *Righteous Victims: A History of the Zionist-Arab Conflict, 1881–1999.* New York: Knopf.

Mu'allem, N. 1999. "Palestinian Israeli Civil Society Co-operative Activities." Paper presented to the workshop "Peace Building Between Israelis and Palestinians," November 27–28, Helsinki.

Mufson, S. 2008. "Nigeria's Oil Morass." *Washington Post,* February 1.

Müftüler Baç, M. 1999. "The Cyprus Debacle: What the Future Holds." *Futures* 31(6): 559–575.

Musah, A-F. 2003. "Privatization of Security, Arms Proliferation, and the Process of State Collapse in Africa." In *State Failure, Collapse, and Reconstruction.* Ed. J. Milliken, 157–178. Oxford: Blackwell.

Mustapha, A. 2003. "Ethnic Minority Groups in Nigeria: Current Situation and Major Problems." Paper presented to the Commission on Human Rights Sub-commission on Promotion and Protection of Human Rights Working Group on Minorities, ninth session, May 12–16, Geneva.

Nagarikko Pahalma: Naya Nepal (New Nepal: Peoples Initiative). 2004–2006. Kathmandu: NESAC. Compilation of papers and proceedings of two National Peoples Conferences, November 2004 and June 2006.

Nami, E. 2006. "Achieving Reunification Through Economic Parity." Paper presented at PRIO Cyprus Center's second annual conference, November 22, Nicosia, Cyprus.

Nan, S. 2008. "Shifting from Coherent Towards Holistic Peace Processes." In *A Handbook of Conflict Analysis and Resolution.* Ed. D. Sandole et al., 383–395. London and New York: Routledge and Taylor and Francis.

National Planning Commission, Government of Nepal. 2003. *The Tenth Plan (PRSP) 2002–2007.* Kathmandu: Government of Nepal.

———. 2007. *Three-Year Interim Plan Approach Paper (2064/65–2066/67).* Kathmandu: Government of Nepal.

National Planning Commission, Government of Nepal, and UNDP. 2006. *Millennium Development Goals Needs Assessment for Nepal.* Kathmandu: National Planning Commission, Government of Nepal, and UNDP.

Nazzal, N., and L. Nazzal. 1997. *Historical Dictionary of Palestine.* Lanham, MD: Scarecrow.

Necatigil, Z. 1997. "Judgment of the European Court of Human Rights in the Loizidou Case: A Critical Examination." *Journal for Cypriot Studies* 3: 147–171.

Nefissa, S. B. 2007. "The Reactivation of Arab Civil Society and the Demand for Democracy." In *The State of Resistance: Popular Struggles in the Global South.* Ed. F. Polet, 67–71. London: Zed Books.

Nepal South Asia Center (NESAC). 2002. *Review of Poverty Alleviation Initiatives in Nepal.* Report submitted to UNOP Malaysia.

Nesiah, V. 2002. "Politics of Peace Talks: Framework of Conflict Resolution." *Daily Mirror,* November 26.

Neubert, D. 2001. "Die Globalisierung eines Organisationsmodells: Nicht-Regierungs-organisationen in Afrika." In *Interkulturelle Beziehungen und Kulturwandel in Afrika.* Ed. U. Bauer, H. Egbert, and F. Jäger, 51–69. Frankfurt A. M.: Peter Lang.

Northern Ireland Council for Voluntary Action (NICVA). 2004. *Telling the Story of Peace II: An Assessment of the Impact of PEACE II Funding in Strabane, East Belfast, and Cavan.* Belfast: NICVA.

———. 2005. *State of the Sector Report IV.* Belfast: NICVA.

———. 2006. *Policy Manifesto.* Belfast: NICVA.

Norton, A. R. 1995. Civil Society in the Middle East. Leiden, New York, and London: E. J. Brill.

NOVIB (Nederlandse Organisatie Voor Internationale Bijstand). 2002. *Donor Assistance Toward Somalia and Somaliland: Development Policy and Coherence.* Nairobi: NOVIB Somalia. Available at www.somalicivilsociety.org/templates/oxfamtemp/downloads/Donor%20Study%20Report%20SP.pdf.

———. 2003a. *Mapping Somali Civil Society.* Nairobi: NOVIB Somalia. Available at www.somalicivilsociety.org/index.php?option=com_content&task=view&id=19&Itemid=49.

———. 2003b. *Strengthening Somali Civil Society Organizations, Symposium Report.* Nairobi: NOVIB-Somalia. Available at www.somali-civilsociety.org/templates/oxfamtemp/downloads/conferencenew.pdf.

Nusseibeh, S. 2007. *Once upon a Country: A Palestinian Life.* New York: Farrar, Straus and Giroux.

Obi, C. 2004. *The Oil Paradox: Reflections on the Violent Dynamics of Petro-Politics and (Mis) Governance in Nigeria's Niger Delta.* Occasional Paper no. 73. Pretoria: Africa Institute.

———. 2005. "Oil and Federalism in Nigeria." In *Nigerian Federalism in Crisis: Critical Perspectives and Political Options.* Ed. E. Onwudiwe and R. Suberu. Ibadan: Program on Ethnic and Federal Studies (PEFS), Department of Political Science, University of Ibadan.

———. 2007. "The Struggle for Resource Control in a Petro-State: A Perspective from Nigeria." In *National Perspectives on Globalisation.* Ed. P. Bowles et al. Hampshire, UK, and New York: Palgrave Macmillan.

———. 2008. "International Election Observer Missions and the Promotion of Democracy: Some Lessons from Nigeria's 2007 Elections." *Politikon* 35(1): 69–86.

Öcalan, A. 1999. "Statement by Abdullah Öcalan on His Abduction from Kenya on November 26, 1999." Available at www.hartford-hwp.com/archives/51/162.html (accessed February 13, 2008).

OECD-DAC. 2005. *Paris Declaration on Aid Effectiveness.* Paris High Level Forum on Joint Progress Toward Enhanced Aid Effectiveness, February 28–March 2. Paris. Available at www.oecd.org/dataoecd/11/41/34428351.pdf.

Office of the Prime Minister and Deputy Prime Minister, United Kingdom. 2005. *A Shared Future: Policy and Strategic Framework for Good Relations in Northern Ireland.* March. Available at www.asharedfutureni.gov.uk/gprs.pdf.

Ohanyan, A., and J. Lewis. 2005. "Politics of Peacebuilding: Critical Evaluation of Interethnic Contact and Peace Education in Georgia-Abkhaz Peace Camp, 1998–2002." *Peace and Change* 30(1): 57–84.

Okonta, I. 2006. *Behind the Mask: Explaining the Emergence of the MEND Militia in Nigeria's Oil-Bearing Niger Delta.* Niger Delta Economies of Violence Working Paper no. 11. Institute of International Studies, University of California–Berkeley; United States Institute of Peace, Washington DC; and Our Niger Delta, Port Harcourt, Nigeria.

———. 2007. *Niger Delta: Behind the Mark. Ijaw Militia Fight the Oil Carte.* World War 4 Report. Available at http://ww4report.com.

———. 2008. *When Citizens Revolt: Nigerian Elites, Big Oil, and the Ogoni Struggle for Self-Determination.* Trenton, NJ, and Asmara: Africa World.

Olesen, A. 1995. *Islam and Politics in Afghanistan.* Richmond, UK: Curzon.

Oliver, Q. 1998. *Working for Yes: The Story of the May 1998 Referendum in Northern Ireland.* Belfast: The "Yes" Campaign.

O'Malley, B., and I. Craig. 1999. *The Cyprus Conspiracy: America, Espionage, and the Turkish Invasion.* London and New York: I. B. Tauris.

Omeje, K. 2005. "Oil Conflict in Nigeria: Contending Issues and Perspectives of the Local Niger Delta People." *New Political Economy* 10: 3.

Organization for Security and Cooperation in Europe (OSCE). 1999. *Welcome to the Evolution: Observations on the Development of Bosnian Human Rights Organisations.* December. Sarajevo: OSCE.

Orjuela, C. 2003. "Building Peace in Sri Lanka: A Role for Civil Society." *Journal of Peace Research* 40: 195–212.

———. 2004. "Civil Society in Civil War, Peace Work, and Identity Politics in Sri Lanka." Ph.D. diss. Department of Peace and Development Research, University Göteborg, Sweden.

———. 2008a. *The Identity Politics of Peacebuilding: Civil Society in War-torn Sri Lanka.* New Delhi: Sage.

———. 2008b. "Reaping the Harvest of Peace? Politics of Reconstruction During Sri Lanka's 2002 Peace Process." *Critical Asian Studies* 40(2): 211–232.

Ottaway, M. 2003. "Rebuilding State Institutions in Collapsed States." In *State Failure, Collapse, and Reconstruction.* Ed. J. Milliken, 245–266. Oxford: Blackwell.

Owen, T. 2004. "Human Security—Conflict, Critique and Consensus: Colloquium Remarks and a Proposal for a Threshold-Based Definition." *Security Dialogue* 35 (3): 373–387.

Özbudun, E. 1981. "Turkey: The Politics of Political Clientelism." In *Political Clientelism, Patronage, and Development.* Ed. S. N. Eisenstadt and R. Lemarchand, 249–268. Beverly Hills, CA, and London: Sage.

Paffenholz, T. 1998. *Konflikttransformation durch Vermittlung. Theoretische und Praktische Erkenntnisse aus dem Friedensprozess in Mosambik (1995–1996).* Main: Grunewald.

———. 2000. *Construire la Paix sur le Terrain.* Mode d'emploi, Groupe de Recherche et d'Information sur la Paix et la Sécurité (GRIP). Bruxelles.

———. 2001a. "Western Approaches to Mediation." In *Peacebuilding: A Field Guide.* Ed. L. Reychler and T. Paffenholz, 75–81. Boulder: Lynne Rienner Publishers.

———. 2001b. "Designing Intervention Processes: Conditions and Parameters for Conflict Transformation." In *Berghof Handbook for Conflict Transformation.* Ed. F. Ropers, 151–169. Berlin: Berghof Research Center for Constructive Conflict Management.

———. 2001c. "13 Factors of Successful Mediation in Mozambique." In *Peacebuilding: A Field Guide.* Ed. L. Reychler and T. Paffenholz, 121–127. Boulder: Lynne Rienner Publishers.

———. 2003. *Community-based Bottom-up Peacebuilding: The Development of the Life and Peace Institute's Approach to Peacebuilding and Lessons Learned from the Somalia Experience (1990–2000).* Uppsala: Life and Peace Institute.

———. 2005. "Peace and Conflict Sensitivity in International Cooperation: An Introductory Overview." *Internationale Politik und Gesellschaft* 4/2005: 63–82.

———. 2006a. "Civil Society Functions in Peacebuilding and Options for Coordination with Track 1 Conflict Management During Negotiations: Theoretical Considerations and a Short Analysis of Civil Society Involvement During Negotiations in Guatemala and Afghanistan." Presentation at the forty-seventh annual convention of the International Studies Association, San Diego.

———. 2006b. "Community Peacebuilding in Somalia—Comparative Advantage of NGO Peacebuilding—The Example of the Life and Peace Institute's Approach in Somalia (1990–2003)." In *Subcontracting Peace: NGOs and Peacebuilding in a Dangerous World.* Ed. O. Richmond et al., 173–182. Alderhot, UK: Ashgate.

———. 2006c. "Peacebuilding: A Task for Development Cooperation." *Journal für Entwicklungspolitik (JEP)* 22(3): 6–34.

Paffenholz, T., and L. Reychler. 2006. *Aid for Peace: A Guide to Planning and Evaluation for Conflict Zones.* Baden-Baden: Nomos.

Paffenholz, T., and C. Spurk. 2006. *Civil Society, Civic Engagement, and Peacebuilding.* Social development papers, Conflict Prevention and Reconstruction paper no. 36. Washington, DC: World Bank.

Paffenholz, T., M. Damgaard, and D. Parasain. 2004. *UNDP: Support for Peace and Development Initiatives in Nepal.* United Nations Development Programme unpublished review report.

Pahis, D., and E. Lyons. 2008. "Choosing and Evaluating Solutions to the Cyprus Conflict: Are They Emotional or Cognitive Judgments?" Paper presented at the International Society of Political Philosophy thirty-first annual meeting, Paris.

Paige, J. M. 1998. "Coffee and Power: Revolution and the Rise of Democracy in Central America." Cambridge and London: Harvard University Press.

Palestine-Israel Journal of Politics, Economics, and Culture. 2001. Special issue: *Education in Times of Conflict* 8(2). Available at www.pij.org/current.php?id=18.

Palestinian Center for Policy and Survey Research. 2003. Opinion Poll on Geneva Initiative. Available at www.pcpsr.org.

Panday, D. R. 2006. "Nepal's Social Movement Makes a Difference." *Nepal Monitor: The National Online Journal.* Available at http://www.nepalmonitor.com/2006/12/social_movement_civil_society.html.

———. 2008. *Nagarik Andolan ra Ganatantrik Chetana.* Kathmandu: Fineprint.

Papadakis, Y. 1998. "Greek Cypriot Narratives of History and Collective Identity: Nationalism as a Contested Process." *American Ethnologist* 25(2): 149–165.

Papic, Z. 2001. "The General Situation in B-H and International Support Strategies." In *International Support Policies to South-East European Countries: Lessons (Not) Learned in B-H.* Ed. Z. Papic, 15–37. Sarajevo: Muller.

Pappe, I. 2006. *The Ethnic Cleansing of Palestine.* Oxford: Oneworld Publications.

Parajuli, R. 2004. *Maoist Movement of Nepal: A Selected Bibliography.* Kathmandu: Martin Chautari.

Paris, E. 1961. *Genocide in Satellite Croatia, 1941–1945: A Record of Racial and Religious Persecutions and Massacres.* Chicago: American Institute for Balkan Affairs.

Paris, R. 1997. "Peacebuilding and the Limits of Liberal Internationalism." *International Security* 22(2): 54–89.

———. 2004. *At War's End: Building Peace After Civil Conflict.* Cambridge: Cambridge University Press.

Paris, R., and T. Sisk. 2008. "The Future of Postwar State-building: To Retreat, Reinvest, or Rethink?" In "Introduction," *The Dilemmas of Statebuilding: Confronting the Contradictions of Postwar Peace Operations.* Ed. R. Paris and T. Sisk. London and New York: Routledge.

PASYDY (All Cyprus Trade Union Forum) Website. 2008. Available at www.pasydy.org/forum.html.

Patrick, I. 2001. "East Timor Emerging from Conflicts: The Role of Local NGOs and International Assistance." *Disasters* 25(1): 48–66.

PDH (Produraduria de los Derechos Humanos). 2004. *Informe de Muerte Violenta de Niñez, Adolescentes y Juventud.* Guatemala. Available at www.pdh.org.gt/html/Informes/especiales/MN2003.pdf (accessed December 19, 2006).

———. 2006. *Características de las Muertes Violentas.* Guatemala. Available at www.pdh.org.gt/files/inf_especiales/Caracteristicas_de_las_muertes_violentas_PDH.pdf.

Peacock, S., and A. Beltrán. 2003. *Hidden Powers: Illegal Armed Groups in Post Conflict Guatemala and the Forces Behind Them.* Washington, DC: Washington Office on Latin America Special Report.

Pearce, J. 2005. *Security and Development: Between Structure and Agency.* Presentation at the EADI's (European Association of Development Research and Training) eleventh general conference, titled "Insecurity and Development—Regional Issues and Policies for an Interdependent World." September 21–24, International Congress Center, Bonn.

———. 2006. "Case Study of IDRC-Supported Research on Security Sector Reform in Guatemala" (manuscript). Final report. Bradford.

———. 2007. "Violence, Power and Participation: Building Citizenship in Contexts of Chronic Violence." Working Paper no. 274. Brighton: Institute of Development Studies, University of Sussex.

Pearson, B. L., and L. Robertson (Management Systems International). 2008. *Evaluation of Civil Society Programs in Bosnia Herzegovina, February 17–March 2, 2008.* Washington, DC: US Agency for International Development.

Pejanovic, M. 2002. *Through Bosnian Eyes: The Political Memoirs of a Bosnian Serb* Sarajevo: TDK.

Peled, Y., and D. Navot. 2005. "Ethnic Democracy Revisited: On the State of Democracy in the Jewish State." *Israel Studies Forum* 20(1): 3–27.

The "People's Voice" Initiative. 2002. Available at www.mifkad.org.il.

Perera, J. 2005. "NGOs on JVP's Firing Line Primarily Due to Support for Peace." Article distributed by e-mail. May 9.

Perry, V. 2003. *Reading, Writing, and Reconciliation: Educational Reform in Bosnia and Herzegovina.* Working Paper no. 18. September. Flensburg: European Center for Minority Issues.

Pew Research Center. 2008. *Global Economic Gloom—China and India Notable Exceptions.* Report by the Global Attitudes Project. Available at http://pewglobal.org/reports/pdf/260.pdf.

Pickering, P. M. 2007. *Peacebuilding in the Balkans: The View from the Ground Floor.* Ithaca and London: Cornell University Press.

Pinkney, R. 2003. *Democracy in the Third World.* Boulder: Lynne Rienner Publishers.

Platis, S. 2006. "Presentation of Economic Results from Both Sides of the Dividing Line." Paper presented at the PRIO Cyprus Center's second annual conference, November 22, Nicosia, Cyprus.

PNGOs (Palestinian NGO Network). 2000. *Palestinian NGO Network Conditions Cooperation with Israeli Organizations.* Announcement by the General Assembly of PNGO. Ramallah: PNGOs.

PNUD (Programa de Naciones Unidas para el Desarrollo). 2003. *Segundo Informe Sobre Desarrollo Humano en Centroamérica y Panamá.* San José: PNUD.

———. 2007. *Informe Estadístico de la Violencia en Guatemala.* Available at www.undp.org.gt/data/publicacion/Informe%20Estadístico%20de%20la%20Violencia%20en%20Guatemala%20final.pdf.

Pollack, A., ed. 1993. *A Citizens' Inquiry: The Opsahl Report on Northern Ireland.* Dublin: Lilliput.

Ponciano Castellanos, K. 1996. "El Rol de la Sociedad Civil en los Procesos de Paz de Guatemala y El Salvador. Procesos de Negociación Comparados." INCEP (Instituto Centroamericano de Estudios Politicos) Panorama Centroamericano. Temas y Documentos de Debate no. 64, julio-agosto, Guatemala.

Posner, D. N. 2004. "Civil Society and the Reconstruction of Failed States." In *When States Fail: Causes and Consequences.* Ed. R. I. Rotberg, 237–255. Princeton: Princeton University Press.

Pouligny, B. 2005. "Civil Society and Post-Conflict Peacebuilding: Ambiguities of International Programmes Aimed at Building 'New' Societies." *Security Dialogue* 36(4): 495–510.

"Promotion de la Paix et Coopération Internationale: Histoire, Concepts, et Pratique, 2006." In *Annuaire Suisse de Politique de Développement* 25(2): 19–47. Berlin: Berghof Research Center for Constructive Conflict Management.

Pugh, M. 2004. "Peacekeeping and Critical Theory." *International Peacekeeping* 11(1): 39–58.

Pusic, E. 1975. "Intentions and Realities: Local Government in Yugoslavia." *Public Administration* 53(2): 133–152.

Putnam, R. 1993. *Making Democracy Work: Civic Traditions in Modern Italy.* Princeton: Princeton University Press.

———. 2000. *Bowling Alone: The Collapse and Revival of American Community.* New York: Simon and Schuster.

———. 2002. *Democracies in Flux: The Evolution of Social Capital in Contemporary Society.* Oxford, UK: Oxford University Press.

Qasem, R. 2008. "Against Normalization." *Alayyam Newpaper* (Ramallah), July 13.

Radikal. 2005. "Orhan Dogan: Ocalan Bir Gun Serbest Kalacak." August 15, p. 6.

———. 2007. Kerkük'e karşı Diyarbakir'a karışırız. Available at www.radikal.com.tr/haber.php?haberno=217846 (accessed April 24, 2008).

———. 2008. *Kürt Sorunu Dizisi.* March 3–7. Available at www.radikal.com.tr.

Rashid, A. 1998. "Pakistan and the Taliban." In *Fundamentalism Reborn? Afghanistan and the Taliban.* Ed. W. Malley, 72–89. New York: New York University Press.

Ray, J. 1998. "Does Democracy Cause Peace?" *Annual Review of Political Science* 1: 27–46.

Refugee Policy Group. 1994. *Lives Lost, Lives Saved: Excess Mortality and the Impact of Health Interventions in the Somalia Emergency.* Washington, DC: Refugee Policy Group.

REMHI (Recuperación de la Memoria Histórica), Oficina de Derechos Humanos del Arzobispado de Guatemala, ed. 1998. *Guatemala—Nunca Más.* Guatemala: FeG Editores.

Republic of Cyprus, Department of Antiquities. 2008. "The Looting of Cultural Heritage in Occupied Cyprus. Available at www.mcw.gov.cy/mcw/da/da.nsf/DMLlooting_en/DMLlooting_en?OpenDocument.

Research and Documentation Center. 2007. *Human Losses in Bosnia and Herzegovina 91–95.* Sarajevo: Research and Documentation Center. Available at www.idc.org.ba.

Richmond, O. 2001. "Rethinking Conflict Resolution: The Linkage Problematic Between 'Track I' and 'Track II.'" *Journal of Conflict Studies* 21(2): 109–132.

———. 2002. *Maintaining Order—Making Peace.* London: Palgrave Macmillan.

———. 2005. *The Transformation of Peace.* London: Palgrave Macmillan.

———. 2008. "Reclaiming Peace in International Relations." *Millennium: Journal of International Studies* 36(3): 439–470.

Richmond, O., and H. Carey. 2006. *Subcontracting Peace: NGOs and Peacebuilding in a Dangerous World.* Aldershot, UK: Ashgate.

Risse, T., and U. Lehmkuhl. 2006. *Governance in Areas of Limited Statehood—New Modes of Governance?* SFB-Governance working paper series, no. 1. DFG Research Center (SFB).

Ropers, N., and T. Debiel. 1995. *Friedliche Konfliktbearbeitung in der Staaten—Und Gesellschaftswelt.* Bonn: Dietz Verlag.

Rosen, Y. 2006. "Does Peace Education in the Regions of Intractable Conflict Change Core Beliefs of Youth?" Paper presented at the International Conference on Education for Peace and Democracy, November 19–23, Antalya, Turkey.

Ross, B. 2007. "News Exclusive: Online Interview with a Terrorist." *ABC News,* January 3. Available at http://abcnews.co.com.

Rotberg, R. I. 2004. "The Failure and Collapse of Nation-States. Breakdown, Prevention, and Repair." In *When States Fail: Causes and Consequences.* Ed. R. Rotberg. Princeton: Princeton University Press.

Rouhana, N. 1997. "Power Asymmetry and Goals of Unofficial Third Party Intervention in Protracted Social Conflict: Peace and Conflict." *Journal of Peace Psychology* 3: 1–17.

———. 2008. "Reconciling History and Equal Citizenship in Israel: Democracy and the Politics of Historical Denial." In *The Politics of Reconciliation in Multicultural Societies.* Ed. W. Kymlicka and B. Bashir, 70–93. Oxford: Oxford University Press.

Roy, O. 1986. *Islam and Resistance in Afghanistan.* Cambridge, UK: Cambridge University Press.

———. 1994. *Afghanistan: From Holy War to Civil War.* Princeton: Darwin.

———. 2004. "Development and Political Legitimacy: The Cases of Iraq and Afghanistan." *Conflict, Security, and Development* 4(2): 167–179.

Rüb, F. 2000. "Von der Zivilen zur Unzivilen Gesellschaft: Das Beispiel des Ehemaligen Jugoslawien." In *Systemwechsel 5. Zivilgesellschaft una Demokratische Transformation.* Ed. W. Merkel, 173–201. Opladen: Leske Budrich.

Rubin, B. 1995. *The Search for Peace in Afghanistan: From Buffer State to Failed State.* New Haven: Yale University Press.

———. 2007. "Saving Afghanistan." *Foreign Affairs* 86(1): 57–78.

Ruffin, H., and D. Waugh, eds. 1999. *Civil Society in Central Asia.* Baltimore: Johns Hopkins University Press.

Rummel, R. 1979. "Understanding Conflict and War." In *War, Power, and Peace.* Vol. 4. Beverly Hills, CA: Sage.

———. 1997. *Power Kills: Democracy as a Method of Nonviolence.* New Brunswick, NJ: Transaction.

Rupesinghe, K. 1995. *Conflict Transformation.* London: St. Martin's.

Rupesinghe, K., ed. 2006. *Negotiating Peace in Sri Lanka: Efforts, Failures, and Lessons.* Vol. 2. Colombo: Foundation for Co-existence.

Russett, B., and H. Starr. 2000. "From Democratic Peace to Kantian Peace: Democracy and Conflict in the International System." In *Handbook of War Studies.* Ed. M. Mildarsky, 93–128. Ann Arbor: University of Michigan Press.

Rynhold, J. 2005. "Religion, Postmodernization, and Israeli Approaches to the Palestinians." *Terrorism and Political Violence* 17: 371–390.

Sabah. 2006. "Plan Adım Adım." Available at http://arsiv.sabah.com.tr/2006/09/29/gnd133.html (accessed February 13, 2008).

Sáenz de Tejada, R. 2004. *¿Victimas o Vencedores? Una Aproximación al Movimiento de los Ex PAC.* Guatemala: FLACSO Guatemala.

Saferworld. 2008. "What We Do in Somalia." Available at www.saferworld.org.uk/pages/somalia_page.html.

Saikal, A. 2005. *Modern Afghanistan: A History of Struggle and Survival.* London: I. B. Tauris.

Salamon, L. M., and H. K. Anheier. 1997. "The Third World's Third Sector in Comparative Perspective." Working papers of the Johns Hopkins Comparative Nonprofit Sector Project No. 24. Baltimore.

Salamon, L. M., et al. 1999. *Global Civil Society: Dimensions of the Nonprofit Sector.* Baltimore: Johns Hopkins Center for Civil Society Studies.

Salem, W., and E. Kaufman. 2006. "Palestinian-Israeli Peacebuilding: A Historical Perspective." In *Bridging the Divide: Peacebuilding in the Israeli-Palestinian Conflict.* Ed. E. Kaufman, W. Salem, and J. Verhoeven. Boulder: Lynne Rienner Publishers.

Sali-Terzic, S. 2001. "Civil Society." In *International Support Policies to South-East European Countries: Lessons (Not) Learned in B-H.* Ed. Z. Papic, 138–159. Sarajevo: Muller.

Sallon, H. 2009. "Lawyering for the Cause of the Arab Minority in Israel: Litigation as Means for Collective Action." In *Civil Organizations and Protest Movements in Israel: Mobilizations Around the Israeli-Palestinian Conflict.* Ed. E. Marteu, 195–213. London: Palgrave Macmillan.

Samatar, A. I. 1988. *Socialist Somalia: Rhetoric or Reality.* London: Zed Books.

———. 1994. "The Curse of Allah: Civic Disembowelment and the Collapse of the State in Somalia." In *The Somali Challenge: From Catastrophe to Renewal?* Ed. A. I. Samatar, 95–146. Boulder: Lynne Rienner Publishers.

Sandole, D., S. Byrne, I. Sandole-Staroste, and J. Senehi, eds. 2008. *A Handbook of Conflict Analysis and Resolution.* London and New York: Routledge and Taylor and Francis.

Saro-Wiwa, K. 1995. *A Month and a Day: A Detention Diary.* London: Penguin.

Savija-Valha, N. (Program Development Manager, Nansen Dialogue Center, Sarajevo). 2004. Interview by B. Hemmer. April 19. Sarajevo.

Schade, J. 2002. "Zivilgesellschaft." *Eine Vielschichtige Debatte.* Report no. 59. Duisburg: INEF (Institute for Development and Peace).

Scham, P. 2000. "Arab-Israeli Research Cooperation, 1995–1999." *Middle East Review of International Affairs Journal* (*MERIA*) 4(3) (September): 1–16.

Schirmer, J. 1998. *The Guatemalan Military Project: A Violence Called Democracy.* Philadelphia: University of Pennsylvania Press.

———. 2002. "The Guatemalan Politico-Military Project: Whose Ship of State?" In *Political Armies: The Military and Nation Building in the Age of Democracy.* Ed. K. Koonings and D. Kruijt, 64–89. London and New York: Zed Books.

Schlesinger, S., and S. Kinzer. 1985. *Bananen-Krieg. Das Exempel Guatemala.* München: DvT Deutscher Taschenbuch.

Schmeidl, S. 2007. "Civil Society and State-Building in Afghanistan." In *Building State and Security in Afghanistan.* Ed. W. F. Danspeckgruber and R. Finn, 104–129. Princeton: Princeton University, Woodrow Wilson School of Public and International Affairs and the Liechtenstein Institute on Self-Determination Study Series.

Schmid, H. 1968. "Peace Research and Politics." *Journal of Peace Research* 5(3): 217–232.

Schmidt, S. 2000. "Die Rolle von Zivilgesellschaften in Afrikanischen Systemwechseln." In *Systemwechsel 5. Zivilgesellschaft und Transformation.* Ed. W. Merkel, 295–334. Opladen: Leske and Budrich.

Segovia, A. 2004. *Modernización Empresarial en Guatemaia: ¿Cambio Real o Nuevo Discurso?* Guatemala: FeG Editores.

Shah, S. 2002. "From Evil State to Civil Society." In *State of Nepal.* Ed. K. M. Dixit and S. Ramachandran, 137–160. Kathmandu: Himal Books.

Shahrani, M. N. 1984. "Introduction: Marxist 'Revolution' and Islamic Resistance in Afghanistan." In *Revolutions and Rebellions in Afghanistan.* Ed. M. N. Shahrani and R. L. Canfield, 3–57. Berkeley: University of California Press.

———. 1998. "The Future of the State and the Structure of Community." In *Fundamentalism Reborn? Afghanistan and the Taliban.* Ed. W. Malley. New York: New York University Press.

Shankland, D. 1999. *The Emergence of the Alevis: Islam and Society in Turkey.* Cambridgeshire, UK: Eothen.

Shanmugaratnam, N., and K. Stokke. 2006. "Development as a Precursor to Conflict Resolution: A Critical Review of the Fifth Peace Process in Sri Lanka." In *Between War and Peace: Deprivation and Livelihood Revival in Sudan and Sri Lanka.* Ed. N. Shanmugaratnam. Oxford: James Currey.

Sharma, H. 2004. "District Leadership and Governance: A Case of Rupandehi District Development Committee." In *Nepal: Local Leadership and Governance.* Ed. L. R. Baral et al., 148–178. Delhi: Adroit.

Sharma, K. K. 2008. "Wake-Up Call." *Kathmandu Post,* October 24.

Sharma, S. 2004. "The Maoist Movement: An Evolutionary Perspective." In *Himalayan "People's War."* Ed. M. Hutt, 38–57. London: Hurst.

Shikaki, K. 2004. *A Palestinian Perspective on the Failure of the Permanent Status Negotiations.* Palestinian Center for Policy and Survey Research. Available at www.pcpsr.org/strategic/strategicindex.html.

Shipler, D. 1986. *Arab and Jew: Wounded Spirits in a Promised Land.* New York: Times Books.

Shirlow, P., and K. McEvoy. 2008. *Beyond the Wire: Former Prisoners and Conflict Transformation in Northern Ireland.* London: Pluto.

Shirlow, Peter, et al. 2005. *Politically Motivated Former Prisoner Groups: Community Activism and Conflict Transformation.* A research report submitted to the Northern Ireland Community Relations Council, Belfast.

Shrestha, A., ed. 1998. *The Role of Civil Society and Democratization in Nepal.* Kathmandu: Nepal Foundation for Advanced Studies and Friedrich Ebert Stiftung.

Shrestha, A. P., and H. Uprety, eds. 2003. *Conflict Resolution and Governance in Nepal.* Kathmandu: Nepal Foundation for Advanced Studies, in cooperation with Friedrich Ebert Stiftung.

Sieder, R., ed. 1998. *Guatemala After the Peace Accords.* London: Institute of Latin American Studies.

Sikkink, K. 2005. "Patterns of Dynamic Multilevel Governance and the Insider-Outsider Coalition." In *Transnational Protest and Global Activism.* Ed. D. della Porta and S. Tarrow. Lanham, MD: Rowman and Littlefield.

Singer, P. W. 2001. "Caution: Children at War." *Parameters* 36 (Winter): 40–56.

Skocpol, T., M. Ganz, and Z. Munson. 2000. "A Nation of Organizers: The Institutional Origins of Civic Voluntarism in the United States." *American Political Science Review* 94(3): 527–546.

Skuse, A. 2002. "Radio, Politics, and Trust in Afghanistan: A Social History of Broadcasting." *International Communication Gazette* 64(3): 267–279.

Small, M., and J. Singer. 1976. "The War Proneness of Democratic Regimes, 1816–1965." *Jerusalem Journal of International Relations* 1 (Summer): 50–69.

Smith, A. 1904. *An Inquiry into the Nature and Causes of the Wealth of Nations.* Ed. E. Cannan. London: Methuen.

Smith, C. A., ed. 1990. *Guatemalan Indians and the State 1540 to 1988.* Austin: University of Texas Press.

Smith, D. 2003. *Towards a Strategic Framework for Peacebuilding: The Synthesis Report of the Joint Utstein Study on Peacebuilding.* Oslo: Peace Research Institute Oslo.

Solórzano Martínez, M. 2001. "Participación y Democracia en Guatemala." In *Pasos Hacia una Nueva Convivencia: Democracia y Participación en Centroamérica.* Ed. R. C. Macías, G. Maihold, and S. Kurtenbach, 1–55. San Salvador: FUNDAUNGO (Fundacion Dr. Guillermo Manuel Ungo).

Somali Institute of Management and Administration Development (SIMAD). 2006. *Somali Institute of Management and Administration Development: Institutional Profile.* Mogadishu: SIMAD.

SORAR (S Osyal Sorunları Araştırma ve Çözüm Derneği). 2008. SORAR 2007 PKK Workshop (Çalıştay) Raporu-PKK. Available at http://www.sorar.org.tr/Raporlar/PKK_20071130.aspx (accessed February 13, 2008).

Sosyalizm ve Toplumsal Mücadeleler Ansiklopedisi [Encylopedia of Socialism and Social Struggles]. 1988. Vol. 7. Istanbul: Iletisim Yayınları.

Spencer, J., ed. 1990. *Sri Lanka: History and the Roots of Conflict.* London and New York: Routledge.

Sprinzak, E. 1991. *The Ascendance of Israel's Radical Right.* New York: Oxford University Press.

Spurk, C. 2002. *Media and Peacebuilding: Concepts, Actors, and Challenges.* KOFF working paper no. 1/2002. Berne: Swisspeace.

———. 2007. "Media and Civil Society: Clarifying Roles and Relations." Paper presented at the forty-eighth annual convention of the International Studies Association, February 28–March 3, Chicago.

Stakeholder Democracy Network (SDN). 2007. *Further Rigging: Nigerian General Elections, 14 and 21 April, 2007.* Available at www.stakeholderdemocracy.org/index.php?mact=News,cntnt01,detail,0&cntnt01articleid=11&cntnt01origid=65&cntnt01returnid=114 (accessed March 12, 2008).

Stanley, W., and D. Holiday. 2002. "Broad Participation, Diffuse Responsibility: Peace Implementation in Guatemala." In *Ending Civil Wars: The Implementation of Peace Agreements.* Ed. S. J. Stedman, D. Rothchild, and E. M. Cousens, 421–462. Boulder: Lynne Rienner Publishers.

Stavrinides, Z. 2005. "A Long Journey to Peace: The Dispute in the Republic of Cyprus." *Harvard International Review* 27(2): 84–85.

Stedman, S. 1993. "The End of the Zimbabwean Civil War." In *Stopping the Killing: How Civil Wars End.* Ed. R. Licklider, 125–163. New York: Oxford University Press.

———. 1997. "Spoiler Problems in Peace Processes." *International Security* 22(2): 5–53.

Stedman, S. J., D. Rothchild, and E. M. Cousens, eds. 2002. *Ending Civil Wars: The Implementation of Peace Agreements.* Boulder: Lynne Rienner Publishers.

Sterland, B. 2003. *Serving the Community: An Assessment of Civil Society in Rural BiH.* Sarajevo: Daedalus Association for Peace Education Work.

———. 2006. *Civil Society Capacity Building in Post-Conflict Societies: The Experience of Bosnia and Herzegovina and Kosovo.* INTRAC (International NGO Training and Research Centre) Praxis Paper no. 9 (June). Available at www.intrac.org.

Stewart, S. 1997. "Happy Ever After in the Marketplace: Non-Governmental Organizations and Uncivil Society." *Review of African Political Economy* 24(71): 11–34.

Stiefel, M. 2001. "Participatory Action Research as a Tool for Peacebuilding: The WSP Experience." In *Peacebuilding: A Field Guide.* Ed. L. Reychler and T. Paffenholz, 265–276. Boulder: Lynne Rienner Publishers.

Strand, A. 1998. *Bridging the Gap Between Islamic and Western NGOs Working in Conflict Areas.* York, UK: Post-War Reconstruction and Development Unit, University of York.

Strand, Arne, A. W. Najami, and N. Lander. 1999. *NGO Coordination in Afghanistan: An Evaluation Report.* Peshawar/Bergen: Chr. Michelsen Institute.

Strand, Arne, Hege Toje, Alf Jerve, and Ingrid Samset. 2003. "Community Driven Development in Contexts of Conflict." Concept Paper, World Bank. Bergen: Chr. Michelsen Institute.

Stubbs, P. 2000. "Partnership or Colonisation? The Relationship Between International Agencies and Local Non-Governmental Organisations in Bosnia-Herzegovina." Occasional Paper no. 7/2000. In *Civil Society, NGOs, and Global Governance.* Ed. B. Deacon, 23–31. Sheffield, UK: GASSP (Globalism and Social Policy Programme).

Subasic, A., and A. Bulja. 2008. "Bosnia: Unfettered Lives of Crime." *Transitions on Line.* April 4. Available at www.tol.cz.

Suhrke, A. 2007a. "Reconstruction as Modernisation: The 'Post-Conflict' Project in Afghanistan." *Third World Quarterly* 28(7): 1291–1308.

———. 2007b. *The Democratisation of a Dependent State: The Case of Afghanistan.* Madrid: Fundación para las Relaciones Internacionales y el Diálogo Exterior.

Suhrke, A., K. B. Harpviken, and A. Strand. 2004. *Conflictual Peacebuilding: Afghanistan Two Years After Bonn.* Bergen: CMI, and Oslo: PRIO.

Suleman, M., and S. Williams. 2003. *Strategies in Preventing Conflict and Resisting Pressure: A Study of Jaghori District, Afghanistan, Under Taliban Control.* Cambridge, MA: CDA (Collaborative for Development Action).

Sutton, M. 2007. "An Index of Deaths from the Conflict in Ireland (Revised and Updated)." CAIN (Conflict Archive on the Internet) Web Service. Available at http://cain.ulst.ac.uk/sutton/crosstabs.html.

Swedish International Development Cooperation Agency (SIDA). 2005. *SIDA's Policy for Civil Society: The Objective of SIDA's Cooperation with Civil Society.* Available at www.sida.se.

Ta'Ayush. 2008. Arab-Jewish Partnership Website Portal. Available at www.taayush.org.

Tadjbaksh, S., and M. Schöiswohl. 2008. "Playing with Fire? The International Community's Democratization Experiment in Afghanistan." *International Peacekeeping* 15(2): 252–267.

Tamang, S. 2000. "Legalizing State Patriarchy in Nepal." *Studies in Nepali History and Society* 5(1): 127–156.

———. 2002. "Civilizing Civil Society: Donors and Democratic Space." *Studies in Nepali History and Society* 7(2): 309–353.

Tamilnet. 2002. "STF Fire on Demonstration—5 Killed, 15 Wounded." October 9. Available at www.tamilnet.com/.

Tami Steinmetz Center for Peace Research, Tel Aviv University. 2008. Website available at www.tau.ac.il/peace.

Tamimi, A. 2007. *Hamas: A History from Within.* Northampton, MA: Olive Branch.

Tamm, G., et al. 2004. *Life and Peace Institute's Projects in Somalia and the DRC.* SIDA Evaluation 04/36. Stockholm: SIDA. Available at www.sida.org.

Taraki, L. 1997. "Palestinian Society: Contemporary Realities and Trends." In "Palestinian Women: A Status Report." Presented at the Women's Studies Program. Birzeit: Birzeit University.

Tate, N. C., and T. Vallinder. 1995. *The Global Expansion of Judicial Power: The Judicialization of Politics.* New York: New York University Press.

Tawil, S., and A. Harley. 2004. *Education, Conflict, and Social Cohesion.* Studies in Comparative Education. Paris: UNESCO.

Thapa, D., ed. 2003. *Understanding the Maoist Movement of Nepal.* Kathmandu: Martin Chautari.

Thapa, D., with B. Sijapati. 2003. *A Kingdom Under Siege: Nepal's Maoist Insurgency, 1996 to 2003.* Kathmandu: Printhouse.

Thier, A. J., and A. Ranjbar. 2008. *Killing Friends, Making Enemies: The Impact and Avoidance of Civilian Casualties in Afghanistan.* USIP Briefing. Washington, DC: United States Institute for Peace.

Thomas, R. G. C. 2003. "What Is Third World Security?" *Annual Review of Political Science* 6: 205–232.

Tilly, C. 1975. "Reflections on the History of European State-Making." In *The Formation of National States in Western Europe.* Ed. C. Tilly, 3–83. Cambridge: Harvard University Press.

———. 1985. "War Making and State Making as Organized Crime." In *Bringing the State Back In.* Ed. P. B. Evans, D. Rueschemeyer, and T. Skocpol, 169–191. Cambridge, UK: Cambridge University Press.

———. 1990. *Coercion, Capital, and European States, AD 990–1990.* Oxford, UK: Basil Blackwell.

Tocci, N. 2002. "Cyprus and the European Union Accession Process: Inspiration for Peace or Incentive for Crisis?" *Turkish Studies* 3(2): 104–138.

———. 2004. "EU Intervention in Ethno-political Conflicts: The Case of Cyprus and Serbia-Montenegro." *European Foreign Affairs Review* 9: 551–573.

Tribal Liaison Office (TLO). 2007. *Report on the Jirga for Peace, Security, and Reconciliation.* Kabul: TLO.

Trouval, S., and W. Zartman. 1985. *International Mediation in Theory and Practice.* Boulder: Westview.

Tschirgi, N. 2004. *Post-Conflict Peacebuilding Revisited: Achievements, Limitations, Challenges.* Report prepared for the WSP International/IPA Peacebuilding Forum Conference, October. New York: International Peace Academy.

Turkish Cypriot Civil Society Organizations Directory. 2007. Nicosia and Limassol: The Management Centre and Intercollege.

Turkish Cypriot Human Rights Foundation. 2009. Website available at www.ktihv.org.

Turkish Republic Northern Cyprus Presidency. 2008. Website available at www.kktcb.eu/index.php.

Türkiye'de Vicdani Retlerini Açıklayanlar. 2008. Website available at www.savaskarsitlari.org/arsiv.asp?ArsivTipID=2.

UCA (Universidad Centroamericano) et al. eds. 2001–2004. *Maras y Pandillas en Centroamérica.* Vols. 1–3. Managua: UCA Publicaciones.

Ukeje, C. 2001. "Oil Communities and Political Violence: The Case of Ethnic Ijaws in Nigeria's Niger Delta." *Terrorism and Violence* 13(4): 15–36.

Ukiwo, U. 2003. *The Executive Report of the Food Security Assessment.* New York: United Nations.

———. 2005. *World Summit Outcome 2005.* New York: United Nations.

———. 2007. "From 'Pirates' to Militants: A Historical Perspective on Anti-State and Anti–Oil Company Mobilization Among the Ijaw of Warri, Western Niger Delta." *African Affairs* 106: 425, 587–610.

United Nations. 1995. Supplement to "An Agenda for Peace." [Position paper of the Secretary-General on the occasion of the fiftieth anniversary of the United Nations.] New York: United Nations.

UNDP/UNOPS (United Nations Development Programme/United Nations Office for Project Services) Bi-communal Development Program. 2005. *Cypress Tree Project—An Initiative for the Rehabilitation of Cemeteries.* Available at http://mirror.undp.org/cyprus/projects/project_details.asp?ProjectID=44.

United Nations Assistance Mission to Afghanistan (UNAMA). 2007. "Calls for Increased Efforts to Protect Civilians." Press release, August 13. Available at http://unama.unmissions.org/default.aspx?/news/_pr/2007/UN/07aug13-UNAMA-PRESS-RELEASE.pdf (accessed March 4, 2008).

United Nations Development Program (UNDP). Website (Bosnia and Herzegovina) available at www.undp.ba.
United Nations High Commissioner for Refugees (UNHCR). 2003. *UNHCR's Concerns with the Designation of Bosnia as a Safe Country of Origin.* Sarajevo: UNHCR.
United Nations Organization on Drugs and Crime (UNODC). 2007. *Crime and Development in Central America. Caught in the Crossfire.* New York: United Nations. Available at www.unodc.org/pdf/Central%20America%20Study.pdf.
United Nations Peacekeeping Force in Cyprus (UNFYCIP). 2008. Website available at www.unficyp.org.
United Nations Secretary-General (Boutros Boutros-Ghali). 1992. *An Agenda for Peace: Preventive Diplomacy, Peacemaking, and Peace-keeping.* New York: United Nations.
United Nations Secretary-General (Kofi Annan). 2001. *Prevention of Armed Conflict: Report of the Secretary General.* New York: United Nations.
———. 2003. "UN System and Civil Society—An Inventory and Analysis of Practices." Background paper for the Secretary-General's Panel of Eminent Persons on United Nations Relations with Civil Society. New York: United Nations.
———. 2005. *In Larger Freedom: Towards Development, Security, and Human Rights for All.* New York: United Nations.
United Nations Verification Mission in Guatemala. 2000. *Bosnia and Herzegovina Human Development Report: Youth.* Sarajevo: UNDP.
———. 2003. *Youth in Bosnia and Herzegovina 2003: Are You Part of the Problem or Part of the Solution?* Sarajevo: UNDP.
———. 2005. *Report of the Secretary General.* A/59/746 18.3.2005. New York: United Nations.
———. 2006. *Human Development Report, 2006.* New York: UNDP.
———. 2006a. *Establishing an Integrated Citizen Security Policy in Guatemala (POLSEC).* End-of-project report. Available at http://pdf.usaid.gov/pdf_docs/PDACI866.pdf.
———. 2007a. *National Human Development Report: Social Inclusion in Bosnia and Herzegovina.* Sarajevo: UNDP.
———. 2007b. *Annual Report, Nepal.* Kathmandu: UNDP.
———. 2007c. *Reducing Socio-Economic Differences in Southeast Anatolia.* Available at www.undp.org.tr/Gozlem2.aspx?WebSayfaNo=31 (accessed July 9, 2008).
United Nations Special Committee on Palestine (UNSCOP). 1946/1947. *Report to the General Assembly (A/364).* Official Records of the Second Session of the General Assembly, Supplement no. 11.
United States Agency for International Development. 2005. "Increased Development of a Politically Active Civil Society." Available at www.usaid.gov/our_work/democracy_and_governance/technical_areas/civil_society.
United States Central Intelligence Agency. *World Factbook.* (2006.) Available online at https://www.cia.gov/library/publications/the-world-factbook/geos/cy.html.
United States Institute of Peace (USIP). 1998. *Bosnia to Form a Single Truth Commission.* Washington, DC: Peace Watch.
———. 2003. *Can Faith-Based NGOs Advance Interfaith Reconciliation? The Case of Bosnia-Herzegovina.* Special Report no. 103. Washington, DC: USIP.
Upsalla Conflict Data Program (UCDP). 2008. *Definitions.* Available at www.pcr.uu.se/research/UCDP/data_and_publications/definitions_all.htm.
USAID/BiH (United States Agency for International Development/Bosnia-Herzegovina). 2004. *Civil Society Assessment: Final Report.* Sarajevo: USAID/BiH.
Usher, G. 1995. *Palestine in Crisis: The Struggle for Peace and Political Independence After Oslo.* London: Pluto Press, in association with the Transnational Institute and Middle East Research and Information Project.

Uvin, P. 1998. *Aiding Violence: The Development Enterprise in Rwanda.* West Hartford, CT: Kumarian.
Uyangoda, J. 2001. "Sri Lanka's Left: From Class and Trade Unions to Civil Society and NGOs." In *Sri Lanka: Global Challenges and National Crises.* Ed. R. Philips, 187–215. Colombo: Social Scientists' Association and the Ecumenical Institute for Study and Dialogue.
———. 2008. "Transition from Civil War to Peace: Challenges for Peace-building in Sri Lanka." In *The Paradoxes of Peacebuilding Post-9/11.* Ed. S. Baranyi, 179–210. Vancouver: University of British Columbia Press.
van Bruinessen, M. 1992. *Agha, Sheikh, and the State.* London: Zed Books.
"Van Providence Action Plan for the IDPs Service Delivery." 2006. Available at www.undp.org.tr/demGovDocs/VanActionPlanEng10.10.2006.doc.
van Tongeren, P., M. Brenk, M. Hellema, and J. Verhoeven. 2005. *People Building Peace II: Successful Stories of Civil Society.* Boulder: Lynne Rienner Publishers.
Vandenberg, M. E. 2007. "Peacekeeping and Rule Breaking: United Nations Anti-Trafficking Policy in Bosnia and Herzegovina." In *Human Trafficking, Human Security, and the Balkans.* Ed. H. R. Friman and S. Reich, 81–95. Pittsburgh: University of Pittsburgh Press.
Varshney, A. 2002. *Ethnic Conflict and Civic Life: Hindus and Moslems in India.* New Haven: Yale University Press.
Vela, M., A. Sequén-Mónchez, and H. Antonio Solares. 2001. *El Lado Oscuro de la Eternal Primavera. Violencia, Criminalidad y Delincuencia en la Posguerra.* Guatemala: FLACSO Guatemala.
Volkan, V. D. 1979. *Cyprus—War and Adaptation: A Psychoanalytic History of Two Ethnic Groups in Conflict.* Charlottesville: University Press of Virginia.
Voltmer, K. 2006. "The Mass Media and the Dynamics of Political Communication in Processes of Democratization: An Introduction." In *Mass Media and Political Communication in New Democracies.* Ed. K. Voltmer, 1–20. London and New York: Routledge.
Waldman, M. 2008. *Falling Short.* ACBAR Advocacy Series. Kabul: Agency Coordinating Body for Afghan Relief (ACBAR).
Walter, B. 1997. "The Critical Barrier to Civil War Settlement." *International Organization* 51(3): 335–364.
Wanis-St. John, A., and D. Kew. 2006. "The Missing Link? Civil Society, Peace Negotiations: Contributions to Sustained Peace." Paper for the forty-seventh annual convention of the International Studies Association, San Diego.
War-torn Societies Project (WSP). 2001. *Rebuilding Somalia: Issues and Possibilities for Puntland.* London: HAAN Publishing.
Wardak, M., I. Zaman, and K. Nawabi. 2007. *The Role and Functions of Religious Civil Society in Afghanistan: Case Studies from Kunduz and Sayedabad.* Kabul: CPAU (Cooperation for Peace and Unity Afghanistan). Available at www.cpau.org.af.
Washington Office on Latin America (WOLA). 2000. *Rescuing Police Reform: A Challenge for the New Guatemalan Government.* Washington, DC: WOLA.
Webb, K., V. Koutrakou, and M. Walters. 1996. "The Yugoslavian Conflict, European Mediation, and the Contingency Model: A Critical Perspective." In *Resolving International Conflict: The Theory and Practice of Mediation.* Ed. J. Bercovitch, 171–189. Boulder: Lynne Rienner Publishers.
Weber, M. 1978 [1920]. *Economy and Society.* Ed. Guenther Roth, and Claus Wittich. Berkeley: University of California Press.
Weitz, R. 2007. "Afghan-Pakistani Differences Remain Despite Recent American Initiatives." *Central Asia–Caucasus Institute Analyst,* November 14.

Whaites, A. 1996. "Let's Get Civil Society Straight: NGOs and Political Theory." *Development in Practice* 6(3): 240–244.

Whitfield, T. 2008. *Masala Peacemaking: Nepal's Peace Process and the Contribution of Outsiders.* New York: Conflict Prevention and Peace Forum.

Wickramasinghe, N. 2001. *Civil Society in Sri Lanka: New Circles of Power.* New Delhi: Sage.

Wilford, R., ed. 2001. *Aspects of the Belfast Agreement.* Oxford, UK: Oxford University Press.

Williamson, A., D. Scott, and P. Halfpenny. 2000. "Rebuilding Civil Society in Northern Ireland: The Community and Voluntary Sector's Contribution to the European Union's Peace and Reconciliation Partnership Programme." *Policy and Politics* 28(1): 49–66.

Wilson, A. J. 2000. *Sri Lankan Tamil Nationalism: Its Origins and Developments in the 19th and 20th Centuries.* London: Hurst.

Wolleh, O. 2001. *Local Peace Constituencies in Cyprus: Citizens' Rapprochement by the Bi-communal Conflict Resolution Trainer Group.* Berlin: Berghof Research Center for Constructive Conflict Management.

World Bank. 2002. *Local Level Institutions and Social Capital Study.* Vol. 1 (June). Washington, DC: World Bank.

———. 2003a. *Enabling Environments for Civic Engagement in PRSP Countries.* Washington, DC: World Bank.

———. 2003b. *Nepal Country Assistance Strategy, 2004–2007.* Report No. 26509-NEP.

———. 2004. *Afghanistan—State Building, Sustaining Growth, and Reducing Poverty: A Country Economic Report.* Poverty Reduction and Economic Management Sector Unit. Washington, DC: World Bank.

———. 2005. *Engaging Civil Society Organizations on Conflict-Affected and Fragile States: Three African Country Case Studies.* Washington, DC: World Bank.

World Movement for Democracy. 2007. "Građansko Organizovanje za Demokratiju (Citizens' Organization for Democracy [GROZD]), Interview with Milan Mrdja, Program Manager." In *What's Being Done on . . . Effective Networking?* Available at www.wmd.org/wbdo/wbdoEffNet/cod.html.

Xenias, A. 2005. "Can a Global Peace Last Even If Achieved? Huntington and the Democratic Peace." *International Studies Review* 7(3): 357–386.

Yavuz, M. H., and N. A. Ozcan. 2006. "The Kurdish Question and Turkey's Justice and Development Party." *Middle East Policy* 13(1): 102–119.

Yeğen, M. 2007. "Turkish Nationalism and the Kurdish Question." *Ethnic and Racial Studies* 30(1): 119–151.

Yesilada, B., and A. Sözen. 2002. "Negotiating a Resolution to the Cyprus Problem: Is Potential European Union Membership a Blessing or a Curse?" *International Negotiation* 7(2): 261–285.

Yiftachel, O. 2006. *Ethnocracy: Land and Identity Politics in Israel/Palestine.* Philadelphia: University of Pennsylvania Press.

Zakhilwal, O., and J. M. Thomas. 2005. "Afghanistan: What Kind of Peace? The Role of Rural Development in Peace-Building." In *The Paradoxes of Peacebuilding Post-9/11.* Ed. S. Baranyi, 147–178. Vancouver: University of British Columbia Press.

Zartman, I. 1989. *Ripe for Resolution: Conflict and Intervention in Africa.* New York: Oxford University Press.

———. 2000. *Traditional Curses for Modern Conflicts: African Conflict "Medicine."* Boulder: Lynne Rienner Publishers.

Zepeda López, R., et al. 2004. *El Espacio Político en Que se Construye la Paz.* Colección Cultura de Paz No. 7. Guatemala: FLACSO Guatemala/UNESCO.

The Contributors

Roberto Belloni is associate professor of international relations at University of Trento, Italy. Previously he was research fellow at the Belfer Center for Science and International Affairs/Program on Intrastate Conflict and Conflict Resolution at Harvard University (2002–2004) and a lecturer at Queens University Belfast (2004–2008). He has published extensively on peacebuilding, democratization, and civil society, including the volume *State Building and International Intervention in Bosnia.*

Kaja Borchgrevink is a researcher at the International Peace Research Institute in Oslo, focusing on the Afghan peace process after 2001. From 2001 to 2006, Borchgrevink worked with civil society development in Afghanistan and Pakistan for the United Nations and the Aga Khan Foundation. Recent work includes studies of the role of religious actors in Afghan civil society, the Afghan justice sector and the relationship between modern and traditional law, and the transnational aspects of religious education in Afghanistan and Pakistan.

Ayşe Betül Çelik is assistant professor at Sabanci University in Istanbul, Turkey, where she teaches political science and conflict resolution. She is an expert on interethnic conflict resolution and dialogue.

Rhoderick Chalmers has been working for the International Crisis Group in Nepal since February 2004. He has produced reports on several aspects of Nepal's conflict and peace process, including Maoist strategy and internal politics, the various negotiations and peace agreements, and the 2008 constituent assembly elections.

Esra Çuhadar is assistant professor at the Department of Political Science at Bilkent University in Ankara, Turkey. Her research interests include international mediation with a special focus on Track 2 processes in the Israeli-Palestinian and Cyprus conflicts, evaluation of peacebuilding and conflict resolution programs, and political psychology of conflicts.

Kjell Erling Kjellman is a sociologist and senior researcher at the International Peace Research Institute in Oslo. He currently works on a variety of issues related to postwar reconstruction and peacebuilding, particularly those related to state–civil society interaction, landmines, and cluster munitions.

Ibrahim Farah is a Ph.D. candidate and part-time lecturer at the University of Nairobi's Institute of Diplomacy and International Studies. He has worked with various aid agencies for the past eighteen years on relief, rehabilitation, and development work in Somalia.

Sari Hanafi is associate professor of sociology at the American University of Beirut and editor of *Idafat: The Arab Journal of Sociology*. He is also the author of several works on Palestinian refugees, economic sociology, and sociology of migration.

Kristian Berg Harpviken is director of the International Peace Research Institute Oslo (PRIO). Harpviken is a sociologist whose research interests include the dynamics of civil war, transnational communities, and methodology in difficult contexts. His book *Social Networks and Migration in Wartime Afghanistan* was published in 2009.

Bruce Hemmer is a Ph.D. candidate in political science at the University of California, Irvine, where he is a fellow with the Center for the Study of Democracy and the Center for Citizen Peacebuilding. He has several years of practical experience in peacebuilding and democratization in Bosnia and Herzegovina, Kosovo, and Ethiopia with the Organization for Security and Cooperation in Europe (OSCE) and several NGOs.

Darren Kew studies the connection between democratic institution-building in Africa and the development of political cultures that support democracy. Kew has worked with the Council on Foreign Relations' Center for Preventive Action to provide analysis and blueprints for preventing conflicts in several areas around the world, including Nigeria, Central Africa, and Kosovo.

Andreas Kotelis is a Ph.D. candidate in the Department of Political Science at Bilkent University in Ankara, Turkey. His research interests are Greek-Turkish relations, especially focusing on Track 2 and multitrack diplomacy.

Sabine Kurtenbach is senior researcher at the Institute for Latin American Studies at the German Institute of Global and Area Studies in Hamburg and an independent consultant for development cooperation. Her research interests include postwar societies, peace processes, causes and dynamics of violence and armed conflict, democratization, civil-military relations, civil society, and youths.

Ken Menkhaus is professor of political science at Davidson College, where he has taught since 1991. He specializes in the Horn of Africa and has focused primarily on development, conflict analysis, peacebuilding, local governance, and political Islam, including both academic research and policy work.

Cyril Obi is coordinator of the Research Program on Post-Conflict Transition, the State, and Civil Society in Africa at the Nordic Africa Institute in Uppsala, Sweden. He is on leave from the Nigerian Institute of International Affairs, Lagos, where he is an associate research professor.

Camilla Orjuela is a researcher in the School of Global Studies at University of Gothenburg, Sweden. Her research focuses on identity-based conflicts, conflict resolution, diaspora politics, civil society, development assistance, postwar and postdisaster reconstruction, and Sri Lanka.

Thania Paffenholz is lecturer for peace, conflict, and development at the Graduate Institute of International and Development Studies. She also works as an adviser to the United Nations, the Development Assistance Committee of the Organization for Economic Cooperation and Development, and various governmental and nongovernmental organizations. Her research concentrates on peacebuilding and in particular the following aspects: conflict analysis, international peacemaking strategies, the role of civil society, evaluation, the conflict-development nexus and the role of development actors, and the critical analysis of the aid system.

Shane Quinn has been working as program adviser with the Life and Peace Institute since 2003, where his work has mainly focused on the Horn of Africa and Central Africa.

Hassan Sheikh worked with UNICEF as an education officer in south-central Somalia. He founded the Somali Institute of Management and Administration Development, whose main purpose was to produce mid-level administrative technicians for the postconflict reconstruction of Somalia. He led the formation of a Somali Civil Society Forum, a conglomerate of networks, coalitions, and action groups engaged in different sectors.

Christoph Spurk is a media researcher and teaches media and development in the Institute of Applied Media Studies at the Zurich University of Applied Sciences Winterthur, Switzerland. As head of the research unit Media in International Cooperation, he conducts research on the influence of mass media on the democratization process and the development of civil society in developing countries, as well as on the role of journalism in conflict and peacebuilding.

Index

About the Book

Responding to the burgeoning interest in the role of civil society in peace processes, this groundbreaking collaborative effort identifies the constructive functions of civil society in support of peacebuilding both during and in the aftermath of armed conflict. The authors also highlight the factors that support those functions and the obstacles to their fulfillment. A comprehensive analytical framework is applied to eleven country cases, not only allowing comparative analysis but also providing a new tool for further research.

Thania Paffenholz is lecturer in peace, development, and conflict studies and senior researcher at the Center for Conflict, Development, and Peacebuilding at the Graduate Institute of International and Development Studies in Geneva. She is coauthor of *Aid for Peace: A Guide to Planning and Evaluation for Conflict Zones* and coeditor of *Peacebuilding: A Field Guide.*